*The French Resistance*

# The French Resistance

 Olivier Wieviorka

*Translated by* Jane Marie Todd

*The Belknap Press of Harvard University Press*

CAMBRIDGE, MASSACHUSETTS

LONDON, ENGLAND

2016

Originally published in French as *Histoire de la Résistance, 1940–1945,*
© Perrin, 2013

*Library of Congress Cataloging-in-Publication Data*

Names: Wieviorka, Olivier, 1960– author.
Title: The French resistance / Olivier Wieviorka ; translated by Jane Marie Todd.
Other titles: Histoire de la Résistance English.
Description: Cambridge, Massachusetts : The Belknap Press of Harvard
    University Press, 2016. | "Originally published as Histoire de la Résistance :
    1940–1945"—Title page verso. | Includes bibliographical references and index.
Identifiers: LCCN 2015037898 | ISBN 9780674731226 (alk. paper)
Subjects: LCSH: World War, 1939–1945—Underground movements—France. |
    France—History—German occupation, 1940–1945.
Classification: LCC D802.F8 W53513 2016 | DDC 940.53/44—dc23 LC record
    available at http://lccn.loc.gov/2015037898

Book design by Dean Bornstein

FOR PASCALE AND SOPHIE

# CONTENTS

# ABBREVIATIONS

| | |
|---|---|
| ACP | Assemblée Consultative Provisoire d'Alger (Provisional Consultative Assembly of Algiers) |
| AID | Agence d'Information et de Documentation (Information and Documentation Agency) |
| AMGOT | Allied Military Government of Occupied Territory |
| AO | Action Ouvrière (Workers' Action) |
| AS | Armée Secrète (Secret Army) |
| BBC | British Broadcasting Corporation |
| BCRA | Bureau Central de Renseignement et d'Action (Central Bureau of Intelligence and Operations) |
| BMA | Bureaux des Menées Antinationales (Bureau of Antinational Activities) |
| BOA | Bureau des Opérations Aériennes (Bureau of Air Operations) |
| BS | Brigade Spéciale (Special Brigade) |
| CAD | Comité d'Action contre la Déportation (Action Committee against Deportation) |
| CAS | Comité d'Action Socialiste (Socialist Action Committee) |
| CC | Comité de Coordination (Coordination Committee) |
| CCZN | Comité de Coordination du Zone Nord (Northern Zone Coordination Committee) |
| CCZS | Comité de Coordination du Zone Sud (Southern Zone Coordination Committee) |
| CDA | Commission des Désignations Administratives (Commission of Administrative Appointments) |
| CDE | Conseil de Défense de l'Empire (Empire Defense Council) |
| CDL | Comité Départemental de Libération (Departmental Liberation Committee) |
| CDLL | Ceux de la Libération (Those of the Liberation) |
| CDLR | Ceux de la Résistance (Those of the Resistance) |
| CDM | Camouflage du Matériel (Materiel Concealment Office) |
| CEES | Comité d'Études Économiques et Syndicales (Committee for Economic and Unionist Studies) |

CFLN  Comité Français de la Libération Nationale (French Committee of National Liberation)

CFTC  Confédération Française des Travailleurs Chrétiens (French Confederation of Christian Workers)

CGE  Comité Général d'Études (General Studies Committee)

CGP  Commissariat Général au Plan (Economic Planning Commission)

CGT  Confédération Générale du Travail (General Labor Confederation)

CGTU  Confédération Générale du Travail Unitaire (Unitary General Labor Confederation)

Cimade  Comité Intermouvements auprès des Évacués (Intermovement Committee for Evacuees)

CMR  Comité Médical de la Résistance (Medical Committee of the Resistance)

CND  Confrérie Notre-Dame (Our Lady Brotherhood)

CNF  Comité National Français (French National Committee)

CNI  Commissariat National à l'Intérieur (National Commission for the Interior)

CNR  Conseil National de la Résistance (National Council of the Resistance)

COFI  Comité de Financement de la Résistance (Financial Committee for the Resistance)

COMAC  Comité d'Action Militaire (Military Action Committee)

COMIDAC  Commission de l'Action Immédiate (Commission of Immediate Action)

COPA  Centre des Opérations de Parachutages et d'Atterrissages (Center for Parachute and Landing Operations)

COSOR  Comité des Oeuvres Sociales des Organisations de Résistance (Charitable Works Committee of the Resistance Organizations)

CPL  Comité Parisien de la Libération (Paris Liberation Committee)

CVR  Combattant Volontaire de la Résistance (Voluntary Resistance Fighter)

DF  Défense de la France

DGSS  Direction Générale des Services Spéciaux (Directorate General of Special Services)

*DM*  Charles de Gaulle, *Discours et messages*, vol. 1: *Pendant la guerre, 1940–1946*

| | |
|---|---|
| DMN | délégué militaire national (national military delegate) |
| DMR | délégué militaire régional (regional military delegate) |
| DMZ | délégué militaire de zone (zone military delegate) |
| EMZO | État-major pour la Zone Occupée (General Staff for the Occupied Zone) |
| FEA | French Equatorial Africa |
| FFC | Forces Françaises Combattantes (Fighting French Forces) |
| FFI | Forces Françaises de l'Intérieur (French Forces of the Interior) |
| FFL | Forces Françaises Libres (Free French Forces) |
| FN | Front National [de Lutte pour la Liberté et l'Indépendance de la France] (National Front [in the Struggle for the Freedom and Independence of France]) |
| FP | Front Populaire (Popular Front) |
| FTP | Francs-Tireurs et Partisans (Free Fighters and Partisans) |
| GMR | Groupes mobiles de réserve (mobile reserve groups) |
| GP | Groupes de Protection (Protection Groups) |
| GPRF | Gouvernement Provisoire de la République Française (Provisional Government of the French Republic) |
| JC | Jeunesses Communistes (Communist Youth) |
| JEC | Jeunesse Étudiante Chrétienne (Young Christian Students) |
| LFC | Légion Française des Combattants (French Legion of Fighters) |
| LJR | Ligue de la Jeune République (Young Republic League) |
| MbF | Militärbefehlshaber in Frankreich (German military command in France) |
| MLN/ MOLIN | Mouvement de Libération Nationale (National Liberation Movement) |
| MOF | Mouvement Ouvrier Français (French Workers' Movement) |
| MOI | Main-d'Oeuvre Immigrée (Immigrant Labor Force) |
| MRP | Mouvement Républicain Populaire (Popular Republican Movement) |
| MUR | Mouvements Unis de la Résistance (Unified Movements of the Resistance) |
| NAP | Noyautage des Administrations Publiques (Infiltration of Public Administrations) |
| NARA | National Archives and Records Administration |
| OCM | Organisation Civile et Militaire (Civil and Military Organization) |
| OMA | Organisation Métropolitaine de l'Armée (Metropolitan Army Organization) |

| | |
|---|---|
| ORA | Organisation de Résistance de l'Armée (Army Resistance Organization) |
| OS | Organisation Spéciale (Special Organization) |
| OSE | Oeuvre de Secours aux Enfants (Society for the Rescue of Children) |
| OSS | Office of Strategic Services |
| PCF | Parti Communiste Français (French Communist Party) |
| POWN | Polska Organizacja Walki o Niepodleglosc (Polish Organization for the Independence Struggle) |
| PSF | Parti Social Français (French Social Party) |
| PWE | Political Warfare Executive |
| RAF | Royal Air Force |
| RG | Renseignements Généraux (General Intelligence) |
| SAS | Special Air Service |
| SD | Sicherheitsdienst (Security Service) |
| SFHQ | Special Force Headquarters |
| SFIO | Section Française de l'Internationale Ouvrière (French Section of the Workers' International) |
| SHAEF | Supreme Headquarters, Allied Expeditionary Forces |
| SiPo-SD | Sicherheitspolizei und Sicherheitsdienst (Security Police and Security Service) |
| SNCF | Société Nationale des Chemins de Fer (National Railroad Company) |
| SNM | Service National Maquis (National Marquis Service) |
| SOAM | Service des Opérations Aériennes et Maritimes (Air and Sea Operations Service) |
| SOE | Special Operations Executive |
| SR | service de renseignements (intelligence service) |
| SRMAN | Service de Répression des Menées Antinationales (Service for the Repression of Antinational Activities) |
| SS | Schutzstaffel (Protection Squadrons, also known as the Black Order) |
| STO | Service du Travail Obligatoire (Compulsory Work Service) |
| UDSR | Union Démocratique et Socialiste de la Résistance (Democratic and Socialist Union of the Resistance) |
| VdL | Volontaires de la Liberté (Volunteers for Liberty) |

*The French Resistance*

UNITED KINGDOM

BELGIUM

*Meuse*

LUXEMBOURG

GERMANY

• Arras

*Rhine*

*Meuse*

*Marne*

• Châlons-
sur-Marne

Paris •

*Seine*

F R A N C E

*Occupied by Nazi Germany*

*Seine*

• Strasbourg

*Moselle*

*Rhine*

Dijon •

*Saône*

*Doubs*

*Loire*

Tours •

• Bourges

Poitiers •

*Cher*

Châlons-
sur-
Saône

SWITZERLAND

Moulins •

■ Vichy

Angoulême •

• Limoges

Lyon •

*Loire*

*Rhône*

*Isère*

ITALY

Bordeaux •

*Dordogne*

VICHY FRANCE/
FREE ZONE

Mont-de-Marsan •

*Garonne*

*Durance*

Bayonne •

SPAIN

• Marseilles

| 100 | 200 Miles |
|---|---|
| 0 | 150 | 300 Kilometres |

*Corsica*

World War II France

- - - - - Demarcation line

Occupied by Nazi Germany

Annexed by Nazi Germany

Occupied by Italy (1940–1942)

Vichy France/Free Zone (to November 1942)

Occupied by Italy (1942–1943)

*Map 1*

# Introduction

On June 20, 1940, Étienne Achavanne, an agricultural worker, single-handedly sabotaged the telephone lines connecting Boos airfield to the German field headquarters in Rouen. The World War I veteran was arrested, then sentenced to death by the court-martial of Rouen on June 24. He was shot on July 6, the first martyr of the French internal resistance.

On December 22, 1940, Lieutenant Commander Honoré d'Estienne d'Orves secretly landed on the Breton coast to establish one of the first Free France intelligence networks, known as Nemrod. Betrayed by his radio operator, he was arrested in Nantes by the Germans, and, after a trial held at the court-martial of Paris, was executed on August 29, 1941. He was the first agent of Free France to fall to the enemy's bullets.

On June 27, 1940, Henri Frenay, a captain in the French army, escaped after being captured in the Vosges. By autumn 1940, he had laid the foundations for an underground organization seeking to continue the fight in captive France. He left the regular army in January 1941. His movement, Combat, would become one of the most powerful underground groups.

Conversely, Louis Rivet, the chief of the army's intelligence service, preferred to remain within the framework of the Vichy regime until 1942. Even while pursuing his official activities, he encouraged the concealment of weapons and made life difficult for the German agents spying in the free zone. At the same time, however, his forces were tracking down Gaullists and British spies. In November 1942, Lieutenant Colonel Rivet left the French metropolis for Algiers, newly liberated by British and American troops. Rather than join General Charles de Gaulle, he immediately placed himself under the orders of de Gaulle's rival, General Henri Giraud, who would take power in North Africa after December.

These actions and so many others belong to what is commonly called the French resistance. Their variety hinders us from proposing a comprehensive definition of a phenomenon that is surely marked by diversity and pluralism. Some major historians have ventured such a definition, however. François Bédarida, for example, characterizes the resistance as "clandestine action conducted in the name of the freedom of the nation and the dignity of the human person by volunteers who organize to fight against the domination (and usually the occupation) of their country by a Nazi or Fascist or satellite or Allied regime."[1] Others dispute such an approach. "Nothing is to be gained by deceiving ourselves about the possibility of totally mastering the concept of Resistance and successfully rendering its reality in a convincing synthesis. The phenomenon, both protean and unique, is of such complexity and such plasticity that it does not adapt well to a mode of conceptualization that resembles a poorly fitting corset," argues Pierre Laborie.[2]

It is true that the infinite variety of modes of engagement and of lived experience makes any generalization misleading. Is it possible, for example, to place under the same banner the maquisard and the distributor of an underground newspaper, the Gaullist saboteur and the nun who secretly conceals Jewish children in her convent? Must we assimilate the isolated act of a farmer who agrees to aid in the transport of weapons received in a parachute drop to the steadfast engagement of the men and women who worked for four years in underground groups? And finally, does the external resistance belong to the same category as the internal resistance? One was conducted openly by men who had decided to join General de Gaulle and to fight under the standard of the Forces Françaises Libres (FFL; Free French Forces), from the desert sands to the Tuscan hills. The other led the struggle in metropolitan France, facing the perils of darkness and secrecy and conducting a shadow war out of uniform. In short, must we speak of "the" resistance, even though treating it as a bloc (to parody Clemenceau speaking about the French Revolution) leads to an erosion of the regional and social differences marking it, so much so that many historians now prefer to use the plural, to speak of "resistances," rather than continue to employ the singular form?[3]

Rather than propose a new definition—hazardous waters where many have foundered—I shall confine myself to putting forward a few criteria that provide the general contours of the internal French resistance.

The resistance is defined in the first place by its actions. Its aim was to do battle concretely with the German occupier, and even its Vichy ally, criteria sufficient to distinguish it from mere opinion. In other words, the act of rejecting the inevitability of the defeat and declaring one's disagreement with Philippe Pétain's regime is not enough to define engagement in the resistance—an engagement embodied before all else in practices, however diverse they might be.

That said, actions cannot be dissociated from the meanings attached to them. A smuggler who transported Jews living in France in exchange for money cannot be considered a resister, even if by his actions he thwarted the genocidal ambition of the Nazi regime. "There is Resistance only if there is consciousness of resisting, whether it expresses willful engagement or entails a Spinozan consciousness of the necessary task," observes Laborie.[4]

Resistance, finally, is predicated on transgression. It stands opposed to the legality imposed by the Reich and its Vichy accomplice. In that respect, it entailed a risk that all accepted and that many incurred, at the cost of their lives.

These criteria give rise to a restrictive reading of the movement that unfolded in captive France from the twilight of the defeat to the dawn of liberation. It is indisputable that the majority of French people rejected both Nazism and the occupation that attested to its reality. It is no less indisputable that, from time to time, some supported the resistance networks or movements. The resistance never could have taken root in France had it not benefited from such cooperation. It is therefore possible to distinguish a "Resistance organization, which obviously comprises only a very small minority, and a Resistance movement, a much vaster social phenomenon. The Resistance movement included all those who performed individual actions and all those whose acts of solidarity were essential to the organized Resistance. The Resistance movement was not at all marginal to the Resistance organization but rather conditioned its existence,"[5] as the historian François Marcot notes.

Distinguishing is not the same as confusing, however. In this book I shall consider the resistance organization, not the resistance movement. As a result, I will deal with the actions conducted by underground organizations (excluding the Gaullist FFL therefore), while endeavoring to respond to crucial questions. I shall examine the connections between the internal resistance and Charles de Gaulle's Free France, the motivations for individual engagement, the social composition of the organizations, the impact of repression, and the military effectiveness of the army of shadows, in order to propose a comprehensive view of the underground fight. But I shall not confuse the assistance occasionally offered by the population with the more steadfast engagement pledged by thousands of French men and women in the underground groups.

That aim, simple in principle, proves to be complex in its realization. For though research on the resistance has proliferated since the liberation, comprehensive assessments are rare. Jean-Marie Guillon and Pierre Laborie note, for example: "The history of the Resistance remains to be written, insofar as the lacunae and lack of balance in that history appear to be considerable, even though it has been observed many times, and on a regular basis, that we know a great deal about little."[6]

In reality, the absence of a comprehensive view raises obstacles for the historian.

Whatever an author's intention, historicizing the resistance saps some of the power from the legend. In retracing sometimes violent struggles between the envoys from London and the men in the movements, I shall shatter the conventional image of a united resistance with no interest in political questions, a resistance that scornfully dismissed power issues. In recalling the Pétainist temptation that motivated some movements—Combat and Défense de la France (DF) to cite only two—I run the risk of destroying the myth of a resistance rising up from the outset against the National Revolution launched by Philippe Pétain. In evoking the anti-Semitism that pervaded certain newspapers, the *Cahiers* of the Organisation Civile et Militaire (OCM; Civil and Military Organization), for example, I distance myself from the allegory of underground forces resolutely fighting the demons of racism.

It has been especially difficult to storm these Bastilles of memory, given that the history of the resistance was for many decades written by people who, in one way or another, had participated in it. They prided themselves on respecting the words of witnesses, without disputing what was said. Henri Noguères, famous for his overview of the resistance, refused to wait patiently for the archives to be opened because "waiting to begin such work until fifty years had elapsed would have meant giving up the idea that this history was not only written but also debated—*and controlled*—by those who lived it."[7] Lucien Febvre made a curious argument: "The historians will say what, as men of the year 2000, they can say, living in the climate of the year 2000. . . . One more reason for us to provide them . . . in all honesty, with our own version of the events, which, of course, they will interpret differently than we do. . . . And we will be unable to say whether they are right and we are wrong. At least our version of the events had living proof. It is countersigned by thousands of sacrifices."[8] The great historian of the Protestant Reformation was professing an odd relativism. Postulating that the truth does not exist, he acknowledged the plurality of interpretations, even while preferring the one that thousands of martyrs are said to have countersigned with their blood. In short, the resistance has inspired—and rightly so—such respect that historians, intentionally or not, have submitted to a form of self-censorship, which has been of little help in historicizing the phenomenon.

Historiographical discourse raises a second problem. It must provide explanations, not stir emotions. Unlike the novelist or filmmaker, the historian refrains from playing on emotions. But the resistance discourages such a cold hard look. The engagement of such noble figures inspires respect and admiration; the torture or death endured by well-known or anonymous heroes cannot leave us indifferent. Yet the historian must not let such reactions sway him. If he did, he would lapse into hagiography and would abdicate the critical faculty at the foundation of the discipline. In fact, even if he wanted to appeal to feelings, he possesses very meager means for doing so. Aleksandr Solzhenitsyn's work will always be a stronger evocation of the Gulag than a book written by an academic. And who could recapture the tragedy and absurdity of the exodus better than Irène Némirovsky?

These remarks do not settle the question, however. To take only one example, any reduction of engagement in the resistance to a series of sociological, ideological, or generational parameters would subordinate it to soulless variables while denying the role that courage, idealism, and fraternity played. Its participants liked to point out, in fact, that the experience eludes all generalization and "remains in great part inaccessible and intransmissible."[9]

Should we approach the resistance through its existence or through its essence (to plagiarize Jean-Paul Sartre)? The first option invites us to grasp it through its achievements, retracing the slow development of a process marked by encounters, sometimes aborted initiatives, and isolated actions. The second encourages us to examine the meaning of a struggle whose ethical dimension is readily accentuated, even as the context in which it was deployed is forgotten. It is impossible, however, to disentangle the two terms. As Bédarida asks, "What makes for the Resistance's power of attraction, what erects it into a model, a symbol, and even a myth, is that therein universalism combines with historicity."[10] If I were to confine myself to spelling out the deeper significance of a struggle, I would run the risk of decontexualizing the phenomenon by cutting it off from its historical roots, to the advantage of an approach that privileges values. Apart from the fact that I would thereby risk lapsing into sacred history, such a choice, though it would provide a certain understanding of the resistance, would not give an explanation of it. And it is the latter choice which constitutes the guiding thread of this book.

My aim thus lies at the crossroads of two contradictory imperatives. I intend primarily to propose a comprehensive interpretation of the internal French resistance, while synthesizing the considerable volume of studies that, for more than half a century, have shed light on it. I propose to give the reader an understanding of what is certainly a complex phenomenon by challenging the legendary aspects and the oversimplifications, even if that means casting an ethically remote gaze on a mythic—not to say mythicized—page of French history. With no trembling of the pen. The resistance fighters braved Nazism without blinking. The resistance has nothing to fear from its historicization.

## Chapter 1

# The Call

By what means might resistance come into being? The army of shadows could have emerged from the depths of French society, which, shocked by the defeat and wishing to do battle with the Nazi occupier, would then have drawn the necessary resources from within itself to lead the struggle. But it could also have resulted from an external appeal: the volunteers might have responded to the instructions formulated by General de Gaulle or by the British authorities. In the first case, resistance would have an endogenous origin, marking the muffled roar of a people who rejected the inevitability of the disaster. In the second case, it would be exogenous, resulting from the appeal de Gaulle launched on June 18, 1940.

"By the will of its author and because of the growing authority he acquired, the Appeal is said to have been a founding act, and doubly so. The founding act of the Resistance, since all the resistance movements and all the acts of autochthonous resistance stemmed, in de Gaulle's view, from June 18. And the founding act of a regime, though it would not come into being for another twenty years," notes historian Jean-Louis Crémieux-Brilhac.[1] The Gaullists propagated that version, believing that the internal resistance could not have developed without the assistance provided by Free France. "In reality, when [ Jean Moulin, de Gaulle's envoy,] arrived in France [in January 1942], everything, or nearly everything, remained to be done," claims André Dewavrin (Colonel Passy), head of the secret services of Free France. "Even the goals of the resistance movements were still poorly defined by their leaders, and the means necessary to obtain results were practically nonexistent. Everything had to be organized. That is, well-controlled troops and forces had to be created from whole cloth and charged with precise tasks or functions, with the assistance of more or less hesitant, more or less disciplined, more or less selfless personalities. Efforts had to be made to methodically introduce order into a heterogeneous mass, where everyone, in order to fight the languor, cowardice, or betrayal of the *attentistes* (the watch-and-wait faction), the collaborators, or the enemy's agents, thought they had to concern themselves with everything at the same time."[2] That view, though quick to glorify the Gaullist legend, does not tally with reality.

Charles de Gaulle set out to keep France as such in the war. That ambition obliged him, first, to do battle with the Vichy regime, guilty in his eyes of having concluded a shameful armistice, a judgment from which he would not deviate. In addition, it impelled him to construct a state entity capable of embodying the legitimacy that Philippe Pétain was arrogating to himself, an imperative that led de Gaulle to rally part of the French empire behind him, so as to acquire the territorial base he was lacking. The term "Free France" came into being on August 29, 1940, after French Equatorial Africa (FEA) and Cameroon joined with de Gaulle. His goal prompted him, finally, to build an army that, fighting on behalf of France and not merely as a legion engaged alongside the United Kingdom, would attest that the country was participating fully in the Allied effort. These imperatives explain why the Appeal of June 18 was addressed in the first place to specialists, French officers and soldiers, engineers, and professional workers in the armaments industries, whom de Gaulle invited to come to England. In reality, few answered the call. By late August 1940, Free France had rallied to its cause only eleven thousand volunteers—excluding colonials.[3] But despite the small numbers, de Gaulle did not consider mobilizing the population of captive France by forging the terms of civilian resistance or by providing the general outlines for armed struggle, for example, a form of guerilla warfare. Far from theorizing the "small war," whose importance had been posited by Carl von Clausewitz, de Gaulle confined himself to re-creating a traditional army on the British archipelago. It would therefore be an exaggeration to consider him the creator, or even the inspiration, for an internal resistance. At least initially, the interest of such a resistance eluded him. But two qualifications need to be added: first, as of June 1940, de Gaulle sought to influence public opinion by broadcasting through the British Broadcasting Corporation (BBC); and second, he created his secret services, headed by Colonel Passy, which encouraged the development of the underground struggle.

## Radio as Weapon

The role of propaganda, especially over the airwaves, had not escaped the rulers of democracies any more than those of totalitarian countries. In the early twentieth century, both relied increasingly on that powerful medium. For de Gaulle, radio constituted the most reliable instrument for popularizing his actions, for undermining the legitimacy of the Vichy regime, and for giving instructions to the population. Through the magic of the airwaves, he was able to reach millions of French people in real time, an influence to which the underground press could not aspire. But though it was imperative for de Gaulle to use the BBC, he also ran into formidable problems.

In the first place, not everyone in France owned a radio set. In autumn 1939, the administration counted 5 million radios, to which some 1.5 million undeclared sets can probably be added.[4] France was therefore not as well-equipped as the United Kingdom (9 million radios) or Nazi Germany, amply provided by Joseph Goebbels's Ministry of Propaganda (13.7 million radio sets in 1939).[5] Although not a luxury item, a radio was far from being a presence in every household. From the start, that situation limited the impact of de Gaulle's words—even though, at the time, people often listened in groups.

Second, the British authorities sought to control their airwaves closely, to keep dissonant, if not discordant, voices from contradicting the policy determined by Winston Churchill. Granted, the British prime minister supported the leader of Free France. He acknowledged de Gaulle on June 28, 1940, as the "leader of all Free Frenchmen, wherever they may be, who rally to him in support of the allied cause,"[6] even before an accord, concluded on August 7, established the legal terms of that acknowledgment. Churchill had no intention, however, of letting de Gaulle do as he liked, an eventuality that might have impeded the British prime minister's strategy toward the Vichy regime. De Gaulle therefore did not have free access to English radio: his communications were subject to prior censorship, and he did not enjoy a monopoly on French speech.

In fact, the BBC offered three types of programs. Until the end of the hostilities, the British had a regular news broadcast (*French News*). In addition, on June 24, the station created a daily thirty-minute program called *Ici la France (France Here)*, assigned to Pierre Maillaud (Pierre Bourdan), a journalist by training. A few weeks later, it organized a new team of announcers, which Michel Saint-Denis (Jacques Duchesne), a nephew of the actor Jacques Copeau, was responsible for recruiting. Duchesne surrounded himself with brilliant companions: Jacques Cottance (Jacques Borel, who broadcast under the name Brunius); Maurice Van Moppès, Yves Morvan (Jean Marin), a London correspondent for the Agence Havas before the war; and Jean Oberlé. James Darsie Gillie, former Warsaw correspondent for the *Manchester Guardian* and the *Morning Post*, was in charge of the entire French branch of the BBC from 1941 to 1944. This programming debuted on July 14, 1940; on September 6, it was baptized *Les Français parlent aux Français (French Speaking to the French)*. The broadcasts made no claim to be speaking *for* Free France.[7] For though Morvan, Van Moppès, and Oberlé were Gaullists, Maillaud and Saint-Denis most certainly were not.

De Gaulle, then, had only a modest slot. In the wake of the British attack against the French fleet at Mers-el-Kébir in Algiers (July 3, 1940), Churchill offered him five minutes a day, to which de Gaulle agreed. De Gaulle assigned Maurice Schumann, a journalist for Agence Havas and an editorialist in several periodicals associated with the Christian Democrats before the war, to be the spokesman for Free France. The first broadcast, on July 18, 1940, opened with the words, "Liberté, égalité, fraternité, this is the voice of the Free French." It took the name *Honneur et Patrie (Honor and Nation)* in late August 1940. From December 9 on, those five minutes were rebroadcast during the noon news, and, in that time slot, de Gaulle obtained five additional minutes in 1941. The Gaullists, then, did not dominate the airwaves. Although the length of the broadcasts in French continued to grow, from thirty minutes in 1939 to two and a half hours in 1940, finally reaching four hours in 1941, de Gaulle had a restricted niche for a long time. In addition, *Honneur et Patrie* had to submit the text of its program eight hours before the broadcast and obtain a stamp of approval from the permanent secretary of the Foreign Office, or from Anthony Eden, secretary of state for dominion affairs, or from Churchill in person. And the English authorities did not refrain from exercising their right of censorship. Although de Gaulle refused to treat Pétain with kid gloves,

London avoided frontal attacks, in view of the popularity of the victor of Verdun. For example, the British blocked an editorial by Maurice Schumann on October 30, 1940, which cited "the unconstitutionality" of the Vichy government.[8] That order to exercise caution vis-à-vis the French State was not lifted until May 24, 1941. Likewise, tensions in the Levant led the British authorities temporarily to ban de Gaulle from the air in September 1941. On the whole, however, "between spring 1941 and autumn 1942, de Gaulle and Schumann, despite frequent recriminations (or because of these recriminations), were ultimately free to say what they liked at the BBC microphone, in exchange for a rare correction of a few words."[9]

Finally, the Vichy and German powers limited the audience for English radio by every means possible. At first, they attempted to jam the broadcasts, but to no avail, since the English were sending out signals on one longwave frequency, one medium-wave frequency, and between three and six shortwave frequencies.[10] The enemy powers also used threats. On May 10, 1940, a German order threatened with prison, hard labor, or even death anyone who listened to non-German radio broadcasts or who peddled radio news hostile to the Reich.[11] That ban was formalized on October 10 by the Militärbefehlshaber in Frankreich (MbF), the military authority in France. In Alsace-Lorraine, those listening publicly to foreign stations were subject to capital punishment beginning in 1941. In the free zone, listening to English radio in public was banned on October 28, 1940, and the ban was extended to the private sphere a year later. Any violation could be punished by a three-month prison sentence and a stiff fine, a sanction increased to two years of detention in October 1941. These threats were sometimes carried out. In January 1941, sixty-two people were arrested in Paris on charges of having listened to a foreign radio station; and in February, twenty-seven were detained on the same grounds. Furthermore, the authorities had no qualms about confiscating radio sets, citing all sorts of reasons. On October 31, 1941, for example, 1,641 radios were seized in the single city of Évreux, in Normandy.[12] Finally, Vichy responded to the pernicious attraction of the BBC by broadcasting entertainment shows on national radio; these were supposed to capture the attention of listeners and provide a distraction, in both the literal and figurative senses of the word.

These measures were insufficient to prevent people from listening, though it is difficult to quantify how many tuned in. One estimate is that 3 million French people listened to de Gaulle in 1942, and that between 70 and 75 percent of the population was receiving the BBC occasionally or regularly by spring 1944.[13] In any event, the authorities complained loudly. For example, the prefect of Ille-et-Vilaine, in Brittany, pointed out "the clear susceptibility of the population to English propaganda" (December 1940). The collaborationists lashed out, accusing "General Micro," as the Vichy regime dubbed de Gaulle, of being in the pay of the Jews or of "Perfidious Albion." In a column in *Le Matin* (July 30, 1941), Paul Allard's humor was heavy-handed: "Dengaulle Fever is caught primarily through the auditory organs. It is usually the result of chronic intoxication by shortwaves. Some patients cannot do without their usual drug and get up at night to drink a cup of 'stupefactive' messages from Radio Londres. It attacks weak natures by preference: nervous women, prepubescent schoolgirls, old men unfit for the new living conditions, uprooted émigrés, and the idle from the unoccupied zone."[14] But these countermeasures were not sufficient to curb the fascination exerted by the BBC in general and by the Gaullist broadcasts in particular.

It is true that, by providing information to the French, English radio lit a backfire in the fight against German and Vichy propaganda. In 1940, the BBC revealed the expulsion of tens of thousands of Alsace-Lorrainians to the free zone and reported the demonstration of November 11, 1940, which had mobilized hundreds of French young people in Paris seeking to commemorate the World War I victory. These reports were meant to be as honest as possible, and not only from a sense of high moral purpose, as Colonel Maurice Buckmaster, head of the French branch of the British Special Operations Executive (SOE), explained after the war: "We needed to instill confidence in the BBC, so that French patriots would accept without question or complaint any directive launched over its airwaves."[15] In the dark night of occupation, the BBC offered a source of comfort, especially since the news was often funny and entertaining. Jean Oberlé distinguished himself by the quality of his caustic slogans ("Radio-Paris lies, Radio-Paris deceives, Radio-Paris is Germendacious"). Reports, sketches, and songs followed one after another, giving the broadcasts a lively and whimsical tone.

The BBC also addressed orders to civilians to fight, though it always took an extremely cautious line: "Stand mobilized, act without exposing yourself too much, and support the Allies."[16]

The Gaullist forces were also circumspect in that regard. They refrained from launching an appeal to demonstrate on July 14, 1940. Only René Cassin, a Free France jurist and World War I veteran, invited his comrades to commemorate November 11, 1940, in front of the monuments to the dead. A line was crossed, however, on December 23, 1940. At that time, de Gaulle urged French people to desert the streets on New Year's Day, between 2 P.M. and 3 P.M. in the free zone, and between 3 P.M. and 4 P.M. in the occupied zone: "Everywhere things must be done discreetly and firmly, so that the mute protest of the crushed Nation may take on enormous scope." That appeal, reiterated many times between December 24 and January 1, was no doubt heeded, though the streets were traditionally not very busy on that day. In January, British radio sent out a musical appeal to "stash pennies" (*planquer les sous*), sung to the tune of "Savez-vous planter les choux?" ("Do You Know How to Plant Cabbages?"). The aim was to keep the Germans from seizing metal coins for their war production.

The first real battle began in that winter of 1941. On January 14, Victor de Laveleye, the Belgian announcer at the BBC, asked his compatriots to conduct a graffiti campaign, propagating the letter V, the symbol of victory (*victoire/Vrijheid*). The campaign was so successful in Belgium, in the Netherlands, and in the French regions of Nord and Normandy, that the French branch of the BBC suggested disseminating the same signs to honor King Peter of Yugoslavia, who in 1941 had resisted the German ultimatum. On May 16, the British formed a V-Committee to coordinate action in the occupied territories.

The success of the campaign surpassed all expectations. V's blossomed throughout occupied Europe. On March 28, 1941, the police in Lille counted—and erased—5,500 V's, 300 Crosses of Lorrain (de Gaulle's symbol), and 14 "Vive de Gaulle"s.[17] In Paris the police tallied about a thousand V's on April 7, 1941.[18] On July 20, it effaced another 4,400, collecting in addition 5,500 V's cut out of paper.[19]

The authorities did not treat that campaign lightly. On May 18, 1941, Admiral Darlan, second-in-command of the Vichy regime, sent out a circular to prefects, instructing them to devote the greatest attention to the phenomenon. The authorities took action. In Lisieux, the municipality sent a car equipped with loudspeakers through the streets of the city, urging the population to obliterate the inscriptions without delay, for fear of German reprisals.[20] Residents were sometimes forced to wash off the inscriptions, and sanctions were also imposed. The city of Moulins had to pay a fine of 400,000 francs; a penalty of 20,000 francs was imposed on Bourg-en-Bresse, along with a curfew between May 12 and July 1, 1941.[21] Goebbels, the Reich's minister of propaganda, made a crude attempt to co-opt the symbol, claiming, against all evidence, that the V stood for "Victoria." The scheme, lacking in subtlety, did not fool many people.

Encouraged by the unexpected results, Free France pressed its advantage, launching a new appeal for the feast day of Joan of Arc: "On May 11 . . . all French people will unite in a single thought: the freedom of the homeland. On that day, from 3 to 4 P.M., they will be on all the promenades of our cities and villages. They will walk by individually, as families, or as groups of friends; they will not form a procession; absolute silence will reign. But by looking one another straight in the eye, they will express through their gaze alone their common will and their common hope." The plan was a great success. In Lille, between five and ten thousand people gathered around the statue of Joan of Arc, after which the German authorities confiscated the radio sets of the city's residents, as well as those in Lambersart and Marcq-en-Baroeul.[22] A hundred thousand demonstrators walked in Bordeaux, eighty thousand in Nantes. In Cannes and in Lyon, however, the crowds were thinner.[23] Other appeals followed on July 14 and November 11, 1941, and were also heeded to varying degrees. On July 14 the subprefect of Bayeux noted: "It seems that the district as a whole rallied behind the watchword. The lieutenant of the gendarmerie, on rounds in the district that day, had that impression. Blue-white-and-red flowers appeared at many windows, and shopkeepers made every effort to arrange their displays of merchandise to invoke the colors of France."[24]

All in all, the results produced by the BBC were uneven. In calling on the French people to demonstrate, it showed the limits of the influence exerted by both the Germans and the Vichy regime. The BBC made the brewing discontent appear obvious, simultaneously undermining the legitimacy of the French State and increasing the stature of General de Gaulle. At the same time, however, radio as a weapon could not really mobilize the French people in their struggle against the occupier. But what could the BBC have done? Any call for guerilla warfare in 1941 would have been delusional: the Allies could neither arm civilians nor set military objectives, particularly since they feared exposing the people to bloody reprisals. The British leaders took the measure of that impasse, wondering whether it was appropriate to link propaganda to action in the occupied countries. That question would persist until the Normandy landings on June 6, 1944. In other words, the influence of English radio, assuredly great, must not be confused with its effect, which was undeniably limited. The BBC created a breeding ground favorable for resistance, which it endowed with significance and a broad, meaningful historical perspective. Conversely, it could not structure the underground struggle on its own.

The Gaullist secret services set out to do so in their own way.

## The Advent of the Gaullist Secret Services

Charles de Gaulle's goal of keeping France in the war was easier to define than it was to achieve. Those who enlisted in the FFL were too small in number to play a major role, particularly since the British carried out few operations before 1942, apart from the intervention in Crete in 1941 and the war conducted in Africa, especially Tripolitania. In 1940, moreover, there was no hope of mobilizing the masses to engage in what would have been an uncertain struggle. Intelligence, by contrast, was a promising field of intervention. At the time, "it was absolutely vital for the English to know the Germans' intentions as early as possible and to collect the maximum amount of information on their plans for invasion."[25] The Gaullists could play their part in that.

In 1940 Colonel Passy set about endowing Free France with a *service de renseignements* (SR), an intelligence service. Nothing predestined him for that role. Born in 1911, Dewavrin eventually became a professor of fortifications at the military officers' training school of Saint-Cyr and participated in the Norway Campaign. Repatriated to England, he chose to rally behind General de Gaulle, who, on July 1, 1940, entrusted him with the leadership of the Second and Third Bureaus, the bureaus traditionally in charge of intelligence and operations. Lacking any experience in the area, Passy compensated for his youth with his dynamism and undeniable charisma. After meeting Passy in London in December 1942, Paul Paillole, head of the French State's secret services, would confide: "I am struck by the abundance and self-assurance of his words. His voice is serious, agreeable. His blue eyes are young. A certain premature baldness mitigates the impression of youth."[26] Passy immediately set to work. First he had to clarify his objectives, then define the cooperation he intended to establish with the British, and, finally, specify the relationship he wished to maintain both with the Vichy authorities and with the French population. "In reality, from the very beginning, the Second Bureau was supposed to be an intelligence service. The role of a Second Bureau is to prepare a general report summarizing information for the general staff to assist it in establishing contacts related to operations," he explained after World War II.[27]

Originally, de Gaulle thought that North Africa would go over to the resistance, which led him to give precedence to that theater of operations. As historian Sébastien Albertelli notes, "The Second Bureau wanted to create a 'secret movement of a military nature,' which, 'on a signal from General de Gaulle,' would seize the levers of power and lead military groups, formed to mount the 'resistance against the enemy forces.' One of the first tasks of the agents of the Second Bureau would be to inform London of the possibilities for the unloading, transport, distribution, and upkeep of materiel, and then to constitute secret arms depots. The resources deployed—about ten agents, including four radio operators—attest to the importance that the leaders of Free France and the British granted to the realization of that ambitious program."[28] Agents were sent to both Morocco and Algeria in September, but their adventure quickly met with failure. Twenty-four of them were promptly detained by French counterespionage units, and four were brought before the military tribunal. After that disaster, the Second Bureau threw down the gauntlet.

Passy's secret services also turned toward metropolitan France, in the first place to the occupied zone. Several missions were organized, both to collect immediately usable intelligence and to create "networks meant to last."[29] These ventures were not easy to conduct. Agents were usually sent out on fishing boats, for example, the *Marie-Louise*, which patriotic sailors such as Arsène Celton agreed to place in the service of

Free France. Envoys from London, having no radios at the time, were sometimes equipped with carrier pigeons to transmit the information collected—a chancy practice to say the least.

Jacques Mansion, in August 1940 the first agent of Free France to cross the Channel, brought back maps of the enemy's plan of action in September and left in place a few informers, but his mission led to no results more tangible than that. On the night of August 3, 1940, a speed-boat dispatched two agents, Maurice Duclos (known as Saint-Jacques) and Alexandre Beresnikoff (Corvisart) to the area of Saint-Aubin, in Normandy, to collect intelligence about the enemy's activities, to recruit correspondents, and to facilitate the escape of technicians to be used as bargaining chips with the British. In late 1940, finally, Lieutenant Commander Estienne d'Orves went to France to establish contacts, pick up reports, and inspect the organizations formed by his predecessors. A student at the École Polytechnique and a graduate of the École Navale, this devout Catholic had rallied behind General de Gaulle in September 1940 to continue the fight. Yearning to act, he landed in Brittany on December 22 to establish the Nemrod network. He was immediately betrayed by his radio operator, Alfred Gaessler, a petty officer in the Free French naval forces, and was arrested on the night of January 21, 1941. Sentenced to death after a trial held between May 13 and 26, 1941, he was executed at Mont-Valérien on August 29, earning the dubious distinction of becoming the first agent of Free France to be shot by the occupier.

The groundwork laid by Gilbert Renault (Rémy) proved more promising. Born in 1904, Renault came to be associated with the royalist group Action Française and worked as a film producer. On June 18, he had reached Lorient on the Breton coast. After embarking on a trawler, he arrived the next day in Le Verdon, in the Gironde estuary, and immediately set off for England. Later returning to France via Spain, the talented organizer recruited a number of informers in Bordeaux, Bayonne, La Rochelle, and La Pallice, before extending his network to Brittany. Jean Fleuret, head of the pilots at the port of Bordeaux, who had been dismissed at the Germans' request, lent his assistance. So too did Philippon, a lieutenant from Brest who believed that transmitting information to London was not incompatible with the oath he had taken to Marshal Pétain. Rémy also relied on Jacques Pigeonneau, the French consul in Madrid, who allowed him to dispatch the first messages. Rémy in addition recruited Louis de La Bardonnie, a landowner in Dordogne, who had been associated with Action Française before the war. For a time, La Bardonnie kept the transmitter nicknamed Roméo at his La Roque Castle and placed in Rémy's service the little group he had formed at the time of the defeat.

In addition, a few pioneers made direct contact with the Gaullists. For example, Jean Herbinger, a forty-year-old industrialist, went to Lisbon to establish connections with Free France. Upon returning to France on October 5, 1940, he set up a network, the future Mithridate-Raspail, specializing in military intelligence about Italy and Sardinia. The network had at its disposal transmitters in Saint-Raphaël, Genoa, Cagliari, and Bastia.

By late 1941, the Second Bureau had only imperfectly fulfilled its mission. In the first place, a number of networks had been dismantled by the agents of repression. The French police arrested Pierre Fourcaud (Lucas) in Marseilles, and the Germans crippled the Saint-Jacques network, which had been operating in the occupied zone. Not content to execute Estienne d'Orves, they also made use of his radio operator, who until November 1941 poisoned the French intelligence services.

In all, by late summer 1941, 35 missives totaling 910 pages had been transmitted to London via Spain. But the bulk of the effort had been supplied by Rémy's organization, the only one that was really functional. In actuality, the question of how to transmit information had not been resolved. Transmitters were rare: before May 1941, only Roméo was active. And they frequently broke down, a nagging problem that would be only partly solved over the course of time.

## Perfidious Albion

For obvious reasons, the Second Bureau had to cooperate with its British counterparts, whether they belonged to the Intelligence Service (MI6), the Security Service (MI5), or the SOE created by Winston Churchill to "set Europe ablaze." That cooperation began under favorable circumstances. As Colonel Passy recalls, "We constituted a reserve force of men, in many cases courageous men, who, thanks to the chaos produced by the defeat, could return to their own country to observe the enemy, his plan of action, and his movements there. As for the English, they possessed all the indispensable material resources: money, radio sets, false papers, means of transport, correspondents in neutral countries, and so on. Like the blind man and the paralytic, we therefore had to join forces."[30] That collaboration, however, was less affable than Passy suggests in retrospect.

The interests of Free France and those of the United Kingdom did not, in fact, completely coincide. The priority of the British was to pursue the war, which sometimes led officials to seek an understanding with Vichy. Furthermore, de Gaulle intended to seize power upon liberation, whereas the SOE exhibited a staunch apoliticism.

Given these parameters, British leaders at first endeavored to conduct an intense propaganda campaign, both to popularize their fight and to undermine the authority of the occupiers and increase resistance from the defeated populations. In addition to using radio as a weapon, they proceeded to issue many tracts and newspapers, which were dropped throughout Europe by Royal Air Force (RAF) planes. The French theater was given clear priority. In 1941 the British dropped 36.4 million copies of their press materials on France,[31] while exercising caution in their instructions for action. Encouraging intelligence and sabotage, they promoted passive resistance in the factories but refrained from calling for strikes, whose repression would have struck hard at civilians.

Apart from these exhortations, London sought primarily to establish networks that would report to the MI6 or to the SOE, which, founded in July 1940 and attached to the Ministry of Economic Warfare, had two aims. First, the SOE was supposed to encourage and fuel the spirit of resistance in occupied Europe, a task that would very quickly be assumed by its propaganda branch, the Political Warfare Executive (PWE). Second, it intended to select a small, well-trained cell of men able to support the Allied landing and weaken the enemy's potential. Churchill, swayed by memories of World War I, tended to underestimate the economic might of the Nazis, which he thought he could undermine by bombing or sabotaging their industrial plants.[32]

Beginning in 1940, then, the special services, with the SOE in the lead, took action, dispatching missions or setting up networks. In November of that year, Operation Shamrock culminated in success. Six agents placed under the command of Lieutenant Minshall landed by submarine on the island of Groix, seized a tuna boat, and persuaded half the crew to cooperate. Having identified the procedures that the German submarines followed for entering and leaving the estuary, they then brought the boat back to Falmouth.[33] Several later operations would benefit from that information. In addition, on April 25, 1941, a small commando was dispatched near the Canet pond. Bitner (Kjanowski) was supposed to canvass the Polish community of Nord, and another man, Rizzo, was to set up an underground escape and communications channel. The person who received them, Albert Guérisse, a Belgian military doctor, then set up the Pat O'Leary network, which would exfiltrate some six hundred men, including many pilots.[34] The SOE used the airways as well. The first parachute agent was no doubt Georges Bégué (Georges Noble), who jumped on the night of May 6, 1941, near Châteauroux. Lodged at the home of the Socialist deputy Max Hymans, he recruited two agents, Renan and Fleuret, and placed himself in the service of Pierre de Vomécourt, who had himself been parachuted into France on the night of May 10. De Vomécourt had rallied behind London in June 1940, but, after being dismissed from the Free French services, he had opted for the British secret service. Upon arrival, de Vomécourt enlisted his two brothers, Jean and Philippe, then set up an intelligence network, Autogiro, which he financed in part with his personal fortune.

A few French men and women also sought contact with the British services. Claude Lamirault, a fierce nationalist in his leanings, had joined the army before the war and volunteered to work in the intelligence services. After leaving for Gibraltar when the armistice was signed, he contacted MI6. He was parachuted into France on January 11, 1941, with a transmitter and 50,000 francs. Recruiting from among his family—his wife first, then his in-laws—he rapidly went to work with an embryonic network created in Bordeaux in October 1940 by the British secret services. That network possessed, among other things, a Parti Communiste Français (PCF; French Communist Party) base at the Soeurs-de-Sainte-Agonie convent, located on rue de la Santé in Paris. In the relative calm of that holy place, the mother superior, named Henriette Frede, and nine nuns transmitted messages to London, concealing in the attic of the sacristy transceivers that provided a liaison with the British capital. Fairly quickly, the group came to specialize in military intelligence, especially regarding aeronautics, a question that obsessed Great Britain for obvious reasons. The network soon expanded to Brittany, Normandy, and Châteauroux. In October 1941, an airplane picked up Lamirault, carrying the reports for July, August, September, and October, which no one had been able to transmit. Dropped into France by parachute again on December 8, 1941, he brought with him four transmitters and money, greatly expanding his organization, Jade-Fitzroy, at that time.[35]

In any event, by late 1941 the British services had recorded only limited success. F Section (which did not work with the Gaullists) had sent two dozen agents to France, four of whom had a transceiver at their disposal. But by December, a third of them had been arrested on the most varied grounds. Xavier, a radio operator for Pierre de Vomécort, parachuted in on July 9, 1941: he was recognized near Avranches by a police officer, who arrested him on the spot. Xavier had to finish serving a sentence on rape charges, a punishment that had been cut short by the arrival of the Germans. The members of the Corsican Mission, launched near Bergerac on the night of October 10, were welcomed by the Socialist deputy Pierre Bloch but were rapidly taken in for questioning, which led to a spate of arrests, including that of Georges Bégué. The achievements were far from justifying these heavy losses. F Section claimed responsibility for the derailment of two or three trains; its men also managed to destroy a few railroad repair shops in Le Mans and to decrease production at a tank factory in the Paris region. Pierre de Vomécourt, an inspector for the Société Nationale des Chemins de Fer Français (SNCF; French National Railroad Company), also succeeded in diverting convoys headed for Germany by sending them in the wrong direction. And that was all.

Bad luck partly explains these results, which were modest to say the least. But in addition, SOE strategists did not always display exemplary discernment. For example, the first parachute mission, near Limoges on the night of June 12, 1941, included two containers loaded with weapons, plastic explosives—and limpet mines, surprising for a region hardly known for its maritime activity. Above all, the secret services in general, and the SOE in particular, suffered from a lack of support.

It was not that the men were ill-equipped for their task. Until June 1943, training began with a military and physical session lasting two to four weeks, which sometimes took place in Inchmery House, Hampshire. This was followed by paramilitary training, dispensed over three to five weeks near Arisaig, not far from Inverness, Scotland. Novices learned to kill, to read a map, to march for long stretches, and to use plastic explosives. A poacher taught them how to live off the land. Then came a course in parachuting, taught at the Ringway Airport in Manchester. Every trainee made four or five jumps, one of them at night. They completed their training near Beaulieu, where instructors revealed the techniques of the underground, including coding and decoding, and a former burglar taught them the secrets of safecracking and lockpicking. Agents then headed for operational transit schools, where they awaited their missions, sometimes for many weeks.[36]

But the means were cruelly lacking. Some military leaders refused to agree to the necessary efforts, motivated by a combination of moral hesitancy and strategic considerations. "I think that the dropping of men dressed in civilian clothes for the purpose of attempting to kill members of the opposing forces is not an operation with which the Royal Air Force should be associated," explained Charles Portal, chief of the Air Staff of the RAF, to Gladwyn Jebb, assistant undersecretary in charge of the SOE. "I think you will agree that there is a vast difference, in ethics, between the time-honoured operation of the dropping of a spy from the air and this entirely new scheme for dropping what one can only call assassins," he added.[37] Portal also explained to H. N. Sporborg, assistant to Colin Gubbins, head of the SOE, that his work was a gamble that "may give us a valuable dividend or produce nothing. It is anybody's guess. My bombing offensive is not a gamble. Its dividend is certain; it is a gilt-edged investment. I cannot divert aircraft from a certainty to a gamble which may be a gold-mine or may be completely worthless."[38] During the war, the shortage of airplanes would hamper the actions of the special services. The results of the SOE in France, disappointing overall, thus led the British to relaunch its cooperation with Free France.

## Cooperation

To a certain extent, the Intelligence Service had paved the way, for better and for worse. Headed by Stewart Menzies and his assistant

Claude Dansey, MI6 had two irons in the fire. A first branch, assigned to Commander Wilfred Dunderdale, worked on France; but, far from cooperating with Free France, it did not balk at working with the Vichy intelligence services. By contrast, a second entity, headed by Commander Kenneth Cohen, was created to cooperate with Colonel Passy, but it never really managed to formalize an agreement. The British Intelligence Service promised to assist the Second Bureau in sending agents to France, and Passy agreed in return to communicate the intelligence his networks collected.[39] But relations rapidly grew strained. The Gaullists nursed three grievances. Deploring the inadequacy of the resources granted to the underground struggle and reproaching the British for keeping the FFL away from North Africa, they also suspected, not without reason, that their allies were attracting to their own services French volunteers who had come to England.

Relations were just as complex with the SOE, where many high officials cultivated a virulent anti-Gaullism. Until autumn 1941, the SOE was divided into two branches. At first, SO1 was in charge of propaganda directed at the occupied countries. It acquired full autonomy in August 1941, at which time it became the PWE. By contrast, SO2 (called SOE) had a military aim, which ought to have facilitated cooperation with Passy's services. Such was not the case, however. The services of the SOE, with the exception of propaganda, initially gave precedence to Poland, not France. In addition, the British Intelligence Service was reluctant to share resources and rejected all subversive action, which, were it to escape its control, would threaten its intelligence activity. Finally, the French theater was within the jurisdiction of F Section, headed by Maurice Buckmaster as of November 1941, and F Section did not intend to give precedence to collaboration with the Second Bureau.

Despite these obstacles, Passy went along with the British. The SOE initially agreed to provide parachuting and sabotage training for fourteen men—not without ulterior motives. In October 1940, Frank Nelson, executive director of the SOE, explained to his subordinates that "the ideal is to allow the Gestapo and the de Gaulle Staff to think that we are co-operating 100% with each other—whereas in truth, whilst I should wish you to have the friendliest day to day relationship and liaison with the De Gaulle people, I should wish you at the same

time to tell them nothing of our innermost and most confidential plans."
And he added: "This co-operation however—to put it quite brutally—
must be one sided; i.e., I should wish our F Section to be fully cognisant
of everything that the de Gaulle people are doing, but I do not wish
the de Gaulle organisation to be in the least cognisant of anything that
S.O.2 are doing."[40]

These reservations, however, did not prevent the two parties from
organizing joint missions. In March 1941, a commando was dispatched
to Vannes to attack the bus carrying the crews of the German Fighting
Squadron 100. That group would take off from the Meucon military
base, spot the British objectives by night, and drop incendiary bombs,
whose glow then guided the bombers that followed. On March 15, five
Frenchmen dressed in uniform (to satisfy Portal's request) parachuted
in; but, noting that the crews were traveling in cars, not in a bus, the
members of Operation Savannah, as it was called, disbanded to collect
intelligence. On the night of May 11, 1941, a small team, composed of
three Frenchmen—Forman, Varnier, and Cabard—parachuted in to
destroy the transformer in Pessac, which was feeding electrical current
to the railway line for Bordeaux. The operation was postponed, then
completed on the night of June 7. Six out of eight transformers were
destroyed and were not repaired until early 1942, forcing the Germans
to put steam trains back in service. In addition, work at the submarine
base in Bordeaux was interrupted for several weeks. As a penalty, the
commune of Pessac had to pay a fine of a million francs. The saboteurs,
joined by Joël Le Tac, a young law student who had rallied behind Free
France in 1940, afterward left for Spain.[41]

These encouraging results led to closer cooperation between Gaullists and the British, a venture that fell to the newly created RF Section of the SOE. Placed under the management of Eric Piquet-Wicks
and supervised, then headed, by J. R. H. Hutchison and later by L. D.
Dismore, this section was supposed to rationalize subversive actions.
The Gaullists and the British would make joint plans, validated by both
parties, who would rely on preexisting groups that had been unable to
act for lack of materiel. These metropolitan cells would be assisted by
two men (including a radio operator) detached for two months, with
Passy providing the personnel. Several missions were thus dispatched,
especially to the occupied zone. The Torture Mission, defined on

June 13, 1941, had the aim of assisting the group set up by M. Frémont, a farmer from Caen. But Cartigny, one of the two men who were dropped by parachute on July 5, was arrested. He was denounced and then executed in April 1942. The other man, named Labit, managed to get to the southern zone.

All in all, that cooperation rested on "unequal foundations: not only did SOE leaders have veto power over the missions proposed by the [French intelligence service], but they alone, outside any Gaullist control, coordinated the paramilitary activities undertaken in France, some through F Section, others through RF Section. In their desire to obtain the means to act, the leaders of Free France had no other choice but to accept such conditions, which, however, would quickly become unbearable for them."[42]

## What about the French?

It did not take long before the envoys from London, pursuing military action for the most part, discovered that small resistance groups, not satisfied with forming, also wanted to act. In France, many men and women considered civilian action a stopgap measure, a substitute for armed action, which was judged impractical at the time. The underground newspaper *France Liberté* declared, for example: "90 percent of the French people are ready to march. Bring them together, give them weapons. All they ask is to serve, to obey; but may the orders be of consequence, may they have some usefulness, so that the sacrifice we are resolved to make will not be in vain."[43] Similarly, radio listeners wishing to act applied pressure on the BBC. One listener said, "Yes, tell us what can be done. On the walls, it's taken care of. Tracts, it's done. But that is not enough, we must wipe out the traitors."[44] André Weil-Curiel, a young lawyer who had been sent to metropolitan France, noted: "All the men coming to see me and all the men I met with were anxious to do something, but at the same time they seemed disoriented in the emerging world of underground war. They did not know what to do exactly and had a touching desire not to thwart London's plans in any way."[45] Henry Hauck, labor adviser to General de Gaulle, therefore suggested that Free France rely on the Socialists and on union activists. He recruited the former secretary of the Savoy Confédération

Française des Travailleurs Chrétiens (CFTC; French Confederation of Christian Workers), a survivor of the Norway Campaign named Léon Morandat (Yvon). Yvon's mission would be to establish the necessary contacts in the French metropolis with Catholic youth organizations, popular democrats, and trade unionists belonging both to the CFTC and to the redder Confédération Générale du Travail (CGT; General Labor Confederation).

But the right-wing and even antirepublican culture of some members of the Second Bureau doomed the undertaking. Rémy, for example, refused to canvass former labor leaders, whom he likened to "degenerate politicking worms, schemers, constantly tacking between the swill of their emoluments, their gratuities, and their commissions."[46] As a result, Yvon did not parachute into France until November 1941.

Colonel Passy's men, by contrast, proved to be more interested in the possibilities offered, or so they believed, by the Vichy regime. Some, like Pierre Fourcaud, a World War I officer, hoped to establish ties with the intelligence services of the French State or with resistance movements that did not reject Pétainist ideology. Far from avoiding that orientation, Passy regretted de Gaulle's intransigence. "What a unifying role we could play with the good French people of France!" he lamented.[47] On June 20, 1941, on the Bristol airfield, he welcomed Colonel Groussard, former head of the École de Saint-Cyr, who was trying to encourage resistance in the metropolis, while still holding a post in the Vichy state apparatus. Groussard proposed that a liaison be established with Free France via Alfred Heurteaux, leader of a small network in the orbit of the somewhat right-wing resistance movement the OCM. Hence, the SR "would never completely break away from the idea of making use of people of goodwill who might come forward within the Vichy government. Nevertheless, over the course of the summer, the increased repression and its extension to anti-German personalities who had been close to the power structure until that time convinced him that he ought at all costs to avoid revealing himself to men whose loyalty would always remain in doubt."[48]

Such strange bedfellows sparked the fear of Passy's assistant, André Manuel: "In official circles, in the Second Bureau, and even within the police, our agents encounter a great deal of kindness. They take advantage of that climate to conduct their actions almost out in the open.

They are known to the Vichy police, identified by the Gestapo. They all know one another and form a team, with all the advantages and disadvantages of a team: the advantages of solidarity, enthusiasm; the disadvantages of reciprocal knowledge of all activities and contacts. Their solidarity is their downfall, when the Vichy government, moving forward with collaboration, puts its police in the service of the Gestapo. That moment has arrived; their carelessness has made them conspicuous, and little by little, one after another, they are being neutralized."[49] As a result, Passy soon recommended the greatest caution vis-à-vis the special services of the French State.

Overall, Free France struggled to come up with the terms of battle in its awkward early stages. In the first place, it suggested to volunteers that they join Free France to fight in uniform out in the open. But that option was not appealing in every case. The prospects for warfare remained so uncertain that even the volunteers in England languished, weapons at their feet. For example, Daniel Cordier, who joined the FFL from the very start and would become Jean Moulin's secretary, noted: "For the first time in my life, I am occasionally close to despair. After the breach in summer 1940, I no longer understand why I joined this army, that is how ridiculous my activities have become. I left everything behind to avenge the homeland and, after a year of hope and hard labor, I end up training young recruits. Exile and inaction make for an explosive cocktail. I experience inaction as an injustice."[50] Many could not imagine being engaged anywhere but in metropolitan France, refusing to don the colors of exile. In addition, getting to London after the defeat involved an odyssey rarely crowned with success. In Var, 138 people who attempted the journey in the first half of 1941 were arrested by the police.[51] As a result, only a handful of volunteers joined the FFL in 1940.

It was also difficult for Free France to mobilize the population by integrating them within the framework of its networks. It did give precedence to the recruitment of amateurs, which could broaden its base while assembling all the volunteers who wanted to fight the occupier. But that decision was not the expression of an ideological choice. De Gaulle primarily wanted the navy to remain apart from the secret services. Its leader, Admiral Emile Muselier, was dynamic and energetic, a staunch republican, but handicapped by his sulfurous reputation as an opium addict. Furthermore, he displayed a healthy appetite for power, which de Gaulle intended to thwart by refusing to let the French navy be involved in intelligence. Overall, only a minority of French men and women joined a network. As Claude Bourdet, the future second-in-command of the Combat movement, explained in a definition that has become famous: "A *network* was an organization created in view of a precise military task, primarily intelligence, secondarily sabotage, and frequently as well the provision of avenues of escape for prisoners of war, and especially, for pilots who fell into enemy hands—'channels,' as they were called."[52] Far from engaging in proselytism, these structures recruited only the specialists they needed, whether that "specialist" was a railroad switchman able to track the movements of enemy troops or a civilian employee at the German headquarters who could recopy a map. As a result, these networks could in no case give rise to a mass movement, especially since the Second Bureau was desperately short of resources. Between summer 1941 and summer 1942, its total labor force increased from twenty-three to seventy-seven, with the number of officers growing from ten to nineteen.[53] At least at the beginning, the modesty of its forces kept it from engaging the masses in underground action—even supposing that had been its objective. The same is true for the British secret services.

Finally, radio could sometimes become an instrument for mobilization, especially if Free France was conducting a political action at the same time. Even before Jean Moulin arrived in London in October 1941, de Gaulle was considering that method. Within the Comité National Français (CNF; French National Committee), he created a Commission for the Interior, and on October 8, 1941, submitted a plan to Hugh Dalton, minister of economic warfare and, in that capacity, head of the SOE. De Gaulle wrote: "Military action proper (military intelligence and assistance, preparation of a military organization in place) is currently well under way by the Free France special services in liaison with the British special services. But there are now grounds for undertaking political action, which is and must be distinct from military action and must entail different men and different means."[54] Free France did not have altogether clear ideas on that point, however. Though de Gaulle intended to keep France in the war, he showed little concern for fashioning his battle as an ideological crusade against the

Vichy reaction or Hitler's totalitarianism. Hostile both to the Third Republic and to the political parties, he also refused to commit himself openly, professing an apoliticism that, intentionally or not, favored the unity he was hoping for. It was not until November 11, 1941, that he explicitly embraced the republican slogan "Liberty, Equality, Fraternity," a belated decision that had fueled some anxieties on the left. Similarly, hatred of the French left, harbored by some members in the Second Bureau, kept them from rapprochement with the progressive parties and trade unions. Yvon, as we have seen, had to wait until November 1941 to be parachuted into the metropolis. Finally, and perhaps above all, those in charge of the BBC, whether or not they were Gaullists, feared involving the civilian population prematurely in actions that risked ending in bloody reprisals, without assuring real military gains.

All these arguments lead us to conclude that Free France, even while embodying a political alternative, could not offer the French masses a path to engagement between 1940 and 1941. In its beginnings, therefore, the resistance was an endogenous process emanating from captive France. Civil society had to find within itself the resources necessary to conduct the fight. But were the parties and the labor unions—unlike the army and the churches—in the vanguard of the struggle against the Nazi occupier or the Vichy regime?

## Chapter 2

# Parties and Labor Unions

THE DEFEAT OF 1940 and the continuing struggle, which for a time Great Britain conducted all alone, called for a military response. And from the moment of the collapse, Free France and the networks, whose modest structures were beginning to take shape, endeavored to provide it. But the rout sometimes also gave rise to a response, political in the broad sense of the term, whose aim was to challenge the racist, freedom-killing, antirepublican policy that the Third Reich and Vichy sought to impose. A number of French citizens, in other words, refused to live under the Nazi jackboot, asserting their values against all odds. In that respect, two forces—the political parties and the labor unions—were potentially in a position to act. And yet their response, until 1941 or even 1942, remained timid at best, primarily because of the Vichy conundrum.

The French State, in fact, was confusing the issue—and would do so for a long time. In the eyes of the French people, the regime certainly enjoyed a strong legitimacy. It could invoke both the quasi-plebiscite held by parliamentarians on July 10, 1940, and the patriotic pedigree of its leader, the victor of Verdun. Joining the resistance therefore amounted to stepping outside the law, a risk that Dutch, Belgian, and Norwegian citizens did not face, since their governments had taken exile in London. In addition, Vichy seemed to be sending out signals that were, if not contradictory, then at least ambiguous. At the diplomatic level, Philippe Pétain and his minister of foreign affairs, Pierre Laval, had from the start opted for a policy of collaboration with Nazi Germany, an option solemnly confirmed after their meetings with Hitler in Montoire (October 22–24, 1940). "It is with honor, and to maintain French unity—a unity that has lasted ten centuries—within the framework of constructive activity on the part of the new European order that I engage today on the path of collaboration," the victor of Verdun declared on October 30, 1940.[1] A portion of the French people, however, denied the obvious. They believed that Vichy was playing a double game, that it secretly supported London and discreetly approved the actions of General de Gaulle.

A few indications may have shored up that belief. The dismissal of Pierre Laval on December 13, 1940, was interpreted as an act of resistance against Germany. The continuing presence, until November 1941, of General Weygand, delegate general to French Africa, was also considered a gauge of resoluteness, since the former generalissimo claimed he was doing no more than conforming to the armistice conventions (even as he calmly applied Vichy legislation in the empire). In short, good-hearted souls, by overinterpreting very tenuous signs, could reach the conclusion that Pétain, while protecting the French from the rigors of the occupation, was preparing the Revanche (revenge to recover lost territory, as when France wrested back Alsace-Lorraine from Germany after World War I). That was a complete illusion, but it did not dissipate until November 1942. In greeting the Anglo-American landing in North Africa with cannon fire, the Vichyists confirmed that the neutrality they were applying was asymmetrical at best, since it favored the Germans' schemes. Furthermore, the Reich's invasion of the free zone on November 11, 1942, reduced to nothing the French sovereignty that Vichy had prided itself on defending. But in 1940–1941, the chimera of the double game remained a force to be reckoned with, and confusion reigned in many minds.

On the domestic front, the French State set out to exclude from society the elements that were supposedly undermining it: Jews, Freemasons, *métèques* (a derogative term for foreigners), and Communists. At the same time, it conducted an antirepublican policy, locking up the major leaders of the fallen regime, and transferring or dismissing loyalist public servants—beginning with Prefect Jean Moulin. Promising to restore the state's authority, to reestablish the natural communities constituted by the family, the trades, and the provinces, Vichy advocated a corporatist order, as outlined in the Charte du Travail (Work Charter), promulgated in October 1941. Such authoritarian and reactionary measures disgusted the men and women who identified France as the country of human rights. These policies therefore provided a powerful basis for opposition. Nevertheless, they satisfied a fringe of the general population and of the elites that had long militated for change. The dysfunction of the Third Republic, which had exasperated a portion of society, led a fraction of the political body to demand a reformation of the state, which, delay after delay, had gotten lost in the desert before 1940. Furthermore, the economic crisis of the 1930s had exacerbated xenophobia and anti-Semitism: at the time, some parties and a few leagues were calling for the establishment of professional quotas and the expulsion of undesirable aliens. Many also worried about depopulation and strongly favored celebrating and protecting the family. Finally, the Front Populaire (FP; Popular Front), by revealing the intensity of the class struggle, had fueled a violent anticommunism, prompting a few peace seekers to look for a third way, between the hammer of socialism and the anvil of capitalism. In short, Philippe Pétain's domestic program responded to a political and social demand, which explains in part the plebiscite vote of July 10, 1940.

To be sure, the vote by deputies and senators in the hall of the Grand Casino, which granted the Marshal full powers and gave him the task of revising the constitution, was in large measure the result of panic. Stunned by the defeat, the parliamentarians put all their faith in the man of the hour, whose past—thanks to the memory of Verdun— seemed to offer every patriotic guarantee. It would be wrong, however, to remain satisfied with that misleading appearance. Indeed, the vote of July 10, 1940, was also, and perhaps especially, an expression of support. Pierre Laval, working furiously behind the scenes on behalf of the Marshal, hardly concealed his underlying intentions. "Parliamentary democracy has lost the war; it must disappear and give way to an authoritarian, hierarchical, national, and social regime," he declared on July 6, 1940.[2] A few days later, responding to a question from Pierre Masse, senator from Hérault, he explained: "If you mean by individual liberty the right for all wops [métèques] and foreigners . . . [strong applause], I will explain, for example, that no one may be a deputy if he has not been French for several generations. That is our way . . . of conducting racial policy."[3] Far from being fooled by the Marshal's stars and the warped eloquence of Laval, a number of elected officials—on both the right and the left—truly subscribed to all or part of Vichy's domestic program. That explains the broad consent granted on July 10. The plan for constitutional revision was approved by 570 parliamentarians; 80 voted no, 20 abstained, and 27 legislators embarked on the cruise ship *Massilia*, to continue the struggle in North Africa.

All in all, the presence of the Vichy regime obscured the situation rather than clarifying it. In suggesting to the credulous that it was secretly supporting the Allies and even General de Gaulle, the French State dissuaded potential resisters from taking action, since they did not wish to impede Pétain's secret policy by infelicitous initiatives. Why deny it? That belief also offered a convenient alibi for a watch-and-wait attitude. Pétain, in presenting himself as the architect of a new order, forced the supporters of reactionary national reform into a no-win situation. Should recovery be preferred to the fight against the occupier? Or should the battle against the Germans be given precedence over National Revolution, the new order Vichy planned to enforce? A number of French people did not find that choice obvious. For a time, the personalist philosopher Emmanuel Mounier opted for reform. Conversely, Henri Frenay, the founder of Combat, never compromised his priorities, despite the empathy he felt for the Marshal and for many aspects of his domestic program. Vichy, arising from the defeat but not imposed by the occupier, truly represented a special case in occupied Europe. That also explains the singularity of the resistance, which had to manage the fight against the occupier while at the same time positioning itself in relation to an authoritarian regime. At least in the beginning, the Vichy regime was bathed in an aura that the Norwegian Vidkun Quisling, to cite only one example, would never enjoy. As a result, the French political parties faced a situation that was complex to say the least.

Could—and should—the political parties become the soul of the resistance? Nothing predestined them to fulfill that role. From a functional standpoint, their mission was to organize political debate and participate in electoral races, not take part in a subversive struggle. From a cultural standpoint, the parties, with the exception of the Communists, were particularly ill-equipped to respond to the exigencies of the resistance. The army of shadows preferred the darkness of the underground to the limelight. It required anonymity, not the personalization that ideological battles entail. It was predicated on contempt for, even transgression of, the rules; and in general, militants respect the rules, while parliamentarians make them. In addition, the Vichy regime was quick to place leaders, major and minor, under police surveillance, which kept their freedom of action in check.

The political parties did have a good deal going for them, however. Although their leaders might not have been able to sound the battle cry, they could at least have contested the orientation of the Pétainist regime. They were often well known, sometimes respected, and had been anointed by universal suffrage, which conferred a legitimacy on them that many of the Vichy leaders lacked. They also had at their disposal devoted and selfless militants capable of converting their political know-how into resistance. Granted, not all the organizations had such a pool of militants available; but on the left, the PCF and the Section Française de l'Internationale Ouvrière (SFIO; French Branch of the Workers' International), as well as the right-wing Parti Social Français (PSF; French Social Party), and even Action Française, might for various reasons have been able to brandish the standard of revolt in 1940. Yet such was not the case.

## The Vagaries of the French Communist Party

Until August 1939, the PCF defended a patriotic and prowar position, advocating a policy of standing firm against Nazi Germany. That radical stand coincided with the anti-Fascist line adopted in 1934 which, popular in progressive circles, also served the well-understood interests of the Soviet Union, henceforth aware of the threat of Hitler. As a result, the signing of the German-Soviet Pact on August 23, 1939, was met with disbelief. Apart from the fact that French leaders had not been in on the secret, Stalin's opportunistic about-face placed the PCF in an awkward position, in relation to both a patriotic base disgusted with Nazism and to other political groups, which as a general rule approved of the struggle against the Third Reich. The French authorities reacted with resolve. Not only did they ban the party, as well as the organizations linked to the Comintern, on September 26, 1939, they also hunted down the most prominent militants. Then, on January 20, 1940, they stripped the Communist deputies of their powers. In all, during the first three months of 1940, the government dismissed 2,718 elected representatives, arrested 3,400 militants, and pronounced 1,500 sentences.[4]

The Stalinist leadership believed that the war was being waged between the rival imperialists in Paris, London, and Berlin, and that the
French proletariat need not concern itself with the conflict, except to
oppose it. That belief sowed discord within the party. The exodus of
thousands of militants and elected officials drained the PCF of its
core; and twenty-six deputies, including Marcel Gitton and Jean-Marie
Clamamus, refused to follow the new line. Only a few small groups
remained, in the Paris region and in Nord-Pas-de-Calais. But the
party apparatus resisted. Of the fifty-five members constituting the
Central Committee, fifty-one remained loyal to Stalin. Deputies Jacques
Duclos and Arthur Ramette fled to Belgium on October 2, 1939.
The secretary-general, Maurice Thorez, facing military mobilization,
deserted on the evening of October 1939, heading to Brussels and then
Moscow.[5]

The defeat of June 1940 strengthened the analysis Stalin was giving
of the conflict, which he still considered an imperialist war. But the
leaders of the PCF, convinced that the situation served their interests,
endeavored to instrumentalize the good relations between Berlin and
Moscow. Between June 18 and August 22, 1940, emissaries dispatched
by Jacques Duclos, the No. 2 man in the PCF, negotiated with Otto
Abetz, ambassador of the Reich in Paris, for official authorization to
resume publication of their daily newspaper, *L'Humanité*. In addition,
militants were encouraged to act openly to retake possession of mayoralties and union offices. That legalist approach turned on "a coherent
and classic theoretical model: the imperialist war is rich with revolutionary potentialities, raising, through the void it produces, the question of power and thus the crucial question of a party that can offer
revolutionary hope."[6] This suicidal tactic allowed the French police to
make many more arrests. Between October 1940 and April 1941, the
prefect of Var signed 112 internment orders in his department.[7]

What is known as the Appeal of July 10, 1940, sums up and illustrates that wavering. It was more likely drafted on about July 15 and
distributed at the end of the same month. The appeal denounced the
bankruptcy of the bourgeoisie, proposed the formation of a government
of the people, and called for peace, while adding that "France, still covered in blood, wants to live free and independent. . . . Never will a great
people like our own be a slave people." Calling for the constitution of

a "front of freedom, independence, and the rebirth of France"[8] around the PCF, it in no way constituted an appeal for resistance, despite what Communist leaders later claimed.

The PCF, in fact, was still beholden in its analysis to the Bolshevik precedent of 1917. Following Lenin's example, the party sought to reach a compromise with the imperialist victor and recommended, via the underground *L'Humanité*, fraternizing with German workers in military uniform. It avoided frontal attacks on the occupier, even while sprinkling its statements with patriotic accents, and it relentlessly assailed the Pétainist regime. "The people as a whole, workers and peasants, manual laborers and intellectual laborers, young and old, are subject to the dual oppression of the [Vichy] reactionaries and of the foreign occupation. And it is against the reactionary forces that the people must first strike their blows. It is against Pétain, Laval, and company, the ones primarily responsible for the defeat, the agents of capital and the zealous servants of the foreign authorities, that the people's wrath must be unleashed in all its force and in all its violence," declared Maurice Thorez in September 1940.[9] The PCF, finally, displayed no sympathy for the Gaullist movement. "If Germany's occupation of France is sufficient to prove that Mr. Hitler's 'new European order' would mean a scandalous servitude for France, it is no less certain that de Gaulle and Larminat's movement, fundamentally reactionary and antidemocratic, also has no other aim but to deprive our country of all freedom, in the event of an English victory," wrote Thorez and Duclos in March 1941.[10]

Until spring 1941, the PCF, interpreting the new rules of the game in terms of the class struggle, thus gave precedence to the fight against the Vichy regime over the war against the occupier. As Daniel Virieux notes, "What places the nation in danger, through war, defeat, and occupation, is the 'capitalist regime, generator of poverty and war,' of which Vichy, a 'government of plutocrats and war profiteers,' is the principal guarantee."[11] The PCF, even while applying that line, made every effort to reconstitute an apparatus disrupted by mobilization, defeat, and repression, relying on a new underground leadership assigned to two trusted men: Jacques Duclos and Benoît Frachon, a union activist, who were later joined by Deputy Charles Tillon, future leader of the Francs-Tireurs et Partisans (FTP; Free Fighters and Partisans). At the time, liaison officers and radio transmitters, carefully controlled by

Duclos, ensured communications with Eugen Fried, representative of the Workers' International in Brussels, and Georgi Dimitrov, the Comintern boss in Moscow. The PCF, moreover, organized the fight on the labor union battlefield. It developed People's Committees charged with speaking out in protest, by demanding raises, for example, which caused headaches for the Vichy regime. This also allowed the party to combine the legal and the illegal work of the militants, while at the same time mobilizing them. "The organization of action for the immediate redress of the grievances of the masses rallies them around us and pits them against the bourgeoisie. The labor protest struggle does not impede the political struggle, *it is indispensable to it*, even more in the present situation than in calmer periods. . . . No Communist, no Party organization can fail to take an interest in the labor struggle and, as a result, in the work of the unions," noted Benoît Frachon in early 1941.[12]

The strategy was sometimes crowned with success. On February 5, 1941, the Comité Populaire des Établissements Aéronautiques Gnome-et-Rhône (People's Committee for the Aeronautic Plant of Gnome-et-Rhône) in Gennevilliers obtained a travel allowance of two francs a day, payment for the eighty-hour withdrawal at the June 1940 rate, a bonus of seven hundred francs for young people who earned the Certificat d'Aptitude Professionelle (the secondary school vocational training certificate), the opening of a vocational school, the reopening and heating of the refectory, the opening of a resupply cooperative under worker control, and finally, the provision of hand soap.[13] Along the same lines, the PCF encouraged the housewives' demonstrations that began in winter 1940–1941. About forty of these had occurred by May 1941, all in the occupied zone.[14] That form of opposition "makes it possible to mobilize milieus that exert a clear influence on public opinion, even though they are not very politicized, and which it would be unpopular and difficult to repress, given their sex and the nature of their demands. At the same time, it allows us to keep in the shadows the militant workers called upon by the Communists for tasks requiring secrecy."[15] Communists, finally, did not hesitate to protest openly against the Vichy regime. On November 5, 1940, they staged their own celebration of sorts upon the Marshal's arrival in Toulouse, disseminating issues of *L'Humanité* and *L'Avant-Garde*, thanks to "an ingenious system set up with a rat trap."[16]

All things considered, it is difficult to believe that, by 1940, the PCF had rallied behind resolute resistance to the occupier, whatever it may have claimed after the war. Above all, its strategy adapted to the vacillations of Soviet diplomacy, from which it hardly differentiated itself. In fact, the line it followed between August 1939 and June 1941 would become a Shirt of Nessus for the Communist leaders. After liberation, political adversaries rarely missed the opportunity to remind the "party of the seventy-five thousand executed," as the PCF called itself with some exaggeration, of the German-Soviet Pact and of the party's request to resume official publication of *L'Humanité*. They did not forget that, in a letter addressed to Marshal Pétain on December 19, 1940, five Communist deputies, François Billoux in the lead, had asked for the right to testify against Léon Blum and Édouard Daladier at the Supreme Court of Riom, the tribunal that was to try those supposedly responsible for the defeat.

That said, the party line was by no means unanimously accepted. Faithful to the anti-Fascist postulates of the prewar period, part of the base balked, especially since it shared a robust Germanophobia stemming from the memory of World War I. For example, Communist students participated in the demonstration of November 11, 1940, on the Champs-Elysées, to honor the memory of the victors of 1918. But the PCF and its satellite organizations hardly played a determining role in the organization of the rally. Although about fifty Communist students had gathered on November 8 to protest the arrest of Paul Langevin, a professor at the Collège de France closely associated with the Communists, the idea of demonstrating on Place de l'Étoile actually arose well before that episode.[17] Most of the three thousand-odd participants—a low estimate—who gathered at the Étoile or on the Champs-Elysées were not responding to any order. On the contrary, police reports and statements by the participants insist on the spontaneous character of that display,[18] which ended in the arrest of a good hundred high school and college students. Furthermore, the Communist groups, far from claiming responsibility for that exploit, distanced themselves from it. In December 1940, a long tract, signed by the branches of the PCF and of Jeunesses Communistes (JC; Communist Youth) from the Paris region, hailed the audacity of the students, even while urging them not to be misled: "To assure the independence of France, one must allow this country to be liberated from the subjection of British imperialism. . . . *It is not through war that France will once again become free and indepen-dent, IT IS THROUGH THE SOCIALIST REVOLUTION.*"[19]

The PCF apparatus thus imperfectly expressed the expectations of the base. One fringe of that base, as of 1940, sought to attest to its opposition both to the occupation and to Nazism. Some of the cadres as well did not toe the party line. At the time, the visceral anti-Fascists—intellectuals, Jews, veterans of the Spanish Civil War—used *Les Cahiers du Bolchevisme* to denounce Nazism, a term little used during that period in the Communist underground press. Finally, some high- and mid-level leaders launched calls to fight in 1940. Auguste Havez did so in Nantes in July, as did Charles Tillon in Bordeaux. On the night of June 17, Tillon declared in a tract that "the French people do not want slavery, poverty, or fascism, any more than they wanted the capitalists' war. They have the numbers. United, they will have the strength." In addition, the text called for the constitution of a government "fighting against Hitlerian Fascism and the two hundred families [that is, the largest stockholders of the Banque de France, who supposedly con-trolled the French economy], reaching an understanding with the USSR for an equitable peace, fighting for national independence, and taking measures against the fascist organizations."[20]

Should the claim be made, then, that two lines coexisted within the PCF? That would be a bit hasty. Granted, the tract written by Tillon made Nazi Germany, and not the French State, the principal adversary. In other respects, however, it hardly distanced itself from orthodoxy: it called for the formation of a popular government, suggested reaching an understanding with the Soviet Union—an ally of the Reich at the time—to obtain peace, and breathed not a word about Great Britain. Furthermore, the future leader of the FTP was judged sufficiently loyal to be part of the underground leadership of the PCF, a sign that he was not perceived as a danger or a deviant. His self-criticism, written on October 19, 1952, confirmed a posteriori that the man had remained a "disciplined militant, a dyed-in-the-wool Stalinist, who completely satis-fies his chain of command."[21] "I believe I proved by my attitude and by all my acts that I understood and approved from the first moment, and without any hesitation or reservation, the signing of the German-Soviet Pact, an attitude by which it was possible to judge the Communists in

1939. How could I call into question my own attitude in the course of the events of the war?" he declared at the time.[22]

It is also known that Georges Guingouin launched a call to fight in August 1940. The schoolmaster from Saint-Gilles-les-Forêts, dismissed from his post in October, even broke off his marriage engagement to assume sole responsibility for his actions. He went underground in February 1941 and subsequently played a preeminent role in organizing the Limousin resistance.[23] Guingouin seems to have distanced himself in two respects from the strategy advocated by the PCF leadership. In *Le Travailleur Limousin*, judging that "the liberation of France could come about only through the unity of all the forces that 'resist' the authority of Vichy,"[24] he refrained from criticizing de Gaulle and Britain. Likewise, he disapproved of the return to legality recommended by the senior members of the party. But for a long time, he still enjoyed the trust of his superiors. The rift came as a result of a sanction imposed in 1942, which the interregional supervisor of cadres retrospectively deemed "undeserved, never explained. . . . Indeed, my considered opinion at present [1944] allows me to say with assurance that he is not an enemy of the Party (among other things, he too honorably navigated the difficult waters of the German-Soviet Pact), but an enfant terrible of the Party, and that he is absolutely in agreement with the fundamental principles of the Party's general political line."[25] Conversely, it is certain that, in the summer of 1940, Auguste Havez harshly criticized the orders from the leadership. That alarmed Maurice Tréand, who was in charge of the cadres. He saw to it that Havez was immediately flanked by two assistants, as a means to better control him. In any event, "tracts with a clearly anti-Hitler tone were the result of individual and, with a few exceptions, temporary initiatives: once contact was reestablished with Paris, the central line would be adopted once more."[26]

In short, it would be wrong to say that the PCF apparatus adhered to two different lines. Following a well-proven tradition, the leadership faithfully followed the instructions of the Comintern. Cut off from their chain of command and deprived of information, some cadres, left to their own devices, may have interpreted the party line without always finding the right position, which explains the distortions observed here and there. By contrast, a number of militants, uncomfortable with a position that disowned the anti-Fascist battles of the interwar period, did not hesitate to participate in anti-German demonstrations. Far from responding to orders from the leadership, these militants were acting on their own.

It did not take long, however, for the situation to change, as a result of the deterioration in German-Soviet relations. On September 27, 1940, Germany, Italy, and Japan concluded the Tripartite Pact, joined in November by Romania, which immediately afterward subscribed to the anti-Comintern pact. Stalin, jealous of the Reich's influence in the Balkans, could not accept the extension of Hitler's grip to a region deemed vital to Soviet interests. For the Germans, the trip to Berlin in November 1940 by Viacheslav Molotov, Soviet minister of foreign affairs, confirmed that intransigence. But the Reich took no account of it.[27] Bulgaria joined the Tripartite Pact on March 1, 1941, and the Wehrmacht invaded Yugoslavia, then Greece, in April 1941, intensifying the fears of the Soviet Union.

In early 1941, the Communist press, until then displaying the utmost discretion, accompanied its attacks against Vichy with cutting remarks about Nazi Germany, though it confined itself to making "empty promises rather than concrete decisions to do battle."[28] The Comintern, going even further, enjoined the PCF on April 26, 1941, to form a "broad national front to fight for independence," specifying that "the essential task at present is the fight for national liberation. The fight for peace is subordinate to the fight for national independence. A peace without national liberation would mean the enslavement of the people in France. At the present moment, that fight must have the primary aim of not allowing the people, the territory, and the resources of France to be used in the war between Germany and England."[29] In mid-May, the underground leadership repeated the appeal, urging the creation of a Front National de l'Indépendance de la France (FN; National Front for the Independence of France). This was a fundamental shift: "In May 1941, the national problem was this time connected entirely to the war, imperialist to be sure, but a war whose only explored side was that of Nazi Germany."[30] The PCF, in other words, said it was now ready to fight the occupier—on the condition, however, that it play the leading role.

To conduct its mission of liberation, the FN declared it would "be constituted by the working class of France as its fundamental force, with the Communist Party at its head," ruling out any recognition of

General de Gaulle's authority. "Some French people, suffering to see our country oppressed by the invader, wrongly place their hopes in de Gaulle's movement. To these compatriots, we say that the unification of the French nation behind national liberation cannot be realized behind a movement—REACTIONARY AND COLONIALIST in its inspiration—such as British imperialism." These attacks would continue until June 1941.[31]

A shift is not a break, however, and the PCF continued to give precedence to the unionist fight over armed combat until the start of Operation Barbarossa on June 22, 1941. It strove, for example, to celebrate May Day 1941 in a fitting manner, hanging streams of red flags along the electrical wires of the coal field in Nord-Pas-de-Calais and openly distributing tracts by the thousands. Above all, it encouraged labor protests, the miners' strike being both their apogee and their symbol.

On May 27, 1941, a strike, organized in great part by Auguste Lecoeur, regional secretary of the PCF in Pas-de-Calais (by way of the International Brigades), began at coal mine 7 in Dourges, known as the Dahomey mine. Focusing on material demands—the improvement of resupply practices, the provision of soap, an end to bullying—it rapidly spread to the other sectors, prompting the German forces to patrol the coal field and to make multiple arrests. These measures were initially to no avail: on the morning of June 3, 80 percent of the miners, which is to say nearly one hundred thousand pitmen, stopped working. Women actively participated in the fight, especially by picketing. In response to that mass movement, the Germans intensified the repression, arresting miners at random to spread terror, closing the entertainment spots, and holding up the payment of wages. In the face of these sanctions, the miners resumed their protest on June 7, and by June 10 it had become an all-out strike. All told, the fight would last ten days, benefiting from the support of the Gaullist and socialist elements, "whose patriotism the Communists knew how to rouse."[32] Above all, the strike sparked "a chemical reaction. It linked in a single battle the class struggle and national aspirations, two sentiments that had previously run parallel or even neutralized each other." In demonstrating the collusion of the mining companies with the occupier, moreover, the movement "gave a revolutionary content to revitalized patriotic hopes: national liberation and social liberation became one and the same cause."[33] The hopes raised ought not to overshadow the heavy toll: 450 people were arrested, and 244 would later be deported. In addition, those who suffered in the Nazi camps, or their next of kin, would have to wait until 1962 for the acknowledgment that these were "resistance deportees." Until then, the Ministry of Veteran Affairs maintained that the coal miners had conducted an exclusively corporatist battle.[34]

The PCF, then, far from immediately rallying behind the resistance against the occupier, granted priority to the struggle against Vichy, accompanied by a shift in focus to unionist action. Although at first the PC went easy on the occupier, as the German-Soviet Pact required, it multiplied its attacks in early 1941, then called for the constitution of the FN in May. But it did not throw itself into the armed struggle until after June 22, 1941, the day Hitler sent his panzers to attack Russia.

## The Disarray in French Socialism

The Socialist Party, known as the SFIO, also faced the storm in disarray. Deep divisions had undermined the party during the interwar period. The pacifists behind Paul Faure supported a policy of appeasement toward Nazi Germany, a policy challenged by the advocates of standing firm, who had rallied behind Léon Blum. In addition, relations with the PCF sowed confusion. One side, embracing the FP's line, defended the alliance with the party, while the other side rejected it outright. Blum himself did not enjoy unanimous approval. Although some leaders displayed an attachment to him close to devotion, others hated him, finding fault with his bourgeois lifestyle and sometimes accompanying their criticism with anti-Semitic comments.

The vote of July 10, 1940, revealed publicly the magnitude of the fault lines. Although thirty-six Socialist parliamentarians rejected granting Marshal Pétain full powers, ninety voted for them. Not satisfied with bringing to power a man diametrically opposed to their convictions, a few elected officials also agreed to retain their mayoralties, sometimes out of pure opportunism, sometimes at the request of their comrades. Louis Fieu, a deputy and the mayor of Carmaux (the city of Jean Jaurès), withdrew his resignation in January 1942. The miners' union had asked him to stay in office, "so as not to let a workers' victory over the Legion slip away."[35] Going even further, some Socialist higher-ups participated in the institutions created by the Vichy regime. Nine Socialists agreed to sit on the Conseil National (National Council), the rump parliament invented by Pierre-Étienne Flandin in 1941, even though some, such as Isidore Thivrier, mayor of Commentry, had voted no on July 10. A few leaders, finally, went so far as to rally behind collaboration: for example, Charles Spinasse, Socialist deputy of Corrèze and minister of the economy under the FP. He hoped to "lay the foundations for a new order, in which the ideal of French Socialists, which remains alive in us, will inspire a society which is truly free, because it will be based on the solidarity of interests."[36] A few periodicals played a leading role in the Socialist press of collaboration: *L'Effort*, *Le Mot d'Ordre*, and *Le Rouge et Le Bleu*, headed by Spinasse.

These aberrations, however, are only the trees hiding the forest. As a general rule, fierce repression targeted members of the SFIO. Often dismissed from their mayoralties (Léon Betoulle in Limoges, for example), Socialist elected officials were placed under house arrest (Louis Noguères), locked up without benefit of trial (Léon Blum and Vincent Auriol), and even assassinated (the former minister Marx Dormoy and François Camel, the Socialist deputy from Ariège). Nevertheless, the great heterogeneity of the paths taken by the French Socialists reflected the doctrinal and moral confusion assailing the *vieille maison*, to borrow Blum's famous expression. Undermined by the divisions inherited from the prewar period, the SFIO, for lack of reliable guidelines, had trouble adopting a clear ideological position and establishing a doctrine of action. As Marc Sadoun, observes, "In attempting to apply the classic interpretive schemes—historical materialism or pacifism—to the situation created by the occupation of France, militants ran the risk of misunderstanding a phenomenon that called less for analysis than for will, less for knowledge than for volition."[37] Finally, and perhaps especially, the SFIO had acclimatized itself to the republic, accepting the rules of the electoral game and enjoying the benefits of a network of notables. That democratic culture hardly prepared the party to abide by the laws of the underground. Sadoun again: "Because parliamentary democracy did not totally condition the party's existence, the party could withstand a shift in the institutional context; but because that autonomy was only partial, its ability to adapt was necessarily limited."[38] All in all, therefore, the advent of the resistance was a particularly difficult transition to negotiate, though here it is necessary to distinguish between the individual and the collective.

At the beginning of the occupation, French Socialism made two choices: it decided to reconstitute an underground party, but it refused to create a resistance group proper. At the initiative of Amédée Dunois, a contributor to *Le Populaire*, and of Élie Bloncourt, the deputy from Aisne (and a blind war veteran), a few Socialist leaders had assembled militants in the occupied zone in July 1940. In December, the arrival of Henri Ribière, former associate of Marx Dormoy, made it possible to move forward, but the reconstituted party remained at the embryonic stage for a long time: of the ten regions initially anticipated, only three maintained relations with the leadership in late 1942.

In the south, the (re-)creation of the underground SFIO took the form of the Comité d'Action Socialiste (CAS; Socialist Action Committee), founded on March 30, 1941, as a result of Daniel Mayer's patient efforts. A journalist at *Le Populaire*, Mayer had distinguished himself before the war doing battle against the neo-Socialists and opposing the Munich Accords, while declaring an almost religious admiration for Léon Blum. At an assembly convened in Toulouse on June 21, 1941—and with the support of his wife, Cletta—he succeeded in structuring an underground organization, serving as its secretary-general and naming the regional leaders for the free zone. Although he also stood up to the occupier and the Pétainist regime, Mayer set out first and foremost to resuscitate a political group discredited by the aberrations of the prewar period, traumatized by the defeat, and attacked by the French State. At first, he did not seek to recruit widely, preferring to select loyal cadres.[39] One sign of that aim: at a meeting in Lyon in May 1941, the parliamentarians who had granted full powers to Pétain were expelled. Mayer's underground daily, *Le Populaire*, would note in June 1942: "The CAS—as it stands before you—is not the party of the past. Some of its militants betrayed it. . . . It has deliberately and definitively broken away from those members whose moral or physical courage was weaker than their instinct for immediate self-preservation. It has deliberately and definitively broken away from those of its elected officials who did not display their attachment to the Republic by rising up against the attempts at Caesarism, and who preferred to make a pact with the temporary victor rather than continue the fight."[40]

Nevertheless, the reconstruction of the party was not a matter of course. In the first place, a portion of public opinion objected to political parties in general and to the SFIO in particular. Very often, the FP was deemed responsible for the defeat, which the passage of the forty-hour work week and paid holidays had supposedly made all the more ineluctable, given that some of the supporters of that legislation professed a staunch pacifism. Furthermore, the reconstitution of a political organization did not seem terribly urgent. Many, following Gilbert Renault, known as Rémy, believed the initiative misplaced at a time when the fight against Nazi Germany ought to prevail above all else. "We are already in the process, in this salon, of reconstructing France in the socialist mode. Not being an expert, I shall keep quiet, wondering privately what I have come to do in this assembly, which reminds me quite a bit of an elections committee I happened to wander into before the war, only to immediately run off," Rémy noted in January 1942.[41] The instructions from the CAS could in fact seem surreal: "Start thinking right now about what you will ask of our future Constituent Assembly, the one we will all elect, both men and women, as soon as we can—what, for our part, we intend to propose to it," suggested one of its tracts in May 1941.[42] Such a preoccupation may have seemed premature at the very least. Finally, certain federations loyal to Paul Faure refused to cooperate with the underground party for the duration of the war.

Above all, the underground SFIO did not seek to create its own resistance organization. "We decided not to divide the resistance by creating military organizations," Daniel Mayer explained, looking back. "The ideological foundation of that attitude was confirmed by Léon Blum in a letter he sent to General de Gaulle in 1943, in which he explains that the Socialists intentionally refrained from creating their own military structures. From my present vantage point, I may regret that we were thus not placed at the same level as those who, possessing an armed organization, benefited from the distributions of weapons. In terms of party pride and self-regard, I may also regret that we were not placed at the same level as the organizations possessing military structures." "And yet," he concludes, "in terms of effectiveness, I do not regret refusing to introduce division into the armed resistance."[43] The SFIO would pay a high price for that refusal. "The Socialist current, which sustained the Resistance as a whole, is credited less with aid to the Resistance than with the negative attributes of passivity (if not collaboration), a watch-and-wait attitude, and opportunism, as if it had been motivated only by a concern for the places to be taken upon Liberation," concludes the historian Jean-Marie Guillon.[44]

A few glimmers, however, brighten that rather dark portrait. In the first place, some elected officials tried to rally the troops. In July 1940, Jean Texcier, Socialist militant and journalist, composed thirty-three "guidelines for the occupied," among which were:

2. They are victors. Be courteous with them. But do not anticipate their desires in order to be well regarded. There's no rush. Besides, they would not be grateful . . .

7. Although they think it clever to instill defeatism in the hearts of city-dwellers by providing concerts on our public squares, you are not obliged to attend. Stay home, or go to the country and listen to the birds sing.

8. Ever since you've been "occupied," they parade in your dishonor. Will you stay to watch? Turn your attention rather to the display windows. That's much more moving, since, at the rate they're filling their trucks, you will soon find nothing more to buy . . .

14. Reading newspapers in our country has never been recommended to those who want to learn to express themselves in proper French. Now it's even worse: the Paris dailies are no longer even thought in French.[45]

In September 1940, Jean-Baptiste Lebas, mayor of Roubaix, having just returned from the exodus, began to hold quasi-public meetings that attracted as many as three hundred people. The following month, he produced an underground newspaper, *L'Homme Libre*, which was quickly distributed as far away as Lille and Douai. Above all, Socialists acted outside the framework of their party. A number of militants quickly became involved in political or military resistance. The union activist Christian Pineau founded the Libération-nord movement. Deputy Max Hymans, until his arrest on October 4, 1941, helped SOE agents establish their network. Pierre Bloch accepted delivery of one of the first parachute drops to France on October 10, 1941. And Pierre Brossolette participated in the nascent Musée de l'Homme network. Socialists thus engaged in active resistance from 1940 on; but because they were scattered, the SFIO could not capitalize on the political benefits, during or after the war. By contrast, the ideological base of French socialism—secularism, humanism, social justice, democracy— offered a rallying point for the opponents of the Vichy regime, once the ambiguities of 1940 had dissipated.

## A Divided French Trade Unionism

French trade unionism, traditionally divided between a Christian wing, the CFTC, and a secular movement, the CGT, had long absorbed the shocks of the interwar period. Within the CGT, a violent struggle had pitted the reformists, led by Léon Jouhaux, against the Communist minority, headed by Benoît Frachon, who in 1922 had decided to set out on his own, creating the Confédération Générale du Travail Unitaire (CGTU; Unitary General Labor Confederation). The FP, however, had masked these differences, with the "enemy brothers" opting for reunification at the congress of Toulouse in 1936. The German-Soviet Pact shattered that rapprochement. On September 18, 1939, the Bureau Confédéral expelled militants who refused to condemn the Molotov-Ribbentrop Pact, which gave rise to an inextinguishable hatred between the two camps. The outbreak of the war, the defeat, then the policies of the French State exacerbated these tensions. The Vichy government claimed to be conducting a corporatist social policy, rejecting both the fateful class struggle and the cold egotism of capitalism. In that spirit, the French State promulgated the Charte du Travail in October 1941, which was supposed to refashion social relations by favoring collaboration between labor and management. A few trade unionists, including some prominent ones, believed in these chimeras. Anticommunism, pacifism, and the desire to move past Marxism joined forces at the time, inciting some to support the Marshal's projects. So it was that René Belin, formerly the protégé of Léon Jouhaux and assistant secretary-general of the CGT, agreed to head the Ministry of Labor, a post he held from July 14, 1940, to April 18, 1942.

That strategy, however, did not come close to garnering unanimous support. In the first place, Vichy's ideology could only disgust trade unionists committed to humanist and republican ideals. Its social policy turned out to be just as disturbing, inasmuch as it rolled back major unionist gains. Vichy banned strikes, then, on November 9, 1940, proceeded to dissolve the labor and management confederations. The Charte du Travail instituted a single and mandatory form of trade unionism, thereby upsetting unionists, who embraced both pluralism and freedom.

These threats prompted the qualified representatives of wage labor to raise a solemn protest. On November 15, 1940, twelve union activists published a manifesto that, apart from a few pro forma concessions to the Pétainist authority, unambiguously invoked essential principles. Trade unionism "must affirm respect for the human person apart from any considerations of race, religion, or opinion. It must be free, both in the exercise of its collective activity and in the exercise of the individual freedom of each of its members. . . . In particular, French trade unionism cannot tolerate anti-Semitism, religious persecutions, [prosecution for] thought crimes, the privileges of money. . . . Trade union freedom must include the right . . . to join a union organization of [one's] choosing or to join no organization."[46]

In reaffirming the cardinal principles of trade unionism, the manifesto constituted an act of opposition to the Vichy regime. Signed by nine non-Communist representatives of the CGT[47] and by three in the CFTC,[48] it also symbolized an understanding between the two movements, which, having been on opposite sides in the recent past, now accepted the necessary compromises. The representatives of the CGT agreed to trade union pluralism, dear to the heart of the CFTC; and the Christian trade unionists agreed in return to the term "anticapitalist," which was "unusual for them."[49] The text was sent to the secretaries of the federations and departmental associations as well as to a few prominent personalities.[50] Immediately thereafter, a Comité d'Études Économiques et Syndicales (CEES; Committee for Economic and Unionist Studies), comprising representatives of the CGT and the CFTC, was created to discuss texts and then disseminate them.

A division of labor thus seemed to be taking shape. In its organization, oppositional trade unionism did not intend to do battle against the German occupier, a mission that in its view was the responsibility of the resistance movements. It therefore gave precedence to the fight against the French State, which corresponded to the strategy that Léon Jouhaux had decided on in Sète on August 26, 1940. The secretary-general of the CGT declared at the time that opposition to the Vichy regime had to restrict itself to trade unionism, which did not rule out the practice of infiltrating official organizations. That approach would make it possible both to defend unionist positions and to shield underground activities behind a legal façade.[51] A few contacts were also established with the Socialists. At the same time, many CGT members were activists in the ranks of the underground SFIO.

Christian groups shared that point of view. On July 8, 1940, Jules Zirnheld, president of the CFTC, called on Marshal Pétain to ensure that the future constitution recognize "trade union freedom at every level" and preserve "all the social legislation that did the Third Republic proud."[52] At the same time, Gaston Tessier, secretary-general of the same union, formed a "liaison committee for Christian organizations," linking trade unionists in the free and occupied zones. In conjunction with Christian Pineau's friends, both men signed the manifesto. Granted, the CFTC did not officially oppose the Charte du Travail, preferring to allow members and professional groups to decide for themselves.[53] The CFTC objected to class struggle, and corporatism held some appeal for it. Among the base, a number of militants supported the positions of the episcopate and were wary of the resistance, which they identified with the Bolshevism they despised. At the same time, however, the Charte du Travail remained unacceptable. The single-option and compulsory nature of the organizations the Vichy regime set out to create contradicted two cardinal principles. By threatening the very existence of the CFTC, Vichy led certain cadres to "act in favor of the rehabilitation of the institution of the trade union, even if that meant opting for the 'illegal' path."[54] The base was thus divided, even torn, "between the positions of the Catholic hierarchy and opposition to a 'legality' that violated one of the principal social and republican achievements, the right to join and participate in labor unions."[55]

A fringe of French trade unionism, offended by the ideology and social policy of Vichy, thus stood up to the regime from the start. But its fight was contained within narrow limits. No contact was made with the Communists, for whom these men harbored a deep-seated enmity, reactivated by the German-Soviet Pact. The leaders, moreover, gave precedence to theoretical reflections over practical instructions. They did not, for example, call for strikes—a means that the old unified movement had sometimes chosen. And the fight against Nazi Germany was not a top priority. In addition, the line advocated by Léon Jouhaux was not completely devoid of ambiguity. Although the leader of the CGT condemned the Charte du Travail from the outset, his appeal to members to fill positions in the Vichy government's organizations conferred a legitimacy that resolute opposition would have denied them. The unions, therefore, by no means constituted the spearhead of the organized resistance. Nonetheless, some leaders joined the movements or networks—when they did not create them, as in the case of Christian Pineau, founder of Libération-nord.

## Completely on the Right?

One might have thought that the national right would have held high the torch of resistance. Everything predestined it to perform that role, consistent with its history and ambitions. Manifesting a prickly, often Germanophobic patriotism, it had joined the ranks of the Sacred Union in 1914 and, in general, felt no affection for Nazism, though it viewed sympathetically Italian Fascism and the authoritarian experiments of António de Oliveira Salazar in Portugal and Francisco Franco in Spain. In addition, Action Française had supported the declaration of war, believing it would be a hard fight but that there was hope it would settle "the German problem once and for all."[56] Nevertheless, the Vichy program was too strong a temptation: the movement could not help but support a regime that was in part realizing its own program. In *Le Petit Marseillais* of February 9, 1941, Charles Maurras hailed the "divine surprise," that is, "the way Marshal Pétain assumed that supreme position."[57] Throughout the dark years, Maurras repeatedly called for the repression of resistance fighters and the pursuit of the Vichy regime's anti-Semitic policy. At the same time, he denied the right of the Germans "to meddle in the Franco-French war,"[58] though that position in no way resembled an attitude of resistance. Rejecting both collaboration and resistance, the leaders of Action Française remained loyal to the Marshal through and through,[59] refusing to choose between the Gaullist plague and the Nazi cholera. A few Maurrassians, however, influenced by the master's Germanophobic nationalism, joined the resistance: Pierre Bénouville, future leader of Combat; Daniel Cordier, destined to become Jean Moulin's secretary; and Rémy, founder of the Confrérie Notre-Dame (CND; Our Lady Brotherhood) network. But these free agents were in no way expressing the ideas of their mentor, who was paralyzed by his timeworn hatred, and whose sterile mode of thought certainly inspired Vichy more than it did the army of shadows.

The case of François de La Rocque was entirely different. A fierce nationalist, La Rocque had founded after World War I a rightist veterans movement, the Croix-de-Feu. Forbidden in 1936, it had then become a political party, the PSF, whose ideology was so close to Vichy postulates that the French State directly borrowed from them the motto "Travail, Famille, Patrie" (Work, Family, Homeland). Likewise, Lieutenant Colonel de La Rocque looked favorably on the Marshal and his project of national reform, which in many ways he can be said to have inspired. At the same time, the colonial officer differed from the victor of Verdun in more than one respect. La Rocque disapproved of the clerical orientation Pétain had given to his regime and was far from approving the subsidies paid to Catholic institutions of learning. Furthermore, he did not share the anti-Semitism of the French State. Finally, the Vichy leadership, distrustful of a man whose total obedience was not guaranteed, distanced him from the corridors of power.

The distrust was mutual: La Rocque kept his distance, even while complaining that the Pétainist higher-ups paid him little heed. He was named to the National Council but resigned on July 28, 1941. He proved wary of the Légion des Combattants, an organization that was supposed to include the veterans of World War I and of the 1940 campaign, and which he feared would siphon off members from his old party. In essence, the line he defended was support without participation: "The PSF is to be an organization on the margins of the government, not sharing its responsibilities but contributing toward 'building the future.'"[60] Giving precedence to social over political action, he hoped that the Pétainist program would be applied in a France rid of the occupier, whom he felt no inclination to follow. This was surely a pipe dream. Above all, La Rocque was obsessed with the Communist peril. Fearing revolutionary subversion, he discreetly reconstituted mobile teams to spread propaganda. On the day of liberation, he believed, they would be able to counter the seditious Reds who took their orders from Moscow. "My major concern was to contribute as much as possible to seeing that the patriotic order would reign once the liberation of the territory occurred," he declared in May 1945.[61]

François de La Rocque, indisputably patriotic, moderately Pétainist, and skittish about collaboration, cannot be considered to have been a resister, at least not until 1942. He did not make the fight against Vichy and the battle against Nazi Germany top priorities. Obsessed with the domestic peril and tempted by Vichy's political program, he misapprehended the most urgent problem, granting precedence to domestic political considerations and refusing to consider the struggle against the Reich an ardent obligation. Nevertheless, in 1942 he created an intelligence network, Klan, under the authority of the British Intelligence Service. General Karl Oberg, the Higher SS and Police Leader of France, dissolved the PSF on November 2, 1942. Certainly, members of the PSF distinguished themselves in the resistance or, like Charles Vallin, joined General de Gaulle. But they were in no way giving expression to the line taken by their movement.

All in all, until summer 1941, parties and labor unions were not the inspiration or the driving force behind the resistance to come. Should we even consider them resisters? That all depends, of course, on the meaning of the word. If "resistance" means in the first place participation in the fight against the Nazi occupier, it must be acknowledged that neither the parties nor the unions were initially part of that framework. In giving precedence to the Franco-French problem, they preferred to preserve or to rebuild their apparatus and to position themselves vis-à-vis Vichy rather than fight the German forces. If, by contrast, the fight against the French State is construed as having contributed toward defining one's membership in the army of shadows, especially when it entailed risks and led to repression, then it is possible to say that a significant portion of the parties and unions were an integral part of that battle.

In any event, neither parties nor unions were in the vanguard of the underground struggle. Yet their ideologies ought to have offered reliable guidelines for action. Similarly, their cadres and militants, who had often proved themselves, might have constituted a recruiting pool for the underground groups. Such was not the case. Their often hidebound doctrines made it impossible to identify clearly issues that eluded simplistic categories. Vichy also complicated the situation. Superimposed on the issue of patriotism—the fight against Germany—was a political problem: Should Pétain be supported in his enterprise of national reform or, more cynically, should the state apparatus be infiltrated, at the risk of legitimating a contemptible party by means of that strategy? That question caused rifts within groups, blurred distinctions, and obliged cadres and militants, without clear instructions, to obey their consciences rather than orders. In 1914, parties and trade unions had concluded a truce by joining the Sacred Union. That mechanism was not repeated during the dark years.

When it dawned, the resistance did not rise up from the political world but emerged from the depths of civil society. The resistance was constructed outside the world of politics—if not against it.

## Chapter 3

# Birth of the Movements

WHAT WAS TO BE done? The question Lenin asked in 1902 obsessed the first resisters. For lack of historical precedents, they literally had to invent the terms of their fight. The defeat and its principal consequences—the occupation of the northern zone and the advent of the French State—clearly called for a military response, but the pioneers could not imagine formulating one. How, in the absence of weapons and experience, could they aspire to threaten the Wehrmacht, which in some six weeks had demolished the foremost army in the world? Granted, a few individuals, such as Étienne Achavanne, took action as early as summer 1940. Others, from the start of the rout, set about collecting the weapons abandoned by the French troops, an avenue taken in the region of Soissons, for example, by a small group headed by Henri Descamps, a captain in the gendarmerie. Still others performed many symbolic acts of opposition. On June 23, 1940, Colonel Léonce Veiljeux, mayor of La Rochelle, refused to lower the French flag. But such acts could not claim to reverse the course of the war. "Overwhelmingly," notes historian Julien Blanc, "that defiant behavior had no other objective than to make the occupier feel the extent to which he was in hostile territory."[1] Although such acts attested that a handful of French people did not admit defeat, they remained isolated and were not integrated into an overall strategy capable of threatening the hegemony of the Reich. In order to count, they had to become part of a collective mode of action: only that would make them effective.

Were the resistance movements in a position to take up the challenge and conduct a war strategy? Many pioneers were doubtful. "We did not really have the means for anything but intellectual and moral labor against the Germans, the production of propaganda," notes Christian Pineau in retrospect.[2] But that sense of powerlessness was often combined with moral reflection. In the face of the subjection that the Nazi occupier and his Vichy accomplice were imposing, French society had to maintain its values against all odds. The resistance had to protect the population from a much-feared ideological contagion, while at the same time infusing the war with a significance that World War I had lacked. "At bottom, we always believed that our role was to fight on the domestic front—the front of spiritual resistance to Hitlerism—so that the military victory would not be in vain or tragically illegitimate," the historian and Christian resistance fighter Henri-Irénée Marrou emphasized after liberation.[3] Many movements therefore opted for a civilian strategy, which stemmed as much from the impossibility of taking up arms as from free choice. That "civilian resistance was one of survival, aimed at saving what could be saved, without necessarily waiting for the reversal of military power relations. . . . The aim of civilian resistance was not so much to defeat the occupier—it did not have the means to do so—as to exist beside it, in spite of it, without waiting until the eventual hour of deliverance,"[4] notes historian Jacques Sémelin. A division of labor thus took shape. Free France and the networks would "pick up the broken sword" (in de Gaulle's words) and continue the war against the Third Reich. Although the movements did not rule out that prospect, they also, and sometimes especially, assigned themselves the mission of preserving the identity of a France whose values were threatened, while at the same time protecting the population from the rigors of occupation. That division of labor did not occur without some hesitation. In fact, the "pioneers, even as they were embarking on underground action, were not impervious to doubt. Such doubt never had to do with the political and moral justifications for the struggle. Rather, uncertainty crept in about the practical modalities and the foreseeable consequences."[5]

Several modes of action provided channels for the civilian strategy chosen from the start by a few underground movements. Some set out, in the first place, to raise awareness among civilians about the Nazi peril, a role that fell primarily to the press. Newspapers therefore produced counterpropaganda, which endeavored to refute the views propagated by the victor and his French intermediaries. On a more positive note, they defended the path they were forging, the aim being as much to persuade public opinion as to mobilize it. In producing false identity papers, they also sought to assist proscribed persons—especially

Jews, resistance fighters, and Communists—who were being hunted down by the law.

These polymorphous actions encompassed and combined several temporal registers. The movements, generally led by "new men," looked without charity on the past. They claimed they were liquidating it, transcending it altogether. Over the short term, they applied themselves to managing the best they could the consequences of the defeat, fending off psychological Nazification and preparing for the liberation of a France brought to heel. But at first, their horizon of expectation was not limited to a despised occupier. Shocked by the Third Republic's dysfunction, which according to them had led to the 1940 collapse, they meant to rebuild the country on new foundations. Often, these pioneers were looking far ahead. They assessed the historical risks incurred by the questionable positions their institutions were taking. In the eyes of certain Christian Democrats, for example, the Catholic hierarchy's support of the Pétainist regime risked bringing such discredit to the church in the aftermath of war that its pronouncements would go unheard for a long time to come. Pierre-Henri Teitgen,[6] the founder (with François de Menthon) of the movement Liberté in the southern zone in 1940, would explain: "It was fortunate that a number of Catholics joined the Resistance, so that after the war the church could not be reproached for going over to the National Revolution. [But] that was a secondary motivation. It was not for that reason that we resisted." Claude Bourdet adds: "As for leftist Christians, also 'believers' and therefore not realists, they clung all the more to the Republic, inasmuch as saving Christianity from compromising itself vis-à-vis the right wing was still a very recent undertaking, which the servile attitude of the senior hierarchy [with rare exceptions] now risked making definitively futile."[7] Hence, short- and long-term rationales, universalist ambitions, and partisan concerns combined to favor the creation of movements whose aim from the start was not merely to defeat Germany militarily. A clear disproportion existed, however, between the loftiness and even clarity of the aims pursued and the modesty of the means deployed. The early days were a time for heroic *bricolages* (makeshift solutions), to use the time-honored expression.

## Advent of the Underground Press

For many months, some resistance movements gave precedence to setting up underground newspapers. Beyond the objectives of propaganda and counterpropaganda ascribed to them, newspapers had the advantage of being a fairly easy enterprise to run, all things considered. Granted, the shortage of ink and paper and the close surveillance of printers by the Vichy or German police complicated the task. To cite only one example, on November 26, 1940, the French State prohibited the sale, without police authorization, of duplicating machines, as well as of paper that could be used to mimeograph tracts. But these obstacles were far from insurmountable. All who wished could take up the pen and provide an analysis or express their feelings, provided they had the complicity of friendly shopkeepers and a decent level of education. Likewise, mimeograph printing raised few technical problems and required only a few sheets of special paper. For example, the first two issues of the newspaper *Valmy*, created by Raymond Burgard, a teacher of German at the Lycée Buffon, were printed on a child's printing press. In January 1941, the first print run required a month's work to produce about fifty copies.[8] Finally, small-scale distribution initially entailed minimal risks, whether it was done at random or among close and trusted friends. It is clear, therefore, why several fledgling groups opted for this type of action.

Such was the case, in the northern zone, for Christian Pineau. Born in 1904, he had worked before the war at the Banque de France and then at the Banque de Paris et des Pays-Bas. At the same time, he had become involved in the labor movement, which led to a position as assistant secretary of the Fédération des Employés de Banque (Bank Employees' Federation), associated with the reformists gathered around René Belin, the very anti-Communist second-in-command at the CGT. The two men parted ways in 1940, when Belin agreed to become Marshal Pétain's minister of labor. Pineau had played a preeminent role in drafting the *Manifeste du syndicalisme (Manifesto of Trade Unionism)* and in forming the CEES. Backed by that structure, in December 1940 he launched an underground newspaper, *Libération*. He wrote and published the first sixty-one issues entirely on his own, before leaving to go to London in February 1942. The first edition, composed on a portable typewriter on December 1, 1940, had a print run of only seven copies. These were sent through the mail to friends who owned mimeograph machines, in the hope that they would think to make more copies.

The creation of the organization Défense de la France (DF) came in response to more or less the same rationale.[9] At the beginning of the school year in 1940, Philippe Viannay, a twenty-three-year-old philosophy student at the Sorbonne, decided to take action and confided his intentions to Marcel Lebon, owner of the gas and electric company of the same name. Viannay had a great deal going for him. "Six foot two, a chest measurement proportionate to his waistline, powerful arms, an air of brotherly protection about his entire person. On that score, a voice that, though not very resonant, was warm and almost immediately intimate, caressing you from inside, because of the conviction it carried. But then, I'm saying all that very badly," explains Jacques Lusseyran, a student who joined the DF in January 1943. "What I saw entering was not a man but a force. Nobody needed to tell you he was a leader. He could behave however he liked, sprawl by turns on every chair in the room, pull up his trousers and scratch his legs, become unintelligible because of a belching pipe that got in the way of his speech, run his hands through his hair, ask indiscreet questions, and contradict himself (in the ten minutes of the meeting, he did each of these things several times at least), nobody was paying attention. Upon entering, he had thrown a mantle of authority over your shoulders. You were rolling around in its folds with a happiness you could not control."[10]

Referring to the precedent of *La Libre Belgique*, published under the German jackboot during World War I, Lebon suggested to Viannay that he create an underground paper and promised his financial support. Robert Salmon, a student in the *khâgne*—the second year of preparatory courses for the arts section of the École Normale Supérieure—and Hélène Mordkovitch, a geography student, immediately backed the project, recruiting volunteers among their friends or professional associates, primarily students. By late 1941, the movement had about seventy members ready to produce and distribute *Défense de la France*. Initially, the newspaper was printed on a Rotaprint mimeograph machine, acquired in the name of the Lebon gas and electric company in spring 1941. That machine, baptized "Simone," was installed at a site rented for the occasion, then at the homes of private individuals, before finding refuge, between August 1941 and May 1942, in the cellars of the Sorbonne, for which Mordkovitch possessed the keys. Two original features distinguished the DF from its counterparts. Thanks to Marcel Lebon, the organization possessed substantial financial resources from the start. Furthermore, it refused to use professional printers, preferring to act autonomously. Indeed, though a few militants were trained by professionals, the majority learned on the job, and not without success. The first issue came out in early August 1941, followed by twenty-one more between August 15, 1941, and November 11, 1942. The print run remained relatively modest: three thousand copies for the first issue, five thousand for the following ones, ten thousand for the first half of 1942. Despite these numbers, it was still a small-scale enterprise. For the first twelve issues, the master was made from a typewritten original. The newspaper was difficult to read and ran to only two to four pages. The yellowish paper was of mediocre quality.

Pioneers in the southern zone also opted for the underground press. Small groups, disgusted by the armistice, had taken to meeting in Lyon in the orbit of Antoine Avinin (a militant in the Catholic party Jeune République), Noël Clavier (a metal-shutter sales representative), and the breakaway Communists Élie Péju and Jean-Jacques Soudeille. These currents merged in November 1940 and gave rise to a small team. It called itself "France-Liberté," and its aim was to "fight Vichyist propaganda" and "reestablish the Republic."[11] Joined in February 1941 by Auguste Pinton, a Radical member of the municipal council of Lyon, that embryonic group composed leaflets, then typewritten tracts, which circulated from hand to hand.

Jean-Pierre Levy, a thirty-year-old Jewish commercial engineer from Alsace, had settled in the city known as the "capital of the Gauls" in late 1940. He made contact with the small cell and proposed that it extend its propaganda beyond the department of Rhône. In particular, he suggested shifting from tracts to a newspaper and gradually set himself up as its manager—not without difficulties. Levy, "level-headed and accommodating . . . had elevated himself to that position without necessarily having all the authority or all the skills for it," declares Jacques Baumel, a leader in Combat.[12] "Some were wary and had trouble accepting a single manager, though it was indispensable," adds historian Dominique Veillon.[13] In December 1941, however, the first issue of *Franc-Tireur* came out, five thousand copies printed on a mimeograph machine the movement had procured. The bundles were transported to storehouses. Cyclists with trailers in tow came to pick them up, then distributors handed out the copies in neighborhoods or stuffed them in mailboxes.

The genesis of Libération-sud was more complex.[14] In November 1940, Emmanuel d'Astier de La Vigerie, an École Navale graduate turned journalist, traveled to Clermont-Ferrand. Forty years old at the time, he was very attractive, "rambling, elegant, a little fanciful, a little shady, a sort of decadent aristocrat, 1789 vintage. The man Colonel Passy called an 'anarchist in opera slippers' was primarily an adventurer, a former privateer navy officer who had turned to leftist journalism, to which he brought the extraordinary air of an opium-addicted *condottiere*, a tall skinny body and beak nose, an undeniable charm and a no less undeniable political demagoguery."[15] In the capital of Auvergne, he ran into Lucie Samuel, a teacher with an advanced teaching degree in history; her husband, Raymond Samuel, alias Aubrac, an engineer; and Jean Cavaillès, an assistant professor in philosophy whom Lucie Samuel had known at the Amiens lycée in 1938. The cell, which called itself the "Dernière Colonne," intended to act against Nazi Germany and the French State but hesitated about the means. D'Astier was inclined to favor the use of violence against collaborators, while the Aubracs preferred to act at the political level. The little group sabotaged a cargo of sugar about to leave for Germany from the Perpignan railway station, and perhaps also a few locomotives bound for the Italians in Cannes in November 1941, but these two attempts proved negligible. The group then turned to propaganda. Inscriptions traced in chalk were soon followed by tracts crudely printed by Henri Rochon, a copyeditor at the daily *La Montagne*. On the night of February 27, 1941, the Dernière Colonne decided to strike a major blow, pasting ten thousand handbills in four different versions in six cities of the southern zone. But the police interrogated one of the bill posters, François Franck, and followed the trail back to the source. After arresting d'Astier's niece Bertrande, among others, and threatening her uncle Emmanuel, the police forced the creators of the underground organization to suspend their efforts in March 1941. The group rebounded and decided to launch a newspaper backed by a more structured organization. Between

May and June 1941, Rochon, Cavaillès, d'Astier, and the Aubracs went to work. The philosopher proposed the title, *Libération*, which was immediately adopted. The first issue, set by the typographers of *La Montagne* and printed on paper provided by unionized workers, came out in July 1941, with a print run of ten thousand.[16]

Finally, some in the Christian world were alarmed at the positions adopted by the French Catholic church, fearing that Nazism, which they viewed as a form of paganism, would infect French society. Some chose to act openly. Stanislas Fumet, a man of letters profoundly influenced by social Catholicism, and Louis Terrenoire, a Christian trade unionist, obtained authorization to publish *Temps nouveau*, which came out between December 20, 1940, and August 1941. Likewise, Emmanuel Mounier, the famous personalist philosopher, resumed publication of his review, *Esprit*, not without causing some alarm. "The mere fact of publishing involves you in a compromise of your principles," warned two of his friends, to no avail.[17] On August 20, 1941, Admiral Darlan took it upon himself to resolve the dilemma by banning the review.

Father Chaillet followed a completely different path. He was born in 1900 and was ordained a priest in 1931. A specialist in German theology, Chaillet went to Austria before the war. His travels and theological training thoroughly prepared him to confront the problems raised with increasing urgency by Nazism.[18] Having created a mutual support committee in Lyon for émigrés from Germany and Central Europe, he decided, in view of what he was observing, to put out an underground newspaper to express a Christian point of view on the war under way. As he would report after the war: "I remember my disappointment at the few meetings I was able to organize in Lyon, even in sympathetic circles, like those of *Esprit*. I asked our friends to put an end to their policy of participating in the inner workings of the National Revolution, but to no avail. The illusions about participation were nowhere near yielding to the imperious demands of refusal and the implementation of that refusal. Hatred of Hitlerism was having a hard time offsetting the bourgeois and Christian trust in the myth of the Marshal."[19]

In June 1941, two clerics, Father Varillon and Jean Daniélou, asked Gaston Fessard, a Jesuit, to compose a tract alerting young people to the dangers of Nazism. Fessard entrusted his copy to Chaillet, who immediately seized on the in-depth analysis, which ran to some fifty pages, to use as fodder for the underground periodical he was hoping to create. With the cooperation of Louis Cruvillier, director of propaganda at *Temps nouveau*, and of Henri Frenay, who was prepared to finance and print the new underground paper, Chaillet was able to publish the first *Cahier du Témoignage Chrétien (Journal of Christian Witness)* in late September or early October 1941. At the last minute, he substituted the term "Christian" for "Catholic" in the paper's name, in order to affirm the "joint witnessing of Catholics and Protestants, united as brothers in the same faith in Christ, to strike out against lies and violence with the imperatives of the Word of God, which is Truth, Justice, and Liberty."[20] Printed on Joseph Martinet's presses with a run of about five thousand, the newspaper, bearing the headline "France, Beware of Losing Your Soul," stuck to a resolutely anti-Vichy and anti-Nazi line. "Adherence to the 'new order' is in reality an acknowledgment of the value of the spiritual principles of the National Socialist 'conception of the world,' according to which Europe will in the future have to organize itself under Germany's domination," explained Gaston Fessard. "Collaborating with the Marshal's government=collaborating with the new order= collaborating with the triumph of Nazi principles. . . . Catholics and Christians of France must therefore expect to be slandered, dragged through the mud, imprisoned, and even to suffer a worse fate, in proportion to their courage and fidelity to Christ," he concluded, before challenging the sacrosanct principle of the respect due legal authority. "As if the most sacred obedience did not always have a limit, that of sin!"[21] Thanks to that opinion column, for four years the Christian world would be able to counter Nazism and Pétainism with the force of its word.

As these examples suggest, the press became the matrix of movements that were destined to prosper. In fact, the print media obliged promoters to clarify their thinking, define their strategy, and speak clearly to the general public, who had to be persuaded before they could be mobilized. In demonstrating to the French people that the morose resignation Philippe Pétain invited them to adopt did not constitute the only path, the underground press restored a lost political complexity and allowed them to make choices and no longer simply submit. "Printing important news which Vichy ignored or refused to publish was a vital activity if the image of reasonableness and good sense was to be wrested from those who had accepted the Occupation and divisions of France. The *status quo* of 1940 had to be made to appear unnatural, irrational, and reversible if opposition was to appear normal, rational, and practical," British historian H. R. Kedward points out. "News-sheets were a major way in which they gave a rationale to their actions."[22] Newspapers also made recruitment easier. Facilitating contacts, they "served as a witness, by which it was possible to assess the feelings of those one hoped to make sympathizers; they were also the first means of action, and for many militants the only likelihood of practical action for many long months."[23] In offering material proof that an organization existed, they could not fail to impress the potential recruit, especially since the distribution of a banned newspaper was not exempt from risks. In fact, the perils surrounding "manifestations of dissident thought confer a prestige and credibility that go well beyond ordinary demonstrations. In that sense, the freedom to speak under threat precedes and authenticates, by that very means, what it authorizes itself to say."[24] In fact, the movement sometimes employed ruses to reinforce that feeling. *Franc-Tireur*, for example, refrained from numbering the first editions it brought out. "What will it look like if we publish only issue 1?" Jean-Pierre Levy quipped to Antoine Avinin. The movement did not begin numbering its papers until issue 8.[25]

Above all, a newspaper created a dynamic. It forced participants to develop logistics for writing it, printing it, and then distributing it. As a result, it opened up a range of possibilities. After giving its militants false identities, the movement could consider, in a second phase, offering them to other groups—Jews or evaders of the Service du Travail Obligatoire (STO), for example. Similarly, having created irregular groups to guard warehouses and printing offices, it could later assign them other missions, such as sabotage. "Hence a logic was set in motion that carried us along, or rather, carried us away, and obliged us to respond to the many questions that the very development of that logic raised. The newspaper was no longer an end in itself but rather a support," Philippe Viannay notes in retrospect.[26] Finally, printed matter reinforced the cohesion and identity of an organization which, as the underground required, constrained its members to isolation: "The solidarity of complicity was created among all who received it. Although it was not possible, as in peacetime, to distribute membership cards or hold public meetings, [the issues of the newspaper] were a bond, the recurring concrete sign among our militants that they belonged to our movement, whose name was easily forgotten, since it vanished behind that of the newspaper," adds Henri Frenay, founder of Combat.[27]

The unexpected development of an underground press would not erase the doubts that assailed the pioneers. Claude Bourdet, the second-in-command of the same movement, notes acerbically: "Was it necessary to take risks to distribute that pathetic literature? Some wondered."[28] Others, disagreeing with that form of action, resigned from organizations they thought were dedicating themselves to childish pursuits. André Gayet, a militant in France Liberté, left the movement because he believed that "it is not with paper that we will win the war."[29] Colonel Passy, head of the secret services of Free France, was not far from sharing that view. In addition, not all the underground papers had the glorious fate of *Libération* or *Franc-Tireur.* Three small groups launched *La Bretagne enchaînée (Brittany in Chains),* disseminated in 1941 and early 1942. But after eight issues, the venture was abruptly suspended. Likewise, and also in Brittany, *En Captivité,* a Gaullist and Anglophile paper, lasted only from November 24, 1940, to mid-1941.[30] Repression in particular stopped some initiatives in their tracks. In October 1940, Raymond Deiss, an Alsatian publisher of patriotic music, brought out *Pantagruel,* composing its sixteen issues on his own. Printed on the presses of his publishing house, it attained a print run of ten thousand.[31] But the arrest of its founder marked the end of this underground newspaper in October 1941. Deiss was interned in Germany, then beheaded in Cologne on August 23, 1943. Finally, though the engineer Robert Reyl gathered together a few people of good will and brought out a modest newspaper, *Liberté,* in Sèvres, its creator soon turned toward activity in a network, condemning his paper to silence.[32] The underground press, in other words, did not guarantee its creators would be successful. Furthermore, it did not constitute the only path open to the movements. Some opted for other modes of action.

## Expanding the Range of Possibilities: The Northern Zone

Some groups, without rejecting propaganda, refused to consider it the exclusive focus of their action. For example, in 1940 an active circle was constituted at the Musée de l'Homme around the librarian, Yvonne Oddon, and two Russian researchers, Boris Vildé and Anatole Lewitsky. That little group entered into contact with cells that wanted to do something: FFL, led especially by Jean Cassou, Agnès Humbert, and Claude Aveline; Vérité Française, overseen by Colonel Maurice Dutheil de La Rochère; and a mutual support association for colonial fighters, which provided cover for the underground actions of Paul Hauet, a retired soldier, and Germaine Tillion, a young ethnologist. In autumn 1940, these small groups coordinated their actions. Some worked to facilitate the escape of prisoners of war, especially colonial soldiers interned in metropolitan France. The captives would simulate various illnesses and would be taken to the military hospital of Val-de-Grâce. Dr. Lucien Grumbach, assigned to the laboratory of bacteriology, would falsify test results: "The sputum contains tubercle bacillus, the stools parasites or redoubtable germs, such as the dysentery amoeba and bacillus, analyses confirm the existence of syphilis and malaria."[33] Others transmitted intelligence to the Allies via American or Dutch diplomats posted in Vichy. The Musée de l'Homme group also launched an underground newspaper, *Résistance*, publishing five issues between December 15, 1940, and the end of March 1941. The copies were sent primarily through the mail, thanks to a file of four hundred names that Agnès Humbert concealed under the carpet of her apartment building, between two floors.[34] The movement, infiltrated by two double agents, Albert Gaveau and then Jacques Desoubrie, was almost dismantled in late 1941, but a few pioneers—such as Pierre Brossolette and Paul Hauet—escaped the clutches of the Germans. A trial held in February 1942 would lead to death sentences for ten members, seven of whom (including Vildé, Lewitsky, and another man, Nordmann) would be executed. Yvonne Oddon, Agnès Humbert, and Germaine Tillion would suffer the ordeal of deportation.[35]

Similarly, a small cell formed in autumn 1940 around Maxime Blocq-Mascart, who before the war had been vice president of the Confédération des Travailleurs Intellectuels (Confederation of Intellectual Workers), an association created in 1920 with the aim of defending the rights of authors by distinguishing them both from laborers and from managers. They recruited from that pool André Sainte-Lagüe and Aimé Jeanjean, an attaché to the finance committee in the Chamber of Deputies, who had formerly belonged to General de Gaulle's cabinet. At the same time, another group formed from within the Confédération Nationale des Classes Moyennes (National Confederation of the Middle Classes), in which Jacques Arthuys, director of the Cazeneuve lathe company, had been an activist before the war. Assisted by his secretary, Vera Obolensky, the industrialist spelled out the missions of his organization in November 1940. He sought simultaneously to create channels to assist proscribed persons in getting to the free zone, to publish letters to the French people to raise awareness, to set up an intelligence service, and to recruit from military circles, an ambition granted a certain validity by an encounter with Colonel Alfred Touny during a veterans' reunion in Saumur. In December 1940, the two groups merged, creating the OCM. It was headed by Jacques Arthuys, until his arrest on December 21, 1941. In reality, the two organizations complemented each other: "Blocq-Mascart's group was made up of cadres with no rank and file. The Arthuys group would provide the means to constitute one."[36] Built on the military model, the movement comprised a First Bureau, in charge of general organization, and a Third Bureau heading up operations, both directed by Jean Mayer. Colonel Touny managed the Second Bureau, dedicated to intelligence, with Blocq-Mascart keeping Civil Affairs for himself. It was not long before the OCM began incorporating other small groups: the circle within the Ministry of Public Works, to which André Boulloche and Georges and Raymonde Ricroch gravitated; and the coterie that, with Claude Bellanger, had in 1940 been the driving force behind the Centre d'Entraide aux Étudiants Mobilisés et Prisonniers (Mutual Assistance Center for Mobilized Students and for Prisoners). Likewise, it established ties with the Hector network, headed by Alfred Heurteaux.

From spring 1941 on, however, the founders disagreed about strategic orientations. Colonel Touny wanted to devote himself exclusively to the battle against the occupier, while Blocq-Mascart advocated thinking about the political future postliberation. That conflict was resolved only imperfectly. It is true that the OCM focused quite quickly on intelligence, which continued to be transmitted to the Vichy services until the return of Pierre Laval in April 1942. The group concealed weapons and set up escape routes. But though the movement decided fairly soon not to publish an underground newspaper, it succumbed to the temptation to produce theoretical texts ("The Fight for Liberation," in January 1941; "The Opposing Forces," in February 1941; "A Portrait of the Resistance," in January 1942), subsequently collected in its *Cahiers*, whose first issue came out in June 1942.[37]

In the same way, Maurice Ripoche, a forty-five-year old industrialist, attempted in summer 1940 to rally a few people of good will to fight the Germans. A former World War I fighter pilot, he recruited from military circles, the air force in the first place. His approach was shared by Roger Coquoin, head of the laboratory at the Hôtel-Dieu Hospital, who contacted veterans from the regiment in which he had fought in 1940. As historian Henri Noguères notes, "His idea at that moment was to form a sort of reserve army that, procuring arms by salvaging everything it was possible to salvage . . . would once more be in a position to take part in the fight, as soon as the enemy army's luck had turned."[38] In autumn 1940, a manifesto, *Français, nous serons ceux de la libération (French People, We Will Be Those of the Liberation)*, spelled out the orientations and ambitions of the movement that would take the name Ceux de la Libération (CDLL). The information it collected was then sent through the intelligence services of the Vichy regime and, especially, through the Army Air Force Intelligence Services (SR Air), which at the time were in contact with the British Intelligence Service.

## In the Southern Zone

The two principal movements in the southern zone, Libération-sud and Franc-Tireur, had both formed around an underground newspaper. The organization launched by Captain Henri Frenay in late 1940 responded to a completely different ambition.

Henri Frenay, born in 1903, had opted for a military career. After attending Saint-Cyr, he served in Syria, in the Rhineland, then in the Alps, and entered the École Supérieure de Guerre in 1935. He was Catholic and politically conservative. In 1935 he met Berty Albrecht, who was engaged in the feminist and anti-Fascist struggle, and she revealed the reality of Nazism to him. In 1937–1938, he volunteered to study at the Centre d'Études Germaniques in Strasbourg to improve his knowledge of Hitler's Germany. He fought during France's campaign in the redoubt of the Vosges, was forced to surrender in June, then escaped, traveling south on foot for two exhausting weeks to reach Lyon, then Sainte-Maxime, where his mother lived. Assigned to the garrison bureau in Marseilles and resolved to act, he repeatedly established contacts with people he happened to meet. He was "a blond man, small in stature, robust, with blue eyes behind large horn-rimmed glasses, a square, almost protuberant chin, and a very large nose in a lively, open, and determined face. You were immediately struck by the force of his conviction (not to mention his powerful handshake) and by his precise eloquence, which could not be resisted for long. He possessed in the extreme the talent of persuading, of taking his interlocutors much further than they may have initially wanted to go," remembers Jacques Baumel.[39] Frenay enlisted a colonial infantry lieutenant, Maurice Chevance, "a simple, solid, tenacious man, in short, a perfect officer in the African army,"[40] and reestablished ties with a reservist physician, Marcel Recordier. Above all, he designed an organizational scheme in which, looking back, he took "a certain pride."[41]

In Frenay's view, every resistance fighter first had to join the Recrutement, Organisation, Propagande (Recruitment, Organization, Propaganda) section of his organization. Later, he could choose to remain in that all-purpose induction structure, could opt for the SR, or could join Choc, a paramilitary organization. Frenay's movement thus combined three dimensions from the outset: propaganda, intelligence, and armed action, whether that meant attacks in the short term or the more distant prospect of liberation. But let there be no mistake: whatever his theoretical plans for the future, "propaganda was truly the backbone of all the actions Frenay took to spin his web, at least until summer 1941."[42]

Frenay, appointed in mid-December to the Second Bureau, exploited the intelligence he gathered to put out a *Bulletin d'information et de propagande (Information and Propaganda Bulletin)*, with the assistance of Berty Albrecht. The sheet circulated under the table. But the atmosphere reigning both in Vichy and in the military led him to leave the army in early 1941. He devoted himself full time to his movement, baptized the Mouvement de Libération Nationale (MLN or MOLIN).

Thanks to his contacts with the armistice army, Frenay continued his intelligence activity and, with the support of Robert Guédon, a former classmate from the École Supérieure de Guerre, began to consider expanding his organization to the northern zone. Through Guédon, he met Pierre de Froment, who was in contact with Jacques-Yves Mulliez. Since early 1941, Mulliez, the son of mill owners and himself a reserve officer, had been distributing an underground paper, *Les Petites Ailes du Nord et du Pas-de-Calais (The Little Wings of Nord and of Pas-du-Calais)* in the two northern departments. It had a modest print run of about five hundred.[43] The two men agreed to extend the influence of that underground newspaper, renamed *Les Petites Ailes de France*, by producing two editions, one for the free zone under the direction of Frenay, the other for the northern zone, for which Guédon was responsible. Joseph Martinet agreed to print the southern edition, renamed, after a police raid, *Vérités (Truths)* in August 1941. "We've already changed our location, we have to change our aliases and the type of paper we're using, so why not change its name?" Frenay asked.[44] Seventeen issues would be published before November 1941, at which time the name *Combat* was adopted.

As the weeks went by, therefore, the MLN assumed a clear structure and was joined by select recruits. Varian Fry, a liberal journalist, had been assigned by an American group sponsored by Eleanor Roosevelt to assist in the emigration to the New World of prominent personalities threatened by Nazism. After arriving in Marseilles, Fry was supported by a small staff that included Stéphane Hessel and Jean Gemähling. In October 1940 Gemähling, an Alsatian engineer, set up an intelligence channel that worked for Frenay's organization. But his incarceration between November 1941 and March 1942 suspended his activities.[45] In January 1941, Claude Bourdet, an engineer by training, agreed to oversee the Alpes-Maritimes region and quickly came to serve as Frenay's assistant on political questions. Bourdet was a man of extraordinary qualities. "I don't believe I'm being indiscreet in mentioning what he told me one day, after the war, about his notion of existence," says Philippe Viannay, who met him in late 1943. "It was that of a chevalier: living his life without constraints, taking the agreeable things that pass within reach, accepting few obligations but constantly justifying his freedom through his courage in the service of the weak and for the great causes of the moment. . . . The man was quite tall and frail, with an assured gait, swaying slightly in back, an extremely slender head with a bird's profile, topped by a black hat, his body wrapped in a large gray coat. His face, less creased with bitterness than it is today, sometimes had a roguish expression. His voice was slightly rasping."[46]

In June 1941, Jean-Guy Bernard and André Bollier, two students at the École Polytechnique, joined the movement. Thanks to Emmanuel Mounier and Stanislas Fumet, Father Chaillet agreed to write the newspaper's religious column under the pseudonym "Testis." And La Laurencie, a reactionary general who was nonetheless in favor of the resistance, supported the venture financially, immediately contributing 100,000 francs.[47]

Two Christian Democratic university professors, Pierre-Henri Teitgen and François de Menthon, also decided to launch an underground newspaper. Assisted by a few friends who shared their sensibility—Marcel Prélot, René Capitant, and Alfred Coste-Floret—they managed to print the first issue of *Liberté* on a mimeograph machine. Ten issues appeared between November 25, 1940, and October 1, 1941. With the help of Marseilles printers, the periodical attained an impressive print run of forty-five thousand. The movement grew over time, attracting the assistance of prominent personalities, often inspired by social Christianity. Edmond Michelet, a sales representative, took charge of Brive; Charles d'Aragon, a landowner, of Tarn; the jurist André Hauriou and Dr. Victor Parent were in charge of Toulouse; the Germanist Edmond Vermeil, the jurist René Courtin, and the historian Marc Bloch headed up the Montpellier region. A thirty-five-year-old lawyer, Jacques Renouvin, also set up irregular forces that took action against hotbeds of collaboration.[48]

After many meetings, Henri Frenay and François de Menthon decided in early November 1941 to merge their two organizations. Liberté and the MLN thus gave rise to the Mouvement de Libération Française (French Liberation Movement), piloted by a six-member steering committee, three members from each movement. The organization structured itself around the districts that Frenay had devised a few weeks earlier. R3 (Montpellier), R4 (Toulouse), R5 (Limoges), and R6 (Clermont-Ferrand) were assigned to Menthon's friends, while R1 (Lyon) and R2 (Marseilles) remained within the former MLN. *Liberté* and *Vérités* both disappeared, replaced by a new paper, *Combat*, which bore the subtitle "Organ of the Mouvement de la Libération Française."

Jacqueline Bernard and René Ferrière (Cerf) became its editors in chief, while André Bollier took charge of printing the newspaper, whose name would eventually come to designate the movement itself. "I feel a profound joy. We are showing by example the path of unity; others behind us will follow it," concluded Henri Frenay with a certain bombast, happy to be celebrating that merger.[49]

Franc-Tireur, Libération-sud, Combat, Témoignage Chrétien in the south; the CDLL, DF, Libération-nord, OCM, and FN in the north: the map of the major resistance movements was thus fixed by mid-1941, or even late 1940. In large part, it bore the mark of the division between the two zones. Because of the German presence, underground groups in the occupied zone generally concerned themselves at an earlier date with a war strategy, to fight the occupier militarily. That perspective was less present in the free zone, where Vichy's claim to legitimacy carried more weight, impelling the movements to conduct more political actions and to give precedence to propaganda, at least at first. The risks were also lower in the south, a situation that no doubt contributed toward creating a less charged climate in Vichy France than in the occupied zone, where the Germans were gunning down their enemies without qualms. The resistance could thus develop more easily in the free zone, though the Pétainist police did not hesitate to send those who opposed the regime to its jails. These differences would erode over time, but they would never totally disappear.

In any event, and with very rare exceptions—notably, Ceux de la Résistance (CDLR)—no new groups would make inroads in the underground after 1941. The movements that had emerged paid a low entry fee. A mimeograph machine, a few thousand francs, a great deal of courage and goodwill were sufficient to make them viable. These organizations became more solid quite quickly, however. They extended their branches and came to possess fairly significant infrastructures, whether acquired through complicity or through purchase. Newcomers, by contrast, would have had to line up considerable material and human resources from the start, which was not easy, given the shortages that prevailed in the dark years. Whether they wished it or not, the major movements thus held a monopoly on underground political action, especially since, apart from the PCF, the parties remained relatively sluggish, and General de Gaulle did not possess good go-betweens in the metropolis, at least at the start.

The pioneers acted on the basis of different premises: some gave precedence to the circulation of the underground press, while others opted for military action. These principles, however, did not create any "path dependence," to borrow a concept popular among sociologists. The movements were able to emancipate themselves from the frameworks set in place by the creators and to achieve a certain flexibility. The OCM combined military and civilian action from the outset; but the DF, centered on a periodical, embarked fairly quickly on the manufacture of false papers, the creation of irregular groups, and then the formation of maquis. Libération-nord, long focused on its newspaper, followed a parallel path. The movements were in sync with society, as much an emanation of it as its guide, and displayed a real versatility. They evolved with the circumstances, including the progress of the conflict and political changes, without becoming locked into rigid systems. That ability to adapt explains why their organizations persisted, even prospered, despite the harsh context of war and occupation.

The tendency for a movement to become a monopoly actually increased over time, because of the magnetic pull that larger organizations exerted over more modest groups. In accordance with a process destined to become entrenched, movements large and small joined together, as the examples of the OCM and Combat, but also of the Musée de l'Homme constellation confirm. Hence, the major movements exerted a centripetal force that cumulatively reinforced their power. Conversely, the organizations going it alone—and there were some—were doomed to marginality.

The movements covered the entire ideological spectrum, from the far left (embodied by Libération-sud) to the right (represented, for example, by the OCM). They could thus lay claim to representing the real country, providing the muzzled public with the means to express its opinions. Not all defended the same values, however. The banner of resistance concealed tremendous divisions, offset by real points of consensus.

## Perfect Agreement?

In the first place, the movements all believed that the war, far from being over, had to go on. That assessment, however, was not based on a geopolitical argument comparable to the global view of the conflict that Charles de Gaulle had developed in the Appeal of June 18. Rather, it was based on an almost mystical faith: "We told ourselves, of course, that the victory of the Allies was likely, and we even managed to believe it; but that was like the faith of a believer, which rests on an inner conviction, but which from the outside looks like autosuggestion," admits Claude Bourdet.[50] "I was convinced that the Creator could not abandon France. I had faith in Providence, but I thought we had to help him all the same. We therefore had to fight," explains Paul Dungler, an Alsatian industrialist and creator of the 7e Colonne d'Alsace (Seventh Column of Alsace) movement.[51] The formation of movements, in other words, did not result from a strategic calculation—the idea of contributing to the Reich's ineluctable defeat—but was based on a moral approach in which patriotism played an essential role. The idea that France might disappear from the map of great nations was intolerable. As Alban Vistel, a member of the Libération-sud movement, explains: "The humiliation of defeat proves to be less and less bearable, it assails the individual's pride, a pride whose existence might have been unsuspected until then. But beyond the individual, a collective past and a history fall apart, the national community seems to be deprived of a future. Then the old patriotism surges up again, having timidly effaced itself behind the irony of easy times, becoming once again a value when the Homeland is in its death throes."[52]

That revived patriotism was fueled by a traditional form of Germanophobia. "Only one enemy, the Boche, and with him all who help him and appeal to him," proclaimed General Gabriel Cochet, who on September 6, 1940, exhorted the French people to prepare for the Revanche.[53] The underground newspapers, to give added force to their words, served up outdated stereotypes, declaring that "the Germans are a lying, deceitful, plunder-hungry race,"[54] or proclaiming that "Germans have a herd mentality, following their leaders like so many sheep."[55] This hatred, sometimes combined with or intensified by a loathing of Nazism, led to the denunciation of the collaboration and of collaborators, who, in selling out the nation, risked "molding a France that is a traitor to its history, a traitor to the revolution, a traitor to its destiny, borrowing its doctrines and its orders from the enemy that struck it down."[56]

At a completely different level, the denunciation of Germany and of its accomplices was accompanied by harsh criticism of the Third

Republic and its elites, who were deemed responsible for the defeat. As Alban Vistel claimed: "No one disputed the fact that the games the parties were playing, having become an end in itself, offered nothing but a caricature of parliamentarianism, or that the former political world had ultimately lost touch with reality. Bitter experience taught a lesson that was not to be forgotten." This position was more or less shared by all the movements.[57] While remaining faithful to democratic ideals, the underground groups frequently lapsed into antiparliamentarianism, reinforced by their hostility toward the parties. That harsh view was a justification to think ahead to the postwar period. Believing that men as well as institutions had fallen short of their duty, the movements reflected on the future, portraying themselves as the successors of the elites, whom the defeat, and then their attitude during the dark years, had disqualified. "What is now certain is that, to face an extremely grave situation, the men we will need are not those currently in power, who, with a few exceptions, are the same ones who drove us to catastrophe. Too attached to the ways of the past, they cannot even conceive of the duties incumbent upon them or of the methods that must be adopted," Henri Frenay declared in May 1941.[58] *Franc-Tireur* explained in its first issue of December 1941: "After the war, we want to found a new regime, a synthesis between authority and freedom, a true democracy unburdened by the hot air of the parties and the control of trusts and rich lobbies. We want neither a military dictatorship nor a religious dictatorship nor a proletarian dictatorship nor a capitalist dictatorship."[59] Even early on, then, political ambitions lay at the heart of the movements, whatever many of the leaders may have claimed after the war. Despite the evidence, they were quick to declare that "they were not engaged in politics."[60]

Finally, the early groups remained rather discreet on the subject of General de Gaulle and Free France. At best, they displayed indifference, at worst hostility. In summer 1941, Frenay summed up his position as follows:

1. Considered overall, we believe that De Gaulle's movement is a mistake. We are convinced that you defend your country better by staying than by leaving.
2. We condemn the often-unjust policy that attacks our government and especially the Marshal.

> ... The Mouvement de Libération Nationale has no connection to
> Gaullism and receives no orders and no subsidies from London. It will
> never receive any.
> ... It acknowledges that in the early days of its action, Gaullism is con-
> ducting an action parallel to our own against the common enemy. It
> knows that after the victory our objectives may be different.[61]

*Libération*-nord did not evoke "the Rebel" (one of de Gaulle's nick-
names) until February 1941, and then only to immediately add that,
upon liberation, "the French will choose the leaders required at that
time."[62] And *Défense de la France* waited until January 25, 1942, to make
mention of de Gaulle. The memory of the Dreyfus Affair dictated that
the leftist organizations be wary of an unknown officer who kept quiet
about his political orientations and preferred the military motto "Honor
and Homeland" to the republican triptych "Liberty, Equality, Fraternity." The movements fighting on national soil were contemptuous of
men who had left the metropolis, believing, like Danton, that you do
not take the homeland with you on the soles of your shoes. De Gaulle
was readily likened to an émigré, an injurious comparison to the French
émigrés who had fled to Coblenz after the Revolution and plotted
against the regime in 1791–1793. A number of writings therefore insisted, by way of contrast, on the roots of the movements in French soil.
*La Reconquête (The Reconquest)*, for example, which Alban Vistel launched
in November 1940 before he joined Libération-sud, noted that "this
tract does not come out of the sky but out of the soil of France. It is the
expression of French souls."[63] In addition, connections with London
were not requisite, at least in 1940–1941, especially since the British
withdrawal at Dunkirk and the Royal Navy's attack on Mers el-Kébir
had left a few marks. De Gaulle, moreover, did not wish to finance
movements, often centered on propaganda, that felt no need to coordinate their embryonic military action with the Allies. From that standpoint, non- or anti-Gaullism truly cemented a passive consensus.

## Clashes

Although united by patriotism, sometimes by antiparliamentarianism,
and always by an anti-Nazism mixed with Germanophobia, the movements were divided on essential ideological and strategic choices. For

example, only some of them rejected anti-Semitism from the outset. Quoting Goethe, *Pantagruel* pointed out that "racial hatred is the vice of the rabble."[64] The *Manifeste du syndicalisme français* recalled that "in no case, under no pretext, and in no form can French trade unionism allow distinctions between persons based on race, religion, birth, opinion, or wealth."[65] Others adopted a less clear-cut position. Although *Libération-sud* denounced the anti-Jewish statute in August 1941, it subsequently remained quiet on that subject until February 1942,[66] and denounced the Banque Worms, directed "100 percent by Israelites, who naturally evade the anti-Semitic laws."[67] A few movements even proved to be openly anti-Semitic. In his manifesto of October 1940, Maurice Ripoche called on people to "complete the work of liberation by ridding the Nation of inept and blowhard politicians (good or bad), of stateless Jews."[68] In February 1941, *Les Petites Ailes de France* declared that "in June, the FFL, who for their part are not playing politics, retreated to England, as did a clique of Communist and Freemason Jews and intellectuals. The latter are obviously not involved with the FFL, but strike bargains with the [British] Islanders. . . . All [Édouard] Herriot's riffraff and his clique can thus place Joan of Arc and Robespierre side by side, or shout hip hip hooray!!! for the Jews, the Communists, or the Freemasons, and the announcer of the FFL, waiting his turn at the microphone, cannot say a thing about it."[69] The OCM believed that "there may be a Jewish question to be considered."[70] And *Défense de la France* adopted a convoluted position. "The French will never abide the laws of exception against some citizens," wrote Philippe Viannay. "Let there be no doubt that the problem of foreigners is a terrible problem, that France must defend itself against the invasion of Israel or any other invasion. The fifth column is proof of that. The quality of French citizen must be an honor to which few foreigners can lay claim. They must be integrated only after proving themselves. But let us not go back to the Flood to determine who is French!"[71]

As historian Pierre Laborie concludes: "In the minds of certain leaders of the movements, the idea—exploited by Vichy—clearly persisted that the presence of the Jews raised a real problem for the nation. In this dark zone, one can make out, poorly concealed behind the flimsy screen of an ambiguous discourse, unquestionable signs of ordinary anti-Semitism."[72] Such a position is all the more surprising in that Jews often held leading positions in these movements, whether Libération-sud or the DF. It simply confirms, by its very banality, that the resistance, being an emanation of society, sometimes reflected social prejudices. This position had real repercussions, however. It led the army of shadows to take little interest in anti-Semitic persecution, which was never a priority on its list of urgent concerns.

Vichy drew a second demarcation between the movements, for reasons stemming as much from ideological sympathies as from strategy. From the start, a few movements identified the French State as an enemy from which they expected nothing. *Libération*-nord, *Franc-Tireur*, *Résistance*, and *Libération*-sud, however, refrained from attacking Philippe Pétain to avoid alienating public opinion, which was believed to be in favor of the victor of Verdun. "Be circumspect for the time being when speaking of that old dimwit of a marshal. We all know what that two-bit Franco is worth; all the same, many people have not had their eyes opened yet. It's up to the future to enlighten them. But we risk doing damage to our cause in educating them too brutally," explained Agnès Humbert of the Musée de l'Homme group, when with her companions she came up with the line the newspaper *Résistance* would take.[73]

The other organizations adopted a more circumspect position. In the first place, the Marshal inspired respect by virtue of his glorious past, which, combined with his aura, bestowed a kind of infallibility on him. "He has only the interest of France at heart. He is moved only by what is truly French. He knows how to discern with a very sure instinct what is good or bad for the country in the course of events. A large share of his activity consists of observing," declared Philippe Viannay, for example.[74] But beyond that simple equation between the man and the nation, the reforms undertaken by the Vichy regime were appealing to some of the movements. "We are passionately committed to the work of Marshal Pétain," wrote Henri Frenay in a manifesto published in November 1940. "We subscribe to all the major reforms that have been undertaken. We are filled with the desire that they be lasting and that other reforms come to complement that achievement. It is with that goal in view that we are part of the Mouvement de Libération Nationale."[75] Many other organizations shared that approach, including the CDLL and even the OCM. A few movements, finally, believed or pretended to believe that Vichy was playing a double game, apparently collaborating with the Reich but secretly supporting Free France and/or the United Kingdom.

Such a position is bewildering today, when the hypothesis of a secret complicity between London and Vichy is supported by only a handful of people longing for the return of Vichy France. But in 1989, the publication of Henri Frenay's *Manifeste* caused a stir. A number of former members of Combat went so far as to question the veracity of the document and the honesty of its discoverer, Daniel Cordier. Why hide the fact? That controversy now seems quite pointless. In the first place, Frenay never concealed his pro-Vichy leanings, which are obvious to anyone who reads his memoirs. Above all, and whatever the judgment made about these positions, the movements never erred in identifying the most urgent matter. While fighting the occupier, they constantly declared that domestic reform could not occur under the German jackboot. Frenay himself insisted on that point: "The necessary National Revolution will not come about so long as Germany is able to dictate its will. Chronologically, that National Revolution will come after National Liberation, whose aim is to kick the Boche out of France."[76] In a sense, that position had no practical consequences in the northern zone, where the influence of the Vichy regime was practically nil. We may regret that certain movements were not more clear-sighted about the French State. But it must be said that their ideological complicity never diverted them from their primary mission: resistance. Therein lies, no doubt, the opposition between these Vichy resistance fighters and the "resisto-Vichyists."

## The Resisto-Vichyists

Many French people, in venerating the victor of Verdun, embraced some of his political options and credited him with resistance sentiments. A fringe of the army and a portion of the Vichy state apparatus shared that view, supporting the National Revolution but energetically condemning collaboration, sometimes interpreted as a ruse that would allow France to plan the Revanche. Unlike the Vichy resistance fighters, who, even while defending all or part of the Marshal's domestic program, constructed their action outside or even against the French State, the resisto-Vichyists meant to exploit the resources it offered. Thus, "the resisto-Vichyists were authentic resisters and authentic Vichyists, and that dual identity lay at the heart of their singularity."[77]

Some therefore attempted to provide the United Kingdom, and then the United States, with intelligence, while making life difficult for the spies from Germany or Italy who infiltrated the free zone or the colonies. So it was with the secret services. Before the war, they had reported to two military bureaus: the Second Bureau synthesized the information collected by the intelligence services, while the Fifth Bureau conducted more active investigations. The armistice conventions made it necessary to rethink that system. The Germany and Mediterranean sections went underground, sheltered behind the legal façade of a company, Technica, for which Lieutenant-Colonel Baril took responsibility. The organizations reporting to the Fifth Bureau were assigned to Colonel Rivet, who headed what were now considered unofficial intelligence services (SR), both Colonel Perruche's SR Terre (Land) and Colonel Ronin's SR Air.[78]

These intelligence services continued their espionage activities, even those directed at Germany. Colonel Ronin's SR Air, organized around a head office known as "La Centrale," had eight regional subbranches (Vichy, Limoges, Lyon, Marseilles, Perpignan, Casablanca, and Tunis), which focused primarily on Axis air and sea traffic. For example, agents were placed on German military bases, and an Alsatian secretary even worked at Le Bourget. In addition, the radio monitoring group, which reported to the Ministry of Posts and Telecommunications, managed to install monitoring posts distributed all along the demarcation line, from which SR Air decrypted and processed intelligence. Colonel Ronin's men, finally, sought information about the German order of battle to the west and about the aeronautics industry. Through Captain Lacat and Lieutenant Rauscher, installed in Tunis, a liaison was established with Malta, which made it possible to transmit to the British the intelligence collected about Mediterranean traffic. Other contacts facilitated these liaisons, even at the highest echelons, since Winterbotham (head of the Air Section of the British Intelligence Service) and Ronin were in continuous communication between 1940 and 1942. London even went so far as to provide radios to its French counterparts.[79]

In addition, a counterespionage service was created on September 8, 1940. Under the authority of Colonel Rivet, assisted by Colonel Paillole, it assumed a threefold mission: to protect the armistice army against Axis agents, to provide cover for the underground organizations of the intelligence service, and to exploit intelligence. Two branches co-existed: the first was underground, operating under the official cover of rural workstations, with intelligence as its top priority;[80] the second, acting openly through Lieutenant Colonel d'Alès's Bureaux des Menées Antinationales (BMA; Bureau of Antinational Activities), set out to hunt down the enemies of France. These bureaus arrested collaborationists and agents in the Abwehr, the German army's espionage service. Between January 1941 and June 1942, 194 individuals suspected of spying for the Reich were interrogated and handed over to the courts, and thirty Abwehr agents were sentenced to death.[81] At the same time, however, the BMA energetically tracked down Allied agents, supporters of the FFL, and Communists: 173 Gaullists and 443 Communists were sanctioned, and about ten faced the firing squad.[82] In the words of British historian Simon Kitson, the position of the SR can be summed up as follows: "France is alone. She has many enemies, among them 'Perfidious Albion,' which has betrayed her. But the number 1 enemy is Germany, and the liberation of the country remains the top priority. As a result, we can take advantage of contacts with the English to obtain intelligence about the Germans, though trust in the English remains very limited. There is no question of working hand in hand with them; rather, we must draw the maximum profit from contacts, while handing over to the English the minimum information necessary to maintain that connection."[83]

Apart from collecting intelligence, some military circles also intended to prepare for the Revanche by concealing materiel and drawing up plans to mobilize conscripts when the time came. On September 6, 1941, General Bergeret, secretary of aviation, formed a commission headed by General Rozoy, which was supposed to establish a new doctrine of use for the air forces, in view of the defeat French aviation had suffered. But its work was hardly conclusive. In fact, the report simply repeated the old Vichy refrains, lamenting the pacifism and moral decline of the prewar period, while condemning the poor quality of the materiel. In the same vein, the Third Bureau, in charge of operations, discreetly reconstituted itself (on September 8, 1940) and developed a backup plan for North Africa. But the results of these cogitations remained modest at best.[84] More concretely, General Colson, minister of war in July 1940, General Picquendar, chief of staff, and General Frère, in command of the military region of Lyon, ordered the concealment of weapons. Colonel Zeller, head of the First Bureau of the army general staff, therefore assigned one of his subordinates, Major Mollard, head of the materiel section, to "gather together and maintain armaments and materiel in camouflaged warehouses in the free zone, very often in the homes of private individuals."[85] In 1941, the Camouflage du Matériel (CDM; Materiel Concealment Office) is believed to have stockpiled a total of sixty-five thousand individual weapons and four hundred cannons, as well as munitions and transmission equipment. The collection phase was completed in spring 1941, and Mollard and his men (perhaps three thousand civilians and soldiers in all) then took on the job of maintaining the materiel. Vehicles were concealed at transport companies, called Sociétés XV.[86]

A few leaders, finally, endeavored to prepare for a mobilization that, at the opportune moment, would support an Allied landing. Colonel Revers, chief of staff to General Requin at the time, was in command of the second group of divisions. "Drawing up the list of favorably disposed reservists," he set out to study "the possibility of doubling our four small divisions, thanks to the concealed materiel, so that instead of four small divisions we would have eight, no less small, granted, but eight nonetheless."[87] General Verneau, second-in-command and later chief of staff, was more ambitious: he contemplated how to raise 150,000 men. Comptroller General René Camille, named to head a national bureau of statistics in the Ministry of Finance, invented an ingenious system of perforated cards to identify trained reservists and those assigned to the war industries, while at the same time keeping a list of former members of Chantiers de la Jeunesse (Youth Work Camps). "Most of the time, however, the potential 'mobilized' were merely names on file cards, and nothing guaranteed they would join the movement when the time came,"[88] observes historian Johanna Barasz. On top of it all, for the 1941 census, supposedly of "professional activities," Carmille inserted the question: "Are you of the Jewish race?" As it turned out, the renowned statistician, even while continuing his resistance activity, had offered his services to the Commissariat Général aux Questions Juives (General Commission for Jewish Questions), to "uncover those who have not made their declaration, to monitor the state of assets and their possible transfer, and ultimately to get an accurate picture of the Jewish problem."[89]

Some, finally, strove to infiltrate the state apparatus of the Vichy regime in the purest conspiratorial tradition of the French far right. Georges Groussard, former director of Saint-Cyr, formed a Centre d'Informations et d'Études (Information and Study Center) at the request of the minister of the interior, Marcel Peyrouton. This was designed to centralize intelligence regarding antinational activities. Portrayed by its creator as a resistance bureau, that center included future soldiers in the army of shadows (Stanislas Mangin) as well as supporters of ultracollaboration (Joseph Darnand, Joseph Lécussan),[90] which casts doubt on the purity of its intentions. In actuality, it engaged in "more than a thousand denunciations—often accompanied by proposed punishments and internment—of Communists, Gaullists, members of the former republican parties, Freemasons, Jews, and agents of the [British] Intelligence Service,"[91] clearly demonstrating its political leanings. Above all, it had an armed branch, the Groupes de Protection (GP), which became famous for arresting Pierre Laval on December 13, 1940. The Germans immediately demanded the dissolution of that sulfurous militia, which prompted Groussard to negotiate with London in June 1941. The officers of the GP, he declared, could take charge of the resistance in the metropolis and provide intelligence to London. These plans, however, went unheeded, given that Admiral Darlan imprisoned Groussard on July 15, 1941.

General La Laurencie, for his part, took on a dual mission: to remain faithful to Marshal Pétain even while embodying a political alternative to the Vichy government. A supporter of the strict application of the armistice, he rejected the prospect of a *pax germanica*. On May 2, 1941, he wrote to Admiral Darlan: "In fact, I am hoping for the victory of England, and furthermore, I believe in that victory. . . . The victory of Germany, whatever they say, ensures servitude for many long generations. For despite the promising prospects of a 'collaboration,' which, moreover, has never been clearly defined, I have no confidence in the generosity of our conquerors."[92] Contacting breakaway parliamentarians such as Henry Lémery, La Laurencie sought to be anointed by the resistance movements, hoping both to federate them and to cash in on their legitimacy. In November 1941, the general held a first meeting, attended by Henri Frenay and by two Americans: Colonel Legge, military attaché in Bern, and Allen Dulles, director of the Office of Strategic Services (OSS). In December 1941, a further meeting brought together Frenay and Emmanuel d'Astier de La Vigerie, both of whom vacillated between the desire to make the fiery general "the banner" of the movements and the fear of giving up their authority.[93] Talks were abruptly cut off. Questioned about the fate he reserved for Charles de Gaulle after the war, La Laurencie replied: "We will give him amnesty."[94] Coming from a general officer who had sat on the military court charged with trying de Gaulle, a court that had sentenced him to death, this was a rather startling statement. Combat waited another two months before urging its militants to break off all contact with the general, and Frenay met with him again. But La Laurencie's moment had passed. The rapprochement he agreed to bring about with Gaullism occurred too late not to be suspect in the eyes of Free France's emissaries. In addition, he had shown himself too greedy in aspiring to become head of the movements "when they offered him, at best, the role of a standard-bearer."[95]

General Gabriel Cochet more or less shared the same orientations. On June 17, 1940, the general urged his men not to consider the defeat definitive, encouraging them to conceal weapons. He gave many public lectures and later circulated texts signed with his name, calling for resistance but glorifying Philippe Pétain. The Pétainist authorities tolerated his activity for a time, since it kept up the morale of a badly shaken army. But that activity became "intolerable as soon as he began to denounce the policy of military collaboration implemented in the wake of the Paris protocols."[96] Cochet was arrested on June 21, 1941, then released. Again taken in for questioning on September 6, 1941, he managed to escape on November 26, left France via the Pyrenees in January 1943, and joined General de Gaulle, but not until March. As historian Bénédicte Vergez-Chaignon notes, "The resistance the general was proposing—which he was in fact one of the first to propose—did not constitute itself against Vichy but outside or next to it, by force of circumstance. Cochet did not feel he had diverged from the government line, even less that he had broken away from it. It was Vichy that would rank him among the dissidents."[97]

It is well established that Pétain and high officials tolerated, even covered up, that type of behavior. Georges Loustaunau-Lacau, for example, received 100,000 francs to set up a network, and Frenay benefited from information provided by loyalist soldiers. But the resisto-Vichyists in no way embodied an alternative policy secretly supported by the French State. In actuality, the authorities did not intend to give up their collaboration with Nazi Germany. Vergez-Chaignon explains, "At best, they were approved of only in private. Hence that proliferation, even at a high level, must not create the illusion of an organization decided on by the government and deliberately in violation of the armistice convention."[98] To its misfortune, the resisto-Vichyist movement did not know of, or did not want to understand, the indissoluble bond between the French State's domestic program and its diplomacy: only the alliance with the Reich could ensure the continued existence of the Pétainist regime, which, to maintain itself, had to satisfy the conqueror at all costs. Captain Frenay, by contrast, perceived that reality clearly. Taking an "armistice leave" on January 24, 1941, he lucidly articulated the terms of the debate: "The authorities are not in control of their decisions, since they are under German supervision and they govern only half of France, namely, the free zone. In the shadow of the elderly marshal, factions are fighting for power. We know them: the anti-German faction; the watch-and-wait faction—or rather, the opportunistic faction; the collaboration faction. There is no doubt that the instruments of power are in the occupier's hands. It is therefore the collaboration camp that will prevail."[99] But it was not until 1942 that the scales fell from the resisto-Vichyists' eyes. The invasion of the free zone on November 11 would lead some to break away from the Marshal, others to follow him, but none of their efforts would lead to significant resistance. "So much energy expended to 'put the French army back in the war' and so little to create, in Vichy, the political conditions allowing that resumption of fighting," sighs historian Henri Noguères.[100]

What is worse, the belief in the double game seriously handicapped the army of shadows by depriving it for two full years of the cooperation that some war professionals might have lent it. As historian Claude d'Abzac points out, the subtle strategies of the armistice army, rather than preparing the way for the resumption of combat, resulted primarily "in keeping hundreds of fiercely anti-German officers obedient to Pétain, officers who might have been tempted by General de Gaulle's appeals. In fact, if Pétain was playing a double game, then the inferiority of Free France was glaringly obvious. The hero of June 18 was no longer anything but a troublemaker, a divider, who had not understood the true path of resistance. In raising the shield of the Revanche, the Vichy army denied its rival on the other side of the Channel all reason for existence and deprived it of a great part of its power of attraction."[101]

Vichy thus slowed engagement in the resistance, while seriously dividing the movements. Some tried to act by exploiting the state apparatus; others, even while manifesting Pétainist sentiments, acted outside the system. A few organizations simply disregarded it. Libération-sud, to cite only one example, never sought to associate itself with the French State, giving precedence to a radically different strategy. D'Astier de La Vigerie preferred under the circumstances to rely on leftist circles to expand his influence. Making contact with the Socialist Daniel Mayer in spring 1941, he persuaded the SFIO to assign him its troops. Similarly, in late summer he met with the trade unionist Léon Jouhaux, to "make Liberation a great leftist movement, which Socialists, Communists, the CGT, and the CFTC labor unions will join and where they will work together." Although the secretary-general of the CGT refused to work with the Communists, he did agree, at a second meeting, to the principle of an organic understanding between the resistance group and the militants in his bureau, who were opposed to the National Revolution. As a result, Julien Forgues would represent the union in Libération-sud's leadership. All in all, the agreement "gave that small, almost familial group considerable possibilities."[102] The newspaper would offer one of its four pages to the union, while cadres of merit—Marius Vivier-Merle in Lyon, Robert Lacoste in Thonon—would place themselves in the service of the movement, joined by the leaders of the SFIO: Augustin Laurent, Just Evrard, André Philip, and Pierre Viénot, to cite only a few.[103]

Despite their fragility, the resistance movements were therefore a reality, albeit an embryonic one, in late 1941. Handicapped by the conundrum of Vichy, lacking material resources, gravely divided on certain ideological options, they nevertheless formed a potential base from which to take action, which would gradually increase in strength and credibility. They would, in fact, manage to embody an alternative to

Vichyist renunciation, to establish themselves as partners of Free France, to influence the French people through their words, even when they could not mobilize them against the occupier and the Pétainist regime. Having arisen outside the major French institutions—army, churches, parties, labor unions—that might have structured them, they revealed above all the vitality of a society that, unable to rely on historical precedents, knew how to literally invent the terms and forms of combat. Granted, it is important not to overstate the case. In 1941, the resistance remained a tiny minority within the country, and groups targeted by the authorities disappeared. The movements nevertheless prospered, thanks to the men and women they would manage to bring together.

## Chapter 4

# Engagement

THE ENORMOUS QUESTION of how and why people joined the resistance naturally represents a key issue, but its complexity and political sensitivity are such that historians have been in no great hurry to shed light on it. For many years, Gaullist and Communist recollections, flying in the face of the evidence, claimed that the bulk of the French people had been involved in the army of shadows and had fought the German occupier. Whether or not the French people, in the innermost depths of their consciences, believed in that legend remains unverifiable.[1] In any event, the climate hardly encouraged Clio's disciples to dispute something so self-evident that it was taken for established truth. In the society of "Les Trente Glorieuses," the thirty prosperous post-World War II years, involvement in political parties, trade unions, or associations was such a vibrant reality that it was possible to believe by analogy that such active citizenship had also marked France in the dark years. For all these reasons, researchers were hardly eager to investigate a field so pocked with land mines—and one that was infertile to boot.

For their part, historians were and are reluctant to propose rational explanations for engagement. The motivations that impelled a person to join an underground organization arose in their view from individual determinants. Any rational explanation would therefore betray the meaning, and therefore the essence, of a battle conducted for motives irreducible to any generalization. According to them, the sociological variables or ideological choices enlisted to understand the sacrifices of the revolutionaries of 1848, the Communards, or the Algerian insurgents cannot be applied to French resistance fighters, whose heroism, veiled in mystery, resists any interpretive scheme. Pierre Laborie concludes that resistance "is par excellence a web of intertwined engagements and singular paths that find their true meaning only in the collective dimension of action and in the solidarity formed through a shared experience. That experience was without peer for those who lived it and, to repeat a comment heard a thousand times over, will remain in great part inaccessible and intransmissible."[2]

To reflect on the reasons for joining, one must also define the resistance—a risky enterprise. François Bédarida categorized it as, among other things, a "secret, underground action,"[3] but it is easy enough to invalidate that claim. The miners' strike of May–June 1941 and the housewives' demonstrations in 1942, to cite only two counter-examples, were certainly acts of resistance, but there was nothing secret about them; they were performed openly. "In the end, there are better things to do than to exhaust oneself chasing after the mirage of a rigid definition of the Resistance, which is of no great interest and lies partly beyond reach," concludes Laborie.[4]

That statement does not solve the problem, however, since whatever the criteria or the definitions selected, two major theses stand at odds with each other. For some, resistance was far from a minority phenomenon; on the contrary, it concerned society as a whole. The members of the scholarly board that presided over the publication of the *Dictionnaire de la Résistance* declare: "To reduce the majority of the population to a resigned, even complicitous mass accommodating itself the best it could to the Occupation obscures one major fact: the Resistance was a social process. It could exist, live, and develop only within the dynamic of the connections established within and with French society."[5] Historian Bernard Comte points out: "The sermons of the ecclesiastic who reiterates to his flock the condemnation of Nazi neopaganism, the allusions made by a teacher in front of his class—are these not acts of resistance, even if their authors do not participate in any organized action? What are we to say, finally, about those who sympathized with the actions of the occupier's adversaries without ever taking action, for lack of opportunity, ability, or courage? Resistance is both spirit and action, but sometimes the one does not lead to the other."[6] François Marcot adds: "One must not conceal the fact that counting the number of resistance fighters often entails an instrumentalization put to various purposes: to call into question the representativeness of the Resistance by insisting on their small number; to place on a pedestal an elite, to which you yourself belonged; even more often, to condemn the general attitude of the French population."[7] And he goes on: "To say that resistance was only a minority phenomenon is a truism that can fuel a very cynical view of behavior and human passivity. But that sort of judgment, implicit or not, hardly allows thought to move forward and leaves aside another question, infinitely more difficult to resolve: in twentieth-century French society, is not the Resistance a privileged moment of citizen involvement in the affairs of the nation?"[8]

So be it. But the argument can just as easily be reversed: to assert the large-scale engagement of French people in the army of shadows and to exalt "the general attitude of the French population," to emphasize the effect "of a social movement of uncommon magnitude in contemporary France," is also an instrumentalization that absolves the French people of the sin of a watch-and-wait attitude[9]—a temptation from which neither the Gaullists nor the Communists have broken free. Furthermore, that view is disputable both historically and morally, since it collapses different levels of merit or elevates acts of opposition into heroic feats. It is reminiscent of the words ruthlessly penned by Jean Anouilh in a play titled L'orchestre (The Orchestra; 1962). It contains the following dialogue:

MME HORTENSE: I've got patriotism in my blood! During the war, when I was out of work, I turned down a season in Vichy. And I know some people who did not have such scruples, who even played for the occupier!

SUZANNE DELICIAS: Your insinuations can't touch me. It's true I played in a Paris beer hall in 1940, but it was an orchestra of resisters. Whenever German officers were in the room, we signaled one another to play off-key. And that took a certain courage! We were at their mercy, they could have denounced us, because all those people were musicians.[10]

In a more professional context, Raul Hilberg, the great historian of the Shoah, also objected to an overly generous conception of Jewish resistance. "If heroism is an attribute that should be assigned to every member of the European Jewish community, it will diminish the accomplishment of the few who took action."[11]

It is clear, then, why many have preferred to emphasize that the army of shadows was a minority, readily assimilated to "a small team," to borrow the words of Claude Bourdet, second-in-command of the Combat movement.[12] "We survived on France's complicity. That of

France as a whole? No. Of the part that sufficed," proclaimed André Malraux in 1975,[13] adding that, on June 6, 1944, Charles de Gaulle "had fewer volunteers under his command than Vichy had gendarmes."[14] Charles d'Aragon recalls: "As for the aging witness that I myself am, when he takes inventory of his most distant memories of the Resistance, what he finds in the first place is an impression of solitude. I see again what southern France, Vichy France, was at the time. To be opposed at the time was to condemn oneself to isolation, to be at odds with the majority. At least, that is what I felt and which, no doubt, I would not have felt had I lived as a protester within a people in revolt."[15] And that member of Combat concludes: "There always comes a time when one's fate passes from the realm of history to the realm of gerontology. That is the realm of the former resistance fighters. Generally, they don't age well. But the resistance does. It dons again the rags in which it had been bedecked in the name of some sort of corrective devolution. It appears less and less to be the act of a people unanimous in its revolt. More and more, serious books show it for what it was, namely, a minority movement whose perilous and multifarious existence long unfolded within an environment marked by the majority's incomprehension and hostility. To reiterate that is not to dispute (on the contrary) the merit of all those, killed or still surviving, who participated in its battles and its work."[16]

The opposition between these two views certainly points to ideological orientations at odds with each other. Some, refusing to sell the working classes short, celebrate the muffled roar of a people fighting against a despised occupier. Others deplore the passivity of a society quick to "accommodate itself"[17] to the German presence. It can also lead to a distinction between a "Resistance organization" and a "Resistance movement" encompassing, as François Marcot suggests, "all those who performed individual actions and all those whose acts of solidarity were essential to the organized Resistance."[18]

In networks and in movements, even in parties or underground labor unions, engagement was characterized by its duration, its intensity, and its repetition. The men and women so engaged can therefore be considered members of the resistance. By contrast, the term "member" cannot be used to characterize participants in the resistance movement whose engagement remained brief, occasional, and limited.

But that does not mean that the historian ought to neglect them. As Marcot observes, "An entire history could be written about that resistance outside the Resistance. It constituted the base of the Resistance, its deeps roots in the population, and to say that it was only an appendix would be to diminish it, since it increased the effects of the Resistance when it did not quite simply condition the latter's survival. Such individual and sporadic resistance was immersed in a climate of complicity with the organized Resistance. It provided the intelligence that prevented arrests, the material assistance (lodging, food, liaisons) that facilitated the struggle, the moral support that sanctified the value of the organized militants' engagement and justified the sacrifices they agreed to make."[19] Participation in the resistance movement, however, cannot be placed on the same level as engagement in the resistance organization, which is my sole concern here.

## Identifying the Enemy

Joining the resistance was predicated on a cluster of conditions. Through their struggle, resisters set out to defend humanistic, republican, or patriotic values. "The Resistance is in the first place a patriotic struggle for the liberation of the homeland. [It] is also a struggle for human freedom and dignity and against totalitarianism," writes Henri Michel.[20] The resistance thus represented an ideological battle to begin with, but without being partisan. In fact, a person did not have to have been active in a party to embrace a few essential principles—on the contrary, perhaps. As political analyst Marc Sadoun points out, referring to the SFIO: "In attempting to apply the classic interpretive schemes—historical materialism or pacifism—to the situation created by the occupation of France, militants ran the risk of misunderstanding a phenomenon that called less for analysis than for will, less for knowledge than for volition. . . . The Resistance, a spontaneous, un-thought-out, even irrational phenomenon, closed its doors to militants who confronted the event from the shelter of their doctrinal certainties."[21] Many pioneers had not been political activists before the war, as suggested by the examples of the leader of Franc-Tireur, Jean-Pierre Levy, or the founder of Combat, Henri Frenay. But revolt could draw its motivation from various sources, from patriotism to anti-Fascism. This explains the political diversity—implicit or overt—of the underground organizations. Nevertheless, the defense of these principles required that resisters identify the enemy who was threatening their integrity. Yet, as paradoxical as it might seem, that recognition did not come about automatically.

Granted, many French people were united in their hatred of Germany. The Franco-Prussian conflict of 1870, then World War I, had spurred a deep-seated Germanophobia, which many of the older generation disseminated, especially within their families. "I threw myself into the Resistance because, at home, I was already being told stories of the war of 1870–1871," recounts Maurice Jeanmougin, a resistance fighter from Franche-Comté. "The Prussians had taken my grandfather and great-grandfather hostage near Belfort. And then they escaped near Auxelles because the francs-tireurs, the FFI[22] of their time, had attacked the column. Then they lived a few days with these francs-tireurs as a maquis, and after that, they came home."[23] Likewise, the Alsatians "from the interior," who had chosen France as their homeland in 1870, felt no great love for Germany. "My mother," recalls Jean-Marie Delabre, a member of the DF, "had lived in occupied Lorraine during her childhood, and that marked her a great deal. She had a hatred of the Prussians. She always told me that, in Thionville, when an officer passed on the sidewalk, the Lorrainians had to get out of his way. So we were raised in an anti-German tradition."[24] The northerners were still traumatized by the memory of the brutal occupation they had endured between 1914 and 1918. Many veterans of World War I, finally, shared a profound Germanophobia.

Added to that traditional hatred of the Boche was a rejection of Nazism. Alerted by *L'Aube* and *Temps présent*, the Christian Democrats harbored no illusions about the Hitlerian peril, which they equated with neopaganism—a message relayed through their youth organizations, such as Jeunesse Étudiante Catholique (JEC; Catholic Student Youth).[25] Thousands of Germans (including some thirty thousand Jews), who had fled the Reich between 1933 and 1939 and taken refuge in France, also informed the citizenry of that country about brownshirt totalitarianism, especially when these Germans were taken in and treated like guests—by Berty Albrecht, for example, a close friend of Henri Frenay. Others who traveled to Germany saw firsthand the face of the new order. During the 1930s, the philosopher Jean Cavaillès went often to conduct his research there. These trips, "as well as the German newspapers, especially those of the National Socialist Party, allowed him to stay informed about the political changes in that country and, for example, to learn of the existence of the concentration camps in August 1936."[26] He was far from alone, as evidenced by the example of Pascal Copeau, future leader of Libération-sud, a correspondent in Berlin for *Le Petit Journal* from April 1933 to November 1936, and by that of the Jesuit Father Chaillet, founder of Témoignage Chrétien. A specialist in German theology, Chaillet went to Austria several times, before and after the Anschluss. He immediately understood "the forms and methods of the persecutions."[27] Finally, the Luftwaffe, during the Spanish Civil War, in Poland in 1939, and then on the Western Front in 1940, had displayed unusual violence, as indicated by the bombings of Guernica, Warsaw, and Rotterdam. Its brutality did not bode well for clemency from the victors. German philosopher Walter Benjamin, unable to cross the Spanish border into Portugal, committed suicide in Port-Bou on September 26, 1940, marking with his death the defeat of thought. He preferred to die rather than fall into the hands of his compatriots, from whom he feared the worst, and not without reason. Many resistance fighters, in short, shared the view of Claude Bourdet: "The ignorant madness of Nazi racism and the disaster suffered by German society and culture were the determining factors for me; when I came back to France, I was a staunch antifascist."[28]

Not all French people shared these fears, however. Many misapprehended the reality of Nazism and initially celebrated the victor's "disciplinary action." Others, shaken by the German-Soviet Pact and the defeat of 1940, had their doubts. Deputy Renaud Jean, though a staunch Communist, pondered certain questions while locked up in La Santé prison: "Is the political and economic system of Nazism, as we have repeated for years, a new form of capitalism (better adapted to the new conditions), or, despite the slogans, a revolutionary system akin to Bolshevism?"[29] Nearly a dozen Communist parliamentarians opted for a nationalist communism of collaboration,[30] which can be explained only in part by political opportunism. The necessity of proceeding to a doctrinal stance, whose urgency was signaled by the Molotov-Ribbentrop Pact and the defeat of 1940, no doubt mattered as much to them as the desire to fall in line with the victorious camp. Similarly, Operation Barbarossa impelled some nationalists to embrace the Reich's cause in June 1941. They preferred to defeat Bolshevism rather than fight Nazism alongside the Reds.

On a completely different level, the victor of Verdun's accession to the highest office in the land dissuaded sincere patriots (at least for a time) from becoming involved in the resistance, especially when they shared his political views. They chose to bank on domestic reform rather than fight the occupier. To cite only one example, Captain Pierre Dunoyer de Segonzac ran the École d'Uriage, set up to train the cadres of the French State; but after its dissolution on January 1, 1943, he joined the resistance. Referring to the man who called himself *le vieux chef,* "the old leader," Claude Bourdet points out: "It was tempting, for people in whom political illiteracy and a certain mysticism were closely associated, to retreat to 'sacred France' and to imagine, in the Marshal's shadow, a sort of social brotherhood turning its back both on the French Revolution and on capitalism, like a mythic Middle Ages, revisited and idealized."[31] In short, Vichy led many astray by obscuring the hierarchy of priorities. Without it, "recruitment for the Resistance would have immediately been easier and more widespread."[32]

Not all French people, then, recognized Germany, and especially Vichy, as an adversary to be destroyed. As a result, early experiences during the prewar period, which were certainly diverse, played an essential role in preparing individuals to identify their enemy. The Christian Democrats—through their press, their Parti Démocrate Populaire (Popular Democratic Party), and their youth organizations—offered sure guidelines to their members, alerting them early on to the Nazi peril. Furthermore, they felt little sympathy for Marshal Pétain and embraced "the Republic all the more fervently inasmuch as the salvation of Christianity from its moral compromises with the right was still a very recent venture, which the servile attitude of the senior hierarchy . . . now risked making definitively futile."[33] The long list of Christian Democrats who engaged in anti-German activities in Free France or in captive France (Georges Bidault, Alfred Coste-Floret, François de Menthon, Pierre-Henri Teitgen, Maurice Schumann, and others) confirms that view. Likewise, the SFIO and the PCF quickly came to oppose the French State, whose orientations were diametrically opposed to their values. Granted, some leftists, such as the Socialists Paul Faure and Charles Spinasse, or the union activist René Belin, supported the victor of Verdun. Others opted for collaboration, such as the former Communists Marcel Gitton and Jean-Marie Clamamus. But they were the exception rather than the rule. Right-wing nationalism, finally, had long mistrusted Germany, an attitude that ought to have led its supporters to refuse to come to an understanding with the victor. Some immediately took that tack. The nationalist Henri de Kerillis, who had never stopped inveighing against the rebirth of Prussian militarism, left France in 1940 to join General de Gaulle. He too was an exception. The early resistance, then, was often built on militant practices forged during the interwar period. "It was in fact on that experience that the pioneers relied, first, to react to the shock wave of June 1940 . . . and then, to begin looking for how they could express and propagate their defiance," as Fabienne Federini writes.[34]

And yet, pacifism, anti-Communism, and the desire to remedy the dysfunctions of the Third Republic in order to rebuild France led some to align themselves with pro-Vichy, even collaborationist, positions rather than to join the resistance. In short, what mattered, even more than ethical, moral, or political values, was the ranking given to each one. This shows just how arbitrary any cursory classification would be. To understand the resistance in its diversity, we must begin with individuals more than ideologies, especially since the same doctrinal foundations could lead to opposing engagements, depending on the political and moral priorities each person chose. Henri Becquart, deputy of Nord, and Philippe Henriot, representative of Gironde, both members of the very reactionary Fédération Républicaine (Republican Federation), certainly shared an ardent patriotism, a virulent anti-Communism, and a passionate faith; they also agreed with Vichy's political agenda. Nevertheless, Becquart, who in 1936 had ignominiously accused Roger Salengro of desertion during World War I, broke with Marshal Pétain in 1940. He wrote to the Marshal on October 1, 1940: "In the current circumstances, foreign policy governs everything, and the most excellent measures adopted by a government whose foreign policy offends national feeling are inevitably swept away in the same explosion on the day the country recovers its independence. The policy of groveling before Germany has thus doomed to failure your efforts for internal reform."[35] After Montoire, Becquart went even further, sending Pétain an explicit telegram: "Do not dishonor France. British victory probable. Sign nothing that would hinder it. Resist. Everything can still be saved. My respects."[36] Conversely, Henriot became deeply involved in collaboration, joining the Milice (Vichy's paramilitary police) and becoming a redoubtable firebrand at Radio-Paris. Becquart placed national independence and the fight against Germany at the top of his priorities; Henriot, by contrast, believed that the anti-Bolshevik crusade had to take precedence. The same dichotomy existed on the Catholic right. Pierre Dunoyer de Segonzac and Henri Frenay had the same political horizons. But *le vieux chef* embarked on the adventure of Uriage, while Frenay, even while protesting his respect for the Marshal, founded a resistance movement in 1940.

That said, many French people, while sharing the same disgust for Germany and/or Nazism, refused to participate in the struggle. The mechanisms leading to action coincide only imperfectly with the formation of an opinion: an individual might reject a policy without seeking to oppose it concretely. To take the next step, one had to agree to the terms of engagement, which was no easy matter.

## What Sort of Effectiveness, and for What Battle?

Joining the resistance meant pledging one's life, a peril of which the resistance fighters were fully aware. The action taken therefore had to be worth the risks; in other words, the participants had to deem such action significant. That criterion remained subjective, however. For some, the distribution of an underground newspaper was a childish gesture, because a war is won at gunpoint. Soldiers, for example, rarely opted for that strategy and preferred to put their energies into intelligence, sabotage, or the formation of the Armée Secrète (AS). The Organisation de Résistance de l'Armée (ORA; Army Resistance Organization), which was created after the invasion of the free zone, judged it pointless to publish a newspaper. Others, on the contrary, believed in the power of the word. Faithful to the message of the Bible, Christians weighed the importance of words and judged that the battle could also be won in hearts and minds. "As at the dawn of every genesis, the first and only recourse is the Word. One must emerge from one's lonely dereliction to go toward others. It is impossible that others are not waiting for the words that will create another world," notes Alban Vistel, a member of Libération-sud.[37] Catholics therefore played a preeminent role in the media, both on the air (Maurice Schumann) and in the underground press (Coste-Floret, Teitgen, Menthon, Viannay, and others).

Some resisters did not even believe they could reverse the fortunes of the war with their fight. That concern was beyond their ken. Seeing themselves instead as witnesses, they sought above all to show the world that free souls were rejecting the inevitability of the new order. As the Jesuit Yves de Montcheuil explained upon liberation: "One must not measure the value of their acts merely by their material efficiency. They will have saved the honor of France by showing that the country did not belong to those who wanted to place it in the service of injustice, by bearing witness that France did not wait passively for deliverance but fought to regain its freedom."[38] Many did not think they would live to see the liberation of France and agreed, not without a certain bombast, to sacrifice their lives on the altar of witnessing. "I invented many deaths for myself," recounts Paul Michel-Villaz, a member of the DF. "Superb ones. I had prepared myself for all eventualities. I was absolutely certain I would not weaken at the last moment. Above all, I did not want to cry or beg. No one would lead me like a beast to the slaughter. I had gone to great lengths to prepare for my death. I was sure I would have a fine death."[39] Others, like the future filmmaker Claude Lanzmann, were somewhat oblivious in their behavior. As he confides in his memoirs: "I performed many objectively dangerous actions during the underground urban struggle, but I reproach myself for not having performed them in a state of full consciousness, since they were not accompanied by an acceptance of the ultimate price to be paid in case of arrest: death. Would I have acted if I had taken the entire measure of the action beforehand? And even if you claim that unawareness is also a form of courage, to act without being internally ready for the supreme sacrifice amounts, in the end, to amateurism. That's what I continue to tell myself even today. The question of courage and cowardice, as you've no doubt understood, is the guiding thread of this book, the guiding thread of my life."[40]

In other words, not all resistance fighters necessarily sought to strike the Nazi war machine, nor did they count on reversing the course of the war by their actions. Bourdet notes, "To embark on that adventure, where the reasons for hope were hardly solid, was already a difficult choice. But you also had to have the sense that you could in fact achieve something real, do something useful and effective. At the beginning, however, nothing seemed less certain. What we called 'movements' or 'organizations' were a few isolated cells within the great tide of resignation. We did not have money or weapons. Our underground 'newspapers' were pitiful bulletins, two pieces of letter-size paper containing almost nothing you couldn't hear on the BBC. More than that, at the start so few copies were printed that you heard rumors of them more than you read them."[41]

Others, such as André Malraux, challenged that approach. The author of *Les conquérants (The Conquerors)* joined the army of shadows belatedly, a choice that remains something of a mystery. The leader of the España Squadron lacked neither panache nor physical courage—he had shown that during the Spanish Civil War. Likewise, he enlisted in the French army in 1939, though he had received a deferment in 1922 and had been discharged in 1929.[42] Although hungry for fame, Malraux refrained from publishing for four years under the Nazi jackboot. And, having been close to the Communist Party before the war, he displayed no indulgence toward Vichy. These elements ought to have led him to join early on, especially since his two half-brothers were fighting in the British Special Services. That was not the case, however. In Malraux's eyes, only war counted, but the Francoist victory and the defeat of 1940 had disillusioned him. The historian Jean Lacouture comments: "He had fought in Spain to win. He had lost. He had fought in France, and he had lost. Action was not debased in his eyes; but he was weary of it, disconcerted, more full of questions than of certainties."[43] Above all, worn out from embracing lost causes, he believed neither in the virtues of propaganda nor in the efficacy of terrorism, whose pernicious character he described in his novel *La condition humaine (The Human Condition)*. Terrorism could lead to an orgy of violence, which became "a fascination" for Malraux's character Chen.[44] "In murder," Malraux added in *L'espoir (Man's Hope)*, "the most difficult thing is not the killing. The most difficult thing is not to become debased."[45] Rather than participate in a fight he considered fruitless, even dangerous, he believed it was better to wait until the French could again assume battle formation.

Only then would action be meaningful. Malraux therefore dismissed all the emissaries who proposed that he enlist, Claude Bourdet first among them: "To begin with, the writer snorted, one of those powerful and unexpected snorts for which he later became famous, but which at the time impressed me even more. Then he said: 'Have you got any money?' It was almost like asking a Christian when he had last seen Jesus Christ. I stammered some kind of excuse, some pitiful explanation. Another snort, another question: 'Have you got any weapons?' More stammering, combined with a few hopes, in the form of more or less optimistic predictions, vague as to the place, the time, the nature. 'All right,' said Malraux, 'come back and see me when you have money and weapons.'"[46] In March 1944, the writer finally joined the southwestern Forces Françaises de l'Intérieur (FFI; French Forces of the Interior), showing that, on the eve of the Allied landing, he gave precedence to the military option rather than a civilian strategy.

The sense of effectiveness, subjective and dependent on personal feelings, varied over time. Armed action appeared futile in 1940; it became urgent in 1944, especially after the Normandy landing. The "September resisters," those who enlisted after June 1944, have been the occasion for much mockery. It must be conceded, however, that actions that appeared suicidal at the start of the occupation became self-evidently clear upon liberation. Such engagement, moreover, was not without risk. The summer of 1944 was the bloodiest period of the repression: 42 percent of the death sentences—94 percent of them targeting resistance fighters—were pronounced in 1944, and the month of June took the highest toll.[47] In addition, 21,600 non-Jewish men and women were sent to the camps between June 6 and late November 1944, constituting more than a third of nonracial deportees. More than one in two belonged to the resistance and suffered punishment for that reason.[48] Whatever the view taken of men considered eleventh-hour workers, it must be said that they paid a heavy tribute to the god of war.

## A Matter of Self-Interest?

The auspicious fate enjoyed by a few personalities of "resistance high society" (the expression coined by Georges Altman, editor in chief of Franc-Tireur)[49] has given credence to the idea that the resistance was a profitable investment. The political fortunes of Maurice Bourgès-Maunoury, Jacques Chaban-Delmas, and François Mitterrand, to cite only three illustrious lives, suggest that the army of shadows guaranteed the limelight to several of its members. By that measure, engagement in the resistance could be interpreted as an opportunistic decision that allowed its leaders to pursue a diplomatic career upon liberation. Charles d'Aragon looked with amusement on these very real maneuvers: "In 1942, the comings and goings of the future power elite were taking precise shape. Ordinary French people did not suspect it, but for the best-known resistance fighters, the future was bright. Their eyes were on both the 'blue line of the Vosges' and on the lofty heights of the national palaces. From the depths of my own obscurity, I always saw my leaders and friends advancing, one foot on the road of suffering and peril, the other on that of imminent victories."[50]

On a completely different level, joining the resistance has sometimes been portrayed as a way to escape the grip of repression. Those wishing to avoid the STO supposedly found safe refuge in the French mountains, while Jews had every interest in placing themselves under the protection of the resistance to flee their tormentors. Whether motivated by opportunism or dictated by an imperative to survive, engagement in the resistance would have corresponded in such cases to a well-understood defense of one's own interests. But that view is contradicted by the facts.

In the first place, underground organizations did not have the material resources to take in proscribed persons. They were in fact swamped in the winter of 1943, when thousands of STO evaders rushed to the Alps, hoping to find protection and assistance. Three-quarters of the young people who fled the STO actually preferred to hide on farms, among family or friends, even in their own homes, rather than face the perils of the underground.[51] After all, participation in the resistance posed a real danger, whereas, if an STO evader was arrested, he risked at the very most being immediately sent across the Rhine. "Everywhere, almost systematically, the evaders who were discovered were simply sent to Germany without punishment or particular discrimination. Imprisonment or internment time rarely exceeded four weeks," explains historian Raphaël Spina.[52] "It must therefore be admitted: only a minority of evaders were truly and actively hunted down.

Only a minority suffered the wrath of Vichy's repression, which, moreover, entailed only limited risks."[53] By contrast, a maquisard who was captured faced deportation, if not the firing squad.

Similarly, it was safer for a Jew to hide than to engage in combat activity, which brought him to the attention of the authorities. Of the 991 Jews from the coal field of Lens studied by Nicolas Mariot and Claire Zac, 487 were arrested and 467 deported to the east.[54] But many others left, in two major waves: from late 1940 to early 1941 and then in summer 1942. The free zone was a relatively safe sanctuary when compared to the occupied zone: three-quarters of the Jews who crossed the demarcation line survived, whereas 62 percent of the Jews who remained in the occupied zone were arrested and deported.[55] Crossing the border also offered "a clear chance of survival." Fifty-four Jews from Lens chose that route[56] and managed to take refuge in Switzerland. Few, conversely, opted to join the resistance. When they did so, it was generally after they went underground rather than before. For example, Sylvain Auslender succeeded in hiding and was hired by the Bureau Central de Construction between February 1943 and February 1944, before joining the ranks of the local resistance. Similarly, Kalman Wittenberg left Lens in May 1940, then became a military leader of the resistance in Tarn.[57] But these examples are the exception: unlike exile or concealment, engagement in the resistance was rarely a survival strategy.

In the end, the illustrious fate of a few resistance fighters should not overshadow the fact that such activities led to the death of many men on whom a radiant future shone. Jacques Bingen, Marc Bloch, Pierre Brossolette, Jean Cavaillès, Jean Moulin, and others would have continued promising careers after the war had they not decided to become engaged at the risk of their lives. It was more profitable, in other words, to remain on the job, though that might entail making a few token gestures to the army of shadows toward the end. Such was the choice made by the historian Lucien Febvre. He continued to teach at the Collège de France and directed the revue *Les Annales*, from which, in fact, he ousted its cofounder, Marc Bloch.[58] Bloch, a Franc-Tireur leader in the Lyon region (R1), was arrested and tortured, then shot on June 16, 1944. Febvre's conduct was deemed so shocking that students from the École Normale booed him during his Sorbonne classes after liberation.[59]

Maurice Papon, secretary-general of the prefecture of Gironde, after playing a role in the deportation of Bordeaux Jews, began a successful career that took him to the Paris prefecture of police, then to the hallowed halls of several ministries. Jean Moulin, by contrast, met the tragic fate we all know. Arrested by Klaus Barbie, head of the Gestapo in Lyon, he died after suffering atrocious torture inflicted during his transfer by train to Germany.

It is true that the occupation opened vast vistas for the ambitious. As Fabienne Federini puts it succinctly: "There was a social interest in not protesting publicly, in keeping quiet about the situation that proscribed persons faced. That interest was shared by all those in the social space, at every level, who took advantage of the physical or symbolic disappearance of their direct rivals in order to attain a social position corresponding to their aspirations."[60] The example of Jean-Paul Sartre confirms that view. Granted, the author of Les Mots (The Words) founded a short-lived resistance movement called Socialisme et Liberté, but he put an end to it rather quickly: "In his view, the risk incurred appeared disproportionate to its effectiveness."[61] Conversely, the dismissal in 1941 of his Jewish colleague Henri Dreyfus-Le Foyer opened up a spot for him to teach at the Lycée Condorcet; his decision to accept the position marked the distance "between the moral rigor he applied to others and his own practical attitude toward life."[62]

Such observations invite a forceful shift in perspective. Far from reckoning on a benefit to be gained from joining the struggle, resistance fighters faced a threat to their professional, social, and personal situation. Many suspended their studies, quit their jobs, and disrupted their family lives. Like many militants, they neglected "the present to better assure the future," and expressed a collective identity while suppressing "their personal characteristics."[63] Whereas the Vichy regime embodied betrayal, and the French people, suffering from want, withdrew to the private sphere, the resistance fighters placed the collective good at the heart of public life. That logic led them to give precedence to the medium term over the short term and obliged them to abandon their personal interests. The desire to protect specific interests, however, sometimes increased the will to fight the occupier or the Vichy regime. The Christian Democrats assessed the perils the French Catholic church faced in supporting the French State. Through their fight, they hoped to preserve the chances of Catholicism when the war was over, demonstrating by example that not all believers had been marred by the Pétainist adventure. Similarly, many of the members of the OCM (Jacques Arthuys, for example) had been activists before the war in organizations that claimed to represent the middle classes. They dreamed of a third way that would renounce the ravages of collectivism and the excesses of liberalism, a dream that the polarization brought about by the FP had supposedly shattered. They therefore hoped to make their voices heard upon liberation and to send packing both the Communist left and the conservative right.[64] The early publication of the OCM's *Cahiers* attested to that ambition. Engagement in the resistance sometimes paired the defense of political interests with the primacy of the public interest. But (though this is subject to verification), the pursuit of individual benefits, which were in fact only hypothetical, played a marginal role at best, and in any case, a belated one.

Likewise, geopolitical speculations rarely motivated engagement in the resistance. Although de Gaulle based his approach on a visionary analysis—namely, that the war would necessarily become global— resistance fighters did not usually undertake a rational examination of the situation to discern which camp would prevail.[65] Alban Vistel confides: "At a time when there is no horizon left, the lure of success or of a reward, even in the afterlife, can be only a futile pursuit on which one cannot dwell. Action in the interest of atonement bore within itself its own end, in an asceticism that had its source in the very depths of the individual. Salvation of one's people, of one's national community? No doubt one thought about it, but only as a vague possibility. In reality, a man confronted himself in absolute solitude and with no space in front of him except the space he would be able to conquer. If the idea of salvation crossed his mind, it brought no comfort, since that salvation could be nothing but the affirmation of his own worth."[66] Strategic prognoses therefore played no role, at least until 1942. Vistel continues: "Every promise seemed pointless, and the most learned analysis of the geopolitical data would have led only to a comfortable absenteeism."[67] Usually, resistance fighters joined up not because they judged that the Reich was destined to be defeated, but because an inner urge impelled them to act. Their response was more emotional than rational. The unpredictability and brutality of the defeat had been a shock. The presence of an occupier close at hand on a daily basis, and who came to occupy the most ordinary places—high schools, hospitals, restaurants, movie theaters—intensified that shock. Events serious or minor added up over the dark years and could impel the population to perform actions that were not necessarily filtered through reason. Paul Béquart, a member of the DF, explains: "In front of the statue of Montaigne, hence at a certain distance from Boulevard Saint-Michel, I heard people singing 'La Marseillaise.' They were rounded up by the Germans, preceded by the Feldgendarmerie. Perhaps they would be shot momentarily or in the next few hours? When I heard them, my decision was virtually made. I could not go on feeling like I was doing nothing in the face of that. That's a character trait, emotional or psychological as you like, which has always remained with me and which I understand better today. Personal decision making is connected to something very individual, which is that I cannot be a bystander to a social action once it elicits an emotional reaction in me."[68]

The decision to join the resistance thus drew from two different but complementary sources. The will to defend principles threatened by the new circumstances of the year 1940 combined with the desire to react against a situation perceived as intolerable. That engagement occupied the dual register of conscience and emotion. These two necessary conditions were not sufficient, however. The battle the resistance fighters were preparing to wage also required practical skills. At the same time, resisters had to remain true to their principles.

## Modes of Action

In situations of dissent, "people tend to act within known limits, to innovate at the margins of existing forms, and to miss many opportunities available to them in principle," writes historian and sociologist Charles Tilly.[69] That is, everyone possesses a "limited repertoire of collective action" that defines all the means of protest available.[70] In order to act, militants therefore had to make use of a certain range of practical know-how, which did not always correspond to advanced skills. Any individual, for example, could distribute underground newspapers or tell an "honorable correspondent" the exact nature of the German railroad convoys streaming past his windows. The transformation into a saboteur or a radio operator, by contrast, required training inaccessible to most people.

Involvement in the resistance thus placed individuals in a situation of inequality. Professional skills and political training before the war provided some with extensive resources. A Communist engaged in activities since the 1920s had mastered the technique of distributing tracts, knew how to organize a strike or demonstration, and possessed military training—if, like Henri Rol-Tanguy, he had fought in the International Brigades during the Spanish Civil War. A typographer knew all the mysteries of printing and page layout. By contrast, a young student at the Sorbonne had very little to offer, apart from his capacity to write and think. That inequality in terms of practical knowledge or expertise played an ambivalent role, since it could either hinder or spark engagement. Some, yearning to act, wondered what role they could play in an underground organization. Others, possessed of a wealth of talents, could instantaneously place their skills in the service of the army of shadows.

These initial inequalities eroded over time, however. Many tasks required only limited skills. The Gaullist secret services in general and Colonel Rémy in particular relied on ordinary people to set up their networks, though they were met with skepticism from the British, who preferred to use dedicated spies. Rémy, for example, recruited a wine merchant, Lavédrine, who for professional reasons often had to go to Saint-Nazaire, where the Germans were setting up a submarine base. "He has no map of Saint-Nazaire except a little sketch, torn from a post office calendar," wrote Rémy. "We have agreed that, on the pretext of visiting his clientele, he will go regularly to Saint-Nazaire, and I will let him know what information interests us."[71] Movements and networks sometimes organized training for their members. The printer Jacques Grou-Radenez taught Charlotte Nadel and several other members of the DF the skills of typesetting and letterpress printing. Professional practices were occasionally adapted to suit the unusual conditions of the German occupation. Jean Pelletier (Jim), for example, recruited an architect, René Bourdon, and assigned him the task of finishing and then printing up the plans collected by the CND network.[72]

Similarly, ancient traditions were reactivated and adapted to fit the new circumstances of the war and the occupation. In Provence, rural

resistance fighters identified with the "social bandit" model.[73] Chari-
vari, a medieval tradition of mock wedding serenades that developed
into a noisy response to any unpopular situation, experienced a revival.
In May 1941, about twenty youngsters between fourteen and eighteen
starting singing "L'Internationale" in the village of La Cadière in Var,
then sounded the priest's alarm bell.[74] The Protestants of the Cévennes
embraced a very ancient tradition, which made it the "duty of each
church to protect the persecuted and to assist them," prompting them
to look after those in need and to take them in.[75] The song "La Com-
plainte des maquis cévenols" (The Lament of the Cévennes Maquis)
explicitly recognized that lineage:

> The proud children of the Cévennes,
> Defectors and maquisards,
> Show they have in their veins
> The pure blood of the Camisards.[76]

Smugglers, in the habit of secretly crossing the Swiss or Spanish
border, metamorphosed into rescuers. The SOE Vic network employed
their services, through the Spanish republican general known as
Martin.[77] And poachers, accustomed to defying the state's authority,
helped people cross the demarcation line on trails they had been using
for a long time. In the Jura, several acted "out of the atavistic instinct
that so often drives the rural Sequani to go against the order imposed
by others and predisposes them to hunt or poach, to smuggle, or to
choose marginalization," historian François Marcot points out.[78]

On the whole, however, their actions ran up against formidable obstacles. With the exception of military specialists in espionage, founders
of the movements and networks literally had to invent the forms of their
engagement. That required an especially fertile imagination, since they
could rely neither on historical precedents nor on institutional structures with a tradition of struggle behind them: initially, neither the
army nor the parties nor the trade unions called on people to do battle.

In view of their deficits, the first resistance fighters often believed
that their incompetence prevented them from finding a useful role in
the army of shadows. Many would have much preferred to go to Britain
and to fight in uniform. Regular war belonged to familiar intellectual
frameworks; it was the most obvious way to overcome the Reich and to

avenge the defeat of 1940. And it required no particular aptitude, except that of a soldier. Several pioneers attempted to join Charles de Gaulle. Henri Gorce-Franklin, future leader of the Gallia network, tried to reach Spain in summer 1940, but to no avail; in January 1941, Pierre Bénouville went to North Africa in the hope of fighting alongside the British, before returning to Combat; Antoine Avinin made many attempts to cross the Mediterranean, but finally joined the Franc-Tireur movement. The act of joining the internal resistance organizations was thus often experienced as an engagement by default. Not all pioneers wanted to conduct the struggle in the metropolis and were delighted when they could finally wage open warfare. "To set out against the enemy, weapons in hand and in broad daylight, was for a fighter in the Armée Secrète a joy verging on intoxication," admits Pierre Bénouville who, after working in the underground as part of Combat, joined the Italian theater of operations.[79] Conversely, a few pioneers made a deliberate choice to remain in the metropolis. "If I leave France, they'll say I deserted. I believe that the French people will be grateful after the war to those who shared their dangers and their woes," the union activist Léon Jouhaux declared to Christian Pineau, who was urging him to go to London.[80] All in all, the modest skills the resistance fighters believed they possessed for waging their battle tended to be a hindrance rather than an asset.

In addition, the terms of the struggle had to be consistent with—or at least not in contradiction with—the values the resistance fighters were defending. Several forms of action proved problematic, in the first place the execution of individual soldiers. Advocated by the Communist movement from August 1941 on, that method profoundly shocked a fringe of the Catholic world, faithful to the biblical dictum "Thou shalt not kill." In March 1944, when Philippe Viannay published an editorial titled "The Duty to Kill" in *Défense de la France*,[81] a few troubled militants sought out the advice of Father de Montcheuil. The Jesuit priest explained at the time that killing under conditions of war was not a crime but the way to fight injustice.[82]

On a less tragic note, some practices upset resisters whose upbringing was at odds with the demands of the underground struggle. Men and women raised to assign the utmost value to truth, honesty, and discretion now had to lie, steal, and spy—a metamorphosis that was not at all easy. They also had to learn to violate laws that, as good citizens, they had respected without a second thought before the war. At times, the rules of the underground life posed a few special problems, and some had difficulty adjusting to them. "General Delestraint, who had taken General Desmazes as his assistant, arrived with him one day for a meeting, which was to be held in an apartment. First on the landing, then outside the door of the room where people were waiting for them, they had exchanged a thousand courtesies: 'Be my guest, my dear general,' 'After you, my dear general . . .' After which, General Delestraint, upon entering the room, introduced himself: 'I am Monsieur Vidal.'"[83]

Members and their organizations were thus in a dialectical relationship. As a general rule, individuals did not choose their training. "The new arrival necessarily found himself compelled to participate in the activities of a network or a movement that he had not really chosen," Henri Noguères explains.[84] "How many French people during those dark years waited in vain for the opportunity to become associated with one or another of our networks!" adds Colonel Rémy:

> It was best not to imitate that retired old navy officer in Toulon—the father of one of our officers in the Free French naval forces—who was desperately seeking a "contact." Finding an underground publication slipped furtively into his mailbox from time to time, he got the idea of drawing up a list of his friends and acquaintances. Beginning with the letter "A," he sent them the seditious paper in a sealed, stamped envelope, with his visiting card stapled to it. His ploy went on for several weeks, during which time he received no response. Even more surprising, no one came to arrest him. He had run through more than half the letters of the alphabet when a friend came by and knocked on his door, dragged him to the most remote room in the house, and exclaimed, "Have you gone nuts?" "Why do you say that?" "You're not crazy to send stuff like that with your visiting card attached? Do you think that's how it works?" "How it works where?" "In our networks, you imbecile!" "Eureka!" cried the old officer in front of his dumbfounded friend. "Eureka! I have my contact!"[85]

But the reverse was equally true: the organizations had to show extreme caution in their recruitment efforts. Infiltration of the underground organizations was the preferred means the authorities used to break up the resistance. The Combat movement in the Lyon region, probably in the second half of 1942, made an effort to set down a few rules:

> There is no diploma for courage, for sincerity, for enthusiasm, for simplicity, for discipline, for open-mindedness, or for self-denial. Certificates and titles are not a diploma for intelligence. Yet it is those qualities that make a man worthy of the name, that distinguish the true revolutionary from the loudmouth demonstrator.
>
> Also, do not judge a man on the basis of his friends' praise. They will tell you: "So-and-so is a terrific guy." It's possible. *Look at him.* Consider his gaze, his handshake, his appearance, his way of speaking, even more than the great deeds he may have performed in the civilian or military arena.
>
> Finally, put him to the test for some time. Entrust modest missions to him at first, then missions of gradually increasing importance. Carefully verify his discretion and the appropriateness of his relationships.[86]

The decision to stay in an organization required a minimal consensus about the strategy being followed. In cases of dissent, the militant could either express his disagreement or resign,[87] and these two responses usually occurred one after another. André Brunschwig (Bordier), for example, disapproved of Libération-sud's support for the strikes launched in the Lyon region in late 1942 and then joined Libération-nord. Likewise, Jean Cavaillès preferred to abandon Lucie Aubrac's movement to conduct more military action within the framework of the Phalanx Zo network. Jacques Lusseyran, refusing to confine himself to distributing a newspaper, a line advocated by Pierre Cochery, left Les Volontaires de la Liberté to join the DF. Although it is difficult to evaluate the statistical evidence, dozens of resisters changed organizations when they believed they did not correspond, or no longer corresponded, to their expectations. The liberation of North Africa in November 1942, the presence of General Giraud, then the arrival of General de Gaulle in Algeria in May 1943 reinforced the attraction that Free France and regular war had exerted for a long time. For good reason, it seemed less difficult to cross the Pyrenees via Spain and join the resurgent French army or the FFL than to cross the English Channel. Some twenty-three thousand volunteers successfully made that southern journey.[88] Some, no doubt, had already fought in the army of shadows, though for lack of statistics it is impossible to say how many.

We do know at least that active military personnel represented 18 percent of the men who traveled through Spain to North Africa in 1943 and 1944, a sign of the pull exerted by General Giraud for a time.[89] In addition, 5 percent of the members of the DF left the group between 1941 and 1944. Sometimes they had lost contact or feared for their safety, but sometimes they enlisted in the FFL. Twenty-four individuals (out of a total of some three thousand members) made that choice.[90]

By contrast, some resistance fighters worked simultaneously for several organizations, combining, for example, a movement and a network. The underground groups had to take their members' expectations into account or risk eroding their numbers. The formation of irregular groups, such as the maquis in 1944, was one of the ways to satisfy a hunger for action that the civilian strategy did not allow. Indeed, the taste for adventure also had a certain weight—sometimes a significant one—in decisions about which organization to join.

## Everyday Life

Unlike the poilus during World War I, whose experience is encapsulated (perhaps wrongly) in trench warfare, resistance fighters faced the ordeals of the conflict in diverse ways. A member of the Glières maquis had little in common with an agent in the CND, a militant of Libération-nord, or someone who conducted air operations.

This diversity can be explained in part by how willing a resistance fighter was to take risks. Some people joined the army of shadows without feeling any particular inclination for the transgressive behavior and perils that life underground required. Others, by contrast, enthusiastically embraced a life of adventure. Many, obsessed by the heroic stories about World War I, impressed by the feats of aviators during the interwar period, or in awe of the sagas of the great colonizers had their own dreams of taking up the torch. "Between the age of eight and nine," recounts Marlyse Guthmann, a resistance fighter in the DF, "I read *Marushka*, a book that told the heroic story of a little girl in Russia. And I always identified with that little girl. My brother and I used to say: 'We'll never have the chance to be heroes.'"[91]

"To be honest, I must admit that I am and remain a born adventurer. My sudden passion for philosophy is only spiritual adventurism."

So wrote Boris Vildé, one of the leaders of the Musée de l'Homme group, on September 18, 1941, in the journal he kept in prison. "That demon of curiosity is precisely the mark of adventurism. Love of the unpredictable. When I used to play chess, I would often make a rash move: not for lack of ability or from mental laziness, but quite simply to see what effect it would have and how I would manage (usually, in fact, I extricated myself very well, and I especially liked to win hopeless matches).

"Same thing in life: I push myself on purpose into grave or desperate situations to see how I will get out of them, or how life will go about resolving a complicated situation. It's wonderful to have arrived at a point where only a miracle can save you (especially if you're not always sure the miracle will happen)."[92]

Different personalities and character traits account for why the resistance was experienced by some as asceticism, while others enjoyed more profane pleasures. As Rémy tells it, in January 1943, assigned to bring Fernand Grenier back to London to seal the PCF's commitment to join Fighting France, he equipped himself with an enormous azalea:

> "Excuse me?" the Communist deputy retorted.
> "An azalea. You know, a large plant in a pot, with white or pink flowers."
> His eyes got big.
> "It's for the boss's wife," I told him in confidence.
> "Who?"
> "Madame de Gaulle!"
> Grenier stares at me, looking upset, clearly taking me for a madman and no doubt wondering to himself how our adventure is going to play itself out. It wouldn't take much for him to return to the platform, but the train is already moving.[93]

In other words, the Communist deputy had only a moderate taste for adventure:

> Rémy informs me that the parcel that so intrigues me is an azalea. A large plant with white flowers in a pot, for "the boss's wife." And he explains: Madame de Gaulle.
> I retort: "But you're not taking to heart the advice you gave me: no baggage. In my briefcase, I have a shirt, a razor, a towel, and that's all. . . . If you want to bring flowers from France to Madame de Gaulle, a bou-

quet of violets or mimosa flowers slipped into the pocket of your coat would have the same significance . . ."

. . . We Communist resistance fighters had also committed reckless acts, and our time in the underground exacted a high cost. But whims like Rémy's, as late as January 1943, when our arrival in London was so important for the unity of the Resistance, were beyond my understanding.[94]

Did engagement in the resistance, transgressive by nature, require strong, even atypical personalities? Claude Bourdet thinks so: "All those men were nonconformists in one way or another, hard to manage, sometimes 'tough customers,' sometimes 'eccentrics.' None corresponded to the usual image of the good citizen concerned about what people will say and respectful of the established order."[95] But the sociology of the resistance belies that statement.

Whether life was conceived as an adventure or as a duty, it continued to make its own demands. Despite the weight of his responsibilities, Jean Moulin conducted a complicated love life during the dark years, seeing a beloved mistress and trying to seduce another woman while being hunted by the Gestapo.[96] Philippe Viannay and Hélène Mordkovitch married in the midst of the war and produced a child, Pierre, born on July 14, 1943. Lucie Aubrac was pregnant when she reached England, having helped her husband, Raymond, escape. She gave birth to her daughter Catherine on February 12, 1944.

Beyond temperament, material conditions shaped the relationship the secret resistance fighters maintained with the world of the underground. A handful of militants, working in the networks or belonging to the upper echelons of the hierarchy, could sometimes enjoy the good life. Disregarding security orders, they frequented black market restaurants and pursued multiple love affairs. The small SOE team that blew up transformers in the Bordeaux region in spring 1941 returned to Spain, having spent 250,000 francs in two months, leaving "a trail of broken glass if not of broken hearts behind them."[97] Similarly, Colonel Rémy, in possession of a great deal of money, went to the best restaurants, living the dark years in style. In 1942, to mark the expected success of an attack (which would fail) against German troops parading down the Champs-Elysées, he reserved a table at Ledoyen.[98] On May 15, 1942, he dined at Prunier, a restaurant where he was a regular.[99] And on Tuesday, June 9, 1942, after a series of hard blows, including the likely betrayal of his radio operator Capri, he sought solace at Schubert on boulevard du Montparnasse, with his agent "Champion," accompanied by his wife. "The food at Schubert is excellent," he writes. "The hostess, who has a very distinguished bearing and says she is from Kharkov, uncorks a bottle of Hungarian wine. I ask the pianists to play us the Spanish music I like so much. They run through the best-known tunes by Albéniz, Granados, and Falla."[100] "Rémy could spend on a single meal what we had to live on for a month," Fernand Grenier comments ruefully.[101]

For the majority, by contrast, day-to-day life was a trial, and there was nothing fun about it. Resistance fighters spent long hours in crowded trains, rushing from one meeting to another. They covered unbelievable distances on bicycle. "Oh, the cycling world has not recorded our names or our performances," recounts Rose Fernandez, a resister from the Aude department. "Yet how many of us had legs that logged impressive numbers of miles, which I refuse to add up? To provide fresh supplies for comrades imprisoned at Saint-Sulpice, we biked to Lauragais in search of provisions. To bring clean linen and news to our comrades hidden away in every corner of the department, to make our connections, to carry letters, to pedal without letup on roads crisscrossed by German troops and their Feldgendarmerie: that was our obscure and inglorious lot."[102]

Underground agents lived in modest and poorly heated apartments, renting a *chambre de bonne* (furnished room) here, a bed with a local resident there. They moved frequently to escape the zeal of the authorities. "In the space of a few months, we had a small worker's flat, dark and freezing-cold, on rue des Varennes in Vierzon; a barn in Sonnac where, as soon as the light went out, large rats would come up onto the bedspread; several hotel rooms in Capdenac-Gare and in Fondamente, rented for the regional PC[F] . . . and, in Montpellier, not far from the Peyrou, the beautiful bourgeois home lent to me by 'my director' [that is, by Montagnac, general director of the Office des Céréales]," recalls Henri Noguères, member of the Mouvements Unis de Résistance (MUR; Unified Movements of the Resistance).[103] For reasons of security or convenience, adds Francis-Louis Closon, an envoy from London, "I'd go from one place to another. I lived in a Parisian pied-à-terre on the ground floor, overlooking the courtyard of a grand building on boulevard Haussmann. I lived there without heat for one cold, terrible winter, with no way of warming myself when I jumped out of bed in the morning, except to dive into the bathtub and rub myself raw with a scrub brush under cold water, which has a numbing effect. I went out red, warm, and covered in sweaters. Transformed into an insulation cooker, I retained a tolerable warmth."[104] Despite his power and his plentiful funds, Jean Moulin lived very modestly and was stingy about subsidizing his collaborators. When his secretary, Daniel Cordier, sheepishly admitted on November 22, 1942, that he had had a second bicycle stolen, Moulin announced icily, "Well then, you'll go on foot!"[105]

Being in the resistance was also stressful. In the first place, resistance fighters had to divest themselves of their former identities, usually adopting carefully chosen pseudonyms. Some opted for all-purpose names, like the Communist Georges Marrane (Léon). Others saw to it that their new identity alluded to their duties (Vélin [Vellum], for the printer André Bollier), to history (Kléber for Jean-Jacques Chapou, Fouché for Francis-Louis Closon), or to geography (Vercors for Jean Bruller). Some pseudonyms promoted an agenda (Indomitus for Philippe Viannay), and a few resisters were not averse to irony. Maurice Kriegel, for example, wanted to call himself Warlimont, after the Wehrmacht general, but a misspelling made him go down in history as Valrimont. The Gaullist secret services baptized their agents assembly-line style, first with the names of metro stations (Saint-Jacques, Passy, Corvisart) and then, for regional military delegates sent to the metropolis from September 1943 on, with geometrical terms (Hypothénuse, Droite, Polygone, Circonférence). Some had trouble giving up their identity; others were delighted to do so. "The norm, the rule, was to no longer bear one's own name, to no longer have any social position, to no longer seek one," acknowledges Jean Cassou, a member of the Musée de l'Homme group. "Since others had come to terms with my appearance, I could blossom in the company of men who were no longer anything but themselves, who no longer carried any baggage with them except the single conviction that had put them there."[106]

They also had to adopt a rigorous discipline, constantly make sure they were not being followed, never blindly trusting those around them. Francis-Louis Closon recounts: "Systematic mental gymnastics allowed me to empty out my memory. I never knew anything but the indispensable; the detailed security system I diligently maintained became a reflex.

Getting home always required a large number of precautions. When I was in a car in the metro, I arranged to be right next to the exit. At the last moment, as the doors were closing, I would slip out in a rush, like a scatterbrain who has almost missed his stop. When I was alone on the platform, I could make sure I was not being followed. I let two trains go by and then I went on my way, my mind at ease."[107] "In June 1943," confides Henri Guillermain, an operations officer, "I spent four full nights going between landings, parachute drops, inventories, the transport of arms, etc., sleeping only sixteen times [that month].With special lozenges dropped by parachute, I managed to go four days and three nights without sleeping, but after forty-eight hours, I acquired a sneaky headache I could not get rid of, despite the aspirin tablets."[108] As Henri Noguères remembers, "In Lyon, capital not only of the Resistance but also of the Gestapo and the Milice, it was always a test of nerves to exit the Gare de Perrache between a double line of *miliciens*. And that test was repeated often."[109]

Even the intrepid Rémy sometimes cracked. As he ruminated in June 1942:

> For more than a week, I haven't come home without the conviction that I was going to be arrested during the night. Something has snapped in me. I am guided by a sort of fatality. I've thought a lot about leaving my apartment, but I haven't had the courage to do it. It seems to me I would be letting down my friends who have been arrested. And then, I've gotten used to this space, where [my wife] Edith has lived for a few days. And besides, I'm tired.
>
> If I have to be caught, too bad. Or maybe it's all to the good. This constant anxiety, the screeching brakes I hear in the night that make me rush out onto the balcony—not to escape, I've reconnoitered the place and I don't have a chance—but simply to look, to see the car that will enter the square, not too fast, that will stop downstairs by my door, those men who will get out, who will be up at my place in a minute.[110]

The resistance fighter moved in a schizoid atmosphere. Claude Bourdet recalls: "Most of the time, I lived completely underground. Of the people I knew, I saw only a small number of trustworthy friends. But from time to time, I treated myself to a back-to-normal evening, I assumed my old identity, I went out to dinner with my father, or sometimes, when my wife was in Paris, I went to the theater with her. Even so, most of the time, I went around with a pistol hidden in the sleeve of my jacket: experience had shown that comrades owed their salvation to the ability to shoot first."[111] Daily life was rarely exhilarating, and the repetitive tasks were unpleasant. "Early on, I had the impression that the Resistance was turning me into a kind of petty bureaucrat and party official, something between a subprefect stuck in a lousy job and a vice consul in an underprivileged country," notes Charles d'Aragon.[112] Bourdet confirms: "Until my arrest, my own life was basically that of a functionary of sorts, a bureaucrat composing circulars and sitting on committees. Nothing distinguished you from an ordinary bureaucrat, except the precariousness of your situation, a certain way of glancing right and left when leaving one place to go to another, and often the presence of an automatic pistol under your left arm."[113]

Although funds from London allowed a handful of *condottieri* to live their epic adventure with plentiful resources, the vast majority of the resistance fighters experienced cold, hunger, fear, deprivation—and boredom. Engagement in the resistance therefore cannot be explained solely by the desire to lead an exciting life that broke free from the monotony of days. On the contrary, the trying conditions of the underground ought to have dissuaded volunteers from embracing a fate that promised more thorns than roses. That was not the case, however, since the resistance offered volunteers personal fulfillment. "Never were we freer than under the occupation," wrote Jean-Paul Sartre when the war was over. Many in the underground could have endorsed that apparently paradoxical statement, if only because, through their struggle, resisters lived in harmony with their principles. Jacques Bingen, an envoy from London, wrote before committing suicide to avoid betraying his comrades under torture:

> Morally speaking, I want my mother, my sister, my nephews, my niece— she knows it already and will serve as a witness—as well as my dearest friends, both men and women, to really know how phenomenally happy I have been these last eight months.
>
> There is not one man in a thousand who, for eight days of his life, experienced the extraordinary happiness, the feeling of satisfaction, that I have felt constantly for eight months.
>
> No suffering will ever be able to take away the gain in joie de vivre that I have just experienced for so long.[114]

But the resistance also allowed men beaten down by history to regain control and to affirm the triumph of their independence over the inevitability of the facts. "All my novels exude the horror of History, that hostile, inhuman force that, uninvited, invades our life from the outside and obliterates it," confides Milan Kundera.[115] Engagement in the resistance reversed that perspective by offering rebels the possibility of intervening in the march of time and of restoring the primacy of the will over the imperiousness of fate. To a lesser degree, it also granted the minority of women who entered its ranks the right to participate in a civic space from which they were excluded, since the French republic had not granted women the right to vote. That affirmation was also generational: some younger members wanted to show they were equal to the victors of World War I, others to demonstrate, in the face of the resignation of their elders, that they were taking over from a generation in decline.

Understood from the individual standpoint, engagement in the resistance was thus the result of a complex combination of factors. The desire to fight to preserve values judged essential played a key role. It must be acknowledged, however, that, more than the principles themselves, what mattered most was their ranking—the priorities that individuals set for themselves. That said, neither ideology nor ethics can on its own explain the decision to act. As British historian H. R. Kedward points out, patriotism is a "concept which runs throughout the history of Resistance, turning the wheels of explanation." "Many who use it unthinkingly forget that patriotism in 1940 was the justification for many points of view, not least support for Pétain. . . . There is an implicit assumption in this 'essentialist' approach that the defeat and Armistice of May–June 1940 carried, or should have carried, the same emotional charge for all French people; and that it was possible for individuals of totally different backgrounds and interests to react in the same patriotic manner."[116] In short, factors other than love of country conditioned engagement. The enemy had to be identified, which was not necessarily an easy matter. Resistance fighters also had to think that their action had a certain effectiveness, a notion that eluded all objectification. Volunteers had to accept the nature of struggle proposed by their organization, even if that meant making the necessary adjustments over time, whether by forcing the movement or the network to change, making other commitments in the underground, or even leaving their own group to join Free France. Finally, the gift of oneself corresponded to personal aspirations that cannot be reduced to the hope for material gain. Through their fight, volunteers sometimes satisfied their taste for adventure but, more generally, they made their lives consistent with their principles, by responding to the dictates of their conscience.

These individual motivations are irreducible to any unifying scheme, as the diversity of experiences confirms. Must we therefore give up the idea of any further generalization? Not at all. The resistance was not a faithful reflection of French society. Political organizations, leading lights, and social classes contributed unevenly to it, as evidenced by the heterogeneity of its composition, which evolved with the progress of the war.

## Chapter 5

# Game Change

ON JUNE 22, 1941, Adolf Hitler sent his panzers to attack the Soviet Union, a decision that turned the military situation upside down. The Reich, after recording spectacular successes on the new eastern front it had opened, had to stop its advance in the winter, on the doorstep of the Soviet capital of Moscow. It also failed to seize Leningrad, the birthplace of the October Revolution. After resuming the offensive in spring 1942, the Wehrmacht suffered the disastrous capitulation at Stalingrad on February 2, 1943, then fell to the Red Army's tanks at the Kursk salient in July of the same year. Napoleon's Russia campaign had sounded the death knell of his imperial ambitions; Hitler's now demolished the hegemonic designs of Nazi Germany. But it would take many long months for Stalin's troops to travel the thousands of miles between the quays of the Moskva and the banks of the Spree.

To the west, the lines were also shifting. On December 7, 1941, Japan launched a surprise military strike on the U.S. naval base at Pearl Harbor, Hawaii, which brought the United States into the conflict. Faithful to the pledge he had made to Winston Churchill, Franklin Roosevelt followed the "Germany First" strategy, giving precedence to the European theater of operations over its Asian counterpart. When the foremost economic power in the world joined the war, the balance of forces changed substantially. That very day, Charles de Gaulle, leader of Free France, declared to the head of his secret services, Colonel Passy: "Now the war is won once and for all! And two phases are in the offing: the first will be the rescue of Germany by the Allies; the second, I fear, will be a great war between the Russians and the Americans . . . and as for that war, the Americans run the risk of losing it if they are unable to take the necessary measures in time."[1]

These two dramatic events changed the course of the war, suddenly making the defeat of Nazi Germany, previously considered inconceivable, possible and even probable. As a result, they completely altered the context of the resistance. Until 1941, underground fighters had little hope of playing a significant military role in the conflict, except by assisting a beleaguered Great Britain as far as their meager resources allowed. The logic that guided the resistance fighters, with the exception of the networks and some movements, was to bear witness. They did not imagine they could weaken the Reich's military supremacy. The intervention of the American giant and of the Soviet titan radically modified their prospects. The resistance could now expect to assume an active military role, if only by relieving pressure on the Red Army's troops to the east.

These developments also invalidated the basic premises of the Vichy regime, which suddenly found itself in an awkward position. Philippe Pétain had been banking on a German victory; over time, that certainty eroded. He had also sworn to protect the French people from the rigors of the Nazi occupation, yet that burden continued to grow heavier. In launching the National Revolution, he had promised a new era, but he spent most of his energy sowing discord, persecuting his real or supposed enemies. Hence the Jews were the object of two laws of exclusion, the first enacted in October 1940, the second in June 1941. Communists were rooted out and interned in camps or prisons. Republicans, often dismissed from their mayoral duties, were frequently imprisoned; and the leaders supposedly responsible for the defeat were handed over to the court of Riom in February 1942.

These measures were hardly embraced by the populace, which became so restive that, on August 12, 1941, the chief of state spoke out against the rising "ill wind." While making it clear that "a long interval will be needed to overcome the resistance of all these adversaries of the new order," the victor of Verdun announced that he intended, "from now on, to destroy their efforts by decimating their leaders." Far from leading to a surge in popularity, that hard line eroded the regime's credibility and revealed its authoritarian, anti-Semitic, and collaborationist reality in an ever harsher light. It therefore led a large portion of French society and of the resistance, until then inclined to place their trust in Pétain, to break ranks with him and to set their sights on Free France, which was gaining in credibility. Granted, many still put their money on the double game that the World War I hero was supposedly playing and distrusted the man of June 18. De Gaulle projected a certain

ambiguity and for many months kept quiet about the political direction he had in mind for the country. There was nothing equivocal
about his patriotic and moral orientation, however, and they attracted
growing sympathy.

In any event, the new course of the conflict and the hard line the
Vichy authority had taken brought clarity, simplifying the choices available to a society still staggered by the defeat and sometimes quick to
subscribe to the French State's promises. That clarification came about
unevenly, however, varying by milieu, group, and political entity. The
PCF was particularly swift at taking the measure of the upheavals
caused by Operation Barbarossa.

## The Communists Change Course

Until spring 1941, the PCF, held hostage by the German-Soviet Pact,
had preferred to reserve its barbs for the Vichy regime rather than
attack Nazi Germany, by pen or by sword. It had encouraged protest
movements, urging its cadres and militants to act openly, at least at first.
It was not long, however, before that strategy evolved. By mid-April
1941, the Communist press had taken a harsher tone vis-à-vis the Reich,
calling for the French people to stand up to the occupier. Henceforth,
"it is not enough to posit that, from the standpoint of the people, the
patriotic battle is justified; rather, the patriotic battle is itself the foundation of the people's struggles."[2]

That shift corresponded in part to the Comintern's wishes. On
April 26, 1941, a telegram from the Communist Internationale, signed
by its chairman, Georgi Dimitrov, and by two French leaders, Jacques
Duclos and André Marty, invited the people to achieve national unity
by "excluding all traitors and defeatists" and to form a vast Front National de Lutte pour la Liberté et l'Indépendance de la France (FN;
National Front in the Struggle for the Freedom and Independence of
France). The following May 15, the party's underground leadership repeated that watchword: "Fighting for creation of that large national
liberation front, Party is ready to support any French government, any
organization, and all men in the country whose efforts move toward a
true struggle against invaders and traitors."[3] But Jacques Duclos ac-

companied that about-turn with one reservation: "The French nation cannot unite in the cause of national liberation behind a movement of reactionary and colonialist inspiration, such as that of British imperialism." Accordingly, he called for "the nationalization, without compensation, of the banks, insurance companies, mines, railroads, and large capitalist companies." These demands did not appear in the telegram sent by the Comintern.

In spring 1941, therefore, the PCF adopted a less equivocal position: the fight for national liberation now prevailed over protest movements. Emerging from its isolation, the party called for national union. The invasion of the Soviet Union on June 22, 1941, naturally accelerated that development, which the Comintern encouraged. On June 31, Dimitrov ordered the Communist leadership to disrupt "by any means possible production of arms. Form small detachments for destruction of the war factories, naphtha storage tanks, bridges, railroads, roads, telegraphic and telephone communication systems. Prevent by any means transport of troops and arms."[4] On August 9, a new message sent to Duclos affirmed that "situation allows and requires ever more energetic actions and creation national mass offensive movement against invaders. . . . That accelerates creation in France conditions for victorious national war of liberation, indispensable therefore to begin preparations practice masses for such an imminent prospect. Requires examining practically questions weapons, armaments, organization armed groups and armed actions."[5]

The PCF, in changing its orientation, was thus responding to the wishes of the Soviet Union. In the weeks that preceded the German attack, Moscow likely sought to put pressure on Berlin, which refused to recognize Soviet interests in the Balkans. During the disastrous first months of Operation Barbarossa, the Comintern hoped to weaken German military potential by disrupting its rear lines, if only by derisory means. That national strategy did not contradict the aspirations of the French Communists. The confusion caused by the pact and by the strategy followed between August 1939 and May 1941 had greatly disturbed the rank and file, which had left in droves. In returning to an anti-Fascist and patriotic line, the party thus fulfilled the expectations of many militants. The reversal that occurred in spring 1941, however, did not magically discharge all debts or suddenly solve the three problems facing the Communists: how to restructure its organization, rethink its modes of intervention, and secure the union it desired.

## A New Organization

Although the PCF had gone underground when it was banned in September 1939, it still had to adapt its structures to the new conditions of the struggle. Militarily, it had little weight. Granted, its Organisation Spéciale (OS), charged primarily with keeping the peace and enforcing the law, had developed a military branch, the Travail Particulier or Travail Partisan (Special Work or Partisan Work), at the urging of Charles Tillon. Likewise, in summer 1941, the JC had created an offshoot, the Bataillons de la Jeunesse (Youth Battalions). The Main-d'Oeuvre Immigrée (MOI; Immigrant Labor Force) also had an armed branch, the OS-MOI, created that summer as well. But the proliferation of these bureaucracies must not mislead us. The PCF suffered greatly from a shortage of men and resources. Between August 1941 and March 1942, the Bataillons de la Jeunesse, in their bastion in the Seine department, cumulatively signed up only thirty-six men, before definitively collapsing.[6] And the OS-MOI troops never had more than a few dozen partisans.

In early 1942, these three organizations, previously autonomous, merged into the Francs-Tireurs et Partisans (FTP). The advent of that group was mentioned for the first time in *L'Humanité* in February of the same year. It was headed by a national military committee: Charles Tillon, the commander in chief, and Eugène Hénaff (later replaced by René Camphin) were in charge of manpower; Albert Ouzoulias was responsible for operations; and Georges Beyer was head of armaments and intelligence.[7] But the apparent rigor of that organization chart must not mask the PCF's desperate straits: for many long months, the armed struggle it claimed to be waging rested on the shoulders of a few volunteers. In Ille-et-Vilaine, the OS is reported to have had fifty-eight members active in June 1941. Although forty-five FTP were recruited between July 1941 and December 1942, forty-nine were arrested during the same period. In all, only fifty-four militants remained active in December 1942.[8]

In its civilian actions, the PCF, true to its traditions, multiplied its satellite organizations, which allowed it to reach different social milieus but spared it from giving too red a hue to the engagement of volunteers. The physicist Jacques Solomon, for example, founded and ran *L'Université Libre*, a publication for intellectuals. But the FN, created in May 1941, constituted by far the movement destined for the brightest future. Open to all, it embodied in theory the national unity now advocated by the PCF. A manifesto addressed to both the occupied and unoccupied zones circulated in July 1941. A committee for the southern zone, launched in November 1941, enjoyed the support of the journalists Yves Farge and Georges Bidault, even though they did not belong to the party.[9] In the same vein, the FN expanded and multiplied its professional organizations. For example, the Germanist Daniel Decourdemanche (Jacques Decour) headed a group of writers, and the poet René Blech led an artists' group.

That unification strategy produced limited results, however, until at least late 1942. This was because the PCF, though it praised the merits of unity, refused to relinquish its independence. The party meant to maintain control of the FN and confined itself to recommending the unification of the base. An aggravating circumstance: its unified approach upset some militants. That summer, it is true, *Les Cahiers du Bolchevisme* called on its readers to overcome their hesitations: "If any member of the Party claims to find certain alliances repellent, it will not be difficult to see that, in reality, that repugnance serves only to hide a passivity unworthy of militants in our Party, at a time when everything commands us to fight."[10] But part of the Communist world had trouble accepting that reversal. Martha Desrumeaux, the Communist chief in the department of Nord, recalls: "It took two days to convince me that we had to work with the Gaullists. I didn't want to do it. Not that I was sectarian, but I had a grudge against them."[11] Similarly, the resistance movements, especially in the northern zone, were wary of the sudden ecumenism. Although Joseph Beaufils (Joseph), an emissary of the PCF, met with Philippe Viannay in October 1941, no cooperation was established between the FN and the DF. The confederated union activists were also distrustful of the unified groups. Léon Jouhaux, during his meeting with Emmanuel d'Astier de La Vigerie in late 1941, even stipulated that his friends would join Libération-sud only if the movement agreed not to cooperate with the Communists.[12] Free France proved cautious, though François Faure, Rémy's assistant at the CND, entered into discussions with Jean Jérôme, an important PCF cadre, in March 1942. And Jean Moulin—through Georges Marrane, former mayor of Ivry—reestablished contact with the PCF between June and mid-July 1942. Pierre Brossolette, another emissary of the Gaullist intelligence services, resumed that mission beginning on July 24.

Although Charles de Gaulle advocated the broadest unification possible, he still had every intention of being personally in charge. In London on September 24, 1941, he created the CNF, an embryonic provisional government claiming to represent the real France. By proposing a less politically freighted alternative, that initiative could not fail to keep in check the FN's pretensions to embody national unity. The obligatory conclusions were drawn in *L'Humanité* on October 2, 1941: "What we need is the unity and action of the French people alongside other peoples in chains, alongside the English, alongside de Gaulle's troops, and alongside the heroic soldiers of the Red Army."[13] That said, there was a huge gulf between the acknowledgment of General de Gaulle, on the whole formal and symbolic, and the will to cooperate with the groups in London or with the internal resistance. It would take a long time for that gap to narrow, particularly since the underground forces by no means agreed with the modes of struggle defended by the PCF and its satellite organizations.

## Actions

The PCF had focused primarily on propaganda and on protest movements—strikes and especially demonstrations—as its fields of action. The invasion of the Soviet Union intensified that dynamic. Although labor conflicts weakened after the harsh repression of the miners' strike, demonstrations resumed, with patriotism giving a new coloring to class issues. Thirteen processions celebrated Bastille Day on July 14, 1941 (twelve of them in the occupied zone),[14] and the housewives' movement resumed in winter 1941–1942, affecting twenty-four departments. On May 31, 1942, a young Communist teacher, Madeleine Marzin, stirred up women "assembled in large numbers on rue de Buci [in Paris], outside a warehouse of merchandise destined for Germany. She urged them to help themselves to canned goods and sugar. Turning words into action, she began to hand them out. The police charged. The three young FTP assigned to protect her struck back. An exchange of gunfire followed. Madeleine Marzin and her three bodyguards were arrested and handed over to the special court set up by Vichy."[15] On August 1 of the same year, Lise Ricol, the wife of Artur London, roused to action passersby on rue Daguerre. "The tracts and flyers hurled into the crowd fell like rain, immediately disappearing into pockets and bags. A resounding 'Marseillaise' rose up," and the "virago of rue Daguerre" took advantage of the disorder to make herself scarce, even managing to shake off the two police officers trying to take her into custody.[16]

These demonstrations mobilized women and children, borrowing from the repertoire of food riots, but they tended to end in failure. Prefects alerted mayors that the calmest municipalities would be given precedence over the more unruly ones,[17] providing an incentive for the most docile citizens. But in publicly displaying the existence of discontent, that form of protest did have the advantage of "bringing it to light without drawing manpower away from other fronts."[18]

For in fact, the PCF was expanding its repertoire of action. It attacked the occupier or collaborators, striking individuals directly. On August 21, 1941, Pierre Georges (Fabien), a young Communist, murdered Alfons Moser, a midshipman in the Kriegsmarine, whom Georges had selected at random at the Barbès-Rochechouart metro station. The following October 20, a commando sent to Nantes, composed, notably, of Gilbert Brustlein and Spartaco Guisco, executed Lieutenant Colonel Karl Hotz, head of the German military headquarters of Loire-Inférieure. In Bordeaux the next day, Pierre Rebières took down Hans Gottfried Reimers, legal adviser to the military administration. The PCF also targeted collaborators. On November 21, a commando, including, notably, Fabien, attacked the Rive Gauche bookstore, an intellectual showcase for collaboration; and on January 10, 1942, two militants, Tondelier and Tardif, blew up the Paris headquarters of the Rassemblement National Populaire (National Popular Rally), a collaborationist group run by Marcel Déat. The PCF also did not forget "renegades" who had gone over to the enemy. It published eleven blacklists comprising 1,058 names in all,[19] and created a group with about thirty members, the Valmy battalion, specially designated to "liquidate the traitors." On September 4, 1941, that group killed Marcel Gitton, who, after breaking away from the party in November 1940, had joined the collaborationist camp. On April 28, 1942, it mounted an assault on Jean-Marie Clamamus, a senator and the mayor of Bobigny, which he survived.

What, exactly, did the PCF leadership expect to gain from that type of action? Jacques Duclos, though not a consummate military strategist, no doubt grasped that the attacks would not change the course of the war. That was in fact the assessment of the German military. "In none of these cases," noted Otto von Stülpnagel, military commander for France, "is it proven that other strata of the population participated in these attacks. Furthermore, it can be stated that these groups of terrorists belong to a restricted circle of Communist criminals—young people in particular—who are prepared to do anything."[20] But these attacks did relieve pressure on the beleaguered Red Army, albeit on a very modest scale. In actuality, however, the Communist leaders' primary objective was domestic. In inciting the Germans to carry out a bloody repression, they hoped to win the public's support, by revealing the true face of an occupier praised until then for its self-discipline.[21] In setting in motion a cycle of attacks and reprisals, they hoped to increase recruitment, as the Communist Georges Beaufils candidly acknowledged. Colonel Rémy had protested: "So you think it 'pays off' to get five or ten of your people shot, in exchange for taking a revolver or a carbine?" "Yes," retorted Beaufils, "because with the announcement that five or ten of our people have been shot, we sign up fifty or a hundred new members in the FTP."[22] Alexander Bogomolov, Soviet ambassador to London, told Christian Pineau the same thing: "It rouses the hesitant from their apathy. The people do not forgive the execution of innocents."[23]

Despite the moderation recommended by Otto von Stülpnagel, the Germans, acting on Hitler's express orders, did have dozens of hostages shot, causing a profound emotional reaction in the country. Admiral Darlan and his minister of the interior, Pierre Pucheu, personally drew up the list of the unlucky souls to be led to the guillotine or the firing squad. These Vichy officials thereby discredited themselves, confirming in stark terms the collaborationist compromises of the regime. It is equally possible, however, that public opinion, while scathing toward the executioners, believed that innocent civilians were paying too high a price and held the Communists responsible for that bloodbath. The PCF's underground press, in fact, initially refrained from claiming responsibility for such exploits: the regional Communist newspaper in the north even attributed the attacks to score-settling among the Germans themselves.[24]

De Gaulle took a clear-cut position, which he expressed on October 23 at the BBC, after the attacks in Nantes and Bordeaux. "If the Germans did not wish to meet their deaths at our hands, they had only to stay home and not make war on us," he acknowledged. Then he added: "But there is a tactic to war. The war of the French people must be waged by those to whom that responsibility falls, namely, myself and the Comité National. . . . And at present, the instructions I have given for the occupied territory are not to kill Germans openly. There is one very good reason for that: at this moment, it is too easy for the enemy to retaliate by massacring our momentarily disarmed combatants."[25] On the whole, the non-Communist movements agreed with that approach. Henry Frenay writes in his memoirs: "It is only too true that war kills innocents. But as for signing their death warrant by my own decision, as it were, for the sole benefit of increasing the fighting spirit of the population and without any notable damage to the enemy . . . I will never consent to that."[26] Individual attacks therefore remained the exclusive preserve of the Communist movement.

At times, this strategy caused discord in the ranks. Although used during the darkest hours of tsarism, notably by the young Stalin, it was not in fact part of the traditional arsenal of Marxism-Leninism, which preferred to put its money on the masses rather than on individual acts. Some Communists also found it painful to kill, as Albert Ouzoulias, head of the Bataillons de la Jeunesse and later of the FTP, confided in retrospect: "Comrades would refuse to execute a German soldier, who could be a comrade from Hamburg, a worker from Berlin. An officer could be an anti-Hitler professor. At most, they agreed to kill an officer in the Gestapo. But our comrades did not yet understand that the best means to defend our country at war was precisely to kill the maximum number of German officers. That would hasten the end of the war and of a tragedy affecting a large number of peoples, including the German people. At that moment, internationalism meant killing the greatest number of Nazis possible."[27]

The method followed also raises a few issues in retrospect. In the first place, the PCF seemed more inclined to attack French people than to strike out against Germans. Within a few months, the Valmy battalion had killed eleven nationals and had wounded forty-four, but it did not attack the occupier until summer 1942.[28] Second, the death toll from that armed struggle was modest at best. Between June 22, 1941, and December 31, 1942, only twenty-five Germans perished in the Seine department comprising Paris and its outskirts.[29] And finally, far from serving the cause of unity, these actions had deleterious effects on the internal resistance. As Jean-Marc Berlière and Franck Liaigre point out, "The Communist Party styled itself the champion of the all-out fight. The actions performed by its militants, the sacrifices to which they agreed, and its discourse in favor of immediate action pointed up the deficiencies, the supposed shilly-shallying, of the other components of the Resistance."[30] It is true that the Communist leadership thought in political, not military terms. The sacrifices its militants agreed to make allowed it not only to substantiate the occupier's barbarism but also to attract new recruits and to embarrass the movements, stigmatized by their watch-and-wait attitude. Charles Tillon confirmed that interpretation after the fact. "De Gaulle's order corresponded to a certain watch-and-wait state of mind and greatly reinforced it. But experience tells us that the internal Resistance was right never to conform to the high-and-mighty instructions. That would have meant postponing for three years the organization of the guerrilla war, until the Allied landing."[31] The attacks thus increased tensions both within the internal resistance and between metropolitan France and Free France. For in fact, the Gaullists, like the movements, embraced completely different positions.

## Gaullist Adjustments

Free France had initially focused its attention on the secret services, headed by Colonel Passy. That orientation, though maintained, nevertheless underwent a clear modification in 1941. The Second Bureau, run by André Dewavrin, was created in 1940 and grew in the months that followed. A counterespionage service, assigned to Roger Warin (Wybot), was added to the three original sections—Intelligence, Actions, and Code—in late 1941, and the service was renamed the "Bureau Central de Renseignement et d'Action Militaire" (Central Bureau of Intelligence and Military Action) in early 1942 (later called simply the Bureau Central de Renseignement et d'Action, or BCRA). In July 1942 André Manuel, head of intelligence, took charge of a bloc operation ensuring coordination between sections. On September 19, 1942, he was named official assistant to Colonel Passy. That reorganization was accompanied by an increase in personnel, from twenty-three to seventy-seven individuals between summer 1941 and summer 1942; the number of officers grew from ten to nineteen during the same period.[32] The recruits included distinguished men, such as Fred Scamaroni, a young civil servant who had joined the cause in 1940, and the German-born Stéphane Hessel, a student at the École Normale Supérieure who arrived in London in 1941 after assisting Varian Fry and his escape network. Nevertheless, that progress was altogether inadequate and, between 1940 and 1944, the shortage of manpower was a recurrent problem. For lack of men and resources, R Section, the intelligence division, could send only five agents into the field monthly before February 1943. In all, scarcely more than four hundred men—a tiny number—were dispatched to the metropolis prior to the Normandy landing on June 6, 1944.[33]

In reality, volunteers were not beating down the door. Despite the spy novels popularized by the writer Pierre Nord, war out of uniform suffered from a sulfurous reputation. Furthermore, soldiers in the army of shadows were not protected by the Geneva Conventions. In October 1942, Hitler issued an order that members of sabotage teams, armed or unarmed, in civilian dress or in uniform, be handed over to the security services of the SS (the dreaded Sicherheitsdienst, or SD) and executed, a provision that applied even to the agents in the British commandos of the Special Air Service (SAS).[34] That measure could not fail to dampen enthusiasm, especially since the forms of combat—solitary and anonymous—were hardly attractive. As Colonel Passy told Jean Moulin's future secretary, Daniel Cordier, when he proposed to join up: "You will not have the moral support that the regular army offers you, that of being surrounded at every moment by your comrades in arms. You will live alone, you will take your meals alone, etc. You are going into seclusion. No Sundays, no Saturdays, no leaves. You are on the front twenty-four hours a day, because the police and the Gestapo will hunt you down day and night. You can be arrested by day or by night. . . . Once you are arrested, you will be interrogated and tortured to extract the information you possess."[35]

But some recruits who had languished in Britain for many months, having been denied the possibility of facing the Germans on the battlefield, did volunteer. Cordier explained to his future superior: "With my comrades, we waited for the invasion of England, in order to do battle with the Germans. Our officers promised us we would go off to fight as soon as we were technically prepared. We did what was asked of us, training, then the platoon. A year after I joined, I'm still here. For that reason, I am volunteering to join the BCRA."[36] Zeal was not enough, however. During the first half of 1942, more than two volunteers out of five were judged unfit for underground action and sent back to their original units. The selection process suffered from a lack of professionalism. It was not until late 1942 that the British established tests reliable enough to select fit recruits, reducing the margin of error from 10 to 1 percent. Furthermore, the regular units, which also faced manpower shortages, balked at giving up their specialists. They denied three-quarters of the requests made by the BCRA, which can hardly be said to have enjoyed the support of the leader of Free France. As historian Sébastien Albertelli points out: "The interest de Gaulle showed in underground action never reached the level that the leaders of the BCRA expected. They did not understand why he refused to grant them top priority in recruitment."[37]

Despite these weaknesses, the BCRA pursued its actions, meeting with uneven success. Its key component was Colonel Rémy's network. In January 1942, it took the name "Confrérie Notre-Dame" (CND; Our Lady Brotherhood). Its leader declared: "France was placed under the protection of Our Lady by its kings and did not come out the worse for it. Why should I not do the same on a more modest scale? In fact, do not the bonds that unite us make us a true brotherhood?"[38] In any event, the CND provided invaluable intelligence, which allowed the British to surmise that the battleship *Bismarck*, the jewel of the

Kriegsmarine—which the admiralty had lost track of—was returning to Brest. The Royal Navy was therefore able to sink the ship on May 27, 1941. In addition, René Dugrand, a worker at the Société Nationale des Constructions Aéronautiques du Sud-Ouest (National Society of Aeronautic Construction in the Southwest), refused to go on strike on November 11, 1941, despite pressure from his comrades. He took advantage of that work stoppage to remove a sample of a metal manufactured specially for the Luftwaffe, concealing it in a slit he had made in the heel of his shoe. Later assigned to the company's division of plans and drawings, he would deliver aeronautical documents of interest to the British.[39] On January 24, 1942, the CND also gave the British the information that allowed a commando to destroy the radar station of Bruneval, on the Channel (February 27–28, 1942), and to bring back for examination pieces taken from the site. Upon his return to England in late February 1942, Rémy also brought back the plans for the submarine bases in Brest, Bordeaux, and Saint-Nazaire.

More generally, Colonel Passy's services had received 700 telegrams in 1941; they processed 920 in 1942, and the pieces of mail rose from 1,145 to 2,360 between those two dates.[40] Sabotage missions, authorized by de Gaulle in January 1942, were a less resounding success. The BCRA could claim responsibility for only one large-scale action, Operation Pilchard. On May 10, 1942, a commando of three men—Bodhaine, Clastère, and Gaudin—destroyed the towers and the main antenna of Radio-Paris in Allouis, in the Cher department, The attack interrupted for twelve days the jamming of radio waves from foreign stations and suspended the collaborationist broadcasts for the same period of time.

The modesty of the BCRA's resources limited its ambitions. To carry out his actions, Colonel Passy had to cooperate with the British services, while also relying on the forces in the metropolis engaged in the underground struggle. He explored these two paths simultaneously.

## SOE, F Section

The cooperation between the BCRA and the British secret services was never fully satisfactory to either party. Winston Churchill, though he supported Free France, repeatedly became annoyed with Charles de

Gaulle, whose haughtiness and rigidity disturbed him. As British historian M. R. D. Foot points out, "Resolute intransigence was the only attitude his keen sense of honour allowed him to adopt, but it did not make for any sort of smooth working."[41] Nevertheless, the tension between these two personalities cannot be reduced to a clash of volatile temperaments. Even though they were allies and fiercely determined to bring down the Third Reich, each of the two leaders was intent on defending his respective national interests. That resolve led to confrontations in Africa and the Middle East.[42] The British prime minister, while less indulgent than the U.S. president (who had dispatched a close friend, Admiral Leahy, as ambassador to Vichy), refrained from burning all bridges with the French State. He agreed to ease the maritime blockade that had cut off the French metropolis from its empire and to receive emissaries dispatched by the Marshal. These measures could not fail to antagonize de Gaulle. In the same vein, Churchill always opted for the broader perspective, preferring to strengthen his "special relationship" with Roosevelt rather than undermine it by supporting the demands of Free France, especially since de Gaulle was not an easy partner. "The hardest cross I have to bear is the Cross of Lorraine," Churchill is said to have declared. Finally, and perhaps especially, the FFL fell far short of their promises. In September 1940, the Dakar escapade had quickly failed; and volunteers were not exactly pouring in between June 1940 and November 1942. In 1941–1942, the Vichy army attracted nearly four times as many young Frenchmen as the FFL; the Légion des Volontaires Français contre le Bolchevisme (Legion of French Volunteers against Bolshevism), created in summer 1941 to fight on the eastern front, drew in slightly more than eight thousand in twelve months, which is to say, almost twice as many as the FFL over the same period.[43] As historian Jean-François Muracciole sums it up, "For Great Britain, which until late 1942 had its back to the wall in a struggle to the death against Nazi Germany, support was counted first by the number of divisions involved. How could someone claim to embody French legitimacy when he was incapable of rallying [the colonies of French West Africa] or of attracting more than two hundred French people a month, when several million soldiers were killing one another on the eastern front?"[44] Even French aviation did not particularly distinguish itself. In September 1941, the Free French Air Force had 186 pilots lined up, but Czechoslovakia had contributed 546 to the RAF, and the Poles more than 1,800.[45] In view of these parameters, the British hedged their support for the Free French secret services, initially preferring to count on their own forces.

The SOE comprised two divisions, one of which, F Section, acted in total independence from the BCRA. But its groups experienced serious setbacks in both the northern and southern zones. Pierre de Vomécourt, founder of the Autogiro network, was sent to London, then parachuted into France on April 1, 1942. He was taken into custody by the Gestapo on the 25th. He managed to convince his judges to treat him as a prisoner of war, and, with his comrades, was interned in Colditz Fortress, from which he eventually returned. In addition, a team composed of Denis Rake (Justin), Édouard Wilkinson, and Richard Heslop formed in summer 1942. But on August 15, Rake and Wilkinson were arrested in Limoges during a routine stop. Two stupid details gave them away. Although they claimed to have met for the first time that same day, both men were carrying "plenty of brand new unpinned thousand-franc notes, numbered in a single consecutive series; and their identity cards, ostensibly issued in different towns, were made out in the same handwriting."[46] They would finally be released by the prison warden, whose heart was with the Allies. A fourth agent, Benjamin Cowburn, had parachuted into France on the night of June 1. But left to himself, he could do no more than ask a few friends to introduce abrasives into the machines at an airplane engine factory and oversee an attack on several electrical lines extending out from Éguzon, in the Indre department. He subsequently decided to return to England.[47] Promising inroads were made in the Bordeaux region, however, where Claude de Baissac, a Mauritian, arrived by parachute on July 30 near Nîmes and laid the foundations for the Scientist network.

In the free zone, the SOE managed to organize the escape of agents who had been arrested the previous autumn in Marseilles. About ten men in the Mauzac internment camp—including Pierre Bloch, Georges Bégué, and Michael Trotobas—managed to escape at dawn on July 16 and were able to return to service.[48] Trotobas parachuted into France again on November 18, 1942, and established himself in Lille, creating the Farmer sabotage network. In addition, Victor Hazan, an agent who had arrived in France on the night of May 1, set about training a few men to handle British weapons and explosives—especially plastic explosives, which were not very widespread at the time. In autumn and winter 1942–1943, he trained more than ninety instructors to teach the elementary uses of submachine guns, pistols, and explosives.[49] As this assessment suggests, apart from a few seeds that had only to take root, F Section of the SOE met with mixed success. The disastrous Carte affair hardly improved matters.

In 1940, André Girard, a painter, set decorator, caricaturist, and adman all at once, who had taken refuge in Antibes, set up the Carte network.[50] Girard was averse to propaganda, which he found useless and too politicized for his taste. He therefore focused on military action. At the time of the defeat, he recruited willing souls in Antibes to form a military organization. Maurice Diamant-Berger (alias André Gillois), the writer Joseph Kessel, his nephew Maurice Druon, Jean Nohain, and Claude Dauphin backed the venture. Girard also canvassed officers in the armistice army, well aware of their state of mind, since he had performed his military service at Saint-Cyr during the interwar period. Military circles, in turn, were drawn to Girard, who manifested a vigorous apoliticism, defended Pétain while attacking Laval, and condemned Montoire but professed a firm anti-Communism. A few contacts were also established within law enforcement: both Commissioner Dubois, head of Sécurité du Territoire (Homeland Security) in Nice, and Commissioner Achille Peretti, head of the Nice police force, offered their assistance. In 1942 Carte undoubtedly had about a hundred agents, attracted by a very simple program: intelligence and preparation for D-Day.

After Georges Bégué's arrest, Lieutenant Basin (Olive) provided liaison between the network and the SOE. At the time, Girard proved to be extremely shrewd. Far from begging for funds from the British services, he turned them down, haughtily declaring: "No one, not you and not us, can ensure funds sufficient to pay the costs of all our men."[51] Basin was impressed and hastened to write up favorable reports about the powerful network. Peter Churchill (no relation to the prime minister), a new envoy from the SOE, arrived in France on the night of January 9, 1942, carrying 700,000 francs, destined in part for the promising group. His report was so laudatory that, after his second mission between April 1 and April 20, 1942, two radio operators were placed in the service of the network, an unprecedented privilege, given the scarcity of "pianists," as they were called. In spite of everything, London remained on its guard and demanded that an officer be sent to Great Britain to provide information. Henri Frager, Girard's second-in-command, was dispatched to the British capital. Painting in glowing terms an enormous organization ready to assist the Allies during the landing, he also asked for five minutes on the BBC to counter or nuance Gaullist propaganda—a request that the British, annoyed by de Gaulle, eagerly welcomed. In late July, Frager returned to France with Nicholas Bodington at his side. Carte demanded fifty thousand Sten submachine guns and fifty transceivers. Taken in by the bluff, the man from the SOE could not praise the network enough. Bodington wrote to his superiors: "The Carte organization must be considered both civilian and military. [It] was constituted with the greatest care by specialists, under conditions of extreme secrecy. Carte has nothing in common with a group of amateurs."[52] The British secret services later noted: "Carte is either a cover for the armistice army created for its secret organization, or a private initiative pursuing the same goal."[53]

These reports explain the poisonous charm the organization exerted over the British. Thanks to that network, they believed, the United Kingdom would have at its disposal an army ready to go. "What made people in London take CARTE so seriously was its military flavour," M. R. D. Foot points out.[54] Above all, London would be able to bench de Gaulle, allowing it "to counterbalance, from France, the influence of the Gaullist Resistance, which accounted for a large share of the general's legitimacy," historian Thomas Rabino confirms.[55]

Under such conditions, the SOE could not fail to increase its support. In August 1942, the organization had received nearly 2.5 short tons of weapons; in 1943, it accepted 116 tons,[56] plus substantial financial assistance beginning at the same time. A million francs were deposited monthly with Baring Brothers, which credited the accounts of Lombard Odier Darier Hentsch et Cie. The Genevan bank ultimately turned the funds over to French establishments. Last but not least, the SOE sent instructors. On October 2, 1942, the felucca *Seadog* delivered Major Goldsmith (Valentin, Jean Delannoy), who proceeded to teach recruits the art of explosives, then took a tour of the region.

From then on, the organization thrived, increasing the number of its branches on the Côte d'Azur, in Provence, and in Isère, and recruiting prominent personalities, notably, Pierre Bénouville (known as Guillain de Bénouville). Jacques Baumel met him at the time and describes him as follows: "He was a small man with an oddly youthful appearance—he looked much younger than his twenty-six years—despite displaying early signs of baldness. He had a touch of dandyism, belied by his eyes, which stared at you without blinking. Extremely piercing eyes. He looked like what he was, a 'hussar' avant la lettre, a young, right-wing intellectual, author of a biography of Baudelaire and monographs on Pascal and Stendhal, combined with a soldier who had continued to fight despite the signing of the armistice. He is said to have been taken prisoner with the sixty survivors of an irregular force of eight hundred and forty men and to have escaped twice."[57] The arrival on the scene of Bénouville, a former member of Action Française, a tough Pétainist who had gone to North Africa to assist the Allies (he was arrested, then acquitted),[58] confirms the attraction the network exerted over a certain far-right milieu, Vichyist but Germanophobic, patriotic but hostile to de Gaulle. In late August 1942, Carte likely had three thousand agents, three hundred of them remunerated. Above all, it had a radio station, Radio-Patrie.

The status of the station was at the very least dubious. It was supposed to broadcast from the occupied metropolis and, in order not to involve His Majesty's Government and to circumvent the accords that bound the United Kingdom to Free France, it did not report to the BBC. It took advantage of that relative independence to broadcast, beginning on October 4, 1942, patriotic propaganda delivered by André Gillois and Claude Dauphin. Not content to ignore General de Gaulle, it sowed confusion by presuming to address instructions to the resistance movements. "Radio-Patrie wanted to capitalize on the growing popularity of General de Gaulle, to be put to use later for ends that he would not have approved," notes Rabino.[59] Carte thus became the linchpin of the SOE's anti-Gaullist strategy. The material support the British promised was supposed to ensure them control "of a hub of resistance with both military and political importance. As such, the absence of relations with de Gaulle constituted an indispensable precondition."[60] Carte, possessing substantial resources, was also able to siphon off manpower from the movements by promising weapons and money to militants. In Cannes, some men abandoned Combat to join Carte.

A gulf existed, therefore, between the weakness of the network and its leader's bravado. The conclusions were ultimately drawn, however. Worried at seeing no results forthcoming, London authorities demanded that André Girard give an accounting. After first putting them off, he flew to England on February 21, 1943. His interlocutors then discovered the wide scope of the disaster. In early April, the British told him that they no longer wanted to work with him and forbade him from returning to the French metropolis. His assistant, Henri Frager, picked up the pieces. The British and the French assumed joint management of Radio-Patrie, beginning on January 21, 1943. The SOE had been blinded by its own anti-Gaullism, as this affair confirms. This explains why Colonel Passy's secret services had encountered the greatest difficulty in their efforts to cooperate with the SOE's RF Section.

For lack of agents, the British had to count on French assistance to conduct their actions in metropolitan France. From that standpoint, cooperation with the BCRA opened up welcome prospects. In May–June 1941, it led to the creation within both organizations of a liaison division. In theory, French and British officers jointly devised plans, which were submitted to the SOE and approved by General Petit, de Gaulle's chief of staff. Preexisting local groups would carry out these plans, with technical assistance from two men, including a radio operator, detached for two months. But these principles were at odds with the inequity in power relations. As Albertelli observes: "Not only did the SOE leaders have right of veto over the missions proposed by the intelligence service, but they alone were responsible, without any Gaullist oversight, for coordinating the paramilitary actions undertaken in France, some by F section, others by RF section. In their desire to obtain the means for action, the leaders of Free France had had no other choice but to accept such conditions, which, however, quickly became intolerable to them."[61] Then, in June 1942, de Gaulle demanded that Free France and the BCRA be included in the Allies' plans, at a time when plans for the landing in Europe were underway. Alan Brooke, chief of the imperial general staff, replied curtly that the coordination of subversive actions in Europe lay solely within the SOE's jurisdiction, which in essence deprived the Gaullist secret services of any access to the Allied high command.[62]

In short, Franco-British coordination of underground actions was going nowhere. That did not prevent the BCRA from giving greater attention to the underground groups developing in metropolitan France.

## Free France and the Movements

From 1941 on, the Gaullist secret services concerned themselves with establishing liaisons with those resistance movements that appeared most substantial to them. Two emissaries sent to France had tested the waters. Joël Le Tac explored the possibilities in the southern zone, and Jean Forman took an interest in the Liberté movement. On the basis of their experience, the two Free France agents suggested dividing up the work. Operations would be planned in London, and the movements would be in charge of executing them. Propaganda, in the service of action, would strengthen the sympathy of the masses for the Allies but would avoid involving them in premature and risky operations. Finally, liaison officers and radio operators would provide backup for the underground groups.

The two men were sent back to France to test the viability of that plan. Accompanied by René Périou, a radio operator, Forman was dropped by parachute on October 13, 1941. A day later, Le Tac and his radio operator, Alain de Kergolay, were dropped on the Breton coast.[63] At that juncture, on October 20, 1941, Jean Moulin arrived in England.

Jean Moulin came from a republican family and served as chief of staff to Pierre Cot, minister of the air force during the FP government. In 1937, he had begun a brilliant career as a prefect. In 1940, in charge of Eure-et-Loir, he refused to "sign a protocol accusing the Senegalese troops of atrocities against the civilian population (the rape and murder of women and children)," which the Germans falsely accused them of committing, in revenge for their resistance during the taking of Chartres.[64] Thrown into a prison cell, Moulin attempted suicide. After being dismissed from his duties by the Vichy regime on November 2, 1940, he made the decision to go to London. Before leaving, he took stock of the resistance forces, in both the northern and southern parts of the country. On September 9, 1941, he left France, stopping in Marseilles, Barcelona, and Lisbon. Then he flew out on a seaplane to Bournemouth, touching down on October 20. On the 24th, he met with Colonel Passy. Received by de Gaulle the next day, Moulin presented the main lines of a "report on the activity, plans, and needs of the groups formed in France in the aim of national liberation," which he had written during his prolonged stay on the banks of the Tagus River. Although it is not clear what exactly happened during these conversations, "the result, at least, is known: an immediate understanding between the two men, who had nothing in common except their patriotic loyalty and government service," as Daniel Cordier comments.[65] In particular, Moulin was able to inform de Gaulle of one fact: the growth of the resistance movements throughout France.

## The Movements in the Northern Zone

The resistance movements had become more structured and had extended their branches beyond their region of origin or core focus. While continuing to publish their newspapers, they were broadening their repertoire of action and clarifying their political positions.

In the occupied zone, Libération-nord conformed to that development process.[66] The movement, officially created in November 1941, appointed a steering committee in December. Its powers should not be overstated, however. Alya Aglan points out that "neither at the top nor at the bottom of the movement was there any real hierarchy, each component conducting the action it judged to be a priority. The leadership of Libération-nord had no clear boundaries and remained subject to the fluctuations produced by the shifting power relations within its steering committee. It functioned in a truly democratic manner."[67] She concludes: "With too many or not enough leaders, Libération-nord did not look at the time like a truly organized movement, but rather like the expression of a conjunction of interests, whose diversity constituted both its richness and its principal weakness."[68] In any event, the movement took root, especially in the Paris region and in peripheral or border regions, notably Nord, where the memory of the first German occupation had remained keen. Exploiting the recruitment channels of the CGT, the CFTC, the SFIO, and the Freemasons, it fell largely under the domination of Léon Blum's party, after Henri Ribière, a Socialist high official, succeeded Christian Pineau in spring 1942. Although the newspaper played an important role, until 1943 it still had modest dimensions. Its circulation remained small (350 in spring 1942, 1,000 at the end of that year), and, for a long time, it was written solely by Pineau. Jean Texcier, assisted by Jean Cavaillès, later took over the paper and opened its columns to other contributors. Along the way, the movement clarified its line. In spring 1941, it openly took a position against Philippe Pétain, whom it had previously avoided attacking directly. It supported de Gaulle, while refraining from displaying an unconditional Gaullism. That consensus, however, masked a fundamental disagreement between Pineau and Cavaillès. Refusing to confine the movement to intelligence and to politics or trade unionism, the philosopher Cavaillès, hired by the Sorbonne in August 1941 and immediately put on the steering committee, sought to involve the organization in sabotage and in the formation of paramilitary groups.[69] He was heeded in part: an officer, Colonel Zarapoff, agreed to take charge of the movement's military organization. By contrast, the newspaper only belatedly mentioned armed struggle as a mode of resistance, recommending it for the first time in early 1943.

The DF pursued a parallel development, giving precedence to its newspaper and professionalizing its staff. The printing works, located in the cellar of the Sorbonne until September 1942, was complemented in February 1942 by a typesetting shop, concealed in a *chambre de bonne* at 41 rue du Montparnasse. The development of these infrastructures favored the growth of the newspaper: between August 15, 1941, and November 11, 1942, it came out nearly twice a month, with twenty-one issues appearing during that time. And its circulation continued to rise, from three thousand copies in summer 1941 to ten thousand in mid-1942.[70]

The newspaper, composed by about ten authors, set out to counter Vichy and German propaganda by taking the side of Great Britain and pointing out the Reich's military and economic setbacks. It also denounced German looting and the de facto annexation of Alsace and Moselle. Above all, it strove to rally the population by evoking Nazi barbarism. Its rejection of Hitlerism rested primarily on a traditional

Germanophobia that portrayed Hitler's coming to power as the logical outcome of German history.

The movement's line regarding the French State was less clear. While rejecting collaboration, it credited Philippe Pétain with resistance sentiments, judging that "the Marshal is only continuing to do what he has always done: resist, safeguard French interests."[71] It also agreed with some of his domestic policies, while finding it unacceptable that the Vichy program should be applied under the jackboot. "Everything the government can produce at present is stillborn. Everything it offers will later be said to have been brought in on 'The Foreigner's Wagons.' And so, good things will be repudiated, while bad ones will be revived."[72]

To be sure, several members in the movement disputed that line, such as the second-in-command, Robert Salmon. Philippe Viannay, however, stuck to his position against all odds until November 1942. In fact, Viannay had trouble emancipating himself from a familial culture marked by anti-Semitism, conservatism, and Catholicism. As he would later acknowledge: "I can only admire those who chose at a glance, in both their hearts and their minds, the most direct route, especially when they did not originally have the background predisposing them to do so."[73] Furthermore, his seniors—Marcel Lebon foremost—believed in the Marshal's double game and influenced him in that direction. In any event, the leadership refused to become divided on a problem judged secondary: the position taken toward the French State in no way determined the conditions for its actions. As a result, it was not until November 1942 that the position toward Vichy was modified.

That ambiguity did not prevent the DF from methodically continuing its expansion. It assigned Suzanne Guyotat, a librarian in Lyon who was a friend of the Viannay family, the task of implanting the movement in the southern zone. Thanks to Hélene Roederer, a young student, and Francis Cleirins, a Belgian refugee, the movement was able to distribute its newspaper in the Lyon region, in Loire, Drôme, and Ardèche. It also spread to Nord, Loiret, Normandy, and Poitou. The DF thus ensured its growth by sending emissaries to the provinces, taking advantage of contacts established here and there, and incorporating small local teams. Its numbers remained modest, however (230 militants on October 1, 1942), with the lion's share in the Paris region: 75 percent of the recruits were operating in Île-de-France at the time.[74]

The low rate of recruitment can be explained in part by the limited modes of action proposed. Apart from distributing its underground newspaper, the DF had difficulty sending clear instructions to the population, and from the outset that reduced its capacity to mobilize them. Its powerlessness was partly the result of an ideological choice. The spiritual struggle was recommended as the most important form of combat: "TO RESIST IS ABOVE ALL TO DEMONSTRATE TO THE INVADER THAT HE IS UP AGAINST A SUPERIOR CIVILIZATION THAT HE WILL NOT BE ABLE TO ABSORB," Robert Salmon (Robert Tenaille) propounded in the columns of *Défense de la France*.[75] For many long months, therefore, the movement confined itself to moral exhortation, urging the French people to hold on to their dignity: "The German should be able to say upon his return: 'France refused to give herself to me, she shrank from my touch. Even the prostitutes fled me in disgust, and the boudoirs of courtesans were closed to me.'"[76] Following that line, it called on each individual to engage in an examination of conscience, a secularized form of expiation that would make the light shine forth: "Every individual, in and of himself, must be a center of resistance, a fulcrum, a rock capable of withstanding the storm in isolation. . . . Young man of France, it is first and foremost to that interior work that I invite you. When, at the price of fervent struggles . . . you have become the captain of your soul, then you will be free and ready to serve. . . . And when there are many of you like that . . . then, like a building whose every stone voluntarily holds together, France will be rebuilt in an indestructible manner."[77] The movement, in other words, did not manage to elaborate concrete methods for engagement. Ultimately, it confined itself to committing volunteers to spread the good word and inviting the French to adopt a civic attitude. But these watchwords were not quite enough to spark enthusiasm. A number of organizations ran up against that impasse: the inability to spur forms of protest apart from the dissemination of propaganda.

*La Voix du Nord* confirms this pattern. It was created in 1941 by Jules Noutour, a Socialist peace officer dismissed by the mayor's office of Lille, and Natalis Dumez, the former Christian Democratic mayor of

Bailleul. The first issue of the newspaper came out on April 1, 1941. *La Voix du Nord* sought to respond to separatist activities encouraged by the occupier that threatened to remove Flanders from the French sphere of influence and to incorporate it into the Reich. The underground newspaper also followed in the wake of the illustrious publications printed clandestinely during World War I. Distributed in the two north-ernmost departments, *La Voix du Nord* saw its circulation rise to about 2,500 copies by September 1942.[78] For many months, the movement, clearly handicapped by the arrest of Natalis Dumez on September 7, 1942, confined itself to disseminating the paper, before moving on to other pursuits in 1943.

By contrast, other groups in the northern zone continued to locate the struggle in the military realm. Such was the line followed by CDLL. That movement did not begin to publish a newspaper until May 1943, giving precedence to military action, thanks to its ties to Vichy's SR Air and also to the activities of Georges Savourey, head of the intelli-gence service. In 1942 the movement added a system of escape routes for exfiltrating Allied aviators.[79] In the same vein, it organized both irregular groups from Champagne, which were supposed to act imme-diately, and reserve troops, set to intervene during the Allied landing. But the movement suffered a series of hard blows. In October 1941, its leader, Maurice Ripoche, barely escaped arrest and took refuge in the free zone, which deprived the movement of an energetic chief. In March 1942, Georges Savourey was taken down in turn, prelude to the elimination of almost all the leaders of the movement.

The OCM attempted to act on both the political and the military level, having imposed a bureaucracy on itself early on. Maxime Blocq-Mascart headed the civil bureau. Jacques-Henri Simon (Sermoy), a lawyer in the Council of State, took charge of external relations in summer 1942; and Jacques Rebeyrol, also an attorney, oversaw political action and propaganda. The movement then became involved in col-lecting intelligence, a mission initially entrusted to its Second Bureau, then, beginning in spring 1943, to its offshoot, the Centurie network. In January 1941, André Boulloche, an engineer from Ponts et Chaussées (Bridges and Roads), joined the OCM and co-opted his former boss, Pierre Pène. Boulloche, however, preferred to become engaged with the FFL and left France in November 1942, leaving Pène to organize the

Aisne and Ardennes departments. Relying on contacts he had at Ponts et Chaussées, Pène formed groups able to transmit intelligence—about the German bunkers built in Margival, for example. Several groups, formed spontaneously in the southwest, also became associated with the movement in 1942, under the leadership of André Grandclément. He organized the collection of intelligence on the air bases and ports of Bordeaux and La Pallice and set up escape channels via Spain to exfiltrate resistance fighters and Allied soldiers.[80]

The OCM refused to create a newspaper, believing that such an activity threatened the safety of its members. It nevertheless intended to bring its influence to bear on the political future of France and was therefore led to clarify its position toward Philippe Pétain. Some of the views it had taken indicated a real proximity to Vichyist ideology. In its first *Cahier*, for example, the movement pointed out that "anti-Semitism . . . in its attenuated form, remains almost universal, even in the most liberal countries. This leads us to presume that it does not have a purely imaginary basis." "Jews in commerce and finance, or in the liberal professions, arouse envy," it added. That prompted the group to recommend two measures: "Disperse the Jews to facilitate assimilation, and put a halt to immigration."[81] In June 1942, however, the movement broke ranks with Pétain, emphasizing that "the cover he gives to everything disapproved of by public opinion has destroyed his moral prestige. His harsh measures against the Resistance have destroyed his prestige as a leader. His errors in assessing English weakness and German strength have destroyed his reputation for clear-sightedness. His inability to promulgate a well-constructed constitution and legal framework has undermined his political authority. His choice of men has annihilated hopes for reform."[82] At a completely different level, an OCM commission prepared the draft of a constitution. It stipulated in particular the election of the president of the French republic by universal suffrage. There would also be regional chambers, and groups representing the major professions would contribute half the votes toward the election of deputies. A senate would oversee the acts of the government, but the president would be able to dissolve it. Finally, a supreme court would rule on the constitutionality of laws.[83] The OCM thus combined military and political actions. Its vitality undoubtedly made it one of the most important movements in the northern zone. Should it be credited, however, with eighty thousand members in spring 1942, as Maxime Blocq-Mascart claimed upon liberation?[84] In view of studies of other underground organizations, that estimate seems high, but at present there are no statistics available to correct it.

## The Movements in the Southern Zone

In the south, the growth of Libération was aided by the ties the movement had established with leftist groups. In spring 1941, Daniel Mayer agreed to join Emmanuel d'Astier de La Vigerie's organization and to place his troops under its control, but without acknowledging that it held any monopoly over members of the CAS. Similarly, the union activist Léon Jouhaux, despite his initial reluctance, adopted a holistic approach governed by two principles: "Obedience to the Gaullist symbol; noncollaboration with the Communists."[85]

That dual alliance facilitated the influx of experienced cadres from both the CGT and the SFIO. In late 1941, the formation of a steering committee made official the representation of the CGT, the CFTC, the CAS, and of Yvon Morandat. But that committee rarely met and, from autumn 1942 on, played an increasingly limited role. In fact, political and union leaders now wanted their organizations to appear ex officio in the underground struggle. Libération-sud, following its own path, was also inclined to mark itself off from its former partners. It curtailed the practice of automatically accepting members from leftist organizations. Prominent recruits nevertheless joined the movement. In summer 1942, a journalist, Pascal Copeau (Salard, Corton), who had attempted in vain to join the FFL, reestablished ties with d'Astier de La Vigerie, after being interned in the Miranda camp in Spain and sentenced to a month in prison. Copeau, son of the founder of the Vieux-Colombier theater, had known d'Astier de La Vigerie before the war at the magazine *Vu et lu (Seen and Read)*, and was immediately integrated into the leadership. Jacques Baumel explains: "More than an organizer, Copeau was a born politician with all that entails: conviction but also know-how, a taste for intrigue, an aptitude for making shrewd moves and for quickly understanding power relations."[86] Copeau soon became second-in-command of the movement.

Pierre Hervé (Arnaud, Chardon), national secretary of Étudiants Communistes (Communist Students) in 1937, had first been an activist in the Communist ranks. He then helped organize the Free University in the Paris region. Arrested on June 11, 1941, he was acquitted, but was kept in a holding cell as an administrative internee. He managed to escape the Palais de Justice on the night of July 8, 1941. Since his cover was blown in the north, he went to the free zone with his wife, Annie, and there met up with Lucie Aubrac, whom he had known at JC. After joining Libération, he became head of the Lyon region (R1).[87] Maurice Kriegel (Fouquet, Valrimont) and Alfred Malleret (Baudoin, Bourdel, Joinville), both Communists, also became associated with the movement; Serge Asher (Ravanel), a young student at the École Polytechnique, joined in early September 1942. During and after the war, that Communist presence appeared suspect. The membership of individuals who concealed their Communist ties was seen by many as covert infiltration. The movement not only structured itself from the top down but also rooted itself in its base. It expanded along the Mediterranean coast, in Savoy, Rhône-Alpes, Languedoc, and Limousin; and, following a tested formula, it sometimes incorporated smaller groups. In Toulouse, a team baptized "Liberté, Égalité, Fraternité" was thus integrated into d'Astier de La Vigerie's organization. Colonel Georges Bonneau, one of its founders, became head of the region of the Midi (R6). Libération-sud thus radiated outward to the unoccupied zone as a whole.

The movement put forth an original political line from the start, declaring a pronounced anti-Vichyism. It invited its readers to "choose between struggle and inertia in the wake of a ruler who, for us, will never be anything but a traitor."[88] Although the newspaper did not mention General de Gaulle's name in the first four issues of 1941, it was the first to embrace the Rebel as a symbol, hailing in particular his clear-sightedness as a military leader. "For us, even while reserving our freedom for the future, we note that at the present hour there is only one movement, that of Free France, only one leader, General de Gaulle, symbol of French unity and French will," it affirmed on February 15, 1942.[89] However sincere, that decision to rally behind the Gaullist cause also allowed Libération-sud to mark itself off from its rival Combat, whose Gaullism came later and was more lukewarm.

Libération-sud developed that line and propagated it among the population, meeting with some success. Although only four issues appeared between July and December 1941, fourteen came out between January and September 1942. Circulation increased from twenty thousand in September 1942 to between sixty thousand and a hundred thousand between December 1942 and July 1943, thanks to the assistance of Édouard Ehnni, secretary-general of the Livre CGT (the union for workers in book publishing, printing, and distribution) in Lyon, who divided up printing responsibilities among his colleagues.[90]

But it did not take the movement long to extend its activities beyond the narrow sphere of propaganda. It established a service providing false identity papers, entrusted to Pierre Kahn-Farelle, a thirty-six-year-old manufacturer. In 1942, the service employed a dozen permanent workers. In addition, a political action section covered everything falling outside military missions and propaganda. Run by Jacques Brunschwig, then by Pascal Copeau, it primarily promoted worker action. It invited the fifteen to eighteen thousand militants, who, it said, belonged to professional cells, to engage in undetectable sabotage, "feasible for anyone, and whose results stem from the inventiveness, logic, and assurance of the person performing it."[91] Finally, a paramilitary sector was assigned to the engineer Raymond Aubrac, who set out to form irregular groups, to collect intelligence, and to identify drop zones and landing fields.

That strategy sparked debate and tensions. The strikes that erupted in Oullins and then in the Lyon region in autumn of 1942 caused a first rift between those advocating support for the social movements (Pascal Copeau, Lucie and Raymond Aubrac) and those promoting a more cautious line (Robert Lacoste, Jacques Brunschwig). The conflict led to the departure of Brunschwig, who also found Copeau's ascent difficult to bear and preferred to join Libération-nord. A second disagreement— between Paul Schmidt, the liaison officer dispatched by the BCRA, and the movement's leaders—centered on military action. Schmidt deplored the fact that "the old prewar hatred against all things military persists. Events force people to think about it, but you sense it is done reluctantly, that only reluctantly was the decision finally made to organize this branch."[92] In short, the leaders of Libération-sud were hardly enthusiastic about military action. Believing it was only "one means of action in the political realm," they maintained that it ought to be subordinated to the political.[93] Laurent Douzou deems that a smart approach: "There was a risk that the secret operations against the occupier would be considered a matter for specialists, which, however unorthodox, remained military by their very nature. But the work of establishing a new society was something from which no one could be excluded for lack of skills or experience. It was an activity that, though poorly defined in the present circumstances, was familiar and of interest to the entire nation."[94] Granted, Libération-sud, like many groups, was very poorly equipped to wage a military fight; its paltry resources and know-how hardly encouraged it to take that path. But in any event, the group undoubtedly preferred to focus on the liberation rather than on victory. D'Astier de La Vigerie and his friends, in establishing connections with the CAS and the CGT, were obviously positioning themselves for the postwar period, when they hoped to play an active role. From that standpoint, military combat, as useful as it might be for bringing down Nazi Germany, contributed nothing toward the construction of power relations that, upon liberation, would herald brighter days ahead. It is clear, therefore, why combat remained a secondary aspect for these leaders.

Franc-Tireur developed along similar lines, at least in part. Jean-Pierre Levy set out to expand his movement to the southern zone as a whole, beyond its birthplace in Lyon. Like his counterparts in the northern and southern zones, he relied in the first place on people of goodwill. For example, in Saint-Étienne, he entered into contact with Jean Nocher, a journalist at *La Tribune républicaine*. Nocher had formed a small group, Espoir; in 1942, it merged with the Lyon group, and Nocher became department chief for Loire. Efforts to tap promising political or social groups furthered that geographical expansion. Auguste Pinton was assigned the task of attracting Radicals; Antoine Avinin canvassed the circles of the Ligue de la Jeune République (LJR; Young Republic League), the precursor to the Christian Democratic Party. Pierre Eudes, secretary-general of the Strasbourg chamber of commerce, which had taken refuge in Lyon, concerned himself with the Alsace-Lorrainians who had fled to the Rhône region. That expansion, however, had real limits: Rhône-Alpes remained the movement's power base from start to finish.

As with the DF and many other organizations, Franc-Tireur's newspaper favored the growth of underground groups more by its form than by its content. "Even more impressive than content was the regularity of publication," notes the historian Dominique Veillon.[95] As a result, the movement devoted enormous resources to propaganda, especially since shortages complicated its task. To be sure, stationers, such as Darblay in Bellegarde, sometimes handed over all or part of their stock; the RAF sometimes delivered containers loaded with paper, for example during the parachute drop of August 26, 1942, in Puy-Saint-Romain.[96] But it was sometimes also necessary to turn to the black market. Also, since Franc-Tireur declined to set up its own printing facilities, it relied on printer friends; for a time, that function was performed by Louis Agnel in Miribel. In any case, the print run increased substantially, from six thousand in December 1941 to fifteen thousand in the first three months of 1942, reaching thirty thousand in November 1942.[97] Thirty-seven issues appeared between December 1941 and August 25, 1944, a rate that was "monthly, as far as possible, and by the grace of the Marshal's police," as the newspaper's banner announced.

That said, did the newspaper constitute an appropriate instrument for mobilization? In informing its readers about the realities of the war, Vichyism, and Nazism, it indisputably played a role in enlightening the public. From that standpoint, the presence of professional journalists offered a guarantee of quality. For example, Georges Altman, editor at the *Progrès de Lyon*, joined *Franc-Tireur* in March 1942, allowing the paper to benefit from the intelligence he gathered through his professional contacts. But the share granted to news in the strict sense tended to decrease, taking up 29.1 percent of column space in 1943 versus 56.6 percent in 1942. Like its counterparts, *Franc-Tireur* had difficulty competing with the BBC; it therefore gradually abandoned information in favor of ideas. Plans for the future increased in importance (2 percent of column space in 1942, 24.5 percent in 1944),[98] a sign that the movement was intent on presenting the political future of its dreams. It will come as no surprise, finally, that early on *Franc-Tireur* adopted a clear line, in contrast to the ambivalence of *Combat* and *Défense de la France*. In January 1942, the newspaper announced loud and clear its rejection of the leader of the French State. "If Laval and the others were able to wallow as they pleased in treason, it is because Marshal Pétain, acting as chloroform to the French resistance, covered all their acts, even the worst ones, with his name and his stars," it asserted.[99] In March 1942, it took the side of the man of June 18: "Inasmuch as General de Gaulle has publicly pledged to return liberty to the country and to allow it to choose its own destiny, he alone appears qualified to ensure the continued existence of the state."[100]

Neither propaganda nor the clarity of its positions was sufficient to win over the population, however. Like many underground groups, Franc-Tireur confined itself to immaterial exhortations. "Civil servants, workers, industrialists, farmers, with all your strength organize the passive Resistance. Take the opposite course from all of Vichy's decisions, make the exercise of power impossible, everywhere and every day," it recommended in April 1942.[101] In autumn 1942, the movement began to call on people of goodwill to gather together, without offering them any great hope: "Weapons will arrive in time, at a time when we need them."[102] A few concrete instructions were sometimes formulated, however. "Railroad employees, send the cars off on the wrong course as they are leaving the station. Workers especially, sabotage work in your factories, forget to grease the parts. Everyone, try to steal war materiel," the newspaper suggested in September of the same year.[103] But if these exhortations instilled a certain state of mind, they were by all appearances insufficient to induce civilians to join the struggle.

Nevertheless, the movement gradually broadened its repertoire of actions, without having theorized its practices from the outset, as Combat had done. "Unlike Henri Frenay, who was deliberate in his actions, Jean-Pierre Levy and the steering committee were impelled to adapt by necessity and circumstance," writes Veillon.[104] Necessity and circumstance proved fruitful, however. In 1942, for example, the movement set up specialized services: propaganda was entrusted to Georges Altman and Élie Péju; Jean-Pierre Levy personally took charge of intelligence. In addition to collecting economic or military information occasionally provided by sympathizers, the service could count on the assistance of Adolphe Moulon, who, thanks to two teams of postal workers, intercepted letters addressed to the Légion Française des Combattants (LFC; French Legion of Fighters) and then to the Milice, or to the bureaus of the STO. Above all, the movement set up irregular groups under the command of Benjamin Roux. Through an SOE agent known as Alain, it received a parachute drop on May 28, 1942, which supplied it with arms and munitions. That manna from heaven was quickly exhausted, however: between 1940 and December 1942, the RAF carried out only seven or eight operations, whose spoils had to be divided up among the three major movements in the southern zone. Yet the modesty of its resources did not prevent Franc-Tireur from taking action. On the night of November 2, 1942, eleven simultaneous explosions targeted collaborationist kiosks and shops in Clermont-Ferrand, Lyon, Limoges, Périgueux, Roanne, and Vichy. Likewise, on December 24, a small team blew up the France-Rayonne factory in Roanne, which was manufacturing guncotton for the occupier. It should be added, to complete this overview, that an exfiltration channel between Périgueux and Spain was created in 1942. It allowed 120 Jews and soldiers to escape before it was dismantled in March 1943.[105] Franc-Tireur thus managed to broaden the range of its interventions, though its results, especially as regards intelligence and sabotage, must not be overestimated, particularly in comparison to the Combat movement.

## Combat's Moment to Shine

By late summer 1940, Henri Frenay had laid the foundations for his future organization, an undertaking that attested both to his talents as a visionary and to his obsession with organization, of which his comrades would enjoy making fun. At the time, the movement was structured around three major axes. General Services dealt with false identity papers, social services, finances, liaison, and housing. Political Affairs was in charge of the recruitment-organization-propaganda axis, as well as intelligence. Finally, Military Affairs managed the irregular groups, the AS, and Résistance-Fer (Resistance Rail); beginning in 1943, it also supervised the maquis. Over time, then, Combat broadened its practices. In mid-February 1942, responding to a suggestion made by Berty Albrecht, it created a social services department to assist the families of those arrested for underground activity. In 1942 André Plaisantin, along with Marcel Peck, head of the Lyon region, proposed that the movement's cells be regrouped by administration and profession within a single structure, the Noyautage des Administrations Publiques (NAP; Infiltration of Public Administrations). In the

PAS-DE-CALAIS

NORD

SOMME

SEINE-INFÉRIEURE

AISNE

ARDENNES

A

●Amiens

OISE

MARNE

MEUSE

MOSELLE

MANCHE

CALVADOS

EURE

Paris

SEINE-ET-MARNE

Châlons-sur-Marne

C

MEURTHE-ET-MOSELLE

BAS-RHIN

FINISTÈRE

CÔTES-DU-NORD

ILLE-ET-VILAINE

MAYENNE

ORNE

SEINE-ET-LOISE

AUBE

HAUTE-MARNE

VOSGES

HAUT-RHIN

MORBIHAN

Le Mans

SARTHE

EURE-ET-LOIR

LOIRET

YONNE

HAUTE-SAÔNE

TERRITOIRE DE BELFORT

M

LOIRE-INFÉRIEURE

MAINE-ET-LOIRE

LOIR-ET-CHER

P

CÔTE-D'OR

Dijon

D

DOUBS

VENDÉE

DEUX-SÈVRES

INDRE-ET-LOIRE

VIENNE

INDRE

CHER

NIÈVRE

R5

SAÔNE-ET-LOIRE

JURA

CHARENTE-INFÉRIEURE

HAUTE-VIENNE

CREUSE

ALLIER

PUY-DE-DÔME

LOIRE

RHÔNE

AIN

HAUTE-SAVOIE

R1

CHARENTE

Limoges

Clermont-Ferrand

Lyon

SAVOIE

B

DORDOGNE

CORRÈZE

CANTAL

HAUTE-LOIRE

ISÈRE

Bordeaux●

GIRONDE

LOT

AVEYRON

LOZÈRE

ARDÈCHE

DRÔME

HAUTES-ALPES

LANDES

LOT-ET-GARONNE

TARN-ET-GARONNE

R3

GARD

VAUCLUSE

BASSES-ALPES

R2

ALPES-MARITIMES

R4

GERS

TARN

●Toulouse

Montpellier●

HÉRAULT

BOUCHES-DU-RHÔNE

VAR

BASSES-PYRÉNÉES

HAUTE-GARONNE

HAUTES-PYRÉNÉES

ARIÈGE

AUDE

Marseilles●

PYRÉNÉES-ORIENTALES

100          200 Miles

0          150          300 Kilometres

CORSE

**Military Regions of the Resistance**

| A | Military region |
| ● | Staff headquarters |
| — | Regional boundaries |
| ......... | Departmental boundaries |
|  | Northern Zone |
|  | Southern Zone |

*Map 2*

summer of that year, Claude Bourdet took up the idea and extended it to the entire region and to every administration. The movement's collusion with employees in the civil service allowed it to obtain useful intelligence, while also identifying future administrators for the postliberation period. But there was a flip side to the coin: "We would thereby provide alibis for a certain number of fans of the double game."[106] In summer 1941, Frenay had also come up with the idea of organizing his movement on the basis of the regional map devised by the Vichy regime. R1 comprised the ten departments in the Lyon region; R2, the seven gravitating around Marseilles; R3, the six in the environs of Montpellier; R4, the nine in the Toulouse region; R5, the nine in the Limousin zone; and R6, the five radiating out from Clermont-Ferrand.[107]

The expansion reflected Frenay's inventiveness. But it was also an expression of the desire to build a national movement, extending to both the southern zone and the northern zone. In January 1941, that mission was assigned to Robert Guédon, a classmate of Frenay's at the École de Guerre. Guédon relied particularly on Jeanne Sivadon, director of the École des Surintendantes d'Usines, a women's school that trained social workers, and on Pierre de Froment, who had formed groups in Vierzon and Amiens especially.

The results, however, were disappointing. An agreement was reached with Jacques-Yves Mulliez to distribute *Les Petites Ailes de France*, but the northern branch underwent a crisis in late 1941. Profoundly shaken by the death of his wife, Robert Guédon, the target of a police manhunt, kept his distance from the organization. "He is not around very much, and since he's the one who pulls all the strings, the groups receive few directions. They have the impression—exaggerated no doubt, but depressing—that they are stuck in neutral, and therefore that they are taking great risks for nothing," wrote Frenay.[108] Frenay decided to go to Paris to handle the situation. In early January, he created a steering committee for the northern zone, headed by André Noël and Élisabeth Dussauze. But in February 1942, about twenty arrests, resulting from the betrayal of a double agent, Henri Devillers,[109] dismantled the organization, which was never able to rise from its ashes. In summer 1942, one of the surviving members, Jacques Lecompte-Boinet, a civil servant and the son-in-law of General Mangin, made contact with

Frenay, then with his second-in-command, Bourdet. But the three meetings that took place ultimately convinced Lecompte-Boinet "to break any ties of allegiance with Combat."[110] Assisted by a young lawyer, Pierre Arrighi, he then set up an intelligence network, Manipule, entrusted to Robert Reyl and Jean Roquigny. Reestablishing connections with Guédon's and Froment's former groups, he also constituted a movement, which in early 1943 baptized itself "Ceux de la Résistance" (CDLR; Those of the Resistance), without maintaining any organic connection to its parent organization. The MLN had been the only organization to attempt to establish itself in both zones, and the venture quickly failed. "When I go back in my mind to that last quarter of 1941, what I recall in the first place are the efforts we expended to unite the forces of the budding Resistance in the two zones," notes Frenay, not without sadness.[111]

In the south, by contrast, the final results were less disappointing. It is true that the MLN enjoyed two advantages there: high-quality recruits on the one hand, and a dynamic of unity on the other. From December 1940 on, Berty Albrecht lent effective assistance. In 1941 Claude Bourdet (Aubin, Lorrain) implanted the movement in Alpes-Maritimes, before becoming Frenay's second-in-command. Maurice Chevance (Bertin, Barioz, Thuillier, Vilars) was in charge of Provence. While building a haulage company for colonial officers, he contributed both to the development of the movement and to its financing, thanks to the extraordinary success of his business, which came as a surprise to him. Through Albrecht, two students at the École Polytechnique joined the small team in 1941. André Bollier (Vélin, Carton) took charge of printing the newspaper; his classmate Jean-Guy Bernard, after leaving for Toulouse to develop the organization there, became its secretary-general.

Although, in great part, the analysis of Combat's social composition remains to be done and cannot be attempted here, three observations are in order. The movement recruited broadly from the ranks of the army, both renegade soldiers and others. Given Frenay's background, that is hardly surprising. Women also played an important role. The professions they had chosen before 1939, especially as factory welfare officers (*assistantes sociales*), paved the way for their emancipation, while demonstrating their predisposition for altruism. They were well prepared to participate in the resistance. Several members of the MLN, finally, had been active during the interwar period in parties on the margins of the Third Republic, either Jeune République or Frontisme, the leftist group founded by the Radical Gaston Bergery. This may explain the movement's success in propagating an ideology that rejected both Communist barbarism and the cold egotism of capitalism. All in all, it was able to rely on cadres of great merit, many of whom paid for their engagement with their lives.

In addition, the MLN grew stronger by taking a unified approach, which corresponded to Frenay's aspirations. Granted, not all underground leaders shared that faith. Paul Dungler, a former leader of Action Française in Alsace, who had long been alerted to the Nazi danger, founded a network in his home region, the 7e Colonne d'Alsace (Seventh Column of Alsace). He refused outright to merge with the MLN. According to Frenay, Dungler told him that "his group is exclusively Alsatian, not even Lorrainian. As such, it has specific problems that would get lost in a vast movement."[112] Likewise, the founder of Combat encountered the reluctance of the head of Libération-sud, whom he apparently met for the first time in August 1941, through Louis Terrenoire. While admitting "the necessity of coordinating the efforts of 'Libération,' 'Liberté' and the MLN, at the word 'merger,' he loudly protested. There can be no question of that, since the political content of our organizations is not the same. Conversely, he wishes, like me, to be in contact with de Gaulle in the near future."[113] In fact, the two men were opposites in every way. As Jacques Soustelle explains: "Exaggerate Frenay's traits and you get Murat; exaggerate [d'Astier de La Vigerie's] and you get Fouché. Frenay acted by grappling with reality, bringing people together, appealing to the emotions and to faith; d'Astier, by inventing slogans, assembling staffs, opening dazzling prospects for intrigue and power to those he wanted to tempt. One roused devotion, the other, complicity; while the former, passionate about plans and projects, retained from his military career an inclination for organization charts and pyramid hierarchies, the latter, a dilettante who went from the navy to occasional journalism, preferred committees where his genius for maneuvering could thrive."[114]

The mistrust between d'Astier de La Vigerie and Frenay would never dissipate. The self-designation of *Libération* as the "Organ of the

Directorate of French Liberation Forces," announced on the front page under the newspaper's name, shocked the head of Combat, since it implied that the periodical represented the underground forces as a whole.[115] It outraged him that, in May 1942, his rival could go to England and present himself as the delegate for all the movements in the free zone. Conversely, the Marshalist and somewhat right-wing complexion of the early Frenay could only antagonize d'Astier de La Vigerie, who was firmly entrenched on the left. The question of a merger, however, would continue to arise. It was only provisionally resolved over the course of time.

Frenay had better luck with the Christian Democrats, who had founded Liberté in 1940. The merger between the MLN and Liberté resulted in the creation of the MLF, a designation that was abandoned rather quickly in favor of the name of their joint newspaper, *Combat*. One sign of its growth: a year after its creation, the newspaper relied on fourteen printing offices in the southern zone,[116] and its circulation reached about forty thousand in May 1942.

Combat therefore became a relatively powerful organization, thanks to its founder's qualities as a visionary. In December 1942, 102 permanent employees were working in its services, absorbing a perpetually expanding budget. The movement made do with twenty to thirty thousand francs in late 1941, while in 1942 it devoured two hundred thousand francs a month. That bottom line, however, though certainly flattering, must not be allowed to obscure the crises the movement faced until 1942.

Frenay, as noted earlier, rejected neither Marshal Pétain nor the reforms he aspired to impose on the country. Like many men on the right, he also professed a vigorous apoliticism. But as the resistance developed in the southern zone, the movements were forced to take a stance against Vichy, a dilemma that the northern groups, confronting the German occupier directly, were spared. "One of the weaknesses of Frenay's action at that time," his biographer Robert Belot points out, "was that he had trouble finding a political formulation for his ideal, one that could be a credible alternative and could be translated into reality. It was in that respect that his contempt and distaste for public affairs were a handicap, hindering him from becoming the man of action he wanted to be."[117] Frenay's ambivalence, in addition to handicapping his movement by preventing it from formulating a clear line that would rally people to his cause, dulled his political senses. In the end, it ensnared him.

After the series of arrests resulting from the betrayal of the double agent Devillers, the Vichy authorities, acting through Berty Albrecht, asked to meet with Frenay. On January 27, 1942, the movement's steering committee accepted the principle of such a meeting. On January 28, Frenay began discussions with Henri Rollin, assistant director at Sûreté Nationale (National Security), followed the next day by talks with Pierre Pucheu, minister of the interior. The two men agreed to meet again, and that interview took place on February 6, 1942. One last conversation between the resistance fighter and the minister occurred on February 25. These curious negotiations lead us to wonder what goals the two parties were pursuing. Frenay was obviously trying to gain some time and was hoping, thanks to the truce granted by the Vichy authorities, to reconstitute an organization badly shaken by the winter arrests. As a matter of fact, the French State refrained from prosecuting the members of the movement, ordered the resistance fighters who had been taken into custody released on bail, and suspended the proceedings against them.[118] As Claude Bourdet points out, "materially, the operation was a complete success for us. For nearly two months, until late February . . . police activity against us slowed, which allowed us to reconstitute the apparatus, to designate new leaders, to change offices, mailboxes, pseudonyms, etc. . . . Unfortunately, the results from a moral standpoint offset the positive results. Information from Pucheu's services was leaked to the other movements, probably more to fabricate a favorable image of Pucheu throughout the country than to cause trouble among us."[119] Actually, the minister's aim was undoubtedly to divide his adversaries[120]—and he achieved his goal. "These conversations, which to many people looked like overtures to an armistice or offers of peace, struck a terrible blow to the unity of the Resistance," Colonel Passy notes. "The talks between 'Libération' and 'Combat'—undertaken several weeks earlier—regarding an eventual merger between the movements immediately came to an end. Violent tensions, further exacerbated by the venomous remarks of Frenay's rivals or enemies, arose between the two movements . . . benefiting only the enemy and his lackeys."[121] These morally inauspicious talks were exploited by *Libération*, which criticized them in veiled terms on March 1, 1942, and again on March 20: "Among the French who are fighting the Germans, there are sincere, courageous men, who believed, however, that they could negotiate with the government, thinking they could outmaneuver it. They will be duped by Vichy and abandoned by their troops."[122] Frenay had to tour the southern zone and explain to a shaken base the ins and outs of that sorry episode. All in all, the affair demonstrates that Frenay, even in early 1942, still did not identify Vichy as an enemy. He broke away only with the return of Pierre Laval in April 1942. At that time, Frenay conspicuously kept his distance from the Marshal. In an article published in *Combat* in May 1942, he addressed Pétain as follows. "You had a choice: give in or walk away. You should have walked away and left to others the task of delivering our country. You prefer to remain, no longer in half-freedom but in complete slavery, in order to sponsor treason. Everything is clear now, the Pétain myth is dead. Your stars are being snuffed out."[123]

That rift, however, did not prompt him to rally wholeheartedly behind Gaullism, for two major reasons. First, the methods of the man of June 18 hardly appealed to Frenay, persuaded—like many resistance fighters—that the struggle had to be waged on French soil. Second, the hostility that the leader of Free France manifested toward the head of the French State annoyed Frenay for a long time: "De Gaulle left to continue fighting. Is he right? History will decide. I do not say he is wrong, very much on the contrary, but please, let him stay and let us leave him there. As a combatant, he is within his rights to criticize certain acts of the government that may impede his action. But I am sure that, as a Frenchman, he wants nothing to do with the division of France."[124] At a more profound level, the two leaders disagreed on many points, and their temperaments could not fail to lead to confrontations. "In fact, [he] did not feel 'Gaullist' right away. He was a somewhat self-educated Republican, still subject to the influence of his military and familial background," comments Claude Bourdet—demonstrating a marked aptitude for understatement.[125] That reluctance by no means disappeared. It explains in part the continuing disputes between Henri Frenay and Charles de Gaulle.

It is fair to say that, on the eve of the Anglo-American landing in North Africa in November 1942, the internal resistance had grown stronger. Its birth and development owed very little to Free France, however, whatever may have been written after the war by the upholders of Gaullian orthodoxy. On the contrary, everything suggests that the movements were able to grow by exploiting the anger roused by the occupation in the north and by the Vichy regime in the south. Until 1941, London offered them neither resources nor a moral framework, particularly since some underground groups refused to break ranks with the Marshal and rejected the possibility of fighting anywhere besides metropolitan France.

In addition, the underground groups were able to broaden their repertoire of actions, producing false identity papers, setting up irregular groups, and embarking on immediate action. Many, however, were unable to get past the aporia of moral protest, confining themselves to exhorting the French to adopt a civic attitude. True, the leaders were struggling to invent the terms of a resistance practice, since they were unable to assign militants practicable and concrete objectives. In 1942, it would no doubt have been a pipe dream to call for national insurrection or even generalized sabotage, given the power of the occupier and the lack of resources. Moreover, certain options were beyond the parameters of the army of shadows. Although it was able to form a secret army meant to assist the Allied forces in the course of a future landing, the decision to intervene on the European continent remained the exclusive preserve of Anglo-American leaders. Finally, rank-and-file militants possessed limited skills, which circumscribed the type of actions they could conduct, at least at first. Granted, the diversification within the various movements broadened the potential range of their interventions. But that process, slow and irregular, affected only a handful of volunteers enlisted in the irregular groups and other armed organizations. The revolution set in motion by the creation of the STO can be assessed by that measure: the resistance was suddenly able to assign its members concrete and accessible goals, while all of a sudden having a mass of volunteers at its disposal.

Note, moreover, that the internal resistance, even before Jean Moulin's arrival on the scene, was moving toward unity, though by diverse paths. Some movements absorbed groups seeking the support of more powerful organizations. Liberté and the MLN, for example, believing there was strength in numbers, undertook to merge or federate. Finally, the large organizations, especially in the south, considered coordinating and even uniting their actions, despite their mutual distrust. The unification process, far from having been set in motion by Moulin, thus preexisted his arrival. But his appearance on the scene had the dual effect of accelerating that process and of responding more clearly to the question of what ties ought to bind the internal resistance and the external resistance.

Within that configuration, the involvement of the political parties complicated the situation. In fact, the rebirth of the SFIO and the engagement of the PCF in the underground struggle deprived the movements of the political monopoly they had sought to claim. As a result, they were torn between two contradictory objectives: ally themselves with powerful partners or limit their ambitions. Whatever their qualms, the movements would now have to negotiate with the political parties, which many held in contempt. That aspect, however, had little weight in the face of de Gaulle's claim to legitimacy. The underground groups now had to reckon with Free France, though they considered it both a rival and an ally.

## Chapter 6

# Rallying behind de Gaulle

UNTIL LATE 1941, Free France ignored the possibilities the resistance movements offered. "Until that time," Charles de Gaulle demonstrated "little interest in the active resistance and even in political action in France. Collecting military intelligence and radio propaganda took precedence," writes historian Jean-Louis Crémieux-Brilhac.[1] The man of June 18, moreover, maintained a cautious silence about his political program, both for reasons of ideology—the mistrust the political parties inspired in him—and for tactical reasons: the desire to unite the majority of French people.

It was not long, however, before the situation evolved. Some Gaullist personalities suggested seeking support from unionist and Socialist circles, an option advocated by Henri Hauck, de Gaulle's labor adviser and a former member of the CGT and the SFIO. Hauck persuaded de Gaulle to recruit Léon Morandat (Yvon, Léo, Arnolphe)—a member of the CFTC, who found himself in Great Britain after fighting at Narvik—for the political leadership and to send him on a mission to France. But Morandat's departure was delayed because of opposition from Colonel Passy and several of his agents, Rémy first and foremost. The formation of the CNF on September 24, 1941, changed the game plan, since it led to the creation of a Commissariat National à l'Intérieur (CNI; National Commission for the Interior), under the leadership of André Diethelm, former cabinet chief to Georges Mandel. As inspector of public finances, Diethelm had been sent to Portugal by the Vichy regime, and he took advantage of his mission to Lisbon to join up with de Gaulle in August 1941. The following month, the general made him minister of the interior. A division of labor thus seems to have been taking shape. Placed under the jurisdiction of General de Gaulle's private staff, the SR would conduct military operations; the CNI would supervise political action by organizing its own missions directly with the SOE. De Gaulle personally approved that setup. On October 8,

1941, he submitted a plan to Minister of Economic Warfare Hugh Dalton, whose ministry oversaw the SOE. "There is now reason to undertake political action, which is and must be distinct from military action and must involve different men and resources."[2] Soon thereafter, on the night of November 6, 1941, Morandat parachuted into France to establish contact with Catholic and unionist circles and to form propaganda networks in the southern zone.

The CNI, however, disappointed the hopes it had raised. It managed to set up only three missions. True, de Gaulle rather naïvely believed that the SOE would back his efforts. But the British government was hardly eager to support the Rebel's political action, especially since the British special services considered him a dictator in training. Furthermore, André Diethelm was lacking in energy and initiative. And, because there was a shortage of liaison officers, relations between the CNI and the BCRA deteriorated. The two services engaged in a ruthless struggle to recruit the best people (including Jean Moulin) and made little effort to coordinate their activities, at the risk of undertaking "parallel, uncoordinated actions targeting the same people or organizations" in the French metropolis.[3]

## Moulin's Arrival on the Scene

These rivalries opened the way for Jean Moulin, to whom de Gaulle entrusted major responsibilities upon the former prefect's arrival in October 1941. Nevertheless, it is not possible to attribute to Moulin a decisive role in the new approach taken by Free France. For though his appearance on the scene was a major event for Colonel Passy's men, "that was because Moulin, far from upsetting the plans the service had been working on for months, supported them with authority. At the time, to Passy's great dismay, de Gaulle was showing little enthusiasm for underground military action." The former prefect, "surrounded by the aura of his authority," was able to convince the leader of Free France of the validity of the plans being made by the Gaullist intelligence service.[4] He was, it seems, all the more convincing in that the major movements of the southern zone had begun to coordinate their actions, an advantage in de Gaulle's view—and also a potential risk. Indeed, "de Gaulle feared that a military power outside his control would emerge in France, one that would erect itself into an autonomous force or would take its orders directly from the Allies."[5] To ward off that threat, Passy, on the pretext of separating the political from the military, suggested "transforming the movements into 'recruitment and screening centers,' on behalf of a command of which they were in fact dispossessed."[6] He also advised decentralizing the movements. As Sébastien Albertelli points out, "These plans attested at once to the fear already inspired by the movements, to the little importance that [the Gaullists] intended to attach to the efforts [that the movements] had already agreed to make toward structuring themselves, and, all in all, to a profound ignorance of their nature. They did not augur well for the relations that would be established between the Resistance forces operating on either side of the Channel."[7]

Moulin therefore parachuted into France on the night of January 1, 1942, charged with a complex mission. He was supposed to impel the three large southern groups to intensify "current propaganda action"[8] and to set in place, at the highest echelons, the division between the political and the military.[9] Although no merger of the paramilitary groups belonging to the underground organizations was envisioned, their centralization and coordination would fall within London's purview. Finally, Moulin was to achieve unity of action among the resistance groups in the south, which meant persuading them to recognize General de Gaulle's authority. Two men, Raymond Fassin and Hervé Monjaret, accompanied him. They were supposed to be in charge of liaisons between London and Liberté, but upon their arrival they discovered that that movement had merged with the MLN to become Combat. From June 1942 on, Paul Schmidt and Michel Brault (Jérôme) would act as liaison agents for Libération-sud; Monjaret began working for Franc-Tireur that summer.

Moulin had three bargaining chips with which to impose his views. First, he could finance movements that had previously been living off their sympathizers' generosity. Originally allocated a budget of 3 million francs, by January 1942 he had handed over 250,000 francs to Frenay.[10] That was clearly a large sum, but not at all comparable to the funding for the networks, which received a monthly bonanza of 3 million francs. In General de Gaulle's view and in that of his subordinates, the intelligence the networks were delivering to Free France justified that preferential treatment. Pierre Fourcaud, for example, gave the networks 1,725,000 francs in June 1941.[11]

Second, Moulin guaranteed the movements a direct liaison with London, though the value of that asset should not be overestimated. His transmitter was damaged when he was dropped by parachute and would not be repaired until February, and radio contact did not become regular until April. Mail service also proved unpredictable. Moulin's first report, dated March 1, was transmitted by the British legation in Bern and did not arrive in London until April 7. The next two reports, written in late March and sent through Switzerland, reached England only in May; because of a problem with the code, they were not deciphered until early June.[12] About ten radio operators were dispatched from England, but in many cases they were arrested as soon as they arrived.

Third, General de Gaulle's envoy enjoyed enormous prestige, to which Frenay was not unresponsive: "In the little kitchen where we are talking, we are all of a sudden transported to another world. We literally drink up his words. It is scarcely believable that the man was over there only a few days ago, while that voice we pick up from England seems at once so close and so far away."[13]

Moulin gave top priority to persuading the three southern movements to pledge their allegiance to General de Gaulle. In January 1942, Libération hailed "the great French leader," and Franc-Tireur acknowledged that he was "the only one qualified to ensure provisionally, with the government, the continued existence of the state."[14] Combat, by contrast, waited until March to declare its adherence.

General de Gaulle's envoy also created services in common. The Bureau d'Information et de Presse (Press and Information Service), launched in April 1942, was entrusted to the Christian Democrat Georges Bidault. Its aim was "to supply the press of Free France with information coming from the underground movements of the metropolis, and vice versa."[15] The Comité Général d'Études (CGE; General Studies Committee), founded in July 1942, initially had four members— Deputy Paul Bastid, the senior official Alexandre Parodi, the union activist Robert Lacoste, and the law professor François de Menthon. It was supposed to plan the measures to be taken upon liberation. Finally, the Service des Opérations Aériennes et Maritimes (SOAM; Air and

Sea Operations Service), established in November 1942, identified parachute drop zones and landing fields and oversaw the departure and arrival of agents by air and by sea.

These initiatives served the cause of efficiency by sharing services that the movements had previously provided haphazardly. But they also tended to give added weight in the French metropolis to Moulin and the Free France delegation, by granting them total or partial control over information, liaisons, and the political future of the resistance. Within a few weeks, in any case, General de Gaulle's envoy had made a great deal of progress: he had formed joint services and had symbolically rallied the southern movements to Free France. But his actions were still dependent on the changes unfolding at the same time in the northern zone.

## Christian Pineau's Journey

Until 1941, Charles de Gaulle had observed a cautious silence about his political intentions. That reticence worried a fringe of the internal resistance, who, while looking favorably on Free France, wondered about the vitality of its democratic roots.

In winter 1941 Pierre Brossolette, a high-ranking Socialist militant,[16] had joined the Musée de l'Homme cell. After the dispersal of that group, he joined Rémy's network, the CND, where he ran the press and propaganda division. He therefore had connections with London. In January 1942 he supported the proposal of Christian Pineau (Garnier), who had suggested going to England to meet with de Gaulle. Before his journey, the head of Libération-nord consulted the principal leaders of the resistance in the north and south; they too were anxious to understand the intentions of the man of June 18. They all asked for a manifesto from de Gaulle spelling out his war aims.

Pineau, received by de Gaulle in March 1942, was both impressed and disappointed. "It was certainly one of the most emotional moments of my life. I was a little intimidated, since I wasn't expecting that at all. I was a good little union activist who knew his field. I was a good economist, but there was nothing heroic about me. And yet General de Gaulle, with a grand gesture, said to me: 'Now, talk to me about France.'"[17] Conversely, "no questions about the Resistance; no personal questions. It would have been trite to ask me whether I'd had a good trip, but that trip was like no other, for me at least. Maybe it merited an allusion."[18] Above all, de Gaulle set out his conditions: "I really do want to entrust a letter to you for your friends, but don't ask me to approve what I have condemned many times, a Republic without authority, a regime of party rule."[19] The first version of the manifesto was therefore far from what Pineau had expected. Two sentences in particular shocked him: "A moral, social, political, and economic regime abdicated in defeat; another was born of capitulation and feeds on it. The French people condemn both of them." The head of Libération-nord took offense. "It is an injustice to put the Third Republic and Vichy on the same level, and it will be cruelly felt by the men who are being persecuted by the current regime because they refused to join the new order," he later commented.[20] De Gaulle nevertheless refused to make any changes—until Pineau was about to depart. At the airfield, a motorcyclist brought him a new version, which more harshly condemned Vichy, attenuated the criticisms of the Third Republic, and promised a new national and international order.

Upon his return to metropolitan France in April, Pineau handed over the manifesto to Moulin, so that the movements in the free zone could disseminate it. They complied, but not without accompanying that publication with a few reservations. *Franc-Tireur*, while reaffirming its support for General de Gaulle, noted, for example: "We would be against him if, once this liberation is achieved, he envisioned a dictatorship—contrary to what he has always asserted—which we would no more tolerate from a general than we have accepted it from a Marshal."[21] The reaction of the political parties was cooler: Could they abide the Vichy regime being placed on the same level as the Third Republic, whatever the flaws of the defunct regime?

In mid-1942, London had thus managed to enhance the services of its delegation and to win, from the movements and the parties, an acknowledgment of General de Gaulle's authority, though not full acceptance of it. By contrast, the cause of unification was going nowhere. Although, thanks to the SOE, Emmanuel d'Astier de La Vigerie had managed to travel aboard a submarine to London, arriving in May 1942, his discussions with Colonel Passy and General de Gaulle did little to hasten the unification of the southern movements. In addition, the separation of the political from the military that Free France was demanding left the leaders of the internal resistance perplexed. As Frenay recalls, it was easy to "designate leaders at the national, regional, and departmental level, but the closer we got to the rank-and-file militant, the more difficult—and ultimately impossible—it became to set in place the separation that had been asked of us."[22] Despite this reluctance, Moulin managed to convince d'Astier de La Vigerie and Levy to accept the principle of a single secret army. They subscribed to that principle on the condition that Frenay not be given command of the AS. In October 1942, its leadership fell to the retired general Charles Delestraint (Vidal). A number of questions were left hanging, however, and Moulin suggested that the leaders take a trip to London to settle them. On September 26, 1942, d'Astier de La Vigerie and Frenay therefore arrived in the British capital after a long journey, interrupted by a stop at Gibraltar.

## Summit Talks

Three items were on the agenda for the negotiations conducted in the different services of Free France: the unification of the three southern movements, the formation of the AS, and the acknowledgment of General de Gaulle's authority. After d'Astier de La Vigerie rejected a merger, a compromise was reached. Based on a suggestion that the Socialist André Philip had made in July 1942, it was decided that a Comité de Coordination (CC; Coordination Committee) would synchronize actions, dividing up the tasks among the three major groups in the free zone. That agency would prepare "the cadres for the liberated country, up to the regional and departmental levels." At the political level, it would present "suggestions to the Comité National [CNF]" but would apply the directives it received, "after first being consulted." That solution only imperfectly addressed the problems. At the base, it left "the field open to recruitment by each of the movements, to their rivalry at every level, and therefore to conflicts."[23] Similarly, "the overlap between the political and the military in the committee's operation transformed a disagreement at the political level into a refusal to obey at the military level."[24]

Talks, however, ratified the principle of the AS, and Delestraint officially received its command. All the movements would place their paramilitary forces in the AS, which would carry out actions in two ways. In the short term, it would avoid "engaging troops and elite cadres in hopeless operations, putting them at risk of being wiped out prematurely." The primary objective was still "to paralyze the German operation through a general action launched at the opportune moment after the Allied landing."[5] In anticipation of D-Day, however, nothing prevented the AS from using the professional cells and irregular groups for occasional missions—sabotage operations or attacks, for example.

Frenay and Levy, in accepting in principle both the CC and the AS, recognized de jure the leader of Free France's authority. But that acknowledgment was by no means unconditional, as Frenay (Charvet) reminded General de Gaulle at the dinner they shared on November 16, 1942, before the head of Combat returned to metropolitan France:

> "General, the actions we are conducting in France have two indissociable aspects, which, however, are different in nature. On the one hand, in the secret army and the irregular groups, we are soldiers and, as such, part of an overall plan of action. Our tasks during the landing will be assigned by the inter-Allied staff and by yourself, and, it goes without saying, we will obey.
>
> "In other respects, we are citizens, free in our thoughts and acts. We cannot relinquish that freedom of judgment, which means that, in this area, we will obey your orders or we will not obey them."
>
> "Well then, Charvet, France will choose between you and me," de Gaulle concluded.[26]

Despite the hesitations and ulterior motives of each of the protagonists, the movements in the free zone had recognized the preeminence of Free France, while moving toward unified action. In the north, the final results proved to be more uneven.

## Rallying in the Northern Zone

In March 1942, François Faure (Paco), a member of the CND, had an interview with a representative of the central committee of the PCF. Having boarded the same Lysander flight as Christian Pineau, he arrived in London with the news that the Communist FTP had on principle rallied behind Free France. De Gaulle accepted their support, on the condition that the CND be firmly separated from the Communist organization. Upon his return, Faure transmitted the instructions he had received in London, which Colonel Rémy passed on to Georges Beaufils. The Communists would form an intelligence network called "Fana," which would provide information to the BCRA via the CND. Free France had thus established contact with the PCF, but the relationship was mediated by Rémy, who in fact played a political role for which he had no authorization.

Pierre Brossolette, a member of the CND, sought not only to influence the policy that Free France was conducting toward captive France but also to promote the coordination of the internal resistance under London's leadership. Possessing, in Jacques Soustelle's words, "a vigorous talent and an incisive dialectic,"[27] he hoped to persuade as many people as possible to rally behind Gaullism, believing that "General de Gaulle symbolizes the France that has not despaired, that did not accept defeat."[28] "A Gaullist who did not idolize de Gaulle, since his critical faculties were clearly above average," he was convinced "that only the general could unite the French people, behind resistance in the first place and reform in the second," Soustelle writes.[29] In December 1941, he sent several reports to London to "inform the BBC's French broadcasts."[30] On the night of April 27, 1942, he flew to England and placed himself in the service of the BCRA. At the time, he suggested entrusting the leadership of underground actions "either to a committee, where several men or several services could pool their intelligence and their points of view, or to a man more freshly arrived from France, one who possessed a great deal of dynamism, authority, and political experience."[31] He was thinking at the time of the Socialist André Philip.

Although Brossolette, a Socialist, and the more conservative Passy came from completely different backgrounds, the two men got along immediately. The head of the Gaullist secret services therefore agreed that his new friend would go back to France, with the assignment to rally prominent personalities to Free France. "They therefore hoped to get the silent majority in occupied France not only to acknowledge the Allies but also to embrace 'Gaullism,'" explains historian Guillaume

Piketty.[32] In fact, Brossolette had no trouble winning over two Socialists who reached London via Lisbon in July 1942. Immediately upon his arrival in London, Louis Vallon, a student from the École Polytechnique who had worked at Radiodiffusion Française, was named head of the newly created political section of the BCRA; Deputy André Philip became minister of the interior.

With the arrival of these two men, the SFIO unofficially rallied behind Free France, though it is true that some Socialists in London disputed Charles de Gaulle's authority. They belonged to the Jean-Jaurès circle dominated by Louis Lévy, a journalist at the Socialist daily *Le Populaire*, and by Georges Gombault, former editor in chief of the leftist weekly *La Lumière*. These Socialists considered de Gaulle a Fascist, since "no French personality possessing a mandate or representing political groups" supported him.[33] Léon Blum did not see things that way and said so loud and clear. In 1942 he wrote to his London friends, exhorting them to support the man of June 18: "The interim government will be able to form only around a single man, a single name, that of General de Gaulle. He was the first to rouse the desire for resistance in France and he continues to personify it. . . . I am not unaware that there are apprehensions about General de Gaulle, even mistrust of him—rumors circulating about his old political connections and about some in his current entourage, an aversion on principle to any power that is personal in appearance and military in aspect. But I do not share that type of concern."[34] In May 1942, Blum dispatched the Socialist deputy Félix Gouin as the SFIO's representative vis-à-vis Free France, completing a move that Pierre Brossolette had gotten under way.

The SFIO's decision to rally behind Free France was no small matter. Under Daniel Mayer's leadership, the party had rebuilt itself and had recovered some of its constituency. In December 1941, a report on thirty-one departments in the southern zone estimated its membership at 11,239, which is to say, 15 percent of its 1938 membership in these same districts.[35] Based on these data and on a secret report internal to the party, it is possible to estimate that, overall, it had about 28,000 members at the time. Compared to its 280,000 members before the war, that is a paltry number; but, when contrasted to the modest battalions that the other underground forces had assembled, it is not insignificant, especially given that the SFIO had been banned. In addition, the SFIO had considerable political capital. Léon Blum's voice had great authority. It could be heard both in the United States and in the United Kingdom, where the Labour Party and the trade unions respected the leader of the FP.

Finally, the prestige of the Socialists was singularly enhanced by the trial of Riom. The Vichy regime had come up with the idea of bringing before a special tribunal those supposedly responsible for the defeat of 1940, in order to embarrass them. The trial opened on February 19, 1942, and brought charges against Édouard Daladier, Léon Blum, and General Maurice Gamelin, as well as smaller fish such as Guy La Chambre, former minister of aviation, and Robert Jacomet, former comptroller general of army administration. Although Gamelin, La Chambre, and Jacomet opted for silence or a timid defense, Blum and Daladier fought every step of the way, embracing without shame the achievements of the FP and pointing out not only the incoherence of the accusations but also Marshal Pétain's implication in the country's lack of military preparedness. That turn of events greatly annoyed Adolf Hitler, who was furious to see the debates center not on the responsibility for the outbreak of war but on the causes of the defeat. The trial, widely covered by the underground press and by the major foreign media, confounded the accusers. On April 14, 1942, Berlin compelled Vichy to end the farce.

The SFIO, its prestige restored, had risen from the ashes. It was therefore a major asset in the Gaullist strategy, especially since Léon Blum was through and through a loyal partner of Free France. In November 1942, he sent a note to London for Franklin Roosevelt and Winston Churchill, calling for de Gaulle to seize the reins of the country upon liberation. "In a France brought to its knees by an incomprehensible disaster, strangled by a dual oppression, he is the one who gradually, day by day, revived national honor, love of freedom, patriotic conscience, and civic-mindedness. It is around his person and his name that groups from every background and of every nature, which now constitute a substantial bloc, have joined together. Without him, nothing would have been possible. He has rekindled and maintained the flame, has breathed life into the spirit. He alone can embody, in its common feelings and its collective will, France delivered; he alone possesses the authority necessary to grapple with the urgent tasks of the first moments." Blum concluded: "You serve the cause of democratic France by helping General de Gaulle to assume the attitude of a leader from this moment forward."[36]

Pierre Brossolette was less successful in bringing right-wing elements over to Free France, even though the future of Colonel de La Rocque's PSF occupied all his attention. Before the war, this group had enjoyed great influence, but it had adopted an ambivalent attitude toward the Vichy regime. Should it therefore be ignored, or should efforts be made "to absorb it into the national movement"?[37] By all appearances, Brossolette leaned toward the second option. He strove to realize it upon his return to France, by maneuvering to get Charles Vallin to rally behind de Gaulle.

Vallin, deputy of the Seine department and a prominent leader in the PSF during the 1930s, fought courageously in the 1940 campaign, then accepted high-level responsibilities within the French State. In particular, he had a seat on the Conseil de Justice Politique (Council of Political Justice), a special tribunal charged with assessing the responsibility of the leaders of the Third Republic. A member of the governing body of the LFC, an organization of veterans of World War I and of the 1940 campaign, he was also named to Vichy's National Council. Most certainly patriotic, he gradually came to understand that Vichy was misguidedly pursuing collaboration and considered breaking away from the regime. He had, however, made many pledges to the French State. That complicated the situation: Should de Gaulle accept the return of lost sheep to the fold? The leader of Free France, in displaying his liberality, would broaden his base of followers, would prove his desire for unity, and would delegitimate Vichy by depriving it of part of its support. But in welcoming compromised men, he offered them the possibility of easily clearing their names, while perhaps too quickly forgetting past compromises.

On the night of September 5, 1942, Pierre Brossolette and Charles Vallin boarded a felucca at Narbonne-Plage, which transferred them to a vessel headed for Gibraltar. An airplane transported them from Gibraltar to Bristol, and from there they reached London. The vice president of the PSF initially received an enthusiastic welcome, especially since, calling on people to "choose between the spirit of Vichy and the spirit of Verdun,"[38] he directly invited them to rally behind Charles de Gaulle, without seeking to exonerate Marshal Pétain. It was not long, however, before that ecumenical atmosphere dissipated. Leftist circles, the Jean-Jaurès group in the lead, denounced the arrival of a Fascist: Vallin reinforced the image they were forming of General de Gaulle.[39] Paradoxically, "the general outcry occasioned by Vallin's arrival owed at least as much to the anti-Gaullism of these men on the left as to their hostility toward Vichy."[40] The uproar was such that de Gaulle promptly dispatched the PSF leader to sub-Saharan Africa for a lecture tour, immediately calming the situation. The operation, built on morally questionable foundations, had thus failed. It brought de Gaulle no real political benefit, particularly since Vallin's defection had sown confusion in Vichy and within PSF circles. For in the meantime, Colonel de La Rocque had informed his members of his "formal and unreserved condemnation" of the operation.[41]

By autumn 1942, therefore, the connections between Free France and captive France had grown closer. In the south, the three principal movements had agreed to coordinate their actions, while placing themselves under de Gaulle's leadership, a process initiated in large part by Moulin. In the north, unification remained in limbo, but the contacts established through Brossolette had begun to rally the SFIO, a process made official by Gouin's mission in May 1942. The internal resistance and the external resistance, which had each pursued its own path until that time, were now converging. Nevertheless, the events of November 1942 weakened that evolution even as they accelerated it, a paradox that requires clarification.

## The Ambiguities of Autumn 1942

On November 8, 1942, an Allied expeditionary corps under the command of General Dwight D. Eisenhower landed in Morocco and Algeria. Although they were hoping to be welcomed as liberators, the U.S. troops were met with gunfire by the Vichy forces and lost 526 men in battle. They quickly managed to secure control of the two territories, however, greatly assisted by a small group of conspirators, who, on the night of November 7, had seized the nerve centers of Algiers. Control of North Africa offered the Allies an ideal base from which to threaten Italy and southern France. Hitler, believing that Vichy would not withstand an Anglo-American offensive on the southern coast of France, invaded the free zone on November 11, 1942, to ward off that peril, shamelessly violating the armistice conventions. Philippe Pétain refused to respond, however. The French fleet, rather than join with the Allies, scuttled its ships on November 27; the land forces stood by, weapons lowered. With one exception: General Jean de Lattre de Tassigny ordered a response. He was arrested, convicted by the national court of Lyon on January 9, 1943, and sentenced to ten years in prison. He refused to escape, proclaiming at the time: "No, no, I will not escape, I trust in the Marshal's justice."[42]

These two events brought dramatic changes, first and foremost by making it necessary to designate the authority that would exercise power in the liberated empire. The Americans played it by ear. Taking advantage of the unexpected presence in Algiers of François Darlan, who had been dismissed from his government post upon Laval's return to power (April 1942) but had subsequently been named commander in chief of Vichy's military forces, they named him high commissioner for France in Africa. Had the admiral sincerely changed sides and agreed to support the Allies, alleging Marshal Pétain's "private assent"? This thesis has been advanced by the defenders of the so-called double game, who—flying in the face of the evidence—claim that Vichy, far from collaborating, secretly supported London and Washington. The claim does not stand up to scrutiny, however. In fact, Darlan had ordered the loyalist troops to respond to the Allied landing; he waited until November 10 to suspend hostilities; and it was only on November 11 that he commanded the Toulon fleet, under Admiral de Laborde, to cast off. Furthermore, he told Laborde to head to French West Africa, which was free of Anglo-American troops, rather than the Maghreb. It should be noted for good measure that the admiral refrained from abrogating the anti-Semitic, anti-Communist, and antifreedom laws of the French State.

Public opinion, both French and foreign, was outraged that such a compromised figure could become proconsul in the empire with the assistance of the United States. The "Darlan deal," as it was called, created a huge backlash, though it made it easier for the empire—French West Africa especially—to rally behind the Allies. A group of young people took on the task of resolving the conundrum. Fernand Bonnier de La Chapelle, a young royalist chosen by lot from among his companions, assassinated the admiral on December 24, 1942. Had he acted under General de Gaulle's orders, given that the small circle of resistance fighters was composed primarily of Gaullists? Was he trying to serve the cause of the comte de Paris, pretender to the throne? Both these hypotheses have circulated, but neither has been confirmed. In any event, Bonnier de La Chapelle was rapidly tried and sentenced to death, taking the secret with him to his grave. General Giraud's time had come.[43]

Henri Giraud, an army general, had been taken prisoner in May 1940 and was then transferred to the Königstein Fortress, near Dresden. On April 17, 1942, he managed to escape on his own, descending by rope the eight hundred feet of the steep cliff on which the former medieval fort turned prison was perched. Once installed in the free zone, Giraud was contacted by U.S. agents, who were seeking a prestigious leader to rally the Army of Africa to its cause. Dispatched to Gibraltar, the general reached Algiers on November 9 and accepted from Darlan the command of the armed forces. After the admiral was assassinated, the members of the Imperial Council chose Giraud as high commissioner. The Americans could only be delighted by that decision: it shut out de Gaulle and offered them a man who would docilely execute their orders. Giraud, in fact, confined himself to asking for the rearmament of the French units and refused to "play politics."

The appointment of Giraud complicated matters, however. Granted, it strengthened national unity and the unification of the resistance by attracting patriots who, while supporting the Marshal's domestic policy, rejected collaboration. By that measure, it increased the number of right-wing adherents to that camp and militarized them, providing them with the reinforcement they were counting on from the Vichy forces. It is true that some in the military now succumbed to the attraction of a general who, proclaiming his apoliticism, sought only to rebuild the French army, and who had "only one aim—victory," to borrow the title of Giraud's memoirs. But the sudden arrival of this hero on the political scene also reshuffled the cards. It threatened to marginalize de Gaulle, especially since the Königstein escapee, backed by the Americans, refused to negotiate with the man of June 18. The prospect of de Gaulle's marginalization was particularly disturbing in that Giraud shared many Pétainist political views. Hence he kept the laws of the French State in place, even introducing harsher provisions in some cases. For example, Jewish soldiers and officers were not allowed to serve in the Army of Africa's combat units. Likewise, political detainees, first and foremost the Communist parliamentarians in the Maison-Carrée prison, were kept locked up. That program could only cause revulsion in a large portion of the internal resistance. It also raised alarms in their ranks. The risk was that Giraud, in situating himself "between Vichyism and Gaullism,"[44] would appeal to a part of French society that found the third way he was opening up attractive. To all appearances, that path threatened democratic and republican values. "To those who had believed they were building, or at least protecting, the Revanche under the aegis of the head of state, [he] offered an alternative solution that entailed neither a breach nor apostasy," as historian Bénédicte Vergez-Chaignon observes.[45] The threat turned out to be serious, to say the least.

## The Military in Confusion

The threat was all the greater in that the invasion of the free zone had on the whole been met with timorous reactions on the part of the army. When the Germans invaded the free zone, the loyalist forces did not mount any resistance. General Revers, whose heart was with the Allies, reports: "We had about fifty thousand to sixty thousand men with very inferior armaments and no tanks—or practically none. We had planned . . . to withdraw, and to fight if need be. But we knew very well that that we could not hold out for long or be effective. In short, we could not prevent the invasion. A resistance of that type against the German onslaught could be envisioned only if we were certain of external support in the short term. But we did not have that certainty."[46] Above all, Philippe Pétain's decisions deprived "his followers of the opportunity that some had so often dreamed of: the possibility of fighting the Germans with the Marshal's full agreement."[47] They caused a severe crisis within the armistice army. Dissolved in short order, it lost "the illusion of rebuilding, with what it believed to be the Marshal's tacit support, an army rendered powerless by the provisions of the armistice." Above all, it lost "all reason for existence."[48]

Some officers, moreover, had built up secret arms depots in the hope that the concealed materiel would be of service during the Revanche. That hope was cruelly dashed: the Vichy government ordered the weapons handed over and, with very rare exceptions, it was obeyed. "At that moment, great fear took hold throughout the southern zone," explains Colonel Mollard, who was head of the CDM at the time. "It was a race to see who could get rid of the weapons and materiel the fastest. . . . Even those who didn't dare declare their depots shouted out in cafés: 'I have a depot, and I will not declare it,' so that their neighbors would spread the word and discharge them of all responsibility."[49] Officers often refused to give arms to the resistance fighters who demanded them and even handed weapons over to the enemy.

Raymond Aubrac, in charge of military affairs for Libération-sud, reported to General Revers as soon as the southern zone was invaded. The general "received [him] in his dressing gown and informed [him] that he [Revers] was obliged to obey Admiral Darlan, being his assistant."[50] Aubrac, in no way discouraged, forced his way in to see a colonel in Grenoble, whose men were loading crates of materiel onto Italian trucks. "He listened to me with surprise, then anger," Aubrac writes. "Invoking the duty to obey received orders, he told me that I could consider myself lucky to be allowed to go free. I took off without further ado, free but unarmed."[51] Colonel Mollard justified that failure in retrospect: "The CDM is reproached for having dumped the arms, for letting themselves be divested of them. But in November and December, what organization could have absorbed all the secret materiel brought to light on November 8 and the following days, in order to equip the groups anticipated by the secret mobilization? Who offered to help us conceal all that materiel again? No one. We were asked for pistols, one or two weapons here or there, but not for all of it, since no organization with troops existed as yet in the southern zone."[52] A few operations succeeded, however. In Toulouse, Colonel Noetinger handed over concealed materiel to Libération; Lieutenant Colonel Delaye, commander of the artillery park in Grenoble, gave a few weapons to Alain Le Ray, the first military leader of the maquis of Vercors.

Sixteen and a half short tons of armaments were also delivered to the maquis of Cantal, and twenty-two and a half tons to those of the Montagne Noire.[53]

In all, the complexity of the situation does not allow for any Manichaean version of the facts. "In the urban area of Lyon, the Armée Secrète (AS) was apparently somewhat negligent, doing a cursory sorting of the arms, leaving the ripped-open crates in place. In Valence and Grenoble, the operation did not take place. There was blame on both sides, since, in the first case, the AS had not budged, and, in the second, the colonel in command of the army depot had not wanted to hand over the caches and had delivered them to the depot occupied by the Italians," writes Johanna Barasz.[54] Paul Paillole, head of counterespionage, estimates that overall, "the Wehrmacht and the Abwehr in the free zone would seize a third of the arms depots. Another third would be destroyed. Another third would be recovered in various ways by the resistance organizations and the Organisation de Résistance de l'Armée (ORA)."[55] In any event, "mistrust and indecision deprived the resistance of armaments. But it was the decisions made by the Vichy government and its determination to apply them that resulted in the delivery to the enemy of the weapons carefully stockpiled for the Revanche, and in their use against the Allies."[56]

That relative failure confirms that the military, even when hostile to the occupier, could not emancipate itself from the model of traditional warfare or break its ties completely with Vichy legality. In its view, weapons were supposed to equip units in uniform duly mobilized by a legitimate power—by preference, Marshal Pétain. In no case were they to be used by groups engaging in sabotage and guerrilla actions. Furthermore, war professionals felt nothing but scorn for supposedly politicized movements composed of amateurs—an aggravating circumstance. They therefore refused to arm them, a fortiori when they suspected them of being motivated by revolutionary sentiments. Finally, the culture of obedience of the French army hardly predisposed it to embrace the cause of dissidence, especially since, in many respects, it shared the reactionary principles of the French State. Cynics will add that the events of November 1942 offered the army a convenient alibi to justify its watch-and-wait attitude. It was certainly easier to claim to be preparing for the Revanche, citing the Marshal's secret wishes, than to go over to the underground struggle, at the risk of destroying one's career. "Officers, worried about their future, clung with fierce intransigence to the oath to the head of state they had taken and to the mystique of discipline. That intransigence, however, attested less to their conviction than to their confusion," writes Vergez-Chaignon.[57]

Some did choose the arduous path of transgression, however. They might have rallied behind de Gaulle by joining the AS, which suffered from a cruel lack of competent military cadres. But few officers took that step. Indeed, the attraction of Gaullism quickly dissipated. "In fact," writes Barasz, "it rested on two essential promises: first, liaisons with London and the Allies; and second, the structure of a preexisting organization, namely, the Armée Secrète. The prospect of liaisons went nowhere, while contact with the AS revealed to the military that the organization was much less advanced than it had imagined."[58] When all was said and done, the resistance movements distrusted the French army. In addition to the fact that the army hardly distinguished itself during the campaign of 1940, it had been little engaged in the struggle before November 1942. It also seemed to harbor a culpable attraction for Marshal Pétain.[59] The leaders of the AS did not necessarily oppose the arrival of a few officers, but these new arrivals would be obliged to accept the conditions of the resistance and to integrate fully into its structures.[60] Soldiers therefore preferred to fight under the colors rather than condescend to join the organizations of Fighting France— the name adopted by Free France on July 14, 1942—or of the internal resistance.

Before leaving for Gibraltar, General Giraud had entrusted the command of the metropolitan forces to General Frère, who had made a name for himself in 1940. On August 2 of that year, he had presided over the permanent military tribunal that had issued a death sentence in absentia to "the general-staff certified infantry colonel in retirement de Gaulle Charles."[61] Frère was put in charge of the Organisation Métropolitaine de l'Armée (OMA; Metropolitan Army Organization), soon renamed the "Organisation de Résistance de l'Armée" (ORA; Army Resistance Organization). The aim of this underground organization was to federate all soldiers who were determined to act. That said, the ORA did not define itself "as the army's resistance but as the army in resistance."[62] Assisted by Colonel Zeller, Lieutenant Colonel

Pfister, and General Verneau, under the nominal command of General Giraud, it declared its apoliticism and opposed "immediate action, while preparing for D-Day."[63] From that standpoint, the events of November 1942 in no way changed the modus operandi that these soldiers proposed to adopt.

Those in charge of the Vichy secret services assessed more quickly the upheaval caused by the latest events. Since 1940, they had actually pursued conflicting policies. On the one hand, they had thwarted German agents and collaborationists and had assisted their British counterparts by transmitting information to them, thus serving the war effort of the United Kingdom. But, on the other, they had brutally hunted down Gaullists and Communists, and had hounded the agents of His Gracious Majesty operating in the metropolis, whose amateurism they condemned.

The scales were not balanced, however. Although no references can be found of "gestures of kindness on the part of the special services toward arrested German agents, by contrast, the Allied or Gaullist agents arrested were fairly often the object of a certain benevolence and sometimes of assistance."[64] Whatever their ideological preferences, the heads of the secret services granted priority to the fight against Germany. They therefore reacted swiftly. Colonel Rivet, head of SR Guerre, and Colonel Ronin, his opposite number at SR Air, after being alerted by their colleagues in the British Intelligence Service of the imminence of the Allied landing, flew off to Algiers on November 5 and 6, respectively. Forgotten by his colleagues, Colonel Paillole, head of counterespionage, crossed the Spanish border on his own the night of November 28, 1942, hidden in a locomotive tender, where a "flask of rum" allowed him to withstand the assault of the cold.[65] He went first to London, where he met with Colonel Passy on December 27, then landed at the Algiers airport on January 2.

On January 30, 1943, thanks to these colonels who had rallied to the cause, General Giraud was able to merge the three SR branches—Air, Land, and Sea—into a Direction des Services Spéciaux (DSS; Directorate of Special Services). He entrusted its keys to Georges Ronin. The heads of the special services were making an unambiguous choice: to fight Germany under the banner of General Giraud. That kept them from rallying behind de Gaulle, for whom, in reality, they felt little sympathy.

As far as the Allied cause was concerned, General Giraud's sudden appearance on the scene had three positive aspects. It helped the Allies rally the empire; it delegitimized the Vichy regime, which was deprived of part of its conservative supporters; and it prompted a portion of the army—troops stationed in Africa, the secret services, the forces remaining in the metropolis—to join the dissidents. The Americans, moreover, could rejoice at having proposed a serious alternative to Fighting France. There was a flip side to the coin, however: the American and British public had trouble understanding the support given to a general who was both dull-witted and reactionary. And the Giraudist authority, instead of unifying the French people, sowed the seeds of division, even within the resistance. Indeed, the underground forces, far from blindly supporting Charles de Gaulle, sometimes adopted a convoluted position, out of ideological conviction combined with strategic concerns.

## The Internal Resistance's Attitude toward Giraudism

Recall that some of the movements, while denouncing collaboration, had not rejected the Vichy regime en bloc and distrusted General de Gaulle. Giraudism allowed them to sever their ties to the French State while maintaining their distance from Fighting France. In January 1943, the DF suggested to de Gaulle that he "rally his troops under the command of his senior."[66] Subsequently, seven movements—including the DF, Franc-Tireur, Libération-sud, and Combat—asked that the two generals unite their efforts "just as the combatants in the interior have united. To de Gaulle, the government he already represents in the eyes of France and abroad—to Giraud, the conduct of military operations."[67] In appearance, this position was reasonable. It belonged to the logic of sacred union and took into account the reality of a power relation that in early 1943 favored the Königstein escapee—vigorously supported by the Anglo-Americans—at the expense of the man of June 18. But two flaws undermined that position: it overlooked the reality of the policy Giraud was conducting in the empire, and it fell far short of an enthusiastic Gaullism. One sign of the distrust the man of June 18 inspired in the PCF: it initially strove to maintain a balance between the two generals.

Although Jean Moulin had met with Communist leaders during his stay in Paris between July 2 and 19, 1942, that connection had not led to any results. Conversely, Colonel Rémy, having returned to Paris, set about reestablishing his ties with Communist representatives. Appointed to assist the FTP in creating their Fana intelligence network, which the Gaullist secret services agreed to support, he began political negotiations, deliberately exceeding the scope of the instructions he had been given. In late November, he met with Fernand Grenier, deputy of Saint-Denis, and, despite Colonel Passy's reiterated opposition, set about to take him back to London, "filled with the certainty that he was performing a historic act."[68] On January 11, 1943, the two men reached England; their arrival would have a profound impact. "In the terrible period of isolation that Fighting France was going through, the trip made by a personality such as Grenier, and the official adherence of the Communist Party, considerably strengthened General de Gaulle's national and international prestige, though it had the disadvantage of increasing the distrust of the English-speaking Allies and the fears harbored in North Africa," writes Daniel Cordier.[69] De Gaulle, moreover, was fully cognizant of the importance of the event. In a letter to the central committee of the PCF, sent on February 10, 1943, he hailed "the Communist Party's adherence to the Comité National, which [Grenier] brought to me in your name, and the delivery to me, as commander in chief of the Fighting French Forces, of the valiant groups of Francs-Tireurs that you have constituted and led."[70] At a time when Giraud seemed to be prevailing, the PCF's decision to rally behind de Gaulle gave him a trump card. At the same time, however, it erected new obstacles.

In the first place, the sincerity of the PCF's adherence to Fighting France remained enigmatic. A few days after the interview between Grenier and Rémy, Georges Beaufils, a senior official in the FTP, submitted minutes to the head of the CND. In a disturbing tone, they reported "an interview that took place between a representative of the Fighting French Forces and a delegate of the central committee of the Parti Communiste Français." While manifesting his agreement

on principle regarding national liberation and the fight against the occupier and Vichy, Beaufils placed the PCF and the Forces Françaises
Combattantes (FFC; Fighting French Forces) on the same level: "National insurrection will be planned in close collaboration between the
PCF and the FFC, in keeping with the agreement that it will be up to
General de Gaulle and the PCF to reach, as soon as circumstances allow
them to meet."[71] The party, in other words, presented itself as the equal
of Fighting France. By all appearances, it intended to "produce a bipo-
larization of the Resistance, with the Communists controlling the internal Resistance, leaving leadership of the external Resistance to de
Gaulle."[72] In portraying itself as the only real partner of Free France,
the PCF was trying to become the exclusive representative of the
metropolitan resistance. The text made no allusion to the other underground groups, not even to the forces more or less controlled by de
Gaulle and his delegate, Jean Moulin.[73] That ambition led the party to
give equal weight to de Gaulle and Giraud, since the division between
the two generals had the secondary effect of increasing its own influence. Without breaking ranks with the man of June 18, who was hailed
in *L'Humanité* on January 21, 1943, the party thus maintained its
connections to the Königstein escapee, especially after February 5,
1943, when he released the twenty-seven Communist parliamentarians rotting in the Maison-Carrée. And to better demonstrate its neutrality in the quarrel between the two rivals, the PCF sent Deputy
Henri Pourtalet to Giraud as its delegate. "Since two generals wanted
to work for the liberation of France, it was natural that our Party,
which had already sent a delegate to the general in London, should
send another to the general in Algiers," Jacques Duclos explains.[74] The
PCF was still faced with a harrowing dilemma: Should it support de
Gaulle, at the risk of being swallowed up by a national coalition, or scale
back its ambitions to assure itself a better position?[75] In winter 1943,
that alternative was far from clear-cut.

The adherence ex officio of the PCF consolidated the reintroduction
of the political parties into the game, a trend that had begun with the
SFIO. These parties, it should be said, had bad press both in the French
metropolis and in London. In a forceful article published in the Gaullist newspaper *La Marseillaise* on September 27, 1942, Pierre Brossolette had sounded their death knell: "In the past, the French assembled

in political parties based on their affinities, and opposed one another in different parties on the basis of their aversions. At present, sympathies and antipathies, friendships and scorn, play out on a different register."[76] But once the SFIO and the PCF, as such, declared their presence alongside General de Gaulle, it became difficult, not to say impossible, to deny that privilege to other groups, radical or conservative. "Whether desired or not, a dialectic of democratic legitimacy was under way,"[77] notes Cordier. De Gaulle would therefore have to respond without delay to the questions raised by the adherence of those enemy brothers, the Socialists and the Communists.

In early 1943, therefore, Fighting France was in a paradoxical situation. It had succeeded, primarily thanks to Jean Moulin and Pierre Brossolette, in establishing contact with some of the movements and political parties of captive France and had obtained, if not their submission, then at least their adherence. The Allies' game, however, gravely threatened Fighting France's position, by supporting General Giraud in defiance of democratic values. By all appearances, the deciding match would be played in the international arena. But the growing influence of the metropolitan resistance conferred an essential role on the movements and on the parties—assuming that the same battle was being waged on both sides of the Channel.

## Chapter 7

# Fighting the Same Battle?

WERE THE INTERNAL RESISTANCE and the external resistance fighting in unison? Their rapprochement, which began to take shape in 1942, suggests so; but the conflicts between the two spheres belie it. Free France was preoccupied above all else with keeping France in the war and winning the battle of legitimacy—based on the sacrifices made on the field of honor—in order to win recognition from London, Moscow, and Washington. The movements, while dreaming of ousting the occupier from France, were also or especially concerned with influencing the populace, protecting them from the rigors of occupation, and immunizing them against the ideological project of the French State and the Third Reich. Beyond their differences, these objectives created zones of convergence: to begin with, the desire to convert the French people to the virtues of anti-Nazism and anti-Pétainism, as a prelude to their mobilization in the army of shadows.

## Convince and Mobilize

Both Free France and the movements sought to influence public opinion. They hoped thereby to point up the unpopularity of the German occupier and to delegitimize the Vichy regime and Pétain, who was still popular in 1942. Whereas the resistance fighters of the interior wished by that means to break through the isolation they were suffering, de Gaulle wanted to assess the influence of the BBC and its capacity to impose orders on civilians. The battle, far from being reduced to ideological issues, thus took on concrete aspects. By underscoring the misdeeds of collaboration, the resistance reminded people of the French State's responsibilities. It thereby gained the cooperation of patriotic civil servants within the administration who were disgusted by the policy announced at Montoire. The French people, in responding to the appeals launched from London by taking to the streets, proved to Roosevelt that de Gaulle, who was being portrayed as a dictator in training, had the trust of the masses. Unlike espionage or sabotage, moreover, the expression of disapproval required no specific skills, and the risks incurred, though not nonexistent, were limited.

The movements thus focused on their underground newspapers, while Free France multiplied radio broadcasts to captive France. Above all, the two forces fought hard to get the French out into the streets. Until 1942, demonstrations came either in response to spontaneous initiatives or to orders launched from London. But the processions on May Day and Bastille Day in 1942 resulted from instructions issued by the movements, amplified by the propaganda services of Free France. It was the Mouvement Ouvrier Français (MOF; French Workers' Movement)—an organization of trade unionists from the CGT and the CFTC who opposed the Vichy regime—that proposed the commemoration of Workers' Day, a suggestion taken up in London by the CNF. The appeal, diffused through the major organs of the underground press in the southern zone (*Libération, Franc-Tireur, Combat, L'Humanité*), was relayed by the BBC beginning on April 25, 1942. "French people, on May 1, 1942, as you did on May 1, 1941, you will look one another straight in the eyes, on the public squares of our cities and towns. And that look will suffice—under the sign of Labor as under the sign of Joan of Arc—to express our common will and our fraternal hopes," Maurice Schumann, the spokesman for Free France, announced on April 28, 1942.[1] And de Gaulle personally spoke out, asking that all French people walk "silently and individually in front of the statues of the Republic and in front of our city halls and town halls. All will be united in the will to ensure that the nation's liberation, greatness, and security emerge from this war, along with the conditions for a free, dignified, and secure life for every French worker, to which he has the right as a man, and which he has so nobly merited as a Frenchman."[2]

The French rose to the challenge, despite the fears of some leaders. "If we failed, that failure would be keenly felt by our militants and trumpeted as a victory by Vichy," Henri Frenay recalls.[3] "If it was a fiasco," adds Yvon Morandat, "we were going to prove in the eyes of the whole world that the French people were not following de Gaulle and the Resistance."[4] These worries proved to be unfounded. In the capital of the Gauls, "by six twenty P.M., Place Carnot is swarming with people around the statue of the Republic. And the crowd is arriving from every direction. At first, it's a dense and silent throng, which slowly gathers, 'meets up.' . . . Young men climb onto the rim of the large basin surrounding the statue. Suddenly, there is a smattering of 'bravos': an old laborer in overalls places the first bouquet at the feet of the statue, and bunches of lily-of-the valley rain down. And all at once, a powerful, tremendous 'Marseillaise' bursts forth, stunning the officers—in fact good-humored—who are overrun by the crowd. Oh, how the 'Marseillaise' of freedom is sung, with what joy those shouts ring out, unheard for two years!"[5] Free France agents estimated that fifty thousand people demonstrated in Lyon, thirty thousand in Marseilles, ten thousand in Montpellier, twenty thousand in Paris, and three thousand in Bordeaux[6]—even though, to limit the risks of German repression, the appeal had explicitly targeted only the southern zone. The case should not be overstated, however: although twenty-three demonstrations took place in eighteen French departments,[7] several other departments, such as Isère, remained totally calm.

That success prompted a recurrence on July 14, 1942. The movements once again coordinated their actions with the Gaullist services to celebrate triumphantly the national holiday. Appeals launched in tracts or in the underground press were complemented by orders broadcast over the airwaves of the BBC, between four and eight times a day until the crucial date. Maurice Schumann exclaimed: "French people of the unoccupied zone, fly the flag on July 14; who would dare reproach you on the national holiday? French people of the unoccupied zone, walk along the major arteries of your cities in the afternoon, displaying the tricolor. French people of the unoccupied zone, at six thirty in the evening on July 14, assemble in great numbers and sing 'La Marseillaise.' It is a national duty to demonstrate on July 14. May the French people rise to their full height on that anniversary of their first victory."[8] For eleven major cities, Schumann also named the places where the gatherings were to occur. German or Vichy authorities attempted, through an impressive deployment of officers, to prevent them, but in vain. Tens of thousands of people assembled in sixty-six processions (forty-four in the southern zone), making for a truly remarkable day.

Free France and the movements had thus managed to work together to invite the French people to put their patriotic feelings on display.

That mobilization found rich soil in which to take root. The vast majority of the population rejected collaboration and were viscerally opposed to Germany. By 1941, "it was obviously against the occupier, and the negative representations he crystallized, that national sentiment was reconstituting itself,"[9] as historian Pierre Laborie points out. As of 1942, "detachment and the opposition to Vichy's policies, the rejection of collaboration, the visceral hostility toward the Germans" were the driving forces of public opinion.[10] These feelings created a propitious context for demonstrating one's hatred of the occupier and of the occupation, though the scope of that phenomenon must not be overestimated. The veneration that Marshal Pétain still enjoyed could lead to abstention, especially since demonstrating entailed real risks in the free zone and even greater ones in the occupied zone. The risks were considerable in Haut-Rhin and Bas-Rhin and in Moselle, three departments the Reich had annexed. The demonstration in Lyon on March 18, 1942, held to protest the concert given by the Berlin Philharmonic, resulted in between fifty and sixty arrests.[11] In Marseilles, collaborationists from the Parti Populaire Français (French Popular Party) opened fire on the procession passing along rue Pavillon on July 14, killing two women.[12] On the same day in Hochfelden, in Bas-Rhin, the crowd laid down flowers in front of the monument to the dead; the Germans responded by establishing martial law and deporting 160 young people.

Nevertheless, patriotism cemented a consensus that united all opponents, Communists included, though for a time the PCF had been tempted to go it alone. The demonstrations took place in a syncretic republican time, combining the memory of the French Revolution and the republic—as July 14 required—with the social hopes of May Day, not yet a public holiday. Beyond the ecumenism to which it attested, the plan of action was ultimately in de Gaulle's hands. The BBC gave him a powerful instrument for mobilization, and the underground press could not compete. Above all, the man of June 18 addressed "every French person, using the conventions that govern the relationship between a head of state and the citizens," issuing invitations for "demonstrations that aspired to be a form of restoration of the legitimate state."[13]

Did these displays have any effectiveness? The measures taken by the Germans and by the Vichy police would lead one to think so, though it is not possible to gauge. But declaring one's opposition to Germany or to the French State did not necessarily mean one was ready to join the resistance. In other words, there was a gap between opinion and action. The establishment of the STO narrowed that gap.

## The Issues Raised by the STO

In 1941, Nazi Germany faced a labor shortage resulting from the large number of contingents mobilized in its armed forces. In all, 18.2 million Germans served in the military,[14] both to ensure control of the increasingly vast territories Nazi Germany occupied in Europe and to decide the outcome of the war against the Soviet Union. The growing demands of the Wehrmacht incited Berlin to use all means at its disposal. To replace the men sent to the front, the Nazi regime used as slaves concentration camp inmates and prisoners of war interned in the stalags. It also strove to tap the civilian labor force in the occupied countries.

In France, the German authorities proceeded with caution, initially relying on volunteers. In July 1942, more than seventy-six thousand French people were working across the Rhine. That is not a negligible figure, but it fell short of German and Vichy expectations.[15] In a speech on June 22, 1942, Pierre Laval therefore recommended the establishment of the Relève (replacement system): in exchange for three qualified workers sent to Germany, one prisoner of war would return home on furlough. But the response disappointed the hopes of Berlin and Vichy: only forty thousand workers (thirteen thousand of them specialists) chose to participate in the swap.[16] The Vichy regime, under German pressure, was therefore obliged to use strong-arm tactics. On September 4, 1942, it promulgated a law "on the utilization and deployment of labor," which obliged all young men between twenty-one and thirty-five to perform work the government would judge necessary, "in the higher interest of the nation." Although the law did not explicitly require that they go to Germany, it also did not rule out the possibility. Some three hundred thousand people—that is, nearly half of those conscripted within the framework of the STO—crossed the Rhine to fulfill that obligation.[17]

As of September 1942, therefore, a grave threat loomed over the lifeblood of the country. Its first target was the working class, whose contribution to the Reich's factories was crucial. But politics as well as economics were at stake. The growth of the PCF and the spontaneous outbreak of strikes at the start of the FP government had conferred on the proletariat a central place in French society. The revolutionary spark might rise up from the toiling classes, which made them an object of vigilant interest, whether or not the prospect of a new October Revolution inspired fear. Since the industrial revolution, the fate of the workers had been a focus of attention, giving rise to proworker sentiments in leftist organizations and among some elites in management, the clergy, and the intelligentsia. Each group in its own way was anxious to improve the lot of the very poor. But fears also focused on young people, who had achieved a certain autonomy before the war. The rise of movements both secular (the nondenominational scouts) and Catholic (the various youth groups: JC, JEC, Jeunesse Agricole Catholique [Young Catholic Farmers], and Jeunesse Ouvrière Chrétienne [Young Christian Workers]) channeled that independence.[18] In targeting two particularly vulnerable categories—the young and workers—comprising millions of individuals, the STO immediately became a burning issue.

It was so in the first place for the workers themselves, whose conditions deteriorated continually over the dark years.[19] Factory workers had been suffering from a high unemployment rate, though it fell quickly in the second half of 1940. Above all, they faced severe material hardship. Victims of scarcity, especially in the urban areas, and of an inflation rate that outstripped wages, they struggled to sustain themselves. In Isère, 75 percent of a typical household budget went for food.[20] By 1942, the wages of Gard miners had lost a third of their purchasing power.[21] In the region of Montbéliard, employees of the Peugeot factories, tormented by hunger, went so far as to threaten farmers when they did not get what they asked for.[22] Working conditions also deteriorated, primarily because of the pressure exerted by the occupier's greed. At Peugeot, the work week was 28.5 hours in September 1940; in December 1942, it surpassed 52 hours.[23] The three thousand workers in the SNCF shops in Oullins, in the Rhône department, were working 60 hours a week in April 1943.[24] At the same time, safety conditions worsened. In Nord-Pas-de-Calais, mortality rates in the coal mines increased by 60 percent over the course of the war. The mining companies listed 161 deaths for the period between 1935 and 1938, but counted 266 for the years 1941–1944.[25] These drastic living conditions gave rise to a muffled discontent, which was amplified by the STO. Almost all workers rejected the prospect of forced labor, which does not mean that, in doing so, they opted for the underground.

The French have invented a romantic image of the working class during World War II. That image was nurtured by the PCF, which endlessly repeated the famous line François Mauriac wrote during his time in the underground: "Only the working class *as a bloc* has remained faithful to the desecrated homeland."[26] The facts, however, partly belie that optimistic claim. In actuality, the law "on the requisition and deployment of the labor force"—soon followed on February 16, 1943, by summonses to report to the STO, sent out to young men born between 1920 and 1922 (three age cohorts)—did not instantly cause a revolt: 450,000 Frenchmen set off for the Reich between October 1942 and March 1943.[27] Fritz Sauckel, general plenipotentiary for labor deployment—nicknamed "the slave driver of Europe"—had every reason to be satisfied. The first action he spearheaded (June 1–December 31, 1941) fulfilled 95.9 percent of its objectives; the second (January 1–March 1, 1943), 100.1 percent; the third (April 1–December 31, 1943), 76.98 percent. In all, the first three actions had a compliance rate above 91.58 percent.[28] It was only in summer 1943 that a "real collapse in the number of departures" began to occur, "despite all the means implemented by the Germans and the Vichy regime."[29] The last action (January 1–June 23, 1944) recorded a 95.05 percent noncompliance rate. But that does not mean that all the STO evaders went over to the resistance.

True, the idea of going to Germany was so unpopular that acts of opposition, largely spontaneous, impeded the process as early as autumn 1942. Three modes of action were enlisted at the time. First, there were strikes. On October 15, 1942, the Maréchal de Saint-Priest factories staged a work stoppage to oppose the departure of some four hundred wage workers.[30] In addition, at least sixteen anti-Relève strikes broke out in the southern zone—in Limoges, Tulle, Tarbes, and Béziers, among other cities—between October 21 and November 5 of the same year.[31] In the SNCF depots of Oullins, a flare-up occurred when a call-up list with thirty-seven names was posted on October 12, 1942. Almost all the workers walked out, and the movement spread throughout the region, mobilizing twelve thousand strikers. On October 21, the list and others were removed, and most of the 343 people who had been arrested were released.[32] Furthermore, when the Franco-German commission appeared at the Peugeot factories to enlist 1,590 workers, 4,690 employees scattered and a strike broke out, obliging the Germans and factory management to announce the "temporary suspension" of the impressment.[33]

Second, there were demonstrations. In the coal fields of Gard, these multiplied on November 24 and 25, 1942, to express opposition to the departures.[34] A convoy was supposed to leave Montluçon, a small city in the Allier department, on January 6, 1943. The resistance was alerted and, Communists in the lead, it called for a protest. At about 12:30 P.M., as the train was entering the station, a crowd—probably two thousand people—massed outside, then invaded the rail yard, the ticket office, and the platforms. The police and the gendarmerie did not budge. The locomotive stalled, and most of the conscripts got out of the cars, as the mobile reserve groups and the German forces moved in. The train ultimately departed at 2:45 P.M., taking with it thirty-seven men who had not escaped. During the night, many evaders were apprehended, and on January 8 about a hundred men left in a new convoy, while twenty-six rebels were interned in the camp at Saint-Paul-d'Eyjaux.[35] Finally, on March 9, 1943, Jean Chapus, the stationmaster in Romans, in the Drôme department, warned Captain Vincent-Beaume, the local head of the MUR, that a train would carry off three hundred conscripts the next day. The same evening, the workers assembled around the factory exit. Then the demonstration moved to Place d'Armes, arriving at 6:30 P.M. Between six and seven hundred demonstrators sang "La Marseillaise," then "L'Internationale." The next day, Romans was plunged into a general strike. At noon, two to three thousand people invaded the rail yard, and women lay down on the tracks. Once again, the mobile reserve groups brutally imposed order, and the convoy took off after a five-hour delay. In what was a relatively rare phenomenon, local society had not confined itself to protesting but had taken action, urged on by the resistance.[36]

Third, some civil servants endeavored to undermine the STO, legally or illegally. In September 1942, Jean Isméolari, chief inspector at Labor, set up at his own initiative four appeal commissions, which

reached full capacity in March 1943. Focusing on medical, social, economic, and special cases, they legally exempted some thirty thousand
called-up workers. Isméolari's methods were original, since he never
sought to increase the number of STO evaders. His actions spared them
the torment of going underground for an indefinite period of time; and
it spared the resistance the heavy burden of men in need of provisions
and arms.[37]

Such shows of opposition, however, must not be granted excessive
importance. On the whole, the working class displayed a limited fighting
spirit. In Isère, "apart from hunger, nothing seems able to shake off
what we would be tempted to call worker apathy."[38] The exigencies of
survival, as well as the refusal to sacrifice oneself in vain, no doubt explain that languor. In the factories under high surveillance, wage laborers faced great risks. For example, the German authorities, noting
that the productivity rate in Alsace was lower than that in the rest of the
Reich, promulgated an order on June 12, 1942, which increased control
over workplaces. A wage laborer could not turn down a task requested
by his employer; absence without a valid excuse now constituted a
crime; and no labor contract could be broken without the authorization of the Labor Office.[39] The Reich did not hesitate to use strong-
arm tactics to impose its will. The poor reputation of the Bisheim
railroad repair shops, for example, led the Gestapo to arrest 190 Communists or alleged Communists in May 1942, which instantly reduced
the number of incidents.[40] Granted, conditions were particularly tough
in Alsace and Moselle, territories that had been annexed by the Reich.
But discipline in the factories overall was no joking matter for the
Germans. Given these conditions, it is understandable why strikes
were rare and brief, "long enough to be visible, short enough to avoid
reprisals, too limited to make the recruiters back down."[41]

The workers, while refusing to go to Germany, did not balk at
working for the Reich. As historian Jean-Marie Guillon notes, performing labor for the occupier, "even as directly as within the framework of the Todt Organization, was accepted inasmuch as [it] quickly
appeared unavoidable as a means to escape what was long considered
deportation."[42] Although prepared to some extent to mobilize in order
to avoid exile, workers were not resolved to join the ranks of the resistance or even to sabotage production surreptitiously. On June 30, 1944,

the total value of orders placed in France rose to about 10 billion Reichs-
marks, and deliveries reached 6.2 billion. That production rate illustrates
that "not only did French industry work to a large degree on behalf of
the Germans but also that the majority of German orders placed, not-
withstanding the many obstacles, were in fact filled and delivered before
the end of the Occupation—which leaves the historian to wonder about
the countless accounts of indirect sabotage by means of deliberate slow-
downs, dished up after the fact by the businesses concerned."[43]

Thus, French nationals subject to the STO took paths other than
resistance in their efforts to escape exile. Many made arrangements for
legal exemptions. They enrolled in college or chose protected
occupations—mining, the police force, the army. In all, 418,000 people
were exempted, more than half of those eligible.[44] Others agreed to
work for the Reich, but in France, a solution ratified by the accords concluded in September 1943 between Albert Speer, German minister of
armaments, and Jean Bichelonne, French minister of industrial production. On the eve of the Allied landing, more than fourteen thousand
protected businesses (Sperr-Betrieben) employed nearly a million wage
workers.[45] These refusants, to borrow the term invented by Raphaël
Spina, remained on French soil without suffering the torments of being
outside the law. Only a minority of those eligible evaded the STO in
the strict sense of the term—probably between 200,000 and 350,000
people.[46] Of that minority, perhaps a quarter joined the resistance, the
other three-quarters preferring to take refuge on farms or to hide out
at home or among loved ones.[47]

## Responses of the Internal Resistance

Impressment represented a boon to the resistance. First, it offered the
possibility of issuing a challenge to the Vichy regime on patriotic
grounds, by pointing out the misdeeds of collaboration, which had led
the authorities to hand over its own nationals to the Nazi Moloch, a
unique case in occupied Europe. Second, it resolved the nagging question of manpower by producing a flood of evaders anxious to escape
forced labor. Finally, it allowed thousands of ordinary men and women
to become involved in the struggle as patriots, by putting to use basic
skills: a town clerk could fabricate false identity papers without great

difficulty; a farmer could take in a proscribed person; a doctor could fudge on certificates. The French State recognized the scope of these perils. "STO was never embraced by Vichy personnel with the illusory expectations which had marked the *Relève:* it was quickly seen for what it was, an obligation forced on the vanquished by the victors, and in that light *défaillance* [noncompliance] could be interpreted in the town halls and prefectures and among the gendarmes as a patriotic act," notes H. R. Kedward.[48] The army of shadows, a small minority until late 1942, therefore had hopes of becoming a mass phenomenon.

At the same time, the conversion of STO evaders into resistance fighters was not a matter of course. The army of shadows would have to find a way to manage that sudden influx. How to feed, clothe, and house, not to mention arm, thousands of volunteers? And the movements risked discrediting themselves if they did not successfully cope with the situation. They also had to come up with a doctrine of action. Would they merely hide the evaders, or would they opt for a more radical choice, arming them and turning them into combatants? In all, the STO offered an unhoped-for opportunity to the resistance, which was struggling to recruit and to invent modes of action apart from mere civic exhortation. As a result, "in the southern zone, the passions of the Resistance leaders were roused by that movement of civil disobedience, an uncommon phenomenon in France, which, it was hoped, would modify the human and military potential of the Resistance if, in welcoming these evaders, it integrated them into the combat units."[49]

The movements thus rushed into the breach. Very quickly, they made appeals in their newspapers and tracts for workers to reject the slavery that the masters of the Reich held in store for them. On October 16, 1942, a tract distributed in the factories of the Lyon region prescribed:

> Not one man in Germany! . . .
> You shall not go!
> You shall not work for the enemy. You shall not abandon
> your children, your trade, your house, your country. You
> shall not accept the wretched fate that the accomplices of
> the Boches are preparing for you.[50]

Similarly, *Franc-Tireur* asked "all the people of France to be accomplices in the struggle against deportation."[51] "By every means possible, obstruct the Relève, which is becoming a mass deportation and threatens the country's very existence," ordered *Défense de la France* in February 1943.[52] In addition, a "joint declaration of the French resistance groups" promised:

1. To support the workers in their current actions of resistance in whatever form they take (strikes, demonstrations, etc.) . . . ;
2. To call on civil servants and employers to assist the workers in their resistance to the deportation by sabotaging administrative measures, by procuring food vouchers for the workers who refuse to go, and by helping them by every means in your power;
3. To ask farmers to welcome into their homes workers who do not want to go to Germany, to provide them with shelter, give them work, and allow them to secure their livelihood;
4. To urge the workers able to escape the Relève to join the ranks of the patriotic combat groups, in order to fight the invader and to prepare themselves to support, in the near future, the actions of the troops who will be landing here and will constitute the second European front;
5. To urge the workers already dragged away, or about to be so, to consider themselves a fifth column introduced into the German fortress, and to fight in the factories by sabotage and propaganda, while waiting to revolt when the order is given.[53]

These appeals were heeded in part. The resistance mobilized in support of the evaders, providing them with false papers, for example. At times, it engaged in more spectacular actions. On the night of March 12, 1943, Georges Guingouin's men blew up the railroad viaduct near Bussy-Varache, in the Limousin region, to prevent a trainload of conscripts from leaving.[54] Most important, in late December 1942, a few men "went over to the maquis" (*prirent le maquis*) to escape the STO—a turn of phrase introduced by Michel Brault, a Combat leader. Often taking refuge in Haute-Savoie, in the Alps, these men concealed themselves in mountainous regions and, for lack of being able to fight, struggled to survive. It did not take long for the trickle of maquisards to become a rushing stream. By January 1943, the internal resistance was faced with heavy responsibilities, since these spontaneously created maquis often placed themselves under the orders of the regional leaders of the army of shadows, from whom they expected weapons, provisions, and munitions—all resources in short supply.

Despite their lack of means, the leaders of the southern resistance instantly understood the new and unprecedented prospects opening up to them. Unable to respond to the evaders' expectations at the material level, they set about defining a doctrine of action. In January 1943, Henri Frenay developed a plan that stipulated "the creation of a certain number of redoubts in the Alps, the Jura, the Massif Central, and the Pyrenees, which would be supplied with weapons, equipment, and food via parachute drops. These bases in turn would resupply, within a circumscribed zone, small maquis (a maximum of about thirty men), which would constitute a particularly mobile combat unit. Before the Allied landing, they would limit themselves to sudden and rapid strike operations, rejecting on principle pitched battle." The head of Combat concluded: "The condition for creating these redoubts, of course, was that we receive formal assurances that they would be regularly resupplied."[55]

In April 1943, Frenay considered the matter more thoroughly and composed the directives of the Comité Directeur des Mouvements Unis de Résistance (Steering Committee of the United Resistance Movements). These instructions now distinguished between "two categories of evaders, those who want to hide, who will be assisted, and those who want to fight, who will be integrated into small mobile groups receiving assistance from the population."[56] Immediately thereafter, Frenay created the Service National Maquis (SNM), entrusted to Michel Brault with assistance from Georges Rebattet (Cheval). He also founded a school for cadres, run by Robert Soulage (Sarrazac); in operation by that summer, it trained several hundred students.

Henri Frenay assigned a dual mission to the maquis. They were supposed to provide a hiding place for the bulk of evaders and also to select an elite ready to engage in guerrilla warfare. In Frenay's mind, the maquis served both as places of refuge and as bases of action. They would harass the enemy before the landing took place. His plan therefore combined a civilian and a military dimension. Conversely, it ruled out the possibility of creating immediately mobilizable maquis of thousands of men, assembled in a vigorously defended bastion, to conduct attacks, before launching the final offensive against the enemy forces once the Allied troops had landed. "In my view, flexibility, speed, and mobility were the three basic principles to be observed."[57] That plan stipulated one condition: London would support the rebels by taking care of the necessary logistics. Neither the Gaullists nor the British were prepared to satisfy that requirement—even supposing they had the means.

Jean Moulin pursued a different line of reasoning. After the incidents at Oullins, he proposed a unified struggle against the STO, which would be entrusted to the MOF, created by the trade unions in spring 1942. The resistance movements had protested, fearing they would be excluded from that strategic battle. General de Gaulle's delegate had therefore founded a Comité de Résistance Ouvrière (Workers' Resistance Committee), run by Yves Farge. In the various regions, he implanted Bureaux de Résistance Ouvrière (Workers' Resistance Bureaus), which were supposed to sabotage the "deportation" of workers, to borrow the term used at the time. Representatives of the MOF, of the PCF, and of the three movements in the free zone were supposed to be in charge. That effort was short-lived, however. In reality, the MOF was only an empty shell and did not have the means to take on the struggle against the STO. Combat, then Libération-sud, therefore tackled the question by creating an Action Ouvrière (AO; Workers' Action), charged with, among other things, sabotaging the impressment of French labor.[58]

In any event, the influx of rebels to the Alps radically altered the rules of the game and required that more substantial solutions be proposed. Beginning in early March 1943, the leaders of the internal resistance sent telegram after telegram to alert Fighting France of the gravity of the situation. The steering committee of the MUR cabled General de Gaulle on March 3: "Deported French believe abandoned by Allies . . . Payments foreseen financial resources absurd . . . Without means action resistance deportation organization will pass Communist hands your authority French opinion as whole will be quickly undermined if you do not demonstrate through us in struggle liberation begun we ask English government to understand. . . . If our appeals in vain will order desperate extreme action."[59]

These appeals, however, went unanswered. The Gaullist services played for time, lacking any concrete support from the British, who in fact had been burned by bad experiences. A first attempt at a parachute drop had failed when the liaison agent possessing the coordinates of the field where the containers were supposed to be received was arrested. And a parachute drop carried out by Halifaxes near Annemasse ended in disaster: three aircraft out of six went down, at a time when the RAF had only about fifteen planes to carry out such missions.[60] These failures could only "reinforce the Allied staff's distrust of the improvisation and disorder in the Resistance."[61]

The British authorities would undoubtedly have supported the maquis had they been integrated into the major offensive being planned to destroy Nazi Germany. But strategists were not considering a French landing for 1943 and therefore rejected the assistance of the maquis: "The British government's considered opinion is that the maintenance of an army of forty thousand to fifty thousand men for an undeterminable period of time is impossible, since that permanent support would remove a very large number of [airplanes] from operations."[62] In addition, the rise of the maquis complicated the task of the Anglo-Americans. Generalized insecurity could lead the Germans to increase the number of their divisions to the west, reducing proportionately the chances for a landing in France.[63] Colonel Passy concluded: "The calls for open revolt, for the formation of 'armed bastions,' could therefore be interpreted by our Allies only as an inconceivably frivolous folly or as unbearable pressure to force them to carry out operations without concern for the plans of their military staff."[64]

The British, conducting the war on a European scale, did not plan to launch the assault on French beaches before 1944. They opposed the prospect of a guerrilla war undertaken by the internal resistance, judging it premature. Logically, they therefore refused to provide military support for the maquis, which had to count solely on Fighting France.

## Responses of Fighting France

Yet Jean Moulin, having returned to France, could not offer the movement the hoped-for financial assistance. In March, he carried over the same budget allotted in January and February, without taking into account the new situation created by the STO. The open conflict between de Gaulle and Giraud had increased tensions between Fighting France and the British government, which led Moulin to be cautious. Fearing that London would cut off provisions for the CNF, he chose to manage his reserves carefully. But, once informed of the situation, he changed his mind on March 11, instructing his secretary, Daniel Cordier, to "supply all funds" for the fight against forced labor by drawing on reserves. Part of the funds, however, were handed over to trade union organizations, which were fighting to keep called-up workers from being sent to Germany but did not seek to turn them into resistance fighters.[65]

Even so, the technical obstacles and the desire to hold onto Fighting France's war chest are not enough to explain the position of Jean Moulin, who, at least at first, proved very reserved toward the maquis. He undoubtedly believed that, for lack of British support, the venture was doomed to fail. Perhaps he also feared that Frenay, with the help of that influx of evaders, would form a parallel secret army and would run it via the SNM, which did not answer to the AS. As he noted in a report sent to his minister, André Philip, on June 4, 1943:

> I believe I ought to call your attention to the fact that the leaders of the movements, seeing that the AS is escaping their control to a certain extent, are trying to piece together a different AS with the maquis. In my opinion, there is no contraindication to that, provided that:
>
> 1. certain maquis, which are of geographical or strategic interest for the D-Day action, be under the control of the AS;
> 2. the receipt and distribution of weapons continue to be compulsorily and fully carried out by the AS. It is important, in fact, to avoid the recurrence of certain very regrettable incidents, attributable to the fact that some maquis, having appropriated weapons unbeknownst to the AS, made use of them in a reckless manner, causing very grave reprisals and prematurely exposing the organization.[66]

Frenay, therefore, was not blinded by rampant paranoia when he judged that the delegate of Fighting France suspected him of piecing together, in a roundabout way, a rival AS. The head of Combat also believed that London, by slashing its funding, sought, as he said, to "weaken our movement."[67] The argument may be overstated, given the monies released by Cordier as of March 11, 1943, but it is not without foundation. From January to May 1943, Moulin delivered only 7 million francs to the AS, in contrast to the 4 million francs that the SOAM, a strictly technical service, collected or the "tidy sums" received by the networks.[68]

In any event, neither Moulin nor Fighting France demonstrated an unbridled enthusiasm for the maquis. "If there is one area in which the incomprehension of General de Gaulle's services, both in London and in France, was characteristic, it is in that of the maquis," confirms Claude Bourdet.[69]

That cautiousness only exacerbated the tensions between the internal and the external resistance. Jean-Pierre Azéma, Jean Moulin's biographer, concludes: "The fact that London had proved incapable of facing a situation judged exemplary was therefore blamed on Free France—by the Resistance Movements, of course—and, as a result, on Moulin. What was the use of hanging on to that delegate, who was, moreover, a scold, if he was no longer performing the functions for which he had been taken on, namely, to provide resources?"[70] The resistance therefore came up with its own response, without initially benefiting from the support of the Gaullist services.

## The Growth of the Maquis

The first maquis were formed in late 1942. On December 18, Simon Samuel, a French-Romanian physician, and Louis Brun, a woodturner, both associated with the SFIO and members of Franc-Tireur, reconnoitered the Ambel farm in the Vercors. On January 6, 1943, a first contingent of evaders was installed there. Subsequently, several camps spread across the plateau, which became a place of refuge. Their management and administration were in the hands of Socialist militants.[71] In Haute-Lozère, the first group of rebels hid out in Bonnecombe, in the Aubrac Mountains, in March 1943. It comprised only five immigrant workers from the foreign workers' camp of Chanac, who were "constantly harassed for political reasons, several of them having fought with the International Brigades."[72] Finally, on Easter in 1943, Daniel Trellu, the FN-FTP leader from Finistère, decided to create a small maquis in Châteauneuf-du-Faou, in the Montagne Noire. But by October of the same year, the group had only eight men. In reality, the Communists only half-heartedly supported the maquis, which they suspected of "serving as heralds of the watch-and-wait attitude and of emptying the cities of their active elements, uselessly immobilizing them in the mountains."[73]

These disparate examples confirm that the maquis were initially a spontaneous phenomenon, involving only a minority of evaders. Only 5 percent of them joined the maquis in Doubs, 10 percent in Isère, 17.4 percent in Ariège, 19 percent in Tarn, 20 percent in Jura, and 20.3 percent in Alpes-Maritimes.[74] Overall, between 15 and 20 percent of the STO evaders took to the mountains, that is, a total of thirty to forty thousand individuals.[75]

Nevertheless, accommodating these young people put a tremendous strain on the supply system. A maquis of sixty evaders required eighty-eight pounds of food a day.[76] Local organizers had trouble providing the necessary supplies, which the movements were scarcely in a position to secure. The men therefore roughed it in makeshift shelters and rarely ate their fill. The partisans led by Georges Guingouin, who established themselves in the forest of Châteauneuf in Limousin in the summer of 1943, did not escape that iron law, despite the excellent organization set up by the "Limousin Tito." Guingouin recalls: "Silver birch branches to sleep on, which for the first few days caused bruises, but the sap trench that was supposed to be used as a dormitory had to be abandoned because it was too damp; kitchen utensils are now kept there. An old threshing machine tarp will serve as a roof. A few boards and a few logs make up the table and benches for the open-air refectory. . . . Potatoes and plain water, that was their diet at first, and it was more than Spartan. Unfortunately, they all soon came down with dysentery. The spring from which they drew their drinking water, coming out of the mud in a steep-sided valley that never saw the sun, was polluted."[77] In Jura, "the Francis group's first cabin was put up in the woods of Fontainbrux and covered with a large tarpaulin 'liberated' from a bus in Bellevèvres; its dividing walls, all running lengthwise (like a bus!), are made of hazelnut tree branches arranged closely around a layer of ferns, intended to insulate you from the cold. You sleep on hazelnut tree stakes covered with straw. In the middle is a trench. On either side, the excess dirt forms terraces on which you sleep, eat, and live, since they allow you to stay clear of the rising water and to protect yourself from the cold. Tables and benches are made of wood."[78]

These maquis, as already noted, had the aim of hiding the evaders more than turning them into combatants. In Jura, "few maquis have survived the winter, and their ambitions are limited to a single objective: to keep going. Out of lassitude or caution, the maquisards able to do so went back home or to friends' houses, more hospitable than the snow-covered woods or abandoned farms."[79] A few examples contradict that statement. In the Dordogne Valley, rebels established the armed camp of Le Chambon in March or April 1943, at the initiative of members of the AS.[80] And in December 1942, Pierre Dalloz devised a plan for "the military utilization of the Vercors."

Dalloz, an architect and site inspector, had the intuition in 1941 that the Vercors offered great strategic possibilities. In December 1942, he hatched a two-stage plan. Initially, the plateau would become a base defended by a deployment of irregular groups. Later on, the Allies would be able to send troops into that bastion and create, on the enemy's rear lines, "a powerful fortress from which raids could be launched under excellent conditions, on industrial regions and major communication routes."[81] In 1943, that plan was brought to Yves Farge, who transmitted it to Jean Moulin. General de Gaulle's delegate accepted it and handed over an envelope containing twenty-five thousand francs. General Delestraint, head of the AS, was persuaded by the project, now called the "Plan Montagnards" (Mountaineers' Plan). He submitted it to de Gaulle and to the BCRA, who gave their consent. On February 25, the BBC broadcast the message "The mountaineers must continue to climb the peaks." A small team that included, notably, Alain Le Ray, an officer in the mountain infantry and the son-in-law of François Mauriac, ascended the plateau,[82] and a "combat committee" formed between early March and early April 1943.

The Gaullist authorities were thus quick to approve a plan whose viability appeared at the very least uncertain. That haste can no doubt be explained by the small number of maquisards involved, the overtly military character of the operation, and the synergy with the Allied strategy it promised, especially since Dalloz agreed from the outset to London's supervision and ignored the authority of the movements. Moulin therefore devoted considerable resources to the maquis of the Vercors. Over four months, it received 4,609,750 francs, whereas the AS as a whole was paid only 6,166,000 francs during the same period— "enough to fuel rumors about the 'upper-crust' maquis and the recriminations of some, particularly at Combat."[83] At first, however, the investment produced only a bitter harvest. The first committee, victim of the repression, vanished in spring 1943. But a second committee, including, among others, Alain Le Ray, Eugène Chavant, and Jean Prévost, replaced it in late June.

The formation of the first maquis ended in spring 1943. All in all, the results were mixed. Having emerged from a refusal to submit to forced labor, they provided an alternative to the hundreds of thousands of young people threatened by the STO. Thanks to that sudden influx, the internal resistance expanded its recruitment and opened prospects for concrete action accessible to thousands of French people. The movements, in taking charge of that plan of action, had a hard time channeling the flood, which tested their capacity to protect civilians while at the same time mobilizing them. Simultaneously, the resistance, which had tended up to that point to be urban, now began to be ruralized. Farming regions and the mountains became the natural refuge of the evaders. The resistance also became nationalized, since the movement affected wide swaths of southern France, aided by its geography, especially the presence of mountain massifs.

Shadows marred that picture, however. Although not marginal, the maquis were a minority phenomenon, since the majority of the evaders preferred to count on their own resources to flee the STO rather than join up. In fact, the movements did not have the means needed to conduct their policy, given that London refused to support insubordination, which was not at all in keeping with its doctrine. The maquis, developing under difficult conditions, had to live off the land. From the start, that situation raised the issue of their relationship to the population: Would the French people, the farmers to begin with, agree to bring them fresh supplies and to support them, at the risk of being left destitute or of attracting the wrath of repression? Finally, the strategy was far from fixed. What would the military role of the maquis be? Should they confine themselves to serving as a refuge or play a more active role, working in synergy with Allied plans? In spring 1943, these questions were far from decided. One point, by contrast, was clear: the STO produced a shock wave in public opinion, which the movements were eager to exploit. But that eagerness stood in sharp contrast to the indifference the organized resistance displayed toward anti-Semitic persecution.

## Chapter 8

# Responses to Persecution
# of the Jews

IT CAN HARDLY be said that during World War II the resistance was preoccupied with rescuing the Jews. Its indifference fueled and continues to fuel suspicion. Are we to consider silence the price to be paid for the primacy of the political or armed struggle waged against the occupier? Or are we to read it as the sign of the ideological proximity of a portion of the underground forces to the Vichy regime? In either case, the Jews of France could only rarely count on the army of shadows to save them from death, even as the Germans and the French State, beginning in 1940, unleashed a racial persecution campaign targeting that community, which in 1939 was estimated at 330,000 members.

## Racial Persecution

On September 27, 1940, the occupiers ordered a census of the Jews residing in the occupied zone, a measure that, on June 2, 1941, the French State extended to the free zone and the French empire. Furthermore, the Vichy regime set about excluding Jews from the national community. On July 22, 1940, a commission began to review the naturalization proceedings that had occurred since 1927. Out of a total of 195,000 people, 15,000 of them—including 6,000 Jews—were obliged to reassume their original nationality. On October 3, 1940, a first legal statute drew up a long list of prohibited occupations, which a second statute, on June 2, 1941, clarified and expanded. The law banned Jews from the public sector and from the media; it made the exercise of the liberal professions and access to higher education subject to very low quotas.[1] The French and German authorities also dispossessed the Jews of their property, a means to eliminate the supposed influence they exerted on the national economy. In both the south and the north, therefore, their businesses were entrusted to temporary administrators, who took over their management in a process called "Aryanization," codified by the law of July 22, 1941. In addition to these acts of exclusion and dispossession, internment and then deportation measures were taken. On October 4, 1940, a law authorized prefects to intern "foreign nationals of the Jewish race . . . in special camps." In November 1940, some 26,000 foreigners who had taken refuge in the southern zone were languishing behind barbed wire, and that figure rose to 35,200 in December of the same year, before dropping subsequently.[2] In the north, a first wave of arrests targeted more than 3,500 Jews, most of them Poles, on May 14, 1941. They were taken to the Pithiviers and Beaune-la-Rolande internment camps in the Loiret department. Two roundups followed in August and December 1941. Foreign-born Jews could also fall under the provisions of the law of September 27, 1940, if there were "too many of them in the national economy" and they found themselves "unable to return to their country of origin." Subject to forced labor and harsh disciplinary conditions, they were assigned to foreign laborer groups (groupements de travailleurs étrangers), where Spanish Republicans, German political refugees, and Polish Jews worked side by side, until the Vichy regime decided in 1941 to form "homogeneous Jewish groups," also called, oddly, "Palestinian groups."

The Nazi regime did not seek merely to persecute the Jews of Europe by excluding them from national communities, depriving them of every means of existence, and subjecting them to humiliating and barbarous treatment. As of 1942, it also planned for their systematic destruction, a process of extermination already well advanced in Eastern Europe. The first convoy bound for Auschwitz left France on March 27, 1942; seventy-three more followed.[3] The trains transported more than 76,000 Jews to the death camps, from which only a handful of survivors—2,600—returned.[4] That annihilation was planned, premeditated, and organized by the Third Reich, but it benefited from the zealous cooperation of the French State, which placed its administration in the occupier's service. Granted, Vichy refused to compel the Jews to wear the yellow star in the free zone or in the empire, as they were ordered to do in the occupied zone on May 29, 1942. Likewise, it distinguished between French Jews, whom it theoretically refused to hand over to the Nazis, and stateless persons and foreigners, whom it shamelessly delivered to them. Conversely, it undertook to put the Jews of France on file, to identify them, exclude them, and dispossess them. Its police force and its gendarmerie conducted the roundups and guarded the internment camps. An aggravating circumstance: in early July 1942, Pierre Laval suggested, "for humane [sic] purposes, that children, including those under sixteen, be permitted to accompany their parents" to the Nazi camps, a requirement that the Reich had not formulated.[5] The Vichy regime thus bears a heavy responsibility for the murder of some 80,000 Jews.[6] The arrest of the Jews by the French services made it possible to obtain a higher number of deportees than the occupation authorities could have achieved on their own. As Serge Klarsfeld points out, their manpower was inadequate for accomplishing that mission.[7]

Vichy had two objectives, in fact. Determined to collaborate with Berlin, it intended at the same time to maintain its sovereignty, which led it to consider the Jews bargaining chips in the negotiations it was conducting with the Reich. Simultaneously, it pursued its own anti-Semitic policy. The first measures—and the statute to begin with—far from coming in response to an order from the Germans, as many Jews believed at the time, were adopted in complete autonomy. The desire to settle the so-called Jewish question was in fact a pillar of the national revolution desired by the Pétainist regime.

In reality, the anti-Semitism that thrived during the dark years had taken root in rich soil. During the 1930s, France's economic and political crisis had reactivated racist and xenophobic prejudices inherited in part from the nineteenth century. In that gloomy economic climate, some accused the Jews of dominating certain professions and of practicing unfair competition. Others attributed to these supposed heralds of anti-France responsibility for parliamentary decline or suspected them of fomenting revolutionary unrest with the backing of Moscow, accusations that intensified when Léon Blum came to power in 1936. A few voices suggested that the Jews were pushing for the war against Hitler to defend their persecuted coreligionists. Many, finally, believed that the Jews were unassimilable by their very nature because they belonged to a stateless people, an orientation reinforced by endogamy. "In the synthesis of structural cultural codes of the 1930s, the identification between Jew and foreigner had taken root: the Jews were not—could not be—French like other people; the spirit of discrimination had set in," notes historian Renée Poznanski.[8]

A fringe of the internal resistance and some men in Free France subscribed to these stereotypes, which were shared by a portion of the French people. For example, the jurist Pierre Tissier, General de Gaulle's companion in London, refused Léon Blum's adviser Georges Boris free access to the general in 1940; in a book published in 1942, he suggested that "the Jews who have only recently acquired French nationality and who are not assimilated [should be] subject to the same restrictive measures as the other recently naturalized and unassimilated French people."[9] In September 1941, the resistance fighter Henri Frenay claimed that "a Jewish problem" was developing on two distinct levels:

> The problem of the recent immigration of foreign Jews. The problem of Jewish capitalism, of Jewish finance, which had assumed an intolerable place in the national economy.
>
> A) This problem will have to be solved within the general framework of a statute on the basis of which naturalizations will have to be reviewed.
>
> B) The second problem will also have to be considered within the general framework of the financial oligarchies, whose power had become so great that they were becoming an obstacle to the will of the state. In that regard, Jewish capitalism was particularly dangerous because particularly powerful.
>
> Hence, the solution to be given to the Jewish problem will be a French solution, which can and must take into account the civilian or military service that some have rendered to our country, their country.[10]

## Timid Reactions

With very rare exceptions, therefore, the organized resistance did not engage in the battle against anti-Semitism. Apart from the fact that some of its members were not immune to racist prejudices, the resistance showed caution for strategic reasons. Because it suspected, and not without reason, that part of the public was in the thrall of anti-Semitic demons, it avoided going against the current, not wishing to alienate the French people. For example, in its issues of August 21 and 28, 1941, *L'Humanité* denounced the execution of Szmul Thyszelman and Henri Gautherot, but two weeks later, "Szmul" had metamorphosed into the less Jewish-sounding "Simon."[11] The internal resistance and Free France also feared that, were they to support the Jews, they would be validating the Nazi propaganda that condemned the war as Jewish. The BBC, which closely monitored the Gaullist broadcasts, was also afraid it would alienate the Arab-Islamic world if it granted too much importance to the anti-Semitic persecution. And finally, many resistance fighters did not perceive the singularity or the gravity of the threat. Faithful to the egalitarian conception of the republic, they refused to establish a distinction—and a fortiori a hierarchy— among victims, at a time when France as a whole was under the occupier's yoke. *La France continue*, an underground newspaper founded by Henri de Montfort, railed against anti-Semitism, while at the same time emphasizing that it felt "the same respect for all martyrs of German oppression, whoever they may be. [We are] firmly resolved to avenge all of them equally when the impending German defeat allows us to settle all accounts, and on a grand scale."[12] Voices of protest were therefore rare.

Several beliefs or ideologies could encourage groups to wage that battle, however. Marxism, for instance, had always considered "anti-Semitism to be an invention of the reactionaries, in order to prevent the workers from uniting against their class enemies, the capitalists."[13] The Communist press therefore condemned the exclusion measures, whether these took the form of despoiling merchants, dismissing Jewish teachers, or applying the *numerus clausus* to universities. Further, it blasted the exhibition "The Jew and France," held at the Palais Berlitz in Paris between September 1941 and January 1942, which was designed to illustrate the supposed Jewish invasion of national life. The PCF also supported the publication of the Yiddish periodical *Undzer Vort (Our Word*; in all, eighty-nine issues appeared during the occupation), which fought the anti-Jewish policy and reminded its readers of the necessary solidarity between the Jews and French society. Ideology continued to assert its rights, however. Newspapers evoked the class struggle that was splitting the community apart and attacked prominent Jews. They also expressed unconditional support for the Soviet Union.[14] "An attentive reading of the publications of the MOI, in both Yiddish and French, shows . . . that the Jews' fight is always circumscribed by that of the

Communists and that the analysis of anti-Semitism is modeled on that given by the Communists," writes historian Annette Wieviorka.[15]

Christianity offered a more ambiguous theological framework. A long tradition equating the Jews with the people who killed Christ had fueled hostility toward the children of Israel, whom the church set out to convert. At a more secular level, the majority of senior members in the Catholic hierarchy supported Philippe Pétain, who, they hoped, would restore God's place in the commonwealth and would eliminate the contentiousness that had existed between the throne and the altar under the Third Republic. Conversely, the Catholic world could appeal to Jesus's Jewish origins and invoke the commandment to love one's neighbor as a means to staunchly condemn the persecution striking the People of the Book. In addition, many believers, not without reason, equated Nazism with paganism, which could only incite them to reject both Hitlerian ideology and the collaboration advocated by the Marshal.

In fact, several Christians raised their voices to repudiate anti-Semitic persecution. In May 1941, for example, the Jesuit theologian Gaston Fessard protested the distribution of the film *Jud Süss*, which he called "so anti-Christian and so un-French."[16] But it was primarily Témoignage Chrétien that took on the task of embodying that repudiation. In November 1941, Father Pierre Chaillet, alongside three Jesuit theologians—Gaston Fessard, Henri de Lubac, and Yves de Montcheuil—decided to found a periodical expressing a Christian point of view of the war. The Protestant minister Roland de Pury and Christian intellectuals such as Robert d'Harcourt, Joseph Hours, and André Mandouze participated in that movement. In addition to nearly a dozen voluminous *Cahiers*, it published the *Courrier français du Témoignage chrétien (French Correspondence of Christian Witnessing)*, which was not as thick but had a more substantial print run: in 1944, 200,000 copies of issue 12, devoted to the massacre at Oradour-sur-Glane, were printed.

Témoignage Chrétien, refusing to become involved in politics, wanted to make the voices of Christians heard "in their own realm, which is where God and his Justice reign. No expediency, no carnal fear can exempt them from bearing witness, an act they must perform in opposition to the caricature of Justice, the caricature of truth, the caricature—alas!—of honor," Father Fessard explained.[17] That mission made it imperative to reveal the profound nature of Nazism, which, "radically opposed to Christianity . . . everywhere it dominates . . . unleashes a persecution outwardly less violent but more dangerous and even more complete than Communism."[18] It led the movement to condemn collaboration, "the slavery of the vanquished by the victor, who doles out his constraints, his 'generosity,' and his punishments depending on whether the slave yields more or less, whether he accepts wholeheartedly or halfheartedly his de facto situation. And adherence to the 'new order' is in reality an acknowledgment of the value of the spiritual principles of the National Socialist 'conception of the world,' according to which Europe will in the future have to organize itself under Germany's domination."[19] Finally, that mission led to the denunciation of anti-Semitic persecution, to which the movement devoted its sixth and seventh *Cahiers*, in April–May 1942. "Christians, we have the urgent duty to bear witness before all our brothers, following the imprescriptible principles of our faith, that anti-Semitism is incompatible with Christianity. In bearing witness against anti-Semitism and for truth and justice, we bear witness to Christ. No temporal authority can exempt us from that witnessing, no spiritual authority can reproach us."[20] In that spiritual crusade, Témoignage Chrétien took the measure of its solitude in view of the silences of the Catholic hierarchy, but it evaluated its mission in historical terms: "On the day of Hitler's defeat, which for our joyful anti-Semites of today will no doubt be a day of 'national' mourning as well as a bitter disappointment, when the people, liberated from servitude, will tally up these years of woe and glory, our testimony will be credited to the account of the French tradition, which will not have proved unworthy of its past spiritual achievements or had any doubts about its future."[21]

Finally, the republican, patriotic, humanistic, and democratic tradition offered frames of reference for opposing state anti-Semitism. In its early days, the resistance made moderate use of that tradition, preferring to attack the problem from the periphery rather than aiming at its heart. For the most part, the resistance limited itself to condemning the hatred contained in propaganda that ran counter to the national tradition but avoided dividing public opinion. It also denounced the first roundups and the disastrous internment conditions in the camps. In February 1942, for example, *Libération*-sud railed:

The French must say it again and again, must shout it. Some want to reduce their homeland to the foulest barbarism. Thousands of poor souls
are hunted down, arrested, starved, and killed, among other things, for
the crime of having been born Jewish. The Israelite's situation in the occupied zone is a true hell. The Drancy and Compiègne camps are full of
Jewish prisoners taken hostage. In Paris several hundred disabled and
decorated Israelite veterans have just been arrested. Ninety-five Israelite
hostages were massacred by machine gun in Paris.

Is it acceptable to hear some pseudo-French say: "After all, they're
only Communists or Jews"?[22]

These protests, however, remained rare, at least until mid-1942. As
Poznanski notes, "the Resistance movements," in choosing caution, "re-
nounced the role of ideological or spiritual leadership on the question
of anti-Semitism, preferring to bow to tendencies they suspected were
strongly implanted in public opinion."[23] In that realm, the struggle
was first waged by a fringe of the Christian world and by a part of the
Communist sphere. In the northern zone, the Communist review
*L'Université libre*, founded in 1940 by Jacques Decour, Georges Politzer,
and Jacques Solomon, was for many months the only publication in occupied France to use antiracist propaganda and to openly oppose all
discrimination, including that against foreign Jews.[24] In the south,
*Courrier français du Témoignage chrétien* was the only organ of the press
to grant a preeminent place to the issue.

## From Assistance to Rescue

As writers wielded their pens on the ethics battlefield, some men fought
on more concrete fields of action. In the first place, Jewish organizations worked hard from summer 1940 onward to set up programs of
assistance. What was known as the Rue Amelot Committee, which
combined Bundist, Socialist, and Zionist groups as well as the Oeuvre
de Secours aux Enfants (OSE; Child Rescue Network), opened four
dining halls, a health clinic, and a clothing shop to assist a population
suddenly reduced to poverty by exclusion and despoliation. Even while
maintaining a legal façade, the Comité Juif (Jewish Committee) also
assisted individuals coming into the free zone, hid children in foster
families, and offered material aid to proscribed persons.[25] In addition,

some organizations worked to alleviate the conditions of captivity reigning in the camps of the southern zone. The Nîmes committee, which brought together Jewish and Christian organizations under the presidency of an American named Donald Lowry, took charge of co-ordinating assistance to the interned. The Comité d'Aide aux Réfugiés (Refugee Aid Committee), a Jewish organization, also helped refugees in the southern zone. Likewise, the Comité Inter-mouvements auprès des Évacués (Cimade; Intermovement Committee for Evacuees), founded by Protestant movements in 1939 to support Alsace-Lorrainian refugees, focused on the fate of captives. While setting up missions in most of the camps, it also sought to exfiltrate internees and slip them secretly into Switzerland. The OSE, finally, took care of children, whether interned in the camps or separated from their parents. In late 1941, it managed seventeen houses (including three in the northern zone) and during that year oversaw the fate of 6,700 children. As the threat became more real, it gradually entrusted them to foster families rather than keep them in group homes.[26]

The intensification of the anti-Semitic persecution made it evident that the Jews of France were in mortal peril. At that time, the imperative to rescue people under threat by concealing them took precedence over assistance or social welfare—whose aim was simply to relieve the distress of proscribed persons. Certain organizations sought to save the Jews from the peril lying in wait, either by encouraging them to leave or by hiding them. German domination of the continent and the United States' entry into the war made emigration highly uncertain, however: Spain and Switzerland were the only possible destinations. But 6,449 people did manage to take the path of exile between 1940 and 1942.[27] Most in the Jewish community who escaped death, however, did so by hiding, thanks to the assistance provided by thousands of French people. Nonetheless, they needed to feel they had support, even though "the idea was commonly accepted that immigrants, not exclusively but especially Jews, posed a serious problem for the state."[28]

From that standpoint, the obligation to wear the yellow star, imposed in May 1942, then the roundups of summer 1942—starting with the terrible Vel' d'Hiv roundup of July 16 and 17—sent a shock wave through the public. As the police prefecture admitted in a report of July 17, 1942:

Although the French population is fairly anti-Semitic on the whole and in a general way, it judges these measures harshly, considering them inhumane.

The reasons for that disapproval rest in great part on the rumors currently circulating that families would be dislocated and children under ten handed over to public assistance.

It is the separation of children from their parents that most affects the French masses and produces reactions that find expression in harsh criticism of the government and of the occupying authorities.[29]

In fact, as Poznanski points out, "the deeply distressing scenes that unfolded in the occupied zone and then in the southern zone moved the population. The terrible ordeals imposed on very small children, victims of an incomprehensible obduracy, erased many prejudices or relegated them to the shadows."[30]

That distress was expressed, relayed, and amplified by four prelates in the southern zone, who vigorously protested the anti-Semitic persecution. Despite his physical condition, Monsignor Saliège, archbishop of Toulouse—"whose malady was crushing a body that was already squat by nature, keeping him helpless in a chair, paralyzed from the mouth down"[31]—sent out a pastoral letter, which was read in churches on August 23, 1942.

Children, women, men, fathers and mothers, treated like a vile herd; members of a single family separated from one another and packed off to an unknown destination: such is the sad spectacle that these times hold for us.

. . . Jews are men and women. One cannot do just anything to them, to those men, those women, those fathers and mothers. They belong to humankind; they are our brothers, like so many other people. A Christian cannot forget that.[32]

Monsignor Théas, bishop of Montauban, Cardinal Gerlier, archbishop of Lyon, and Monsignor Delay, bishop of Marseilles, had letters in the same vein read out in their dioceses, causing a considerable stir. Indeed, "it was the first time since 1940 that a public personality had openly criticized the government."[33] The French State attempted in vain to silence the prelates, asking prefects, for example, to exert pressure to dissuade them from speaking out. In fact, the state lucidly assessed the danger: these stances legitimated the assistance that civilians were able to offer the Jews by justifying them on theological and moral grounds. They therefore erected new obstacles on the path to collaboration and the maintenance of order.

In any event, reactions became sharper as of 1942. They sometimes came as an urgent response to a situation judged unacceptable. General Saint-Vincent, military governor of the Lyon region, refused, for example, to provide soldiers to maintain order as 650 Jews were being taken from the city. He was immediately forced into retirement.[34] Above all, the rescue of Jews tended to become better organized over time. Although the Éclaireurs Israélites de France (EIF; Israelite Scouts of France) remained within the law, three paid employees—Henri Wahl, Ninon Weil-Hait, and Denise Lévy—helped Jews escape their tormentors, a movement that expanded after Darquier de Pellepoix, commissioner for Jewish Questions, dissolved the EIF on January 5.[35] In the same way, the minister André Trocmé, founder of the Chambon-sur-Lignon secondary school in the Cévennes, lodged hundreds of Jews (probably some 2,500) in his institution and in foster families, assisted by Cimade, ministers from the neighboring parishes, and some mayors, who provided false identity papers.[36] In Lyon, Amitié Chrétienne (Christian Friendship), a joint organization of Catholics and Protestants, also took action. Placed under the protection of Reverend Boegner and Cardinal Gerlier at the instigation of Father Chaillet, Father Glasberg, and Jean-Marie Soutou, among others, it spent lavishly to keep children from being deported. Notably, it hid 108 children after the major roundup of Vénissieux in August 1942.[37] Religious communities also played a crucial role. By late 1942, the institution of Notre-Dame-de-Massip, in Capdenac (the Lot department), had taken in six children from the Toulouse region, then added forty from Mende, Clermont-Ferrand, Brive, Albi, and Rodez in October 1943, and fifteen more in 1944. Responding to the request of the office of Catholic charities in the archdiocese of Toulouse, Sister Denise Bergon and Marguerite Roques saved eighty-three people in all, giving them shelter at the convent.[38] Finally, the OSE expended a great deal of energy to save children. Georges Loinger, leader of the Burgundy network, got some across to Switzerland between September 1943 and July 1944.[39]

That said, most Jews were rescued by ordinary people outraged by the fate reserved for these men, women, and children. The Yad Vashem memorial in Israel has distinguished about two thousand Righteous among the Nations in France,[40] but that designation honors only a minority of the thousands of anonymous people who aided proscribed persons to hide or to cross the Franco-Swiss border. Let us not overstate the case, however, by likening Jews to minors unable to take their own fate in hand. Many escaped on their own, enlisting family members, professional contacts, or friends to ensure their safety, often in the free zone, in the Italian occupation zone after November 1942, and in Switzerland. Several Jews from Lens, for example, paid smugglers to get them to the Confederation without the support of any organization. In addition, a number of Jews fought in the resistance movements, networks, and Free France organizations, though they never attempted to reorient "the policy of their movements toward action aimed at saving the Jews."[41] In all, the mobilization of the Jews and of a portion of French society prevented the architects of the Final Solution from achieving their ends, as the rates of deportation suggest. Whereas the Reich, assisted by the Vichy authorities, succeeded in deporting 41,951 Jews in the last eight months of 1942, that figure fell to 17,000 in 1943, then to 16,000 in 1944.[42] In all, 11,600 Jewish children were subjected to the hell of deportation, while 72,400 escaped death.[43]

Nevertheless, the French obeyed the dictates of their hearts or of their reason more than they deferred to instructions from London or the internal resistance. To be sure, some newspapers began in 1942 to call for people to choose life in the underground. *Undzer Vort* recommended in March 1943: "Do not wait at home for the Nazi bandits. Take every measure to conceal yourselves. In the first place, find safe haven for the children, with the assistance of the French population standing with you. Secure your own safety, join a patriotic combat organization to strike the bloodthirsty enemy. In the event that you are caught by the Nazi brutes, resist by every means, barricade the doors, call for help, fight the police, what do you have to lose? Conversely, you may save your life. *You must look for every means and everywhere for an escape.*"[44]

But neither the BBC nor the underground press placed the fight against racial deportation at the top of its priorities, even though the CNF had officially taken a stand on August 7, 1942: "Before public opinion in the free countries, it denounces the unheard-of infringement on the sovereignty and honor of France by a government under the foreigner's orders. It declares that the Vichy government, in making itself guilty on Germany's orders of such a monstrous violation of the right to asylum, of human rights, and of the French moral and legal tradition in its entirety, destroyed with its own hands the fiction of its autonomy and reduced to nothing its claim to represent France, in the eyes of nations still concerned for the values of our civilization."[45] The identity of the victims was not clearly stated, however, and the CNF instrumentalized the race issue to undermine the legitimacy of the French State. In addition, whenever a Jew was murdered, the BBC immediately cited the same fate inflicted on a Christian. "In many cases, that obstinacy in designating the victims while obliterating precisely what had turned them into victims kept it from recognizing the singular fate of the Jews of France," Poznanski writes.[46] Above all, the term "deportation" gradually came to designate the dislocation of called-up workers. Beginning in 1943, the fate of the Jews vanished little by little from the media, including the Communist media, and interest focused on the STO. The fight against anti-Semitic persecution had mobilized Jewish and Christian organizations, but the internal resistance movements and the Free France organizations remained largely apart from that process.

In reality, anti-Semitism had by no means completely disappeared, despite the storm that swept away the Jewish community of France. In a report prepared for de Gaulle in February 1943, Henri Frenay recommended that the general avoid being *"the man who brings back the Jews. Although it is our duty to eliminate any 'racial' distinction, we must in practice take into account the attitude of the population, which has in fact changed in the last two years."*[47] In September 1943, the Christian Democrat François de Menthon, minister of justice, reminded René Cassin, a jurist of Fighting France, that he was in favor of preserving the naturalization review commission established by Vichy. "The naturalization of dubious Israelite elements, too numerous in the years preceding the war, has provided a pretext for anti-Semitism, which may raise a certain problem on the day of our return." Disavowed by a decision of the law committee, he strove in an application decree to prevent the automatic reintegration of Jews and even proposed validating the denaturalizations declared by the French State, even if that meant authorizing an appeals processes.[48] Prejudices certainly died hard.

It should be noted, therefore, that the resistance remained silent even as genocide on an unprecedented scale was being perpetrated, despite a proliferation of signs that increasingly reduced the scope of ignorance. That silence, concludes Poznanski, "contributed toward making the exclusion of the Jews commonplace. Without venturing to discern the effect on public opinion that an uninhibited Resistance leadership might have had—one that from the start pronounced itself against any measure of persecution against the Jews—we may observe the extraordinary impact of the handful of pastoral letters read from the pulpit in summer 1942: on the Jews, whom they comforted; and on public opinion, whose outrage they legitimated and thus strengthened, paving the way for rescue operations."[49] The voices of these prelates had great influence, but they remained a very isolated case. The rising eminences or established figures of the intelligentsia, from André Gide to Jean-Paul Sartre to Paul Claudel, opted for silence. Nor did the party bosses of the republic distinguish themselves for their courage or lucidity. The only audible cries calling for people to fight against the persecution came from the church, despite its being discredited by association with the Vichy regime.

## Chapter 9

# The Internal Resistance in 1943

From the beginning to the end of the war, the relationship between the internal resistance and Free France was marked by ambivalence and complexity. Both forces were fighting for the same goal—to hasten the victory of the Allies and the liberation of France—which required a coordination of their efforts, since in unity there is strength. But they had less admissible ulterior motives. Whereas Charles de Gaulle wished to control the movements, both to increase the effectiveness of the army of shadows and to consolidate his own power, a large portion of the internal resistance rejected that control, demanding that the man of June 18 treat them as equals, not subordinates. That gap explains both the points of convergence and the clashes between captive France and Free France. The orientation toward unity was strong enough to assemble the underground forces in the Conseil National de la Résistance (CNR; National Council of the Resistance), under the shadow of the Cross of Lorraine. The council met in Paris on May 27, 1943, chaired by Jean Moulin for the first (and last) time. But the movements, jealous of their independence, shook off the yoke many times, exacerbating tensions with the London services. True, the internal resistance had increased extraordinarily in power. Aware of its strength, it now refused to be considered a secondary partner, especially since the tide was turning. After the Soviet victory at Stalingrad in February 1943, the invasion of Sicily, then of Italy, and the fall of Mussolini in July 1943, all signs pointed to a more or less imminent Allied landing in France. The resistance would obviously have a role to play in the liberation of the country, a prospect that conferred a new importance on it.

## Rise in Power

The movements, having arisen spontaneously from the defeat or the occupation, developed without any support from existing structures and invented their own modes of intervention. Over time, however, they managed to acquire a solid armature. The improvisation of the heroic days was followed by more extensive organization.

As a general rule, a steering committee (*comité directeur*—a designation used by all the movements) now attended to their fate. The steering committees were able to assemble representatives of the principal political partners, always around a strong personality. In the case of Libération-sud, for example, these consisted of the CGT, the CFTC, and the CAS.[1] That system also inspired Libération-nord, whose leadership committee in early 1942 was composed of Henri Ribière, Christian Pineau, Jean Texcier, and Louis Vallon, all Socialists; of Gaston Tessier, representing the Christian trade unionists of the CFTC; and of Pierre Neumeyer and Louis Saillant, on behalf of the Communist and Socialist trade unionists of the CGT.[2] The growth of the organizations and their geographical expansion also prompted the leadership to improve coordination and the effectiveness of their fight. Pierre Gacon, head of the Rhône-Alpes region, therefore joined the steering committee of Franc-Tireur in 1943. In the same vein, Suzon Guyotat, in charge of building up the DF in the southern zone, was co-opted by its leadership. Other movements, conversely, preferred looser methods of operation. Jacques Lecompte-Boinet, the leader of the CDLR, rejected an "overly hierarchical organization, which seemed dangerous to him in the northern zone. He wanted a flexible, fragmented organization composed of very small groups—between six and eight members— whose leaders would be linked to a regional chief, who would himself be in contact with the national leader."[3]

In the south, the creation of the MUR in January 1943 superimposed a new command structure at the top decision-making level. In its first phase, the steering committee, chaired by Jean Moulin, was composed of Henri Frenay, commissioner of military affairs (AS, irregular groups, maquis); Emmanuel d'Astier de La Vigerie, commissioner of political affairs; and a representative from Franc-Tireur (Jean-Pierre Levy and later Eugène Petit [Claudius]), who served as commissioner of intelligence and material resources and was also in charge of relations with the prisoners' movements.[4] Although each group held onto its own newspaper and the services associated with it (printing works, typesetting shop, distribution network), their other organizations merged, dispossessing the "steering committees of their decision-making power at the MUR level."[5]

The multiplication of services made it necessary to modify the organization charts. The CDLR thus created a liaison and false papers service in March–April 1943, as well as the AO service to assist STO evaders and to organize sabotage operations. Until late 1942, the DF was informally managed by a small group of pioneers under Philippe Viannay. The creation of new branches—false papers, distribution, irregular corps—led to a reshuffling of its staff. Charlotte Nadel in typesetting, Jacques Lusseyran and Jacques Oudin in distribution, and Bernard Lebon in false papers were invited at that time to join an inner circle. Its formal structure should not be exaggerated, however. "Everything was discussed without an agenda. Events, de Gaulle, Pétain. Jokes circulated," reports Robert Salmon, a member of that three-person leadership team. "To my great distress," recounts Jean-Daniel Jurgensen, the third man of the troika, "the committee meetings took place at night. By midnight or one o'clock, I increasingly had a tendency to agree with Philippe [Viannay], so that we could go to sleep. It was a very quirky type of atmosphere, very cordial. You shouted a little, you discussed, you dealt with a pile of details."[6]

That convivial ambience, however, should not veil the reality, even the violence, of the disputes, though as a general rule the leaders were firmly at the helm. "Nothing was more hierarchical than the Resistance. No society was more stratified than that half-underground society," recalls Charles d'Aragon, Combat's departmental leader for Tarn.[7] The decision-making process, democratic in its essence, "lapsed into a system that was truly monarchical in coloring, if by that one understands government by a single person surrounded by advisers," historian Laurent Douzou points out.[8] The preeminence of the leader was all the greater, given that the need for secrecy tended to keep the number of meetings to a minimum. The steering committees usually played only a limited role, therefore. From autumn 1942 on, the Libération-sud committee, for example, was gradually left out of decision making: the representatives of the political world and of the trade unions wished to reclaim their independence, and the movement followed its own path.

The power of the leader was sometimes disputed, however. Jean-Jacques Soudeille, for example, accused Jean-Pierre Levy, who had met with General La Laurencie in spring 1942, of presenting Franc-Tireur with a fait accompli and reproached him for his dictatorial tendencies. He then resigned from the steering committee. Likewise, Jean Cavaillès, a supporter of military action that was rejected by the unionist cadres of Libération-nord, left the movement's leadership in July 1943, preferring to keep supreme control over intelligence and immediate action via the Cohors network.[9] Finally, as previously mentioned, the turmoil produced by his meetings with Pierre Pucheu obliged Henri Frenay to undertake a tour of six regions in the southern zone to reassure regional cadres, shaken by what they saw as an unacceptable compromise of principles. The power the leaders possessed, far from being absolute, was thus limited by the consensus that the adopted strategy was required to inspire. Otherwise, opposition could lead to clashes, sometimes to rifts, based on personal disagreements or rivalries.

Discord was particularly keen within the leading circles of the MUR. There, essential differences in approach were mixed up with power issues. Frenay, head of the most powerful movement, had a hard time agreeing to sacrifice his preeminence on the altar of unity. The appointment of service directors and regional or departmental leaders therefore led to conflicts, especially with Moulin and d'Astier de La Vigerie. That antagonism cannot be reduced to a clash of egos, however, given that disagreements on strategy played such a prominent role. Moulin, for example, advocated separating the political from the military and demanded control of the AS. Frenay, sometimes backed by d'Astier de La Vigerie, refused to let the command of the AS slip from the hands of the internal resistance. He rejected the disassociation between civilian and military actions and requested that decisions be made in the metropolis, as close to the ground as possible, not in London, which was too far from the theater of operations. "That debate, often stormy and painful, would be repeatedly addressed at several meetings of the steering committee,"[10] writes Alya Aglan, but no compromise satisfactory to all parties was ever reached.

Weakened by resignations or arrests, the steering committees were often reshuffled over the four long years of the occupation. Although, in all, ninety-two people composed the "Center" of Libération-sud during the dark years, of the seven original members in 1940, none remained active in 1943. Of the ninety-two, fifty-six left the inner circle before liberation: forty-one of them were arrested, but fifteen left for other reasons,[11] a significant proportion. In addition to personal disagreements and differences, there were the ravages of the repression. In March 1943, Maurice Ripoche, head of the CDLL, was arrested; his replacement, Roger Coquoin, was gravely wounded by a bullet when he was detained in December 1943. Gilbert Védy (Jacques Médéric), assigned to replace him, was intercepted by the French police immediately upon his arrival, on March 21, 1944. He committed suicide by swallowing his cyanide pill.[12] And finally, Colonel Ginas, the last leader of the CDLL, was arrested in 1944, an epilogue to a long run of bad luck. Historian Henri Michel concludes: "It is difficult to find a greater hecatomb of leaders."[13] The DF, conversely, managed to hold on to almost its entire leadership staff between 1941 and 1944. In that regard, it was the exception rather than the rule.

In any case, by mid-1943 the movements had succeeded in imposing a structure on themselves. Equipped with a capable and solid organization, they also expanded geographically. In the south, the three principal movements emancipated themselves from their original bastions between 1940 and 1942 and took over other zones, a dynamic amplified by the creation of the MUR. Henceforth, departments and regions were under a three-member directorate comprising one representative from Combat, one from Franc-Tireur, and one from Libération-sud. Combat obtained command of five of the six regions, while the Lyon region (R1) was granted to Libération, which initially named Alfred Malleret (Joinville) as its leader. He was succeeded in January 1944 by Auguste Vistel (Alban). The dynamic set in motion by the founding of the MUR was undoubtedly productive, but it was also uneven. In the Massif Central (R6), the stability of the core leadership that coalesced around the physician Henry Ingrand, regional leader of Combat, served well the activism of the MUR as well as their recruitment. In Provence-Côte d'Azur (R2), by contrast, the arrests made by the German and Italian services between March and May 1943 decapitated the command of the MUR, only recently set in place, undercutting its efforts to establish itself.

Until early 1944, geographical expansion in the north came solely at the initiative of the movements, which were not overseen by any federative structure. The DF, to increase its ascendancy, sent emissaries to the provinces of Brittany and Franche-Comté. Between 1942 and 1944, therefore, the DF managed to attract some eight hundred members in Brittany[14] and about five hundred in the eastern region—not insignificant figures.[15] The OCM decided to designate a leader for each department, then for each region. Marc O'Neill attended to the fate of the Paris region, Roland Farjon to Nord-Pas-de-Calais, and Colonel Rollot and André Grandclément implanted the movement in the Bordeaux region. In April 1943, Maxime Blocq-Mascart's organization claimed nearly five thousand men in the Paris region[16] and 2,200 for that of Reims,[17] numbers that, while indicating real growth, are undoubtedly subject to correction. The CDLR, finally, developed in Normandy, Champagne, and Franche-Comté. In Lorraine, that group benefited from the integration in late 1943 of the small Défense de la Patrie movement, negotiated by one of its organizers, Jean Braun (Durthal, Aumont).[18]

The major underground groups, then, far from following the precepts of Malthusianism, deliberately opted for expansion. They even exerted a real attraction over the more modest movements, which were vegetating for lack of means or dynamism.

Several organizations asked to be incorporated into more powerful movements. In December 1942, Voix du Nord, shaken by a series of arrests and out of resources, had its organizational structure subsumed by Libération-sud and its intelligence service by Libération-nord, before falling entirely under the control of the northern movement. Nevertheless, Voix du Nord preserved the autonomy of its newspaper and its activities in the department of Nord, where it had originated.[19] Small groups were likewise incorporated into the DF in Brittany and Poitou, a process that sometimes gave rise to fierce debates, as confirmed by the schism that occurred within Volontaires de la Liberté (VdL; Volunteers for Liberty).

In May 1941, a few students, from the Henri-IV and Louis-le-Grand lycées in particular, had formed the small organization of VdL, which they planned to devote exclusively to propaganda. They believed, in the words of one of its organizers, Pierre Cochery, that it was imperative not to embark on a form of activism "beyond our capacities, which does not entail on our part the contempt felt for other people by intellectuals with soft hands. Every man to his business."[20] True to that line, the VdL printed several thousand copies each of some one hundred bulletins between May 1941 and August 1944. But some militants, yearning to do battle, contested that approach. In January 1943, about forty members decided to break away and negotiated their integration into the DF, while the remainder followed the original line, alongside Jean-Louis Bruch and Pierre Cochery.

The major movements, though exerting a real appeal, sometimes also suffered the effects of centrifugal forces. In March 1942, Georges Dunoir and his friends left Franc-Tireur; they had demanded a right to inspect the content of the newspaper and a harder anticlerical tone, which Jean-Pierre Levy rejected. As a result, the dissidents left to found a periodical, *Le coq enchaîné*,[21] which published eleven four-page bulletins between April 1942 and liberation.[22]

The internal resistance thus put its money on spatial expansion, driven by its most valorous branches. But it could never really abolish the effects of the demarcation line. Henri Frenay had dreamed of establishing himself in the northern zone; although his efforts quickly fizzled, it was not until "March 1943 that the rift would be altogether clear and definitive, known and accepted."[23] Similarly, the two Libération movements attempted to cooperate, banking on the proximity of their steering committees and on the ideological similarities between them. In early August 1942, they established weekly contact with each other, and their association, previously confidential, was made public on December 10, 1942. But instances of synergy remained limited, and in that undertaking Libération-sud had no better luck than its rival Combat. In all, the expansion process never went national, but the extension of the services of the internal resistance at that time strengthened the geographical dominance of the movements.

## From Specialization to Versatility

In many cases, these movements had risen up around an underground newspaper, and at first they bolstered their production and distribution systems. In early 1942, Léon Morandat (Yvon) took charge of printing and distributing *Libération-sud*, then passed the reins to Jules Meurillon. He relied on a network of printing offices that in 1943 agreed to devote five or six days of continuous work to producing each issue, in response to growing demand. In September 1943, the movement even spent 116,000 francs to acquire its own printing works in Auch. The quality of the printing was also becoming more professional: the newspaper was now typeset on zinc plates produced by Francisque Vacher, a photoengraver at *Le Progrès de Lyon*.[24] Likewise, in March 1942 Franc-Tireur entrusted the fate of its newspaper to Georges Altman, a journalist at *Le Progrès de Lyon*, who, assisted by Élie Péju, oversaw its content, production, and distribution. *Combat* continued its development with the help of André Bollier (Vélin), who took over the printing. He first availed himself of the services of professional printers, who made up a "single issue, typeset in Lyon, then sent in the form of photoengraved zinc plates," which were easily transportable. Intent on maintaining his autonomy, Bollier acquired a first printing press in November 1942, followed in April 1943 by a Minerva pedal-powered press, which was installed on rue Viala in Lyon.[25] The founding of the MUR did little to modify that system; each group retained control over its newspaper and the services associated with it.

In the north, the DF had opted for autarky and continued to take that path. In April 1943, the movement acquired a Teisch, a powerful printing press, kept first in a garage on rue de Sèvres in Paris and later, in July 1943, set up at the Labordière factory run by the parents of two of its members, Denise and Marie-Solange Rousseau. When not in service, the machine, placed in the mail room, was covered with an enormous crate maneuvered by a system of pulleys. Thanks to the printer Jacques Grou-Radenez and Alain Radiguer, manager of the Caslon Foundry, the DF acquired a Crafftmann press in 1943. It was installed in a closed washhouse on rue Guémenée in Paris, owned by an eighty-four-year-old woman named Mme Cumin. In spring 1944, the DF purchased "La Grosse Margot," a press weighing more than six and a half tons. It was hidden in a house rented for that purpose on rue Jean-Dolent, in the fourteenth arrondissement. For reasons of security, the movement was also careful to keep its printing works separate from its stereotypy and typesetting shops, a system that allowed it to maintain its production capacities nearly intact until liberation.[26]

To protect its members from the wrath of the repression, the movements came up with the idea of providing them with false identity papers. At first, they simply exploited the complicity of civil servants or town clerks. In Drôme, for example, a dispensary provided supplies to Franc-Tireur, whose local team was composed largely of municipal employees.[27] But the increase in manpower, the proliferation of arrests, and soon, the threats to the Jews and the workers called to serve in the STO led the movements to shift gears. In the south, Libération created an ad hoc service, which, beginning in 1942, developed under the guidance of Pierre Kahn-Farelle, a thirty-six-year-old Parisian manufacturer, and put a dozen paid employees to work. With the creation of the MUR, it was turned into a National Identity and False Papers Service, which served all the federated movements.[28] In the north, the DF had entrusted the task of establishing a forgery shop to a couple, Monique Rollin and Michel Bernstein, in February 1942. The beginnings were arduous to say the least, even though Bernstein, a Parisian bookseller specializing in social and economic history, would have been familiar with printing procedures. The letters were traced in ink to be duplicated in a loop, then transferred onto a gelatin plate. But that process allowed the production of only fifty documents a week. In addition, the intensification of repressive measures made it necessary to supply other documents in addition to identity cards, such as certificates of employment or demobilization, *Ausweises* (permits to cross the demarcation line), and driver's licenses.

These requirements led to the use of a photoengraving system. The procedure consisted of producing photo enlargements of the models to be reproduced. From them, the photoengraver produced a negative impression on a zinc plate, putting the designs or enlargements in the required format. The engraving was then etched with nitric acid. The plates were sent to the printing works to be put on paper, and the documents were stamped at the forgery shop. Seals were made from a rubber imprint taken from the plate.

This technique, though simple in principle, proved complex in its application. A photoengraver had to be found, different stamp models acquired, and sheets of rubber obtained in sufficient quantity. These obstacles were gradually removed, however. A photoengraver named Émile Courmont agreed to support the movement. Marcel Guichardot, another photoengraver, drew up the designs. Georges Boisseau, assistant to the mayor of Clichy-sur-Seine, wrote to many communes on flimsy pretexts and, in their responses, they always affixed their official seal. Alain Radiguer of the Caslon Foundry supplied rubber, types, and a vulcanizing press. The blank forms and the stamps needed to produce identity cards could be freely purchased in tobacco shops. The DF was therefore able to meet the increase in demand. In July 1943, Philippe Viannay ordered 125 stamps a week from Rollin and Bernstein; in August, he required 200. In the course of the dark years, the forgery shop produced some 12,000 units in all, which satisfied growing demands in terms of both quantity and quality. The movement provided vehicle registration documents and driver's licenses, certificates from employers and student IDs, and both census and demobilization certificates. Bernstein forged mayor's seals and German eagles, the stamp of the police prefecture and of the German military headquarters. He even went so far as to fabricate a Philippe Pétain postage stamp so that newspapers could be sent free of cost.

Forgers had to proceed methodically. As Francis-Louis Closon, an envoy from London, explains: "The place of residence had to be verifiable and necessarily different from the place we used as an office, where a police search could uncover damning documents. The identity in the strict sense did not matter very much, except that the name and birthplace had to correspond to vital statistics records held in a town clerk's office. The practice of listing birthplaces outside France, in overseas territories or in towns whose registry offices had been destroyed by the war, was already overused by the Resistance and sparked doubts among police officers in the know."[29] Monique Rollin and Michel Bernstein prevailed over these obstacles, but they had to impose an iron discipline on themselves. Between February 1942 and June 1944, Bernstein left his apartment only about ten times and limited his contacts to the bare minimum. Only Génia Gemähling, secretary-general of the DF, provided the couple with fresh supplies; Rollin was in charge of delivering the stamps and of maintaining relationships with suppliers.[30]

The movements also developed their intelligence services (SR), to guarantee their own security and to offer the Allies information on the Germans' military plans and France's domestic situation. In May 1942, Franc-Tireur created an SR headed by Jean-Pierre Levy in person. Jean Gemähling assumed the same role at Combat, but, upon his arrest, had to suspend his activities between November 1941 and March 1942. He returned to that work after he was released, assisted by the writer Benjamin Crémieux. When the MUR were founded, Gemähling assumed leadership of the SR for the three federated movements and organized it into three branches: the SR-Mil collected military documentation relating to the Germans; the SR-Pol gathered information of a political nature; and the SR-Sec[urité] formed "a sort of counterespionage network" meant to protect underground groups from the rigors of the repression, by warning them of possible arrests, for example.[31]

As a general rule, the northern movements allotted a major role to intelligence. At the OCM, Lieutenant Colonel Touny, then Marcel Berthelot (Lavoisier), an agrégé in German, who, as former attaché to the French embassy in Berlin, had seen with his own eyes the misdeeds of Nazism, centralized the information they were transmitting to the Allies. Until March 1942, Georges Savourey ran the SR of the CDLL; he was particularly effective because he was able to work in concert with the French State's SR Air. Intelligence played a more marginal role in Libération-nord and the DF, which, at least in the beginning, gave precedence to a civilian strategy. As Christian Pineau, founder of Libération-nord, explained in 1942: "In fact, military resistance requires a hierarchy, a discipline, a discretion incompatible with the very notion of a mass movement. It can use only men who are able to move around, to fight, and to run relatively high risks. And it can use only a small number of them. Political resistance, by contrast, does not require any hierarchy, beyond a very broad structure. It leaves a great deal of individual initiative to each person. . . . Military resistance and political resistance must therefore have separate organizations, which does not mean that there is no link between them. . . . We therefore leave the task of organizing military resistance as defined above to the Fighting French Forces, but it is our responsibility to organize political resistance."[32]

The movements also worked hard to set up irregular corps to attack the occupier or collaborators. Benjamin Roux was in charge of these groups at Franc-Tireur, and they apparently comprised five hundred men in spring 1943.[33] Raymond Aubrac commanded the paramilitary sector on behalf of Libération-sud, and Jacques Renouvin did the same at Combat. In fact, Renouvin had several qualifications for assuming that role. A militant of Action Française and a former member of its youth organization, the Camelots du Roi, he had publicly slapped Pierre-Étienne Flandin, who, after the Munich Conference, had sent a telegram of congratulations to the four signatories, including Adolf Hitler. Renouvin, a participant in the Liberté movement in the Montpellier region, organized surprise attacks, slashing handbills and destroying newspaper kiosks, before putting his talents to use in Frenay's service.[34] The northern movements were not to be outdone. Jean Cavaillès, upon his return from London in early 1943, created an immediate action division for Libération-nord. "On seeing his calm face, his smile, his bearing—that of an intellectual accustomed to contemplation—who would have guessed that that man, frail and pensive in appearance, claimed the honor of the most dangerous missions, took charge of sabotage and daring assaults, wore grooves in the roads of the occupied zone with his bicycle?" asks Jacques Soustelle, who saw him in London, after first associating with him at the École Normale Supérieure.[35]

A few groups also worked to mobilize members of the working class, to draw them into the struggle and then sabotage the Relève. In July 1942, Combat assigned Marcel Degliame (Fouché, Dormoy), a former member of the CGTU and the PCF, the task of developing AO. Because of the connections it had established with the CGT and the SFIO, Libération-sud in particular was on the leading edge in that respect. The Political Action service, run by Jacques Brunschwig and later by Pascal Copeau, implanted itself in business ventures: it claimed to have between fifteen and eighteen thousand members in its professional cells in early October 1942.[36] The two services merged upon the founding of the MUR in 1943.

It should be added that all the movements set up social services, financed in part by monies received from Free France, to assist families who had been affected by the arrest of a loved one. Agnès Bidault took on that responsibility for Combat, Génia Gemähling for the DF.

In mid-1943, the movements could look back proudly at the progress they had made in less than three years. Having imposed an organizational structure on themselves, they had succeeded in expanding geographically, though the demarcation line that still separated the northern zone from the so-called free zone left its mark. Their field of action had also grown, as reflected by the increase in the number of branches. In December 1942, Combat had 102 paid employees, remunerated in part with money supplied by Jean Moulin and distributed among fourteen specialized services.[37] Franc-Tireur paid salaries to about 50 militants for the duration of the war.[38] The internal dynamic of the movements and their determination to adapt to the context also led them to broaden the range of their actions, as the example of false papers confirms. Before long, the forgery shops, which were originally intended to protect the militants, began to produce documents on a larger scale, to assist proscribed persons (Jews, dissidents, STO evaders) in fleeing their tormentors. Initially built up around one or two objectives—to inform public opinion, for example—the movements gradually embraced the full range from civilian resistance to armed struggle. The DF, which at first confined itself to distributing a newspaper, thus created a false papers shop, before agreeing to engage in more martial practices. Conversely, the CDLL, though reluctant to "play politics," decided not only to publish an underground newspaper from May 1943 onward but also to participate in the political process that de Gaulle set in motion in 1943 in preparation for liberation.

Qualms persisted, to be sure. The CDLR declined to create a newspaper and limited itself to distributing its *Bulletin*, which came out between spring 1943 and liberation in 1944, to members only. Likewise, Éditions de Minuit confined itself to publishing clandestine texts. Created in 1942 at the initiative of the writer Pierre de Lescure—who before the war had moved from Catholic and nationalist circles to leftist milieus—and Jean Bruller (Vercors), an illustrator trained in book production, the publishing house set out to assemble "the largest number possible of French writers with a worldwide reputation, to affirm the French spirit of resistance to Nazi domination," as Jacques Debû-Bridel, a member of the CNR and the Comité National des Écrivains (National Writers' Committee), recalls.[39] Above all, it sought to reconcile the contradictory demands weighing on men of letters: to resist, but without betraying the hopes of the prewar period or the rules of art.

In February 1942, the publication of its first opus, Vercors's *Le silence de la mer (The Silence of the Sea)*, amply fulfilled these aspirations. The message of that book, in fact, corresponded to the literary world's horizons of expectation. "The nonviolent attitude it extolled respected their pacifist propensities, a legacy of the 1930s. Nevertheless, *Le silence de la mer*, an underground publication, illustrates an oppositional attitude and is indisputably related to 'war literature,'" as historian Anne Simonin writes.[40] In depicting a father and daughter who, forced to lodge a cultivated German officer in their home, take refuge in silence, Vercors managed to get around two dead-ends. As Simonin points out, he "invented a mode of writing at the very moment when everyone agreed that belles-lettres were in a state of total collapse, and when the collaborationist press did not hesitate to attribute a 'share of responsibility for our disaster' to literature. In that context of military occupation, in the face of that orchestration of the impasse of French letters, *Le silence de la mer* offered a twofold hope: the possibility of an art that showed concern for humanity and that was also respectful of aesthetics. It proposed a model of *littérature engagée* that, though not perfect, was at least acceptable from a literary standpoint."[41] She adds: "Because it marked the advent of an underground publishing house, *Le silence de la mer* not only consecrated an attitude, it not only offered a model of *littérature engagée*, it was also an incitement to action, to the engagement of the writer."[42]

In all, fifty-one writers, including many stars in the firmament of letters (Louis Aragon, François Mauriac, Julien Benda) cooperated with Minuit, which brought out about twenty carefully edited volumes. *Le silence de la mer*, despite its influence—it met with success when it was published in England—had to face the ire of the Communists. Because it proposed a strategy antagonistic to the armed struggle that the PCF was defending, it was considered "a work of propaganda" and for that reason was violently attacked, all the more so because Fighting France showered it with praise.[43]

It is no exaggeration to say that versatility gained ground everywhere, and many resistance groups wishing to hasten the liberation sought to offer diverse modes of engagement. But did they achieve their aims?

## The Court of Public Opinion

As already noted, the movements had three goals, whether or not they formulated them consciously: to inform the public in the aim of ultimately mobilizing them; to protect civilians from the rigors of the occupation; and to facilitate militarily the victory of the Allies. In mid-1943, these three objectives were achieved in part—beginning with the first.

The movements influenced public opinion thanks to the spectacular development of their press. Professionalization of the printing process and organized distribution allowed them to attain print runs all the more impressive in that the scarcity of ink and paper, not to mention the repression, did not facilitate their task. The print run of *Franc-Tireur*, for example, jumped from 6,000 in December 1941 to 50,000 in January 1943, before reaching about 100,000 in September of the same year.[44] *Libération*-sud went from 20,000 copies per issue before September 1942 to an average ranging from 60,000 to 100,000 copies between December 1942 and July 1943, finally reaching between 120,000 and 150,000 copies between July 1943 and March 1944.[45] By 1942, *Combat* had a print run of 300,000 copies.[46] The same increase occurred in the northern zone. Although *Libération*-nord remained at a relatively modest level (50,000 copies in 1942), *Défense de la France* enjoyed remarkable success, surpassing 100,000 copies in 1943 and, for its issue of January 15, 1944, attaining a print run of 450,000—a record unmatched in the annals of the occupation.[47]

These figures, however, do not allow us to gauge the real impact of the underground press on public opinion. The voice of the BBC was no doubt more forceful, since millions of French people listened to it religiously. It also had a wider impact; in instantly reaching everyone, it unified the population. Finally, it was faster, since the airwaves were able to immediately announce news that the underground press, captive to its twice-monthly (at best) publication schedule, circulated more slowly. The leaders of the movements quickly realized that they could not rival the BBC or the Swiss airwaves in the area of information. They therefore opted for complementarity rather than competition.[48] The proportion devoted to news tended to decrease: military news occupied only 10 percent of column space in *Défense de la France* between August 1941 and October 1942[49] and disappeared altogether with the twelfth issue. By contrast, the underground press provided information that the radio stations could not or would not broadcast. For example, it was able to show photographs of General de Gaulle to the French people, who knew his voice but not his face. In November–December 1942, moreover, de Gaulle was taken off the air[50] to prevent his comments from interfering with the Anglo-American strategy in North Africa. And in May 1943, the BBC refused to air Jacques

Soustelle's press release announcing the creation of the CNR, which made it clear that the internal resistance was refusing to subordinate the man of June 18 to Giraud.[51] The underground press was quick to relay that news. It clearly took de Gaulle's side and kept quiet about some of its writers' reservations concerning the general. Likewise, it explained the ins and outs of the Algiers imbroglio to a French public largely uninformed on the matter. In fact, both media developed that complementarity. Newspapers regularly mentioned the wavelengths of the different radio stations,[52] while the French broadcasts provided voices from captive France to a wide audience.[53]

Rather than put their money on news, then, the underground newspapers took on the role of an opinion press. The gradual clarification of their ideology served that aim. Whereas some—whether for tactical reasons or out of ideological complicity—had avoided frontal attacks on the Vichy regime and the victor of Verdun, as of 1941 in some cases and 1942 in others, their criticism became relentless. Forthrightly evoking the Marshal's venerable age, they demythologized his role during World War I and recalled his defeatism. *La France continue* noted, for example: "In 1916, he wanted to evacuate Verdun, which was saved solely by Joffre's will; he wanted to abandon the English and to order the withdrawal of our troops in spring 1918; on March 27, he requested the opening of peace talks."[54] "Pétain has never stopped betraying. He is not a senile old man, he is a witting traitor," concluded *Franc-Tireur.*[55] Conversely, the resistance newspapers rallied behind de Gaulle and marginalized his rival Giraud. "The resistance fighters do not understand that, for the French, de Gaulle is not an undisputed leader," the OCM noted sharply in September 1943.[56] Such political clarification no doubt consolidated the audience that the underground newspapers enjoyed. The resistance now embodied a clear political alternative, especially since its message resonated with the aspirations of the public, hostile to collaboration and to the ideological orientations of Vichy. Yet the French people, though they increasingly put their faith in General de Gaulle, sometimes maintained their respect for the person of Marshal Pétain.

The underground press was heeded all the more in that it usually avoided misrepresenting the facts. Granted, it did not altogether avoid certain exaggerations. In August 1942, *Combat* claimed to have "tens of thousands of Frenchmen and Frenchwomen" in its "civilian army."[57]

*Franc-Tireur* compared Lyon and Paris to "those Balkan villages in a state of permanent riot, perpetually plotting, where the overwhelmed police pursue investigations, conduct raids, carry out searches, and make arrests without ever putting an end to that underground mobilization, to that plotting without end."[58] At that date, May 6, 1944, such a statement attested to a robust optimism. On the whole, however, the movements' newspapers showed caution. They avoided lapsing into triumphalism and spreading false news, at least in part making a virtue of necessity.

True, their credibility was at stake. The underground press could not too visibly distance itself from the BBC, which, in its effort to gain followers, had as early as 1940 refused to lapse into overblown propaganda. Resistance fighters rejected the brainwashing associated with World War I, which they remembered with deep dismay. Furthermore, the desire to tell the truth whenever possible was part of two cultures to which the bulk of the internal resistance belonged. In the first place, the republican model had insisted on citizen education and had denounced hypocrisy and lying on moral grounds. The republic wanted to convince, not to indoctrinate, and some of the movements subscribed to that principle. In addition, Christianity equated the victory of Christ with the triumph of Truth, a legacy that certain underground groups meant to carry on. Telling the truth was therefore an urgent obligation, especially since the French State and the Nazi regime were shamelessly lying. And a truthful discourse could also prove profitable. "Although a lie reproduced in millions of copies retains a certain power, it is enough at least that the truth be spoken for the lie to recede," noted *Combat* in March 1944.[59] In all, strategic imperatives and political cultures came together to reject the excesses of propaganda, even though the movements had no fear of being disbelieved. The internal resistance knew it would be understood, inasmuch as its members by the thousands were taking considerable risks: their courage and sacrifices validated its word. "I believe only those stories whose witnesses would be willing to be slaughtered"—Blaise Pascal's statement, used as a motto for *Défense de la France*, had the value of a pledge.

The underground press, moving away from a purely informative approach and assuming its role as an opinion press, also set out its postwar plans. In debating the future of France, it revived democratic debate, which had been stifled by the Reich and its Vichy ally, all the while popularizing themes—from the nationalization of industries to Sécurité Sociale (Social Security)—that would organize public debate in the second half of the twentieth century.

These elements suggest that the underground press was indisputably listened to—but was it heard? Although it is difficult, not to say impossible, to answer that question, a few hypotheses may be ventured.

In the first place, the underground press played a role in delegitimizing the French State by providing its readers with arguments that formalized in ideological terms the population's reaction against collaboration and Vichy policy. In popularizing the figure of General de Gaulle and in laying out the major reforms that the country ought to undertake upon liberation, it also presented a credible and reassuring political alternative, which guaranteed that the country, once rid of a despised regime and occupier, would not fall into anarchy or chaos. In disseminating instructions for action, in particular by calling on readers to reject the STO and to join the maquis, the resistance newspapers also assigned individuals concrete objectives capable of mobilizing them. And because its distributors were in contact with the French people, the underground press provided willing individuals direct access to the movements, facilitating enlistment. It therefore opened down-to-earth and accessible prospects for engagement to thousands of people whose only qualification was their dedication.

That capacity to mobilize should not be overestimated, however. Granted, the occupier ultimately failed in his efforts to recruit for the STO. But it is difficult to credit that failure exclusively to the underground press, since the BBC also called on people to refuse to subject themselves to forced labor, which thousands of French young people wanted to evade in any event. Similarly, the demonstrations on July 14, 1942, were a success more thanks to the appeals launched over the Gaullist airwaves than because of the mobilization—limited all in all—of the resistance newspapers.[60] On the whole, then, the underground papers played an important role in recruiting volunteers, delegitimizing the French State, and consolidating consensus around the resistance and General de Gaulle, but they were far from the only architects of that success. The political parties also contributed to it, as far as their resources allowed.

## A Socialist Revival?

The political parties, discredited by the defeat and by the scuttling of the Third Republic, had remained listless until 1941. But under the leadership of Daniel Mayer, the SFIO gradually reformed itself, reconstituting its organization and restoring its image thanks to the energetic defense put on by Léon Blum at the trial in Riom. In December 1942, the party already counted about 28,000 members, a number that rose to perhaps 50,000 by 1943.[61] The CAS, unlike its Communist rival, refused to create a vassal movement, concerning itself primarily with action at the political level. In the short term, it sought to distance itself from the few Socialists tempted to collaborate or to support the Vichy regime, and to that end undertook a vigorous purge. In the medium term, it intended to play a prominent role in liberated France, thanks to restored structures and a renovated program. Hence the party "established an artificial division of action [and] gave precedence to the modes of intervention most closely associated with its traditional activities" but refused "to sabotage or harass the enemy."[62]

In view of that aim, the CAS set about clarifying its doctrine. It argued for government intervention in the economy, while hesitating both on type (nationalization or full state control [*étatisation*]?) and on scope (should the banking sector be included or not?). Furthermore, it demanded reform of the constitutional framework and recommended a de facto unicameralism, a reduction of presidential power, and a proportional system of representation. At the diplomatic level, it suggested rejoining the League of Nations, which the establishment of a true decision-making power would allow France to improve.[63] These themes were not new, of course: the underground SFIO confined itself to updating measures the SFIO had advocated during the interwar period, without undertaking a doctrinal renewal. Unlike in the 1920s, however, it abandoned the lofty heights of idealism: it agreed to take up themes previously barred by the neo-Socialists, and above all, to consider itself a government party.[64]

To disseminate its ideas, the CAS relied on its underground press, despite its difficult beginnings. In the north, *Socialisme et Liberté*, a modest newssheet published in December 1941, was at first its only standard bearer. But the CAS later managed to revive *Le Populaire*: the first issue came out in the southern zone on May 15, 1942, and *Social-isme et Liberté* soon became its northern edition. A few titles *(Le Popu-laire du Centre, L'Espoir de Provence)* completed at the regional level that national deployment. On the strength of the some 150,000 copies it dis-tributed in 1944 (including 95,000 copies of *Le Populaire*), the press assured the SFIO a growing audience.[65] It thus participated in delegiti-mizing the Vichy regime and shored up democratic debate by guaran-teeing socialist themes a certain visibility, though this was partly obscured by the trying conditions of the underground. A few clouds darkened the future, however, and prevented the SFIO from ap-proaching liberation in serenity.

In the first place, the underground SFIO had a complicated rela-tionship with the resistance movements. While hailing the part they were playing in the struggle, it denied them the right to a political role after the war, a mission that, it said, fell to the parties. Léon Blum wrote with the utmost firmness to General de Gaulle in March 1943: "Un-derstand very clearly, I beg of you, that the resistance organizations that have emerged on French soil at the sound of your voice will be unable to take the place of [the parties] to any degree. When France has re-covered its sovereignty, when stability has been restored, the usefulness of these organizations will be exhausted. . . . As far as I'm concerned, I would see nothing but dangers if the resistance organizations, once the task for which they were created has been accomplished, were to sur-vive in their current form. Either syndicates of outdated and selfish in-terests such as the veterans associations of the last war or paramilitary militias, an object of dread for any republic: such would be nearly the only choices open to them."[66]

The movements, taking the opposite tack, regarded the parties harshly. They are "discredited, because all without exception, after jeal-ously maintaining unity on minor problems, divided on the one truly vital question: French resistance or abdication. Let us keep them from spewing their old poison," admonished the *Cahiers politiques* in August 1943.[67] The movements thus aspired to supplant groups discredited by incompetence and dreamed of reshaping the political field upon liber-ation. The war, they noted, had made it possible to separate the wheat from the chaff. The parties were distinguished by their absence in the army of shadows, while the movements, having surged up out of nowhere, had brought to the fore an elite whose courage, they said, made it worthy of seizing the reins of power when the time came.

In addition, the resistance fighters were constructing a new political reality. They had proved they were able to bring about national union because, they claimed, they had integrated individuals from every background, transcending the sterile divisions of the past. The resistance newspaper *Libérer et Fédérer* thus wanted "a new, young, and popular movement arising from the ordeal and from hope ... which would assemble the bulk of those who until now have remained outside any movement, workers and farmers, manual laborers and intellectuals, former militants and members of no political party, Catholics and free thinkers."[68] Although certain movements had at first refused to become involved in politics, the dynamic set in motion by Free France ultimately doomed that abstention policy. Free France surveyed the underground groups about the men who should lead the country upon liberation and about the reforms to be undertaken. In doing so, it required them to choose. If they abstained, they would be favoring the return of the old parties—an appalling prospect in their eyes. The movements had only one option, therefore: to enter the arena.

This political awakening led some movements to enter into conflict with the SFIO. Combat, Franc-Tireur, Libération-sud, and others were in fact fighting over the same ground as the Socialists, never imagining they could venture into preserves that, they thought, the PCF had well in hand. An aggravating circumstance: for better or for worse, they all defended the same political orientations, in brief, a democratic socialism. Rivals as much as partners, they therefore tended to deny one another the right to exist,[69] which could only increase the tensions within the internal resistance.

The SFIO also had a complicated relationship with Free France and General de Gaulle. It is true that, in 1942, Léon Blum had made his decision and called for his followers to support without hesitation the man of June 18. He had sent Félix Gouin as a delegate to the general to assure him of his (Blum's) support and to facilitate ties between the Socialists and the Gaullist camp. The deputy from Bouches-du-Rhône was given the task of overcoming the intransigence of the Jean-Jaurès circle in London. For though Socialism rallied unconditionally behind Gaullism, Socialists did not, at least until 1943.

## Evolution of the French Communist Party

The PCF also grew stronger in the first half of 1943. At the impetus of Auguste Lecoeur, regional secretary for Nord-Pas-de-Calais before the war, it adopted a more organized structure and codified strict rules of security. Lecoeur prohibited meetings in public places and increased compartmentalization, not hesitating to have leaders tailed in order to denounce their carelessness. "From that moment on, the militant had to make sure that he was not being followed or watched. Increasingly, meetings would take place in the countryside, obliging militants to travel long distances on foot or by bicycle to the areas around Paris. In addition, compartmentalization increased: no more overlapping assignments, no more militants responsible for multiple sectors," writes historian Stéphane Courtois.[70] Despite the downfall in early 1943 of Pierre Brossard, head of cadres, who was living under his own identity and from whose home the French police seized a trunk containing the life histories of several hundred leaders,[71] the apparatus subsequently remained intact overall until liberation.

Having regained part of its power, the PCF maintained complex, predominantly hostile relations with the other resistance groups. In 1942 it had established ties with Free France, but it avoided making a choice in the war of the kepis, giving equal weight to de Gaulle and Giraud. Similarly, it kept its distance from the CAS. Denouncing its watch-and-wait attitude, it rejected the FP strategy that its rival was proposing, preferring to support "a national conception," which led it to "broaden the struggle to every stratum of the population opposed to collaboration and the Vichy government."[72] In marginalizing the SFIO, it hoped to ensure its monopoly over working-class and leftist representation within the alliance with the so-called bourgeois resistance.

That strategy granted a key role to the FN. Less rigid than the PCF, it claimed to welcome all French political orientations. Its steering committees, formed in the north in February 1943, in the south in March of that year, included personalities from the most varied backgrounds. Hence Georges Bidault (Combat), Yves Farge (Franc-Tireur), Louis Martin-Chauffier (Libération-sud), Michel Zunino (dissident SFIO), and Justin Godart (Radical Party) sat on the committee in the southern zone. Its leader, Pierre Villon, explained: "I made every effort to find men of unquestionable merit, of a quality that was so to speak national, representing every opinion, to really reflect national unanimity, in order to express their common will in directives to the entire Front National and, beyond it, to all French people."[73]

On the strength of the diversity it embodied, the FN aspired to take charge of underground actions in metropolitan France. In January 1943, Fernand Grenier suggested that a "national committee of Fighting France (delegation in France)," an offshoot of the FN, should coordinate the resistance groups of captive France,[74] an idea adopted in a manifesto of April 1943: "The Front National collaborates with all the resistance movements in each of the zones and, at the same time, with the national committee in London under General de Gaulle's authority and General Giraud's forces. The Front National seeks the union of all the resistance movements, whatever designation they may adopt, into a single large cluster of national liberation forces under a single leadership."[75] The PCF was thus banking on a division of labor: Giraud or de Gaulle would be in charge of external operations, and the FN would be in command of actions in the metropolis. On February 5, 1943, L'Humanité, combining words and actions, launched the slogan "Unite, Arm, Fight" and called for the constitution "everywhere of Front National committees comprising all patriots." Yet the FN, even while declaring its openness, was merely an outgrowth of the PCF. Hence, in Var, "it exists only where the PCF exists and only because some of its militants dedicated themselves to its creation."[76]

The PCF also intensified its union activism, its ardor all the more pronounced in that the armed struggle it advocated was sometimes unpopular and cut it off from the population. In addition, these activities decimated its cadres, though protest actions also allowed it to promote new elites. Furthermore, the fight against the STO had tended to be the prerogative of the movements, which were on the leading edge in constituting the maquis. That undercut the monopoly that the party claimed to have on the working class.[77] All these factors incited the PCF to take action. On the one hand, it militated for the reunification of the CGT, which had been divided since the German-Soviet Pact of 1939. Negotiations opened in January 1943, but came to a standstill as a result of the changes occasioned by the context. A number of leaders were in hiding, others had been interned, while still others were putting their money on legal action, all of which complicated the process. But on April 17, 1943, the Le Perreux accords sealed the reunification of the two branches of the CGT. It was not until August 1943, however, that an underground labor bureau was in operation.[78]

The PCF and its satellite organizations also encouraged protest actions. They demanded pay raises and a better resupply system and encouraged the movements seeking to sabotage the STO. On March 18, 1943, for example, they launched a strike at the Vermorel factory in Villefranche-sur-Saône. Hence, as Jean-Marie Guillon points out, "the Communists fed off discontent but knew how to give it a form of expression, to offer it prospects, to make themselves the spokesmen for the workers, which neither the official union activists nor the Socialists knew how or were able to do."[79] He adds: "By means of mass actions, the Communists resituated and reactivated the social struggle within the framework of the national struggle."[80]

The PCF, finally, worked hard to popularize its watchwords by developing a powerful underground press. *L'Humanité*, for example, brought out 383 issues prior to the liberation of the capital. It sometimes produced regional variants of its Paris version and probably had a print run of about 200,000.[81] Likewise, the FTP in the northern zone set up an organ of the press, *France d'abord*, 62 issues of which were published between January 1942 and 1944.[82] More specialized periodicals complemented these offerings. *La Pensée libre*, a ninety-six-page magazine for intellectuals launched by Jacques Decour, Georges Politzer, and Jacques Solomon in February 1941, vanished with its founders' deaths, but *Les Lettres françaises* succeeded it in September 1942.[83] *La vie ouvrière*, an organ of the CGT, survived throughout the dark years; its two editions—one in each zone—amounted to 230 issues between August 1940 and 1944.[84] The party also strove to create a regional press. The FN, for example, published *Le Pays Gallo* in Brittany, which the unified printing works printed up in Fougères and Rennes.[85] The PCF and its associated groups, in managing to express its ideas in the midst of the occupation, also played a role in fueling political debate, even if that meant polarizing it. That tactic sparked the distrust of certain groups, Combat above all.

Not all the movements of the internal resistance shared Frenay's visceral and often passionate anti-Communism. But some Communists had secured solid positions within Libération-sud, and that fueled suspicion both during and after the war. Had these militants cut the strings that attached them to their former party, or were they practicing infiltration? Those in question, Pierre Hervé, for example, always said they remained autonomous vis-à-vis the PCF. He declared in the 1970s: "'Valrimont' [Maurice Kriegel] and 'Joinville' [Alfred Malleret], conducting their actions to attract the notice of the Party, wanted to 'organize' us, enlist us, and place us directly under the Party leadership. Many hesitations arose for the Aubracs and for me. 'Joinville' became the Party's intermediary, so there was an internal conflict, a covert struggle. We were not registered members of the Party. We believed its position within the Resistance was good, but inside the movement we believed that we had to be allowed to act effectively and freely. That meant there were a few meetings with 'Valrimont,' 'Joinville,' Aubrac, and me. After that, the intrigues of 'Valrimont' and 'Joinville' eventually led me to take my distance. I thus left for Toulouse."[86]

That version hardly corresponds to the reality, however. Documents used by historian Daniel Virieux demonstrate that several Communist leaders in Libération-sud remained in contact with the PCF during the dark years. A note from Georges Marrane, creator of the FN in the southern zone, specifies that "it is 1 [Raymond Aubrac] who brought 2 [Pierre Hervé] into Libération and put him in charge of C [Toulouse]. In C, we already had friends, including 2 [Maurice Rousselier], 3 [Jean-Pierre Vernant], 4 [Victor Leduc]."[87] Another report recalls that, in November or December 1940, Lucie Aubrac had asked for "contact with the Party. In agreement with 21 [Victor Michaut] and the cadres, she abandons her trip [to the United States, where she had the opportunity to go], and I use her with her husband in the propaganda apparatus. . . . During these eighteen months of absence, she tells me that, with her husband, they had become, in agreement with the Party, leaders in Libération. Hence, she could put me in contact with the Party."[88] Pierre Hervé also said in May 1943: "Now that we have 2 heads of unified regions and the assistant to the head of political affairs who are T [Communists], and now that, if you can provide us with men, we will have one or two others, we can influence the political line taken by the Resistance. Will we take no interest in it? . . . I think that would not be taking advantage of the possibilities being offered us."[89] "On the subject of our friend, member of the steering committee in the MUR, the documents he has transmitted to us are interesting, and I would like to know whether, in modifying them a little, it would be possible to use certain information without blowing his cover," wrote Jacques Duclos to Pierre Villon. He concluded: "As for control of that guy [Pierre Hervé] . . . I think you can control him yourself, and he will have to consider you his Party leader, with whom he must work and to whom he must be accountable."[90]

Despite their denials during and after the war, some leaders suspected of philo-Communism thus maintained relations with the PCF under the occupation. Certain historians have underestimated the effects of these elements. Laurent Douzou argues: "Leaders with a Communist past were 'kept in line' by the PCF, to which they transmitted reports, at least as of 1943, [but] the content of the few texts leaked from the archives held by the PCF suggests that their connections to the Communist apparatus were not extremely close. Based on the current state of the sources, the thesis of Communist infiltration reflects less the reality of things than the force of the ideological struggles for which the history of the Resistance has been the battlefield, beginning in the underground period and since Liberation."[91]

That dual membership remains problematic, however. At the level of morality, to which resistance fighters attached the highest importance, the dissimulation deceived men and women who granted their comrades in arms their full and complete confidence. From the political standpoint, it could create conflicts of loyalty. For if the aims of the movements were at odds with those of the PCF, the philo-Communists ran the risk of giving precedence to the PCF and of secretly undermining the positions their movement was defending. Of course, the ties between the Communist leadership and the comrades engaged in the resistance groups were tenuous, especially given the constraints dictated by life underground. But these men, most of them well-tested militants, had no need for precise instructions about "working toward the Party," to parody the expression that historian Ian Kershaw applied to the Führer. These maneuvers, in any event, increased tensions between the movements and the Communist sphere.

Many men within the internal resistance cultivated a profound anti-Communism before the war, which was further fed by the German-Soviet Pact and the line followed by the PCF between 1939 and 1941.

Their hostility was above all ideological: rejecting Marxist-Leninism and dialectical materialism, they also condemned Stalinist totalitarianism. The PCF's alignment with the positions defended by Moscow also fueled suspicion. "We have not forgotten the past attitude of the French Communists, or rather, their attitudes, since they changed as often as the twists and turns of Stalin's tortuous policy required," *Franc-Tireur* noted in February 1942.[92] The strategy chosen, in short, gave rise to profound disagreements. In addition to condemning the attacks against the occupation forces, the movements refused to be placed under the supervision of the FN, which, especially in the southern zone, had at most modest battalions lined up in 1942 and even 1943.

Nevertheless, more genial feelings gradually reduced that animosity. The feats of the Red Army sparked admiration. The dynamism and the spirit of sacrifice of the Communist fighters prompted the underground press to hail them. "Your martyrs, Communist comrades, are our own, they are those of France as a whole," wrote *Libération*-sud in July 1943, for example.[93] Some groups also argued for cooperation with the PCF in the name of realism, so as to strengthen the effectiveness of the underground struggle. And a few hoped that the Communists, once integrated into a national union, would serve the cause of social progress without seeking to impose their dogma by force of arms. All in all, as historian Henri Michel summarizes it, "the movements felt a profound need to cooperate with the Communist Party in the Resistance; without it, the common struggle would be missing part of the working-class forces; independent of it, the resistance struggle would suffer from a lack of coordination. But they had contradictory feelings toward the Communist Party: superiority by virtue of anteriority but also admiration combined with fear. . . . They admired the courage, the organization, the know-how of the Communists; they feared their political objectives upon Liberation."[94]

All things considered, the development of the movements and the rebirth of the SFIO and the PCF restored a hidden democratic political life that, at the risk of clashes, debated the shape that the postwar period would take. That dynamic also made it possible to influence public opinion, by showing that a changing of the political guard was being planned during the dark years. That process did not go smoothly, however. It created tensions at the top, between parties and movements with different visions of the postwar period. They often acted as rivals, even adversaries, rather than as partners. It also raised the crucial question of the relationship between London and the metropolitan groups, a decisive issue complicated by the Gaullist camp's constant perplexity about the operational capacities of the internal resistance.

## Operational Capacity

More than ever, the movements sought to act militarily. In addition to their irregular groups, they had devoted members spread across entire regions, which allowed them to organize their actions around three priorities: intelligence, sabotage, and the exfiltration of Allied combatants—airmen shot down in France, for example.

The movements developed their intelligence activities at different rates. Pierre Arrighi fairly early on collected information for the CDLR on the German presence in the Paris region. In March 1943, René Duchez, a house painter working for the OCM, stole from the offices of the German military headquarters he was repainting the blueprint for the fortifications to be built in Calvados.[95] Pierre Bernard (Le Kid, Robin), head of an irregular group for the DF in Brittany, distributed topographical maps to his men, so that they could record the enemy installations they spotted. Militants from Franc-Tireur transmitted the plans of the airfields and mobile bridges that the Germans had installed in the Valence region. And in Var, as in other departments, a service of the FTP, which formed in the second half of 1942, communicated military intelligence to the Allies.

Underground groups also embarked on sabotage, giving preference to economic targets (factories and arsenals) and railroads. In July 1943, Arrighi, then one of the leaders of the CDLR, along with a small team, set out to paralyze the Amiot factories at Colombes, which were manufacturing Junker airplanes for the Luftwaffe. "But the saboteurs were novices, and not all the explosives went off, having been clumsily primed. The fire that broke out was quickly brought under control," historian Marie Granet writes.[96] In Burgundy, Courvoisier, regional head of the OCM, organized a railway sabotage in summer 1943 that killed twenty-six in the German ranks and wounded about sixty.[97] On the night of July 9, the FTP unbolted rails in Noyal-Vilaine, in the Ille-et-Vilaine department. A train loaded with soldiers on leave derailed and was then hit by another train, which increased the number of casualties: eight dead, thirty seriously injured, and several slightly injured. In all, the reports of the gendarmerie listed five railway sabotages in that department between August 7 and 22, 1943.[98]

But railway traffic was by no means the sole objective. On February 17, 1943, the Lyon teams of Franc-Tireur destroyed two Gestapo goniometric vehicles, which were locating transreceivers belonging to the resistance. The same month, Roger Crivelli managed to blow up twenty-three engineering trucks loaded on train cars parked at the Roanne station, despite the German guards standing watch. Crivelli, a twenty-three-year-old cement worker, was single-minded in his approach. While working at France-Rayonne, he distinguished himself on November 11, 1942, by flying an enormous tricolor flag atop the factory's chimney.[99] Georges Guingouin's men also took action. On May 8, 1943, they sabotaged the Wattelez factory in Le Palais-sur-Vienne, which specialized in the regeneration of rubber.[100]

The movements also engaged in direct attacks. The Communists, for example, waged assaults on the occupation troops. On August 5, 1942, the FTP-MOI threw a hand grenade into a group of Luftwaffe soldiers training at Jean-Bouin Stadium in Paris, causing eight deaths.[101] On August 8, 1942, five Germans were wounded in an attack targeting the Hôtel Bedford, which housed several services of the occupation authorities.[102] In Brittany, the FTP also went on the offensive in the second quarter of 1942 and in early 1943, waging multiple attacks with explosives against buildings occupied by Germans in Quimper and Brest, then in Saint-Brieuc and Guingamp.[103] And thirty-six actions were conducted in late 1943 by the four units of the FTP-MOI in Paris, fifteen of them by the Jewish unit.[104] But not all the attempts were crowned with success: on May 28, 1943, the regional Commissariat aux Questions Juives (Commission on Jewish Questions) in Rennes succeeded in defusing a bomb sent through the mail. And on September 4, 1943, a team of the FTP attempted in vain to take down the divisional superintendent of Renseignements Généraux (RG; General Intelligence) in Vieux-Vy-sur-Couësnon (Ille-et-Vilaine department) and was immediately arrested.[105]

The resistance thus increased the number of its actions, though the case should not be overstated: in many regions and in many movements, the armed struggle remained if not marginal then at least a minority phenomenon. It grew nonetheless. As of 1943, notes Jean-Marie Guillon, the armed struggle "took root as the preeminent form of action to be waged or planned, even though, until shortly before liberation, it was not in fact the paramount activity of most resistance fighters."[106] The resistance thus took a more martial turn, as confirmed by the example of Var. The army of shadows conducted fourteen actions a month before November 11, 1942, but forty-seven a month in the following years; 54 percent of the acts of resistance occurred between November 11, 1942, and June 6, 1944. And though propaganda represented 74 percent of subversive activity before the invasion of the free zone, it decreased at that time to 38 percent, while direct action leapt from 2.8 percent to 42.8 percent between the two periods.[107] In all, 230 attacks and sabotage operations had occurred in the Provençal department by June 6, 1944. Economic targets in the broad sense (mines, arsenals) made up the lion's share (31 percent), followed by railroads (30 percent) and attacks against places frequented by the occupier (23.5 percent).[108]

Attacks against people remained the exception rather than the rule, however. In the Seine department, twenty-five Germans were killed between June 22, 1941, and December 31, 1942.[109] But "despite these attacks, and the illusions and legends that were spread after the war, despite what may have been written and read on the subject, Paris remained a haven of peace for German soldiers, who, only too happy to escape the eastern front, stayed there in complete tranquility."[110] Similarly, though the occupation armies in Var were more frequently targeted than collaborators (65 percent of the attacks against persons), these assaults produced only a dozen victims, with the collaboration camp recording nine dead or wounded.[111] Indeed, the resistance fighters sometimes preferred French targets to German objectives. Of the 138 attacks counted by the prefect of Haute-Saône in October–November 1943, only 12 were directed against the German army. And of eight murders committed in those same two months, only three were motivated by patriotism. In Vanne (Haute-Saône department), for example, two resistance fighters executed a couple of retired farmers "for reasons unrelated to the Resistance."[112] The statistics must not mislead us: the chaff was sometimes mixed in with the wheat.

In any case, the transition to a form of armed struggle encountered serious obstacles. In captive France, the lack of arms and explosives kept the movements in check, and the difficulty of liaisons with London prevented them from transmitting under good conditions intelligence collected in the field. On the other side of the Channel, Free France, while hailing these initiatives, sometimes deplored their anarchical development and demanded that they be integrated into an overall military strategy. Let us wager that General de Gaulle's services, in rationalizing these actions, counted on reaping the benefits to increase the Rebel's legitimacy in the eyes of London and Washington.

In other words, everything militated in favor of coordination. The BCRA undertook to make it a reality.

# Chapter 10

# The Long Road to Unity

In early 1943, Fighting France set out to unify the internal resistance. The prospect of a landing incited it to place resistance troops in battle, insert them into the Allies' strategic plan of action, and obtain the arms necessary to carry out the missions that would be entrusted to them. At the same time, the need to thwart General Giraud's political aspirations obliged Fighting France to mobilize support in captive France that would allow General de Gaulle to strengthen his legitimacy in the eyes of the Allies. That dual imperative impelled de Gaulle to send emissaries to the metropolis to hasten what was now an essential union. These missions were undertaken in part by Colonel Passy's secret services, which endeavored first to reorganize the networks' activities.

## Professionalizing the Networks

Since its first faltering steps in 1940, the BCRA had gained real experience. Its networks now supplied the Allies with a bounty of intelligence. The BCRA had received 920 telegrams in 1942; 3,000 were delivered to it the next year. And the mail it received increased just as significantly, from 42 to 167 pieces in the same period.[1]

Even while developing its own networks, the BCRA sought primarily to rationalize and professionalize the actions of the internal resistance movements. Two obstacles stood in its way. First, the unpredictability of liaisons with Britain prevented the BCRA from communicating the intelligence collected and from receiving arms, money, and materiel. Second, because their fields of activities had both a civilian and a military aspect, the underground groups, inadequately compartmentalized, proved to be vulnerable to the repressive forces. This threatened the position of Fighting France, whose credit rested largely on its capacity to provide the Allies with intelligence to be used in waging the war.

The BCRA therefore strove to improve transmissions between Free France and captive France. For the southern zone, it considered sending sixteen operators, each equipped with three radios, one of which would be specifically dedicated to the movements. Nothing came of the idea, however, for lack of qualified personnel. Combat, Franc-Tireur, and Libération-sud therefore continued to rely on the men London had dispatched to establish liaisons, until the creation of the CC made that presence unnecessary. In November 1942, Fassin, Schmidt, and Monjaret created the SOAM, charged with seeking out and approving landing areas for agents dispatched to France or exfiltrated to England. A patrol boat, fishing boat, or even submarine was then sent out by night to Langrune (Côtes-du-Nord), Douarnenez (Finistère), or Plouha (Côtes-du-Nord). By means of a dinghy, the men would reach the craft, located between 460 and 2,600 feet off the coast, and then immediately set off.

The SOAM also identified landing fields and parachute drop sites. As a general rule, either its agents or local resistance fighters would scout their region to find the appropriate place. The site had to be away from the cities and major traffic routes, out in the open, and easy to spot by RAF pilots. The field was then identified on a Michelin map and its location transmitted to London, which decided whether or not to approve it. If approved, the site received a code name. A message sent over the BBC announced to resistance fighters that an operation would take place the following night. A letter, transmitted in Morse code by a light signal, indicated to the pilot that the ground team was ready to receive the agents or containers.[2] Several dozen fields were approved in this way, but not all were used. In January 1943, the SOAM became the Centre d'Opérations de Parachutages et d'Atterrissages (COPA; Center for Parachute and Landing Operations), still under the authority of Jean Moulin.[3]

The north, by contrast, remained uncharted territory, though Colonel Rémy, in his personal style, established contacts between Free France and the occupied zone. Having returned to France in October 1942, Rémy was given the assignment of setting up an État-major pour la Zone Occupée (EMZO; General Staff for the Occupied Zone). He recommended relying on the OCM and suggested naming one of its leaders, Colonel Touny, to be in charge of the EMZO. That proposal was unacceptable to the BCRA and to General de Gaulle. In essence, it amounted to ensuring a hegemonic position to one movement, the OCM, contrary to the unification policy favored by London.[4] It also threatened the Gaullist camp's dream of a merger among paramilitary groups: the movements would certainly have refused to place their troops under the command of a rival group. In short, "the OCM was demanding nothing less than the monopoly on Gaullist representation in France," a particularly exorbitant demand, inasmuch as Touny openly declared Giraudist sentiments.[5]

Rémy had exacerbated the situation by continuing to negotiate with the PCF, in defiance of instructions and without informing his chain of command. Impressed by "the guts, ideals, and spirit of sacrifice of its troops,"[6] the political neophyte met with Fernand Grenier on November 28, 1942, and managed to take him back to London on January 11, 1943. Although the official adherence of the PCF considerably reinforced General de Gaulle's prestige,[7] the rapprochement between Fighting France and the party rested on shaky foundations, particularly since it gave the advantage to the PCF without binding it to the Gaullist camp.

## The Brumaire-Arquebuse Mission

These botched initiatives led the BCRA to retake control. It therefore dispatched two prominent emissaries to the metropolis in early 1943. Pierre Brossolette (Brumaire) was supposed to:

1. Proceed, in the ZO [occupied zone], to the strictest separation possible between everything having to do with intelligence on the one hand, and, on the other, with civilian and military action.
2. Proceed to the inventory of all the forces that . . . can play a role in the national uprising in view of Liberation. . . .
3. Seek out . . . the cadres for a provisional administration of the ZO on the day of Liberation.[8]

Three objectives were also assigned to Colonel Passy (Arquebuse):

a) he will determine the measures to be taken regarding the rationalization of operations of the different intelligence networks;

b) he will enter into contact with all the Resistance groups in the Z.O., in order to coordinate military action within the Z.O. and between the two zones;

c) he will study the conditions under which the constitution of a central steering committee charged with resolving all civilian questions might go forward.[9]

The Brumaire-Arquebuse mission thus combined a military dimension (to separate intelligence work in the movements from civilian and military activities) and a political dimension (to choose the future administrators of liberated France and form a central steering committee in charge of civilian questions). Passy was responsible for "conversations relating to questions of military action or intelligence"; Brossolette for "all discussions dealing with political action."[10]

These objectives bore within them the seeds of conflict. In 1942 Jean Moulin had done some of the groundwork in the northern zone, thanks especially to Henri Manhès, whom he had known before the war and dispatched to the north as his delegate. But de Gaulle had not defined which zone ought to fall to Moulin and which to Brossolette, even though the two men were secretly in competition. Brossolette, who considered the northern zone his "preserve,"[11] could not fail to take a dim view of Moulin's intrusion on his lands. Nevertheless, it would be "wrong to believe that the two were motivated by the trivial aim of claiming their turf: at the time, the Resistance was as yet nothing but a high-risk adventure, as the common fate of these two men so ominously demonstrated."[12] More fundamental differences intensified that personal rivalry: Moulin, observing the revival of the political parties in captive France, was thinking about ways to link them to Fighting France; Brossolette, by contrast, was hostile to them.

Everything, therefore, was impelling Brossolette to act quickly, before Moulin set his sights on the northern zone. He militated for Passy to be dispatched to the metropolis, to ensure himself strong support; and he set off without waiting for Moulin to return to Britain, a sign that he preferred to have a free hand rather than discuss with his rival the plan to be applied, and in General de Gaulle's presence. Brumaire thus arrived by Lysander on the night of January 26, 1943; Arquebuse parachuted into France on the night of February 26. As the latter re-called: "I went in to say my goodbyes to General de Gaulle, who, after giving me his final instructions, shook my hand and said: 'Try not to get caught!' 'I'll try, General,' I replied; and I left, fortified by that comforting viaticum."[13]

In compliance with the orders they had received, the two men sought, in the first place, to separate as completely as possible the intelligence networks from the action organizations, to create new intelligence networks, and to establish their transmissions on a "rational and solid" foundation.[14] After long and bitter negotiations, Passy and Brossolette achieved their aims. The northern movements agreed to create autonomous structures devoted exclusively to the collection of information. Networks therefore emerged from the major movements—Centurie for the OCM, Manipule for the CDLR, Turma for the CDLL.

The reorganization corresponded to a philosophy that had been established long before. In 1942 Christian Pineau, during his visit to London, had responded positively to the entreaties of the BCRA and created two networks out of Libération-nord: Phalanx, in the southern zone, specialized in economic and political intelligence; Phalanx ZO in the occupied zone, entrusted to Jean Cavaillès and Jean Gosset, gave precedence to economic and military aspects—as the German presence required. That body, soon renamed "Cohors," emancipated itself completely from its southern counterpart in February–March 1943.[15] In the same way, in 1942 the FTP turned their intelligence service, Service B, into a network, which, renamed "Fana," established closer ties with the BCRA in spring 1943.[16] Colonel Passy's services also focused their efforts on the free zone. During the Pallas mission (November 23, 1942–January 27, 1943), André Manuel, Passy's second-in-command, looked into the possibilities existing in the south and urged the movements to form networks devoted exclusively to collecting intelligence. To that end, Henri Gorce (Franklin), head of the Gallia mission, sought to impel the MUR to better organize their intelligence services. Gorce, however, arriving in France in a Hudson aircraft on the night of February 14, 1943, received a cool welcome. He suggested that the MUR specialize in military intelligence, that they transmit to him personally the information they collected, and that they incorporate their agents into the Free Fighting Forces. Henri Frenay and Jean Gemähling expressed their hesitations at a meeting held in April or May 1943. Apart from the fact that they feared a takeover by the BCRA, they were afraid that, in revealing the identity of their men, their security would be compromised by leaks, always a possibility. Gemähling also pointed out that specialization on the part of resistance fighters ran the risk of impoverishing their collection of intelligence, since they gleaned political as well as military information.[17] As a result, the MUR's intelligence service held onto its autonomy at first. It ultimately attached itself to the Gallia network, however, which Gorce had set up at the same time, and its men were registered with the BCRA. Brossolette and Passy, during their own missions, really did nothing more than spread throughout the northern zone an overall system that had begun to be implemented in 1942.

Passy also sought to resolve the thorny question of transmissions. "As soon as I arrived in France," he recounted, "I realized that the possibilities for creating new intelligence networks were practically limitless, but that the principal obstacle standing in the way of their sound exploitation would be the problem of transmission. We had only a very small number of radio operators in London who could organize and run a transmission network, and an equally small number of agents equipped with the British permits needed to create and exploit properly an operational network. In addition, asking intelligence networks still being formed to take on the heavy task of liaison and transmission would raise the risk of a long process of trial and error, multiple failures, and serious accidents."[18]

The head of the BCRA circumvented that difficulty by creating two radio power stations that would transmit to London the information collected by the networks. The Coligny station, run by Jean Tillier (a member of the CND), Tillier's wife, Monique, and Olivier Courtaud, would thus work for the CND, Centurie, Cohors, and Fana. Prometheus, under the direction of two of Colonel Passy's close friends, Guy Duboÿs (Chevalier) and Jean Guyot (Gallois), would act on behalf of Manipule, Turma, Legio, Velites, Luth, and Curie.[19] These stations were supplied with relatively substantial resources. For example, Prometheus had a receiving set, six transmitters, and four broadcast transmitting stations, and apparently received 200,000 francs a month. In addition to establishing radio connections, these power stations also allocated the budgets of the networks attached to them.[20] Prometheus, while continuing to perform its missions, changed its name several times to keep the repressive services off the scent, calling itself "Parsifal," then "Phidias," and finally "Praxiteles."

These measures increased the effectiveness of the networks, despite the repression targeting them. For example, Manipule and the subnetworks attached to it transmitted intelligence about the Villacoublay air base, requisitioned by the Germans, and about certain factories in the Paris region (Caudron, Farman, Berliet, and others). Paul Lemarchand (Jacqueline), a navy veteran, rejoined La Royale in July 1943, in order to conduct surveillance on movements at the Brest naval base. He communicated to the Allies the numbers on the submarines and the technical modifications made to them.[21] In all, the plan conceived by Colonel Passy proved its effectiveness, though centralization made the system vulnerable to the assaults of the repression.

Brossolette and Passy approached similarly the coordination of military action in the northern zone, which corresponded to both the letter and the spirit of their mission. Colonel Rémy had sought—in vain—to form an EMZO. The Brumaire-Arquebuse mission took on that high-stakes assignment. Fighting France had to know how many fighters the movements could allot for the liberation of the country, so that it could adjust its strategy and instructions for action. It also had to "provide the Allied governments with precise and solid data if [it] wanted them to take the potential of the Resistance into consideration."[22] That imperative explains why the SOE sent Flight Lieutenant Forest Yeo-Thomas on temporary assignment to Colonel Passy, to report to his superiors on the realities of the French resistance. Finally, Brumaire and Arquebuse were hoping to get the paramilitary elements of the resistance groups to work together or even merge, even though they saw lucidly that "at the present time, given the disparities among the various groups, that merger [is] not immediately realizable."[23]

It was not in fact realized. In the first place, Passy and Brossolette were obliged to dispel the dreams of the OCM created by Rémy's rash promises. They explained to its leaders that there was no question of granting them the privilege of creating the EMZO. "The general ruled out the possibility of having one movement be in charge of the paramilitary forces of the other movements," as Daniel Cordier notes.[24] The leaders of the OCM were intelligent enough "not to get angry."[25] In addition, the two emissaries managed to unite the leaders of the movements' paramilitary groups into an unofficial military coordination committee and to win their agreement on a certain number of principles—in particular, to put a brake on immediate action.[26] Progress was therefore made on this issue, which would ultimately be the responsibility of Jean Moulin and General Delestraint; but at the military level the results remained modest. In fact, a far more urgent question had captured the attention of the emissaries from London.

## The National Council of the Resistance

The silent struggle between the movements and the parties, and the activism of the PCF, had alarmed the Socialists, who feared they would be sidelined because they had no resistance movement of their own. In May and June 1942, two plans drawn up by three Socialist resistance fighters—André Boyer, Gaston Defferre, and Boris Fourcaud— suggested that a political advisory committee be formed, made up of representatives of the parties, the labor unions, and the resistance movements. The express hope was to hasten the unification of the resistance forces; the unavowed intention was to deprive the movements of the monopoly on representation to which they were laying claim. Jean Moulin, judging that the time was not right, declined that offer on June 22, 1942, and confined himself to forming a general study committee charged with enlightening General de Gaulle about the reforms to be achieved upon liberation.[27]

Two events relaunched the Socialists' plans, which de Gaulle, distrustful of the parties, had originally refused to approve. In November 1942, the Anglo-American landing in North Africa initially sowed confusion, since Washington supported Admiral Darlan, and then, after he was assassinated, General Giraud. Franklin Roosevelt had in fact long wagered on Philippe Pétain, hoping—utterly in vain—that Vichy would ultimately go over to the Allied camp. Even when that illusion was dashed, the White House did not support de Gaulle, whom it saw as a dictator in training. To win the battle of legitimacy, therefore, de Gaulle had to prove to the world that the lifeblood of the country was with him, beginning with all the major French political currents. If the parties as a whole rallied behind him, he would garner democratic support, and the adherence of the leftist groups in particular would allow him to obscure his conservative image. Otherwise, there was the risk that the old parties would organize outside the framework of Fighting France, which would erode his credit and damage his ability to exercise power both during and after the war. That peril was not imaginary. In November 1942, the underground newspaper *Le Populaire* proposed the creation of "an executive committee of the French Resistance," which would combine movements, labor unions, and parties to agree on a plan of action. Upon liberation, moreover, it would advise Le Connétable (the Supreme Commander), as de Gaulle was called.[28] In December Daniel Mayer, with Léon Blum's backing, once again went on the offensive, appalled by the constitution in the southern zone of the CC, "which gave the movements complete freedom of action, to the detriment of the parties." He was also annoyed that an anti-STO tract distributed in the Lyon region bore the signature of the PCF but not that of the CAS.[29] On January 4, 1943, he proposed the formation of a Comité Exécutif de la Résistance (Executive Committee of the Resistance), which was ratified by Christian Pineau, a union activist and the head of Libération-nord.

Fernand Grenier's arrival in London caused further alarm and opened a Pandora's box: "It was becoming difficult to neglect the viewpoint of the non-Communist groups, especially the Socialists, who understood immediately that the PCF, in a position of strength, would seek to short-circuit them."[30] The CAS threatened that if the Gaullists refused to create an ad hoc power organization, Léon Blum's friends would take "every measure necessary" to create a structure "that would bring together all the Gaullist political elements of the Resistance." In addition, the committee threatened to order the militants "to resort to purely Socialist resistance action."[31] It was "dangerous, even unrealizable, for the political resistance to be centralized by a Comité de Coordination consisting solely of the leaders of major movements in the [free zone]," concluded Christian Pineau in his political report of January 15.[32]

Moulin did not ignore these warnings. Following the advice of André Manuel, who was with him in the southern zone at the time, on December 14, 1942, he recommended the creation of a Conseil Politique de la Résistance (Political Council of the Resistance), composed of parties, movements, and unions. "The resistance movements, strong as they may be, are not the entire Resistance. There are moral forces, labor forces, and political forces that have remained outside the movements but which must and will play a role in the establishment of the new institutions," he asserted. He specified, however, that the conduct of operations would remain in the hands of the CC.[33] Hence de Gaulle's fear that a committee lying outside his authority would come into being under Socialist leadership, and his need to defeat Giraud by proving that France as a whole recognized his own authority, led the leader of Fighting France—at the urging of Moulin and Pineau—to accept the formation of a "Conseil de la Résistance" (Council of the Resistance; Moulin omitted the term "National" from its name at the time to avoid confusion with the CNF).

The "new instructions" for Moulin on February 21, 1943, drawn up by Jacques Bingen, outlined the form the council would take. It would ensure "the representation of resistance groups, resistance political organizations, and resistance labor unions" and would form "the embryo of small-scale national representation, General de Gaulle's political council upon his arrival in France."[34] A permanent five-member commission, "chosen exclusively from among the movements . . . would become the directorate for the Resistance, with the ability to lead it at the national level."[35]

That plan sparked strong opposition, however. In both the north and the south, the resistance movements balked. Still distrustful of the parties, wishing to reconstitute the political field upon liberation, they feared they would be dispossessed of the leading role they had assumed in the underground struggle. In a memorandum of April 1943, Emmanuel d'Astier de La Vigerie warned: "The movements, which set up the resistance and which are in charge of the executive function, will not abide the creation of a superexecutive body in which the militants of the Resistance would be in the minority, and thanks to which the partisan organizations would retake the levers of power, in order to sate the hunger of the old party cadres for consideration and for future authority."[36] To a certain extent, Pierre Brossolette shared these worries. In January 1943, he had rallied behind the idea of incorporating the political parties into a political committee,[37] but he later changed his mind, ruling out the possibility of a council including both party delegates and representatives of the major national currents.[38]

Other questions arose, less central but still important. Did the imperative for national unity dictate that all the parties be included, or should only the groups engaged in the underground struggle be selected? Jean Moulin was an advocate of the first option, but he excluded Colonel de La Rocque's PSF. True, some of the leaders of that party had adopted an ambivalent attitude, often supporting Pétain even while rejecting collaboration. In addition, the Vallin operation, overseen by Pierre Brossolette, had been a fiasco, which hardly militated in favor of opening the council to representatives of that nationalist right-wing current. The place that ought to be allotted to the Communists gave rise to fierce debates as well. Although no one contested the right of the PCF to a seat on a future CNR, Jean Moulin refused to allow its outgrowth, the FN, to be part of it, a move that would have doubled the number of votes held by Maurice Thorez's comrades. Furthermore, it was not at all self-evident which movements would be selected, especially in the northern zone.

The process outlined in London therefore gave rise to many reservations, even in the ranks of Fighting France. That explains why Moulin was granted broad powers to implement it. His sphere of influence was initially limited to the southern zone, but on February 10 he became the sole representative of General de Gaulle and of the CNF in occupied France, which placed him above Pierre Brossolette and Colonel Passy. Granted, the three men were supposed to conduct negotiations jointly, but Moulin was obviously in charge. A telegram to Brumaire and Arquebuse on March 12 drove the point home: "Rex [Jean Moulin] has full powers for any decision concerning the occupied zone as well as the unoccupied zone, in liaison with London."[39]

But Passy and Brossolette disregarded both the "new instructions" and the broader powers entrusted to Moulin—he held the rank of minister—even though these two developments were brought to their knowledge. To give fate a helping hand, they decided, before Moulin returned to London, to present him with a fait accompli. The maneuver may have seemed perilous, but Brossolette took his chances. "He had observed that, when someone forced de Gaulle's hand, he resigned himself in silence, so as not to attract attention to that questioning of his authority. As for Moulin's reaction, it would probably remain muted as well, since the decisions made in the general's name in the presence of the resistance fighters could not be called into doubt, given the risk of destroying the credit of Fighting France. Finally, whatever might happen, Brossolette knew he would be covered by the presence of his superior at his side," writes Cordier.[40]

Passy and Brossolette thus hastened to create a Comité de Coordination Zone Nord (CCZN; Northern Zone Coordination Committee). Its first meeting took place on March 26, 1943. Granted, that decision did not expressly contradict the instructions of February 21. Historian Guillaume Piketty observes: "As later events would prove, it in no way prevented the eventual creation of a single national leadership for the Resistance, placed under the authority of Rex [Jean Moulin], that is, of General de Gaulle."[41] But that hasty creation did not correspond to the mandate Brumaire had received. "Nowhere in the orders given to Brossolette, Passy, or anyone else is there any trace of instructions drawn up *before* Brossolette's departure on January 27 and prescribing the creation of a Comité de Coordination Zone Nord," observes Cordier.[42]

It is true this plan had many perverse effects. It perpetuated the division of France into two zones, whereas Moulin was advocating unification. It presented General de Gaulle's delegate with a fait accompli, which compromised the coherence and cohesion of the actions of the emissaries from London. It brought the FN onto the CC in the northern zone, from which it had been excluded in the southern zone, thus favoring the overrepresentation of the Communist elements. Finally, it complicated the future creation of the permanent commission and thereby prevented the emergence of a "single and national leadership for the Resistance, directly controlled by General de Gaulle."[43] Moulin, meeting with the two men from the BCRA at the Bois de Boulogne on March 31, 1943, could only endorse that diktat, to keep Fighting France from displaying its divisions in front of the representatives of the internal resistance. As a result, he took part in the meeting of April 3, which made official the CCZN. But he hardly accepted the situation, especially since Brumaire and Arquebuse had begun negotiations regarding the composition of the future CNR, again without waiting for Moulin.

During the first session of the CCZN, the two men from the BCRA had relied on the movements to ensure that, in place of the parties, the "fundamental nuances of the French spirit" (Communism, Socialism, freethinking, Catholicism, and nationalism) were represented, and that the principle of a permanent commission was rejected.[44] At a time when de Gaulle was soliciting the support of the parties as such, that minimalist formulation could not have conformed to his wishes. The BCRA therefore sent a telegram indicating that the system of "spiritual families" was impracticable. André Philip, commissioner for the interior, also backed Moulin's position in a note:

1. It is indispensable from the international standpoint that we be able to present ourselves with the support of the political groups, which, for the British and the Americans, represent the sole expression of French public opinion.
2. Once the Communists act in the capacity of a party, it is impossible to prevent the others from doing the same, insofar as they have succeeded in setting up a true resistance organization.[45]

It is thus easier to understand the rage that took hold of Moulin on March 31, when Brossolette, in defiance of orders, informed him of the "majority's preference for the representation of the fundamental 'currents' of French thought."[46] The confrontation between the two men was violent, and it intensified their mutual distrust.

The insubordination of Brumaire and Arquebuse did not prevent the CNR from moving forward, however. Moulin, a shrewd tactician, suggested at the April 3 meeting that the delegates be called upon to represent not the parties but "sectors of opinion." That allowed him "if not to win the adherence of the movements' leaders, then at least to ensure that they would not oppose the constitution of the Conseil National de la Résistance and that they would work with it."[47] At the end of bitter negotiations, Moulin managed to overcome hesitations and obstacles and formed the council. After infinite precautions were taken, it met on May 27, 1943, in the apartment of René Corbin—who had previously worked with Pierre Cot—on rue du Four in Paris. The council ultimately represented eight resistance movements: CDLL (Roger Coquoin), CDLR (Jacques Lecompte-Boinet), FN (Pierre Villon), Libération-nord (Charles Laurent), OCM (Jacques-Henri Simon), Combat (Claude Bourdet), Franc-Tireur (Eugène Petit), and Libération-sud (Pascal Copeau). The major political currents were represented by

delegates from the PCF (André Mercier), the SFIO (André Le Trocquer), the Radical-Socialists (Marc Rucart), the Popular Democrats
(Georges Bidault), the Alliance Démocratique (Joseph Laniel), and
the Fédération Républicaine (Jacques Debû-Bridel). The labor union
seats, finally, were held by Louis Saillant for the CGT and by Gaston
Tessier for the CFTC. According to Moulin, the session was particularly emotional, unfolding "within an atmosphere of patriotic union
and dignity, which I feel obliged to emphasize."[48]

## The Limits of Success

It is quite obvious that Jean Moulin, prevailing over the obstacles in
his path, achieved an extraordinary result: he succeeded both in uniting
the internal resistance and in getting it to accept General de Gaulle's
oversight. Hence the motion introduced on May 27, 1943, by the Christian Democrat Georges Bidault called for the future provisional government to "be entrusted to General de Gaulle, who was the soul of
the Resistance during the darkest days and who, since June 18, 1940, has
never stopped preparing, in complete lucidity and in full independence,
for the rebirth of the destroyed Homeland and of the republican liberties that were trampled."[49] The motion passed unanimously, even though
the Communists, in keeping with their balancing act, attempted to call
for a reconciliation between Giraud and de Gaulle. The remarks of
Pierre Villon, representative of the FN, caused such an outcry that he
ultimately fell in line with his peers.

The resistance would therefore march in lockstep, in contrast to the
rifts that tore many other countries apart. In Greece, the army of
shadows was so split between the Communists and the nationalists that
a civil war, latent during the dark years, erupted in 1946. In Yugoslavia,
the violent struggle between Tito and Mihailović ended in a total victory for the Communist elements. And in Italy, King Victor Emmanuel
III and his prime minister, Marshal Pietro Badoglio, were unable to
achieve national unity after Mussolini was deposed on July 25, 1943,
and the armistice with the Allies was concluded on September 3 of the
same year. From that standpoint, France was truly an exceptional case:
the achievement of the "unifier," to use historian Henri Michel's term,
held in check the centripetal tendencies of the French resistance, obliged

it to seek minimal forms of consensus, and allowed it to present itself as a homogeneous whole, all the more so in that it was embodied in one man, Charles de Gaulle. United behind the tutelary figure of the man of June 18, the resistance had the appearance of a credible changing of the guard, especially since it avoided the trap of uniformity. It included the entire political spectrum but did not require that these "families," certainly diverse, keep quiet about their differences.

Naturally, the creation of the CNR offered de Gaulle an important asset in his quarrel with Giraud. Chaperoned by Jean Monnet, whom the Americans had opportunely dispatched as a political adviser, Giraud tempered his Pétainist zeal. On March 14, 1943, he even pronounced what he called, with some ingenuousness, the "first democratic speech of his life." He had not turned over a new leaf in his old age, however, and his conversion to democratic ideals was lacking in conviction, as confirmed by the analysis he formulated for his representative in Spain in April 1944: "General de G . . . is the dictator of the future, with a [general staff] of Communists, Socialists, and Jews. He will constantly be obliged to make pledges to the left, while anticipating being eaten alive by his followers. General G[iraud] did not want to stand beside such a staff. He is convinced that France wants nothing to do with a dictator or with the popular front. He is very sincerely republican, but with a republic of clean people and no Jews."[50] There was a risk that the agreement between the two generals would fall apart, especially since the Americans, backed by the British, persisted in supporting Giraud.

On February 23, 1943, however, de Gaulle sent Giraud a memorandum that proposed not only to constitute a "central provisional authority" but also to form an "advisory authority of the French resistance. That council might be formed, for example, by proxies sent to the metropolis as delegates by the resistance organizations and the fighting forces."[51] On March 16, Giraud replied by inviting de Gaulle to meet with him. But the negotiations went nowhere. Moulin, learning from the BBC that de Gaulle was supposed to go to Algiers, on May 8 sent him a précis to provide him with information. In particular, he said that for the members of the future CNR, "de Gaulle's subordination to Giraud as military chief will never be accepted by people of France who demand swift installation provisional government Algiers under presidency of de Gaulle with Giraud as military chief."[52]

That announcement was premature to say the least, since at that date, May 8, the CNR had not yet met: it would have its first plenary session on the 27th. But Jacques Soustelle took it upon himself to transmit it to the press service of Fighting France, which quickly issued a press release, on May 14, 1943. That bending of the truth angered some Gaullists, who feared that negotiations with the Giraudist camp would be derailed. Moulin himself denounced the procedure: "This incident, which occurred just as I was asking the members of the Conseil de la Résistance to hold their organizational meeting, did not fail to cause me serious concerns."[53] But Algiers was well worth the trouble, and de Gaulle was able to demonstrate to the restive Allies, if only by trickery, that France as a whole had united behind him. "The voice of France in defeat, but rumbling and self-assured, suddenly drowned out the whispers of intrigues and the palaver of plots. At that instant, I was the stronger for it, even as Washington and London were realizing the import of the event, without pleasure but not without lucidity," he later recalled.[54] On May 17, Giraud invited de Gaulle to come to Algiers and to form the central French authority with him. The constitution of the CNR, though announced prematurely, had offered de Gaulle the boost he needed to take the first steps toward assuming power.

## Clouds on the Horizon

Conversely, the question of who would command the AS was a long way from being settled. Although the powers of General Delestraint (Vidal), named head of the AS in November 1942, had been extended to the northern zone in February 1943, the southern movements, Frenay in the lead, continually disputed Delestraint's authority. "They believed they had been deceived, and they found distasteful what they considered to be maneuvering because, in the guidelines that created the Armée Secrète in the southern zone in November 1942, it was stipulated that the Comité de Coordination would serve as a go-between vis-à-vis de Gaulle. [Delestraint's] promotion, occurring at the same time as the dramatic emergence of the maquis . . . sparked a crisis," Cordier writes.[55] In fact, the transformation of the Comité de Coordination Zone Sud (CCZS; Southern Zone Coordination Committee) into the steering committee of the MUR changed the game plan, since the organization originally in charge of conducting underground action had turned into the governing body of the three movements in the free zone. As a result, General de Gaulle, via Delestraint, secured direct command of the AS, a dispossession Frenay could not accept. In addition, the creation of the CNR and Delestraint's promotion suddenly shifted the center of gravity of the army of shadows from Lyon to Paris. That transfer abruptly granted "an essential political importance to the movements in the occupied zone and relegated the Armée Secrète in the free zone to the role of auxiliary. Frenay not only had no authority over the paramilitary forces in the northern zone but was also viewed with the greatest distrust in that zone."[56] It is therefore clear why certain leaders of the internal resistance continually contested the Gaullist organization chart. Believing that the separation between civilian and military actions was absurd—militants could engage in political propaganda while at the same time collecting military intelligence—they also denounced the authoritarian conception of obedience defended by Moulin. For example, Frenay wrote to Moulin: "For us, discipline is made up of trust and friendship. There is no subordination in the military sense of the term. There was no way—and we have seen this many times—to impose a leader at one level in our chain of command. What is possible in a regiment or a prefecture is not possible here."[57] "With respect to discipline," retorted Moulin, who remembered the fratricidal rifts of the Spanish Civil War, "no organization, not even a revolutionary one, is conceivable in which everyone has his say at every level."[58]

Compulsory obedience was also repulsive to the Communists. At the meeting of April 12, 1943, Moulin had remarked that "since they were incorporating their action groups into the Armée Secrète, they were becoming military units that were required to simply obey. The representatives of the Francs-Tireurs et Partisans, surprised by that rigid conception and offended by some of the terms used (notably, Rex had let it slip that they had to 'click their heels'), decided that, under those conditions, they would have to refer the matter to their steering committee, which, however, would never agree to abandon immediate action."[59]

As a result, in April Moulin cut off the funds being paid to the FTP. But that retaliatory measure did not resolve two basic questions. In the first place, should immediate action be accepted? The emissaries of Fighting France settled the matter, requiring that the Communist groups execute as their top priority the missions London would assign to them; in all other respects, they would still have complete freedom of action. But that fragile compromise did not answer a second question: Would the Communists conduct themselves as loyal allies? The response was not self-evident, especially since Pierre Brossolette's maneuvers had resulted in two seats being allocated to the Communists on the CNR, one for the party, the other for the FN, giving them added weight.

The inclusion of the political parties on the CNR also posed a problem. That plan favored the unification of the army of shadows and the rebirth of democratic life, particularly since de Gaulle had pledged to convene a Consultative Assembly in Algiers. But it ended up depriving the movements of the political monopoly and of giving a boost to groups discredited both by the defeat and by their uneven participation in the underground struggle. Cordier observes: "The Communists and the Socialists would have occupied a preponderant place after Liberation. . . . As for the rightist parties and the moderates, they were not saved from their insolvency by their participation on the CNR. . . . It was the very texture of the movements that prevented them from playing a political role, for which (contrary to what the ambitions of their leaders suggested), they were not made. The CNR was the symbolic indicator of that failure, not its cause. The future proved that."[60] The analysis is not baseless, but it fails to take into account one major fact: when liberation came, General de Gaulle was the first victim of the parties whose rebirth he had promoted! If de Gaulle, supporting the resistance groups with his prestige, had relied on them to offer a political outlet for wartime Gaullism, the situation might have been very different. Over the short term, the support of the parties was fundamental in winning the battle of legitimacy; over the medium term, it ill served the man of June 18, who in 1946 was the victim of groups he had reinstated, but whose disgrace was embodied in his epic career.

Finally, to Moulin's great dismay, the CNR left out some groups that were not without merit. "Very important groups were left off the Comité de Coordination and now demand with great insistence their place on that committee. Such is the case for Résistance . . . for the Cercle . . . and for Défense de la France, whose newspaper, it seems, is the largest in the northern zone. . . . All these movements complain about being left out and steadfastly request a revision of coordination," he protested in May 1943.[61] Pierre Brossolette and Colonel Passy had chosen three simple criteria for defining a movement: it had to consist of a newspaper, an intelligence network, and a paramilitary group. Given the rules laid out, the marginalization of Résistance and the DF was in no way shocking. But the application of these parameters had been selective: for example, neither the CDLR nor the CDLL had newspapers. Nonetheless, the partiality was not political by any means. It demonstrated that, for Passy and for Brossolette, the military prevailed over the civilian, which left little hope for groups that, like the DF, gave precedence to civilian action. That principle had an unexpected consequence, however. To look good in London's eyes, the civilian movements acquired paramilitary groups, and the military groups, such as the CDLL, embarked on propaganda activities, which increased the versatility of the underground groups.

Even while leaving many thorny questions hanging, the constitution of the CNR strengthened both the unification of the resistance and its subordination to Fighting France. That positive evolution, however, spurred the rise of a minority opposition. The irredentism of certain movements and the ambiguous position of the PCF undermined the process, introducing fissures that would only widen in the second half of 1943.

## Chapter 11

# Caluire and Its Repercussions

THE FORMATION OF the CNR on May 27, 1943, marked a major milestone. Within less than a month, however, the plan of action conceived by Jean Moulin collapsed, having fallen victim to the blows of the German repression and to the strategy consequently deployed by his rivals, whether they belonged to the movements or to the BCRA. The May meeting on rue du Four saw Jean Moulin's apogee; the ambush at Caluire on June 21, 1943, sounded his death knell.

On that day, the men of the SD—the Nazi security services—led by Klaus Barbie, the head of their Lyon unit, arrested General de Gaulle's delegate at the home of Dr. Dugoujon in Caluire, a suburb of Lyon. The affair has for many years been the object of debates and controversies, which cannot be entirely explained by Moulin's prominent role in the Gaullist hierarchy. Many obscurities remain, and though historians as a whole agree on a plausible scenario, the lack of evidence prevents us from irrefutably assessing the responsibility of each person caught up in the machinations of spring 1943.

On May 7, 1943, the Milice had arrested a militant from the France d'Abord movement, who, without being brutalized, had given up six "mailboxes." Located in various places, these were used as an underground postal system for resistance fighters, who deposited documents—papers, reports, circulars—that others then picked up, sometimes several times a day. They could be actual mailboxes, but at times shopkeepers agreed to receive or deliver letters that the resistance fighters handed over to them. Such was the case, for example, of Le Voeu de Louis XIII bookstore on rue Bonaparte in Paris, which rendered that service for the DF. In any event, on May 27, 1943, General Delestraint (Vidal), head of the AS, arranged to meet René Hardy (Didot) at La Muette metro station on June 9. The note announcing the meeting was placed in a box at 14 rue Bouteille in Lyon, which the Germans had under surveillance.[1] When the general walked into the metro station, the

Germans stopped him and immediately took him to Gestapo head-quarters on avenue Foch. It was a major catch: the AS had lost its leader.

Unaware of the tragedy that was about to play out, René Hardy left Lyon for the capital on June 7, 1943. It might be helpful to recall his life history, given the essential role he played in the Caluire trap. Hardy, a former cadre in the SNCF, had attempted in May 1941 to leave France and join up with de Gaulle. He was arrested and sentenced to fifteen months in prison. During his time behind bars, he met Pierre Bénouville, a future member of Combat. In December 1942, Jean-Guy Bernard introduced him to Henri Frenay, who, won over by his talents as an organizer, put him in charge of Résistance-Fer. In early May, Delestraint co-opted Hardy for his general staff and assigned him to draw up a plan to sabotage the railroad network. When the Allies landed, this plan (eventually known as Plan Vert) was supposed to paralyze enemy troop movements through a series of attacks. Hardy was therefore going up to Paris to make available to Delestraint his address book, and especially, his contacts at the SNCF, and to plan the expansion to the occupied zone of the NAP, in conjunction with Bernard.[2] In addition, he intended to work out—also with Bernard—plans for a few actions.

On June 7, Hardy took the Lyon-Paris train departing at 9:50 P.M. The neighboring compartment was occupied by two men: Robert Moog, an agent from the Abwehr detached to the SD, and Jean Multon (Lunel). They were on their way to arrest Delestraint. Multon, the secretary of Maurice Chevance-Bertin, leader of the MUR for Bouches-du-Rhône, had been arrested in Marseilles on April 27, 1943. Having been "turned" by the Germans, he placed himself in their service, which resulted in the arrest of more than a hundred people. Hardy understood, by the astonishment on Multon's face—a reaction Moog did not fail to notice—that he had been recognized. But rather than cut short his trip, he preferred to continue on. Nevertheless, he entrusted Lazare Rachline, a resistance fighter he happened to run into on the station platform, with the task of warning Pierre Bénouville that Multon had seen him. At 1:00 A.M., the Germans—as might have been feared—arrested Hardy at the Chalon-sur-Saône station. Rachline, upon arriving in the capital, saw to it that Bénouville was informed.

On June 10, René Hardy, incarcerated in the Chalon-sur-Saône prison, was handed over to Klaus Barbie, who had found among Hardy's things a letter addressed to his prisoner's fiancée, Lydie Bastien. The head of the Lyon SD then convinced Hardy to work for the German secret services. Barbie had a formidable means for applying pressure, since Hardy was madly in love with Lydie Bastien, whom Daniel Cordier, Jean Moulin's secretary, describes as a "quivering beauty." The Germans, Hardy would explain, "let me know that, since I seemed to love my fiancée very much, if they learned that I belonged to the Resistance as they believed in the first place, or if I disappeared from it, they would arrest the Bastien family and my fiancée as hostages."[3] Did the Gestapo agent realize the importance of his catch? Had he recognized Hardy as Didot, a prominent leader in the army of shadows? The question remains unresolved, since Hardy always claimed that Barbie released him without knowing he was the head of sabotage operations.[4] In any case, the resistance fighter was freed, having promised Barbie he would do his bidding. Was this a fool's bargain? Perhaps. "It cannot be completely ruled out that Hardy, whose best quality was not his modesty, after agreeing to 'work for Barbie,' believed he was sharp enough to deceive someone who at the time was only a minor lieutenant. To play for time, he might actually have delivered the draft of 'Plan Vert' to him, but without 'giving up' the meeting in Caluire, to which he might have been unwittingly and unknowingly followed," writes historian Jean-Pierre Azéma. But that, explains Azéma, is simply a "minimalist explanation,"[5] inasmuch as the Flora report, a German document from that era, explicitly lists Hardy as "a double agent."[6]

Hardy, having recovered his freedom, once again established contact with his comrades, Pierre Bénouville in particular. Did Bénouville know that Hardy had been arrested, albeit briefly, by the Germans? Hardy claimed he did, and Bénouville ultimately acknowledged as much.[7] That point, minor in appearance, is not at all secondary, and this knowledge played a decisive role in the following days. Moulin was shaken by Delestraint's arrest and immediately understood the consequences. "I have kept the arrest of Vidal [Delestraint] secret. There is not a minute to lose. Everything can still be repaired," he wrote in a letter to General de Gaulle on June 15. "But no one in London and Algiers must know about it, especially not the leaders of the movements."[8] The leaders of Combat, however, were quickly informed of the tragedy and realized the opportunities that were opening up. With

Delestraint sidelined, they could retake control of the AS, of which they believed they had been unjustly dispossessed. Moulin got wind of the threat. To ward it off, he came up with the idea of replacing Delestraint in the AS with two interim leaders: Raymond Aubrac would be in charge of the northern zone, while Colonel Schwarzfeld, head of the Lyonnais movement France d'Abord, would take the southern zone. A meeting of the paramilitary leaders of the MUR was supposed to validate that plan. It was scheduled for June 21, in Dr. Dugoujon's office in Caluire.

The meeting therefore had key importance, since a replacement for General Delestraint would be approved at it. There was also a risk it would get out of hand, given that the leaders of Combat intended to assert their rights, even if that meant confrontation. For that reason, Moulin planned the meeting with care, getting together with participants multiple times beforehand to win over to his views some of the leaders of the movements (Copeau and Aubrac for Libération-sud and Claudius-Petit for Franc-Tireur, for example). The leaders of Combat were not idle either; they sought to stymie General de Gaulle's representative and his allies by turning out in large numbers.

At that point, Henri Aubry, Delestraint's chief of staff, decided to ask Hardy to attend the meeting in Caluire. Aubry, a lieutenant in the Colonial Army, had been recruited by Combat; Frenay then assigned him to assist Delestraint, so that Combat would have a reliable man in the AS hierarchy. But in bringing Hardy along to Caluire, Aubry committed three errors. In the first place, the most elementary caution dictated that Hardy be quarantined, whether or not he was suspected of having been turned by the Germans. Had he not vanished for more than a week? Second, the rules of security formally prohibited "bringing a third person, whoever that might be, to a meeting with someone."[9] And third, Moulin was not notified that Hardy was coming, despite the fact that Moulin had distrusted him "ever since he learned of [Hardy's] reappearance in Lyon after days of absence."[10] By that measure, Aubry acted, at the very least, with extreme recklessness. Furthermore, his was a repeat offense. He had known that the mailbox containing the message about the rendezvous with General Delestraint at La Muette station had been uncovered, yet he failed to advise Moulin of that fact, indirectly precipitating his arrest.

Aubry probably acted under the orders of Bénouville, who felt real enmity for Moulin, a sentiment that Moulin returned in kind. No doubt believing that Aubry would not be up to the task, he likely suggested relying on Hardy, "a nasty fellow always ready with a reply."[11] Hardy, without having been invited, was therefore foisted on the meeting in Caluire by two Combat leaders.[12] Was Hardy tailed, or did he give up the meeting to the Nazis, as Edmée Delettraz suggests? A double agent, Delettraz worked both for Colonel Groussard, a Vichyist who had gone over to the resistance, and for the Gestapo.[13] Hardy always denied he was a traitor, pointing out that no Combat leader was arrested subsequently—which is correct but does not constitute absolute proof of his innocence: "There is no dearth of examples of resistance fighters 'controlled' by the German services to whom no arrest is imputable, simply because the Gestapo or the Abwehr expected something different from them."[14]

In any case, the end result was the same. At about 3 P.M., two Citroëns let out seven or eight men from the SD in front of Dr. Dugoujon's house. The Germans immediately arrested everyone they found suspect, patients as well as resistance fighters, not hesitating to rough them up, particularly Henri Aubry, Bruno Larat (head of the COPA), and André Lassagne, a member of Libération-sud. Hardy, by contrast, managed to get away by knocking down the guard who held him by a *cabriolet*, that is, a chain twisted around the prisoner's wrist. The favorable treatment Hardy enjoyed (he had not been handcuffed) and the relative ease of his escape only increased the suspicions surrounding him. Injured, he was transported to the Antiquaille Hospital, then transferred to the detention facilities in the Germans' Croix-Rousse hospital. He escaped on August 3, once again without major difficulties.[15]

All in all, the Lyon SD had made a good haul, seizing prominent leaders of the resistance: Raymond Aubrac and André Lassagne from Libération-sud, Henri Aubry from Combat, Colonel Schwarzfeld from France d'Abord, Bruno Larat from COPA, and, above all, Jean Moulin. He was not immediately recognized, though the SD learned that same day that they had Max in their custody. Barbie, aware of their resistance activity, thus went at the prisoners without mercy, torturing Larat, Lassagne, and Aubry at length. Aubry was particularly brutalized: "At noon, I was again taken to Montluc [prison], where I was put up against a wall. After I was chained to it, four soldiers came in, stood in front of me, and, on the order of my interrogator—who, after making it clear to me that, since I would not give up the steering committee's box, I was going to die—commanded his four men, in German: 'Aim,' and then 'Fire.' After that first volley of shots, which surrounded me on all sides, the interrogator said, in response to my astonishment at finding myself alive: 'The first time was for fun, now it's for keeps: Will you say where the steering committee's box is?' When I again replied that I did not know, they proceeded to repeat that horrible comedy four times. After the fourth volley, I was knocked unconscious by an extremely violent blow with a rifle butt."[16] It was probably on June 23 that Barbie uncovered the identity of Rex.[17] He tortured Moulin abominably and had him transported, in critical condition, to Paris, most likely on June 28, before transferring him to Berlin, probably on July 8. Does the abuse inflicted by the Gestapo agent account for Moulin's death? Or did Moulin prefer to commit suicide rather than talk under torture, a hypothesis substantiated by his first suicide attempt in Chartres in 1940? It hardly matters. "One certainty remains, the only one of importance for history: Jean Moulin was one of the very few resistance fighters who did not yield under torture," Daniel Cordier says in tribute. "It is even possible that, immured in his silence, he did not give his true name or acknowledge his role in the Resistance. The survival of his fellow fighters, all of whom were left in peace, and the testimony of his tormentor are proof of that: 'He confessed nothing,' Klaus Barbie would say. For once, he certainly told the truth."[18]

The Caluire affair has not yielded up all its mysteries—far from it. The historian is at a loss to assess accurately René Hardy's responsibility, especially since he, prosecuted in 1947 and again in 1950, was twice acquitted. Whatever the truth, one fact is obvious: "Arrested, interrogated, and released by the Lyon Gestapo, he deliberately concealed the truth from all the Resistance leaders and resumed his underground activities," historian Henri Noguères notes sharply.[19] But whether Hardy was ensnared or gave up the meeting, Aubry and Bénouville are not exempt from all responsibility. Nothing obliged them to invite Hardy, whose presence was not required, and whose disappearance and sudden resurrection were an argument for caution. In that case, let me repeat, "instructions dictated that Hardy be sequestered and that he not participate in any meetings at all."[20] The two members of Combat thus took a reckless risk, especially since, by his own admission, Bénouville was not unaware that his former prison mate had been arrested by the Germans. The high stakes—the command of the AS—no doubt explains why that risk was taken, particularly given that the two men harbored few warm feelings (an understatement) for General de Gaulle's representative.

Moulin's tragic death deprived Fighting France of a loyal public servant. "In terms of the history of the Resistance in France, Jean Moulin's arrest not only turned a page but also concluded the second act of the drama. No doubt the internal French Resistance, on which Jean Moulin's personality had left an indelible mark in eighteen months' time, would never again be what it might have been without Jean Moulin. But, once he was dead, it would also never again be what it might have been with him," writes Noguères.[21] His death inaugurated an era of turmoil and upheaval. But the most urgent matter was to replace Rex.

## An Impossible Legacy

Let us recall that Jean Moulin occupied three posts concurrently: he was the national commissioner, and he also chaired both the CNR and the steering committee of the MUR. He therefore played a preeminent role in the institutions of the internal resistance and in the hierarchy of Fighting France, maintaining relations between the two and ultimately guaranteeing their cohesiveness. Replacing him would be complicated to say the least. Moulin's successor would have to be approved both by the movements and by the Gaullist authorities, which, given the tensions between them, was no easy matter. There was no obvious candidate, no one with the charisma of Rex, no one boasting his record of service. In addition, Herculean labors awaited Moulin's replacement: naming General Delestraint's successor, establishing the AS on firm footing, spelling out the strategy the AS would implement to assist in the liberation of the country, and finally, guaranteeing General de Gaulle's power without arousing the hostility of the underground organizations. At a time when the Allied landing, heretofore hypothetical, was becoming a reality, action now had to combine civilian

and military aspects: as one might expect, that enormously complicated the situation.

A temporary solution was required at once. Claude Bouchinet-
Serreulles (Sophie, Scapin, Clovis, Sauvier), second lieutenant in the
cavalry brigade in 1934 and a commercial attaché to Berlin before 1939,
had joined Free France in July 1940, at the age of twenty-eight. He had
served in de Gaulle's cabinet for more than two years.[22] Yearning to
act, he asked to be sent to the French metropolis. The general, tired of
putting him off, finally gave in. Bouchinet-Serreulles was thus dispatched in a twin-engine Hudson on June 16, 1943, to assist Jean
Moulin, who considered entrusting the delegation's military affairs to
him. The tragedy of Caluire put an abrupt end to that plan. As soon as
Moulin's arrest became known, Bouchinet-Serreulles offered to step in
on an interim basis, while at the same time urgently calling for "a high-
ranking leader to take the situation in hand."[23] Pierre Brossolette,
with Colonel Passy's backing, immediately proposed himself as a candidate, with the dream of succeeding his rival, whom fate had provi-
dentially gotten out of the way.

It is true that Brossolette had solid qualifications. Extremely intelligent, well-versed in the arcana of the internal resistance, he also enjoyed the full confidence of Passy, head of the BCRA. But he had
aroused strong feelings of hostility within the movements, which had
not forgiven him for the favorable treatment enjoyed by the OCM. In
addition, his mordant pen had swelled the ranks of his enemies, wounded
by the barbs of his caustic wit. Above all, de Gaulle could not imagine
entrusting the keys of the delegation to a man who had continually dis-
obeyed him. How could he make Brossolette his representative and
the chair of the CNR, when, in Cordier's words, Brossolette had "criticized his directives, publicly fought against the plan for the CNR that
Moulin was in charge of implementing, and finally, torpedoed the creation of the permanent commission, de Gaulle's quintessential instrument for controlling the Resistance? Through that appointment, could
de Gaulle, in publicly disavowing Moulin, disavow his own policy?"[24]

The prospect of his appointment therefore caused a general outcry.
Within Fighting France, André Philip, commissioner for the interior,
challenged it, backed by his right-hand man, Georges Boris, and by
André Manuel, Passy's assistant. Within the movements, François de

Menthon, founder of Liberté and a member of the Comité Général d'Études (General Studies Committee), as well as Gilbert Védy (Jacques Médéric), leader of the CDLL, rejected it as well. After a struggle, the BCRA reached a compromise. It reaffirmed the separation between the two zones, giving Claude Bouchinet-Serreulles responsibility for the steering committee in the north and putting Jacques Bingen in charge of its southern counterpart. Pierre Brossolette would be sent to France in September, with the task of settling the questions left hanging: naming the chair of the CNR; introducing Pierre Marchal, military delegate for the northern zone, to the movements; and guiding the first steps of Émile Bollaert, who, as Guillaume Piketty notes, was named "representative for the Comité Français de Libération Nationale on the Conseil de la Résistance Française" on September 2, 1943.[25] Far from being named as Moulin's heir, Brossolette was thus vested with a "simple and limited mission." But he "hoped to take advantage of his knowledge of the underground struggle, and of his special relationship to the BCRA, to set himself up as the 'mentor' of the new delegate general and to take the helm. In fact, he found there a role for which he had a fondness, that of éminence grise."[26]

Bollaert's inexperience was of assistance in that plan. A former prefect dismissed by Vichy, the patriotic and republican high official had no experience in the underground or in the resistance. As a novice, he therefore fell under the sway of his adviser. After a detour to Algiers, where he met with de Gaulle, Pierre Brossolette, flanked by Forest Yeo-Thomas, landed on a field outside Angoulême on the night of September 18, 1943. The two men immediately set off for Paris.

## The Nerve Center of the War

Just as Moulin's death gave Brossolette a boost—or so he hoped—it also opened un-hoped-for prospects to the movements. They had not welcomed supervision from London in general and the growing power of its delegate in particular. But Moulin had the means to command respect, since the financing of the movements depended on him.

Until 1942, the underground groups had relied on the generosity of their members or on the largesse of their patrons to provide for their operations. Over time, however, such funding proved to be inadequate.

The growth of the organizations made it necessary to hire permanent employees who, since they often quit their previous jobs, had to be remunerated, unless they were in possession of a personal fortune. The Vengeance movement, for example, paid its national leader, Victor Dupon, 7,000 francs a month. In July 1942, a decree defined the status of resistance fighters: permanent employees (P2) were entitled to a salary; agents who kept their professional employment (P1) received an allowance; and occasional workers (PO) also received compensation if necessary. In the Cohors network, the pay scale ranged between 3,000 and 5,500 francs a month,[27] not insignificant figures, given that the average minimum wage was between 1,050 and 1,700 francs a month.[28] In addition to payroll expenses, for which the underground groups were responsible, there were the investments necessary for their operations: the purchase or rental of offices, printing works, bicycles, and trucks—not to mention printing costs. Between 1942 and 1944, the price of a metric ton of paper rose from 25,000 to 60,000 francs;[29] in 1943, it cost the newspaper *Libération*-sud between 100,000 and 130,000 francs to print 130,000 copies, not counting the resistance fighters' salaries.[30] Finally, social services required growing expenditures to assist families forced into a downward spiral by the arrest of one of their members. All together, Combat spent between 20,000 and 30,000 francs a month in 1941, 200,000 francs a month in 1942, and between 5 million and 7 million francs a month in 1943. The propaganda-distribution service of Libération-sud consumed 300,000 francs a month in early 1943, but 900,000 francs in 1944.[31] In October 1943, the CDLR, with a civilian budget of 673,000 francs, allotted 300,000 to the fight against the STO, 87,000 francs to the NAP, 60,000 to the secretarial office, 50,000 to social services, 25,000 to worker action, 20,000 to false identity papers, and the rest to local groups.[32]

Increasing expenditures thus obliged the underground groups to abandon the improvisation of the early days and to secure regular financing. The aid Free France provided as of 1942 was therefore welcome. Jean Moulin, who parachuted into France in 1942, brought large sums of money on his first mission, and, between January and October of that year, a total of 12 million francs passed through his hands.[33] Between January and May 1943, Libération-sud received 1.5 million francs, Franc-Tireur 600,000 francs, and Combat 2.5 million francs.

The political parties were also subsidized—the CAS for the southern zone was allotted 200,000 francs—as were the unions: the CGT took in 300,000 francs in March 1943 and 2 million in April.[34]

The support from London, though of decisive importance, had three drawbacks. In the first place, payments were sometimes interrupted for material reasons. The disastrous climatic conditions of winter 1943–1944 limited the number of planes that could travel between England and France, so much so that, in January, 77 million francs were held up on British air bases.[35] Containers loaded with bills sometimes fell in the wrong place, and dishonest agents were also known to claim their share. Between March and September 1943, André Boyer, head of the Brutus network, discovered that 600,000 francs had disappeared;[36] and in December of the same year, of the million francs intended for the southern zone delegation, 230,000 went missing.[37] The unexpected interruption of payments threatened the very survival of the underground organizations, an alarming situation. Second, the distribution of funds provided Jean Moulin with a means for applying pressure, which he did not refrain from using. In April 1943, he ordered his secretary, Daniel Cordier, to suspend payments to the Communist FTP. Third, the distribution of the allocations overall gave rise to bitter recriminations, each group judging itself wronged when compared to its neighbor. In fact, Moulin "distributed the money he received, if not at whim as leaders of the MUR accused him of doing, then at least—and this is certain—as he chose."[38]

The subsidies from Fighting France thus came into play in contradictory ways. They favored the development of the internal resistance, whose growth would otherwise have been impossible. At the same time, they placed it under London's control, threatening its independence and even its survival, when connections were interrupted. In February 1943, the establishment of the STO reaffirmed that paradox: it strengthened the southern zone movements, which emancipated themselves from Gaullist oversight by creating or supporting maquis, despite Moulin's hesitations. But these movements "were unable to manage such masses of fighters without London's support, its financing, and the constant parachute drops of equipment and weapons. In fact, the new Armée Secrète was completely dependent on Free France."[39] That led London to tighten its control.

Some groups strove to break free of its grip. Several organizations could quite simply do without Gaullist assistance, because they worked for the British services, the SOE in particular. The wealth of the SOE was a source of wonderment: the agents of F Section alone, which was totally independent from the BCRA, had an overall budget of 34 million francs in 1942. The same section injected some 400 million francs into its networks between 1941 and 1944, obviously a substantial amount.[40] Similarly, in 1944 the Americans had a war chest of 37 million dollars earmarked for the French resistance.[41] The abundance of financial resources made it easier to steal away agents who, in the face of Free France's poverty, preferred to work under the Allied banner rather than the tricolor flag. Jean-Pierre Levy, head of Franc-Tireur, resisted these siren calls, but he had some difficulty convincing his men: "When I told militants not to frequent black market restaurants, where agents of the [British Intelligence Service] readily invited them, and not to smoke the English cigarettes being offered them, they chafed. I tried to calm them down by explaining the risks they were taking by frequenting black market restaurants—which you could of course forgive in courageous young people who were hungry and could not be satisfied with the food provided by their ration cards. I sometimes had trouble, especially with André Girard in the Cartel network, who, richly supplied by the SOE, was not above promising the moon, painted in glowing colors, and denigrating the services of Free France."[42] But whereas Levy rather quickly broke off the tenuous ties he had established with the British services, Henri Frenay solicited American support, thus precipitating the "Swiss affair."[43]

## The Swiss Affair

In November 1942, Philippe Monod, the head of Combat for the Alpes-Maritimes department, happened to run into Max Shoop in Cannes. Shoop was head of the Sullivan and Cromwell law firm, where Monod had worked before the war. Using Shoop as a go-between, Allen Dulles, director of the U.S. OSS for Europe, suggested that Monod cooperate and proposed an apparently advantageous deal: Combat would provide military intelligence to the Americans, who in return would supply money, transmission capacities, and means of distribution. The substantial sum of 10 million francs was mentioned at the time. In April 1943, an agreement negotiated by Pierre Bénouville was reached. A delegation headed by General Davet, with the assistance of Philippe Monod, represented the MUR (primarily Combat in actuality) in Switzerland. The major leaders of the MUR were informed of that initiative, but Jean Moulin was not notified. When he learned of it in late April, he vehemently disapproved. "You are really stabbing de Gaulle in the back," he exclaimed.[44] Moulin then set about to isolate Frenay. He called a meeting of the steering committees for the three major movements in the southern zone, laying out the situation and urging them to dissociate themselves from Frenay—which they did, but cautiously. Pascal-Copeau, the second-in-command at Libération-sud, adopted a nuanced position. He pointed out that it was not necessarily imperative "to abandon the liaison with Bern," adding: "But I believe we have insufficient control over the matter and run the risk, as we did when this began, of again being presented with extremely dangerous faits accomplis."[45] In London, Colonel Passy ordered his British and American counterparts to abandon these unofficial talks. The British Intelligence Service and the SOE backed him up, fearing that the OSS would take over the French resistance.[46] Passy then suggested that the money promised to the MUR be entrusted to a representative whom Moulin would dispatch to Switzerland.[47] Naturally, that solution did not satisfy Frenay. For a time, he even considered seceding, before finally coming around.

Had Henri Frenay intended to double-cross Charles de Gaulle? That interpretation certainly seems extreme: the head of Combat, loyal to the man of June 18, had fended off the Giraudist temptation. But he clearly intended to restore the balance in a power relation that was not working to his advantage, believing that London ought to treat the movements as equals, not as subordinates. The Swiss channel primarily allowed him to circumvent Rex, whose authority he rejected, and to obtain the funds Moulin was haggling over. "Rightly or wrongly, he had persuaded himself that Moulin was engaging in a form of blackmail of the movements, by keeping them in a situation of chronic insecurity," Jacques Baumel writes.[48] The maneuver directly targeted Moulin: by confining him "to the role of observer or ambassador, [the men of Combat] seized his position as financier and supplier of arms and of liaison agents with the Allies. It would now be [they] who would establish the external liaisons for the Resistance and who would provide the movements with arms and money."[49] Moulin, notified at a late date, reacted violently, to the point of portraying in overly stark terms a maneuver that threatened to dispossess him of his authority. In a letter to General de Gaulle, he went so far as to claim that Frenay "is negotiating with the Americans and of necessity with Giraud,"[50] an abridgement that was both hasty and fallacious. At a time when de Gaulle and his rival were crossing swords, that venomous remark could only antagonize the leader of Fighting France. Did Frenay in fact intend to place himself under Franklin Roosevelt's orders? Not at all. But he was naïve to a fault, not understanding his interlocutors' calculations. In obtaining military intelligence through a channel other than the BCRA, the Allies would be able to disregard Fighting France and would weaken the position of General de Gaulle, whose credit rested in great part on the information that Colonel Passy's services were collecting. Are we to conclude that the Americans, here as elsewhere, sought to weaken the leader of Free France? Daniel Cordier believes so: "It is instructive to observe that, once de Gaulle's agreement on the American course of action in Switzerland was obtained, but only on the condition that money be paid to his representative and that the Americans not have direct access to the intelligence, their generosity suddenly ran dry. They did not offer or distribute another penny to the Resistance. That was truly proof (if any were needed) that their offer was not as disinterested as Bénouville and Frenay claimed."[51] For historian Robert Belot, however, that suspension of funding proved "the honesty of the Americans," who refused to interfere "in Franco-French affairs and to annoy de Gaulle."[52] That analysis is open to dispute, given the hostility Roosevelt felt toward de Gaulle and the obstacles he continually placed in his path.

In brief, the Swiss affair can probably be summed up as follows: Frenay, grappling with grave financial difficulties produced by the young people flooding into the maquis, believed he could finance his movement by relying on the Americans. He did not think he was betraying de Gaulle, whom he publicly supported, but he intended to restore the balance in a power relation that had been tipped by the clout Moulin had acquired. He was undoubtedly happy to bypass the authority of a hated delegate, to the point of blinding himself to the motives underlying Uncle Sam's generosity. In any event, the Swiss affair exacerbated the conflicts between Combat—and more generally, the movements—and General de Gaulle's delegate.

## The Widening Rift

The disagreements took a heavy toll. The movements, with Frenay in the lead, reproached Moulin for his half-hearted support of the maquis, which were taking in STO evaders. The resistance movements had opposed the creation of the CNR, which according to them favored the resurrection of the political parties. In addition, Frenay had laid claim to the command of the AS, which de Gaulle had preferred to entrust to Delestraint. These differences can be traced back to one basic question: Who ought to be in charge of the resistance? In General de Gaulle's view, the question did not arise. Militarily, the conduct of the war and the necessary coordination with Allied strategy demanded that power be concentrated in his own hands; without a leader, the army of shadows would spread itself thin and its actions would be incoherent and disorganized, which would undermine its effectiveness. Politically, de Gaulle believed that he alone, thanks to the Appeal of June 18, was able to embody the true France. It hardly mattered that the country was occupied. France's identity lay less in a particular plot of land than in a state. That was historically correct. Whereas in Italy and Germany, the nation had preceded the state, France had come into being by means of and thanks to the state constructed by the Capetian monarchy. Although defeated in 1940, France could hold itself together if and only if an embodied state endured, albeit outside the national borders. Furthermore, it was imperative that de Gaulle's sovereignty not be disputed or contested, which meant that discordant voices that would question his authority had to be silenced.

A number of resistance fighters refuted that view. While conceding that the command of the army of shadows rightly belonged to de Gaulle, they believed that the conduct of operations ought to be their responsibility: since they lived in the metropolis, they would be better able to judge the opportuneness of the actions to be conducted. From the political standpoint, they rejected any submission to Fighting France. The resistance was, in current terms, an emanation of civil society; that is, it was composed of citizens who had freely decided to become engaged, at the risk of their lives. Obedience was therefore a matter of consent; under no circumstances could it be imposed. Far from accepting subordination of some kind to General de Gaulle, part of the internal resistance intended to place itself on equal footing with him, as Frenay constantly pointed out. Claude Bourdet sums it up: "In reality, what de Gaulle and his services *absolutely could not abide* was the confirmation of the thesis defended in London by several leaders of the Resistance, and by Frenay in particular, namely, that the Resistance, which had come into being without de Gaulle and had freely attached itself to him, supported him as citizens support their chosen government and not as soldiers obey their unit commander."[53]

The conflict, produced by antithetical conceptions, took an emotional turn, crystallizing in the person of Jean Moulin, who embodied and applied the policy of the foremost personage of Free France. Moulin, inclined toward "authoritarianism,"[54] was not always easy to deal with and tended to be brusque. But most of the tension came as a result of his conflicting functions. As chair of the steering committee of the MUR, he could be considered an ally of the movements; but as representative of General de Gaulle, he embodied London's authority. And Moulin never sought to find a balance between the two. As Bourdet points out, "in his function as arbitrator and chair of the steering committee, [he] found himself in an awkward position, containing contradictions within himself, entrusted with an excessive authority stemming from his duties as arbitrator and thus necessarily led to *impose* points of view that he should only have been able to *propose*."[55] When differences arise, complained Frenay, "he always defends the point of view of the Comité National Français, or what he believes to be its point of view, and never that of the Resistance. He cannot be faulted for that, since he is thereby remaining true to his essential mission; but it makes the antagonism between his two functions glaringly obvious."[56] In 1942, Moulin was still finding his footing and demonstrated a certain flexibility, especially since power relations favored the movements. By 1943, however, he had become more rigid: the fight between de Gaulle and Giraud made it necessary to close ranks, and the funds he had at his disposal allowed him to impose his views.

The major leaders of the movements took advantage of their visit to London to undermine the delegate's authority. On April 13, 1943,

Jean-Pierre Levy, head of Franc-Tireur, and Emmanuel d'Astier de La Vigerie, the leader of Libération-sud, arrived in the British capital, where they were joined by Henri Frenay on June 17. In a memorandum written in April, d'Astier de La Vigerie curtly recapitulated the MUR's demands:

1. The Mouvements Unis, and, in general, the organized resistance wish to assert themselves, organize themselves, and direct their operations on their own.

2. The Mouvements Unis wish to receive directives from their leader, General de Gaulle, but their troops and activities can in no case be placed in the hands of officials *(missi dominici)* with only an occasional or abstract knowledge of the capacities of the resistance as a whole— officials who would decide its structure and would amputate essential elements from it and, on the pretext that they represent the Comité National, would conduct an authoritarian and personal policy.

3. . . . The Mouvements Unis wish to know all the activities of Rex [Moulin] as regards metropolitan France, just as they indicate their own to him, in order to compare and coordinate them.

   The Mouvements Unis wish to know his resources, just as they indicate their own to him, in order to compare and coordinate them.

   The Mouvements Unis cannot place themselves in his hands.

4. The Mouvements Unis demand that the Armée Secrète—commanded by a general officer designated by General de Gaulle—be controlled by the Comité de Coordination, which will have, always and in every form, certain directives to give regarding its structure, its organization, and its use, insofar as that use is related to the resistance and of political interest. . . .

7. The Mouvements Unis . . . demand that an agreement on principle be made to appoint a representative of the resistance in London.

   That representative, designated by the Movements and approved by the FFC, would be in London on a permanent basis, would be heard at the Comité National on questions concerning the resistance; he would collaborate with the different services on all activities concerning the resistance.

8. We do not consider ourselves "petty despots" [*rois nègres*, literally, "Negro kings"], in Rex's expression. We do not consider General de Gaulle a "cash cow," in Rex's expression; in sacrificing our lives, we do not consider the material aid, and more particularly, the financial aid offered us to be fair compensation.[57]

The criticisms hit home to a certain extent. D'Astier de La Vigerie had the ear of André Philip, commissioner for the interior at the time, who had formerly held a seat on the steering committee of Libération-sud. The minister, while confirming Moulin's powers, asked him to slow down centralization—which may have sounded a bit like a repudiation. Likewise, the instructions that de Gaulle sent to General Delestraint on May 21, 1943, incorporated the desires the movements had formulated. Accepting "the principle of immediate actions," they specified that "General Delestraint intervenes in this domain only via very broad directives established in agreement with the Comité de Coordination." His powers were extraordinarily limited: "At the current time, since the army of the interior has not yet acquired its definitive structure, General Delestraint, vis-à-vis all the elements that compose it, has the duties of inspector general, designated to take command of it at the time of the landing."[58] The demands of the movements had therefore been heard in part; at a time when de Gaulle was in bitter negotiations with Giraud, he avoided antagonizing the internal resistance, from which he drew part of his legitimacy.

In Frenay's eyes, however, these concessions remained inadequate. Having arrived in London in mid-June, he set out to topple Moulin and Delestraint. His fellow resistance leaders, however, refused to follow him on that crusade, which became all the more pointless when the arrest of both men deprived it of its objective. The leaders greatly feared the prospect of Frenay dominating the MUR hierarchy, even heading up the AS, and they had strong reservations about his political positions. Frenay, moreover, was by nature unbending; his real visionary capacities—he was one of the few people to grasp as early as 1940 what the future resistance could be—did not tend to foster self-doubt, and that irritated his rivals. In short, many hoped that General de Gaulle would keep him in London one way or another. Pascal Copeau, the second-in-command at Libération-sud, wrote to d'Astier de La Vigerie: "In the somewhat overblown way you know, Raymond [Aubrac] even went so far as to declare that the greatest service that could be rendered to the Resistance at the present time would be to eliminate, by any means whatever, a certain number of elements, beginning with Gervais [Frenay] himself. That is why, after your telegram summoning Gervais to London, we agreed to ask you to arrange that the absence of the head of Combat be as prolonged as possible, even permanent."[59] De Gaulle, shrewd politician that he was, found the appropriate solution: in Algiers, he named Frenay commissioner of prisoners, deportees, and refugees, which kept him from returning and deprived him of his authority over a fringe of the internal resistance.

The arrest of Jean Moulin and of Charles Delestraint, however, allowed the movements to move into high gear and to rescind the concessions Moulin had imposed on them.

## The Central Committee of Resistance Movements

The command of the AS was a recurring bone of contention. In early July, Pierre Bénouville used a meeting of the MUR steering committee as an opportunity to name Colonel Dejussieu (Pontcarral) chief of staff of the southern zone AS. And Colonel Touny, one of the leaders of the OCM, chaired the northern zone Comité Militaire des Mouvements de Résistance (Military Committee of Resistance Movements). As a result, "and until Liberation, de Gaulle, despite his efforts, could never retake direct command of the military forces of the Resistance."[60]

Certain movements, moreover, had never truly accepted the CNR. Capitalizing on the indecisiveness pervasive in London, the CDLR, the OCM, and Combat took swift action. Despite the tragedy of Caluire, and without alerting the interim delegate, Charles Bouchinet-Serreulles, they decided to go forward with a meeting scheduled for June 25, which was supposed to form the Comité Interzones (Interzone Committee). In Moulin's mind, that body would be in charge of resistance actions in the metropolis; ultimately, it would be incorporated into the CNR. The leaders of the movements broke free from that framework and created a Comité Central des Mouvements de Résistance (CCDMR; Central Committee of Resistance Movements) with broad powers. That executive committee "will represent the French Resistance and will conduct every aspect of its actions. It will recognize the CFLN as an organization for waging war, administering the empire, and representing the interests of France with the Allies.[61] For its part, the executive committee will be recognized by the Comité de la Libération as exercising power in France, while awaiting the creation of the provisional government. As such, it will have authority over employees of the state and of the public administrations."[62]

That plan, of course, was unacceptable to Fighting France. Apart from the fact that it deprived Fighting France of all authority over the internal resistance, it entrusted political power to the CCDMR until a provisional government could be installed. Claude Bouchinet-Serreulles, presented with a fait accompli, acted shrewdly. Accepting the committee in principle, he named himself its chair on July 23, 1943, and managed to limit its powers. As he explained: "I have the assembly of the 'Comité Central' reaffirm the existence of the CNR as the supreme advisory organ of the Resistance and clearly limit [its] prerogatives. . . . Its task is to coordinate action until then, without ties between the south and the north. It is agreed, in the course of that meeting, that it will not take the name 'executive,' since the executive function belongs solely to the CFLN, and, in France, to its delegation."[63]

The CCDMR did not last long and never really managed to take root. Composed of the eight movements granted a seat on the CNR, it left out the parties—including the powerful PCF—and granted only what was considered minor representation to the FN. "The 1:7 ratio for the Communist Resistance was absolutely ridiculous and did not represent its real weight in the country," Claude Bourdet writes.[64] That move naturally aroused the immediate hostility of those loyal to Maurice Thorez, and the FN's delegate, Pierre Villon, practiced the "empty chair" policy. The committee, moreover, could not compete with the CNR, whose prestige and legitimacy were increasing. Furthermore, the movements that had been left off the CNR were not invited to join the CCDMR, which eroded its legitimacy to speak in the name of the resistance as a whole. "We committed several errors," acknowledges Bourdet, "the first being not to let in representatives of 'Défense de la France' and 'Résistance,' whose importance, even at that time, already exceeded that of some 'official' movements. But the others did not wish their presence at any cost,"[65] preferring to exclude groups that might overshadow them. The CCDMR thus quickly fizzled out and played a negligible role—with one exception. It created or headed up six commissions that ultimately made a significant contribution. Four commissions focused on the actions to be conducted over the short term. The

NAP, entrusted to Jean de Vogüé, solicited the complicity of public employees. The mission of the Comité d'Action contre la Déportation (CAD; Action Committee against Deportation), headed by Yves Farge, would be to fight the STO. The Commission des Services de Santé (Commission of Health Services), directed by Louis Pasteur Vallery-Radot, arranged health coverage for the resistance fighters—the maquisards especially. Finally, the Commission de l'Action Immédiate (COMIDAC; Committee for Immediate Action) merged the military committees in the two zones and aspired to lead the armed struggle in the metropolis. Two other commissions made plans for liberation. Under Michel Debré, the Commission des Désignations Administratives (Commission of Administrative Appointments) had the task of naming the high officials who would run the state apparatus once liberation came—beginning with prefects and commissioners of the republic. And the Commission du Ravitaillement (Resupply Commission), entrusted to Pierre Miné, would anticipate the thorny question of getting provisions to the civilian population, which would obviously be a crucial issue upon liberation.[66] Without managing to undermine the power of the CNR, the movements thus made a place for themselves in the command of underground action and fully participated in preparing for the liberation.

The movements also made their mark by seizing the chairmanship of the CNR and broadening its prerogatives. On July 14, 1943, the FN achieved passage of an Appeal to the Nation, which had been rejected at the May 27 session: "As the full and sole expression of the Resistance, the Conseil de la Résistance claims over the entire territory the rights and responsibilities of manager and provisional body of national sovereignty. Against the enemy and against treason, the Conseil de la Résistance assumes, in close collaboration with Fighting France, and necessarily in conjunction with the Comité National de la Libération, the mission of inspiring, coordinating, and leading the struggle of the French people on their own soil."[67] The CNR thus aspired, in defiance of the Gaullist stance, to lead the resistance and to embody a share of national legitimacy.

These ambitions found free expression, all the more so in that London was slow to nominate a CNR chair. Claude Bouchinet-Serreulles, pressed by the movements and without instructions, arranged for the members of the council to vote on the matter. Georges Bidault was therefore elected on August 30, 1943. It was a smart choice: the brilliant Christian Democrat, forty-four years old at the time and a member of the steering committees of Combat and of the FN, had full mastery of the arcana of the internal resistance. A close friend of Jean Moulin, he understood London's requirements and was not resolutely opposed to de Gaulle—on the contrary. The procedure, however, contradicted the Gaullist line on many points. In the first place, it entrusted the election of the chairman to the parties and the movements, whereas, up to that time, London had been in charge of appointing him. Moulin chaired the steering committees of both the MUR and the CNR, while at the same time running de Gaulle's Délégation Générale (General Delegation). The three hats he wore reduced the rift between London and the internal resistance. By contrast, there was a risk that Bidault would widen that rift, since, despite his loyalty to de Gaulle, he was above all the movements' man. Moulin's presence had averted the risk of a power structure split between Gaullist legitimacy and that of the army of shadows; the election of Bidault suddenly made that split a possibility, particularly since, on November 26, 1943, he formed within the CNR a permanent five-member bureau (consisting of representatives from the FN, the CGT, the OCM, and Libération-sud, plus Bidault himself). That bureau would make the important decisions, the council being unable to meet in a plenary session. That measure, though called for by André Philip in September 1943, posed a political risk, which would become quite real in 1944. After the Caluire tragedy, the delegation had lost ground that it could not recover.

## Pierre Brossolette's Downfall

Émile Bollaert had been named CFLN representative on the CNR on September 2, 1943. But the Brossolette-Bollaert team did not manage to command authority, particularly because of the opposition of Bouchinet-Serreulles, the interim delegate, and Bingen, the delegate for the southern zone, who arrived on the night of August 15. Beyond issues of personnel and power, two philosophies were at odds. Bingen and Bouchinet-Serreulles were working hard to undermine the authority of the CCDMR, in order to shore up the CNR. That was in line with the Gaullist strategy. Brossolette, by contrast, sought to promote the CCDMR. "Always giving top priority to the Resistance movements, he favored the body that in his view was its most direct expression," his biographer concludes. "He took his distance from Georges Bidault, whose actions he did not find convincing. He also believed he was promoting the actions of an organization whose commissions had been working effectively for three months, as he liked to point out. Finally, he probably calculated that, in putting Émile Bollaert at the head of the Comité Central, he could exert indirect control over it, stand up to the CNR, and shore up his own position."[68] In so doing, Brossolette once again flouted the instructions he had received. Bouchinet-Serreulles, however, stood in his way. The rue de la Pompe affair offered a suitable pretext for getting rid of him.

In summer 1943, the delegation was obliged to welcome new arrivals to Paris, for whom lodging had to be found. A secretary, Jacqueline d'Alincourt (Violaine), overwhelmed by these demands, sublet a room for Colonel Marchal, military delegate for the northern zone, providing her address and true identity. As it happens, the landlady, Mme Sorlin, had connections with the German police. After Marchal dropped off his bags in the apartment, Mme Sorlin went through them and, having found compromising documents, alerted her contacts. Marchal and then d'Alincourt were arrested. At the residence of Violaine, the Germans found rent receipts, including one for the apartment on rue de la Pompe, which housed the delegation's secretarial office. On September 25, the Germans raided the office. Although they arrested nine liaison agents, the damage was limited: only "two light briefcases"[69] were seized, and the detained resistance fighters did not talk.

According to Henri Noguères, that affair was "no more and no less serious than many others in Lyon, Marseilles, and Paris, which had led to a series of arrests and the seizure of important Resistance files."[70] But Bouchinet-Serreulles committed the blunder of including every detail of that drama in his report of October 7, 1943. His honesty proved to be his downfall. "Never before in the history of the Resistance, where such 'affairs,' unfortunately, were common—not to say a daily occurrence—had anyone given an account with such a wealth of details. In London, which generally received succinct information about the worst hits, that report, when compared to the others, created the impression that this was a major catastrophe, especially since Serreulles covered for his subordinates," Daniel Cordier writes.[71]

Pierre Brossolette and Colonel Passy took advantage of that affair to sully the interim delegate's reputation. Brossolette went on the attack: "I have no opinion of Sophie [Bouchinet-Serreulles], on the sort of perpetual scheming to which he stoops, he and the countless committees he chairs, on the triviality of his paramilitary actions, and on his attempt [easily thwarted] to make Baudoin [Bollaert] his puppet. Sophie's office is a nameless bedlam, which arranges meetings and does not keep them, which commits daily errors, which puts everybody on edge, through which nothing can be obtained (out of fecklessness and nastiness both), and which is putting everything at risk through unbelievably careless methods (in that respect, the fact that the archives were ransacked at the same time as the office says it all)."[72]

In early November, therefore, Brossolette—once again accompanied by Yeo-Thomas—seized the opportunity to demand the recall of Bouchinet-Serreulles. The BCRA followed suit, asking its agents to cut off all contact with him. It did not take long for the opposing camp to react. While agreeing that Bouchinet-Serreulles and Bingen would be sequestered, Georges Boris recommended repatriating Bollaert and Brossolette to England. On November 7, the Gaullist authorities ordered the return of all four men.[73] Brossolette made a show of resisting, but it was no longer the moment for insubordination. On November 9, in fact, d'Astier de La Vigerie had replaced André Philip at the Commission for the Interior, and Brossolette thereby lost a prominent ally. In addition, de Gaulle became involved, demanding the immediate recall of Bouchinet-Serreulles and Brossolette. Although Passy agreed to let Bingen serve as interim chair of the General Delegation, he adamantly ordered Brossolette to return with Bollaert, whom de Gaulle wanted to see in Algiers. He also took the opportunity to make it clear to his friend that he could no longer cover for his disobedience.

Believing that air travel would be unpredictable, Pierre Brossolette decided to return to England by sea. Colonel Paillole's special services set up the Jouet des Flots mission, which was supposed to transport not only Brossolette and Bollaert but also two envoys from London and several officers. On February 2, 1944, the men set off, but a leak flooded the engine; the mainsail was torn off in a storm, and the boat drifted, running aground near Audierne. Bollaert and Brossolette hid at the home of a resistance fighter. But on February 3, while riding in a car, they were arrested during a routine stop. Incarcerated in the Rennes prison, they were not immediately identified. In mid-March, however, they were transferred to Gestapo headquarters on avenue Foch in Paris—though only Brossolette had been recognized in the meantime. Brossolette, after being interrogated many times, was taken to a *chambre de bonne*, where, on March 22, he eluded his guards and threw himself out the window rather than talk under torture. He died at ten o'clock that same night.[74] In the shadowlands, he rejoined Jean Moulin, who, like him, had preferred to die rather than run the risk of breaking.

The organization skillfully built up by Jean Moulin did not survive its creator. Part of the internal resistance took advantage of the Caluire tragedy to recover its independence, while the Gaullist camp fought tooth and nail over the inheritance, depriving the delegation of part of its authority, which was already quite weak. As Pascal Copeau would point out, a page had been turned. "The authority of the delegation would be the object of negotiations, and, for all the delegates, even the military ones, the only way to hold on to their authority would be to become in large part interpreters of the real problems of underground action."[75] The bulk of the resistance truly supported General de Gaulle and intended to lend military support to the liberation of the country. Nevertheless, it had no intention of blindly obeying the man of June 18. It wanted to play a prominent role, both politically and militarily. More than ever, therefore, the relations between the two camps were marked by complexity and even conflict.

## Chapter 12

# Power Struggles in Algiers and Their Consequences

IF THE REICH APPEARED invincible in 1940, its defeat seemed assured in 1943. The Anglo-American forces, after landing in North Africa on November 8, 1942, seized Tunisia in May 1943. They landed in Sicily on July 10, then got a foothold on the Italian peninsula, beginning a slow and painful trek northward; Rome did not fall until June 5, 1944. To the east, the Soviets crushed Field Marshal Friedrich Paulus's Sixth Army in Stalingrad on February 2, 1943, then inflicted a strategic setback on the German forces during the Battle of Kursk in July of the same year. In short, Germany, put on the defensive, was tottering. But to bring it down, the Allies would have to land in northwestern Europe, as Stalin was vehemently demanding.

The opportuneness of such a landing sharply divided the general staffs. The British, true to their historical strategies, preferred to strike the enemy at his weak point and, as a result, recommended a strategy of attrition favoring the Mediterranean theater of operations. The Americans, by contrast, suggested attacking the Reich's bastions, which would allow the Allies to prevail once and for all. They therefore overwhelmingly favored the northwestern theater, which would lend decisive support to the offensive that the Soviets would launch to the east. These long debates postponed the western landing. It was not until November 1943 that the decision was made at the Tehran Conference, under joint pressure from the Americans and the Soviets: the Allies would intervene in France in spring 1944.[1] That decision assigned France a determining role, since the fate of the western war would be played out there. The use to be made of the resistance became a burning question: What place ought to be given to the army of shadows within the Allied strategy?

Charles de Gaulle also had questions about the strategy, combined with a certain political bafflement. Everything, to be sure, now suggested that he would exercise power upon liberation. That prospect obliged him to propose unification, to integrate both those longing for the return of the Vichy regime and those who pledged their allegiance to the Red Flag. Otherwise, the country was at risk of collapsing into civil war or of igniting into a new October Revolution. In 1943, that possibility was still only theoretical, however. For the time being, de Gaulle pursued a more mundane objective: to impose his authority alongside Giraud and then to supplant him.

## From Dyarchy to Undivided Rule

Giraud, with the support of the Americans, had attempted to remain in power after Darlan's assassination in December 1942. His complete absence of political savvy and the neo-Vichyist policy he was conducting in North Africa alienated his supporters, however. His Anglo-American mentors acknowledged the obvious: Giraud would have to share power with de Gaulle. On May 30, 1943, the Rebel landed at Maison-Blanche Airport in Algiers, and on June 3, the two men formed the Comité Français de la Libération Nationale (CFLN; French Committee of National Liberation). Dividing up their powers was an arduous task: the copresidents possessed the same rights; and, within the provisional government, harmony cannot be said to have reigned between Giraudist and Gaullist commissioners. But de Gaulle knew how to take advantage of his rival's blunders and to marginalize him little by little. In summer 1943, a specialized presidency was put in place, and on October 2, after the liberation of Corsica, Giraud was forced to choose between commanding the French forces and holding political responsibilities. On November 9, he opted for military action and stepped down from the CFLN. De Gaulle had prevailed: he remained alone at the helm.[2]

The fight for power at the top was far from the only problem. Large swaths of French society had put their trust in Marshal Pétain, even if they had not necessarily subscribed to his reforms. That reality became increasingly obvious in North Africa, where the administration and the Colonial Army were in the thrall of the Vichy regime. De Gaulle had never compromised his principles and, with real panache, had rejected any accommodation with the French State, which was guilty of concluding the shameful armistice agreement with the Reich in June 1940.

But pragmatism was the order of the day. To ensure the cooperation of the state apparatus and its armed forces, the chair of the CFLN would have to keep from appearing sectarian if he wanted to attract the lost sheep led astray by bad shepherds. The imperatives associated with national unity and the conduct of the war led de Gaulle to close his eyes to the past. There were two conditions, however: the men who had succumbed to the Pétainist mirage had to demonstrate an irreproachable patriotism, and they could not have blood on their hands. Even while protecting his right flank, de Gaulle also had to protect his left, to prevent his policy from being contested by forces persecuted by the Vichy regime, which would cry for justice.

To respond to these contradictory demands, de Gaulle created institutions designed to incorporate all political forces. The CNR had partly responded to that aspiration; the convening of a consultative assembly would fulfill it. The idea had been put forward by the jurist René Cassin in 1941. General Giraud accepted it in principle, and the decree of September 17, 1943, made it a reality. The Assemblée Consultative Provisoire d'Alger (ACP; Provisional Consultative Assembly of Algiers), composed of 103 members, included former parliamentarians (20 representatives) and the delegates of the general councils (12), as well as envoys from both the external resistance (12) and the internal resistance (49). The left dominated the ACP, all the more so in that it refused to seat the parliamentarians who had voted to grant Marshal Pétain full powers on July 10, 1940—with the notable exception of the moderate Paul Antier. Charles Vallin, François de Clermont-Tonnerre, and Roger Farjon were thus excluded.[3] In spite of everything, the right made its presence known, particularly since several conservative and moderate parliamentarians—Antier, Vallin, Farjon, and others—had joined Free France after a time.

In addition, de Gaulle carefully refrained from launching a radical purge in North Africa. He did of course put collaborationists and torturers on trial and locked up symbols of the old order: Boisson, the governor of French West Africa; and Flandin and Peyrouton, former ministers of the French State. A few general officers were also imprisoned (Admirals Michelier and Derrien, for example) or driven out of the army (General Barré). Finally, Pierre Pucheu, former minister of the interior, was executed on March 22, 1944, after an expedited trial. On the whole, however, the purge was by no means a bloodbath. "Insofar as it was in de Gaulle's hands, [it] combined leniency and the examples made of major figures," writes Jean-Louis Crémieux-Brilhac.[4] Although limited in scope, the purge was met with overt hostility from many of the supporters of the old regime. As historian Bénédicte Vergez-Chaignon observes, "Quite simply, the fact that someone was loyal to the person and the ideas of Pétain, obeyed the orders of his governments, applied his policy, was not considered an error, even less a flaw. It was normal, and even proper, to have been a Pétainist—and to be one still. . . . The idea spread that the purge was only one manifestation among others of the Gaullists' desire to clean house for their own benefit. A true clique on a quest for power, they had undertaken to do so as soon as they set foot in North Africa."[5] It is therefore understandable why de Gaulle acted with restraint to promote the unification he desired. Even so, the national unity championed at the political level still had to be translated into practice. Given the fractures to be repaired, that desire was not at all easy to fulfill.

## The Choices of the Military

From that standpoint, the armed forces became a burning issue. Some eighty thousand men quartered in Africa made it possible for France to play a role, albeit a modest one, in that theater of operations, a role that would be expanded by the anticipated reintroduction of conscription.

In captive France, many officers had suffered greatly when the free zone was invaded, and they dreamed of taking up arms once again when the time came. The ORA aspired to assemble these willing men. When the Germans arrested its first leader, General Aubert Frère, on June 13, 1943, General Jean-Édouard Verneau succeeded him; but he too was arrested, on October 23. At that time, General Georges Revers took the reins of the organization; but it hardly attracted all the cadres in the Grande Muette. Of the 11,000 officers in the land army who were in the metropolis in November 1942 (4,200 in the armistice army, 2,000 in corps converted to civilian use, and 4,800 who had been released from service), only 1,500 went to North Africa. Although 4,000 more joined the resistance, only 1,500 signed up with the ORA; 1,400 preferred to join the networks, and 1,000 supported other organizations, primarily the AS and the FTP.[6]

Although the ORA had not assembled all military officers, it wanted to support the struggle of resistance fighters and to contribute to the rebirth of the French forces.[7] It proposed, in General Verneau's words, to "establish liaisons with the civilian organizations" and to "join them in the aim of improving military efficiency."[8] Its resources remained limited, however: Revers acknowledged that, at the start of 1943, only a quarter of its members were armed, and the organization possessed fewer than twenty radio sets for the entire territory.[9] It comprised at most a few thousand men in June of that year,[10] certainly a small number for a force that aspired to make a significant contribution to the liberation of the territory. Hungry for action, some even preferred to join the AS, a group that sometimes turned to these war professionals despite their controversial past. In August 1943, Raymond du Jonchay, for example, despite being an ardent Marshalist, became the director of the AS for the Vienne department.[11] In the Jura department, six out of eight FFI district leaders were active military, as was the entire staff of the department, with the exception of its leader, Romuald Vandelle.[12]

Relations between civilian and military resisters were marked by distrust. Naturally, political suspicions had not disappeared. Members of the ORA were suspected of Vichyism; they in turn feared that the Communists would take over the internal resistance. Quarrels about strategy exacerbated these suspicions. The AS made the case for immediate action, while the ORA had misgivings. "The terrorist campaign—derailments, attacks on shops and town halls—ill serves the Resistance, especially vis-à-vis peasants and the middle class," Revers observed in November 1943.[13] But the ORA ultimately rallied behind that strategy, even though guerrilla warfare was not part of its fighting traditions.

Each camp, moreover, accused the other of stealing away its troops—the ORA had the somewhat undeserved reputation of having a wealth of arms. These considerations explain why its inclusion in the internal resistance's hierarchy remained problematic from start to finish. Although an accord concluded with the MUR in autumn 1943 stipulated that ORA officers, without being in command, would become chiefs of staff in the regions, the agreement was unevenly applied. True, the ORA suffered on account of its ambiguous status:

Did it represent the army, in which case it could assist the AS with its advice, or did it constitute a distinct resistance movement? General Revers chose the second option, to break the isolation of an army discredited by its Vichyist orientation.[14] In so doing, however, he entered into competition with the other underground groups, which were upset by the emergence of a new rival. Their fears were only reinforced when Revers attempted to negotiate with the Communists in December 1943. All in all, the role the ORA was supposed to play in the order of battle was not clear-cut. That situation, combined with the small number of the ORA's troops, had the end result of depriving Giraud of a decisive asset.

The question of the secret services appeared in a different light. The intelligence collected in the metropolis was a bargaining chip highly valued by the Allies. It therefore played a prominent role in the negotiations that the French authority conducted with the British and Americans. In addition, the secret services partly controlled the metropolitan resistance. In March 1942, the creation of the Études et Coordination (Studies and Coordination) section had turned the Gaullist BCRA into "a true general staff for underground action in France."[15] Oversight by the secret services brought with it control of all or part of the underground forces, which, with the prospect of liberation, represented a major asset. It is therefore understandable why the Giraudists and the Gaullists were at odds, each group fighting to ensure that the foreseeable merger of these services would be to its own advantage.

## The Tricky Merger of the Secret Services

In this regard, Giraud had a few resources at his disposal. A part of the Vichy intelligence services had been entrusted to him in November 1942, and Giraud restructured its organization. He created the DSS, which he assigned to Colonel Ronin, formerly the head of SR Air. The new Direction des Services de Renseignement et de Sécurité Militaire (DSR-SM; Directorate of Intelligence and Military Security Services) was placed under Colonel Rivet, who had run the Services Spéciaux (Special Services) since 1936. Within that system, the Direction de la Sécurité Militaire (Directorate of Military Security), under the orders of Lieutenant Colonel Chrétien and later of Commander Paillole, enjoyed relative autonomy.[16] Giraud's proclaimed apoliticism reassured these officers. "The Special Services now reported to him, inasmuch as he was the highest military authority. This therefore marked a return to a conventional system, in which the military intelligence services were attached to the commander in chief."[17] The Giraudist intelligence services avoided politics and worked in harmony with the British and Americans, particularly since in North Africa they were all in close quarters on a daily basis.

The merger of the Gaullist and Giraudist secret services remained a possibility, however. A coordination of efforts was obviously required, since disarray could hamper the future liberation of the territory. As one might suspect, any plan to coordinate actions had to grapple with the mutual feelings of hostility between the two camps. Past political disputes had not been settled: the Vichy services had hunted down Gaullist resistance fighters; and during the invasion of the free zone, these services had refrained from releasing those languishing in jail. As a result, "in General de Gaulle's eyes, Rivet's services had irremediably compromised themselves with Vichy."[18] Differences in strategy intensified the ideological quarrels. For Colonel Rivet, "the military intelligence services had to remain under military command . . . even though the intelligence collected would not be exclusively military but also political and economic." De Gaulle, by contrast, believed that the intelligence corps now had to "be attached to the political authority, whatever the nature of the intelligence collected and whatever the diversity of the actors collecting it."[19] It made no sense to separate the political from the military, especially since, as Passy reminded de Gaulle on August 16, 1943, "intelligence and military action could camouflage political activities, for which the British balked at providing specific resources."[20] The Giraudist professionals, finally, took a dim view of the BCRA, holding its amateurism in contempt.

Achieving unity was therefore a battle. At first, each camp dispatched representatives into hostile territory. André Pélabon had joined Fighting France in September 1942, and he went on to manage the North Africa bureau, since he had good knowledge of the region. He was quite naturally sent to Algiers, where, in July 1943, he created the subbranch of the Gaullist secret services.[21] General Giraud in turn dispatched General Mathenet to London, naming him to head a military mission. But the merger was at a standstill, particularly since no one really wanted it, except, of course, as a way to take over the competing service!

De Gaulle then considered making General Cochet head of the services. It was quite a shrewd choice. Cochet, while initially approving of Marshal Pétain's actions, had called for resistance from the start. He was twice arrested as a result. After long weeks of captivity in Spain, he managed to get to England in March 1943.[22] Since his pedigree made him acceptable to both camps, on October 4, 1943, de Gaulle placed him at the head of the intelligence and action services, which linked the BCRA to the DSR-SM. That body was itself subordinate to the COMIDAC, an agency headed by de Gaulle, at which both General Giraud and André Philip held seats. The COMIDAC was supposed to manage all relations with the French resistance.

This encroachment did not satisfy either of the two camps, however, and they resisted Cochet's authority. The new head of services demanded that Ronin submit to him the instructions he was sending to London; Ronin refused and was relieved of his duties on October 14, 1943. With Colonel Passy, it appeared that the game would be more complicated. Cochet demanded effective command of the BCRA, which Passy opposed. But the conflict came to a rapid conclusion. On November 19, 1943, Cochet, sidelined for many long weeks, handed in his resignation; the next day, de Gaulle created a Direction Générale des Services Spéciaux (DGSS; Directorate General of Special Services). He entrusted it to Jacques Soustelle, in whom he had every confidence, and not without reason. In June 1940, the young ethnologist, in Mexico at the time, had rallied behind the Rebel and had immediately organized Free France committees in Central America. In June 1942, he went to London and worked there in the information services alongside Maurice Schumann. The longtime Gaullist thus had a perfect pedigree. He was flanked by another of de Gaulle's trusted friends, Passy, who was named technical director. The DGSS had two bases of operations: the BCRAL in London and the BCRAA in Algiers, run, respectively, by André Manuel and André Pélabon.[23]

The merger threatened the Giraudist services, which refused to be placed under the authority of their enemy brothers. Soustelle relieved Rivet of his duties on December 16 and, using a proven method, in early

January refused to pay his rivals their allocations. But General de Gaulle's opponents persisted. Without giving the president of the CFLN any warning, Giraud sent representatives to France and Spain to organize networks that would be loyal to him. These maneuvers could not fail to irritate de Gaulle. In March 1944, he suspended financing for the Giraudist services and, on April 15, forced Rivet into retirement. The merger of the Special Services thus went into effect in spring 1944[24]—though it cannot be called a victory for the BCRA. In fact, the new commissioner for the interior, Emmanuel d'Astier de La Vigerie—named in November 1943—had every intention of exercising right of access to any operation the resistance would launch upon liberation. Logically, he therefore demanded control of the Special Services; Passy and Soustelle both disapproved. The former head of Libération-sud succeeded in imposing his will, however. In March 1944, a decree stipulated that the COMIDAC, in de Gaulle's absence, would be chaired by d'Astier de La Vigerie, who, moreover, was granted supreme control to allocate the COMIDAC's funds for resistance actions and to dispatch civilian missions to captive France.[25] Passy therefore left the Direction Technique des Services Spéciaux (Technical Directorate of Special Services) to become chief of staff to General Koenig, head of the FFI. "That about-turn," writes Sébastien Albertelli, "allowed de Gaulle to accede to d'Astier's request without depriving himself of Passy's expertise in underground action."[26] In spite of everything, Passy lost a large share of his power in the battle. The underground actions undertaken to liberate the country would obey different rules from those that the founder of the BCRA had dreamed of imposing. Indeed, the path the underground followed, far from being dictated by London or Algiers, would be its own.

## Action

The internal resistance, largely unaffected by the death of Rex, increased in power, further developing its press and false papers shops and militarizing its action. The networks experienced a real expansion. With more areas of engagement and better liaisons, they were now in a position to provide precious intelligence to their principal, the BCRA or the British Intelligence Service. In autumn 1943, Georges Gorse of the Gallia network, for example, recruited Colonel Louis Gentil, director of materiel in Chamalières. Thanks to contacts established with the Service Central des Marchés et de Surveillance des Approvisionnements (Central Service for Markets and for the Oversight of Supplies), Gentil was able to provide his organization with arms and vehicles, which he pilfered from the army. He also recruited active officers, who supplied him with military information. In the same vein, the Dupleix network, founded by Jacques Hirsch-Girin, attached itself to Gallia. Aiming to prevent repression, it warned some two hundred people of threats to their safety. In February 1944, Gallia had seven operational regions and two subnetworks; at the time, it specialized in the pursuit of military intelligence in Brittany and the Paris region.[27]

Along the same lines, Jean Pelletier, a member of the Max subnetwork working under Manipule, took advantage of the positions held by his parents, who were employed as concierges in the building on rue de Presbourg that housed the western branch of the Todt Organization, which was in charge of the Reich's public works projects. Pelletier was able to inform the Allies about the materiel and manpower that the occupier was using in the western region in February 1943. Once a week, he handed over a full suitcase of documents to Pierre Arrighi, head of the network.[28]

One indication of the growth of the networks: the BCRA undoubtedly received more than three thousand telegrams from them in 1943 and more than eight thousand in the first eight months of 1944. The volume of mail increased as well, from forty-two pieces in 1942 to more than one hundred and sixty in the following two years.[29] In addition to military intelligence, there was economic, political, and social information, which allowed the CFLN to form an accurate idea of the state of mind reigning in the metropolis.

The Gaullist secret services and their networks also engaged in direct action. By striking precise targets, they hoped to keep the Allies from dropping bombs, whose inaccuracy caused heavy civilian losses without necessarily obtaining positive results. Hence, on the night of July 26, 1943, a saboteur named Jean-Marie Pellay destroyed the Gigny Dam on the Saône to prevent German warships from traveling on the river to the Mediterranean. Mission Paquebot, as it was called, fulfilled all its objectives, and river traffic was paralyzed for three months.[30]

Raymond Basset and André Jarrot arrived by parachute in August; on the night of September 1, they destroyed several pylons and transformers that fed electricity to the factories of Le Creusot. The success of that operation, baptized "Armada," led the BCRA to repeat it. Once more dropped by parachute in November, the team attacked the Gigny Dam a second time, then, before returning to London in April 1944, set about destroying pylons (187 in all), canals, locks, and locomotives.[31]

The networks that the SOE had set up also got involved in the fight. On October 31, 1943, the Salesman network, run by a journalist named Philippe Liewer, sabotaged the electrical substation of Dieppevalle, a suburb of Rouen. It was paralyzed for six months "by fifteen pounds of well-placed plastic."[32] The network also sank a minesweeper being repaired in a shipyard near the Norman capital by placing a plastic explosive charge in the hull.[33] Michael Trotobas's Farmer network caused a number of train derailments in the Nord department. With about twenty men, it sabotaged the locomotive maintenance facility in Fives, near Lille, on the night of June 27, 1943, destroying 4 million liters of oil and damaging twenty-two transformers.[34] The Parson network, finally, transmitted the plan for the coastal defenses established in Brittany.[35]

Nor did the movements remain inactive. The CDLR group in Épernay derailed a trainload of German soldiers on leave on the night of September 21, 1943.[36] In Ille-et-Vilaine, the FTP conducted twenty-eight actions between February and December 1943, and between January 1944 and the launch of the Allied landing claimed responsibility for eighteen railroad sabotages, twenty attacks on high-tension wires, and nine assaults on collaborators.[37] On November 11, 1943, a demonstration took place in Grenoble around the monument to the mountain infantry known as the Diables Bleus (Blue Devils), to commemorate the victory of 1918. The Germans secured the perimeter and deported 450 residents of Grenoble. In reply, on the night of November 13, Aimé Requet, assistant to the leader of the irregular groups, blew up the Polygone, where artillery and munitions were stored. In retaliation, in late November the Germans and their French accomplices arrested or murdered the principal leaders of the resistance in Isère, including Dr. Valois, head of the MUR in that department. The resistance then responded by blowing up materiel warehoused in the

PAS-DE-CALAIS

**FARMER**

NORD

SOMME

SEINE-INFÉRIEURE

●Amiens

AISNE

ARDENNES

MOSELLE

SILVERSMITH
PEDLAR

MEUSE

**WOODCUTTER**

MANCHE

CALVADOS

EURE

SEINE-ET-OISE

**BEGGAR**

**DONKEYMAN**
**(fragment)**

**SPIRITUALIST**
**MINISTER**

Paris●

MARNE

●Châlons-
sur-Marne

MEURTHE-ET-
MOSELLE

BAS-
RHIN

**PEDAGOGUE**

**RACKETEER**

CÔTES-DU-NORD

ORNE

**HELMSMAN**

**WIZARD**
**(destroyed)**

SEINE-ET-MARNE

**DIETICIAN**

AUBE

HAUTE-
MARNE

**GLOVER**

VOSGES

HAUT-
RHIN

FINISTÈRE

ILLE-ET-
VILAINE

MAYENNE

**PERMIT**

EURE-ET-LOIR

**HISTORIAN**

YONNE

HAUTE-
SAÔNE

**STOCKBROKER**

MORBIHAN

**HILLBILLY**

Le Mans●

SARTHE

LOIRET

**DONKEYMAN**
**(fragment)**

Dijon●

**SACRISTAN**

**CHANCELLOR**

LOIRE-
INFÉRIEURE

MAINE-ET-
LOIRE

**HERMIT**

LOIR-ET-
CHER

**VENTRILOQUIST**

**GONDOLIER**

CÔTE-D'OR

DOUBS

TERRITOIRE
DE-BELFORT

INDRE-ET-
LOIRE

NIÈVRE

**AUDITOR**

**TREASURER**

VENDÉE

DEUX-
SÈVRES

**WRESTLER**

INDRE

CHER

**LICENSEE**

SAÔNE-ET-
LOIRE

**MASON**

JURA

**SCHOLAR**

VIENNE

**SHIPWRIGHT**

ALLIER

**DITCHER**
**ACOLYTE**

**MARKSMAN**

HAUTE-SAVOIE

CHARENTE-
INFÉRIEURE

HAUTE-
VIENNE

**FIREMAN**

**SALESMAN**

CREUSE

**SAINT**

PUY-DE-DÔME

RHÔNE

AIN

CHARENTE

●Limoges

**DIGGER**

CORRÈZE

Clermont-
Ferrand●

**NEWSAGENT**

●Lyon

**PIMENTO**
**(fragment)**

LOIRE

SAVOIE

**TILLEUL**

CANTAL

**FREELANCE**

HAUTE-LOIRE

ISÈRE

GIRONDE

**WHEELWRIGHT**
**(fragment)**

Bordeaux●

**ACTOR**

LOT

DORDOGNE

AVEYRON

LOZÈRE

ARDÈCHE

DRÔME

HAUTES-ALPES

LANDES

LOT-ET-
GARONNE

TARN-ET-
GARONNE

**FOOTMAN**

**PIMENTO**
**(fragment)**

**CLERGYMAN**
**(fragment)**

GARD

VAUCLUSE

BASSES-
ALPES

ALPES-
MARITIMES

**WHEELWRIGHT**
**(fragment)**

GERS

●Toulouse

TARN

HÉRAULT

Montpellier●

BOUCHES-
DU-RHÔNE

**GARDENER**

VAR

BASSES-
PYRÉNÉES

HAUTE-
GARONNE

**DETECTIVE**

AUDE

Marseilles●

HAUTES-
PYRÉNÉES

ARIÈGE

PYRÉNÉES-
ORIENTALES

*J O C K E Y*

100        200 Miles

0          150          300 Kilometres

CORSE

F Section Networks of the SOE

- - - - - Demarcation line

*Map 3*

barracks of Bonne, in the Haute-Savoie department, on the night of December 1, 1943.[38]

The hope of an imminent landing sparked enthusiasm. On February 25, 1944, Léo Hamon slipped into the offices of the STO general commission and burned 200,000 personal information cards. On May 16, 1944, the FTP attacked the four Opel garages of Fougères, in Ille-et-Vilaine, destroying thirty-four trucks and eleven airplane engines, as several thousand quarts of oil and gasoline went up in smoke.[39] The attacks multiplied. On October 6, 1943, Calvet, the director of the German employment office in Annemasse, was killed at his home by two men disguised as members of the Groupes mobiles de réserve (GMR; mobile reserve groups); his counterpart in Saint-Brieuc met the same fate in 1944.[40] For many weeks, Cristina Boïco tailed SS General Julius Ritter, Fritz Sauckel's representative in France. On the morning of September 28, 1943, Ritter was executed by a commando composed of Marcel Rayman and Leo Kneller, with Celestino Alfonso providing cover. On October 10 of the same year, the public prosecutor Lespinasse, who had demanded the death penalty for the FTP hero Marcel Langer, was executed in Toulouse on his way to mass. On October 23, police superintendent Barthelet was assassinated in the same city.[41]

The maquis, for their part, engaged in guerrilla warfare. Georges Guingouin's men, based in the Châteauneuf forest, destroyed the engine of the Limoges–Peyrat-le-Château tramway in early July 1943 and, on the 12th of the same month, severed the underground cable of the Limoges-Ussel-Clermont line. Guingouin recalls: "From that moment on, that superior form of warfare was applied, waged by irregular soldiers: from a home base, raids were carried out by 'flying squads,' which varied in number based on the objective to be realized, from the simple detachment to the company of shock troops to the Ranger battalion."[42] The maquis of Ain destroyed eleven locomotives on the night of January 15, 1944.[43] These groups were not averse to spectacle. On November 11, 1943, Captain Romans-Petit's men paraded in impeccable order to lay flowers at the monument to the dead in Oyonnax, "the victors of tomorrow" saluting "those of 14–18." By means of that display of force, Romans-Petit sought to silence the scandalmongers, who, he writes, were expressing "doubts about the morality of those now called maquisards, and whom Vichy radio portrays on a daily basis as terrorists commanded by faithless and lawless gang leaders. That propaganda has an effect even on those who are favorable to us, but who, far from our zone of action, have no direct contact with us."[44] The demonstration was heavily covered by the media, and the photographs taken on the occasion went around the world.

By no means were all the maquis' actions so symbolic, however. Many groups first raided the storehouses of Chantiers de la Jeunesse (Youth Work Camps), from which they took uniforms, shoes, and supplies. On September 10, 1943, Romans-Petit's men attacked the warehouses of Artemare in the Ain department and, on the 28th of that month, robbed the storehouse of the supply corps of Bourg-en-Bresse. The Estibi maquis launched a raid on the night of January 15, 1944, against the Paulhan factories of Saint-Jean-du-Gard. It seized 1,980 pairs of khaki shorts and 1,455 khaki jackets, as well as 1,640 tent canvases, plus overalls and forestry jackets.[45] The maquis often targeted collaborators (or alleged collaborators) and lived off the land. In Gard, eighty major attacks, apart from railroad sabotages, occurred between November 1942 and December 1943. Although fifteen directly affected German troops, the principal motive of forty-three operations was to steal money or ration tickets, while twenty-two targeted people or buildings associated with collaboration.[46] Jacques Bingen, a delegate in the southern zone, was alarmed by these attacks: "The number of armed assaults is multiplying tragically over the entire territory. One has only to lend an ear in any public place . . . to be convinced of the great agitation that has seized hold of the average Frenchman—a Frenchman who hates the Germans and who is waiting for the Liberation on his balcony or in his cellar. The most preposterous accounts spread by word of mouth; there is talk everywhere of assaults, attacks on isolated individuals, armed robberies. . . . In short, the general impression is that the country as a whole is being held ransom by gangs, and people are beginning to forget that, though some are composed of the dregs of society, others of militia provocateurs, the vast majority, composed of patriots, engage only in well-planned operations directed against the enemy and his accomplices."[47]

Usually, however, inactivity prevailed, and the maquisards, overcome by boredom, lived under difficult conditions. In the small Saint-Adjutory maquis in Corrèze, "about fifteen maquisards in a little wood

near a stream . . . slept in little straw huts. . . . Many boys were sick, af-
flicted with boils and scabies. I remember especially an escaped prisoner of war, covered with pustules," reports a resistance fighter in charge
of inspecting the modest group in July 1943.[48] In Glières in the Haute-
Savoie department, "the days of complete idleness sometimes seemed
very long, so far from everything and everyone. Crossword puzzles or
cards, depending on one's personal preference, songs, and interminable
discussions helped us to fill hours and hours," a former maquisard recalls.[49] Other, better-organized maquis fought more effectively against
idleness, as indicated by the testimony of André Jacquelin, one of the
leaders of the Bir-Hakeim maquis in the southern part of the Massif
Central:

> The day begins at seven, and at eight, after performing our ablutions, it
> is time for limbering-up exercises. . . . The various work details follow
> until ten, then theoretical instruction on the new weapons of every kind
> recently dropped by parachute. At the noonday meal, we share the day's
> menu: very hot soup, beefsteak, mashed potatoes, cheese and fruit with
> boiling coffee to finish up, and a liter of cheap red wine split four ways,
> that was a feast day! A little free time until two, and everyone takes the
> opportunity to write loved ones and do various little chores. At two, the
> field instruction begins: combat exercises, surprise attacks, and so on,
> until five. Then, striking of the colors, followed by mealtime and the eve-
> ning gathering. The leader in each hut presents his team with an idea, a
> subject, focuses and guides the discussion. And the young voices come
> to life. Sometimes it's very serious, other times very light. Or several
> teams get together to put on a play, a variety show, or to go for a hike.
> You improvise, you make do. Out of nothing you make everything. Ini-
> tiative, intellectual and manual dexterity, taste itself, simple good taste,
> all these develop. And the hut is also spruced up during evenings when,
> closed in around the little smoking stove as the autumn wind passes
> through the chinks in the walls, you work for the team's home and to
> protect yourself from the impending cold weather, but also with the pros-
> pect of leaving it soon, in a few months, to take part in the battle for
> Liberation.[50]

These activities, though modest, allowed the maquisards to stave off
boredom. The many ambushes Romans-Petit laid to defend the roads
and disorient the enemy were "above all a kind of reward," he notes,
even though they constituted "a test of endurance against the cold and

against marches," and a "military operation consisting of sudden and sustained firing on German vehicles."[51] Let us not imagine, however, that France was ablaze in 1944. The watch-and-wait attitude sometimes prevailed, the maquisards preferring to prepare for the landing rather than engage in direct action. In Ille-et-Vilaine, for example, the groups in the AS did not commit any attacks or sabotage operations until late May 1944.[52] And in the winter of 1943–1944, the maquis experienced a profound crisis that greatly disturbed Robert Soulage (Sarrazac), head of the national maquis school service, according to a report he sent to Pierre Dejussieu, head of the southern zone AS, on January 27, 1944:

> This crisis manifests itself as a general tendency toward skepticism regarding the possibilities for action and the usefulness of the maquis, as a weariness observable both among the regional leaders and among the troops, as a slackening of discipline, an increase in pointless fights, the breakdown of many camps. The current lack of funds, though temporary, risks intensifying the crisis to the point where the leaders will wonder if it is not their duty to reconsider their position and to give the general order to disperse.
>
> To confine ourselves to the essential, seeking definitive remedies, it is clear there are three deep-seated causes of that malaise:
> —the lack of leaders, a consequence of the officers' treason;
> —the lack of arms;
> —the nonexistence of a principle of organization adapted to the present conditions.[53]

The armed struggle was sometimes coupled with labor protests, carried out primarily by the Communists, who hoped to revive their worker identity and consolidate the role the proletariat would play in national insurrection. "The first condition for enabling the general insurrectional strike is to promote daily action in businesses," *L'Humanité* noted on September 1, 1943.[54] Such action also offered the PCF the possibility, or so it hoped, of "promoting the CGT as the only organization of the working class," and of being in a position to control it once the war was over.[55] Several strikes therefore punctuated the second half of 1943. In Montceau-les-Mines, eight thousand miners staged a work stoppage between October 25 and 29, 1943, to put forward their demands. In Saint-Étienne, ten thousand coal mine workers made the most of Armistice Day in 1943, going out on strike for ten days. Finally, five thousand steelworkers stopped work on September 20, 1943[56]— all signs, among so many others, that anger was coming to the surface and that the PCF was still very much heeded within the ranks of the proletariat.

The resistance thus became surer of itself and more mature. But the means for its engagement in the battles for liberation remained ill-defined, even at the highest echelons. In mid-1943, neither London nor the Allies had yet developed a doctrine for action. One event, though, urged caution on their part: the liberation of Corsica.

## The Corsica Affair

Until November 1942, the war had largely spared Corsica. Two major resistance groups had gradually taken root, however. A partisan of Free France since June 1940, Fred Scamaroni, originally a member of the prefectoral administration, had at the age of twenty-eight laid the foundations for a network, R2 Corse, that was attached to the BCRA. In addition, the FN had taken shape under the leadership of a Communist teacher named Arthur Giovoni and had opened itself to individuals who did not share its leftist views, such as the Radical-Socialist senator Paul Giaccobi and his son François.

The Anglo-American landing in North Africa incited the Germans to invade the free zone, and the Reich offered Corsica as spoils to its Italian ally, who had long dreamed of possessing it. More than eighty thousand Italian soldiers moved in to occupy the Isle of Beauty, enraging the population and triggering action from the resistance. In January 1943, a submarine dropped off Scamaroni and his two radio operators near Ajaccio. But on March 17, agents of Mussolini's secret police arrested one of his two agents, Rossi, who gave up the network: nineteen members of R2 were detained, including Scamaroni. He preferred to commit suicide rather than crack under torture: "I didn't talk! Vive de Gaulle! Vive la France!" he wrote in blood on the walls of his prison.[57]

The sudden death of Scamaroni left the field wide open for the Giraudist camp, which decided to support the only resistance group with any weight: the FN. On April 2, 1943, Giraud therefore dispatched Captain Colonna d'Istria, head of the Pearl Harbor mission, with the assignment to gather the troops and prepare for a landing. At the same time, the submarine *Casabianca*, one of the few vessels left intact when the fleet was scuttled at the naval base in Toulon, traveled back and forth, carrying arms and munitions. The Italian armistice, signed on September 3 but not revealed until the 8th, precipitated matters. On that day, a Comité Départemental de Libération (CDL; Departmental Liberation Committee) gave the order for the insurgency to begin.

Maurice Choury, head of both the FN and the CDL, proclaimed: "Anti-German propaganda must be intensified among the Italian troops, and every possible means employed to get weapons to them. Everywhere and without delay, the battle must be waged against the Germans. Obstacles and ambushes must be set up against them, their vehicles fired on, their movements stopped. They must be exterminated by every means. That military aspect must not lead us to forget its political aspect. The directives received concerning the replacement of the antipatriotic municipal councils, the summary purge, the election of two delegates per village for the departmental assembly, must be applied without delay. Each village must send to Ajaccio, as quickly as possible, not only these two armed delegates but all armed combatants whose presence is not indispensable at home."[58] The struggle was therefore political, but it also occurred within a military context. In fact, some of the Italian troops fraternized with the population, supporting the insurrection; but in reply, the Germans in short order deployed some twelve thousand men to the Bastia region.

This sequence of events baffled General Giraud. In the first place, there was a risk that the adventure would end in a bloodbath, especially since, though the Germans wanted to fight, the Allies, believing the operation premature, refused to support the insurgents. De Gaulle, moreover, had not been notified, and he did not conceal his rage. Giraud, in addition to keeping the insurrection secret, had offered the FN—and thus the Communists—a monopoly on insurrection. Above all, he had deprived de Gaulle of the glory of having liberated the first French department.[59] Giraud was therefore on his own. He sent 109 men from the Third Shock Company, who disembarked from the *Casabianca* in Ajaccio on the night of September 12. They were soon joined by 500 men transported on two destroyers, the *Fantasque* and the *Terrible*. André Philip, commissioner for the interior, though notified belatedly of the operation, managed to send his prefect, Charles Luizet,[60] to the military governor, Amédée Mollard. It was up to these two men to take over the civil and military administrations.[61] In early October, insurgents and regular soldiers seized Bastia. The German forces then evacuated not only Corsica but also Sardinia.

That epic liberation, then, ended in success. But it sounded General Giraud's death knell. Corsica had liberated itself on its own—a little too much on its own, and a little too early, for de Gaulle's taste.[62] He never forgave Giraud for presenting him with a fait accompli. Giraud, as already noted, had to accept limitations on his powers in October, before being excluded from the CFLN on November 9. Until 1944, he confined himself to performing the duties—very limited in scope—of commander in chief.[63]

Above all, the liberation of Corsica had allowed the Communists to control the insurrectional process without respecting the canonical rules of democracy. In the liberated boroughs, elections by show of hand entrusted municipal authority to councils dominated by the FN, an outcome that delighted its leader, Arthur Giovoni. "The plan is being applied in the villages. The Front National groups assemble the population on the village square, declare the disgraced town councils deposed, and proclaim their replacement by patriots whose names must be approved by acclamation," he explained in a report—sent to Moscow no less.[64] For two months, Luizet had to use "endless discussions and a firm hand"[65] to return to forms more respectful of representative democracy. Nevertheless, the prefect abandoned the plan of holding municipal elections. With "the rather impulsive traditions of this region, it would be foolhardy to conduct a municipal election campaign with ten thousand men in possession of submachine guns," his minister, André Philip, argued in October 1943.[66]

Despite the happy ending, the scenario raised questions about the intentions of the PCF. The fear of seeing it seize power upon liberation gnawed at the leaders of the CFLN and those of the internal resistance. From that standpoint, was the Corsica affair an accident or a precedent?

## Communists on the Offensive?

The strategy of the PCF caused bafflement, even anxiety, and not without reason. Indeed, as historian Stéphane Courtois points out, "from June 1943 until Liberation, the PCF conducted two different strategies. The first was official and corresponded to the Party's traditional national dimension: this was a 'sacred union' strategy in view of national liberation. The second strategy went forward furtively and sporadically: to break away and seize power, which corresponded to the Communist dimension of the Party."[67]

Two conditions were required for that dual strategy to succeed: "First, the Party had to be in charge of the internal Resistance; and second, it had to be independent of General de Gaulle's government."[68] The PCF therefore strove to place all the underground groups under the FN's control. But that ambition was met with resolute opposition from de Gaulle, Jean Moulin, and the other metropolitan resistance movements.

Then the party changed its tactics. First, to undermine Gaullist hegemony, it claimed to be giving equal weight to de Gaulle and Giraud. Second and above all, it sought "to monopolize the governing bodies of the resistance in the metropolis."[69] To do so, it attempted to turn the CNR into an organization in charge of the internal resistance—a process facilitated by the separation of the functions once performed by Moulin, who had been both chair of the CNR and head of the General Delegation. It also attempted to put a brake on the constitution of the CDLs, which London began to form in September 1943. The party preferred the Comités de la France Combattante (Committees of Fighting France), whose creation Jacques Duclos had approved with overwhelming support in May 1943.[70] Finally, the PCF encouraged the formation of the Milices Patriotiques (Patriotic Militia), mentioned for the first time in L'Humanité on August 15, 1943, and intended, in Duclos's own words, to form "national army reserves from the working classes, with the FTP constituting their vanguard."[71] These militias would also be able to maintain order on behalf of the CDLs and provide the framework for the levée en masse to come.[72] The party proceeded cautiously, however, since it was obliged simultaneously "to secure a dominant position and to advance as far as possible on the path of its specific policy, but without incurring the risk of challenging the principle of its alliance" with the Gaullist camp.[73]

In fact, these hegemonic claims ran into serious obstacles. Charles de Gaulle was keeping a close watch on the PCF, and he maneuvered with keen political instincts. Anxious to bring about national unity, in October 1943 he considered opening his government to representatives of the PCF, but without submitting to its stringent conditions. He reserved the right to name his own ministers. "For the Communist Party, however, it was a matter of principle to designate for itself the militants who would be part of it," recalls Duclos.[74] De Gaulle also refused to grant the commissioners full powers in their departments or to launch the mass purge the PCF was calling for.[75] Negotiations broke down in November 1943, when de Gaulle rejected their demands; but on April 4, 1944, the PCF gave in, and two Communists joined the CFLN. Fernand Grenier headed the Air Commission and François Billou was named a commissioner without portfolio.

Clearly, there were strong advantages to joining the government. The PCF was thereby able to "rejoin the national community" and benefit from Gaullist legitimacy, while at the same time offering its ministers the means to demonstrate their governing skills.[76] De Gaulle knew how to capitalize on that appealing prospect to impose his views. In addition, he limited the prerogatives of the CDLs, which, when the time came, were to replace the former general councils and to assist prefects and commissioners of the republic with their insight. A commission chaired by Francis-Louis Closon, an envoy from London, named the members of the committees and saw to it that all the major political and moral currents were equitably represented. Otherwise, there was a risk that a dual power structure would emerge upon liberation, one that pitted the representatives of the central state against the legitimacy of the people in resistance, as embodied by the CDLs. Closon was well aware of that danger. He therefore recommended "controlling and overseeing their activity, that is, engaging in a politics of presence, if we wish to keep the committees, on the day liberation comes, from turning into so many local soviets that will dispute the orders of the central authority at a time when obedience is called for."[77] As a result, the regulations of March 14 and April 21, 1944, limited their powers.

The CDLs would remain provisional advisory assemblies, and they would not expand to the municipalities or districts.

Despite these obstacles, the PCF scored a few points. It managed to dominate a few CDLs, by demanding seats for its many satellite organizations—the FN, the CGT, the Union des Femmes Françaises (Frenchwomen's Union). They were successful in the Indre and Alpes-Maritimes departments, where the Communists came to have three out of five votes. While repeatedly calling for unity, the party also took care to hold onto the autonomy of its combat groups. On December 23, 1943, the AS and the FTP merged, creating the FFI, which were made official on February 1, 1944. But that unity remained theoretical, since the FTP's command and organization were still autonomous.[78] Finally, the CCDMR had formed an action commission (COMIDAC) in February 1944, charged with serving as a guide for the FFI. Initially composed of Maurice Chevance, Jean de Vogüé, and Pierre Villon, the commission soon came under Communist control, since, of "the three Vs" that composed it in May 1944, only Vogüé (Vaillant) did not belong to the PCF. Such was not the case for Villon, representative of the FN, or for Maurice Kriegel (Valrimont), a former member of the Communist CGTU and of the Libération-sud movement. Valrimont had succeeded Chevance (Bertin), who left to join Henri Frenay in Algiers in April. The commission, attached to the CNR on May 24, 1944, and renamed Comité d'Action Militaire (COMAC; Military Action Committee), was thus dominated by Communist elements, which gave them a trump card, since the ambition of the COMAC was to take charge of resistance activities in the metropolis. In fact, on May 13, 1944, the CNR granted it "supreme command of the FFI" until the landing, in defiance of the powers de Gaulle had conferred on General Koenig, theoretically the leader of the FFI.[79] Furthermore, many regions were run by a Communist leader, for example Rhône-Alpes (Henri Provisor), Provence-Côte d'Azur (Robert Rossi), and Île-de-France (Henri Rol-Tanguy). "In all," historian Philippe Buton points out, "of the thirty-eight highest posts in the internal Resistance, the Communists occupied twenty—or twenty-two, if one counts the political proximity of the leaders of R3 [Languedoc-Roussillon] and R4 [Midi-Pyrénées]."[80] He continues: "The conspiratorial dimension of these events, however, must not be exaggerated. For the most part, all can be explained quite naturally. The vagaries of the PCF's reconstruction had led former members, cut off from the party, to join the non-Communist movements—especially in the southern zone."[81] Whether premeditated or accidental, the Communist presence at the upper echelons of the resistance hierarchy was real. It alarmed both the Gaullist authority and many of the leaders of the underground groups.

De Gaulle was able to limit Communist hegemony by curbing the prerogatives of the internal resistance and by integrating the Communists within the state apparatus, which forced them to observe a minimal governmental solidarity. In his fight, he also relied on the other parties and on certain movements—with, admittedly, varying results.

The SFIO assessed better than anyone the peril represented by the dynamic strategy of the PCF. In autumn 1943, it therefore militated in favor of unity of action, which would allow it—or so it hoped—to preserve its identity and its strongholds while associating itself with its enemy brother in the struggle. But Daniel Mayer's overtures were rejected by August Gillot. The Communist representative on the CNR explained to the Socialist leader: "We reject anything that could give a class aspect to our current struggle, so as not to provide grounds for division among the French people. Believe me, it is not about undercutting our common goal, which is the fight against the invader. Anything that would appear to be a specifically worker's action would be a pretext for anti-Communist propaganda, which would deal a blow to joint action."[82] The PCF, in a position of strength, thus declined the advances of the SFIO, which lacked any means for applying pressure, since it had no resistance movement comparable to the FN. That led the Socialists to turn to the MUR.

The MUR considered with suspicion the Communist maneuver, which posed the risk of eliminating them in the end. In November 1943, they proposed undertaking negotiations to play the role vis-à-vis the SFIO that the FN had assumed in relation to the PCF. Mayer declined that offer. He declared: "It is only publicly, when legality has been restored, that clarifications and useful conversations between the appointed delegates of organizations can be of some substance. For the time being, it seems to me that the future of such a closer association can be preserved, and people prepared for it, only by creating the climate necessary for rapprochement."[83] In fact, Mayer feared that an alliance with the resistance would distort the Socialist and working-class identity of the SFIO, and that the PCF would bring about a turn to the left. In his view, his party, condemned to intransigence, had no other choice but a unitary strategy, "by means of which it seeks both the place in the Resistance that has been refused it and the revolutionary bona fides it needs."[84]

Some movements, to counteract that refusal, decided to federate. They adopted the same plan that had guided the creation of the MUR and expanded it to the northern zone, but without seeking de Gaulle's approval.

## The National Liberation Movement

Founded in late 1943, the Mouvement de Libération Nationale (MLN; National Liberation Movement) had two principal objectives. In linking two northern zone movements, Résistance and the DF, to the MUR, it sought in the first place to set in motion a dynamic of unification. Its gamble paid off in part, since small groups—Lorraine, Libre-Patrie, and Amis de la Liberté—joined the federation. Conversely, the CDLL, the CDLR, OCM, and Libération-nord refused to join, undermining from the outset the ambition of unity. For the most part, the MLN, placing itself under the authority of the CCDMR, looked forward to the postwar era. It aspired—and this was its second objective—"to organize, from this moment on, the forces of the Resistance in view of establishing the Fourth Republic."[85] In short, it sought to create a party upon liberation.

That objective, however, veiled conflicting strategies. Frenay's friends, Bourdet in the lead, wanted to keep in check the hegemony of the FN. From their standpoint, the incorporation of the right-leaning movements—the CDLL, the CDLR, and the OCM—represented an asset for consolidating the anti-Communist camp. That strategy failed, however, preventing the "restoration of balance in the MUR (where the influence of Libération, a Communist-leaning movement, had become invasive)."[86] In spite of everything, the MLN might become the matrix of the major resistance party Frenay desired, especially if General de Gaulle became its leader upon liberation.

By contrast, fellow travelers of the Communists, who dominated the leadership of Libération-sud, looked on the MLN with skepticism. They were put off by the prospect of a resistance party. Pierre Hervé explained in late 1943: "It would be an association of the entire Resistance, from the OCM to the most 'revolutionary' elements of the MUR. That group would be destined to take the place of all the old, bankrupt parties. As a result, that new party would, at the very least, have the ambition of being the sole party for the bourgeoisie, with a demagogic 'revolutionary' wing. Quite obviously, as in Germany, it would enter into struggle with the former so-called republican parties."[87] The philo-Communist wing did not oppose the formation of the MLN, but it planned to bring the FN into that organization. The plan, considered in 1943, was relaunched in May 1944, but without being realized. The Socialists put pressure on Libération-nord, which was close to the SFIO, not to join the MLN. "As long as I'm here, there will be no understanding between the MLN and Libération-Nord," declared one of its leaders, Jacques Brunschwig (Bordier), to Yvon Morandat.[88]

The fellow travelers, however, were not necessarily thinking of subordinating the MLN to the FN. Granted, Pascal Copeau and Emmanuel d'Astier de La Vigerie refused to declare war on the PCF—in notable contrast to Frenay. Persuaded that it represented the working class and embodied a form of revolutionary messianism, they did not wish to cut off the far-left flank. Copeau explained to Frenay: "The FN exists only because the PC[F] is its backbone and pulls its strings, but that is precisely the reason there could be no political base for the future without a union of which the FN would also be a part. . . . If you do not have total union, you will have the FN on the one hand . . . and, on the other, you will have another union that, whether you like it or not, would, by force of circumstance, have no originality except its lack of collaboration with Communism."[89] At the same time, these strong personalities likely distrusted a party grappling with its Stalinist demons. Thanks to the new blood of the resistance, the MLN would thus allow for the regeneration of a party that, in their eyes, remained that of the working class. In the absence of integrating the FN, they thus pronounced themselves in favor of a new group arising from the army of shadows, one that would work in harmony with the Communists. That major party, "which ought to stand beside the PC[F] and collaborate loyally with it, lies in the zone where the PS, the confederated current of the CGT, and the great majority of the militants in the Resistance as a whole are at present moving. To induce the PC[F] to take an interest, via the FN, in the formation of that association of democratic French forces: therein lies the entire problem of the political future of France," explained Copeau.[90] All in all, these men were making the argument for alliance, not subordination; they overwhelmingly approved harmony, not conflict. In so doing, they displeased both Frenay's friends—advocates of confrontation—and the orthodox Communists, who championed submission to the PCF.

In fact, the creation of the MLN and its possible merger with the FN was problematic within the PCF. "The Communist comrades militating among us, whom we had a tendency to consider 'agents' of the Party in late 1943, were for the most part already strongly contaminated by the 'ecumenical' state of mind I'm referring to," Claude Bourdet observed after the war. "The PC[F] was thus guided toward a path it did not wish to take and, even more seriously, it lost its autonomy in favor of a true unity of the Resistance."[91] Taking note of that peril, the orthodox Communists argued fervently for unity—while secretly torpedoing it. Unsurprisingly, the FN rejected the merger with the MLN. "It said it wanted it, but it did not want it. As a matter of fact, how could it have wanted to entrust its finances to a unified movement? The unified movement was our mystique. It was an ideal without hope," Pierre Hervé acknowledged after the war.[92] Copeau did not admit defeat, however. He requested the intervention of the commissioner for the interior, d'Astier de La Vigerie, and asked him to:

—have Gouin-Le Trocquer give instructions to Socialists, so that they are not held responsible for division Resistance . . . ;
—have Grenier and others put pressure on FN;
—have orders given to FTPF to collaborate effectively with FFI.[93]

That request obviously went unheeded. At the time, the PCF was not considering a merger between the FN and the MLN, which would have deprived it of an essential lever of command. Copeau and d'Astier de La Vigerie were deluding themselves. They misapprehended the essence of the PCF, which intended to retain full control of its apparatus and pledged its unwavering loyalty to Moscow. The commissioner for the interior, despite his charisma and goodwill, did not have the means to reorient the strategy deployed by Jacques Duclos, André Marty, and Maurice Thorez. The unification of the underground movements remained a pipe dream. And the goals pursued by the PCF remained a mystery—until liberation in 1944.

Hence, the political transformations that marked North Africa profoundly modified the rules of the game. The elimination of General Giraud consolidated General de Gaulle's power, accelerated the merger of the secret services, and ultimately clarified the role that the ORA would play in the military liberation of the country. It also radically altered the strategy of the movements, which were forced to rethink their relationship to the PCF and to the Gaullist authority. But other issues were becoming more urgent. The imminence of the Allied landing obliged the internal resistance and the Gaullist authority to prepare militarily and politically for a crucial target date: the liberation of captive France.

## Chapter 13

# In Order of Battle

At the tehran Conference held in the Iranian capital from November 28 to December 1, 1943, the Allies decided to grant absolute priority to Operation Overlord: in spring 1944, the Anglo-American troops would land on the French coast. That target date opened exhilarating prospects, since it heralded the departure of a despised occupier; but it also suggested that hard battles were ahead. From that standpoint, the Glières tragedy in winter 1943–1944 struck an ominous note. It relaunched questions about the relevance of the armed struggle in general and of the maquis in particular.

## The Glières Tragedy

In March 1943, several dozen STO evaders had taken refuge in the Haute-Savoie department. That movement, partly spontaneous, partly encouraged by the PCF,[1] received heavy coverage in the Swiss press, and the story was immediately picked up by the BBC and the underground newspapers. "Savoie, French Alps, Mountain Legion. . . . For how many days have the newspapers and the airwaves, friendly as well as enemy, tossed back and forth these words, these expressions, these images? However hardened the world may be by so many years of horror and heroism, it still shudders, because French people, French young people entrenched in our mountains, are making Laval tremble and the Germans fume," exclaimed Maurice Schumann, spokesman for Fighting France, on March 18, 1943.[2] But despite the requests formulated by the resistance movements, neither the Allies nor the Gaullists supported the maquisards. By contrast, "the publicity provided by the Swiss press, relayed by British radio broadcasts in French, then by Resistance newspapers, gave the impression that Haute-Savoie could serve as a place of refuge for those threatened by the STO."[3] Historian Claude Barbier estimates that, between summer 1943 and the liberation in

1944, between six and ten thousand evaders were in Haute-Savoie, though only a minority had joined the maquis—probably between 1,600 and 2,000 for the second half of 1943.[4]

Whatever their number, that sudden influx placed the resistance movements in an awkward position: they had neither the resources nor the logistics to lodge, feed, clothe, and above all arm the volunteers who presented themselves. The British were refusing to support the maquis in large part because, in September 1943, the final decision to land in France had not yet been made. They decided, however, to dispatch an inter-Allied mission to assess the strength of the maquis and the possibilities they offered. The Cantinier-Xavier mission, sent out on the night of September 21, 1943, gave Jean Rosenthal and Richard Heslop the assignment of evaluating the maquisard potential in Savoie, Haute-Savoie, and Isère.[5] After visiting several camps, the two emissaries returned to Britain on the night of October 16, and then, having made their report, left once more for the metropolis.

In winter 1943–1944, the situation deteriorated in Haute-Savoie. Alarmed by the flood of evaders, the Vichy regime tightened its repressive grip on the department, establishing a state of siege there on January 24. It also dispatched police reinforcements, then the Milice. That hard line made life impossible for proscribed persons, which led the resistance to order several camps set up on the Glières Plateau, essentially as "a place of refuge."[6] The influx of volunteers and the geographical advantages of the site impelled London to make the most of that good fortune and to plan a series of parachute drops to arm the Alpine resistance. Between January and March 1944, between four and five hundred men arrived at the plateau,[7] to hide and to receive the promised weapons. What the officers did not grasp was that these two aims were in contradiction: refuge was predicated on discretion, whereas the delivery of dozens of containers could not fail to attract the attention of the repressive forces. As a result, "dispersal, confrontation, or surrender would be the only means to resolve the dilemma."[8]

Beginning in late January, the Glières maquis adopted a military mode of organization, under the leadership of Lieutenant Théodose Morel (Tom). A graduate of Saint-Cyr and an officer in the mountain infantry, Morel had fought bravely against the Italians in June 1940, then commanded the 27th Infantry Battalion quartered in Annecy.

Transferred to the military academy in Aix-en-Provence to serve as an instructor, he returned to the prefecture of Haute-Savoie after the dissolution of the armistice army. He established contacts with the resistance there, while at the same time agreeing to become departmental commissioner for propaganda for the LFC. A deeply devout man, he undoubtedly had ideological affinities with the Vichy regime, but his patriotism was unwavering. Thanks to his charisma and zeal, he was able to take charge of a maquis that combined Communists and conservatives, without fear that his authority would be challenged.[9]

In January and February, the maquis set up its organization. While training its men, it avoided engaging in guerrilla warfare, which was judged premature. Resistance fighters and the repressive forces thus observed a kind of armed truce. The resistance refrained from acts of glory; and the authorities turned a blind eye to the maquis's stratagems, rather than become involved in an unpopular repression, in which they would also be risking their lives. For three weeks, therefore, the two camps had "a kind of coexistence profitable to both parties: the maquisards enjoyed relative freedom of movement, while the guards [most of whom belonged to the GMR, police forces charged with maintaining order] had the assurance that they would no longer serve as targets for the maquisards."[10]

It was not long, however, before that precarious balance was disrupted. First, three parachute drops on February 14, March 5, and March 11 prompted the Vichy authorities to put an end to the situation. The Germans were particularly worried about the safety of the troops they were sending to get some rest at the region's hotels or hospitals, which had previously been considered secure. Vichy wanted to prove to its master that it had things well in hand. It dispatched the Milice to the scene with instructions to take care of the matter. The maquisards understood the gravity of the threat. But rather than leave the plateau, they chose to remain in place. They wanted, in fact, to take delivery of the weapons, for which they had been waiting a very long time. By that measure, the first parachute drop trapped the resistance fighters "by turning them into guards of a stock of weapons they could not use, since the maquisards had received only light weapons, automatic rifles, and explosives—no machine guns, mortars, or antiaircraft devices, nothing that would have allowed them to hold the plateau against a well-organized assault."[11] In addition, the Gaullist airwaves had transformed Glières into a high-stakes symbol. That obliged the men to stand firm, if not to engage in battle. On February 3, Maurice Schumann launched a call to arms, which he repeated on the 6th:

> Men and women of Savoie, the maquis of Haute-Savoie, the French front where soldiers without uniforms are ready to fight for you and to die in your midst, appeals to you for assistance and solidarity, which can and must make the aggressor retreat.
> It is from the maquis itself that these pleas have just reached us.
>
> 1. You who are armed and inactive, join the maquis of Haute-Savoie immediately. You who are armed and inactive, join any maquis immediately.
> 2. Workers of Haute-Savoie, any time your actions can impede, directly or indirectly, operations that are or will be undertaken against the maquis, stop working, and launch a strike of solidarity with your brothers under attack.
> 3. Savoyard patriots, do not hesitate, any time you can do so without exposing yourselves to pointless risks, to sabotage railroads, highways, and factories whose operation might favor the work of the aggressors.[12]

On March 9, however, the spokesman for Fighting France advised caution. But the damage had been done. The situation reflected the BCRA's strategic dilemma. As historian Sébastien Albertelli writes, "Once the French had finally obtained a massive delivery of arms to the Alps, it was necessary at all cost to keep in place the teams able to receive them; and yet, even though the BCRA was aware that 'national guerilla warfare' had begun between the maquis and the occupation troops, it refused to encourage a premature action."[13] But Jean Rosenthal, envoy of the BCRA, went a step further: he urged the maquisards to fight, rashly promising them paratroopers as reinforcements.[14]

The affair got off to a bad start. On March 1, 1944, Michel Fournier, a medical student aide in the maquis, was arrested by the GMR in defiance of the armed truce in place. The resistance fighters were furious and decided to retaliate by attacking the GMR quartered in the city of Entremont. On the night of March 9, they conducted an assault on the Hôtel de France, with Lieutenant Morel leading the charge. A member of the GMR named Maurice Marlin told the story after the war:

Then I saw Lieutenant Tom Morel arriving. He positioned himself in front of the captain [Lefebvre, the head of the group] and hurled abuse at him: "You broke your word, you're a traitor." At the same time, two maquisards grabbed him from behind and held his arms, while a third took away his pistol, holstered in his belt. Captain Lefebvre struggled in vain, and Tom Morel added: "Now you're my prisoner."

Captain Lefebvre turned red in anger and began to shout: "Me? Captain Lefebvre of the French army, a prisoner? . . . Never."

He then managed to free his right arm and to seize a small .25 caliber pistol concealed in his right puttee.

His face bright red, he shot Lieutenant Tom Morel at point-blank range, hardly more than three feet away.

Mortally wounded, Tom slumped to the ground.[15]

During that tragic night, Glières lost three men, including its charismatic leader, who was replaced by Captain Maurice Anjot on March 18. That carnage played a role in radicalizing positions. On March 2, Jean Rosenthal had sent a message to the BCRA: "We will remain on impregnable plateau with motto: live free or die. We issue a challenge to Darnand, Lelong, Calvey, Racouillard [Calvayrac, Couillard], Battestini. Ready and waiting for these mercenaries of the enemy, the militiamen and police recruited in prisons."[16] Joseph Darnand, chief of the Milice, was itching to fight, in order to prove to the Germans the valor of his men. The occupiers, however, remained skeptical about the military value of that Praetorian Guard. They thus assigned the task of eliminating the maquis to regular troops, General Pflaum's 157th Reserve Division. On March 26, Pflaum launched an offensive reconnaissance mission in the Monthiévret sector. The modest skirmish demonstrated to Captain Anjot the futility of resisting such experienced soldiers. That same evening, lucid and cautious, he ordered his men to disperse. They left the plateau, declining to engage in combat under difficult conditions. Underfed and underequipped, hundreds of men braved the snow and cold to save their lives, the plateau having been surrounded by French and German forces. Their efforts were often in vain: 169 men were arrested at the end of the terrible odyssey.[17]

The Glières death toll was particularly high: in all, the maquis lost 210 men, while the Germans suffered 4 losses at most. Claude Barbier adds: "Nearly one man in two who had been on the plateau between late January and late March 1944 was killed, deported, imprisoned, or sent to a work camp."[18] The sacrifices were all the more heavy for being in vain. The maquis had been formed to receive the weapons for which the resistance fighters were clamoring. In fact, the British dropped 5.5 short tons of arms on February 14[19] and 100 tons on the night of March 10.[20] But because the resistance fighters did not have time to store them or to take them down to the valley, the Germans seized 122 automatic rifles, 3,000 cartridge clips, 1,011 automatic pistols, 722 rifles, 160 revolvers, 2 antitank guns, 2 flamethrowers, 300 hand grenades, and 1 heavy machine gun, not to mention munitions and explosives.[21] Glières was not a battle, since Captain Anjot, on the evening of March 26, had ordered his men to disperse. But the tragedy gave the general staffs pause.

## The Great Divide

Until 1943, the British and the Americans had been skeptical about the military capacities of the French resistance, though they appreciated the value of the intelligence it transmitted through its networks and movements. Between July 1943 and July 1944, the BCRA was the source for between 23 and 45 percent of the reports received by the American secret services based in London, that is, for 1.5 to 4.4 times as much material as that transmitted by the British Intelligence Service. William J. Donovan, head of the U.S. secret services, acknowledged in a report to President Franklin Roosevelt in 1945: "It is estimated that the BCRA provided to the British and American armies, through OSS and British channels, 80% of the intelligence on which the Normandy invasion was based."[22] But the Allies doubted the operational value of the resistance. With very few exceptions, they preferred to bomb the objectives they judged to be critical rather than count on the sabotage teams operating on the ground—even at the risk of increasing the number of civilian casualties. In addition, they did not intend to rely on the army of shadows to wage the battle for liberation. During and after the war, underground fighters denounced that policy, which was surely costly in human lives, claiming that it illustrated the blindness of the general staffs, who were set in their ways and unable to grasp the possibilities opened up by the subversive war. But to understand that attitude, it is necessary to assess the constraints under which the Allies were working.

In the first place, World War II threatened the very existence of every nation-state: Great Britain was brought to the brink of defeat in 1940. British and U.S. leaders, defending their national interests, could not on principle delegate all or part of military operations to forces they did not control, particularly the resistance. As a result, they refused to make the success of their intervention contingent on underground forces of any nationality.

Beyond that question of principle, the leaders also wondered about the reliability of the French resistance. Nothing, for example, guaranteed that the parachute drops would arrive safe and sound. In fact, between one-half and two-thirds of the missions on behalf of the SOE failed because there was no one on the ground to receive the drops, while a quarter to a third of the failures were the result of climatic conditions.[23] Even when the weapons were dropped in the right place, they too often fell into German hands. As a general rule, the British services anticipated a 20 percent loss rate, which included both damage to the containers during their fall and the seizure of goods by the enemy.[24] The Bordeaux region was a case in point. André Grandclément, regional head of the OCM, worked in liaison with a British SOE network. The Gestapo agent Dohse convinced him to work for the Reich, in the interest of fighting Communism. In exchange for the release of his arrested comrades, Grandclément indicated to the Germans where the weapon caches were and allowed them to seize a third of the stock the network had received.[25] The SD also managed to turn French or British agents working for the SOE and to broadcast false information over their radio sets. Even aside from arms, the Germans helped themselves to a total of 8,572,000 francs[26] that had been dropped by parachute, an especially significant amount in that the British had limited resources for their aid missions to the resistance. For the operations in northwestern Europe, the SOE had only twenty-seven airplanes in November 1942, and fewer than forty in spring 1944.[27] In late January 1944, the Allied services and the BCRA in London relied on thirty-three aircraft (including nine American ones) for the parachute operations leaving from England—definitely a small fleet.[28]

330 / THE FRENCH RESISTANCE

In addition, the Allies had no intention of encouraging a premature guerrilla war, which, by keeping German units in France, ran the risk of reducing the landing's chances. In parachute drops, therefore, preference was given to explosives over weapons, especially when the containers were intended for the French networks of the BCRA and not for organizations controlled by the SOE. In September 1943, the BCRA networks thus received more than 13,000 pounds of explosives, while the SOE's groups were given only some six thousand. In all, the resistance was "equipped not to fight but rather to unnerve the enemy through a proliferation of sabotage actions."[29]

Concerns of a political nature made these questions of strategy more pressing. First, the British distrusted the Gaullism professed by the BCRA and reproached Colonel Passy for waging a partisan campaign.[30] The appointment of Delestraint to head the AS had reassured them, inasmuch as the general showed every sign of being serious and apolitical, but his arrest alarmed them and reinforced their "deepest doubts about the military capacities of the Resistance."[31] Second, the Communist conundrum weighed heavily on their minds. Winston Churchill was especially wary when Grenier and Billoux joined the CFLN. "You will remember that we are purging all our secret establishments of Communists because we know they owe no allegiance to us or to our cause and will always betray secrets to the Soviet, even while we are working together. The fact of the two Communists being on the French Committee requires extremely careful treatment of the question of imparting secret information to them," the prime minister recommended to Alexander Cadogan, his undersecretary for foreign affairs, on April 13, 1944.[32]

All in all, there was nothing to suggest that the Allies would support the French resistance, particularly since their strategists harbored few illusions about what the army of shadows could offer the landing. Their leaders, noted the British general William Morgan, who in 1943 was in charge of considering logistics for the landing, "could not be warned in advance of the date and time of the operation. Consequently, no assistance from resistance groups can be expected during the initial assault. After the assault has taken place, however, pre-arranged plans could be put into effect for the demolition of railway communications in certain specific areas and for guerilla activities on the German lines of communication. . . . The assistance of the groups should therefore be treated as a bonus rather than an essential part of the plan."[33]

The situation evolved in early 1944, however. The active preparation for Operation Overlord prompted the Allies to reconsider their position. In January, Emmanuel d'Astier de La Vigerie, the new commissioner for the interior, succeeded in convincing Churchill to increase the deliveries of arms to the underground forces. The British prime minister was all the more easily convinced in that Michel Brault (Jérôme), head of the SNM, was in London and had spoken highly of the action of his groups. Moreover, his statements tallied with the positive assessments Forest Yeo-Thomas had brought back from his tour of the metropolis alongside Pierre Brossolette.[34] "Gentlemen, I have decided to go forward with arming the French patriots," the resident of 10 Downing Street concluded. "Monsieur d'Astier, can you answer for them that they will not turn their weapons against each other and will obey General Eisenhower's orders?" he asked.[35] That agreement in principle did not settle the question of the command, however, or define the doctrine regarding the use of the underground forces—two points gnawing at the British leaders.

The British had always denounced what they considered the excessive centralization brought about by the BCRA and Jean Moulin. They claimed that if the Germans arrested a handful of major leaders, the underground hierarchy would collapse, threatening the execution of the plans in support of the Allies, before and after the landing. The SOE therefore seized on the affair of rue de la Pompe, which had confirmed its alarm. In a memorandum of October 23, 1943, the SOE advised: "The only workable system would seem to be for SOE and the reorganized French Services under the Comite Francais de la Liberation Nationale in Algiers to make contact with groups of resisters at the lowest echelon. . . . It will be necessary to establish communications with them direct, and to see that no communications pass through the already tainted lines of the old structures in FRANCE. Arms and materials . . . must be delivered to them direct and not through the intermediary of the central control. Instructions for sabotage and orders for D-Day will likewise have to pass to them direct, either through the intermediary of an agent sent for the purpose or through wireless, but again not passing through the central control."[36]

The plan of action put forward by the SOE echoed the bitter re-flections of the BCRA. Moulin's arrest and the difficulties in naming his successor had deprived the delegation of most of its prestige and effectiveness. Like it or not, Colonel Passy's services had to resign themselves to abandoning the idea of a centralized command. As Passy explained after the war:

> We could no longer hold onto the notion of centralization, based on the organic development of the Resistance around two poles, Paris and Lyon, which had been in favor six months earlier. It appeared obvious to us that the indispensable coordination of the paramilitary efforts could be achieved only from London. We thus became the apostles of a large-scale decentralization that was supposed to be realized at the regional level first, and then, when possible, at the departmental level. In organizing direct transmissions and operations with the BCRA in each of the twelve regions, we had to make them truly autonomous sectors, capable of plan-ning military action on their own in view of the landing, but above all, able to be self-sufficient when the landing occurred—even if, as antici-pated, internal communications in France were cut off—and to execute the military program established in agreement with our allies, by re-ceiving directly from us the instructions, weapons, and personnel they needed.[37]

## The Regional Military Delegates

The establishment of regional military delegates (*délégués militaires ré-gionaux*, DMRs) was the cornerstone of a supervised decentralization whose terms were set out in the directive of August 25, 1943. According to their historian Philippe André, the DMRs had to "first, organize and coordinate the paramilitary resistance of the movements on that new scale, and second, set in place sabotage plans conceived by the BCRA and approved by the Allies, in view of facilitating a hypothetical landing on the French coast. Their directive therefore defined them both as ambassadors and as technicians."[38] These vague instructions, a source of later conflicts, did not make clear the respective powers of the other envoys from London, for example the operations officers in charge of receiving parachute drops. They also had the potential of worrying the internal resistance, which was quick to suspect London of wanting to control it. The directive thus had the aim of reassuring the resistance fighters, by reminding them that the jurisdiction of the DMRs was "strictly limited to military questions."[39] But the leaders of the army of shadows were not taken in. Maurice Chevance-Bertin, a veteran of the Combat movement and later a member of the COMIDAC of Algiers, bitterly observed:

> The DMRs, in fact, have transmissions, finances, weapons. They have often played the role of arbitrator between organizations. They have for that reason often become the regional chiefs. The powers that are given them in these plans tend to reinforce their command activities.
> *That is a mistake.*
> The morale of the Resistance suffers as a result. *By the position he holds, even a very mediocre DMR has more weight than a regional leader with broader powers.*[40]

At first, the Gaullist secret services did not have the resources to support their policy. Drawing from a limited pool, they preferred to dispatch a few hand-picked men—about ten in mid-September—rather than send inexperienced agents.[41] These officers often had a difficult time, especially since the missions were marked by a real lack of preparation. Maurice Bourgès-Maunoury, DMR of the Lyon region, reported: "We do not have money, weapons do not seem to come when we order them, our cable connection with you is a very uncertain thread that transports questions and answers that never seem to correspond. We might therefore be reduced to calling for discipline, but our position is very poorly defined. Leaving aside the aura, much disparaged, in which the person arriving from the outside is surrounded, we have nothing to contribute but diplomacy, not to say charm."[42] The first wave of DMRs, which encountered hostility from the internal resistance and from many operations officers, was, moreover, swept away in the storms of the repression. By early 1944, of the seven delegates who had been operating in the northern zone, four had been arrested.[43]

The situation improved over time, however. London managed to supply each region with a delegate, either by sending reinforcements from Britain or by naming reliable men in the field. In all, the BCRA dispatched about fifty officers, and, over the period as a whole, about a hundred people performed the duties of DMR or assistant DMR.[44] In addition, as time passed Colonel Passy's services resolved the conflicts about assignments. In April 1944, they decided: "The entire staff sent from London or Algiers is placed under the orders of the regional military delegate, who is therefore able to organize his region without competition among the different elements, whatever their origin."[45] General Koenig, head of the FFI, ratified that principle in May. The chain of command also became clearer. Two zonal military delegates (*délégués militaires de zone*, DMZs), placed on the CC of the internal resistance, performed inspection duties, and a national military delegate (*délégué militaire national*, DMN), Jacques Chaban-Delmas, occupied the top of that pyramid in March 1944. Finally, and perhaps especially, the clashes between the envoys from London and the heads of the internal resistance abated. Although the personal qualities of most of the delegates played a role in that mollification, the considerable resources provided them also helped make their voices heard.

The delegates had two things in their favor. First, their financial resources were increasing. In September 1943, the two DMZs—Louis-Eugène Mangin for the south, Pierre Marchal for the north—had each brought with them 5 million francs. In November, the seven DMRs received 500,000 francs apiece—with the exception of Valentin Abeille, in Brittany, who was granted 2 million francs.[46] These amounts, though large in appearance, were barely enough to cover their setup costs, to which Bourgès-Maunoury in the Rhônes-Alpes region dedicated 62 percent of his early budgets. For example, he spent 26,000 francs to purchase four bicycles and 18,000 francs to buy 200 liters of gasoline.[47] Gradually, however, the situation improved. In June 1944, the DMRs had at their disposal an overall budget of 140 million francs (39 million for the Rhône-Alpes, 10.5 million for Limousin, 12.5 million for Île-de-France),[48] and, at the regional level, they allocated the funds going to the underground groups. To be sure, Jacques Bingen, the eventual successor of Jean Moulin, strove to defend the prerogatives of his delegation by demanding that his service pay out the funds. To no avail. By March 1944, the DMRs were involved in drawing up the budgets and, in April, they were given the responsibility of allocating them to the regions.[49]

Second, the DMRs had good connections with London, thanks to their miniaturized radios, called "midgets." On March 30, 1944, R1

(Rhône-Alpes) and R2 (Provence-Côte d'Azur) received 106 midget radios, but regions P (Île-de-France) and B (Aquitaine) were less well off, with, respectively, 12 and 20 radio sets.[50] The improvement in communications guaranteed that the directives of the BCRA and the Allied staff would be received without delay; above all, it favored parachute drops of weapons. In that respect, the Allies proved to be less stingy. By March, the SOE's F and RF Sections had reaped the benefits of 268 successful operations. That number continued to rise, to 613 in April, 1,010 in May, and 1,263 in June.[51] The resources of the SOE were in fact growing. In February 1944, 74 aircraft were in its service, and in March it received a supplementary allocation of 45 planes operating from England.[52] These efforts made it possible to better arm the French resistance. From January to late May 1944, more than 3,800 tons of materiel sent from England or North Africa were dropped by parachute— enough to arm some 125,000 men.[53]

## Execution of Plans or National Insurrection?

The use to be made of the weapons sparked a lively debate between the advocates of national insurrection and the supporters of strictly military action. Charles de Gaulle had proclaimed on April 18, 1942: "The duty of every Frenchman, the duty of every Frenchwoman, is to fight actively, by every means in his or her power, both against the enemy himself and against the people of Vichy, who are the enemy's accomplices. To those people, as to the enemy, the French have no obligation, except to drive them out and, in the meantime, sabotage their orders and despise their faces. National liberation is inseparable from national insurrection."[54] That formulation, though apparently clear, lent itself to multiple interpretations. De Gaulle wanted the French to participate actively in their liberation to avenge the insult of the 1940 defeat and to offer the Allied armies notable assistance. At the same time, he feared that an insurrection would trigger bloody reprisals or even launch a revolution, which would lay claim to a sovereignty forged in struggle, in opposition to the legitimacy he had acquired through the Appeal of June 18. As a result, he recommended that the insurrection be "of short duration." D'Astier de La Vigerie, the commissioner for the interior, instructed the new delegate general, Alexandre

Parodi: "It must not go beyond three or four days, forty-eight hours if possible."[55]

The Communists did not see things that way. Repeating de Gaulle's words, they argued for insurrection on a vast scale, which would be preceded by strikes and would spread throughout the country. That scenario would accelerate liberation, guarantee national independence, and glorify the role played by the underground groups—the FFI, the FTP, and the Milices Patriotiques above all. Two antagonistic conceptions of national insurrection therefore coexisted. "For de Gaulle," notes Philippe Buton, "insurrection was symbolic; for the PCF, it was strategic."[56] The non-Communist resistance movements tended to embrace the Gaullist conception and insisted on the need to comply with a plan formulated in conjunction with the Allies.[57] In that context, dropping massive quantities of arms raised the risk of insurrection, a possibility that certainly did not fit with the Anglo-American strategy. Their strategists greatly preferred that the resistance confine itself to executing the plans it had set in place.

In April 1943, a planning committee composed of the BCRA and the SOE was created to that end. The French experts, not knowing the time or place of the landing—both were top secret—came up with several plans based on different scenarios. Plan Vert gave detailed indications of the railway lines that the underground fighters would have to cut off. Plan Violet targeted the enemy's telephone and telegraph communications. Plan Tortue (Tortoise Plan) was intended to prevent German tank divisions from reaching the theater of operations. In June 1943, Claude Bouchinet-Serreulles took with him microphotographs of the three plans, which he was to submit to General Delestraint.[58] The DMRs were then given the assignment of implementing them—though they did not learn of Plan Violet until the final days of May 1944.[59]

On the whole, the DMRs carried out their mission brilliantly. In late May 1944, all the regions were equipped with one or several DMRs, with the exception of Aquitaine.[60] The priority of these officers was to prepare the plans—and they succeeded. In R5 (Limousin), Plan Vert was ready to go by May 10;[61] such was also the case in R2 (Provence-Côte d'Azur), except in Bouches-du-Rhône.[62] Of thirty interruptions of rail service planned in R4 (Midi-Pyrénées), twenty-nine were completed by April 7.[63] Along the way, DMRs yielded to the temptation of spontaneous action. In R3 (Languedoc), the delegate Paul Leisten-schneider cut twelve electrical lines between April 23 and May 1 and, between April 15 and April 30, he played a role in destroying eleven locomotives.[64]

The decentralization that occurred in autumn 1943 guaranteed the Allies that the plans prepared by the BCRA and validated by the SOE would be executed, barring a major catastrophe. A few shadows loomed, however. First, there had been heavy losses. Close to a year after the delegation came into existence, twenty-one of its members had been arrested, and many paid for their engagement with their lives. After his arrest, Pierre Marshal, for example, chose to commit suicide, swallowing his cyanide capsule on the stairs of his apartment building on September 23, 1943. Second, clashes sometimes arose between leaders of the internal resistance and their DMR. Relations were tense between Ravanel and Schlumberger in R4 (Midi-Pyrénées), between Guingouin and Déchelette in R5 (Limousin), and between Courson de Villeneuve and Colonel Gaspard in R6 (Auvergne). These inevitable conflicts should not be exaggerated, however. Harmony reigned as a rule, especially since, at the regional level, London sought more to ensure proper execution of the plans than to run the internal resistance. A number of DMRs, in fact, had emerged from its ranks. Louis-Eugène Mangin had fought in the Ali-Tir network, André Boulloche in the Centurie network. Valentin Abeille had been in charge of Combat, then of the AS in the Jura department. Gilbert Grandval, the military leader of the CDLR, was even head of the FFI as well as DMR in the Champagne-Alsace-Lorraine region (C). The success of the DMRs thus lay more in their capacity to execute the plans prepared by the BCRA than in attempts to place the internal resistance under de Gaulle's control, especially since the eclipse of the General Delegation favored the independence that the army of shadows was demanding.

## Death of the Delegation?

Jean Moulin's death had set off a violent fight to designate his heir. Although Émile Bollaert (Baudoin), under Pierre Brossolette's guidance, had been called on to succeed Moulin, the choice elicited no enthusiasm. In November 1943, the Christian Democrat Pierre-Henri Teitgen averred: "Just between us, the successor to Max [Moulin] was really a poor choice. He may be a very good public servant in normal times, but, on the one hand, he knows nothing about the Resistance, and, on the other, he does not seem at all aware of the enormous responsibilities that will fall on his shoulders on the day of liberation. Besides, he seems to be without any political savvy."[65] "In my view, Baudoin [Bollaert] does not have the desired qualifications to perform what ought to be his paramount role. His political notions and methods run the risk of compromising General de Gaulle," confirmed Pascal Copeau, head of Libération-sud, in a letter to d'Astier de La Vigerie, his former boss—now a minister—on January 24, 1944.[66] The duties of the delegation thus fell once more to Claude Bouchinet-Serreulles, assistant to Bollaert for the northern zone, supported in the southern zone by Jacques Bingen, who arrived on the night of August 15, 1943.

And yet Colonel Passy, director of the BCRA, continued to undermine the authority of these two emissaries, who were restricting the power of the Bollaert-Brossolette team. Passy could not come out against the return of his two accomplices, which would end so tragically, but he saw to it that Bouchinet-Serreulles, discredited by the affair of rue de la Pompe, was recalled. Bouchinet-Serreulles, who left France on the night of March 3, 1944, was ordered to justify his actions and was even accused of causing the arrest of Bollaert and Brossolette, an accusation that broke his spirit. The delegation was then entrusted on an interim basis to Jacques Bingen, but neither the BCRA nor the CFLN sent him instructions about what to do.

This dissension greatly weakened the delegation. Georges Bidault, the new chair of the CNR, pointed out in a telegram to Algiers on April 4, 1944: "Not only has the General Delegation of the CFLN suffered for the last nine months from an abnormal situation, but it has also had the greatest difficulties accomplishing its mission, since it lacks the necessary investiture to take a position in its own name and the necessary connections to take a position in your name. Our delegation has been violently criticized for now being in charge only of air and sea liaisons."[67] Francis-Louis Closon, an envoy from London, put things in perspective: "No doubt it was not easy to designate a delegate from Algiers who had both de Gaulle's confidence and that of the movements. But everything occurred as if, after the death of the strongman—which is what Jean Moulin was—a combination of circumstance and will had worked to weaken the delegation." He concluded: "I have no satisfying explanation for that situation."[68]

To break the deadlock, Charles de Gaulle decided to name Alexandre Parodi as head of the delegation. A member of the Council of State and of Libération-sud, Parodi had since 1942 held a seat on the Comité Général d'Études (General Studies Committee)—originally called the Comité Général des Experts (General Committee of Experts)—which Jean Moulin had authorized on July 1, 1942, as a way to prepare for the major postliberation reforms.[69] The appointment of the loyal Gaullist Parodi, however, seemed to mark the disavowal of Jacques Bingen, on whom that heavy responsibility ought to have fallen. In a letter of April 14, Bingen poured out his feelings:

> From October to April, neither the [CFLN], nor its specialized services, nor "friendly" services, have performed even their minimal duty. In six months, there was not a single departure from France by the means that they alone had the responsibility and the duty to put into operation.
> . . . Never did I receive a word of support, never a letter (or cable) of encouragement, official or unofficial.
> . . . In short, I declare the recall of Sophie [Bouchinet-Serreulles] scandalous, and scandalous as well the appointment of 4Tus [Quartus, Alexandre Parodi], not in itself, but Sophie [is] unheeded, even though he was the only one who knew something about something.[70]

That letter would be his last will and testament. Named delegate for the southern zone, Bingen left Paris on the afternoon of May 10. An MLN agent was waiting for him in Clermont-Ferrand. Unfortunately, the agent had chosen for his assistant Alfred Dormal, who was actually working for the Gestapo. Detained at dawn on May 11, Bingen managed to knock out one of his guards and to take refuge under the porch of a house. But a woman walking by pointed out his hiding place to a passing German truck. Bingen swallowed his cyanide capsule and died while being transferred to Gestapo headquarters.[71] Jacques Maillet replaced him in the southern zone, with Roland Pré performing the duties of assistant delegate for the northern zone.

Over time, then, the delegation had lost most of its powers, even its assignments, which were partly taken over by the DMRs. This loss of

clout deprived General de Gaulle of a powerful instrument, all the more
so since he was still a long way from controlling the AS. In July 1943,
Pierre Dejussieu had been named chief of staff for the southern zone
AS, which amounted to transferring leadership of the underground
forces from London to the metropolis. On December 23, 1943, an
agreement between Georges Beaufils (Latour), head of the FTP,
Mangin (Marbot), interim DMN, and Dejussieu (Pontcarral) stipulated
merging the command structures of the AS and the FTP to form a
single organization, the FFI. On February 1, 1944, the CCDMR created COMIDAC, which aspired to take charge of the FFI's actions.
General Revers, representative of the ORA, would hold a seat as "technical adviser," without voting rights.[72] The FFI were escaping Gaullist
oversight.

De Gaulle had believed he could ward off that risk by creating "his"
COMIDAC in Algiers and by making it clear, in his directive of
March 10, 1944, that the rival COMIDAC, which he called the Comité
Militaire National (National Military Committee), "does not constitute a command organization but rather divides inspection and monitoring duties among its members."[73] In addition, General Eisenhower's
delegate on the CFLN, Pierre Koenig—known as the victor of Bir-
Hakeim—received the official command of the FFI in March 1944. But
on May 13, 1944, the metropolitan COMIDAC, renamed "COMAC,"
came under the authority of the CNR and proclaimed itself a "leadership and command organization for the FFI."[74] Two competing authorities, in other words, aspired to lead the FFI into battle, and that
portended serious conflicts ahead. They erupted upon liberation.

That said, the importance of who had military control of the resistance should not be overestimated. De Gaulle accurately assessed the
weakness of the underground forces, which could do no more than provide support for the Allied troops. In the battle taking shape, their
role would be secondary at best, minor at worst, and the conduct of operations, unpredictable by nature, held surprises in store that could
not be foreseen. All in all, military control was secondary; political control was not. And on that point, the president of the CFLN did not
lower his guard.

Politically, the liberation posed three major risks. First, the power
vacuum resulting from the collapse of the Vichy regime could lead to

chaos, if a shadow state did not immediately replace it. Second, the Allies might take over France, either by bringing back the political staff of the Third Republic, or by relying on the Vichy apparatus, or by setting in place an Allied Military Government of Occupied Territory (AMGOT). This last hypothesis belonged to the realm of fantasy, since neither Roosevelt nor Churchill was considering such an extreme measure;[75] but the example of Italy, placed under that humiliating yoke in 1943, stood as a dangerous precedent. Third, the fear of a Communist insurrection could not be completely ruled out, though de Gaulle remained skeptical about the chances of a French-style October Revolution. "We feared the blood of civil war, summary 'liquidations,' as much as the intervention of the AMGOT; we kept our eye on the romanticism of certain resistance fighters and on the domineering will of our Communist comrades," concludes Francis-Louis Closon.[76] Jacques Duclos retorts: "Although some resistance fighters had a tendency to choose their position by taking the opposite view from the Communist Party, the Party had only one desire, only one will: to forge national unity through combat, to advance headlong with ever greater forces into the battle for national liberation, which was at the same time the battle for freedom against Fascist slavery and barbarism."[77] These perils, whether real or imaginary, pushed de Gaulle to build an underground counterstate to ensure his later power.

## The Commissioners of the Republic

De Gaulle's envoys initially concerned themselves with naming the prefects and commissioners of the republic who, once liberation came, would replace the Vichy high officials in the departments and regions. The CGE did the groundwork, assisted by Closon. According to his orders of July 20, 1943, he was supposed to "expedite the process of drawing up a list of future prefects" by serving as liaison with the CGE.[78] In July 1943, Claude Bouchinet-Serreulles created the Commission des Désignations Administratives (CDA; Commission of Administrative Appointments). Under the guidance of the CCDMR and chaired by Michel Debré, the commission was theoretically under the authority of the lawyer Émile Laffon, the "delegate for the organization" sent from London. But in actuality, "the two men seem to have worked in perfect harmony."[79] In conjunction with Closon, the CDA therefore drew up a list of prefects and commissioners, which would be approved by the underground groups before being sent to Algiers.

A first list named forty-one prefects, twelve parliamentarians, six resistance leaders, sixteen high officials, ten members of the liberal professions, seven labor activists, six engineers, and two industrialists.[80] On October 3 the Algiers COMIDAC confirmed the appointments of twenty commissioners and fifty prefects, while officially recognizing the CDA, now entrusted to Laffon and Debré. Arrests and the concern for political balance required the commission to start all over again in 1943 and in 1944. But the two men's patient efforts were rewarded in the end. By March 9, 1944, forty designated prefects had assumed their posts, eighteen knew of their appointments, fifteen still had to be notified, and only fifteen spots remained vacant.[81] On the eve of the landing, only five commissioners of the republic (who acted at the regional level) and eight prefects—especially in the eastern departments—were yet to be named.[82] In May, the designated officials discreetly established themselves in their districts. Émile Laffon called them in or paid them a visit. "He provided them with a dossier we had prepared, which included the [important] texts, certain information about possible contacts with the local Resistance, and a sum of money," his assistant, Jean Morin, reports.[83]

As always, that idyllic picture must be nuanced somewhat. In the first place, the appointment of the lucky few, not surprisingly, caused a few tensions between the Gaullist delegates and the representatives of the internal resistance. "Most of the commissioners and prefects were . . . if not friends, at least men whom Laffon and Debré especially, but also Closon, Parodi, Mons, Leenhardt, or Bidault, had had the opportunity to evaluate," explains historian Charles-Louis Foulon.[84] High officials therefore had an advantage, to the detriment of those with less typical profiles. In addition, the movements did not call for a vigorous purge of the prefectoral corps, which surprised both Laffon and Debré. In a harsh report on September 19, 1943, Laffon wrote: "The staff that was in place on June 20, 1940, and was subsequently dismissed by Vichy, will not necessarily be recalled. The movements asked us several times to keep the prefects still in place today, insisting on the services they rendered to the Resistance. We turned out to be more intransigent than the movements. Those who pursue careers in the prefecture have a particular mindset; their traditional tendency is to betray the government they ought to serve, while making pledges to the political party they sense will win. . . . The return pure and simple of the 1940 personnel raises irrefutable objections. That personnel is on the whole discredited, ruined by years of debasement, unable to grasp the import and the greatness of the reformation required by the liberation of the territory."[85] Finally, a few misfires occurred here and there. In the Toulouse region, the designated commissioner, Jean Cassou, wounded while passing through a German roadblock, had to be hastily replaced by Pierre Bertaux. In Burgundy, Jean Mairey took the place of Jean Bouhey, also wounded before the liberation.

In any case, an administration was suddenly preparing to step out of the shadows. Loyal to General de Gaulle, that administration in spite of everything granted a real place to the internal and external resistance, since resistance fighters—Francis-Louis Closon, Michel Debré, Yves Farge, Henri Ingrand, Alain Savary, and others—received regional commissionships. Although underrepresented, the Communists and fellow travelers were not forgotten: Lucien Monjauvis was installed in Saint-Étienne, Jean Chaintron in Limoges, Jacques Bounin in Montpellier, and Raymond Aubrac in Marseilles.

The decree of January 10, 1944, granted broad prerogatives to the commissioners. They were to "take all measures likely to ensure the safety of the French and Allied armies, provide for the administration of the territory, reestablish republican legality, and satisfy the needs of the population." In addition, they had extraordinary powers in the event that communications with Paris were interrupted. In particular, they had the right to:

1. suspend the application of all legislative or regulatory provisions actually in force, provided they refer the matter to the commissioner for the interior as soon as possible.
2. order all measures and make all decisions necessary to ensure order, the smooth operation of administrations, public services, and private enterprises, as well as the security of the French and Allied armies.
3. suspend from their duties all elected officials and all public servants or agents of the administrations, collectivities, state-owned companies,

public services, or services of public interest, whether controlled or
subsidized, and designate interim replacements . . .

5. pursue or order the pursuit of all criminal investigations . . .

7. make use of all people or resources.[86]

In short, their mandate was more reminiscent of the imperative for
"public safety" set in place by the deputies named by the revolutionary
National Convention than of the more humdrum management of the
prefects of the Third Republic, even though their job title referred
explicitly to the revolution of 1848.

## The Departmental Liberation Committees

Democracy continued to assert its rights, however. In each department,
a Comité Départemental de Libération (CDL; Departmental Liberation Committee), emerging from the darkness of the occupation, would
partly replace "the superannuated general council" and would assemble
"authentic resistance fighters engaged in battle."[87] Its initial assignment
would be to plan and control the insurrection. Then, after the installation of the new powers, it would "assist the prefect,"[88] to borrow the
terms of the decree of April 21, 1944, which organized the postliberation government.

The constitution of the CDLs was an arduous process. The idea
came from the internal resistance, but it was initially up to Francis-
Louis Closon to choose the happy few. Nevertheless, in late January
1944 the CNR formed a commission to move forward with the appointments. Closon managed to snap up the chairmanship[89] and undertook
the arbitration necessary. It was a vast program. The MUR, speaking
through Claude Bourdet, rejected the departmental echelon, preferring the regional level; they challenged the presence of the political
parties, reserving for themselves the right to name their representatives. The PCF's strategy was worrisome. It and the FN "caused incidents when the new committees were formed, demanding a broader
representation of their followers under various names."[90] Closon settled
the matter: he decided to amalgamate resistance forces and political
parties and to turn the CDLs into "instruments that both reveal and
regulate tensions" and that would be able to make the transition from

Vichy to liberated France.[91] He also vetoed the creation of courts-martial in the departments, which "would have been charged with quickly expediting purge cases, of judging the guilty or presumed guilty, of having them executed, of stabilizing the situation in the heat of action, in order to hasten the return to a state of calm."[92]

In constituting the CDLs, Closon could rely on two assistants—Jean Mons for the northern zone, Francis Leenhardt for the southern—and worked in harmony with the commission of the CNR. The repressive forces complicated the task. In Burgundy, three members of the CDL were arrested before liberation.[93] Closon noted that, in Limoges, "a few months after my arrival, the best people on the team fell one after another, sold out by a man arrested by the Germans who had gone over to the Gestapo. He was finally taken down, but too late."[94] In all, "the committees, painstakingly set up, reconstituted themselves with increasing difficulties. After a hard hit, we had to wait for the region to stabilize, to find the men—scattered everywhere—who were still of value, to gradually mend the rent fabric. The new arrivals, courageous as they were, could not help looking over their shoulder. The bright colors of morning did not erase the oppressive twilight of the previous night. They lacked the experience and authority of their predecessors, and fear gave rise to absenteeism."[95] By the eve of the landing, however, the great majority of the CDLs were constituted. When the day came, they would ease the transition from the Vichy power to the authorities of the provisional government of the French Republic.

Finally, the fear that communications between Paris and Algiers would be interrupted led the CFLN to name provisional ministers, given the title "secretaries-general." They would act in an interim capacity, in anticipation of the government's arrival in the capital. The choice of these individuals gave rise to a violent conflict, however. The CGE, tasked with proposing names, sent a list to Algiers without consulting the CNR. The CNR was upset and obtained the right to approve future appointments, a demand unacceptable in General de Gaulle's eyes. General Giraud's expulsion clarified the situation. The order of January 21, 1944, stipulated that the mandate of these nineteen ministers "can and must be conferred on them only by the CFLN."[96] Their mission should not be exaggerated, however: it was limited to taking in hand the ministries and in managing the central administrations in the pivotal period between the enemy's departure and the installation of the provisional government.[97] The stakes remained modest, therefore, but that did not prevent a new conflict from erupting. The Communists were calling for the top ministries. They had to be satisfied with Justice, entrusted to Marcel Willard, and Education, which was awarded to Henri Wallon as a consolation prize. The other posts were granted to major resistance fighters, often those on the CGE. René Courtin received National Economy, Emmanuel Mönick Finance, Robert Lacoste Industrial Production—and finally, François Mitterrand, put in charge of Prisoners and Deportees at the age of twenty-seven, began a stellar career that overlooked a rather Vichyist French youth.[98]

The underground infrastructure would keep France from sinking into chaos or falling under the control of the Allies. It filled the power vacuum by reviving the state. It was a risky gamble, which de Gaulle won. He had truly known how to combine the hard realities of raison d'état with the glittering dreams of a French-style New Deal, and a solid grounding in history with the profound need for renewal, embodied by the resistance.

## Reformation?

For the internal resistance and for the CFLN, liberation, far from being simply the departure of a detested enemy, had to herald change. Charles de Gaulle had exclaimed in Algiers on July 14, 1943:

> The good people who imagine that, after so much blood spilled, so many tears shed, so many humiliations suffered, our country will agree, when victory comes, either simply to return to the regime that abdicated even as its armies were surrendering, or to hold onto the system of oppression and delation built on disaster, these good people, I say, will do well to rid themselves of their illusions. . . . France delivered will have no desire to take the road to the abyss once more, or to remain on the road to slavery. France has chosen in advance a new path.
>
> . . . Yes, after the fall of the system of yesteryear and in face of the indignation of the one that is collapsing, after so much suffering, anger, disgust, experienced by an enormous number of men and women in our country, the nation will want everyone, I say, all its children, to be able

to live and work with social dignity and social security. Without taking away the spur to action provided by initiative and legitimate profit, the nation will know that natural resources, work, and technology—the three elements of prosperity for all—should not be exploited for the benefit of a few. The nation will know to act in such a way that all the economic resources of its soil and of its empire will be put to work, not at the whim of individuals but for the advantage of all. If there are still Bastilles, let them prepare to open their doors of their own volition! For when the struggle is waged between the people and the Bastille, in the end, it is always the Bastille that is wrong![99]

The CGE, originally composed of Deputy Paul Bastid, the labor activist Robert Lacoste, the economics professor François de Menthon, and Alexandre Parodi, a member of the Council of State, gradually expanded to include Pierre-Henri Teitgen, René Courtin, Jacques Charpentier, Michel Debré, and Pierre Lefaucheux. These "nine sages of the Resistance," to borrow historian Diane de Bellescize's expression, secretly produced a series of reports dealing in particular with the economy, the purge, the organization of the press, and institutions. They set out in detail the reforms that ought to be put into effect upon liberation.[100]

The internal resistance, like broad swaths of the French population, shared these concerns. Beyond the military defeat, the disaster of 1940 was interpreted as a sign of national decline, which the crisis of the interwar period had brought to light. During the 1930s, the upheaval in the economy resulting from Black Thursday had seemed to sound the death knell of economic liberalism. The hard times had also increased the hunger for social justice, which the FP had made every effort to satisfy through its reforms.[101] Experts and politicians made the case for renewal, all proposing more or less the same solutions. At the institutional level, several voices were demanding that the Fourth Republic curtail the omnipotence of the legislature and restore the prerogatives of the executive branch. The public authorities, whether through programs or nationalization, would henceforth intervene in the economic sphere, which would be rid of the toxic influence of the trusts. A new press would emancipate itself from moneyed interests. A social security system would protect the French people from illness and take care of them in their old age. Finally, the state would move forward to democratize education and would offer every young person an equal chance in life. These prospects had fueled political debate during the interwar period but had rarely been taken up by the parties, on either the left or the right. Far from creating a consensus, in fact, they had exacerbated divisions.

By contrast, the war and the occupation intensified that desire for reformation, which rested on the pillars of economic modernization and social justice. The resistance was therefore eager to present, in its newspapers or journals, the solutions it was advocating. The program of the CNR, adopted on March 15, 1944, summed up its aspirations.

Émile Laffon, delegate of the CFLN, had submitted a political program to the members of the CNR in July 1943. In particular, it advocated strengthening executive power, socializing certain businesses, and expanding the rights of wage laborers.[102] But that plan had run into the determined opposition of the Communists, who rejected willy-nilly the reduction of legislative power, the restoration of the League of Nations, and nationalization. As for the right, it remained faithful to economic liberalism. Because of the combined opposition of these two groups, the Laffon report was buried. In October 1943, however, the commissioner for the interior decided to survey all the underground groups and ask them to spell out the direction they wanted the country to take upon liberation. Pierre Villon, head of the FN, responded by putting forward a "prospective charter for the Resistance."[103] The Communists could not in fact "perpetually dodge drawing up some kind of program for the future; otherwise, they would arouse persistent doubts about their real intentions."[104] One sign of the importance attached to that text: Villon, for the only time during the occupation, met with Jacques Duclos and Benoît Frachon, so that they could adopt a joint position. The text was delivered to the CNR. Its board, composed of five members—Georges Bidault, Pierre Villon, Louis Saillant, Pascal Copeau, and Maxime Blocq-Mascart—discussed it, amended it, and then, in January 1944, sent it to the other members of the council. After being submitted to the MLN and the SFIO and once again amended by the CNR board, the text, titled "Program of Action for the Resistance,"[105] was unanimously adopted on March 15, 1944.

It consisted of two parts. The first section, which defined an "immediate plan of action," advocated the formation of "fight committees" in cities, villages, and businesses. These committees were to assist STO evaders, track down and punish collaborators, fight against requisitions, and organize patriotic militias throughout the country. The general staff of the FFI was to order its groups "to combat the enemy from this moment on" and to "distribute the unused stores of arms to the groups judged by the general staff of the FFI best able to fight effectively, now and in the immediate future."[106] Hence, though London accepted the principle of immediate action, the text marked an alignment with the positions defended by the Communists, who were quick to denounce the "fear of the people"[107] concealed behind the watch-and-wait strategy. At the time, the Socialists opposed the intensification of direct action, but they were not followed by the other underground groups.[108]

What later generations have remembered about the program are primarily the "measures to be applied upon the liberation of the territory." Apart from the reestablishment of democracy, they stipulated, at the economic level, "stepping up national production . . . along the lines of a plan established by the state," "returning to the nation the monopolized major resources of production, the fruit of work in common, energy sources, the riches below ground, the insurance companies, and the major banks." Social programs were not overlooked. The CNR called for the right to employment, time off, retirement, and job security, for "a major wage adjustment," and, less conventionally, for "a complete social security plan intended to assure all citizens against all social risks."[109]

These proposals were accepted, but not without debate. The PCF was initially hesitant about nationalization, not because it was opposed to the idea in principle—indeed, it had left open that possibility in 1937. But the party considered the term problematic. "Its major flaw is to make the idea of nationalization—appropriation from above—a substitute for the mobilization of the people, confiscation from below," Philippe Buton notes.[110] Jacques Duclos therefore suggested using the expression "return to the nation," which was eventually adopted.[111]

Beyond all these controversies, a notable paradox needs to be pointed out. The program of the CNR became—and in fact remains—sacred for a part of the left, readily inclined to consider it a progressive monument, as suggested by the Time for Outrage movement, launched primarily by the resistance fighter Stéphane Hessel. An attentive reading, however, reveals the limits of the program. For example, voting rights for women were not among the priorities—the Radicals threatened to split off if that measure were adopted.[112] In the empire, the CNR confined itself to suggesting "an extension of the political, social, and economic rights to the indigenous and colonial populations." At a time when the storm was brewing, as proven by the demonstrations of May 8, 1945, in the Algerian cities of Sétif and Guelma, these proposals appeared timid at the very least. Finally, at the economic level, the program by no means represented a theoretical breakthrough, since it simply adopted measures that the SFIO, the PCF, and even the avant-garde circles of the interwar period had advocated: an intervention by the state based on the nationalization/central planning diptych. One sign that the charter did not look very revolutionary to contemporaries: its diffusion in the underground press was "uneven and, on the whole, limited."[113]

Nevertheless, the program marked an advance in two respects. First, it linked the economic and the social. That pairing can hardly be said to have preoccupied the neoliberals and technocrats of the interwar period or of the Vichy regime. Although quick to reflect on the respective merits of central planning and nationalization, they had concerned themselves little with social questions. Second, the program brought about a consensus that extended from the PCF to the classic right. Whereas state intervention had been a factor of divisiveness before 1939, during the dark days of the occupation it united the entire political spectrum. Overall, the CNR's program went down in history not because of the boldness of its views but because of its capacity to bring people together. That reality explains why, in its main lines, it was implemented.

On the eve of the Allied landing in Normandy, the resistance could thus look to the future with relative optimism. In eliminating Henri Giraud, Charles de Gaulle had managed to unify all the underground forces, including the secret services, though outbreaks of irredentism manifested themselves here and there. The army of shadows now possessed a doctrine defining the use to which it would be put. Supplied with plans that would facilitate the liberators' advance, it had finally been equipped with arms, which the Allies were now less stingy about dropping. The CFLN had succeeded in building a counterstate, which, when liberation came, would guarantee a peaceful transfer of power. The resistance had also managed to define a political program, which, though not staggeringly modern, established a consensus that guaranteed its implementation.

But not all fears were assuaged by the passage of time. The Corsica insurrection had inaugurated the era of suspicion by raising fears of a Communist revolution. The Glières tragedy had revealed the military limits of the maquis. The Allied strategy caused alarm, in that it circumvented and arrogantly disregarded Gaullist authority. And though the DMRs provided assurances that the orders given would be executed in the provinces, at the national level the delegation had lost a large share of its power, depriving de Gaulle of essential leverage.

Nothing, in other words, guaranteed that the liberation would unfold smoothly, and many unknowns remained. The future would see to their elimination.

## Chapter 14

# Formez vos Bataillons!

The supreme battle is under way!

After so much combat, fury, sorrow, the decisive shock, the shock so long hoped for, has come. Needless to say, it's the battle of France and the battle for France!

Vast resources for the attack, which is to say—for us—assistance, have begun to surge forth from the banks of old England. Before that last bastion of Europe to the west, the tide of German oppression was arrested not long ago. It is today the home base of the offensive for freedom. France, submerged for four years but not destroyed or vanquished, is on her feet to take part in it.

For the sons of France, wherever they may be, whoever they may be, their simple and sacred duty is to fight by every means at their disposal. The task at hand is to destroy the enemy, the enemy who is crushing and defiling the nation, the hated enemy, the dishonored enemy.[1]

With these fighting words, uttered on June 6, 1944, the very day the Allies stormed the beaches of Normandy, Charles de Gaulle assigned the French an essential role in the liberation of their country. He refrained, however, from defining concretely the form it would take. Three distinct but complementary logical possibilities coexisted. First, the Allies hoped that the resistance would carry out the plans prepared by the Gaullist secret services; second, they were banking on generalized guerrilla warfare, which the maquis in particular were supposed to instigate; and third, de Gaulle and the Communists were counting on a national insurrection, notions of which proved to be diverse, not to say antagonistic, from the first.

### Adjusting the Organization Charts

The BCRA had developed several plans in liaison with the British SOE. But the chains of command remained vague, with each authority seeking to keep supreme control over its secret services. That fragmentation indirectly threatened the effectiveness of the military deployment. It provided no guarantee that the scenarios devised in the London bureaus would in fact be activated. That obliged the Allies to rework the organization charts.

On the French side, the CFLN created the État-Major des Forces Françaises de l'Intérieur (General Staff of the French Forces of the Interior) in March 1944, placing it under General Koenig's command. A World War I veteran, Koenig was still a young man, having been born in 1898. He had joined the FFL in July 1940 and had won glory in the desert sands of North Africa in 1942. His loyalty inspired de Gaulle's full confidence, and his professionalism reassured the Allies, still inclined toward suspicion about the amateurism of the army of shadows. The military leadership of the internal resistance thus fell to the victor of Bir-Hakeim, who established himself in London in 1944. His power was shored up by the control he came to exert over the secret services. A general staff headed by Henri Ziegler (Vernon) had been established within the BCRA that same month; on May 6, it was placed under Koenig's orders.[2]

The Allies too modified their chains of command. In March 1944, to coordinate the actions of their networks, the Americans and the British formed a Special Forces Headquarters (SFHQ) to run their special services—except those that reported to the British Intelligence Service. The SFHQ was directly incorporated into the Supreme Headquarters, Allied Expeditionary Forces (SHAEF), the body that, under General Eisenhower's leadership, supervised preparations for the landing and would later take charge of it. The SHAEF reported to his G3 branch, which was in charge of operations.[3]

That situation, however, resulted in a dangerous dualism, since coordination between French and Anglo-American groups was uncertain. On May 24, Koenig offered to head up a trinational staff, which would be in charge of all the underground forces. That proposal was ratified by the SHAEF on the 30th. On D-Day, Koenig would receive his directives from the Allied high command through the SFHQ and would command the special forces in their entirety. One sign of the confidence the Allies granted him: from June 17 on, he enjoyed the same status as the commanders serving under Eisenhower's authority.[4] In theory, his powers were broad: not only the BCRA but also the F and RF "action" sections of the SOE reported to him. Finally, Allied representatives guaranteed that orders would be properly executed. Hence, Koenig was flanked by Major General Redman on the British side and by Colonel Haskell on the American, while Colonel Buckmaster (for the SOE) and Colonel Van der Stricht (for the OSS) assisted Koenig's chief of staff, Colonel Ziegler.[5]

Once the chain of command was determined, the order of priorities had to be established. De Gaulle laid his cards on the table. In March 1944, the Comité de Défense Nationale d'Alger (Algiers National Defense Committee) defined "the military use of the Resistance during operations to liberate the metropolis." On April 5, that document received de Gaulle's imprimatur.[6] Precedence was given to sabotage, preferably in the rear of the battle zones: the army of shadows was to avoid guerrilla warfare, except under orders, and "always refuse battle against an all-too-superior offensive enemy." Insurrectional actions would be performed, but in the zones farthest from the front. They would rely primarily on the maquis.[7] For the Allies, conversely, the only thing that mattered was the implementation of the plans, the execution of which was precipitated by Eisenhower's anxiety. On June 3, 1944, Eric Edward Mockler-Ferryman, head of Operations Western Europe in the SOE, asked Walter Bedell-Smith, Eisenhower's chief of staff, for his instructions. The response was not long in coming: it was judged indispensable that the maximum effort be made in France on the night preceding D-Day, to ensure the best chances for Neptune, that is, for the landing. But that instruction contravened the plan of the Gaullist secret services, which stipulated that actions be launched region by region as the Allies advanced, in order not to expose the underground forces prematurely. The SHAEF, in ordering an increase in sabotage operations throughout the territory, was hoping to mislead the Germans, to plunge them into uncertainty: Did the Normandy landing herald the invasion, or was it merely a diversion tactic? In any event, in Fighting France the order produced "stupor and incomprehension," to borrow Jean-Louis Crémieux-Brilhac's terms. Koenig and de Gaulle kept quiet, but that pregnant silence did not signify approval of an initiative that raised the keenest fears.[8]

# Resistance Organizations
## Spring 1944

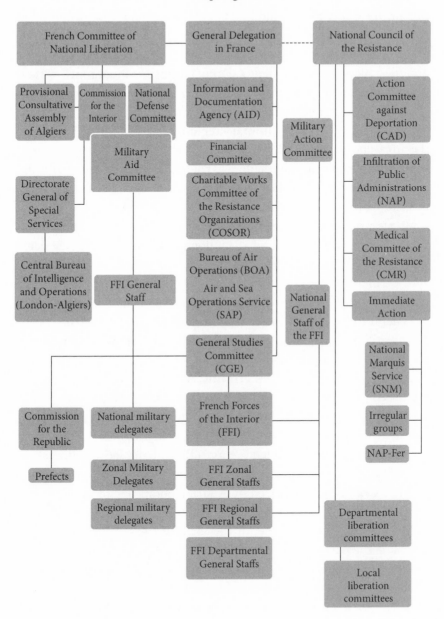

*Figure 14.1*

## Executing the Plans

Beginning at 9:15 P.M. on June 5, the resistance fighters, glued to their radio sets, heard a stream of 210 messages ordering them to take action. Of these, a few verses from Verlaine's "Chanson d'automne" (Autumn Song)—"Blessent mon coeur / d'une langueur / monotone" ("they wound my heart / with a monotonous / languor")—were broadcast twice, alerting the Ventriloque network that it was to act that very evening.[9] More generally, the twelve military regions falling to the FFI staff and the fifty-one networks that reported to the United Kingdom were supposed to implement immediately the plans that the regional military delegates had set in place in the previous weeks.[10] But did the army of shadows have the means to act?

In view of liberation, the resistance was in possession of substantial funds. For the month of June 1944 alone, the regional military delegates received 140 million francs.[11] To maintain "a mobilized force of 280,000 men at 1,500 francs a month," the resistance was allocated 420 million francs in August of the same year, combined with 67 million in general funds, 13 million for the missions planned for that month, and 75 million for the British networks that had been incorporated into the FFI.[12] The money was not flooding in, however. The expenses of the underground groups were growing, particularly because of the influx of volunteers who had to be fed, clothed, and sometimes paid a salary. In addition, difficulties in communication complicated money transfers and made certain zones vulnerable to a shortage of funds. In early 1944, these obstacles led Georges Bidault and Jacques Bingen to create the Comité de Financement de la Résistance (COFI; Resistance Finance Committee). Chaired by André Debray, one of the directors of the Banque de Paris et des Pays-Bas, the COFI took out loans in France in the CFLN's name, in the form of treasury bills or checks drawn on the Banque d'Algérie. The committee managed by that means to raise 614 million francs—while striving to prevent compromised individuals from redeeming themselves at bargain rates for the support they had given Vichy or even Nazi Germany.[13] In any event, affluence replaced penury, all the more so in that the FFI and the FTP were robbing banks and post offices to finance their operations. In Cher, 107 postal stations were robbed between June and September 1944. Upon liberation, the Ministry of Posts, Telegraphs, and Telephones tallied up 4,145 holdups, that is, a dead loss of 166.7 million.[14] A few spectacular heists were pulled off. The director of the Banque de France in Périgueux, fearing that its liquid reserves would be seized by the internal resistance, tried to transfer part of them to Bordeaux; but on July 26, the maquis intercepted the train at the station of Neuvic (Dordogne department) and made off with 2.28 billion francs—an all-time record.[15]

The internal resistance also benefited from plentiful parachute drops. In 1943 it had received 3,000 containers, but more than 50,000 arrived between July and late September 1944.[16] That total conceals serious disparities, however. Region M (Brittany) was well-off, having received 29,029 weapons over the summer; Region C (Ardennes-Alsace-Moselle), with its 2,025 weapons, looked like Cinderella in comparison.[17] True, Region M was close to the front, Region C far away, which explains why the Allies preferred one over the other. Conversely, the balance was restored between the groups serving under the British flag (F Section of the SOE), which had long been favored, and the units that reported to the general staff (supplied through RF Section of the SOE), which had been treated poorly for many months. Between June and September 1944, the first group of organizations obtained 39,116 Sten submachine guns, 12,101 pistols, and 417 bazookas or PIATs (antitank weapons). The second received 38,549 Stens, 6,505 pistols, and 744 antitank weapons.[18] The Allies agreed—finally!—to better equip the internal resistance with war materiel. After June 6, 1944, they proved less sectarian and shared their bounty more equitably. Above all, the French had access to armaments more sophisticated than the rustic Sten. Although that light submachine gun, easy to disassemble into three foot-long parts, was easily hidden and transported,[19] it had a disturbing tendency to jam, and its firing accuracy was limited. Conversely, the allocation of bazookas, mines, and Bren machine guns (6,443) demonstrated that the SHAEF now believed the army of shadows capable of waging the "small war," in Clausewitz's pet phrase.

But the FFI still had to learn how to use these weapons. To that end, the secret services sent trainers to teach them the rudiments of guerrilla warfare. The BCRA dispatched several instructors, some of them women, to reveal to resistance fighters the art of the tripwire and the mysteries of plastic explosives. From April 1 to 17, 1944, for example, Jeanne Bohec (Rateau) initiated the FFI of Côtes-du-Nord in the "manufacture of homemade explosives, those that can be purchased retail and prepared oneself."[20] But the essential role was taken on by the Jedburgh teams.

Devised in 1942 by Colin Gubbins, head of the SOE, and named after a Scottish village, the Jedburgh teams were to be in charge of tactical coordination between the French resistance fighters and the Allied forces. "A team consisting of three men, including a radio operator, would be parachuted in, would establish contact with the local maquis, and would organize drop zones, resupply systems, and training; after that, it would act as a liaison with the regular armies," historian Arthur L. Funk writes.[21] Each team consisted of three officers—French, British, or American—though other nationalities, such as the Dutch, could be co-opted.[22] Historian Philippe André notes: "In zones poorly organized by the local Resistance, the Jedburghs were supposed to constitute maquis, recruit troops. In the well-organized zones, by contrast, the teams often provided logistical and tactical support. They could also be sent to prepare for the arrival of the paratrooper commandos."[23] In June 1944, 93 teams, which is to say, some 280 men in all, were sent into France, including 6 teams to Brittany. By August, twenty-five three-member teams had arrived by parachute, in the west especially. That represented only a quarter of the total number.[24] The strategic blockade that confined the Allies to their narrow beachhead in Normandy, before Bradley launched his offensive on Avranches in late July 1944, explains why the SHAEF was reluctant to deploy its Jedburghs, not knowing in which zone they would be most useful.

In any event, the Jedburghs made every effort to train the FFI and then to implement the plans already in place, with precedence given to cutting off the main railroad lines. Hamish, an officer on the team, boasted about the results obtained: "Upon our arrival [on June 13, 1944], we found between 200 and 300 men, about 150 of whom were armed. When we left the site [on September 24], there were 3,000 men combating in our sector and 1,000 more waiting for weapons. . . . The principal sabotage activity in our sector consisted of continually cutting off the Paris-Limoges railroad line. It was our good fortune to have many excellent French officers who did a magnificent job for us. It is to

Radio-Paris was talking about it, saying of course it was doomed to fail. People on the street were excited and wanted to talk. No one had any details, only tremendous hope. The whole of France was turned toward Normandy."[38] The information even made its way to the concentration camps. "What happiness in our misery," thought Claude Bourdet, interned at Neuengamme. "We were over the moon. We told ourselves we could bear anything now, and that in fact we would soon be freed."[39] Sometimes, however, hope was tinged with anxiety. "We don't remember that day as being joyful, because we were so bent over our task," relates Alban Vistel. "Maybe we sensed it was a harbinger of new tragedies. June looked bright at first. It would later acquire the name 'the month of the executed.'"[40]

In fact, the landing brought an influx of volunteers, who rushed to join the army of shadows. That levée en masse corresponded in part to the plan outlined during the dark days: a flood of volunteers would surge up from nowhere to fight a despised enemy. Men who had been sleepwalking until then were yearning to join the fray, and thousands of willing souls rose to the challenge, responding to implicit or explicit instructions that enjoined them to fight. General Koenig joined his appeals to de Gaulle's exhortations, and Communist calls for action increased. On June 8, the Comité Parisien de la Libération (CPL; Paris Liberation Committee), chaired by the Communist André Tollet, ordered:

> Death to the German invaders.
>
> Gather together in the Francs-Tireurs et Partisans and in the irregular groups within the Forces Françaises de l'Intérieur. May thousands of fighters come out of every street, every house, every factory, and soak the paving stones of Paris with the impure blood of the enemy. May they strike every harder and avoid ever more the enemy's blows. Men and women of Paris: to each of you your Boche, your militiaman, your traitor!

On June 6, 1944, a patriotic frenzy took hold of the country. Colonel Zeller, leader of the ORA, was struck by its fervor on an inspection mission in the southeast. He noted in August: "The FFI, based on the directives given by General Koenig, launched full throttle into actions without restriction, impelled by a magnificent national uprising of the entire population in the rural areas and small towns. But in the minds of most of its participants, those actions were supposed to be short-lived, and the hope of an imminent landing in the southeast gladdened every heart."[41] In fact, the FFI apparently numbered 50,000 in January 1944, but their forces jumped to 100,000 in June, reaching 500,000 by liberation.[42] "Unfortunately," as Philippe Buton points out, "some resistance fighters mistook the landing for the Liberation."[43] The premature launch of a strategy both military and political gave rise to many tragedies.

## The Maquis Arrive on the Scene

At the military level, the strategists in Algiers had considered creating three redoubts where the FFI would confront the occupiers.

In Brittany, the SHAEF entrusted two commando units, placed under the command of Major Bourgoin, with varied and ambitious missions. These forces were supposed to "sever, as far as possible, all communications between Brittany and the remainder of France,"[44] which would delay or even immobilize the some 150,000 Germans quartered in Brittany. They were also supposed to spark "a large-scale revolt" in the region.[45] On the night of June 5, 1944, four advance teams of nine men, commanded by an officer, were dropped by parachute in Côtes-du-Nord onto what was called the Samwest base, near Duault; two others arrived at the base designated Dingson, near Malestroit in Morbihan.[46] The men of Samwest, engaged by the enemy from June 9 on, decided to quit fighting and retreat to Dingson, where the FFI departmental leader, Paul Chenailler (Morice), had gathered his troops at La Nouette farm. The flood of combatants rapidly swelled. On the one hand, Morice had launched a mobilization order on June 6, inviting the units that were forming to go to the Saint-Marcel woods to receive arms and equipment. The venture succeeded beyond expectations. "June 6, levée en masse in Morbihan. There were no longer Communists, workers, members of the liberal professions, fishermen: everyone united to join the maquis, and in the camps we saw the Red Star next to the Sacred Heart, the sons of Chouans making peace with the descendants of Blues," recounts Dr. Mahéo, chief physician of the maquis.[47] Between three and four thousand men received weapons there.[48] On the other hand, the Allies decided to abandon Côtes-du-Nord and to use Saint-Marcel as an entry point for the paratroopers of Major Bourgoin's 4th SAS Battalion, which arrived by parachute on the night of June 9. One hundred and fifty men reached the camp in several waves, which increased manpower but also the risks. Indeed, the comings and goings of the maquisards and the proliferation of parachute drops attracted the attention of the occupier. "Every day, a parade of FFI units was coming to the camp to get armed. They sometimes arrived in very large groups (up to several hundred men), fell into formation, and marched in step around the farmyard, then went to be summarily enlisted, receiving weapons and an FFI armband. They were then directed to the edge of the camp. Paratroopers moved among them, to show them where to place the automatic weapons and to teach them quickly how to handle the new arms; then they returned to their original maquis on one of the following nights," writes historian Roger Leroux.[49]

The Germans decided to put an end to the situation. On the morning of June 18, one of their units attacked the maquis, defended by some 2,400 men. A transmission got through by a stroke of luck, allowing the Allies to dispatch forty P-47 fighter planes, which gave Bourgoin, "too wily a fighter to be rounded up methodically in his heathland base," the chance to order the maquisards to disperse.[50] Thirty Frenchmen died in the battle and, according to the available estimates—which may be exaggerated—the Germans lost between 300 and 560 men, as a result of the air support provided by the Allies and assistance from professional soldiers.[51] But on the following days, the occupation troops returned, finished off the wounded after torturing them, and killed civilians in the surrounding villages and woods. "The eldest of them, a helpless eighty-three-year-old woman, was murdered in her bed. These massacres were committed by the 261st Ukrainian cavalry squadron and the 708th Georgian infantry battalion. As for the soldiers of the Wehrmacht, on June 27, 1944, they burned the châteaux of Saint-Geneviève and Les Hardys-Béhélec, then the farms and villages of Saint-Marcel," writes historian Luc Capdevila.[52] Despite that heavy toll, the operation caused an enormous stir: for the first time, the resistance had kept the enemy forces in check.[53] "By now every Breton who was going to help the allies was anxious to enrol, somehow, behind Bourgoin's liberating army of some four hundred Frenchmen," Foot observes.[54] Nevertheless, Saint-Marcel confirmed "that the armed

struggle could not be organized from a permanent base. The very notion of mobilized maquis arose from a grave misunderstanding of the
conditions facing the Resistance."[55] That tragedy was repeated in a
different form on Mont-Mouchet.

In April 1944, several hundred maquisards were concentrated in Auvergne on Mont-Mouchet, in the heart of the Margeride massif. Even
today, the question of how that group came into being is open to debate.
Some say that the initiative simply translated into action directives
from London, which, via the Plan Caïman devised in March 1944, had
sought to form a "C Force" in the center of France, which the Allies
would support by sending arms and airborne troops. According to that
plan, the resistance forces were supposed to liberate part of the territory; in the event of an Allied landing in the Mediterranean, they were
also to prevent an enemy counteroffensive and cut off the German units
retreating from the Atlantic coast.[56] Others counter that the decision
was made at the regional level by the FFI leader, Émile Coulaudon
(Gaspard), after he had met with Allied agents. In any case, the mus-
tering began in the spring and then picked up speed. Even before June 6,
some 2,500 maquisards, all from the AS and the MUR, had gathered
around the forest house.[57] The concentration of maquisards led to a first
attack by the French repressive forces—the Milice and Legionnaires—
which was repelled on the evening of June 2.

After the landing, the flood of volunteers swelled. General Kurt von
Jesser therefore decided to wipe out the maquis. The attack, waged by
1,800 and then 2,700 men, was launched on the afternoon of June 10;
it lasted until dawn on June 12. Many men managed to flee and to re-
group in the redoubt of Truyère-Chaudes-Aigues, which since June 6
had served as the second assembly center. But on June 20, that base too
was assaulted by German troops, which prompted Coulaudon to give
up any idea of a redoubt. The toll, it is true, was high: 125 maquisards
and more than 50 civilians lost their lives in the first assault alone.[58]
The Germans saw relatively light losses, contrary to a legend quick to
claim that, "since the beginning of the battles," they had suffered "1,400
dead, 2,000 wounded," as Colonel "Gaspard" repeated at a tribute in
1964.[59] "In the days and months that followed, the number of a thousand was put forward, later reduced to two hundred deaths, and finally
to a hundred. The various German archives (Freiburg, Berlin) allow

us to fix the total losses among the assailants at about thirty," concludes historian Eugène Martres.[60] This sad epilogue demonstrated that forces composed of volunteers, however valorous they might be, could not stand up to experienced troops in pitched battle.

The tragic fate of the Vercors provides confirmation of this fact. In 1942–1943, several camps had organized on the mountainous plateau, led by the former Socialist deputy Léon Martin and the Franc-Tireur movement. They provided shelter for the young people fleeing the requisition of labor imposed by the law of September 1942. In December 1942, an architect, Pierre Dalloz, drafted a "note on the military possibilities of the Vercors." He declared that, if there were a landing in the Mediterranean, the site could be turned into an offensive base "in case of a critical situation from the enemy."[61] The scheme, baptized the Plan Montagnards (Mountaineers Plan), was transmitted to Jean Moulin and was supported and financed by London. A committee headed by Captain Alain Le Ray (in the capacity of military leader) and Eugène Chavant (civilian leader) worked to organize the plateau in the first half of 1944 and to turn the evaders into fighters.[62] But did the Plan Montagnards still make sense under the circumstances? To clarify the situation, Eugène Chavant went to Algiers, where Jacques Soustelle, head of the special services, reassured him. "For the first time," recalls Colonel Marcel Descour, chief of staff of the Rhône-Alpes region (R1), "I received a written order from the head of the BCRA [*sic*], in direct contact with General de Gaulle."[63] On the night of June 8, Descour ordered that all means of access to the massif be sealed off and that the men be mobilized as planned.[64] Volunteers rushed in and overall troop strength quickly reached four thousand men.[65] Historian Gilles Vergnon concludes: "The shot in the arm of June 6 was the basis for the mobilization of the Vercors on the 9th, and Descour's decision, which had such far-reaching consequences, was so easily understood by the other leaders only because it seemed to go without saying and to respond to an openly expressed request. It was truly an uprising, or rather, it was the dynamic of an unfinished, uncontrolled uprising of unexpected scope, which shook up all existing structures."[66]

General Koenig, observing that throughout France his orders had sometimes exposed the resistance forces to danger, ordered the guerrilla war curtailed on June 10. His message concluded: "Impossible now to resupply you with arms and munitions in sufficient quantities. Stop. Break contact everywhere as much as possible to allow reorganization phase stop. Avoid large assemblies. Form small isolated groups."[67] The order sowed confusion. Many believed it was a fake. Some, such as Charles Tillon, judged it inappropriate. The head of the FTP believed that the order did not apply to his organization, which was obliged neither to "reorganize itself nor to stop guerrilla warfare."[68] Others had anticipated it. In any case, Colonel Descour refused to modify his plan of action. Wrongly banking on the reinforcements promised by Algiers, he pursued a dangerous strategy, turning a base intended for guerrilla warfare into an entrenched camp. Emerging from the underground to fight in broad daylight, he also launched a challenge to the occupiers, which they could not fail to accept. "The matter at hand was to oblige the groups of partisans operating on the plain to withdraw to the Vercors and there constitute the greatest concentration of armed men ever realized in occupied France," Henri Romans-Petit, head of the maquis of Ain, points out. "That aspiration, which ran up against the opposition of elements outside the Vercors, was based on a political philosophy. The soldiers of the Vercors naively believed they could force the Allies to incorporate the Vercors plan of action into their own by becoming a numerically significant force."[69]

Algiers dispatched some assistance. Several missions (Eucalyptus, Justine) were sent in to aid and train the maquisards, and even—the objective of the Paquebot mission—to create a landing strip on the plateau. On June 25, and again on July 14, the resistance fighters received parachute drops of weapons.[70] But the Germans had no intention of tolerating that trouble spot. After launching a first attack between June 13 and 15, they went on the offensive on July 21, fielding ten thousand men—not including airborne troops.[71] Within three days, the maquis was demolished and suffered heavy losses: 326 resistance fighters and 130 civilians were massacred by the German troops;[72] 35 of the wounded were savagely killed while being treated in the cave of La Luire; civilians and maquisards from Vassieux and La Chapelle-en-Vercors were also subjected to abuse before being brutally exterminated.

Once the assault on the plateau began, the men of the Vercors repeatedly called for help. Eugène Chavant telegraphed on the night of

July 21: "La Chapelle, Vassieux, Saint-Martin, being bombed by the enemy. Enemy troops parachuting into Vassieux. Request immediate bombing. Had promised to hold three weeks; time elapsed since the installation of our group: six weeks. Request resupply of men, provisions, materiel. Morale of the population excellent. But will quickly turn against you if you do not take immediate measures, and we will agree with them in saying that those in London and Algiers have understood nothing of the situation we find ourselves in and are considered to be criminals and cowards. We repeat: criminals and cowards." But his efforts were in vain.[73]

No single cause can explain the tragedy of the Vercors. Certainly, the military leaders, because of their preference for combat in formation over guerrilla warfare, no doubt made an unfortunate choice. But "the voluntary dispersal of the maquis by its leaders, when its forces numbered several thousand men with varying degrees of training and cohesiveness, would have been a high-risk operation with unpredictable results."[74] It is likely that the leaders honestly believed that the Allies would support them. But the Vercors was not part of the grand strategy of the SHAEF or among the objectives of the provisional government of the French Republic in Algiers. That explains why the Gaullist authority took little action to assist the maquis. Fernand Grenier, commissioner of aviation, deeply regretted that fact. The Communist minister, who denounced "the watch-and-wait attitude, a crime against the nation," at a press conference on July 26, repeated his criticism in a letter to General de Gaulle the next day. At the next meeting of the Council of Ministers, the head of the provisional government read the letter aloud and took its author "violently to task":

"You will disavow the letter you wrote. Otherwise, you will leave here, a commissioner no longer."

There are moments in life when one speaks for thousands of comrades. An internal force dictates the words you need. This is one of those minutes. Very pale, I tell the story of how the first FTP originated, of their heroism, their military valor, the fight waged in London to get them weapons, how I had suffered since January 1943 at seeing them constantly underestimated, abandoned in fact, by Fighting France. . . . When I wanted to aid the FFI here, I ran into a wall; and when I learned of the destruction of the Vercors, I was outraged.

Then de Gaulle, overcome with rage:
"You know how to exploit cadavers!"[75]

The head of the provisional government demanded a retraction, and he obtained one. "National interest alone—to maintain the unity of the combatants—guided us in that emotional hour," Grenier concluded.[76] The affair was not over, however. Many veterans of the Vercors judged, and believed for a long time, that they had been betrayed: even though the Gaullist authority had mobilized them within the framework of the Plan Montagnards, it had, according to them, abandoned them at the time of the assault.

The maquis had shone with remarkable brightness at the dawn of liberation, inasmuch as they seemed to announce a levée en masse that, by its spirit, could bring down the occupier. Clearly, the results did not live up to that promise. The three emblematic maquis devised by the Gaullist services played only a limited military role, which also holds for the more modest groups that proliferated before and after D-Day.

Such was the case for the DF. Previously, the movement had pursued a civilian strategy, but on Easter 1944 it decided to switch over to armed struggle and to create a maquis in northern Seine-et-Oise. In August 1944, Philippe Viannay recalled:

My aim in taking that command was twofold.
—I first thought it was desirable for one of the MLN leaders to participate actively in the militants' fight. It is good for soldiers to have close by them those who command them.
—Then I thought that such an experience would allow me to report with great accuracy the difficulties encountered by the FFI command.[77]

The decision did not by any means meet with unanimous approval. Within the steering committee, two leaders, Robert Salmon and Jean-Daniel Jurgensen, judged the approach puerile. Noting that Viannay had no military experience, they feared above all that, in leaving Paris with his troops, the head of the DF would compromise the open publication of the newspaper, which depended on taking the Parisian printing works by military force. Viannay persisted. In February 1944, he was named departmental chief of the FFI for northern Seine-et-Oise. Having the wherewithal to arm about a hundred men, he organized his subregion by bringing in proven militants and by relying on the groups that preexisted his arrival—Élie Quideau and Kléber Dauchel's FFI, and the gendarmes from the brigades of Marines, L'Isle-Adam, Conflans-Sainte-Honorine, and Neuilly-en-Thelle, that is, a force of about three hundred men.[78] On June 19, however, a group hiding in the woods of Ronquerolles (Seine-et-Oise) was attacked. The Germans arrested nineteen maquisards, executed eleven, and deported two.[79] That tragedy led Viannay to modify his strategy. Rather than concentrate his troops in one place, he scattered them. That way, they would be able to wage the guerrilla war that the command was counting on. Between June 9 and August 20, 1944, his forces perpetrated, in all, seven attacks on railroads, eleven roadblocks, five sabotage operations to sever communication cables, fifteen attacks against occupation troops, and a few demolitions—blowing up a footbridge in Conflans-Sainte-Honorine, for example.[80] At the military level, therefore, the results were modest, especially when compared to the losses suffered.

This example, among so many others, invites us to wonder about the appropriateness of the strategy applied in June 1944. Even though the implementation of the plans was a success overall, the burgeoning of the maquis yielded limited results, punctuated by bitter tragedies.

In the first place, the maquis suffered from a lack of coordination with the Allies' grand strategy. The French had not been involved in preparations for the landing and, until June 6, remained in total ignorance in that regard. The Gaullist authorities thus found it impossible to address clear instructions to their troops, with the exception of the plans that had been prepared in advance. As a rule, moreover, the local commands were inexperienced. They rarely had military training, and the conditions of life in the underground did not allow them to train their men for battle, even supposing they had sufficient armaments and munitions. It would therefore appear easy to heap irony on these occasional soldiers and their comic opera officers—but that would be to forget that the bulk of the French people now wanted to fight. Sickened by the occupation, believing that victory was within sight, they became involved at the risk of their lives. Throughout the territory, in other words, the regional commands had to keep the lid on that feverish impatience, which was hard to reconcile with the caution and coolheadedness that war demands. That explains in part the heavy toll exacted from the maquis.

## Taking Power

In the wake of a landing that heralded victory, many French people believed it possible to strike against the representatives of Vichy. On June 6, 1944, maquisards seized Saint-Arman-Montrond, a subprefecture of Cher. The next day, the FTP occupied Tulle, bringing it to heel on the 8th. But on the 9th, elements from the SS Panzer Division Das Reich retook the seat of the Corrèze department. "Enraged at the sight of forty-four corpses of German soldiers from the eighth and eleventh companies of the ninety-fifth regiment lined up in the hospital," they hanged 99 residents from street lamps and deported 149.[81] The city of Guéret, however, escaped that tragic fate. On June 7, the FFI seized the prefecture of Creuse, but the occupiers counterattacked, mobilizing four companies and receiving air support.[82] Nevertheless, they refrained from engaging in reprisals. Military honors were paid to the soldiers, and the wounded, treated decently, were taken to the hospital.[83]

The premature liberation of cities large and small was not the sole prerogative of the Communists; other groups yielded to the same temptation. But the PCF was certainly on the leading edge of that movement. Although not planning to storm the Winter Palace, it intended to create power relations favorable to itself, so as to leave the range of possibilities wide open. On June 6, for example, the leadership of the southern zone FTP ordered the immediate liberation of Savoy, the Alps, the Massif Central, and Limousin, and the seizure of Guéret, Tulle, and Limoges. That order was rejected by Georges Guingouin.[84] The "Limousin Tito" waited until August 12 to seal off the prefecture of Haute-Vienne and entered it only on the 21st, to keep the highly anticipated liberation from ending in a bloodbath. Many leaders, Communist or not, proved equally cautious, both militarily and politically. In Ain, Romans-Petit refrained from engaging his troops in frontal attacks and opted for a mobile guerrilla war that harassed the enemy along the highways or railroad lines.[85] Likewise, the liberator of Oyonnax dissuaded those who wanted to occupy Bourg-en-Bresse from executing their plan. He concluded after the fact: "Granted, we could besiege the city, penetrate it, take many prisoners. But we would have heavy losses and would probably be unable to hold the city, since what can a few heavy weapons do against tanks? It would probably have been recaptured and would have experienced terrible reprisal measures. That operation, very spectacular to be sure, was fraught with too many perils to be attempted. I demonstrated its impossibility to the advocates—some of them unexpected—of that grandstanding, which was not at all key militarily."[86]

The resistance was therefore fully effective when it was run by determined but cautious leaders and when it coordinated its actions with the Allied strategy. But that combination proved difficult to achieve. For though the strategic decisions were made at the top, tactics unfolded at the regional, if not the local level. As a result, the FFI's senior command played only a minor role, especially given the violent conflicts between the COMAC and the FFI general staff.

## Conflicts

The question of who ought to assume operational command of the army of shadows had continually poisoned relations between the Gaullist authority and a fringe of the internal resistance, which demanded that they themselves conduct the operations. That quarrel, sometimes concealed, sometimes open, festered in summer 1944 and pitted the COMAC—headed by the Communist Pierre Villon—against the authorities of the provisional government in Algiers, particularly the civil and military delegations and the FFI general staff.

During a secret session on May 1, 1944, the COMIDAC (soon to be renamed "COMAC") had articulated the problem clearly. Colonel Ely, the representative of Generals Koenig and de Gaulle, recalled that "the FFI command must report to London and Algiers, military questions must be given first priority, and a state of mind must be created that unites the French people in arms against the invader."[87] The members of the COMIDAC retorted that "the FFI must execute the plans prescribed and the missions entrusted by the Allies, but for the resistance, the essential thing is still the possibility of undertaking and realizing operations conceived on its own, designed to liberate all national territory possible by its own actions. To do so, the FFI must be commanded from here, from Paris, and not from London."[88] Three disagreements fueled the conflict, therefore: the COMAC and the Gaullists were fighting for control of underground action; the COMAC advocated "immediate action," whereas the provisional government recommended action in correlation with the Allies; and the COMAC wanted the masses to intervene in the liberation process. "We respected the framework defined by the Allies, but without refraining from intervention by our military forces and generalized popular actions, strikes, for example," recalled Maurice Kriegel (Valrimont).[89] As a result, the scenario worried both the Allies and the Gaullist authority, haunted by the question of reprisals and the eventuality of a Communist putsch.

In June and July, the COMAC strove to impose its views. It therefore rejected the order given by General Koenig on June 10, 1944. On the contrary, it prescribed, on June 14:

> The FFI must prepare themselves at every level for that collaboration with the masses, in view of national insurrection: the increase of *guerrilla action* against the enemy is one of the elements preparing the way for national insurrection; it galvanizes the will for popular struggle. . . . Everywhere that power relations allow, the aim of insurrection must be to rid the country of the invader, to strip the representatives of Vichy of their powers, and to replace them with provisional authorities established and controlled by the liberation committees and, where they exist, by the authorities designated by the provisional government of the French Republic, in order to mobilize all the forces of the liberated region to drive out the enemy from the rest of the territory.[90]

These debates sprang up continually throughout the summer. At the meetings held in June, July, and August, the COMAC made another attempt, but Jacques Chaban-Delmas, the DMN, dodged the issue with consummate skill. The young inspector of finances, born in 1915, had joined the Hector network in late December 1940. In October 1943, he became unofficial assistant to André Boulloche, DMR for the Paris region (P). In spring 1944, the BCRA refused to confirm the nomination of Bourgès-Manoury to serve as DMN, on the grounds of his youth. Mischievously, Bourgès then proposed Chaban-Delmas for the post: a year younger, Chaban-Delmas was unknown in London. In early May, he was officially named interim DMN by the BCRA.[91] The choice proved to be judicious: while rejecting the COMAC's demands, the new DMN avoided breaking off talks with his interlocutors. On

August 7, the COMAC was still exploring avenues to reach an accord with General Koenig. It stated:

1. The supreme command of the FFI on metropolitan territory is exercised by the COMAC, under powers delegated by General Koenig.
2. The execution of General Koenig's orders for implementing the Allies' strategic plans will be given priority by the FFI . . . [92]

But at a time when American tanks were barreling through Paris, these negotiations seemed quite pointless.

The COMAC ultimately received "the supreme command of the FFI over metropolitan territory . . . under the powers delegated by General Koenig" on August 14, 1944,[93] but that compromise was without consequence. First, the COMAC did not have a direct liaison with the Allied general staff, which limited the synergy possible between the advance of the Anglo-American troops and the actions of the internal resistance. Second, the command was in fact decentralized, a tendency accentuated by the powers of the DMRs, dispensers of weapons, money, and liaisons. The Communists, finally, possessed very little leverage. Jean-Louis Crémieux-Brilhac sums it up: "The reality is that they do not have the means to launch, and even less to lead, an insurrection at the national level: lacking means of transmission, which are in the hands of the general delegation and of the regional military delegates, confined within the artificial atmosphere of Paris, having become suspect in the eyes of the Socialists and of the northern zone movements, they have no reliable forces other than those of the Party and of the Francs-Tireurs et Partisans, and their capacity for popular mobilization is limited to the Paris region."[94] In that power dispute, the Gaullists therefore stalled for time, and rather deftly. In fact, time was on their side.

## Breakthroughs

The Normandy landings had gone well on the whole, but the Allies were confined to a narrow beachhead for nearly two months, unable to break through the German defenses. General Bradley finally succeeded in escaping that strategic impasse. Although the offensive should have occurred in the British sector, around Caen, he suggested, in view of

General Montgomery's repeated failures, that the offensive take place to the west, in Cotentin. On July 25, Bradley, backed by Eisenhower, launched Operation Cobra. After a few days of hard fighting, the Americans opened a breach in the enemy defenses on the Saint-Lô-Périers-Lessay line, and broke through to Avranches. In view of their rapid advance, the U.S. command decided to split its troops in two. One part turned around and charged toward Brittany, liberating Rennes (August 4), Nantes (August 11), and Quimperlé (August 13); the other, after trapping part of the enemy forces in the Falaise pocket, rushed due east and prepared to liberate Paris. The British, for their part, headed north and, between September 1 and 5, drove the Germans out of nearly the entire Nord-Pas-de-Calais region. On August 15, a Franco-American expeditionary corps landed in Provence (Operation Dragoon), liberated Marseilles, and began a rapid ascent of the Rhône corridor. With the assistance of the FFI, it thereby managed to seize the capital of the Gauls on September 3.

The shift from a war of position to a war of movement, even pursuit, conferred on resistance action its full significance: the army of shadows could now achieve its potential by linking its operations with the progress of the Allied forces. That move was verified in Brittany that summer. The pitched battle of Saint-Marcel had ended in partial failure, but as soon as the order for general insurrection was given, at 6 P.M. on August 3, some thirty thousand Breton resisters[95] actively joined the fighting. It is true that, decently armed, they benefited from the support of the Jedburgh teams and other operational groups, and from the aid of 150 paratroopers, led by Colonel Eon and assisted by Colonel Passy. These forces were able, in the first place, to liberate certain localities (Loudéac, Saint-Brieuc, Lannion),[96] to mop up in cities after the advance guard had passed through, and to provide intelligence to the Allies. They then took over guarding engineering works—the viaducts of Morlaix and of Plougastel, for example—releasing U.S. forces from that task and thereby allowing them to concentrate on military operations in the strict sense.

This modus operandi was more or less reproduced throughout the territory, especially when, on August 16, Adolf Hitler gave the order for general withdrawal. The Wehrmacht's retreat increased tenfold the ardor of the resistance. In early August, Colonel Zeller, leader of the

FFI for the southeast, recommended that the Allied generals lead a forced march into the Rhône River Valley, in order to seize the poorly defended Alpine massif as quickly as possible.[97] His recommendation was partly taken to heart. As a modest motor brigade dashed across the Alps, the maquisards took action. They forced the Annecy garrison to surrender and captured 3,500 prisoners in Haute-Savoie.[98] Grenoble, which was supposed to fall on November 15, celebrated its liberation on August 22. Likewise, the resistance fighters in the Massif Central hampered the enemy's movements and forced the Germans, caught in a trap, to capitulate in Brive and Limoges. In the southeast, finally, the FFI, led by Serge Ravanel, went on the attack on August 16 and secured the surrender of the enemy troops. By the end of the day on August 24, when most of the Midi-Pyrénées region (R4) was liberated, the army of shadows had captured thirteen thousand prisoners. Finally, several thousand German soldiers quartered on the Atlantic coast retreated to the northeast, hoping to reach Dijon. The bulk of the troops managed to get through the Loire, but some twenty thousand, commanded by General Elster, lagged behind. The Elster column, harassed by the resistance, capitulated on September 10 in the city of Issoudun. Nevertheless, they preferred to surrender to the officers of the regular U.S. Army rather than to the FFI.[99]

The resistance thus participated fully in the battles of summer 1944 and without question hastened the liberation of the country. But as always, one must not go overboard. Granted, as Eberhard Jäckel points out, "the withdrawal of the Germans occurred under the most unfavorable conditions. They were harassed not only by the dangers inherent in any enterprise of that kind but also by a series of other problems, among which politics occupied a substantial place. The task at hand was not only to evacuate a vast enemy territory, one moreover, that was infested with rebel gangs, but also to liquidate, at least temporarily, Germany's French policy."[100] In spite of everything, the retreat was carried out in an orderly fashion. General von Blaskowitz's Army Group G, upon arriving in Dijon from the southeast, saved 130,000 out of 209,000 men.[101] In addition, at least 300,000 men coming from the west managed to cross the Seine in August 1944.[102] For the Reich, the second Battle of France was therefore neither a Verdun nor a Berezina. Indeed, though the Wehrmacht lost the bulk of its materiel, it managed to repatriate most of its forces, which explains how, later on, it was able to resist the Allied forces for more than a year, fighting on two fronts. Furthermore, France was by no means about to go up in flames: national insurrection remained a limited phenomenon in both spatial and numerical terms.

## Insurrection

Although all the resistance forces advocated national insurrection, their notions differed about how it should come about. Whereas the Gaullists and the main movements observed a cautious restraint, starting in June the Communists repeatedly called for uprisings. In addition to the desire to accelerate the occupier's departure and to keep the population from standing passively by during liberation, there was a political objective: "To influence local and national political reality."[103] Insurrection, they hoped, would turn power relations on their head and allow the Communists to impose CDLs, "chosen by the masses" at the local level, at the expense of the members designated by the provisional government—as was the case for the CDL of Agen.[104] But that plan fell far short of being realized. Of 212 cities surveyed by Philippe Buton, 179 (that is, 84 percent) owed their liberation either to the Allies or to the German retreat; resistance fighters therefore played only a modest role.[105] The insurgent cities—Paris, Lille, Marseilles, Limoges, and Thiers—were only exceptions. The City of Light, however, shone particularly bright in that respect.

After the breakthrough into Avranches, the Allies made rapid progress eastward. Having taken Mantes on August 19, they were able to cross the Seine the next day. The Americans, however, were hardly eager to capture the capital. Eisenhower, their commander in chief, reported: "We wanted to avoid making Paris a battleground and consequently planned operations to cut off and surround the vicinity, thus forcing the surrender of the defending garrison." But from inside the city, the resistance fighters forced his hand.[106]

On July 14, the Communist groups had begun to launch calls for demonstrations. It appears they were heeded on a massive scale. The insurrectional movement in the strict sense got under way in early August. In response to an appeal by the CGT, the railroad workers launched a strike order on August 10, which was taken up immediately by postal workers and then, on the 15th, by Paris police officers. On August 18, Henri Rol-Tanguy, head of the FFI for the Paris region, wrote up a mobilization order, which was posted during the night. The next day, the principle of an insurrection received the approval of the delegate general, Alexandre Parodi. Insurrection erupted immediately.

The resistance was at something of a numerical disadvantage, though figures vary depending on the source. On July 3, 1944, the COMAC counted 1,750 armed men for the Paris region (P), plus 60,000 more who could be mobilized.[107] In August, the delegation had a nucleus of 30,000 to 35,000 armed men.[108] After the war, the military authorities acknowledged 28,757 FFI for the Seine department. The most plausible estimate lies within the 20,000–25,000 range. It should be added, however, that not all of these men were armed—far from it. Rol-Tanguy estimated the number of weapons available at six hundred.[109] Conversely, the insurgents could count on the neutrality, even the support, of the forces of law and order—police, gendarmerie, republican guard—which possessed about 20,000 weapons.[110]

The Germans, for their part, fielded about 20,000 soldiers and some 50 tanks.[111] But did they intend to fight to the last cartridge shell? General Dietrich von Choltitz, the new commander of Paris, upon assuming his post on August 9, 1944, realized the futility of defending the capital. In fact, "the Allies had already established bridgeheads on the north bank of the Seine—on both sides of the city—and as a result, had already made the Germans' defense of the river extremely difficult. . . . The German units across the entire front were too inferior in number, too deficient in staff and materiel."[112] The German command therefore preferred to evade the orders given by Hitler, who demanded that Paris be "held at all cost" or "reduced to a pile of rubble."[113] In launching these orders, the dictator primarily hoped to facilitate the withdrawal of his troops and to gain some time, in order to establish defensive positions in the rear. Choltitz began a complicated game with the Führer's headquarters and the general staff of Army Group B, seeking to respect the letter of the orders but only to better emancipate himself from them.

At the same time, tensions were mounting in the capital. On August 19, a small committee composed, notably, of Léo Hamon (CPL),

Roland Pré (General Delegation), and Henri Ribière (CNR), set out to negotiate a truce through the Swedish consul, Raoul Nordling. That initiative was keenly contested by the advocates of insurrection. As Henri Rol-Tanguy and Roger Bourderon put it, the effort "came just in time for those who still feared, as they had always feared, that the insurrection would be unable to hold off the enemy forces, that the Allied armies would not arrive in time, that Paris would be reduced to ashes, and that the social order would be disrupted."[114] Rol-Tanguy therefore ordered the fighting to continue, though he was alarmed at the situation reigning in the city: "Paralyzing the enemy, forcing him back into a few footholds where he would be held up, were objectives the FFI could achieve, but reducing the number of these footholds was not feasible, for lack of semi-heavy and heavy armaments."[115] In short, all parties agreed that the assistance of the Allies was required.

On August 20, Rol-Tanguy dispatched Major Gallois, his chief of staff, to ask for aid from the regular troops. In a letter written on the 21st and transmitted the next day by Juin and Koenig, de Gaulle begged Eisenhower to make haste. Ike complied. On August 23, General Leclerc's 2nd Armored Division moved in; its first troops took their position on the square in front of the Hôtel de Ville the next day. On August 25, the city finally fell. General Leclerc and Colonel Rol-Tanguy accepted the surrender of Choltitz at the Gare Montparnasse. Meanwhile, de Gaulle was preparing his return in minute detail. After stopping by the Gare Montparnasse, he returned to the Ministry of War, which he had left with Paul Reynaud on June 10, 1940. Having saluted the officers at the police prefecture, he ultimately arrived—after these long detours—at the Hôtel de Ville, to meet with the members of the resistance. In a memorable speech, he exulted: "Paris! Paris outraged! Paris broken! Paris martyred! But Paris liberated!"[116] But he declined the invitation issued by Georges Bidault, chair of the CNR, to proclaim the republic. "The Republic has never ceased to be. Free France, Fighting France, the Comité Français de la Libération Nationale have incorporated it one after another. Vichy always was null and void and remains so. I myself am the president of the government of the Republic. Why should I proclaim it?"[117] The apotheosis came the next day, as de Gaulle walked down the Champs-Élysées, hailed by hundreds of thousands of French people, happy to celebrate the liberation and their liberators. "Moved and calm," he later recalled, "I therefore go into the inexpressibly exultant crowd, amid the tempest of voices roaring my name, trying, along the way, to cast my eyes over every wave of that tide—so that the sight of everyone might enter my eyes—raising and lowering my arms in response to the cheers. At that moment, one of those miracles of national consciousness happens, one of those gestures of France, which sometimes, in the course of the centuries, comes to illuminate our history. In that community, which is but a single thought, a single impulse, a single shout, differences vanish, individuals disappear."[118]

The insurrection of Paris—unlike that of Warsaw, which occurred at the same time—ended in a brilliant success. The City of Light recovered its freedom intact, whereas the Polish capital was reduced to ashes by the Germans. The liberation of Paris was certainly a shared victory. It marked the triumph of the internal resistance, which had succeeded in mobilizing the population and had spurred it to fight. The Communists, with Henri Rol-Tanguy leading the assault, also played a dynamic role, but without achieving their end: that of welcoming Charles de Gaulle to a city that had liberated itself.

In the first place, Maurice Thorez's faithful had failed to seize command of the resistance. The CNR's military commission (the COMAC), infiltrated by Communist elements, may have had its authority formally acknowledged on August 14 by the Gaullist officials Alexandre Parodi and Jacques Chaban-Delmas, but that acknowledgment remained merely formal, given that, on August 21, General Koenig became military governor of Paris. Locally, the PCF had, in theory, powerful assets, since the FFI were under the authority of Henri Rol-Tanguy at the regional level, and the CPL was chaired by André Tollet—two figures whose loyalty to the PCF was beyond doubt. But the party did not manage to incorporate the Parisian volunteers into its organizations.

Yet to harness the moral and political benefits of insurrection, the PCF would have had to channel the masses into a group of organizations that it controlled, albeit secretly—Milices Patriotiques, FTPF, Forces Unies de la Jeunesse Patriotique (United Forces of Patriotic Youth). Here again, the reality did not meet expectations. Of some twenty thousand Paris combatants, the Red forces controlled at most four thousand men—a modest fifth of the fighting force.[119] Aware of that shortfall, Rol-Tanguy urged volunteers to enlist. The order of August 18, 1944, prescribed: "All able-bodied Frenchmen and French-women must consider themselves mobilized. They must immediately join the FFI groups or the patriotic militias in their neighborhood or factory."[120] He repeated the order on the 24th: "The commanders of departments must immediately organize the enlistment centers to gather together all volunteers determined to participate in the fight against the Boche."[121] But these directives—which were rarely followed, moreover—arrived too late to reverse the trend. Very early on, the Gaullist leaders took the measure of that powerlessness. On August 11, Jacques Chaban-Delmas, the DMN, explained to London that he "did not believe in any FTP danger. They know they do not constitute all the forces of the FFI or of the Resistance."[122]

But the Gaullist authority had just as much trouble controlling the course of events. The BBC, far from setting things in motion, on August 18 walled itself up, deciding to watch and wait. It avoided giving the Parisians instructions for action. Two factors account for that rift between the tumult in Paris and the silence of the British airwaves. First, the faulty communications between London and Paris prevented the leaders from forming a clear idea of the situation. The telegrams sent by Chaban-Delmas, for example, were decoded with a delay of three, four, even six days.[123] Second and above all, the strike movement seems to have bewildered General de Gaulle. He feared that official support for it would paralyze production vital for the capital (in the energy sector especially). Above all, he was afraid that, if repressive measures were taken, he would be held responsible. People were still haunted by the precedent of 1871, so much so that, on August 23, 1944, de Gaulle exclaimed to Leclerc: "Go quickly. We cannot have another Commune."[124] In reality, the head of the provisional government could not imagine assuming the mantle of Adolphe Thiers by obliging the 2nd Armored Division to engage in a bloody repression of an insurrectional movement. And he could not cut himself off from a process that was obviously popular and widespread. The silence of the radio waves reflected that awkward situation, of which Londoners were perfectly aware. "The absence of instructions for Paris constitutes a grave oversight, given that such instructions are the most urgent ones and the only ones that raise real difficulties," observed Georges Boris on August 11.[125] An anonymous report dated August 14, 1944 (no doubt coming from the Commission for the Interior), specified: "It is to be feared that, if the GPRF [Gouvernement Provisoire de la République Française (Provisional Government of the French Republic)] does not give any indications and instructions to Paris, the movement will be triggered without the authorization of the GPRF."[126] Two factors, however, allowed de Gaulle to keep the upper hand: the dispatching of the 2nd Armored Division and the announcement—deliberately premature— of the liberation of Paris, which the BBC broadcast on August 23, 1944.

Despite the blunders, the insurrection in the capital remains one of the finest pages in the history of that summer of 1944. It earns that place first because of the limited loss of life. According to the estimates, the 2nd Armored Division lost between 76 and 130 men. Within the ranks of the FFI, there were 900 to 1,000 dead. And the Paris population suffered 582 dead and 2,000 wounded.[127] The insurrection also made it possible to celebrate the joint action of the internal and external resistance, bringing together as brothers in battle Rol-Tanguy's FFI and Leclerc's soldiers. Despite the tragedies and suffering endured by civilians, it was also a joyous time for participants. The barricades marked "a return to the sacred past of popular insurrections, they represented a miracle, that of the people restored, the brotherly, egalitarian, heroic, fighting people."[128] Amid the joy of liberation, women and men also delighted in carnal union. As the writer Claude Roy notes: "In the shadows, the whiteness of a bare arm on a half-uncovered breast. A fleeing thigh, furtive as a fish in the dark. And Paris makes love on every lawn, with every nation. And when I say Paris, is it really Paris?"[129] The departure of the despised occupier was also often accompanied by large quantities of libations. By that measure, the insurrection of Paris was truly a liberation in the full sense of the term: of language, of the spirit, and of bodies. As a result, these shared memories coincide only imperfectly with the representations that Gaullists and Communists aspired to impose on them. The order reestablished by the leader of the GPRF—republican though that order was—and its interest in continuing the war were difficult to reconcile with the libertarian euphoria that seized hold of Parisians. And the hedonism of a people living it up corresponded no better to the image suggested by the PCF: that of an insurgent people fighting as brothers to break their chains, but maintaining a seriousness, a sense of self-sacrifice and selflessness.

The liberation of Paris did not end in carnage or a bloodbath. It also did not mark the end of the battles waged by the resistance fighters, in the eastern part of the country especially. But that struggle now belonged to a completely different context, since it was governed by the progress of the Allied troops. The resistance, waging guerrilla warfare, changed in nature. It also turned a new page in its history. By that measure, the Paris insurrection of late 1944 must truly be considered an apogee. The capital was at one with a country that avoided the torments of civil war.

## The Civil War Will Not Take Place

It is commonly accepted that France erupted into civil war in 1944. Upon liberation, it is said, the hour of the Revanche had sounded, with resistance fighters rushing to settle the scores of the war, the occupation, and Vichyism, unleashing the wrath of a purge as bloody as it was blind. This thesis is illustrated, for example, by Marcel Aymé's *Uranus*, published in 1948, and by Claude Berri's 1990 film based on that novel.

Between eight and nine thousand French people were executed without benefit of trial by groups that often claimed to belong to the resistance.[130] But 80 percent of these executions occurred either during the occupation or in the battles for liberation. They therefore were not acts of revenge shadowing a legal purge judged too lenient.[131] They were rather akin to acts of war, their aim being to eliminate figures believed to be dangerous. So it was that Philippe Henriot, whose harangues on Radio-Paris had attracted a large listening audience, was eliminated on June 28, 1944, by a commando of the MLN in his employer-provided apartment in Paris. In a quite different realm, fighters in the resistance—or presumed to be in the resistance—shaved the heads of about twenty thousand women accused of having engaged in "horizontal collaboration" with the occupier (though that charge applied to only half of them).[132] There is thus no denying that liberation France was characterized by great violence.

But that violence was not synonymous with civil war. In the first place, the Vichy regime did not call for the French to fight in summer

1944.[133] Far from urging them to become engaged, Philippe Pétain invited the population not "to commit acts that could lead to tragic reprisals."[134] He repeated that instruction to the men in the LFC, even though they were pillars of the regime: "We are not in the war. Your duty is to maintain strict neutrality. I do not want a fratricidal war. The French must not fight one another, their blood is too precious for the future of France, and hatred can only compromise the unity of our country, which is the gage of its resurrection."[135] In the same vein, the Marshal is known to have sent emissaries to General de Gaulle's representatives, hoping—very much in vain—to hand over his powers peacefully. That pitiful maneuver would have allowed him to legitimate his power a posteriori; the man of June 18 naturally declined.[136] These intrigues nevertheless confirm that in 1944 Pétain preferred an accord to an escalation into civil war. It is true, however, that a minority intended to fight—for example, the Milice and their leader, Joseph Darnand—and were ready to impose their views by blood and by the sword. But they were in the minority and therefore lacked the capacity to lead the masses.

Vichy public officials thus gave in, without making a gallant last stand. The French State disappeared "like the Cheshire cat," to borrow an American officer's expression.[137] Mayors and prefects handed the keys over to their successors, without ever contesting the right of the new elites to replace them. In Paris, Prefect Bussières stepped aside in favor of Charles Luizet. On August 3, a small commando in Rennes, led by Pierre Herbart, arrested the regional prefect, Robert Martin, as well as the prefect of Ille-et-Vilaine, Émile Bouché-Leclercq, without encountering the slightest resistance. The same day, Hubert de Solminihac, a member of the DF, demanded the resignation of the mayor of the city, Dr. René Patay, who complied, handing over his powers to his first assistant.[138] These scenes were more or less reproduced throughout France, and the transfer of power went smoothly—to the surprise of some of those involved. "The serious unrest that some feared, rather than being the rule, was the exception. Bloodshed was very rare," Claude Bouchinet-Serreulles pointed out in a report of September 6, 1944. "With the exception of the Limoges region, where the process was slower, the commissioners of the Republic quickly imposed their authority; everywhere they applied themselves to ensuring the preeminence of civil power over military command."[139] That does not mean that the liberation occurred without a hitch, but it confirms that clashes, conflicts, and tensions remained limited in scope. The legitimacy of the resistance was thus not disputed, a sign that, after four long years of struggle, the French accepted its power. It is true that the resistance fighters had won that recognition at a high cost, especially since, in relation to the population, they represented only a minority.

## Chapter 15

# Social Components

DID FRANCE AS a whole become engaged in the resistance? After the war, the Gaullists and the Communists said so, declaring that the bulk of the French people had contributed to the underground fight. Such a claim is optimistic to a fault. From start to finish, the organized resistance was a minority phenomenon, though thousands of French people occasionally lent a hand. But the groups that composed French society during the dark years took on the underground struggle in disparate ways. Their ideological choices, their interests, and their repertoires of action put them in different situations from which to address the demands of the fight; moreover, the social determinants of engagement were distinct from the cultural factors.

## A Question of Class

To understand the resistance in terms of social class, it is necessary to realize, first, that the repertoires of action of each class, which have differed from one another historically, favored engagement to a greater or lesser degree; and, second, that the essentially different interests of each class could only result in heterogeneous forms of mobilization.

The numbers suggest that the various social milieus were unevenly represented in the struggle. Generally speaking, members of the working and middle classes were somewhat overrepresented when compared to the peasantry. For example, in Manche, though not an industrialized department, the proletariat, which before the war made up only 8.5 percent of the working population, composed 16 percent of underground forces.[1] The same was true for Ille-et-Vilaine (where the relevant figures were, respectively, 9.5 percent and 13.5 percent)[2] and for Calvados (13.5 percent versus 18 percent).[3]

First and foremost, that proportionally greater engagement was an expression of opposition to the policies conducted by the Vichy regime and the German occupier. The French State mistrusted the working class, an incarnation of an urban and industrial civilization it despised. It also believed that that group had been morally corrupted by the class struggle and condemned its predilection for launching strikes, whose harmfulness had been revealed under the FP government. Second, the Germans grossly exploited French industry, which resulted in a deterioration of working conditions. Third, the STO, which targeted industrial wage laborers above all, was considered by them to be an unjust servitude, and not without reason: according to the various estimates, such laborers constituted between 54 and 63.5 percent of those who were called up by the STO, whereas they represented only 31 percent of the working population.[4]

The overrepresentation of the working class, moreover, reflected the weight of the Communists in the resistance fight. The PCF and its satellite organizations mobilized their militant networks to wage their battle. These channels, as it happened, were primarily proletarian, since the party had for the most part recruited from such ranks before the war. From that standpoint, the FP marked a "decisive success."[5] Working-class elements represented 30 percent of the party's cells in October 1938.[6] In the region surrounding Montbéliard, for example, Peugeot workers—under the leadership of the Communist Charles Joly—formed the first resistance groups.[7] The FTP in the Var department relied primarily on the proletariat, which constituted 43 percent of their rank and file and 36 percent of their cadres.[8] That disproportion was relative, however. In Ille-et-Vilaine, workers made up only 22 percent of Communist forces (OS-FN and FTP), even though 78 percent of working-class resistance fighters militated in groups belonging to that sphere.[9]

Finally, the proletariat had a broad set of actions to place in the service of the cause. It had mastered the tactic of demonstrations; and, since the late nineteenth century, strikes had been part of its daily horizon.[10] In addition, the proletariat found violence less objectionable than did "the middle or upper classes, which were more likely to embrace the values of social consensus."[11] In the prewar period, factory workers had become accustomed to a form of brutality, reinforced by a few tough fights (the railroad workers strike in 1920, for example) and by the violence of certain demonstrations, especially in the 1920s. "Ever since the general strike of October 12, 1925, against the war in Morocco—one Communist and one police officer were killed—the two camps had been keeping a count of their dead and wounded, which served to blow up a conflict that each camp hoped to burst to its own advantage when the occasion arose," observe Jean-Marc Berlière and Laurent Chabrun.[12] In the left-leaning outskirts of cities, an incessant guerrilla war had pitted police officers against Communist and CGT militants since the 1920s. "Anything at all was a pretext for confrontation there: the most insignificant demonstration, flowers laid before the monument to the dead, the distribution of tracts, a work stoppage in a factory, the voicing of opinions upon leaving the Renault factory on Île Séguin," add Berlière and Chabrun.[13] Furthermore, strategies intended to slow the pace of work had gradually developed as a form of protest against Taylorism; these could be converted into invisible sabotage operations.

In short, the obstacles to engagement in the resistance carried less weight within the working class than in other milieus, though the attitude of the workers ought not to be idealized. As already noted, strikes remained the exception rather than the rule. Even the tradition known as *la perruque*, whereby workers, on company time, diverted materials to transform them into objects far removed from their original purpose, rarely became a militant practice. In the railroad shops of Oullins, apart from a few "four-pointed nails manufactured to immobilize police or Wehrmacht vehicles, most [of the objects produced] were merely the expression of persistent and mundane concerns."[14] And finally, by no means did the shock produced by the STO prompt engagement in the resistance. At the Peugeot factories, "only German orders ensured employment. Working for Germany was accepted by the workers as a necessary constraint."[15] Jean-Marie Guillon notes in reference to workers in Var, "what they refused to do above all was to leave for Germany or for someplace else in France. The act of working for the Germans, even as directly as within the framework of the Todt Organization, was accepted inasmuch as [it] quickly appeared unavoidable as a means to escape what was long considered deportation." He concludes: "STO evaders did not necessarily avoid working for the occupier."[16]

The middle classes also responded to the call, a fact that belies the negative image sometimes attached to the "new strata" previously celebrated by Léon Gambetta. The resistance has frequently been portrayed as the prerogative of the common people or of their loyal interpreters. It is often thought that, because the resistance was anti-Fascist, anti-Vichy, anti-conformist, and revolutionary, it could only be the antithesis of the petty bourgeoisie.[17] Yet everything indicates that this group, though certainly difficult to define, put its stamp on the underground fight. In the Franc-Tireur movement, shopkeepers and small manufacturers represented 20.5 percent of its forces, middle managers 19.5 percent, and salaried employees 19 percent—with workers remaining a tiny minority (6 percent).[18] Likewise, indications are that Libération-nord consisted for the most part of teachers (50 percent), salaried employees and civil servants (14 percent), and artisans and merchants (9 percent), compared to a modest proportion of workers (16 percent).[19] In Ille-et-Vilaine, shopkeepers and artisans counted for slightly more than 13 percent of resistance forces, even though they represented only about 8 percent of the working population.[20] The so-called upper classes also put their mark on the resistance. "For anyone who knew the resistance or resistance fighters well, what was surprising was not the absence of ministers plenipotentiary or colonels or company directors but rather the large number of them," says Henri Noguères, a resistance fighter and later a historian.[21] Moreover, they took command of the underground groups. Most often, "the resistance hierarchy had a tendency to model itself on the social hierarchy, in keeping with the classic political or associative model of less troubled times."[22]

The overrepresentation can be explained, first, by the ideology motivating that element. The antirepublican and reactionary policy of the Vichy regime could not fail to alienate the fringe of the middle classes that stood behind the liberal, progressive, and patriotic values of the republic. Furthermore, if one concedes that the aspiration for social advancement formed the "hard-core" identity of that class,[23] then it must be noted that the French State shattered that ambition by relying on traditional notables and by heaping opprobrium on senior and junior members of the old order—teachers, for example. Although one portion of the middle classes supported Philippe Pétain, another part was resolutely opposed to him.

The middle classes could also provide useful assistance to the resistance. They were proficient in the written word, which, not surprisingly, fostered the development of the underground press. Those who belonged to the state apparatus were well acquainted with the inner workings of the administration, and their complicity made it easier to obtain false identity papers. Because they were well placed on the social ladder, they had access to intelligence, which they communicated to the Allies. Finally and perhaps above all, their initiative and their intellectual skills granted them a key role in the birth and subsequent growth of the resistance. Indeed, they possessed the ability to "set up organizations, formulate analyses, manage budgets, administer affairs, and lead men,"[24] and in that sense conformed to their historical function. On the leading edge of economic modernization and of the republican regime in the second half of the nineteenth century, they occupied the vanguard in the dark years, supplying it with troops and cadres,[25] especially since their talents and their place in French society brought them to the attention of the underground groups. The NAP, for example, encouraged the recruitment of civil servants, who were invited to play a double game: "Members were delighted to have 'napped' [infiltrated] an entire department in a prefecture and, when the time came, a number of civil servants at every level were happy to be able to say they had been 'napped' . . . though that is very doubtful," recalls Henri Noguères.[26] The PCF, anxious to broaden its base, strove through the FN to break free of its proletarian orientation, expanding to include bourgeois (but patriotic) elements. Its efforts were not without success: in Ille-et-Vilaine, workers represented only 19 percent of FN forces, whereas public employees and shop-keepers or artisans constituted a third of them.[27]

These factors explain why the middle classes "formed the backbone of the Resistance. They created it, shaped it at almost every stage, and led it, particularly at the lower echelons. In its very diversity, the Resistance, throughout most of its branches, was made in their image."[28] That observation is also true for the so-called upper strata. The bourgeoisie rose to the challenge, as many examples suggest. Jacques Bingen, Marc Bloch, Maxime Blocq-Mascart, Émile Bollaert, Professor Robert Debré, and his son Michel all came from its ranks. In view of these examples, writer François Mauriac acknowledged in December 1944: "Granted, I would no longer write that only the working class *as a bloc* has remained faithful to desecrated France. What an injustice to the host of boys from the bourgeoisie who sacrificed themselves and are still sacrificing themselves."[29] That does not mean, however, that everyone in the middle and upper classes joined the army of shadows. Some supported the Vichy regime. "For a long time, the principle of obedience to the legal government in France posed no problem in principle: there was no dearth of reasons for remaining at one's post, and the regime did not refrain from pointing that out," observes historian Marc Olivier Baruch. "A first round of arguments based on the initial choice made by Marshal Pétain—not to abandon populations in difficulty, not to allow anarchy to gain a foothold—was supplemented by later rationalizations built on the notion of the double game: to oppose German pressures from within, to do less harm by staying than by leaving."[30] It is known, moreover, that the middle and upper strata supplied "the bulk of the troops" for the collaborationist movements—71 percent of their members, according to historian Philippe Burrin.[31]

## The Peasantry

The peasantry was underrepresented in the underground struggle. In Aveyron, it contributed only 8 percent of resistance forces, whereas it constituted 57 percent of its working population. The proportions were similar in Ille-et-Vilaine (8 percent to 52.5 percent) and in Calvados (11.5 percent versus 42 percent).[32] Its participation was as low in the networks (2 percent for Manipule)[33] as in the movements (4 percent for Libération-nord,[34] 5 percent for the DF).[35]

It is true that farmers had little motivation to oppose the Vichy regime, which sang their praises and celebrated the virtues of the honest heartland. The German occupation was also less perceptible in the rural areas than in the cities, which limited the visceral reactions triggered by the daily and intolerable sight of the conqueror. Furthermore, farmers were only marginally targeted by the STO: although they represented more than a third of the forces called up (42.24 percent), they constituted 72.25 percent of exemptions.[36] Finally, over the centuries, the peasant world had chosen to express opposition through uprisings (*jacqueries*) or demonstrations, two activities that were of little use in the underground struggle.

The situation evolved over time, however. In the first place, the rural world assisted in hiding proscribed persons, whether Jews or STO evaders. Second, the rise of the maquis ruralized the army of shadows. Whereas "the Resistance never addressed the peasants in 1940 and 1941, it did so in 4 percent of tracts in 1942, 30 percent in 1943, and 22 percent in 1944," notes François Marcot, in reference to the region of Franche-Comté.[37] With the fight against the STO and the correlative development of the maquis, rallying the peasants became an essential issue for the resistance. Nevertheless, it assigned them a passive role, confining them de facto to a support function.

All in all, every element participated in the fight, which made the resistance an interclass phenomenon free of social determinism. At the same time, participation remained uneven. It reflected the diversity of expectations, traditions, skills, and even interests possessed by the various social classes, while also being an expression of the politico-ideological position assigned to them by the French State and the German occupier. Every group, moreover, tended to recruit from its own sphere, exploiting the political, personal, or professional channels of the pioneers, which gave each organization its own identity. In Var, "the Communist pole, with its roots in the working class and in the younger generation, stood opposed to a Gaullist MUR entity with a strong Socialist strain, led by men from the middle and upper classes."[38] The army of shadows, though it combined all classes when considered overall, was thus socially polarized in its organizations.

## Political Cultures

The traditions, modes of militancy, and representations that the political parties had forged over time also shaped engagement in the resistance.

The Communist political culture offered a few advantages for facing the ordeals of the dark years. Secrecy, far from being a cause for concern, was familiar to it. The twenty-one conditions set by the Comintern in 1919 had prescribed the creation of an undercover apparatus that could support a revolutionary culture with a predisposition for plots and secrecy. In addition, the PCF had been banned on September 26, 1939, which had obliged some cadres to work outside the law. Likewise, transgression, on which engagement in the resistance was predicated, was not a departure for the Communists, who felt nothing but contempt for the bourgeois order. And finally, the fiery patriotism expressed in the columns of *L'Humanité* may have corresponded to the feelings of a majority of members, who, though dreaming of an October Revolution, may have remained attached to their country. Nevertheless, the Communists required a few adjustments. It was a time of sacred union, and the class struggle was therefore toned down. In the Peugeot factories, for example, no tracts targeted management or called for raises.[39] And in the coalfields of Gard, protests denouncing the deterioration of working conditions were addressed to the state, which was held responsible for them, not to employers.[40] Of course, these examples should not lead us to idealize management, which sometimes concluded lucrative business deals under the occupation. But on the question of the STO, class interests converged: workers refused to go into exile, and employers were eager to hold on to their labor force to ensure the smooth operation of their businesses. That convergence created a de facto solidarity. In any event, Communist militantism offered its partisans resources that its Socialist rival lacked.

Indeed, the SFIO, while proclaiming itself Marxist, had over time accommodated itself to the republic and accepted its rules, even as it dreamed of changing them. Respectful of laws and of legality, it sought to take power more at the voting booth than on the streets, and it refused to use political violence. In cities and villages, its cadres had set about taking over mayoralties and assuming prominence, a process that accelerated during the interwar period. That undertaking prepared its members poorly for the resistance. "The political culture of the militant SFIO restricted it to the confines of the electoral and parliamentarian struggle," political scientist Marc Sadoun notes.[41] That was understandably the case for the moderate parties of the center left and traditional right, whose prewar culture hardly predisposed them to embrace the adventurous life promised by the army of shadows.

Nationalist militants, by contrast, were better equipped to face life underground. Accustomed to street fighting and often trained to handle weapons, they had sometimes professed a pronounced taste for forming plots, as La Cagoule had brazenly revealed in 1937. Often they persisted in their ways. For example, Colonel Groussard, responsible for the arrest of Pierre Laval on December 13, 1940, attempted to infiltrate the Vichy state, both to chase down the crusaders of anti-France and to induce the state to go over to the Allies. In short, whether they created covens, hatched more or less fantastical plots, or conducted parallel negotiations, these shadowy men thrived during the dark years, placing their conspiratorial talents in the service of the cause. Maurice Duclos, Gilbert Renault, and Pierre Bénouville, formerly of Action Française, had "acquired reflexes for radical protest, even for conspiracies outside the law,"[42] which facilitated their transition to dissidence.

Finally, foreigners were a massive presence in the resistance. It is true that anti-Fascism offered them sure guidelines for action. More than 120,000 Spaniards who had fled the Francoist regime during the civil war still lived in France in 1940. Many joined the army of shadows, especially in the southwest. The anarchist Francisco Ponzan Vidal took charge of a network that specialized in collecting intelligence (transmitted to the British) and in smuggling out underground fighters via the Pyrenees. A majority, marked by their commitment to Communism, joined the Unión Nacional Española (Spanish National Union), formed in November 1942 and dominated by the Reds. In May 1944, this organization formed the Agrupación de Guerilleros Españoles (Group of Spanish Guerrilla Fighters) to muster all combatants, many of whom joined the maquis at that time. These men, while hoping to recapture Spain after the war, also wanted to fight weapons in hand against the Nazi forces that had helped to defeat their republic in 1939.[43]

The Poles, following a different logic, sought to contribute to the defeat of the Reich, which, with the complicity of the Soviet Union, had once again dismembered their country. In 1940 Polish troops had fought alongside the Allies in Norway, then in eastern France. Some of their officers remained in France and founded a resistance network, F2, in the Midi. It worked on behalf of Great Britain, transmitting intelligence on the German military plan of action in particular. Likewise, Alexander Kawalkowski, former consul general of Poland in Lille, in 1940 created the Polska Organizacja Walki o Niepodleglosc (POWN; Polish Organization for the Independence Struggle), which recruited extensively from the Polish community, first in the south and later in the coal mines of Nord-Pas-de-Calais. "Worker solidarity and strong patriotism, inseparable from a fervent Catholic faith,"[44] account for the success of that movement, which on the eve of the landing counted some eight thousand members. The POWN, while transmitting intelligence and engaging in multiple sabotage operations, was counting on playing a role in the liberation of Poland when the time came, once its government exiled in London gave the order. That said, not all the Poles joined that group. Others opted for Communism and from 1944 on enlisted under the banner of the Polski Komitet Wyzwolenia Narodowego (Polish Committee for National Liberation), which treated the POWN like its enemy brother.[45] Foreigners also joined the ranks of the resistance in an individual capacity. For example, Boris Vildé was one of the chief leaders of the Musée de l'Homme network.

This brief overview suffices to confirm the preeminent role played by more or less recent immigrants in the army of shadows, whether they fought in the name of anti-Fascism, out of love for the France of the rights of man, or out of hatred for Nazi Germany.

## Catholics and Protestants

The Christian culture of the French people prepared them to varying degrees to take up arms against the occupier or the Vichy regime.

Catholics proved to be divided. A fringe took no interest in the temporal world, practicing "an inner religion of individual self-improvement and individual generosity, without any interest in public affairs or any control over how they unfolded." Others took the measure of their responsibilities vis-à-vis the commonwealth but felt "a distrust of politics tinged with contempt, resentment, or moralism."[46] That hesitancy hardly led them to get involved. Furthermore, the Catholic hierarchy, anxious to "seize an opportunity for the re-Christianization and moralization of society under a good, legal government, friend of the church," supported the Vichy regime, and that did little to prepare the church to brandish the standard of revolt or to understand what was at stake politically or morally in the war in general and in Nazism in particular.[47] No bishop condemned the STO law on principle, except to portray it as an ordeal. This silence stood in contrast to the position adopted by the Belgian clergy. On March 8, 1942, for example, Cardinal Van Roey, primate of Belgium, sent a letter to Falkenhausen, the military governor, in which he denounced the requirement that miners work on Sundays, as well as the order promulgated on March 6 announcing the "deportation" of Belgian workers.[48] The French high clergy did not take that path. Granted, doctrine commanded obedience to legal authorities, and not all the Catholics were "discerning enough to distinguish between established power and legitimate power."[49]

The *doxa*, or popular opinion, also embraced the possibility of disobeying when authority was insurrectional or illegitimate. The Catholics of Action Française had adopted that logic and refused to bow to the laws of the Third Republic, a regime they judged iniquitous. Some, such as Colonel Rémy, placed honor and pride before obedience, and moral legitimacy above a legality they held in contempt. Political power had little weight when compared to the higher interests of the nation, morality, and religion. As a result, "their Catholic convictions, though not the reason for their choice, were also not at odds with it. Very attached within their milieu to all the values transmitted by their upbringing, they granted strong legitimation to the ethics of honor, duty, and sacrifice and to the rejection of mediocrity and resignation."[50]

The Christian Democrats, obeying a different logic, had also cultivated the virtues of insubordination. In its early days, Action Catholique had fought hard against the Catholic hierarchy. These clashes had "shaped a mode of behavior; this was not the first time [that these men] did not take for gospel truth the sermons of their priest or the instructions of their bishop."[51] Rome had banned Le Sillon (The Furrow)[52] in 1910 and had suspended the progressive periodical *Sept* in November 1937. The Christian Democratic movement, fervently committed to social progress and anxious to reconcile the church with the republic, was thus accustomed to circumventing the authorities, whose pastoral letters they did not intend to follow blindly. Finally, Christian labor activists remained viscerally attached to democracy and to trade union freedom. Vichy, in attacking these two principles, quickly attracted their hostility, though not without rifts, since at the base militants turned out to be divided "between the positions of the Catholic hierarchy and opposition to a 'legality' that violated one of the principal social and republican achievements, the right to participate in labor unions."[53]

The Catholic culture of the interwar period also played a role, in that young people's upbringing predisposed them to perform chivalrous deeds. "The models provided by the edifying literature were a factor, as was sublimation, which helps one to respect the prescribed discipline, especially as regards sexual purity," notes historian Bernard Comte.[54] Likewise, during the interwar period, part of the clergy had disseminated a theology that exalted sacrifice. "He that findeth his life shall lose it: and he that loseth his life for my sake shall find it," declares the Gospel according to Saint Matthew (10:39, King James Version). The JEC relayed that message in its press. "Give us an understanding of our Christ's sacrifice, so that we may be ready for all sacrifices you will ask of us," proclaimed its press organ, *Messages*, in May 1939.[55] That sense of abnegation prepared young Catholics to give up their lives if need be. Finally, the marginality of the struggle, far from being a deterrent, reminded many resistance fighters of the heroic times of the catacombs. "Like early resisters everywhere, they were in the minority, and suddenly, they found themselves transported back to the atmosphere of the early church, part of a single messianic hope," historian Renée Bédarida points out, alluding to the first tentative steps of Témoignage Chrétien.[56]

Militants were also able to place an extensive repertoire of action in the service of the resistance. They believed in the power of the word and offered the underground press their reasoning skills and writing talents. The profoundly Catholic Raymond Burgard, a literature teacher at the Lycée Buffon, was thus the force behind *Valmy*, which a staff from the LJR produced and distributed from January 1941 on. In addition, the charitable traditions of Catholicism equipped the church intellectually and materially to aid proscribed persons. It had solid infrastructures and could easily—but not without risk—conceal weapons or harbor fugitives in its crypts, convents, or schools. The Soeurs-de-la-Sainte-Agonie convent regularly took in Colonel Arnould, head of the Jade-Amilcol network. The Franciscans of the Croix-Saint-Simon stored on its premises medical supplies for the Comité Médical de la Résistance (CMR; Medical Committee of the Resistance). In the small Sainte-Thérèse de l'Enfant-Jésus secondary school in Avon, Father Jacques, immortalized in Louis Malle's film *Au Revoir Les Enfants*, hid STO evaders as well as three Jewish children while he was involved in the Vélites-Thermopyles network.

This form of engagement, however, cannot always be considered an act of resistance as such. As historian Étienne Fouilloux notes, the example of the women's religious communities of Lyon sometimes revealed "less clear-cut motives: a simple duty of charity toward the excluded, whoever they may be, which in 1944 could have been someone suspected of collaboration."[57] In addition, some organizations sought to convert the Jews they were supposed to be protecting. The Finaly children, for example, entrusted to Antoinette Brun by the Notre-Dame-de-Sion convent, were baptized by that fervent Catholic, who refused after the war to return them to their family. For many years she hid them, assisted by the Notre-Dame-de-Sion religious community, which, it should be recalled, had been founded "to bear witness within the church and in the world to God's fidelity to his love for the Jewish people and to work toward the fulfillment of the biblical promises"—in short, to convert the People of the Book.

Catholic values, conversely, could impede engagement in armed struggle. Apart from the fact that it violated the biblical "Thou shalt not kill," it ultimately raised the risk of a rebellion "against the government, which still represents order and authority," while fueling "a civil war, when we do not know what new legality it is preparing for, one imposed, perhaps, by foreigners or Communists."[58] Not all the clergy, therefore, made the same choice as Yves de Montcheuil, who in May 1944 called for young people to participate in national uprising. Even religious assistance to the freedom fighters proved to be problematic, since priests, to practice their ministry, had to ask for the authorization of local bishops. The authorities did not grant it, arguing that they had refused it to the Milice. In June 1944, however, Pius XII agreed at the last minute to have the bishopric provide spiritual assistance to the maquisards.[59] Finally, the demands of the underground struggle gave rise to serious debates of conscience, as suggested by the dialogue between Gilles de Souza (Chambrey), in charge of liaisons with the delegation of the government of Algiers, and Alban Vistel, head of the MUR: "'Alban, I've been waiting for you, because I want to confide to you that I'm struggling with a terrible problem.' Then, without any further preamble, since time was running short: 'If I'm arrested, I'm afraid I'll weaken, I fear I'll talk under torture. Courage must be a difficult thing. So I have my cyanide tablet, but I'm a believer.'[60] 'The mere fact that you are considering the problem with such lucidity and courage proves that you have within you all the resources to emerge victorious from the conflict,' responded Vistel. A few days later, the Gestapo arrested [Chambrey] during a mission in Chambéry. He died by firing squad, without having given up any of the weighty secrets he possessed."[61]

Protestants faced more or less the same dilemmas. They accepted the logic of temporal power and in that sense conformed to the principle articulated by Paul: "Let every soul be subject unto the higher powers. For there is no power but of God: the powers that be are ordained by God" (Romans 13:1). But they could just as easily judge that it was better to obey God than men, a path that the Huguenots had followed in the heroic times of the dragonnades, when Louis XIV attempted to intimidate Protestants into converting to Catholicism or leaving France. In 1943 the Reverend Daniel Curtet reminded his congregation at the Fay church that resistance was imperative in three cases: when the state was not respecting the rights of individuals; when it was not allowing the church to preach freely; and when it sought to be the absolute master.[62] Some regions—the Plateau Vivarais-Lignon, for example—had also shown themselves sensitive to the suffering of others, maintaining a tradition of welcoming outcasts that dated back to the seventeenth century and had been reactivated during the interwar period. The plateau took in both Spanish republicans and stateless persons fleeing Nazism.[63] "In Chambon-sur-Lignon, an astonishing place of refuge on the border of Velay and Vivarais, Huguenot solidarity toward the victims of racist and xenophobic persecutions manifested itself to the utmost," confirms Henri Noguères.[64] But let us not idealize the behavior of the heirs to Calvin. Many Protestants also fell under the spell of the National Revolution, whose anti-alcoholism campaign, moralism, and call for a return to the land coincided with concerns that had found expression between 1918 and 1939. The Reverend Marc Boegner, a member of the National Council, assured Marshal Pétain on many occasions of "his deferential admiration and of his gratitude."[65]

## The Jews

The situation of the Jews in France tended to constitute an obstacle to engagement in the resistance rather than an encouragement. The community, if that term is appropriate here, was in reality profoundly split. French Jews long established in France—a country for which a number of them had fought during World War I—looked down on immigrants who had settled during the interwar period, fleeing the poverty and persecutions they had suffered, in Poland especially. "The French looked upon the new arrivals with condescension, a sense of cultural superiority reinforced by class differences," writes historian Patrick Weil.[66] Whether or not they had been in France for a long time, many Jews wished to assimilate, which led them to keep quiet about their identity rather than to flaunt it. "One serves France by being a good Jew, and one serves Judaism by being loyal to the nation," adds Weil.[67] In that sense, the Jews were responding to the wishes of the comte de Clermont-Tonnerre, who in December 1789 had declared: "One must refuse everything to the Jews as a nation and grant everything to the Jews as individuals." That principle had been followed all the more scrupulously in that, for many Jews, France remained the nation of the rights of man and of the citizen. These Jews therefore complied with its laws and did not think of violating a normative order that guaranteed their freedom. Pierre Mendès France, for example, after setting off on the *Massilia*, could have left Rabat for England by way of Gibraltar rather than risk imprisonment for desertion, of which the Vichy authority accused him. He did nothing of the sort, preferring "to stand fast, being averse to an outcome that would temporarily lead people to believe that he was confessing. How imbued with legalism Maître Mendès France is! How confident in the legal procedures and justice of his country, even though he is well acquainted with all the machinations of the Dreyfus Affair!"[68] Mendès thus submitted to a rigged trial, refusing to hide from his country's justice system and hoping "to denounce the abuse of authority of the military tribunal"[69]—which he proceeded to do. Transferred to Clermont-Ferrand and sentenced to six years in prison on May 9, 1941, he escaped on the night of June 21 and joined the FFL, where he served as navigator in the Lorraine group before becoming a minister under General de Gaulle in Algiers.

From this standpoint, Vichy had disastrous consequences. Many Jews, far from grasping that the French State was conducting an autonomous anti-Semitic policy, believed at first that it was submitting to pressure from the German occupier. For example, Jacques Heilbronner, president of the Central Consistory, declared to his members in March 1941: "The only hope resides in the presence at the head of the state of Monsieur le Maréchal Pétain, with whom I have made many contacts and who gives me hope of reparations one day for the injustice imposed."[70] The members of the consistory assumed that the laws had come in response to "pressure by the occupiers."[71] Many Jews therefore adopted a legalist posture, which led them, for example, to comply with the regulations promulgated by the French State, while agreeing to sacrifice themselves for the common good.[72] "Legalism and adaptation to the new realities therefore dictated the conduct of a not insignificant proportion of the Jews and not only of their leaders," observes historian Renée Poznanski.[73]

Newly arrived Jews did not always share that view. The men and women enlisted in the MOI, an organization created by the PCF in 1924 to welcome foreigners living in France, felt they were Communists above all, and the orders that their press disseminated, in Yiddish or in French, were modeled on those of the party.[74] These men and women "turned to Communism because for the time being it was, if not integration into the nation as a whole, then at least integration into a nonracial group on national soil," points out historian Annie Kriegel.[75] She adds: "These Jews, minority for minority, ghetto for ghetto, danger for danger, death for death, felt something like a liberation and discovered something like a necessary surfeit of dignity in *choosing* to accept a condition that was not initially their own, rather than being condemned, from birth as it were and by an obscurantist decree on the enemy's part, to a condition whose meaning was established not by the interested parties but by their executioners."[76] Granted, fighters in the MOI did not deny that identity. Of the four FTP military units of the Paris region under the authority of the MOI in 1942–1943, the second called itself "Second Detachment of the Jewish Francs-Tireurs et Partisans."[77] But that identity remained secondary, and the motives for becoming engaged did not obey the logic motivating the "Jews of the Republic" described in loving detail by Pierre Birnbaum. In any event, the Jews, whether they belonged to an insular Yiddish-speaking world or identified with the France of the rights of man, tended to downplay their identity during the dark years rather than to emphasize it.

Nevertheless, the persecution they suffered led some Jews to join the fight, to avenge their loved ones, or to combat their executioners. "There were many who made the transition from social action in Jewish circles to military action, from semisecrecy to total secrecy, or who, having seen the members of their family deported, no longer hesitated when they were contacted," writes Poznanski.[78] Robert Gamzon, founder of the EIF, embodied that radicalization. He first opted for legality, opening group homes and rural community centers in the southern zone. Later, however, he went underground. He personally took charge of a maquis in the Tarn department in 1944. At the time, he believed it was essential for the Jews to fight, so that they would no longer be "hunted slaves but men who can hold their heads up high and are ready for battle."[79] In addition, many organizations, such as the Comité Amelot, combined legal and illegal activities. And a large number of Jews joined the internal or external resistance in an individual capacity, a presence brought home by the names Raymond Aron, Raymond Aubrac, Jacques Bingen, Daniel Mayer, and Jean-Pierre Levy. On the whole, however, the legalist mind-set of the Jewish community of France, with the exception of the Communists and Zionists, tended to constitute an impediment rather than a predisposition to engagement in the resistance—at least in the beginning.

## A Question of Generation

Was the resistance the affair of young people? The statistics suggest it was. For example, 75 percent of the members of Franc-Tireur were under forty.[80] And those under thirty represented 62 percent of the forces of the DF.[81] The proportion of young people seems to have been lower in the networks than in the movements, but it was still large. In the Manipule network, 40 percent of agents were under twenty-five, and the average age was 32.5[82]—figures generally comparable to those in Ille-et-Vilaine, where the under-thirty set composed 45 percent of resistance forces, though they represented only a third of the population in the department.[83]

Several elements explain that overrepresentation. The qualities ordinarily attributed to that age group—ardor, selflessness, self-sacrifice—were naturally a major factor. In addition, the young may have been less cognizant than their elders of the dangers they were facing, especially since their physical condition was better suited to the demands of the underground struggle. Furthermore, the resistance allowed them to assert themselves with respect to the older generation. Sons sometimes believed they were taking on the burden of their fathers, whether the latter had been glorious heroes in World War I or the misguided architects of the strange defeat. "Is it our fault if we recruit only amateurs?" Claude Bourdet asked his father in 1942. "It is everyone else's fault, that of our society's leaders, who left the task to men like us, who were in no way prepared for it."[84] Many, finally, could not imagine living in a France dominated by the Germans or envision being subjected to the STO and exposed to political and anti-Semitic persecution. They had little appetite for the future promised them by an octogenarian, Marshal Pétain, with his love of asceticism, expiation, and sport, an unpleasant foretaste of which was provided by the Chantiers de la Jeunesse (Youth Work Camps).

That said, resistance organizations rarely launched appeals specifically targeting young people. When they addressed particular groups, they focused on professional sectors and not on generational distinctions. In the fight against the STO, the resistance appealed especially to workers and employers, sometimes to civil servants, but more rarely to young people, which suggests that they were not a major concern for the army of shadows. The underground groups likely believed it pointless to undertake a battle they believed was won, especially since Vichy, from the Chantiers de la Jeunesse to the STO, aimed more to bully young people than to foster their growth.

Young people's entry into the resistance, however, was not always a sign of revolt. It sometimes capped a "secessionist mode of behavior" begun before the war.[85] Many adolescents or young adults, without opposing their parents head-on, had wanted to take their fate into their own hands, whether by claiming the right to choose their course of study (which parents ordinarily decided) or by spending their free time with their peer group—which explains the success that youth movements had had before the war, especially within the bourgeoisie. Although it is not possible to cite statistical evidence, many resistance fighters had before 1940 frequented these organizations (scouts, JEC), which functioned at the time as a training ground for the resistance.

It should be added that the constraints weighing on this age cohort sometimes produced the opposite effect. Many young people, as they began their adult lives, had to make the painful choice between keeping their jobs or pursuing their studies and joining the resistance. In addition, their limited life experience restricted their repertoire of action and thus their usefulness to the army of shadows. Conversely, the absence of family obligations, sometimes invoked to explain the overrepresentation of the younger generation, did not play the decisive role attributed to it. Indeed, contrary to received wisdom, many resistance fighters had family responsibilities. In the DF, a third of resistance fighters had spouses, and more than a quarter were raising at least one child.[86] In the Manipule network, 54 percent of agents were married and 46 percent were parents.[87] Several famous examples confirm that claim. Claude Bourdet, Marie-Madeleine Fourcade, Lucie and Raymond Aubrac, and Philippe and Hélène Viannay joined up when they already had, or were about to start, a family. And Lise London gave birth to her second child in prison.

## Women's Engagement

The "second sex" did not contribute to the underground fight at a level consistent with its weight in French society. On the contrary, all the statistics confirm the underrepresentation of women when compared to the population as a whole. Such was the case in Franc-Tireur (where women constituted less than 10 percent of forces)[88] and in the DF (16 percent),[89] in Ille-et-Vilaine (13 percent)[90] and in Calvados (12 percent),[91] in the Jade-Fitzroy network (14 percent), and in the Zéro-France network (14 percent).[92]

These low figures have often been attributed to statistical bias. Most often, the estimates are based on an analysis of applications for the postwar card that acknowledged service as a Combattant Volontaire de la Résistance (CVR; Voluntary Resistance Fighter). Women supposedly declined to request the card because, after the war, they did not see themselves as resistance fighters[93] and thus engaged in a kind of self-censorship, or because they were not part of the so-called working population and therefore considered the procedure pointless, since the card recognized service in the aim of providing retirement benefits. Finally, the civilian resistance, in which women were more often involved than they were in armed struggle, was systematically underestimated until the 1980s.[94] Women, in this view, were shortchanged because of the tendency over three decades to represent the underground fight in terms of warfare.

This argument is hardly convincing, however. In the first place, the CVR applications rejected by the ad hoc commissions were not notable for their overrepresentation of women. For example, 12 percent of the applications declined in Calvados had been submitted by women; that figure invalidates the thesis that a misogynist administration refused to give women their due. Second, the figures regarding the proportion of women in the repressed population in no way contradict the statistics overall. Women represented 14 to 15 percent of those deported on the grounds of resistance activity[95] and, for the DF, they composed 16 percent of the forces arrested by the Vichy or German services.[96] If the participation of the two sexes had been equivalent, the repression would also have affected them equally (with the exception of capital punishment, which was reserved for men as a general rule). Such was not the case, however. Are we to believe, therefore, that the French State or the Nazi occupier proved more indulgent toward the fair sex? Such a leniency would be surprising; the Reich sometimes even beheaded women in its jails.

Everything suggests, therefore, that the statistics, far from betraying reality, render an accurate picture of it. The proposition therefore needs to be turned on its head. Statistical underrepresentation, far from indicating an underengagement, would on the contrary express a significant entry of the daughters of Marianne into the civic arena. In prewar France, it should be remembered, women did not have the right to vote. They were rarely active in the political parties: before the war, they represented only 3 percent of the members of the SFIO. Legally treated as minors, they had to have their husband's permission to work outside the home and did not have the right to open bank accounts in their own name. To become engaged in the resistance, they therefore had to overcome many material and cultural obstacles. And they did so: proportionally speaking, their involvement in the resistance greatly surpassed the political engagements to which women had subscribed during the interwar period. Furthermore, as Henri Noguères points out, "recruitment, as life undercover dictated, occurred by means of co-optation. And discrimination, based (most often unconsciously) on a notion of inequality between the sexes, one as old as our civilization and as solidly rooted in the Resistance as everywhere else in France, indisputably played a role in that."[97] As a result, the resistance truly marked "women's entry into a world heretofore reserved for men, that of the fight for the commonwealth."[98]

It took a strong personality to overcome the cultural hurdles that prevented a woman from becoming engaged in the resistance. From that standpoint, a career could be an asset for the future female resistance fighter, though a few qualifications need to be made on that score.

All during the Third Republic, the demographic shift and the French people's attachment to the land resulted in a labor shortage in industry and in the service sector. Employers turned to women to fill that gap. In 1936, 6.5 million women were employed, which is to say, 30.06 percent—46.7 percent if only the working-age population (those between fifteen and sixty-four) is counted.[99] Some, especially those in the working classes, had to earn a livelihood. But others chose to work, seeking personal fulfillment and a path to independence.

Although there are no studies of the subject, many indications suggest that the women from the middle or upper classes who joined the resistance had engaged in a strategy of emancipation even before the war. They had chosen to pursue their education, a decision that was not always viewed favorably by their parents. They had sometimes embraced prominent professions that tended to be male bastions (doctor, teacher, lawyer) or had moved into sectors that the respectable bourgeoisie did not consider inappropriate for its daughters (nurse, social worker). Before 1932, therefore, daughters of engineers or women whose fathers belonged to the upper echelons of the public sector or the administration composed three-quarters of students at schools for training social workers in Paris. In the provinces, management groups, farmers, and artisans produced three-quarters of such students. That sector was strongly represented within certain resistance groups. In the DF, 56 percent of women belonged to such emancipatory professions.[100] Factory welfare officers—what we now know as social workers—such as Berty Albrecht and Jeanne Sivadon, and teachers such as Lucie Aubrac and Claire Chevrillon thus had a prominent presence in the underground groups.

But women from working-class backgrounds also participated in the underground fight. They played an essential role in the housewives' demonstrations and in some strikes. As Lise London recalls, in the very harsh conflict that set Nord-Pas-de-Calais ablaze in May–June 1941, "they led processions, picketed, printed and distributed tracts, put up posters calling for solidarity between the general population and the coal miners; they crisscrossed the countryside, collecting food for the strikers' soup."[101] They also assisted proscribed persons, within the framework of the Cimade, for example. Finally, they very often took on the duties of liaison agent or secretary. Although, before the war, these women had usually been constrained to pursue a career rather than choosing to do so, engagement in labor unions or political militantism paved the way for a first emancipation. Lise London, "la mégère de la rue Daguerre" (the virago of Daguerre Street) studied stenography after earning her *certificat d'études*, which allowed her to become a secretary at the Lyon headquarters of the PCF, and then, after July 1938, to work at *La Voz de Madrid*, the newspaper of Spanish Republicans who had taken refuge in France.[102] Similarly, Catherine Roux's certification as an assistant accountant gave her the chance to escape the factory, to which her family background had destined her. She was hired by a manufacturer of gas stoves. "I had a very comfortable place in the office, and was not overwhelmed with work," recounts the future member of the Combat movement. "But those who worked in the factory did so in conditions that rivaled the 1850s. In winter it was like Siberia; there was only one brazier. Frequently I went there on errands, and when I did, I replaced someone for a few minutes so he or she could warm up near the brazier. The disparity between our situations disturbed me, so I helped them to unionize; there was no union in the shop. Thus, at fifteen I had a union card. Then came 1936, an extraordinary period. We had to learn how to negotiate with management. But in the end, nothing worked, and the workers went on strike. I struck with them."[103]

More women than men were single: in the Manipule network, 57 percent of the men had married, but only 38 percent of the women.[104] The same was true for the DF: although 80 percent of the men over 28.5 years old (the average marriage age for men in 1939) were married, only 45 percent of women over 25.5 (the average for women that year) had tied the knot.[105] This gap no doubt reflects the imbalance in the sex ratio resulting from World War I. But it may also have been a matter of choice. Some women, fully committed to the working world, may have rejected the bonds of marriage, conceived rightly or wrongly as a barrier to their independence. In short, one thing is obvious: women's participation in the resistance was not the first symptom of an emancipation strategy; rather, it was the outcome of such a strategy, capping a quest for autonomy that had begun before the war, whether that process entailed the choice of a profession, involvement in a party or labor union, or even the decision not to marry.

Women's entry into the underground struggle did not bring about any drastic shift in gender boundaries. With a few exceptions, women did not exercise leadership functions. In that respect, Lucie Aubrac, a key figure in Libération-sud, and Marie-Madeleine Fourcade, head of the Alliance network, were isolated cases. "Just as businesses or administrations recruited female personnel only for the positions of secretary, switchboard operator, receptionist, or, in a pinch, ledger clerk, women and girls were brought into the Resistance only to be secretaries or liaison agents," recalls Henri Noguères.[106] The Germans—most of them Communists—who fought in France within the context of Travail Allemand (German Labor) also asked young women to use their charms to make contact with soldiers in public places, so as to understand their state of mind and, if need be, to enlist them.[107] In the underground, therefore, women sometimes put their femininity in the service of the cause. Célia Bertin, recruited by Pierre de Lescure, "started to do what young girls my age who had been asked to help were doing: delivering packages, carrying documents and sometimes radio transmitters." As she tells it, "one day, I came upon a security check when leaving the Métro. I was carrying a radio transmitter in a travel bag. The Gestapo agents were searching everyone and making the men put their hands up. Inwardly terrified, I smiled at the soldier—the first and only time I smiled at a Nazi—and, struggling with my bag, I made as if I had trouble opening the zipper. He smiled back and let me go."[108]

Underground groups thus exploited "the differentiation in the roles attributed to men and women, and in particular the resources offered by baby carriages, grocery baskets, or the charming smile of a young girl on a bicycle, ruses that have become clichés in the collective memory."[109] Alban Vistel's remarks do not contradict that observation. "From the beginning, women sought to do their part, and their deepest calling would continually be to give the persecuted a little of that gentleness that the most prideful or resolute of men knows he can find only in a woman. The social services of the Resistance therefore could not fail to be feminine, created, organized, and performed by women," he declares in his memoirs.[110] In the underground press, women rarely took up the pen. "The men discussed things among themselves, and it did not occur to them to ask the opinion of a woman who happened to be there, who came to make them a sandwich, even if they counted on her for the rest of the underground work," reports Génia Gemähling, secretary-general of the DF.[111] Francis-Louis Closon, referring to a liaison agent named Jean-Marie, confirms: "Like all her female comrades, she did the dirty work, typing letters, fetching this and that, bringing back the mail, connecting one person with another, arranging meetings, collecting our mailboxes—secret or under surveillance—seeking out places to meet, and, when it became indispensable, doing the shopping with real or counterfeit tickets."[112]

Needless to say, women rarely fought Sten in hand. Although the BBC and the movements invited them to join the struggle, "the call to arms addressed to women was symbolic; the partisan organizations primarily directed these volunteers toward the health groups and social services for the maquis."[113] And though Madeleine Riffaud, a member of the FTP, took down a German officer in 1944, she was an exception. In all, "men and women were essentially conceptualized and mobilized as complementary actors."[114] The "small war" was still reserved for the men, therefore, which also explains the underrreporting of Frenchwomen's participation in the army of shadows, given the pre-eminent place the maquis occupy in the statistics. By that measure, the differences observable in the engagement of the two sexes "are only the reflection of those existing in the society of the time: women had slightly less education than men, but above all, they were less well integrated into the world of work and into professional and labor union networks."[115] It is not women's underinvolvement but rather their overinvolvement that should be stressed. The social, political, and cultural context clearly made their engagement more difficult, but that does not mean it was minor, in view of the obstacles that stood in the way of their joining the army of shadows.

"Basically, we were maladjusted," confided Emmanuel d'Astier de La Vigerie in the interview he gave for the 1969 documentary *Le cha-*

*grin et la pitié (The Sorrow and the Pity)*. His deliberately provocative remark implies that resistance fighters, poorly integrated into French society, were fringe elements. All indications attest to the contrary, however. Sometimes married, often settled into their professional lives, equipped with solid ideological guideposts, frequently trained before the war in forms of militantism, soldiers in the army of shadows did not live on the margins of the commonwealth. On the contrary, they formed its core, not to say its *sanior pars*, a view corroborated by the sociological analysis of Free France by historian Jean-François Muracciole[116] and also illustrated in René Clément's 1946 film *Le père tranquille (Mr. Orchid)*. H. R. Kedward adds: "The possession of a strongly self-determining, independent, and combative personality is not inevitably synonymous with maladjustment, either personal or social."[117]

These men and women came from every background: the resistance, then, was an interclass phenomenon. But let us not exaggerate. The underground groups were marked by social polarization, which can be explained by several factors. Organizations enlisted their first members by exploiting the professional, familial, or personal channels of their founders, which limited their recruitment area. Individuals became engaged not only because they had found a contact but also because they more or less conformed to the line the network or movement was defending. As a result, the resistance produced a more limited social decompartmentalization than that which occurred in the trenches of World War I.

Engagement also marked a confluence between individuals and underground organizations. Granted, motivations were fundamentally personal and not the result of social determinism. But they had a collective dimension, which is reflected in the statistics. The social identity of an individual is multiple and varied. A human being belongs to a gender, a social class, and a political milieu—which, whatever the role of free will, shape him or her. These factors explain why few Communist workers could be found in Témoignage Chrétien, and why far-right militants rarely enlisted in the FTP. All in all, choices belonged to a border zone defined by both individual decisions and collective patterns. Although motivations cannot be reduced to a single schema, they do correspond to a general logic.

## Squabbles over Statistics

Ultimately, the sociological data invite us to give a statistical estimate of the resistance forces. As already noted, two opposing views have been put forward. According to some, the numbers currently proposed minimize the engagement of the French people in the army of shadows. Historian Jean-Marie Guillon, for example, challenges analyses based on CVR cards: "Large swaths of the Resistance are left out, especially those of a purely political nature, which were neither the least prompt nor the least important, to say nothing of the modest Resistance, where only those who fell victim to the repression are taken into account and who, were it not for that misfortune, would have been neglected." He concludes, therefore: "we grant no value to the supposed proportion of resistance fighters within a department's total population, as provided by certain studies on the basis of CVR applications."[118] This point of view led François Marcot to distinguish between a "Resistance organization, which obviously included only a very small minority, and a Resistance movement, which was a much more widespread social phenomenon."[119]

This approach, though respectable in principle, postulates too broad a conception of the resistance. In the first place, resistance requires a continuity of action: occasional acts must not be confused with long-term engagement. Providing an evader with a place to stay for one night belongs to a very different logic than setting up an escape channel, and these logics shape engagements without common measure in their motivations and intensity. Furthermore, the risks incurred were most certainly not the same. Such a view obscures the considered and thoughtful choices that led individuals to opt for struggle and to commit most of their energy to it, sometimes at the cost of their lives. Finally, it minimizes the importance of proselytism, a key dimension of struggle in the movements.

These considerations explain why the resistance remained a minority phenomenon from start to finish. The statistics gathered during and after the war provide a few rough estimates. It can be inferred that the underground groups counted "a few thousand" men in late 1940 and a few "tens of thousands" in late 1942.[120] In early 1944, two hundred thousand people, no doubt, were more or less directly engaged in the army of shadows.[121] That figure is far from negligible when compared to the handful of pioneers in 1940 and when the obstacles that stood in the way of the volunteers are taken into account. The French administration, for its part, has acknowledged that by December 31, 1975, it had granted 227,531 CVR cards, a figure that grew somewhat later on, to 262,730 by late 2008.[122] In view of the resistance fighters who were denied cards—for good or bad reasons[123]—and the undercount of the civilian resistance, it is likely that the army of shadow numbered in all between 300,000 and 500,000 men and women.[124] Should it be conceded, however, that that estimate misrepresents reality by underestimating the importance of the "Resistance movement," to borrow Marcot's notion?

The resistance took root in favorable soil. Thousands of French people aided it from time to time or in a more regular fashion. The French people found the occupation difficult to bear, and collaboration was never popular. Likewise, the Vichy regime, having at first held an appeal for a portion of the population, became increasingly intolerable to them. The covert civil war it fomented, its servile cooperation with the Reich, the persecutions it launched against republicans, Communists, Jews, Freemasons, and foreigners gradually alienated some of its supporters. That was especially true since Pétain was unable to protect civilians, who were handed over by their own state to the STO and plunged against their will into a war that, through the Allied bombings, once again struck France. These elements created a context advantageous for the resistance, which over time was able to count on the occasional assistance of people of goodwill.

In fact, relatives, friends, and anonymous souls helped to carry out underground actions. "Of my two parents, my father was a resistance fighter and a member of the Communist Party, so he took in loads of men and women who came to the house. Some may say that my mother did not resist—but who got up in the morning to take care of the resistance fighter who had to leave before daybreak? Who darned the socks and washed the linen of the sleeping resistance fighter? Who prepared the food he would take with him? Who dealt with the police when there were signs of trouble?" inquires Mme Dou.[125] Furthermore, resistance fighters often benefited from the hospitality extended to them for one or sometimes several nights by strangers happy to support the army of shadows. People in the rural areas assisted evaders by hiding them on farms, by putting them to work, and especially, by supplying them with provisions. In the Jura department, the maquis of Lamoura was supported by the Grosfilley family, wholesale cheese makers in Saint-Claude, who regularly went up to the maquis to bring them intelligence or food or even new recruits. "La Fraternelle," the Saint-Claude cooperative, also brought provisions from its various branches and delivered them free of charge to the maquisards hiding in Haut-Jura.[126] "On the whole, it can be averred that the peasants of Jura, with greater or lesser enthusiasm, did not consider it unusual to feed those fighting for a cause that they believed just, or in any case justified by the occupier's demands and then exactions," concludes François Marcot.[127] When the Hudson that was supposed to pick up the Aubracs got stuck in the mud on the Orion airfield on February 8, 1944, it was peasants from the neighboring village of Cosges, in the Jura department, who came over to pull it out. As Lucie Aubrac recounts: "Through the window of the plane, I see a crowd silently getting down to business. The men place themselves under the wings, horses and cattle are hitched to the nose. At the signal 'Heave!' the animals pull, the men lift the wings of the plane with their shoulders. What a procession in the night! The Germans were hardly six miles away."[128] Without that ring of protection, the resistance would never have been able to come into being or to take root. Alongside a resistance organization, then, a resistance movement truly existed as a corollary.

The above remark must be qualified, however. The comforting notion of an underground force moving through the population like a fish through water, to borrow the conventional image, cannot obscure the fact that many fighters were denounced by French people, arrested by the Vichy police, and delivered to the death camps by the SNCF, which was not staffed exclusively by the heroes of the film *La bataille du rail (The Battle of the Rails)*. Furthermore, until summer 1943, those called up by the STO often had to make their way to the Reich, having been unable to find the necessary support in the general population or in the organized resistance. "If the climate had been favorable to the resistance, if all the administrations had been complicitous in botching orders, the Germans would have needed armies of police officers to assemble the convoys of inmates. But in the current situation, the courageous have almost no means left for escaping without papers, without food cards. The country as a whole is nothing more than a quivering mass of protoplasm. Nobody thinks about anything anymore. How will we recover from this shame and degradation?" wondered the writer and teacher Jean Guéhenno in February 1943.[129] Ultimately, the resistance gave rise to fear and anxiety. "Reactions toward the maquis were for the most part unfavorable," Pierre Laborie points out. And he adds: "Approval ratings, never higher than 20 percent [before then], did not surpass 30 percent until after August 5 [1944]. By contrast, a mix of condemnation and hostility remained the attitude of most people until early July, a little later in the Midi around Toulouse."[130] "Although people were hoping for liberation, they were sometimes afraid of fighting and of its consequences, afraid of German reprisals, and perhaps as well of the sanctions imposed by the maquisards against those who gave in to the temptation to protect themselves from the risks of a war too close at hand, by temporarily coming to terms with the enemy," confirms Marcot with reference to Jura.[131]

As a result, there must be no confusing the register of complicity and the register of action, limited offers of assistance and engagement over the long term, the desire to minimize risks and the acceptance of the greatest sacrifices. The resistance movement and the resistance organization arose from the same fertile soil; both entailed the rejection of a hated occupation, gradually combined with rejection of the Vichy regime. But the logic guiding engagement in the two cases was assuredly not the same. The provisions supplied to the maquis by a Glières peasant are not of a piece with the actions performed by Tom Morel. False identity papers delivered once or twice by a sympathetic civil servant are not on a par with the sabotage operation undertaken by André Jarrot. In one case, occasional and intermittent engagement, being less transgressive, was obviously less dangerous; in the other, full and repeated engagement entailed serious risks, the magnitude of which was accurately assessed by the resistance fighter.

## Chapter 16

# The Repression

THE REPRESSION OF the army of shadows by the Vichy regime and by the German occupier must be considered a central issue. First and foremost, it evokes the suffering endured by the resistance fighters who were arrested. They were well aware of the perils to which they exposed themselves in becoming engaged. But though they knew they were risking death, torture, or internment, they could not imagine the horrible realities of the concentration camp hell into which the vast majority of captured resistance fighters were cast. From a different angle, the man-hunts carried out by the police forces of the French State and Nazi Germany raise questions about the perceived threat that the resistance posed to their interests, some shared, some divergent.

## A Threat to the Reich?

The Nazis, far from underestimating the resistance, took it seriously from the start, but their perception of the danger evolved over time. The MbF, the German military command in France which had its headquarters at the Hôtel Majestic, was responsible for the repression in the occupied zone until 1942. In 1940 it did not believe that the se-curity of the troops quartered in France was threatened. Furthermore, it lauded the overall attitude of the French population and noted—not without satisfaction—that the administration as a whole was collabo-rating properly with its services. While pointing out that, after the shock of the defeat, anti-German sentiments and a bitter discontent had developed toward the Vichy regime, it judged that the French gener-ally maintained a watch-and-wait attitude.[1] "In the absence of coherent leadership and organization of the anti-German forces, the country's security is not in danger," it averred in July 1941.[2] That did not prevent the military command, however, from remaining vigilant in the face of even the most tenuous signs of opposition. In movie theaters, for ex-

ample, newsreels exalting the feats of the Wehrmacht did not spark the
enthusiasm of members of the audience, who protested, cleared their
throats, or noisily blew their noses. The occupation authorities therefore demanded that the news be projected with the lights half-lowered,
so that the troublemakers could be identified. Similarly, patriotic
demonstrations—the one in Paris on November 11, 1940, marked a first
apogee—attracted the attention of the occupation authorities, who
demanded that the French government take the most stringent measures. In view of its small numbers, in fact, the MbF relied largely on
Vichy authorities to maintain order. Hence, the repression of the actions attributed to the Gaullist movement, and particularly of the "V"
graffiti campaigns in France during the early months of 1941, gave rise
to "repeated interventions vis-à-vis the prefects."[3]

The military command did not remain inactive, however. While
being cautious about using sanctions as a weapon, so as not to alienate
the population, its services made an ever-increasing number of arrests—1,838 in October 1940, 2,787 in November, 5,005 between
April 15 and May 15 1941[4]—combined with administrative detentions.
Collective punishment was imposed on some municipalities. In October 1940, after the sabotage of several telephone lines, the cities of
Saint-Lô and Évreux were compelled to guard the equipment. Historian Gaël Eismann points out that they were subjected to longer curfews,
a fine, the nightly confinement to barracks of five hundred residents,
and the threat that hostages would be taken if the offense was repeated.[5]
Finally, between June 1940 and the end of July 1942, the German
military tribunals under the authority of the MbF pronounced 162
death sentences against civilians residing in France, 42 of which were
carried out.[6] That heavy toll does not include the judgments of the
courts of Nord-Pas-de-Calais or of the navy and air force, both of which
had their own tribunals.

Beginning in summer 1941, Operation Barbarossa and the shift to
armed struggle by the PCF, initiated by the attack against Alfons Moser,
resulted in an intensification of the repression. The Germans immediately demanded that the French State take drastic measures, and Vichy
complied. The law of August 14, 1941—drawn up on August 22, but
backdated to preserve appearances[7]—created the Sections Spéciales
(Special Sections), special courts charged with repressing Communist

and anarchist activities. These courts flouted the most basic legal requirements. Apart from the fact that their decisions were definitive and not subject to appeal, the Special Sections violated the principle of non-retroactivity. For example, Émile Bastard, André Bréchet, and Abraham Trzebucki, the first three Communist militants to be guillotined (on August 28, 1941), were convicted for acts that had no real relation to the attack on Alfons Moser.[8] In all, between August 1941 and August 1944 in the northern zone, and between December 1942 and August 1944 in the southern zone, the Special Sections pronounced 45 death sentences, 12 of which were carried out.[9]

The French police, goaded by both Vichy and the MbF, therefore hunted down Communist militants, suspected—not without reason—of being the authors of the attacks targeting occupation troops. It was the French police, not the German services, that arrested both the armed Communist groups in the Paris region and the Nantes commando that had taken down Lieutenant Colonel Hotz. But the occupiers, while still intervening repeatedly with the police and French tribunals, which were readily suspected of being lax, increasingly took on directly the hunt for resistance fighters. For example, the German tribunals under the authority of the MbF ordered 493 death sentences between August 1941 and late May 1942, 377 of which were carried out.[10] A show trial at the Chamber of Deputies (March 5–6, 1942) and another at the Maison de la Chimie (April 7–14, 1942) sought to demonstrate the resolve of the occupation authorities and to eradicate the "Red Scourge." The Germans, while exploiting for propaganda purposes the information they had obtained about the armed struggle of Communist commandos, also wanted to show the "rather extensive isolation of the Resistance within the French population."[11] That escalation did not mean, however, that the Nazis feared the French resistance's capacity for harm. "We have not yet observed a unified enemy organization. Investigations of a concerted but limited resistance movement are under way," the MbF noted in a report of summer 1941.[12] Its leaders judged that the danger was less military than political. The outbreak of anti-German assaults worried them only because of the irreducible rift that might open between the population and the occupying power as a result of misguided reprisals.[13]

That concern gave rise to a conflict between the MbF in Paris and the Reich authorities. In response to the proliferation of attacks targeting occupation troops, Berlin demanded that a substantial number of hostages—Jews and Communists especially—be executed. The military commanders, first Otto von Stülpnagel, then his cousin Carl-Heinrich Stülpnagel, balked. On September 11, 1941, Otto even asked to be relieved of his duties, a request granted on February 17, 1942.

During and after the war, that dissension fostered the righteous image of a chivalrous Wehrmacht that, outraged by the brutal methods imposed by fanatical Nazis, had opposed the reprehensible procedures as much as they could. That legend, however, does not withstand scrutiny, though it allowed the leaders of the German military command in France to escape their judges after the Reich's surrender. In fact, its leaders embraced Nazi ideology to a great degree and were not afraid to use an iron fist. Humane motives played only a small role. "What clearly concerned the MbF and its services was less to spare the civilian population of occupied France than to adopt less unpopular measures, first by giving its repressive policy the appearance of judicial legality, and second . . . by externalizing it," comments Gaël Eismann.[14] That said, the MbF hardly overestimated the danger that these attacks represented. Otto von Stülpnagel adamantly repeated in autumn 1941: "I said that, in my view, the bulk of the French population did not participate in these attacks, which tend rather to be executed by small terrorist groups in the pay of England particularly, which pop up in the country here one day, somewhere else the next. . . . I have clearly declared that, given the special situation of France, I was personally opposed to the mass execution of hostages, which would necessarily give rise to an ever-growing resentment on the part of the population and would make any later rapprochement policy extremely difficult, if it did not prevent it entirely."[15] The commander of the MbF thus rejected the mass reprisals Berlin was demanding, not out of humanitarian concerns but because he judged them counterproductive. In placing a pool of blood between occupiers and occupied, they ran the risk of fanning the civilian population's hatred and of compromising the collaboration between victor and vanquished. In early December 1941, the MbF suggested that, rather than execute hostages, it should deport to the east "a large number of Judeo-Bolshevik criminal elements."[16] Otto von Stülpnagel declared that such a retaliatory measure would undoubtedly have "a much more frightening effect on the French population than mass executions," which were beyond their comprehension.[17]

Must it be conceded, therefore, that the PCF's shift to armed struggle marked a turning point in the repressive policy of the Germans? There is reason for doubt. Even before the attack of August 21, 1941, the MbF had been distinguished for its harshness, issuing many death sentences and resorting to retaliatory sanctions that were collective, hence indiscriminate, since they struck innocents. In that sense, summer 1941 radicalized tendencies that had existed in embryonic form in 1940. The thesis of a "cycle of attacks and repression," put forward during and after the war, also calls for qualifications. The idea that the Communists, by their methods, triggered a mutual escalation of terror requires some correction. The execution of German soldiers, a marginal phenomenon, never threatened the security of the occupation troops. Nevertheless, the MbF did not intend to tolerate assaults, however minor, on the order it was seeking to impose. It therefore opted for a strategy of reprisals that belonged less to "'reciprocal terror' than to 'preventive terror,' which the notion of a 'cycle of attacks and repression' does not take into account."[18] Jews and Communists were the first victims, though it is not possible to say that this policy, under the mask of reprisals, served the Reich's extermination plans. In fact, the first convoys of deportees set off even before Auschwitz was up and running. Nothing indicates, moreover, that the leaders at the MbF had been informed in 1941 of the implementation of the Final Solution, though they may have suspected that the deportation of hostages they were advocating would likely end in death. All in all, concludes Gaël Eismann, "nothing at present provides support for the hypothesis that the reprisal convoys announced by the MbF served to 'camouflage' the start of the extermination of the Jews or even to 'link the fight against the Resistance in France to the practice of extermination in the east.'"[19]

## Vichy versus the Resistance

From the outset, the Vichy regime considered the resistance an enemy and treated it as such. In hunting down the Jews and Communists, the French State was seeking above all to fight groups destined for exclusion by its ideology. In that program, the crusade against Bolshevism was a top priority. The French State therefore prosecuted Maurice Thorez's followers with the utmost severity. It relied on the law the

Daladier government had adopted after the signing of the German-Soviet Pact, while at the same time introducing more stringent measures. On September 3, 1940, it extended a decree that allowed it to intern "all individuals dangerous to national defense or public security" under guard in holding centers.[20] Even before Operation Barbarossa, between four and five thousand Communists were arrested and interned.[21] With the German offensive against the Soviet Union and the first attacks perpetrated against occupation troops, Philippe Pétain radicalized that repressive policy.

The fight against the Gaullists took place on a different level. The conflict was based not on ideological antagonism but on different approaches to the war, which Charles de Gaulle sought to continue but which Philippe Pétain meant to renounce. The Rebel therefore represented a real danger to the Marshal. De Gaulle, having come from the army, could reassure conservative circles attached to traditional forms of leadership, especially since, at least at the beginning, he refused to spell out his political orientations. In that respect, he directly threatened the legitimacy of the victor of Verdun, all the more so in that, by calling for unification on the basis of patriotism, he was able to unite various groups and embody a national alternative to the grim expiation promised by the upholders of the National Revolution. The Vichy authorities therefore decreed that the Gaullists be hunted down with the same severity as the Communists, even though their subordinates on the ground showed less zeal in chasing down supporters of the Cross of Lorraine than those loyal to the Red Flag. The MbF found this situation distressing: "The assessment of the French forces of law and order still varies fundamentally, depending on whether it is the conduct of the anti-Communist repression at issue or that of the anti-Gaullist repression."[22] The statistics provide confirmation for that claim. Paris excepted, the security police arrested some twelve thousand people between May 1, 1942, and May 1, 1943; 8,481 were Communists and only 2,137 Gaullists, a significant disproportion.[23]

The resistance posed a threefold threat to the French State. Its actions, whether relatively innocuous or bloody, disrupted public order, which the authoritarian Vichy regime prided itself on ensuring. They also impeded Pétain's beloved National Revolution. The refusal of labor unions to support the Charte du Travail, calls for the restoration of democracy, and protests against the exclusion measures against the Jews thwarted the political aims of the victor of Verdun. Furthermore, the army of shadows, in calling for the sabotage of industrial production, in opposing agricultural requisitions, in encouraging French workers to refuse to participate in the STO, and in attacking the enemy's military plan of action undermined the collaboration on which the survival of the Vichy regime depended. For if the French authorities proved incapable of guaranteeing fresh supplies to the Reich and the security of its troops, there was a risk that Berlin would reduce the margin of freedom for its vassal, who was performing imperfectly the duties his lord had implicitly assigned.

The French State thus espoused contradictory philosophies. On the one hand, objective interests led it to support the occupier's repressive policy. Apart from the fact that the two partners had common enemies—Jews, Communists, resisters—the viability of the regime rested on the goodwill of the Germans, who depended, for the security of its troops, on the French State's ability to maintain order. That imperative made the Vichy leaders zealous. As historian Jean-Marc Berlière observes: "To earn the occupier's trust and to snuff out hot spots of para-police activities, it was necessary to provide gages, to demonstrate the competence, efficiency, and willingness of the administrations and of official services, a logic that implied charging them with specific repressive tasks previously performed by the auxiliary police and the German services."[24] But Vichy also sought to defend its sovereignty tooth and nail, and that sometimes led it to reject the increasing encroachments of the Reich, which exerted pressure on courts believed to be too lenient and ordered the French police to make arrests on its behalf. Pétain, moreover, claimed he was protecting civilians from the rigors of the occupation. Executions of hostages demonstrated the emptiness of that promise, confirming that the Germans were hardly troubled by humanitarian scruples when protecting what they considered their fundamental interests. It is clear, therefore, why the MbF preferred to replace a policy of indiscriminately executing hostages with mass deportations of Jews and Communists: "The MbF knew it could count on the support of Vichy if the repression was oriented primarily toward Communists and Jews and if it spared the rest of the population, including prominent citizens, whom the collaboration policy no longer allowed to be designated as hostages." The repressive policy of the German military apparatus therefore adopted a "more ideologically marked orientation"[25] than it did in other countries of Western Europe, precisely because of the convergence between it and the Vichy regime.

The French State thus conducted a repressive policy that largely coincided with the Reich's objectives. Even before the occupation, the RG had shifted from seeking out intelligence to hunting down the regime's enemies. In March 1940 they created a Brigade Spéciale (BS), given the task of repressing Communist activities; this was supplemented in 1942 by a second BS (BS2), charged with mounting an antiterrorist campaign against all resistance fighters. Between August 1941 and August 1944, these two services arrested 3,200 individuals, which in many cases amounted to condemning them to a dire fate. In fact, of the 1,599 people detained, the BS2 handed over 655 to the Germans, and 216 were executed.[26] In May 1941, the regime also created specialized police forces dedicated to Freemasons, Jews, and Communists. In July 1942, it undertook a first reorganization. The Service des Sociétés Secrètes (Secret Societies Service) disappeared; the Police aux Questions Juives (Police for Jewish Questions) became the Section d'Enquêtes et de Contrôle (Inquiries and Monitoring Branch); and the Service de Police Anticommuniste (Anti-Communist Police Service) was transformed into the Service de Répression des Menées Antinationales (SRMAN; Service for the Repression of Antinational Activities).[27] The regional mobile brigades of the criminal investigation division, which in autumn 1942 became regional brigades for the security police, assisted the SRMAN. According to estimates by Jean-Marc Berlière and Laurent Chabrun, they resulted in more than five thousand arrests.[28] Finally, Émile Hennequin, head of the municipal police of Paris, reactivated Brigades Spéciales (not to be confused with those previously mentioned). Composed of five or six guardians of the peace in civilian clothes, these were supposed to repress the authors of subversive propaganda in every Paris arrondissement and in the outlying districts. "Bonuses rewarded the best, sanctions targeted the lazy, the hesitant, the incompetent," note Berlière and Chabrun.[29]

Vichy, even while forming special units, made every effort to rationalize its repressive forces. The law of April 23, 1941, nationalized the police forces and expanded the system reigning in Lyon, Marseilles, and other large cities to all municipalities of more than ten thousand residents. The regime hoped thereby to professionalize these men, even while strengthening its own grip, since the entire system, now run by the regional prefects, was under the authority of a police superintendent. The French State also possessed conventional forces for conducting the repression. In 1943 it had 113,000 men, including 11,000 in the GMR, precursors of the Compagnies Républicaines de Sécurité (Republican Security Companies), along with 44,000 gendarmes, 17,000 Paris police officers, and 30,000 men belonging to the urban police corps[30]—substantial forces to be sure.

## 1942: A Turning Point

In 1942 the repression reached a turning point, though its importance should not be exaggerated. At the administrative level, the men of the MbF were partly relieved of the policing authority they had exerted, to the benefit of the SiPo-SD. Since 1939 this organization had combined two branches: the first, the security police (Sicherheitspolizei), included both the political police (Gestapo) and the criminal police (Kriminalpolizei); the second comprised the Reich's security services, the SD. It was therefore Himmler's SS, represented as of June 1, 1942, by a "higher SS and police leader" (*Höherer SS- und Polizeiführer*), that took over police authority for occupied France, replacing the military command. The military staff at the Hôtel Majestic found themselves restricted to protecting the occupation troops, while most of the antiresistance fight, the reprisals, and the anti-Semitic persecution were put in the hands of SS general Karl Oberg. Having joined the Nazi Party in 1931 and the SS in 1932, Oberg had occupied various posts in the Black Order, before heading the SS and the police for the Radom district in Poland. From the outset, he renegotiated the collaboration between his services and the French police. The Germans pledged to no longer address orders directly to minor public servants in the Vichy administration. The French justice system retained the exclusive right to judge, in accordance with its own laws, citizens guilty of political crimes or violations of common law but not of acts directly targeting the army or occupation authorities.[31] By the terms of these accords, concluded between Karl Oberg and René Bousquet, head of the French police, in

July–August 1942 (and renewed on April 13, 1943), Vichy hoped to maintain its sovereignty. In return, the occupier received assurances that resistance fighters would be prosecuted, while reserving for itself the right to repress men who directly attacked its troops or facilities. Oberg, named by a decree of March 9, 1942, was personally sworn in by Reinhard Heydrich on May 5. He assumed his official duties on June 1, 1942.[32]

This transfer of power was not a fundamental departure, however. The SiPo-SD and the MbF worked in tandem, especially since in France their personnel at first remained the same; men simply moved— voluntarily it appears—from one administration to the other. Oberg also maintained the main lines of his predecessors' orientations, pre- ferring to deport Jews, Communists, and resistance fighters rather than increase the number of executions. On December 7, 1941, the Night and Fog (Nacht und Nebel) decree, signed by Marshal Wilhelm Keitel, stipulated that those who presented a danger to the security of the German army would be deported to the Reich. Only resistance fighters who seemed sure to receive a death sentence without delay would be judged in France. On August 4, 1942, Adolf Hitler ordered that para- troopers and other saboteurs who were arrested be handed over to the SiPo-SD. On October 10, that enforcement agency apparently acquired the right to make use of administrative detention as it saw fit.[33] Gradu- ally, then, the occupier gave precedence to an extrajudicial repression that exempted it from bringing resistance fighters before tribunals. The radicalization accelerated the elimination of the Reich's enemies and prevented them from attracting excessive publicity. Yet the resistance was still not considered a threat of the first order. Internal security was "nowhere seriously compromised," the German services declared in March 1942.[34] The army of shadows continued to be treated not as a military problem but as a policing question, which, on the German side, fell under the sole jurisdiction of the SiPo-SD.[35]

The situation evolved, however, beginning in 1943. In particular, the prospect of an Allied landing led the Germans to adopt a harder line. They especially feared that the army of shadows, whose actions were multiplying, would disrupt communications between the Atlantic and the Mediterranean. In the desire to eliminate the danger of "armed gangs" before the Anglo-American forces stormed French beaches, the occupier was very determined to use the most brutal methods, for example, the deportation of presumed adversaries as a preventive measure. In 1944 it launched several punitive operations, attacking Henri Romans-Petit's groups in Ain (Operation Corporal, February 5–13), breaking up the Glières maquis (Operation Haute-Savoie, last week of March), crisscrossing Corrèze and Dordogne (Operation Brehmer, March 25–April 15), and finally, returning to Ain and Jura for Bloody Easter (Operation Spring, April 7–18).[36] These offensives, whose chief aim was to wipe out the maquis leaders, also sought to terrorize civilians.[37]

This harder line was partly the expression of the increasingly repressive orientation of Nazi leaders. On February 3, 1944, Marshal Hugo Sperrle, a member of the general staff, had promulgated an extremely brutal decree applicable to France and Belgium. In case of attack, German troops were to respond immediately, if necessary without awaiting the approval of their superiors. The combat zone was to be sealed off, civilians arrested, and the houses from which the shots were coming burned down.[38] On March 4, 1944, Marshal Keitel cracked down even more. All assaults against members of the Wehrmacht were to be considered acts of franc-tireurs, and the perpetrators shot straightaway. "Plainly, the German units were commanded to take no prisoners during battles," writes Eismann.[39] Granted, these instructions were not necessarily followed to the letter, and the occupier did not always engage in barbaric acts. On March 1, 1944, the western command told the Wehrmacht high command that more drastic measures seemed pointless. "Terrorists, saboteurs, those who come to their assistance, their accomplices, and all suspect subjects are already treated with a severity impossible to intensify. The western commander would not hesitate to expand these draconian measures to other groups if they had the slightest chance of success. After long and extensive experience in the west, [he knows] that is not the case."[40]

The year 1944 was nonetheless marked by a radicalization of the repression, in both the SS groups and in the Wehrmacht units. Although it was a unit of the Black Order that set fire to Oradour-sur-Glane on July 10, 1944, causing the death of 642 men, women, and children, all civilians—some of whom were burned alive in the village church—it was a division of the regular army that in late July 1944 engaged in the bloody repression of the maquis of the Vercors. True, General Pflaum, commander of the 157th Reserve Division, had laid his cards on the table in his instructions of July 27: "The task at hand is to make a methodical sweep of the Vercors, to find the bands of terrorists dispersed in their places of refuge, and to exterminate them completely; also to uncover the enemy's stockpiled munitions and supplies, to destroy their lairs and storehouses, in order to make any reinstallation of the enemy in the Vercors an impossibility in the future."[41] The Wehrmacht, in other words, was now following the methods of the SS, targeting civilians as much as the FFI, to prevent the maquis from reconstituting itself.[42]

Several factors explain the radicalization. In the first place, the deterioration of the military situation unleashed the ferocity of the German authorities. At a time when the very survival of the Reich, threatened in both the east and the west, was in the balance, the Germans set out to apply their most barbaric law without qualms. To fight bands in the south, the western command issued the following order on June 8, 1944: "The forces of the Resistance must be destroyed in rapid and wide-ranging actions. To reestablish calm and security, the most rigorous measures are called for. They are designed to intimidate the residents of these perpetually infested regions, to suppress their desire to take in groups of resistance fighters and to be led by them, and finally, to serve as a warning to the population as a whole. In these critical moments, it is indispensable to give proof of an unconditional harshness, in order to eliminate all danger in the rear of the fighting troops and to prevent even heavier bloodshed among the troops and civilian population in the future."[43] In the second place, resistance actions now threatened the security of the troops. Having increased the number of ambushes, the resistance represented a military danger, which the Wehrmacht and the SS had no qualms about eradicating. And the Germans were having no success in controlling the guerrilla war by conventional means. Unable to force the resistance into open battle, they developed tactics meant to render entire regions unusable.[44] In the third place, that brutalization, sometimes (but not always) entailed the application to the western zone of the barbaric methods used in the east. Men and units transferred from the Russian front to the western theater of operations used procedures they had employed against the partisans and the Soviet population. Such was the case for the 2nd SS Panzer Division Das Reich. Created in October 1939 under the name SS-Verfügungs-Division, it fought in the west in May–June 1940, in the Balkans in spring 1941, and then in the Soviet Union during the summer. From the outset, it violated the rules of war based on its ideological view of the enemy and its need to establish its professional reputation. Even so, the eastern campaign had changed its view of things, inciting it to attack populations it believed were supporting the partisans.[45] As one of its battalion commanders summed it up, "civilians in Russia are to be treated first and foremost as declared enemies and not as an innocent civilian population."[46] General Lammerding's men alone murdered more than half the individuals considered francstireurs—4,000 out of 7,900—during operations conducted under the aegis of the military command in France between June 6 and July 4, 1944, and took only 400 prisoners. By contrast, during the same period, the German forces captured 4,800.[47] The operations conducted against the maquis in spring 1944, however, did not make use of any units coming from the eastern front. As Ahlrich Meyer points out, they mobilized only security troops or reserve troops placed under the orders of the military command.[48]

That savagery, far from stemming exclusively from Nazi ideology, had its origins in a mind-set solidly rooted in the German army, if not in the population at large. On the one hand, jurists and the military staff were perpetuating a typically German tradition, that of the *Kriegsnotwendigkeit*—the necessity of war—which granted priority to military imperatives over humanitarian considerations and interpreted human rights in a manner that was minimalist to say the least.[49] On the other, since the war of 1870 the franc-tireur had been viewed as a criminal all the more cowardly in that, far from waging battle openly, he wore no uniform and struck combatants from behind. In Belgium during World War I, "mass executions of civilians and prisoners of war, along with the torching of villages, appeared to German soldiers to be a legitimate way to protect themselves as they advanced. Because it was believed that women and children were taking part in the fighting, they too were often the victims of these reprisal measures."[50] These stereotypes, far from disappearing with the Treaty of Versailles, remained very much alive during the interwar period, perpetuated "in a large body of sensationalist literature and in many memoirs."[51] The writings provided fodder for a mind-set that fueled the savagery perpetrated by Nazi troops in both the west and the east.

Vichy was not to be outdone. Philippe Pétain, observing in 1943 that the French police were showing less zeal, in January created the Milice and, on December 30 of the same year, named its leader, Joseph Darnand, to head the Secrétariat au Maintien de l'Ordre (Office for Maintaining Order). In charge of some 150,000 men, he showed no mercy. Darnand, vested with full powers to repress the resistance by the decree of January 10, 1944,[52] gradually came to control the entire system of repression, from the law and order forces to the judicial apparatus to the prisons. In particular, on January 20, 1944, the regime created courts-martial, charged with sentencing resistance fighters to death in a manner that was expeditious to say the least. The accused had no lawyers or right of appeal, and judges could impose only one penalty: death by firing squad.[53] Some two hundred executions took place within that framework between February and August 1944,[54] and the courts-martial of Paris, Lyon, Annecy, and Limoges stood out for their brutality.

These factors explain why resistance losses were heavier by far in 1944 than during the three previous years.

## The Toll of the Repression

The repression of the resistance became harsher over time, which explains the scope of its losses. In all, the Germans shot slightly fewer than 4,000 people during the occupation, whether they were judged by a military tribunal or murdered as hostages.[55] In addition, 15,000 civilians were killed during fighting between troops and partisans.[56] Finally, 88,000 people were deported on other than racial grounds; 35,000 did not return from the concentration camps.[57] This death toll, presented in its broad outlines, should not conceal the changes that occurred over time or the many factors that motivated the repression.

Overall, then, the repression tended to intensify and to become more complicated, as the occupier expanded his arsenal, adding new repressive instruments to the old. On January 7, 1944, Ambassador Otto Abetz mentioned that 34,977 people had been apprehended by the German police "for actions that were Gaullist, Marxist, or otherwise hostile to the Reich," and that 9,117 had been detained by the French police.[58] But the pace accelerated. For example, 21,600 people were deported to concentration camps between June 6, 1944, and the end of November: nearly 1 in 3 deportations to Germany thus occurred after Operation Overlord.[59] Similarly, executions of hostages and those who had received death sentences, as well as summary executions, had been more or less abandoned, but they resumed in July 1943 and increased in 1944: 42 percent of executions occurred in that one year.[60] Finally, for obvious reasons, most of the resistance fighters who died in battle fell in 1944, in a context now dominated by guerrilla warfare. The MbF claimed it killed 7,900 maquisards during the period between June 6 and July 4, 1944.[61] These data confirm that the Germans gradually radicalized the fight against the army of shadows and that 1944 marked a catastrophic peak in that regard.

The motivations for the repression also changed over time. At first, because of the attacks committed against occupation troops, the Germans placed harsh sanctions on the possession of weapons: between September 1941 and September 1942, that infraction accounted for more than 31 percent of death sentences.[62] They persisted on that path and continued to repress mercilessly resistance fighters engaged in military action, whether they were transmitting intelligence to the Allies or fighting with weapons in hand. Hence, maquisards, "pianists," and intelligence agents risked their lives to a greater degree than underground fighters who employed a civilian strategy. For example, of some 2,000 agents in the CND network, 30 were executed.[63] But the 87 members of the DF who were shot (12.5 percent of the losses in that movement) were executed—and very often tortured—because they were fighting as soldiers and not because they were distributing an underground newspaper.[64] Furthermore, arrested maquisards were usually executed immediately, particularly in the south of France, where the large maquis were concentrated in 1944.[65]

The intransigence of the Germans very often turned into a vendetta. On the eve of defeat, the Nazis made sure to murder in their camps some leaders of the armed struggle, to whom they attributed—not without reason—a role in the defeat. Charles Delestraint, head of the AS, received a bullet to the back of the neck on April 19, 1945, only a few days before the liberation of Dachau. Likewise, deported SOE agents were put to death in two waves: the first occurred in September 1944, the second on March 29, 1945. "On directives issuing directly from Hitler, most of them were hanged . . . with nooses made of piano wire. This was meant to make their deaths as slow and as degrading as could be," writes historian M. R. D. Foot.[66] That brutality does not mean that the Germans were more indulgent toward resisters engaged in a civilian strategy. If a captured underground fighter was not executed, he was usually deported, a fate that befell 47 percent of the members of the DF who had been arrested.[67]

The radicalization of the repression was accompanied by an expansion of its targets. To be sure, resistance fighters composed the bulk of the convoys headed for prisons and concentration camps (not to be confused with the death camps, where the Jews were exterminated). Based on a sample, Jean Quellien estimates that 44 percent of deportees sent to the camps or to German jails belonged to the organized resistance.[68] Of that first group, 37 percent belonged to a Communist organization, 28 percent to one of the movements, and 35 percent to a network.[69] Furthermore, 29 percent, though not belonging to an underground group, were part of the civilian resistance. The most minor of gestures could result in deportation to the camps. One woman was deported for sticking out her tongue at a German officer; a gymnastics teacher, for teaching patriotic songs to his students; residents of Alsace-Moselle, for wearing the Basque beret or singing "La Marseillaise."[70] Naturally, the Germans sanctioned more serious acts by French people, whether they had assisted Allied aviators, supplied the maquis with provisions, or lodged an STO evader. One must not exaggerate, however. Indeed, as Raphaël Spina notes, those deported for taking in an evader "constituted a tiny minority of the victims of repression: for the occupier, those who did nothing more than refuse to work for Germany were only a secondary concern. In the Basses-Pyrénées department, where the resistance was particularly active, only twenty-eight German arrests were associated with the STO—for avoiding service or for harboring evaders. In Vaucluse, only twenty-four evaders were deported."[71] Finally, more than one deportee in four—that is, 27 percent—had maintained no real relation with the army of shadows. Those sent to the camps or to prison included Spanish prisoners of war enlisted in the French army in 1939 (28 percent), victims chosen at random in roundups (25 percent), ordinary criminals (17 percent), hostages (9 percent), and Communists who had not been involved in the resistance (9 percent).[72]

The repression therefore expanded in scope as time went on. While targeting the resistance as its top priority, it gradually came to strike civilians who supported the army of shadows or who might support it. The occupation authorities engaged in indiscriminate roundups in retaliation for demonstrations or attacks. On January 22 and 23, 1943, the Wehrmacht proclaimed a state of emergency in Marseilles, and French forces made mass arrests on the pretext of fighting the resistance. Nearly 6,000 people were detained; 1,642 were handed over to the Germans; and 782 Jews were sent to the death camps.[73] After the demonstration in Grenoble on November 11, 1943, the Germans arrested about a thousand people and deported the able-bodied men.[74] This modus operandi was characteristic of the punitive expeditions organized against the maquis. During Operation Corporal, the 157th Reserve Division killed 20 resistance fighters and 39 civilians.[75] The same unit shot 56 maquisards during Bloody Easter in Saint-Claude and also deported 486 people, half of whom had no connection to the resistance.[76] Of some 15,000 victims of the fight against partisans tallied for 1944, a third did not belong to the army of shadows.[77] This mass terror was combined with more targeted operations. Beginning in 1943, the Germans, alarmed by the deposition of Mussolini, seized individuals whom they feared were dissidents. Parliamentarians (Henri Maupoil, Alphonse Warusfel, Georges Maurice, and others), senior figures of the Vichy regime (General La Porte du Theil, for example), and personalities judged dangerous (Ambassador André François-Poncet) joined hostages whom the Reich had already transferred across the Rhine, such as General Maxime Weygand and Prime Ministers Léon Blum, Édouard Daladier, and Paul Reynaud.

The desire to cut off the resistance from a population judged— rightly or wrongly—to be complicitous with the partisans does not in itself explain the escalation. As of 1943, deportation was also considered an appropriate means for the impressment of slave labor. Faced with a growing shortage of workers, the Reich replaced those who had gone off to serve as soldiers in the Wehrmacht with STO conscripts but also with convicts. Before that time, deportation was a consequence of arrest. But Jean Quellien wonders: "Is it not conceivable that deportation (that is, the need to find labor for the camps) now governed, at least in part, repressive policy and arrests?"[78] That would explain why, in addition to resistance fighters, thousands of people were sent to the Nazi camps on the most trivial grounds. Describing the prisoners in his train car, Claude Bourdet confirms that hypothesis in empirical terms: "They were not resistance fighters for the most part but rather people arrested willy-nilly, rounded up, or residents of villages who were deported simply because there was a maquis in the vicinity. There were also many individuals who had been arrested at the Old Port of Marseilles when it was demolished. 'Arrested' is an overstatement: they were taken, that's all. Among them were pimps, traffickers of various kinds, fellows with shady professions, and also ordinary people, Marseillais who had happened to be there."[79] At a time when Joseph Goebbels had proclaimed "total war," deportation made it possible to replace the millions of men who had left for the front with slaves toiling away in the camps. As of spring 1944, by contrast, deportation belonged to a programmatic repression with the dreaded prospect of the Allied landing in view. In any case, it should be emphasized that resistance fighters constituted three-quarters of the convoys. Whether they were shot, deported, or killed with weapons in hand, they often paid the ultimate price for their engagement.

## Tragic Fates

Arrested resistance fighters faced a long ordeal. As a general rule, they were detained not during a routine identity check but after their organization had been infiltrated by the repressive services. D'Estienne d'Orves, for example, was betrayed by his radio operator, Marty, who had placed himself in the service of the Abwehr. Émile Marongin (Elio), after offering his services to the Germans, joined the DF in early 1943 and brought down forty-eight of its members.[80] Sometimes, an arrested resister "gave up" his group after cracking under torture. It should be pointed out, however, that torture was not used systematically. For example, Claude Bourdet, arrested on March 25, 1944, endured a hail of blows but was not subjected to extreme abuse.[81] Similarly, the resistance fighters in the DF who were arrested as a result of Elio's betrayal were spared being tortured. Others were not so lucky, however, especially if they were Communists or belonged to networks or other paramilitary organizations. Their torturers, whether French or German, hoped to obtain information within the shortest delay. An agent of the BCRA named Stéphane Hessel, apprehended on July 10, 1944, endured the bath torture. After being immersed for the fourth time, he decided to talk, though he still hoped to mislead his tormentors by embroidering on "all the themes of underground activity."[82]

The Germans, whether or not they used torture, managed to turn some resistance fighters. Some merely pretended to place themselves in the service of the Reich. Léopold Trepper, head of the Orchestre Rouge network, worked for the Soviets and was arrested in November 1942. He feigned going over to the other side, allowing his jailers to set up a fake radio message intended to hoodwink Stalin by claiming that London and Washington were negotiating a separate peace behind his back. Having won the confidence of his guards, he managed to give them the slip in September 1943, gaining permission to go into the Bailly pharmacy, then leaving by the back door.[83] Others consented to work for the occupier purely out of greed. Still others acted for political reasons or out of calculation. André Grandclément, inspired by anti-Communist zeal, revealed the weapons caches of the OCM in the southwest in exchange for the release of his men. He also agreed to turn his groups into "maquis blancs," which the Germans hoped would fight Communism after they had gone. He was executed by men of the resistance on July 28, 1944.

Interrogations, often punctuated by violence, were difficult to bear. As a general rule, underground groups asked their members to hold out for twenty-four or forty-eight hours, time to implement security measures. Resistance fighters then played a cat-and-mouse game, trying to release information they hoped would be inconsequential. Claude Bourdet recounts: "I had been identified, but I knew from the organization chart [which I had been able to consult, taking advantage of the absence of my guards] that my duties were not clear in the Gestapo's mind. And I also knew there were enormous holes in their diagram, which one had at all cost to avoid filling. As the interrogation proceeded, as I responded in great detail, all the while carefully avoiding broaching a new subject, I gradually succeeded in portraying my duties as being entirely oriented toward the political problems of the postwar period and the naming of a new administration—which was partly true, but which represented only a portion, and not the most important portion, of my activities."[84] Likewise, Pierre Georges (Fabien), apprehended on November 30, 1942, by a brigade of the 4th Division, was abominably tortured but made every effort to say as little as possible, despite the blows: "Names, facts that the police had known for a long time, inconsequential details about the attacks committed in Paris the previous autumn, then in the summer in Franche-Comté, names of militants shot months before."[85] That strategy produced crises of conscience, however, as Stéphane Hessel acknowledges: "If, when the war was over, I had managed to consult my file with the reports of my interrogations at the Gestapo, would I have been appalled by revelations that might have put my comrades in danger? Would I have been relieved by the innocuousness of my testimony and the subtlety of my ruses?"[86] Others attempted to keep silent under the blows. Contrary to legend, many talked, "which may be more horrible," André Malraux would say, when Jean Moulin's remains were transferred to the Panthéon. Some, like Jacques Bingen and Pierre Brossolette, chose to commit suicide.

After being interrogated, resistance fighters were returned to their cells, at Fresnes, La Santé, or Cherche-Midi in Paris, at Montluc or Saint-Paul in Lyon. If they were executed, they faced the firing squad at Mont-Valérien, at the Souges camp, at Châteaubriant (Loire-Atlantique), at the fortress of Duchère in Lyon, or in the ditches of the citadel of Arras. If they were condemned to deportation, they went to a transit camp: Compiègne-Royallieu and Fort Romainville (for women especially, as of 1943) served the Paris region. Then the long odyssey began. The journey by cattle car went on for several days—forty-eight hours in Christian Pineau's case, seventy-two hours for Claude Bourdet. Upon their arrival in Buchenwald, Mauthausen, or Dachau for the men, Ravensbrück for the women, resistance fighters, deprived of their civilian effects, sometimes beaten, discovered the grim realities of the concentration camp, which, in 40 percent of cases, turned out to be their grave.

## The Resistance Vitiated

Was the repression that the French and German police forces conducted effective? The response to that crucial question depends, of course, on the point of view adopted.

In the struggle they waged against the French resistance, law enforcement services recorded a few successes. In the first place, they managed to dismantle General de Gaulle's delegation by neutralizing Jean Moulin, then Pierre Brossolette, and by seizing the archives of rue de la Pompe, all hard blows from which the resistance never really recovered. Their actions proved equally effective in certain regions. When André Grandclément was turned, the result was paralysis in the Bordeaux region, which, despite the efforts of Claude Bonnier, the DMR, never rebounded from the betrayal. Likewise, several CDLs were wiped out before summer 1944, including those of Haute-Garonne, Haute-Vienne, Seine-Inférieure, and Calvados—and that list is far from exhaustive.[87] A few movements literally lost their heads. For example, all the leaders of the CDLL died between 1940 and 1944. Finally and perhaps especially, the major maquis, from Glières to the Vercors to Mont-Mouchet, were decimated before they were able to take action, with the possible exception of Saint-Marcel, which was, however, assisted by regular soldiers. German historian Eberhard Jäckel concludes: "Nowhere, in fact, did the Resistance or the maquis have a decisive impact on the outcome of the war, and the worries they caused the leaders of the Reich must have seemed very secondary, compared to the situation on the front where the landing would occur"[88]—not to mention the Russian front.

In more general terms, the resistance was not in a position to launch national insurrection, the dream of the PCF and a measure advocated by Charles de Gaulle. And though Paris provided a striking counterexample to that rule, the mobilization of Parisians cannot be compared to that of the Varsovians, who joined the fray by the tens of thousands. The terror inspired by barbaric Nazi practices, whether that meant torture or deportation to the camps, does not in itself explain the cautiousness of French society, which, though it hated the occupier, was often reluctant to fight.

The efficiency of the German repressive services was certainly well served by the Vichy regime. Neither the SiPo-SD nor the MbF possessed sufficient forces to monitor the entire population. After Karl Oberg's arrival in early June 1942, the SiPo-SD depended on only 2,400 men,[89] which rose to 3,000 after the invasion of the free zone.[90] That contingent was too small to control the doings of 40 million French people. As a result, the assistance of the French State was imperative. Vichy did not fail to meet its masters' expectations. It proved particularly harsh toward the Communists, who, as a general rule, were arrested by its police forces. It was also unyielding toward the Gaullists, at least until 1942. After the defeat at Stalingrad, by contrast, the zeal of police officers and judges flagged. The wind was shifting in favor of the Allies, and the men in charge of the repression faced the prospect of having to give an accounting. That cooled their ardor. "Inertia and passivity developed in the course of 1943 among the ranks of the police officers, who were not all enthusiastic about the peculiar nature of their new missions, and especially, were not impervious to the shift in the direction of the war and of public opinion," confirm Jean-Marc Berlière and Laurent Chabrun.[91]

True, the resistance did not hesitate to threaten them. A tract distributed by the MUR in spring 1944 warned: "You are individually and fully responsible before the court of the people of liberated France. We are keeping a meticulous record of the activities of every police officer, gendarme, or other law enforcement agent. Do not say later, when it is too late: 'What could we do? We had orders, and they had to be carried out.'"[92] In addition, the army of shadows sent little coffins to intimidate some collaborators, whom the BBC for its part threatened by name. And the resistance sometimes took action. In Nice, the irregular group of the Armée Juive (Jewish Army) executed one of the White Russians working with the team of physiognomists charged with denouncing Jews in hiding to the SS officer Aloïs Brunner.[93] Jewish resistance fighters threatened and sometimes attacked leaders of the Commissariat Général aux Questions Juives (General Commission for Jewish Questions) in Marseilles and especially in Toulouse, which may have had some impact on "the slowdown of despoliation operations observed in the region beginning in 1943."[94] Information about police officers was also kept on file by the Communists. When Roger Linet (Rivière), leader of the FTP for the Paris region, was arrested, police officers came across a set of index cards bearing their names, which disturbed them: not only had "'traitors' handed over colleagues' names and addresses to the FTP—but their names had just become fodder for the BBC, so that everyone would understand that the bill would come due one day. For a time, that had a chilling effect on the 'thugs.'"[95] The resistance directly targeted informers, police officers, and magistrates judged to be too zealous. On May 31, 1942, two municipal police officers were taken down by a group protecting militant Communist women distributing canned goods seized from an Eco store.[96] On April 10, 1943, Georges Vallette called out to guardians of the peace, directing them toward the attackers of Marcel Capron, a Communist deputy who had gone over to the collaborationist camp and whom the PCF had just executed. Three weeks later, Vallette was murdered in retaliation.[97] In December 1943, police stations, including the one in Quimper, were targeted by the resistance, which subsequently prompted police officers in the prefecture of Finistère to be "discreet."[98] In Lyon, Jacques Faure-Tinguély, a judge in the Section Spéciale, was taken down at his home by an FTP-MOI commando, an event that played a role in "increasing the climate of fear reigning within the magistrature."[99] The resistance, with Communists in the lead, thus made every effort to organize a counterterrorist campaign that would cool the enthusiasm of the forces of law and order.

The rank and file, however, must be distinguished from the higher echelons. Indeed, though agents on the ground proved less inclined to hunt down soldiers in the army of shadows, their leaders demonstrated absolute determination, which found expression in the creation of the Milice. Joseph Darnand did not bother to make distinctions. As he told the Paris press on February 10, 1944: "I do not differentiate among outlaws; we will not differentiate between the murderers and the misguided, once they are determined to resist."[100] Raymond Clemoz, his chief of staff, noted: "Staff morale: staff members are manifestly impressed by the distinction sometimes made between 'good terrorists' and 'bad terrorists.' Nevertheless, they must at all cost be made to understand that the agent on the ground is absolutely incapable of making that subtle and somewhat specious distinction. Any individual not in compliance with orders from the police or the peacekeeping forces must be considered a public enemy and treated as such."[101] In fact, the Nazis distinguished themselves by their barbarism. They made extensive use of torture: it was practiced in Vichy at the Petit-Casino, the Hôtel du Parc Lardy, and the Château des Brosses; in Lyon within the walls of Montluc prison and in the barracks of the Alcazar; in Grenoble in a villa located on rue Henri-Ding; and in Paris at the headquarters of the Milice itself, at 44 rue Le Peletier.[102] The Milice also engaged in massacres, especially after the Allied landing. On Joseph Lécussan's orders, it arrested the Jews of Saint-Armand-Montrond in Cher on the night of July 21, 1944, murdering thirty-six people in all.[103] In addition, the Groupe des Forces de Limoges, commanded by Colonel Mahuet, carried out multiple executions in Limousin, particularly in Magnac-Laval. And the some 250 Francs-Gardes under Chief di Costanzo undertook a reign of terror in Brittany.[104]

Finally, the Germans went fishing for recruits in the waters of collaboration and in the depths of the underworld, seeking devoted auxiliaries. Motivated by a combination of ideology and greed, they ravaged the ranks of the resistance. "Employed by the Abwehr or by SS officers from the SiPo-SD, which engaged in a curious game of one-upmanship in that area, Pierre Loutrel, aka 'Pierrot la Valise,' Abel Danos, aka 'Le Mammouth,' Jean-Michel Chaves, aka 'Nez de Braise,' René Launay, 'Feu-feu le Riton,' 'François le Mauvais,' 'Fredo la Terreur du Gnouff' . . . exchanged ten, fifteen, or twenty years of prison for freedom, cars, plentiful gasoline, weapons, the *carton*—a German police card—and impunity."[105] The French Gestapo on rue Lauriston, headed by Henri Chamberlain (known as Lafont) and Pierre Bonny, a police inspector dismissed for graft in 1935, distinguished itself by the scope of its crimes. But other dens also thrived: the gang of Corsicans on boulevard Flandrin, the Masuy gang on avenue Henri-Martin, the gang of Frédéric Martin, known as "Rudi von Mérode." These groups enlisted "traffickers in the black market, shopkeepers and artisans bankrupted by the occupation, men from the underworld, ordinary prisoners released by the Germans and immediately hired in their service, the unemployed, fanatics, drug addicts, prostitutes, unscrupulous doctors, shady lawyers, snitches by vice or vocation, pimps, art appraisers, bankers, workers, and bosses."[106] Unlike the occupier, they were well versed not only in the language but also in the habits and customs of their country and could more easily infiltrate underground organizations. These zealous auxiliaries were notable for the brutality of their interrogations—Masuy is believed to have invented the bath torture—and the relentlessness of their thieving.

Neither the French State nor the German occupier achieved its ends, however. One thing is clear: the resistance was stronger in 1944 than in 1940, a sign that, despite the blows dealt it, it was able to grow larger and more powerful. In addition, the population viewed it as completely legitimate. Upon liberation, the substitution of the Gaullist power for the Vichy authorities proceeded smoothly, even though the Nazis and the Marshal's henchmen had attempted to criminalize it, portraying it as an underworld dominated by Jews, foreigners, and Communists. From that standpoint, the "red poster," which became the subject of a 1955 poem by Louis Aragon, was a powerful symbol. That poster, put up on walls in 1944 during the trial of twenty-three immigrant Communists—including Missak Manouchian and Joseph Boczor—denounced "liberation by the criminal army." It attempted to exploit the fears of the French population by presenting the resistance fighters as stateless persons from the underworld who used indiscriminate violence. It did not, however, delegitimize the army of shadows, a force that had come of age.

In truth, the resistance had been able to adapt. The loss of the leaders of the delegation led it to decentralize, a move the Gaullist authority had long rejected but which proved its effectiveness during the battles of 1944. In addition, the information supplied to the Allies through the networks or movements grew in importance, as the huge increase in telegrams and pieces of mail received by the BCRA confirms. Finally, the protection provided to the general population made it possible to end STO deportations in summer 1943 and also to save 75 percent of the Jews from death—though that positive outcome cannot be credited solely to the organized resistance.

These successes, however, often left a bitter taste behind. Resistance fighters were hoping that a new France would rise up as a result of their sacrifices. In that respect, many expectations were dashed, and liberation quickly came to be considered an incomplete victory.

## Chapter 17

# Incomplete Victory

AT THE END of the war, resistance fighters were dreaming of a new France, having outlined the form it would take during the dark years of occupation. And in fact, the GPRF took a new path in 1944. The constitutional laws of 1875 were replaced by a new constitution in 1946, and the Third Republic gave way to the Fourth. The winds of reform also seemed to be blowing in French public life, a change symbolized by the victories of the left and the decline of the rightist parties. Furthermore, whereas deflation, crisis, and a preoccupation with preserving economic and social structures had marked the interwar period, it was growth, modernization, and social justice that prevailed upon liberation. It is obvious that, in 1945, France adopted novel approaches in its efforts at rebirth. But that did not signal a victory for the resistance.

## Political Reform

The resistance aspired to play a political role in postwar France, an ambition shared by Charles de Gaulle and by the principal underground movements. On April 20, 1943, de Gaulle had exclaimed on the BBC: "New institutions will be needed to lead and guide this new nation in the future. The collapse of the bodies that claimed to be leading the country was only too clear and ruinous. Everything France will have endured, she will not have endured simply to be satisfied with whited sepulchres."[1] This ambition coincided with the dreams of the internal resistance. "We think it wise to prepare immediately for the reconstruction of French society, if we do not want people more adept than we, who until now have kept their distance from the Resistance, to impose themselves in our place. We think it desirable that the Resistance should rule and lead the Revolution to come. We want the Resistance to usher in the Revolution," *Défense de la France* explained in 1944.[2] But the details still had to be worked out. To move from the shadows into the light, the resistance would first have to organize itself into a party (or parties) capable of playing a leading role in political life and competing in the electoral process. Its men would then have to win the confidence of voters.

Resistance fighters had a sizable advantage when soliciting votes. Even before the liberation of the territory, the Gaullist authority had undertaken a political purge. The decree of April 21, 1944, excluded from the assemblies and from general and municipal councils all figures compromised by collaboration or by support of the Vichy regime, unless they gave proof of their activity in the resistance. The decree of April 6, 1945, relaxed these prohibitive criteria, simply barring members of governments formed after June 16, 1940, from occupying seats on the Assemblée Constituante (Constituent Assembly) and on local councils, along with profiteers, people dismissed from public employment or stripped of the right to practice their profession for at least two years, and finally, national or departmental councilors—unless they had been elected before the war. Parliamentarians who had accepted a position offered by the French State were also excluded. The authorities took a moderate line on the matter of the purge: electoral races were very free at the municipal and departmental levels, but the general elections were closely watched.

The purge, first entrusted to prefects, and later, as of April 6, 1945, to a board of examiners, barred 321 parliamentarians in all—that is, nearly a third of the members who had had seats in the legislature in 1939. When the 173 elected officials who had died of various causes during the occupation are factored in, more than 50 percent were unable to solicit votes from their fellow citizens in 1945. The political parties also eliminated their pariahs. The SFIO ousted eighty-four parliamentarians, the Radical Party about thirty, and the right-wing Fédération Républicaine (Republican Federation) about fifteen. All things considered, these expulsions made it possible to introduce widespread reform of the political institutions by favoring the entry of men from the army of shadows.

The Constituent Assembly elected on October 21, 1945, confirmed the transformation of the political staff. Of 586 deputies, only 121 had held seats before the war.[3] Four-fifths of the constituents therefore crossed the threshold of an assembly for the first time. And the change in personnel was accompanied by a clear political shift. The left dominated, having obtained a comfortable majority. The PCF rounded up 5 million votes and 148 seats; the SFIO, 4.7 million votes and 135 seats. The Mouvement Républicain Populaire (MRP; Popular Republican Movement), which represented the Christian Democratic family, made a good showing (4.9 million votes, 143 seats), whereas the traditional powers were in a state of collapse. The moderates attracted only 2.8 million voters (65 seats), and the Radicals, previously dominant—111 of them had held seats in the Palais-Bourbon in 1939—won only 1.7 million votes and 31 seats. The tidal wave of liberation therefore seems to have engulfed the traditional right and the disciples of Édouard Herriot, trends that the local elections had anticipated: in April and May 1945, the moderate parties had won only 15,655 of the 35,307 municipalities, whereas they had been in charge of 22,685 in 1935. The Radicals suffered comparable erosion (6,436 versus 9,162 in 1935). By contrast, the Marxist parties came out well. The Socialists headed 4,115 councils, compared to 1,376 before the war. The Communists made even more progress: 1,413 town halls hoisted the Red Flag, versus 310 in 1939.[4]

From a political standpoint, therefore, the year 1945 was marked by discontinuity. The old groups vanished, worn down by the crisis of the interwar period and the compromises of the Vichy era. A new political staff took power at both the local and national levels, and the right yielded power to the left, an unprecedented phenomenon during the Third Republic, with the exception of the brief interlude of the FP. In that respect, the liberation was as much a renovation, marked by the emergence of a new political staff, as a revival—the victory of the left. But did these changes really mark the triumph of the resistance? There is reason for doubt.

## The Powerlessness of the Resistance

In actuality, the resistance did not manage to reshape the political field. In terms of political organizations, only one succeeded in forming: the Union Démocratique et Socialiste de la Résistance (UDSR; Democratic and Socialist Union of the Resistance). Granted, the MRP proudly declared its resistance origins, corroborated by the indisputable pedigree of its leaders, Pierre Henri Teitgen, François de Menthon, and Maurice Schumann. But it styled itself more the heir of Le Sillon (The Furrow) and of the defunct Parti Démocrate Populaire (Popular Democratic Party) than that of Jean Moulin or Henri Frenay. Above all, its aim was to reconcile the church and the republic on the basis of social reform, and it followed in Catholicism's wake more than it competed with the army of shadows.

It is true that General de Gaulle, in creating a movement under his banner, might have provided a political outlet for wartime Gaullism. The head of the GPRF refused to take that path, even though Frenay pleaded with him to head up a labor movement: "No, Frenay, I will not do it. That is not my role. I understand your apprehensions, and the spectacle of the current wheeling and dealing in the Assembly and elsewhere is not likely to dissipate it. But believe me, there is only one solution for men like you, and that is to return to the parties and to guide them, transform them, from the inside. . . . All the rest is nothing but illusion."[5] That advice was given to other loyalists, Jacques Chaban-Delmas and Michel Debré, for example, both of whom joined the Radical Party.

The refusal can be easily explained. It would have contradicted de Gaulle's principles to assume leadership of an organization. Such an approach would have led him to take sides, whereas he sought to unite the French people. It would have obliged him to become absorbed in minor squabbles, when he wished to place himself above the fray. And finally, it would have impelled him to head up a group that embraced its resistance past, excluding French people who had not engaged in that glorious fight. But less high-minded motivations also guided him. The man of June 18, believing in his destiny, had doubts about the political mission of the resistance and hence about its capacity to attract the votes of its fellow citizens. Above all, he believed himself strong enough to dictate his law to the parties and to the Constituent Assembly. Events dashed that illusion in short order: on January 20, 1946, de Gaulle had to leave the GPRF, a few months after Churchill, his rival and companion in glory, had done the same in Great Britain.

Only the UDSR, therefore, could claim to be keeping "the spirit of the Resistance" alive. In January 1944, the MLN had paved the way by assembling in a single organization Franc-Tireur, Combat, Libération-sud, Résistance, and the DF. That federation, having refused in January 1945 to ally itself with the Communists of the FN, merged with the Union Travailliste (Workers' Union), which ran the OCM and Libération-nord. From that group, the UDSR came into being on June 25, 1945. The new organization, which declared its fidelity to the ideals of the underground, refused to pledge allegiance to the SFIO or to the PCF. It found itself in an awkward position. In breaking away from the FN, the UDSR shattered the unity of the resistance, which it had claimed to embody. When the MRP laid its hands on the Gaullist legacy, proclaiming itself the general's "loyal movement," it deprived the UDSR of its illustrious patron. Above all, the party was faced with a cruel dilemma. To remain an authentic movement rooted in the underground, it had to shut out French people who had not participated in the struggle; in so doing, it condemned itself to marginality. If, conversely, it were to open its doors wide, it would lose its identity. To win at the polls, the resistance thus had to form alliances, at the risk of losing its way in questionable compromises.

In March 1945, the MLN considered uniting with the SFIO, a principle the UDSR ratified in June. In an ideal world, that plan might have had happy results, producing a symbiosis between the old and the new. More generally, the traditional parties might have been resuscitated, had they opened themselves to the lifeblood of the resistance, and resistance fighters might have benefited in turn from a political tradition and political experience, which they most often lacked. That was in fact General de Gaulle's plan. It failed.

## Sclerosis of the Traditional Parties

The traditional parties displayed a certain wariness toward the resistance elements. Naturally, they feared being dispossessed of their power and were sometimes openly contemptuous of these amateurs, often considered soft utopianists. The PCF, whose underground engagement hardly needs to be recalled, proceeded cautiously. Over time, it excluded or expelled indisputable resistance fighters—Charles Tillon in 1952, Georges Guingouin the same year, and Maurice Kriegel-Valrimont in 1961. The independence of mind of these men, the legitimacy they had acquired during the dark years, or the stances they took after liberation were perceived as threats to the Communist leadership. At the same time, some former underground fighters advanced in the hierarchy, though their progress slowed the higher they went.[6] In any event, the process allowed Maurice Thorez and Jacques Duclos to remain in charge of the "Party of the seventy-five thousand executed," without fearing competition from an elite emerging from the underground.

At the doctrinal level, the resistance did not play any role. According to the PCF apparatus, the defeat of 1940 was a logical and predictable event that confirmed the accuracy of the prewar analysis and the deep-seated origins of a catastrophe that arose in the first place from the economic sphere. By that measure, the resistance could add nothing in terms of theory. It simply fueled the flames of propaganda.[7]

The SFIO, which had supported the alliance with the MLN and had sought to transform itself ideologically, returned fairly quickly to its old ways. A few men who had passed through the ranks of the resistance acquired prominence, however. Gaston Defferre, president of the municipal delegation, captured the mayoralty of Marseilles in 1945,[8] and Jean Badiou held on to the keys to Toulouse.[9] Furthermore, the proportion of resistance fighters among parliamentarians, both on the Conseil de la République (Council of the Republic) and in the Assemblée Nationale (National Assembly), remained very high. But should that be seen as a sign of renovation? In actuality, as historian Noëlline Castagnez points out, "the Resistance was not as powerful a factor in advancement, and therefore in rejuvenation, as the Popular Front elections had been in their time. . . . The list system, in giving precedence to the choices made by militants at the expense of voters, allowed for an endogenous revival. That revival, combined with a bonus given to seniority, put a brake on any rejuvenation via the advancement of young, Socialist-leaning resistance fighters."[10] In addition, those who did advance had frequently been card-carrying members before the war; Gaston Defferre, for example, had joined in 1933. There were few elected officials, therefore, whose politicization dated to their experience in the underground. In that respect, Jean-Daniel Jurgensen and Robert Salmon, who came from the DF and won seats as deputies under the SFIO banner in the first Constituent Assembly, were exceptions. Of all the Socialist parliamentarians of the Fourth Republic, 86 percent were new arrivals. But only 12 percent had joined the party after 1939.[11]

Furthermore, the proportion of Socialist parliamentarians who were women was insignificant: under 3 percent. To that extent, "the war truly constituted a discontinuity, since it led to an unprecedented purge of SFIO cadres and particularly of its parliamentarians; but it was neither the fountain of youth hoped for nor the occasion for a salutary diversity."[12] As for the attempts at doctrinal reform formulated by Léon Blum in *À l'échelle humaine (On a Human Scale)*, they remained a dead letter. The SFIO, burned by the electoral results and in competition with a rapidly advancing PCF, closed ranks, an attitude "ratified by the arrival of Guy Mollet's staff in August 1946, which was convinced that a radicalization of its doctrine would be a gauge of recovery."[13] By June 1946, Blum's party had given up the idea of joining with the resistance forces for the general elections, and it waged the fight under its own flag.

Contrary to received wisdom, the promised reforms were therefore limited: the resistance failed to reorganize the political field of the liberation. Its groups were eclipsed by the old parties, which were well served by the system in place. In fact, the list system gave them a decisive advantage, since only organized groups possessed the resources and experience necessary to constitute complete lists at the national level. By contrast, the resistance organizations were political novices and experienced the greatest difficulties in putting forward hundreds of candidates, especially if their people were unknown to the general public. They were ill served by the municipal elections, hastily called in April–May 1945, which left them little time to organize. And local races were a two-edged sword. Although they made possible the advancement of members of the resistance in an individual capacity, they hastened the collapse of the structures that had emerged from the underground, destroying, for example, the framework of the CDLs and favoring the reconstitution of the parties.[14]

The elites of the underground years can hardly be said to have enjoyed a precipitous ascent. Although some resistance fighters managed to gain a foothold, they were rarely newcomers to politics. Teitgen, Menthon, and Schumann had militated in the ranks of the Christian Democrats before the war. Tillon, in addition to having a militant past, had been a deputy in 1939. Even the UDSR did not escape that rule: Antoine Avinin, Pierre Bourdan, and Eugène Claudius-Petit came from the ranks of the LJR. The resistance, then—though this claim is subject to verification—tended to facilitate the advancement of individuals who had been barred access to power by an earlier generation, rather than actually discovering men born to politics in the convulsions of the dark years.

The hypothesis of the left's victory in 1945 requires similar qualifications, since it is based on questionable postulates. In the first place, the magnitude of the change needs to be reassessed, given that the position of the conservatives had been continuously eroding since 1932. From that standpoint, 1945 simply continued a trend that had begun thirteen years earlier, had developed in the municipal elections of 1935, and had become even more pronounced in the general elections of 1936. Second, the MRP, sometimes categorized as leftist, seems rather to have belonged to the rightist camp, as suggested by its voting base and the strategy it adopted: from the outset, it dismissed the platform of the FP.[15] Third, the traditional right had not totally disappeared. In addition to controlling a not insignificant share of local governments, in 1945 it had sixty-two deputies, a reduced but far from negligible force. Fourth, not all the men who had supported the Vichy regime were discredited by their former associations. Camille Laurens, elected in October 1945, had headed the Corporation Paysanne (Peasant Corporation) between 1942 and 1944; Jean Boivin-Champeaux, president of the Républicains Indépendants (Independent Republicans) group on the Council of the Republic, had reported favorably on the plan granting Pétain constituent power in 1940;[16] and Raymond Marcellin, despite being the number two man at the Institut d'Études Corporatives et Sociales (Institute of Corporate and Social Studies) under the occupation, was elected in Morbihan in November 1946. These factors suggest that, in 1945, the left enjoyed a less complete hegemony over the right than is ordinarily believed. The moderates, including the MRP, won more than 40 percent of the vote in 1945; 49 percent if the Radicals are also counted.

The French, then, did not systematically reject the elites of the Third Republic or the supporters of the Vichy regime in favor of men of the resistance. There is verification at the local level for that claim: 228 candidates who had been declared ineligible were nevertheless elected to municipal councils; 77 were defeated; and 23 opted to withdraw.[17] The populace sometimes retained its confidence in administrators who, they believed, had protected them from the rigors of the occupation. Many French people, moreover, while rejecting collaboration, had continued to feel a certain attachment to the Marshal or had even approved of certain parts of his policy. Why penalize elites, therefore, when overall they expressed feelings shared by the masses? Finally, voters may have preferred to keep on elected officials they knew and who had acquired their trust rather than hand over the keys to unknowns, even those bathed in glory.

This overview gives a good indication of the ambiguities of the year 1945, which combined continuities and discontinuities. In many respects, the circumstances of the liberation produced a shakeup that was experienced as such: the left, a majority in the country, prevailed, and the traditional right had trouble recovering from its social conservatism and its heavy support of the French State. The two major conservative parties, the Alliance Démocratique (Democratic Alliance) and the Republican Federation, collapsed, and Radicalism found itself in a rather bad way. The political class, purged to a certain extent, underwent a substantial renovation, opening its doors to men and a few women, often from the resistance, who until then had occupied the lower ranks. In many respects, a changing of the guard had occurred.

A few gravitational forces, however, kept the liberation within the continuity of national history. On closer inspection, the right wing withstood and adapted to the adversity of the time. The MRP and other groups—the Parti Républicain de la Liberté (Republican Party of Liberty), for example—provide an illustration of that capacity for adaptation. It would therefore be more accurate to speak not of decomposition but of recomposition, a process effective enough to allow the party of law and order to regain power in 1952. By contrast, the groups that emerged from the resistance never managed to reshape the political field. Until the launch of the Rassemblement du Peuple Français (Rally of the French People) in 1947, Gaullism had no political outlet. And the UDSR remained a negligible quantity, though it functioned as a swing vote, able to make or unmake majorities.

In addition, the political class, a prisoner of its culture, refused to change the rules of the game, which served its interests. After four years of Vichy authoritarianism, the Third Republic—so decried in the 1930s—had in fact refurbished its image. Conversely, the French State had illustrated the risks of a strong executive branch, particularly when combined with personal power. On that point, Philippe Pétain stood in the antifreedom tradition of Louis-Napoléon Bonaparte and Georges Boulanger, whom the republicans despised. Why, then, give up a proven mode of governance, especially given that the French, without overwhelmingly approving of it, also did not reject it? The Constitution of 1946 thus reproduced in its main lines the constitutional laws of 1875 and their parliamentary orientation. It was not until 1958 that new rules governing the exercise of power would emerge, to the advantage of the executive branch. The resistance, then, ushered in little more change at the institutional level than it did on the political plane. Was that also the case at the economic and social levels?

## The New Deal

In 1945 the GPRF sought to rebuild the country on new foundations. It began a vigorous policy of nationalization affecting primarily the banking sector, energy (gas, electricity, coal), and later insurance. In some cases, nationalization was a penalty for businesses that had collaborated, for example the Renault automakers and the Gnome-et-Rhône airplane engine manufacturer. In addition, the Commmisariat Général au Plan (CGP; Economic Planning Commission), created on January 3, 1946, elaborated guidelines for pursuing five objectives: "increase production, expand trade, raise productivity to the level of the most advanced countries, assure full employment, and raise the standard of living."[18] Finally, two decrees, one on October 4, 1945, the other on October 19, delineated a social security system. Financed not by taxes but by contributions made by employers and wage earners, the plan covered risks associated with work accidents and illness. It also guaranteed a retirement pension to older workers and gave allocations to families so as to raise the sagging birth rate.

In many respects, these measures constituted a revolution. First, they placed the dual imperatives of modernization and growth at the top of the country's priorities, whereas, under the Third Republic, the political class had tried to strike a balance and maintain the existing economic and social structures. The ruling powers had consistently supported an agricultural sector, consisting of small farmers, that was stuck in the past. The French sense of balance the authorities were fond of exalting was pernicious, since large modern firms drove French industry, while an archaic small business sector held it back. The state, taking its distance from liberalist logic, now agreed to intervene in the nation's economic life and bestowed on it an identity that broke with the image of a country of peasants and shopkeepers.[19] It was not without resources: the control of key sectors—credit and energy—offered the state the leverage it needed to realize the objectives outlined in its plan. And the public authorities did not neglect to focus on the fate of the little people: social security guaranteed all wage earners a minimal protection, which the French, unlike the Germans and the British, had long done without.

That revolution, however, cannot be imputed solely to the resistance. Granted, the program of the CNR, approved on March 15, 1944, had in large measure called for the adoption of such measures. But in no wise did it foresee the means to implement them.[20] In fact, the nationalization of certain sectors was introduced in the Constituent Assembly by the political parties, which applied their program without seeking to execute the plans devised by the resistance. And not all the architects of reform had come from the army of shadows. The CGP, for example, was conceived and run by Jean Monnet. A former cognac dealer, Monnet had been General Giraud's political mentor in Algiers. While displaying an indisputable patriotism, he had maintained no connection to the resistance. The CGP, supported by a host of commissions representing management, wage workers, and the administration, in fact adopted a corporatist perspective. To be sure, Monnet felt no nostalgia for the Marshal, nor did he advocate an authoritarian regime. But all in all, he adopted programs that were more beholden to the debates of the interwar period than to the thinking developed in the underground.[21]

Pierre Laroque, the father of social security, had been an adviser to René Belin, minister of labor for Vichy before Laval's return. He was ousted in December 1940 because of his Jewish origins.[22] He then moved to the free zone, where he participated in the work of the CGE, until, in spring 1943, Jean Moulin sent him to establish a liaison in London between that organization and Fighting France.[23] In other words, Laroque had for a time shared the reformist ambitions of a few circles from the early Vichy period. His thinking, fueled by discussions prior to the war, drew as much from that first experience as from the plans formulated in underground organizations.

The structural reforms of the liberation were thus inspired in great part by solutions sketched out in the 1930s and by projects conceived by men who for a time had been part of the Vichy regime. Of twenty-six leaders in charge of the seven most important modernization commissions of the CGP, ten had worked for the French State's organizational committees, Central Office for the Distribution of Industrial Products, or Ministry of Industrial Production.[24] The resistance and its plans therefore occupied only a marginal place in that grand design, which in fact was unanimously approved. Indeed, though the type of businesses that ought to be nationalized gave rise to violent controversies, the principle of nationalization was not challenged.

Three factors explain the force of that consensus. The crisis of the 1930s, as already noted, had shaken many certainties and had led the political, economic, and labor elites to question the viability of a liberal order battered by the consequences of Black Thursday. In addition, many French people believed that the defeat of 1940 was punishment not only for military failure but also for the bankruptcy of an obsolete economic and social system. Finally, the harshness of the occupation had fanned hopes of better days. The resistance, in reflecting on the forms that the economic and social New Deal ought to take, contributed toward popularizing certain options—above all, the triptych of nationalization, central planning, and social security. And in putting that triptych on the political agenda via the CNR, it strengthened the consensus. Nevertheless, the resistance cannot be considered the sole inspiration for the reforms pushed through upon liberation, which owed a great deal to the spirit of the 1930s, one revisited in view of the ordeals of the war and occupation.[25]

Furthermore, the structural reforms did not meet expectations in many cases. "The manner in which the nationalized sector was finally organized was a compromise that fell short of the high hopes of advocates like Philip and Moch," American historian Richard Kuisel points out. "Neither a uniform nor a unified public sector that could supervise the entire economy emerged. The vision of an interlocking group of nationalized industries run by representative style boards and coordinated by a superministry and a national plan that functioned as the opening wedge for socialism vanished in the process of lawmaking."[26] The left was defeated quite quickly: de Gaulle and the MRP opposed the options it was fighting hard to defend. The members called to participate in the work of the CGP were appointed and not elected. Social security relied on an obliging cooperation between management and wage labor, in a spirit very remote from the class struggle; moreover, it was far from universal, since some professions, managers especially, retained their own systems. As a result, frustrations soon fueled the theme of "the liberation betrayed," to borrow the title of a book published by the Communist Pierre Hervé in 1945. Even the reform of the press that the resistance had set in motion did not escape the disenchantment.

## A New Press?

During the interwar period, the press was characterized by its venality. For many years, it had accommodated itself to government subsidies and, more recently, had accepted funds that the Third Reich and Mussolini's Italy dispensed in the hope of winning over French public opinion. The dark years did little to burnish that tarnished image. The great majority of newspapers followed the directives of the Vichy regime, when they did not swing entirely toward a defense of collaboration. As a result, few papers shut down in 1940 or after the invasion of the free zone in November 1942. Upon liberation, therefore, the resistance demanded a moralizing purge of the submissive press. The crusade veiled more mundane interests. The army of shadows was also seeking to publish openly the newspapers it had been distributing under the jackboot.

In summer 1943, the Commission de la Presse (Press Commission) formulated one plan, while the Fédération Nationale de la Presse Clandestine (National Federation of the Underground Press), founded on September 23 of the same year, elaborated another. In April 1944, the two proposals were sent to Algiers for approval, then returned to the metropolis. Finally, on September 30, 1944, a regulation set the rules of the game. It banned the publication of newspapers created after June 25, 1940, the date the armistice went into effect. Prewar newspapers that had continued to publish more than two weeks after that date in the northern zone, or more than two weeks after November 11, 1942, in the southern zone, met the same fate. Press outlets were impounded; newspapers that had been published underground were allowed to use the offices and printing works of the banned ventures, the minister of information having acquired a right of requisition over these properties.[27]

The purge was conducted efficiently. Collaborationist journalists were severely punished. For example, Robert Brasillach, editor in chief of *Je Suis Partout*, and Jean Luchaire, in charge of *Les Nouveaux Temps*, received death sentences and were executed. In addition, a number of national and regional papers were banned. In 1948 sixty-four newspapers were subjected to total confiscation, fifty-one to partial confiscation.[28] The press was thus thoroughly reformed. Although readers remained faithful to the prewar titles that had escaped the wrath of the repression—*Le Figaro*, *La Croix*, *Le Populaire*, *L'Humanité*, and others—they also discovered a plethora of new newspapers: *Combat*, *Franc-Tireur*, *Le Parisien Libéré*, *L'Aurore*, *Le Monde*, and *Défense de la France* (which soon became *France-Soir*).

Did that devolution create the new press the resistance fighters were dreaming of? There is reason for doubt. In the first place, the law was partial in both senses of the word. The astonishingly brief window of two weeks—November 11–26, 1942—allowed *Le Figaro* to be saved but doomed *Le Temps*, which had waited until November 29 to shut down. In addition, dailies that had come out during the occupation obtained the right to publish once again, whether or not they had been absolved: such was the case for the Catholic newspaper *La Croix*. Furthermore, a grave crisis in 1947 bankrupted most of the enterprises, which were coping with salary raises and a substantial increase in the price of paper.[29] Very often as well, the underground staffs were deeply divided. They disagreed both about the political line their newspapers should take (that was the situation at *Combat*) and about the economic alliances they ought to establish to ensure their survival. For example, some members of the DF, determined to make *France-Soir* a mainstream daily, agreed to sell their shares to the Hachette publishing house. By controlling that periodical, Hachette hoped to gain influence within Nouvelles Messageries de la Presse Parisienne, which was in the lucrative business of distributing newspapers. A minority headed by Philippe Viannay rejected that agreement.

The press that came into being during the resistance thus did not manage to realize its objectives. It ran up against a major contradiction: it wavered between the desire to create a new press and the exacting demands of profitability, illustrated by the rapid disappearance of many papers. Twenty-six dailies were published in Paris in 1945; nineteen remained in 1947, only fourteen in 1952.[30] Many opted for profitability. *Défense de la France/France-Soir* hired Pierre Lazareff immediately upon his return from America, so that he might repeat the success of the prewar *Paris-Soir*. And Émilien Amaury, who took charge of *Le Parisien Libéré*, turned it into a prosperous business. "I had trouble imagining that my interlocutor at the time stood within sight of the Promised Land," Charles d'Aragon reports, evoking an encounter with Amaury that occurred upon liberation. "He must have wandered in the desert for thirty years. If he had endured until our difficult times, it was above all because he had understood one truth: to succeed, a newspaper emerging from the Resistance had to resemble in every particular what it was replacing."[31]

In terms of the press, then, the work of the resistance was remarkably limited and its hopes tarnished. Under the Fourth Republic, newspapers were not particularly illustrious, with one exception: over time, *Le Monde* became a newspaper of record. But killjoys will take pleasure in pointing out that the daily of rue des Italiens, created on December 19, 1944, at the request of the public authorities, did not by any means arise from the underground.

Ultimately, then, the influence the resistance exerted over the political, economic, and social sphere appears to have been much more restrained than is generally believed. More broadly, the resistance embodied a rebellious, humanistic, and chivalrous hope and assigned itself a mission: to defeat the Nazi invader and his Vichy lackey. That mission was accomplished on May 8, 1945. Consequently, the return to normality could only prove fatal to the resistance, at the collective as well as the individual level. Furthermore, the strong personalities of the army of shadows rarely played a major political role in postwar

France. The qualities required for the underground struggle—courage, selflessness, refusal to compromise—hardly predestined them for political skirmishes, which explains the miscalculations that many underground heroes made. Their integration proved to be problematic, especially since French society, wishing to turn the page, was often forgetful about its immediate past.

## Chapter 18

# A Divided Memory

IN CONTEMPORARY FRANCE, the memory of the resistance shines with remarkable brilliance. The political parties regularly refer to that glorious page of national history. Since the liberation, the state has kept its flame alive. Films, commemorative plaques, and museums sustain its memory. The memorial status of the resistance remains confused, however, as demonstrated by the quandaries faced by lawmakers, who in 1945 undertook to define normatively the status of former underground fighters.

## Squabbles about Status

In the immediate aftermath of the occupation, parliamentarians took on the task of guaranteeing a number of rights to veterans of the resistance. But the criteria established upon liberation continually evolved, so much so that five laws defining the status of resisters followed in succession between 1945 and 1992.¹ And yet, needless to say, the practices of the underground fighters who had sabotaged railroads, distributed underground newspapers, or prepared for the reestablishment of republican legality during the dark years did not change after the Reich's surrender. The standards applied in the profusion of laws simply reflected the evolution of representations of the resistance after liberation. The resistance fighter, considered a soldier by default in 1945, became in the late twentieth century a pioneer of human rights.

On March 3, 1945, legislation signed by Charles de Gaulle classified the partisan as a soldier who, "*even though* not belonging to the land, sea, or air armies . . . contributed toward saving the nation."² That conception, in exalting military deeds, minimized political and civilian actions, whether taking the form of strikes, demonstrations, the distribution of tracts or newspapers, or aid to proscribed persons—Jews, for example. That understanding had, it is true, three advantages. First, it did not widen the gap between the combatants of 1939–1945 and their glorious predecessors in World War I. Parliamentarians, in the name of that principle, even refused to concede the specificity of the ordeals suffered in the concentration camps. After all, the poilus too had suffered. As noted by a councilor of the republic, assigned in 1948 to report on the bill defining the status of "resistance deportee," the soldiers had spent "very painful years in the trenches and under shellfire. They fought at Verdun, the Somme, Chemin des Dames; they sometimes went without food for several days."[3] Furthermore, that understanding reinforced de Gaulle's essentially military view of a "Thirty-Years' War," a view that served to "de-ideologize" the conflict, now reduced to the neverending clash between France and Germany. In addition to reinforcing national cohesion by closing ranks around the flag, the exclusively martial definition of the resistance ultimately marginalized the PCF, which repeatedly pointed out the working-class, civilian, and political character of the underground fight.

That conception, which came into being with liberation, took root in the following decades. The cold war and the second Stalinist glaciation of the PCF did little to attract recognition to the merits of the civilian resistance. The minister of veteran affairs, given the task of defending a new law, placed the political (by which we are to understand the civilian) and the military in opposition: "Those who participated in these two forms of resistance incurred risks, one can even say equal risks, but not all were combatants in the same capacity. As a result, the definition of risk cannot be retained. The only one . . . that can be retained is the definition of participation in the combat actions of the Resistance. . . . All those who participated in the military part of Resistance actions during the period stipulated must be considered voluntary Resistance combatants, but . . . conversely, those who participated in the political actions of the Resistance movement do not have the right to that definition."[4]

It should be pointed out that this restrictive conception corresponded to the mind-set of parliamentarians and to the approach defended by qualified representatives of the underground. The National Commission, assigned the task of bestowing the title of resistance deportee, judged that, in many cases, "the actions alleged as grounds for the arrest—aid to Israelites or to STO evaders, offenses to the head of state, membership in a secret society, evasion of the STO, anti-German demonstrations and remarks, insults to the German authorities, possession of a hunting rifle or revolver, and so on—cannot be equated with acts characterized as resistance to the enemy."[5] But within the configuration of the cold war, the aim of that definition was also to marginalize the Communist resistance. For example, the men and women who had been sent to Germany after the coal miners' strike in Nord-Pas-de-Calais of May–June 1941 had to wait until 1962 to be recognized as resistance deportees; until that time, the government believed that "the strike in question was motivated by professional interests."[6] Did not Jean Debeaumarchais, secretary-general of the Fédération Nationale des Déportés et Internés Résistants et Patriotes (National Federation of Deported and Imprisoned Resistance Fighters and Patriots), publicly boast "of having personally obtained the rejection of 75 percent of the requests" for resistance internee-deportee cards made by members of the FN?[7] Ethical grounds and base political motives thus combined to devalorize the civilian resistance.

The situation changed in the 1970s, however. In 1975, to strengthen Franco-German friendship, Valéry Giscard d'Estaing decided to abolish the May 8 national holiday, which commemorated the surrender of the Third Reich. Facing an outcry from veterans, he hastened to satisfy one of their demands. On August 6, 1975, he suspended the deadline that, since Charles de Gaulle in 1959, had prevented resistance fighters from applying for a CVR card. The president, however, mistook haste for speed. In modifying by decree what was a matter of law, he laid himself open to censure from the Council of State, which obliged the government to introduce legislation. New bills, which made significant changes to the conception of the resistance that national representatives had proposed, were therefore brought before parliamentarians in the 1980s. According to de Gaulle, soldiers in the army of shadows had simply done their duty all in all; now, however, the notion of voluntary service prevailed. These men "were truly alone with their consciences, and we can only hail their courage today," noted the Socialist minister André Méric.[8] The resister had been considered a soldier by default; he was now viewed as a human rights militant, fighting not against Hitler's Germany but against totalitarianism. The Socialist minister Louis Mexandeau added in 1992: "In terms of democracy, in terms of human rights, the actions of resistance fighters anticipated as it were what came about at the impetus of France in particular, namely, the humanitarian duty to step in, to intervene. It took sixty years for thinking to evolve and for that duty to be acknowledged. So let us not forget those early pioneers."[9] The laws had once sanctified military deeds; now they revalorized the most humble civilian actions, whether the distribution of an underground newspaper or the rescue of Jews.

The norms promulgated in the second half of the twentieth century did little to clarify the nature of the resistance. Far from establishing an inviolable frame of reference, they shifted over time, putting forward two interpretive models in succession. At first, they privileged a military conception that defined the underground fighter as a soldier battling weapons in hand against Hitler's Germany; later on, they saw him as a militant rising up against totalitarianism. These antagonistic views are surprising, since the realm of law is characterized above all by stability, but they merely reflect the memorial foot-dragging of France during that time.

## Memorial Confusion

Until the dawn of the 1970s, France consoled itself with certainties that can be summed up in three postulates: first, all French people had participated, albeit to an unequal degree, in the underground struggle; second, resistance fighters in the metropolis and combatants in the FFL united as brothers under the tutelary figure of Charles de Gaulle; and third, the Vichy regime had enjoyed no popular support, the populace as a whole refusing to get behind the French State. That irenic discourse inspired both the public authorities and the main political forces.[10] In 1943, the man of June 18 stated that "resistance in its many forms has become the fundamental reaction of the French people. . . . It is everywhere, tenacious and effective: in the organization realized in France itself and unified by our Conseil National de la Résistance, which we salute as brothers; in the factories and in the fields, in offices and in schools, in the streets and in homes, in hearts and in minds."[11] The Communists shared that conception and portrayed the resistance as "the upsurge of a people betrayed, handed over to the enemy by their own elites, the people of the factories and the fields, who had saved

France so many times in its long history."[12] A few variations sometimes broke the monotony of the refrain. The PCF, true to its proletarian orientation, believed that "the working class . . . constituted the vanguard of opposition to the occupiers and their lackeys,"[13] whereas the Gaullists considered the French people a single entity. For example, Colonel Passy claimed in his memoirs that in 1943, "the real France, I could almost write all of France, found itself once again at war against the Axis powers, and the Vichy government no longer represented anything."[14] Likewise, the Communists presented the PCF as the marching flank of the army of shadows, while the Gaullists emphasized the preeminent role played by their leader. But overall, consensus prevailed and received the tacit approval of French society.

The recurrent discourse on the resistance, however, kept the French people from looking closely at the shameful times of a history marked by the terrible defeat of 1940 and the compromises of a state that denied its humanist and republican past in order to conduct an authoritarian, anti-Semitic, and xenophobic policy. At a time when France, after being destroyed, was beginning its reconstruction and was focused on modernization, such a discourse increased national unity, even as it refrained from widening the rift that separated presumed traitors from proclaimed heroes. Furthermore, the heroism of the partisans allowed the "party of the 75,000 executed" to obscure the line it had followed between 1939 and 1941, camouflaging the German-Soviet Pact, the desertion of its secretary-general, Maurice Thorez, the calls for fraternization launched by *L'Humanité* in July 1940, and the condemnation of attacks on individuals by Marcel Cachin on June 11, 1942, in the very collaborationist daily *Cri du Peuple*.

Political groups and the state apparatus made every effort to spread the good word, by several different methods. The names of metro stations and streets paid tribute to resistance fighters, beginning with Charles de Gaulle: in the French empire and in the metropolis, 418 municipalities named a thoroughfare after him between 1940 and January 20, 1946.[15] Likewise, demonstrations and parades multiplied, very often bringing together men from the movements and soldiers from the FFL, for example, during the celebrations of the Appeal of June 18 that took place in Paris on June 17 and 18, 1945. The government, because of the widespread scarcity of materials, refrained from building monuments, but it did construct a few memorial sites. At a ceremony on November 11, 1945, fifteen coffins symbolizing "those who died for France" in World War II were collected at Mont-Valérien, which thereby acquired a preeminent status, further reinforced in 1960 by the renovation of the site.

Above all, films played a role in forging the legend. René Clément's *La Bataille du rail (The Battle of the Rails)* came out in 1946, a symbol of the compromise between the Gaullist movement—embodied by the Résistance-Fer movement and SNCF management—and the Communist camp, represented by the Comité de Libération du Cinéma Français (Liberation Committee of French Cinema) and the Coopérative Générale du Cinéma Français (General Cooperative of French Cinema). Initially, the project was supposed to "adopt the point of view of class struggle and glorify the achievements of the internal Resistance." But when the production group expanded to include the national railroad company and Résistance-Fer, a "unanimous vision" of the railroad community took root. "The contribution of new characters, such as the engineer and the two retirees, contributed toward imposing the idyllic image of a railroad family united from top to bottom, to which railway workers of every age and rank were attached by indestructible bonds," observes historian Sylvie Lindeperg.[16] *La Bataille du rail*, awarded the Palme d'Or at the Cannes Film Festival, was singularly influential. In addition to being considered archival footage on many occasions, to the point of being used in that capacity in numerous documentaries, it was the model for a plethora of films set during the dark years. An overwhelming majority of fictional films begin with a scene of railroad sabotage, *Lucie Aubrac* (1997) and *Femmes de l'ombre (Female Agents*; 2008), for example, despite the fact that the Aubracs—to cite a single example—were never associated with an attack against the railroad lines. *Paris brûle-t-il? (Is Paris Burning?*; 1966), also directed by René Clément, displays the same biases, claiming that the Gaullists and the Communists alone, and with remarkable unanimity, liberated the City of Light in August 1944. Its main aspects are "the reduction of Resistance forces to the Gaullo-Communist actors and an overt irenism that only poorly disguises the imbalance between the two camps."[17] The director proved to be quite accommodating: to satisfy the demands of the Gaullist and Communist enemy brothers, he even eliminated from the screen

Georges Bidault, guilty of having embraced the cause of French Algeria, and Maurice Kriegel-Valrimont, victim of the purge launched by the PCF apparatus in 1960.

This heroic view of the French people was flawed in two respects. First, it distorted historical reality. It reduced the resistance to its Gaullist and Communist components, excluding the heterodox elements represented by the movements, the networks that pledged allegiance to Britain, and even the resisto-Vichyists. In addition, it obscured the impact of Pétainism, which was deliberately disregarded. Second, the primacy it granted to the heroes ignored the victims: Jews, prisoners of war, forced laborers. Although these groups received rights and reparations over time, their disproportionately tragic fate was not incorporated into the national myth, which was dominated, not without ambiguities, by the lofty figure of the soldier in the army of shadows. Furthermore, though the nation as a whole honored these exceptional men, it also watered down their achievements: France in its entirety, it was said, had participated in the battle.

This legend was shattered in the early 1970s. In the first place, Charles de Gaulle's resignation in 1969 and his death the next year weakened what had been taken for gospel, its chief apostle having vanished. His successor, Georges Pompidou, conducted a policy of "national reconciliation," all the more questionable in that it led to the dissolution of the Commissariat Général aux Monuments Commémoratifs des Guerres Mondiales (General Commission on World War Commemorative Monuments) in 1969, to a pardon for Paul Touvier, member of the Milice, on November 23, 1971, and to a ban on the distribution of Marcel Ophüls's 1969 documentary *Le chagrin et la pitié (The Sorrow and the Pity)*, even though French television had commissioned the film. In 1971 Jean-Jacques de Bresson, president of the Office de Radiodiffusion Télévision Française (Office of French Radio and Television Broadcasting), though himself a former resistance fighter, justified his decision by claiming that the documentary destroyed "myths that the French still need."[18] With the repression of Prague Spring (1968) and the publication in France of Aleksandr Solzhenitsyn's *Gulag Archipelago* (1974), the Communists began to have trouble portraying themselves as the heralds of freedom valiantly embodied in the saga of the resistance. All these factors could not fail to whet the curiosity of what had become a suspicious French society. The Pompidou government, people told themselves, had censored *Le chagrin et la pitié* because it contained disturbing truths. They therefore rushed to the two Latin Quarter movie theaters that were showing the inflammatory film. True, Ophüls's work broke with orthodoxy. Focusing on the city of Clermont-Ferrand, it showed that residents, far from having resisted en masse, had spent the dark years in a state of indifference, sometimes supporting Philippe Pétain and in one case even joining the collaborationist camp. The revival of Jewish memory as a result of the shock of the Six-Day War and of de Gaulle's gaffe on November 27, 1967, when he denounced the Jews as "an elite people, self-assured and domineering," also contributed toward toppling the columns of the temple. Even before Vichy's complicity in the deportations surfaced, these events brought back the somewhat forgotten fate of the Jews of France.

The country gradually changed its memorial paradigm. Where once the French people in their entirety had been considered resistance fighters, they now became no less uniformly Vichyist or collaborationist. The figure of the hero had dominated national consciousness; the image of the victim, usually Jewish, now prevailed. If Buchenwald had symbolized concentration camp hell, Auschwitz came to embody it.

These shifts affected the status enjoyed by the resistance in national consciousness. First, discordant voices rose up to remind people that neither the Gaullists nor the Communists had had a monopoly on underground action. In their memoirs, the top leaders of the movements— Henri Frenay and Claude Bourdet, to cite only two[19]—pointed out that they had refused to submit to either London or Moscow. Their voices, though not congruent, shattered two conventional images. In evoking the conflicts between them and de Gaulle or his representative, Jean Moulin, they broke ranks with the myth of an army of shadows that deferred without flinching to the orders of Free France. In recalling that their fight was that of a tiny minority, they sapped some of the power from the legend of a France engaged en masse. These men, in speaking out, unsettled the simplistic interpretation of the dark years and reintroduced complexity. Engagement in the resistance, formerly presented as a duty or as self-evident, was no longer taken to be a matter of course. Far from stemming from a deliberate ideological choice, it may sometimes have been a matter of chance, as suggested in negative terms by the film *Lacombe Lucien* (1974). Louis Malle, in depicting a young man who, after being rejected by a leader of the resistance, joined the Milice, violated the dominant code and elicited strong reactions.

Finally, a few scandals tarnished the haloes of the soldiers in the army of shadows. In 1950 Henri Frenay had accused Jean Moulin of being "the Communist Party's man,"[20] a claim that went relatively unnoticed at the time, but which the head of the Combat movement elaborated further in a book published in 1977.[21] In 1993 Thierry Wolton, a journalist, declared that Moulin had been a Soviet agent,[22] insinuating he had betrayed not only de Gaulle but also his country. These attacks, which received ample attention from certain organs of the press, masked different objectives. A fringe of the internal resistance was settling some old scores. Unable to recover from its political defeat after liberation, it preferred to make accusations against the delegate of Fighting France rather than proceed to a reasonable examination of its impotence. In addition, a portion of the right had never forgiven de Gaulle for his intransigence toward Vichy or for Algerian independence, especially since, on May 13, 1958, the supporters of French Algeria had played a large role in the meteoric rise of the man of June 18. In attacking Moulin, it was actually targeting the former president. In putting his trust in an agent of the Soviet secret services, had not de Gaulle displayed a blindness unworthy of the statesman he claimed to be?

On a different matter, a book published in 1994 cast a harsh light on the "French youth" of François Mitterrand.[23] In revealing that the president of the republic, after escaping a stalag, had worked at the very Vichyist Commissariat au Reclassement des Prisonniers (Commission for the Reclassification of Prisoners) in June 1942 and had had strong affinities for Pétainist ideology, it destroyed the image Mitterrand had patiently built up since liberation. In fact, he had constantly portrayed himself as the herald of an internal resistance that de Gaulle had supposedly sought to take over. Mitterrand had described the time he spent in Vichy and the medal he received from the regime as a ruse that, according to him, had allowed him to wage his resistance fight in the shadows. The journalist Pierre Péan reestablished the brute facts, showing in particular that the Vichyist episode and Mitterrand's engagement in the resistance, far from being concurrent, had actually occurred in succession. These episodes, carefully kept quiet by Mitterrand, weakened the legendary status of the internal resistance by demonstrating, first, that some men had collaborated with Vichy before joining the army of shadows, and second, that the glorious deeds complacently spread by their authors had only a remote connection to historical reality.

A final scandal also contributed toward casting a pall over the situation. In 1997 a book implicitly accused Lucie and Raymond Aubrac of having had a hand in the ambush at Caluire, where it was Jean Moulin's fate to cross paths with the Gestapo agent Klaus Barbie.[24] Without providing support for the hypothesis, the book may have "given the impression that it was trafficking in suspicion, even insinuation."[25] Its author was convicted of libel as a result, but the verdict did not dissipate the malaise. Detractors of the resistance rushed into the breach, hoping that by discrediting the legendary couple, they would deal a blow to the legend. At the same time, Gérard Chauvy, citing the many contradictions in the Aubracs' statements, indicated that they had undoubtedly not told the whole truth. Although they could not be held responsible for Moulin's arrest, they too had built up a legend that took a few liberties with historical reality.

The resistance, previously venerated, now succumbed to an era of suspicion, as reflected in cinematic productions. Until the 1970s, films exalted the heroism of former underground fighters; but beginning with *Lacombe Lucien*, they took a more critical stance. Jean-Marie Poiré's 1982 *Papy fait de la résistance (Grandpa's in the Resistance)* ridiculed Gaullist mythology; Claude Berri's *Uranus* (1990) depicted, in a particularly harsh light, a small provincial town in the grip of a nasty settling of accounts orchestrated by Communist resistance fighters. Jacques Audiard's *Un héros très discret (A Self-Made Hero;* 1996), in telling the life story of an imposter, suggested that posterity may have sanctified false heroes. These productions, whether they reflected collective memory or shaped it, clearly revealed that times had changed. The resistance was henceforth under attack and had to be on the defensive.

Even today, however, the resistance remains an obligatory frame of reference. The left, with Communists in the lead, likes to hark back to the heady times of the CNR program, while the right prefers to invoke General de Gaulle. It is also well known that Nicolas Sarkozy, candidate for the presidency of the republic, then resident of the Elysée Palace, promised to go on pilgrimage every year to Glières, the plateau where a maquis had been quartered in February 1944. Sarkozy, even while granting an important place to the Shoah in his memorial policy—to the point of suggesting, on February 13, 2008, that every fifth grader preserve the memory of a young victim of the Holocaust—sought to valorize the army of shadows, to take his distance from the vision of a generally Pétainist France and hence from "the repentance that wants to keep us from being proud of our country."[26] From that standpoint, the heroism of the former underground fighters could only be an inspiration to a man who, rejecting what seems inevitable, aspired to place volunteer service at the heart of his political action.

Such elements must not conceal the essential, however. At present, the resistance plays only a minor role in the public arena, especially since, as already noted, it contributed only modestly toward restructuring the political field. That isolation might have been beneficial to the resistance if it had continued to occupy the Olympian heights, serving as a moral frame of reference above the parties, like the veterans described by the Czech dissident Jan Patočka. "The solitude of the shaken . . . will not establish any positive program," the philosopher wrote. "Its language will be that of the demon of Socrates: all warnings and prohibitions. It must and can create a spiritual authority, must and can become a spiritual authority capable of impelling the world at war to accept certain restrictions, capable of making certain acts and certain measures impossible."[27] But the former resistance fighters did not take that route. For example, they adopted opposing positions on the question of torture in Algeria.

It should be pointed out that many underground fighters engaged in resistance for political reasons; once liberation came, they had no intention of renouncing the right to take a stand. Furthermore, the great ideological heterogeneity of the army of shadows doomed any effort to adopt common positions on controversial issues, whether the Soviet Union, decolonization, or General de Gaulle's return to power in 1958. As a result, "the political instrumentalization of the memory of the Resistance, in the service of partisan and contradictory aims and irreducible to the clash between Gaullists and Communists, introduces confusion and complicates the process of appropriating collective memory."[28]

These factors have obviously obscured the status of the resistance in people's memories, which generally retain "a confused image of the resistance fighter that combines the secret agent, the sheriff or the outlaw as played by an actor in a western, and the fearless knight beyond reproach, who, submachine gun in hand, blows up an incalculable number of factories and trains."[29] The resistance, with no political party to convey its ideas, subject to attacks by a part of the right wing—which has not fully recovered from its association with Vichy and the loss of French Algeria—is having a hard time ensuring the viability of its memory, all the more so in that myriad groups claim to be preserving it. Fragmentation prevents the emergence of a common commemorative discourse and practice, which, conversely, had shaped the memory of World War I. The death of the last witnesses is also depriving the resistance of voices to embody it. Then too, certain affairs, duly covered by the media, have fueled the inquisitorial tendencies of public opinion, more inclined to be swayed by scandals, perhaps, than to commune on the altar of heroism. Everyone now pays tribute to the resistance, but who would dare claim that it influences the course of public life, imposes its values, structures national memory at a profound level? All in all, the resistance suffers from the confused succession of legal norms that have defined it and from a troubled memorial image. But its inalterable value escapes the grip of these contingencies.

# Conclusion

WHATEVER HAPPENS, THE FLAME of French resistance must not and will not go out," Charles de Gaulle declared at the end of his famous appeal.[1] And in fact, as the days passed, the faint glimmer of 1940 became a brighter light, which illuminated the darkness of captive France. Although weak in the dark days of the defeat, on the eve of liberation the French resistance had managed to become a force to be reckoned with for the German occupier and the Vichy regime. But should it be said, as the Gaullists proclaimed at the end of the war, that the internal resistance developed thanks only to the impetus of Free France?

It should be apparent that such a partisan view calls for a few correctives. Indeed, though the BCRA and the SOE played a decisive role in the birth and establishment of the networks, the movements arose spontaneously, without benefit of London's support, at least until 1942. The same is true for the parties and unions, which discovered the paths of dissidence on their own, when they were ready to take them. By that measure, the resistance truly constituted a phenomenon that originated in civil society and only partly in response to an external force.

The resistance, having arisen from the population at large, had to invent the terms of its battle on its own. In 1940 no institution called for struggle, not the political parties, the labor unions, the churches, or the army. In addition, the army of shadows could not seek inspiration in historical precedents, since the defeat of 1940 and the Vichy regime constituted phenomena unprecedented in the long history of France. As a result, the pioneers had to feel their way around, some placing the struggle against the Reich at the top of their priorities, others preferring to protect civilians from the deceptive charms of Pétainism, if not of Nazism, hoping to convince them and then mobilize them. Along the way, they invented an original type of organization, the resistance movement, which allowed them both to organize volunteers and to spur on polymorphous forms of battle—the underground press, demonstrations, labor actions, irregular corps, strikes, maquis, and others.

The skills required by the underground groups were not within everyone's reach, however. Although some, like the Communists and members of the ORA, had military training or extensive repertoires of action, the majority of volunteers joined the underground with no real experience and proceeded to learn on the job. Some apprenticed with typographers to learn printing, others were initiated into the use of weapons in the maquis, still others undertook on their own to execute Germans. These hurdles and the great risks involved limited engagement in the resistance, especially since the movements and even the networks had difficulty addressing clear instructions for action to the population. During the first months, French society could see little way to fight effectively against its oppressors, particularly in view of the fact that it had legitimate doubts about whether the Allies would be victorious.

From that standpoint, 1942 marked a turning point. With Operation Torch and the victory at Stalingrad, the Reich's defeat became possible, not to say plausible. Pierre Laval's return, then the invasion of the free zone, revealed to those still in doubt the collaborationist and authoritarian orientation of the Vichy regime. Finally, the law of September 4, 1942, on the requisition of the labor force abruptly led thousands of young men to take the path of dissidence, which provided the resistance with a flood of volunteers and with the means to bring society as a whole into the fight against the STO.

But should it be said that French society engaged in general insurrection at that time? That would be a bit hasty. More than six hundred thousand French people reported to German factories. And three-quarters of STO evaders, far from joining the struggle, simply went into hiding. Thousands joined the maquis, however, where the movements—as much as their limited resources allowed—strove first to conceal them and then to turn them into combatants. The influx of volunteers led part of the population to lend increasing support to the resistance, bringing it supplies, providing information, and protecting it from the repressive services. Anonymous people also contributed toward the rescue of 75 percent of the Jews of France—a proportion unmatched in occupied Europe. But the resistance movement, by its very logic, entailed a less radical commitment than that made by the men and women who joined the ranks of the resistance organization. This explains why, from start to finish, the resistance organization remained a minority phenomenon in the country.

The resistance was also incomparably diverse. At first, the movements and networks gave precedence to a specific form of struggle. They were of various political stripes, ranging from the left embodied by Libération-sud and Libération-nord to the right symbolized by the OCM. The internal resistance, in openly declaring its ideology, played a role in restoring democratic debate, which had been stifled by the French State. Its vitality was fostered by the contribution of the parties, which gradually emerged from their languor and from the ambivalence that had taken hold of them with the defeat. Although the pluralism fueled tensions and conflicts, it did not result in divisiveness.

After all, Free France managed to unite the French resistance, an exception in occupied Europe. The movements had already begun the unification process, amalgamating small groups or seeking to form alliances. Charles de Gaulle, by offering the army of shadows money, liaisons, and arms, spurred on unification. His patriotism, his charisma, and the clarity of his positions also turned him into a symbol with whom all resistance fighters could identify, even though leaders often manifested a more restrained enthusiasm than the rank and file. To increase the effectiveness of the underground struggle, to connect it with Allied plans, and to win the battle of legitimacy that London and Washington were fighting to deny him, de Gaulle pressed on. His delegates, Jean Moulin above all, worked to realize unification. At the cost of great difficulties and sometimes sharp conflicts, the wager paid off. De Gaulle, it is true, knew how to make the necessary concessions—clarifying his political views in the manifesto he delivered to Christian Pineau, promising a New Deal, and linking the resistance to the reforms and platforms of the administrators who would govern liberated France. Conversely, he also clashed with the movements: by bringing political parties onto the CNR; by dispatching regional military delegates who were suspected of subordinating the internal resistance to him; by refusing to support the maquis; by rejecting the direct action recommended by the Communist groups; and finally, by aspiring to command from London the actions waged in the metropolis. These conflicts, sometimes heated, never got out of hand, however: the resistance that marched toward liberation under de Gaulle's aegis was truly unified.

Although the resistance played a role in influencing, then in mobilizing and even protecting French society, its military success seems to have been less brilliant. That is not to say that it was negligible, however. Movements and networks fed intelligence to the Allies. They exfiltrated aviators who had fallen in France. They engaged in timely sabotage operations. Above all, the assistance they gave after the landing proved to be of infinite value. The army of shadows lived up to its name at that time, sabotaging the railroad network, committing a multitude of guerrilla actions, and guiding the Anglo-American troops. But that contribution should not be overestimated. In the first place, the Germans never considered the internal resistance a military danger comparable to the situation the partisans created for them in the Soviet Union and Yugoslavia. Yet that realistic assessment did not prevent the Germans from conducting a bloody repression. In the second place, neither the British nor the Americans really counted on the army of shadows, at least before June 6, considering it a bonus at most. That view hardly encouraged them to arm the resistance, which explains the extreme scarcity of its military resources until the upturn of summer 1944. With or without the resistance, the Allies would have landed and achieved victory.

This observation should not obscure something just as essential: without the resistance, the liberation would have taken a very different course. In Brittany, the levée en masse of the partisans favored the progress of the American troops, which advanced at an astonishingly rapid pace, thereby cutting short the suffering of a civilian population exposed to the occupier's savagery. The same was true in the southwest and in the Alps. And finally, the Paris insurrection obliged Eisenhower to modify his plans and to capture the City of Light as quickly as possible, perhaps sparing it the attendant destruction that brought Warsaw to grief.

The legitimacy that General de Gaulle and the internal resistance had acquired also facilitated the transfer of power from a discredited Vichy regime to the administrators emerging from the underground, whose power went uncontested. When the day came, mayors and prefects of the French State gave up their places, not even making a gallant last stand, while the population accepted its new leaders at both the local and the national level. General de Gaulle's patriotic intransigence and the sacrifices the underground fighters had agreed to make guaranteed a peaceful transition, which Greece and Italy did not experience—

to say nothing of the tragedies to come in the countries liberated by the Red Army, rapidly subjected to the iron yoke of Stalinism.

Granted, the resistance as a whole did not manage to make good on its promises. Neither de Gaulle nor the movements succeeded in reshaping the political field upon liberation, and the Fourth Republic looked like the Third's twin. Although France began its reconstruction on radically new foundations, the emblematic reforms were largely inspired by solutions already sketched out during the 1930s, the CNR's program playing only a modest role in the New Deal that structured the Trente Glorieuses. On the memorial level, finally, the resistance did not manage to sway public opinion by imposing its ethic. Former members of the resistance adopted opposing positions on questions as essential as the Soviet gulag and torture in Algeria. These differences may seem surprising: above all, they confirm that the resistance was also a political undertaking that included every point of view, from the nationalist right to the Communist left. Resistance fighters, having contributed to the restoration of democracy, did not intend to abandon, in the name of an improbable "spirit of the resistance," the public arena or to keep quiet about their differences. That freedom was a right; they exercised it.

Should the resistance be reduced solely to its achievements, however? Everything suggests that it exceeds the scope of its actions and of the final outcome. Even as France, plunged into the most terrible defeat of its history, yielded to the Marshal and put up with the Nazis' iron rule, some men and women, rejecting the fallacious evidence of defeat, set out to resist any way they could. They took the honorable path and demonstrated that one France—the true France?—intended to hold the flag up high, preserving its ideals against all odds. To defend those ideals, many died at dawn at Mont-Valérien, in the cold north wind at Buchenwald, in freezing Nazi jails. More than in its program, the resistance survives in these luminaries, whether they bear the name Claude Bourdet, Jean Moulin, or Pierre Brossolette. And that is to say nothing of the anonymous figures in that vast pantheon. Museums, sometimes a few plaques, and often tombs remind us of them. But these men and these women live especially in the traces they have bequeathed to us, in our hearts and in our consciences, because they teach by example the lofty but difficult demands of citizenship.

# NOTES

### INTRODUCTION

1 François Bédarida, "L'histoire de la Résistance: Lecture d'hier, chantiers de demain," *Vingtième siècle: Revue d'histoire* 11 (July–September 1986): 80. [Unless otherwise noted, quoted passages are my translation from the French.—trans.]

2 Pierre Laborie, *Les Français des années troubles: De la guerre d'Espagne à la Libération* (Seuil, 2003; 1st ed., 2001), 75–76. Throughout this book, the city of publication is Paris unless indicated otherwise.

3 Jean-Marie Guillon, "La Résistance, 50 ans et 2 000 titres après," in *Mémoire et histoire: La Résistance*, ed. Jean-Marie Guillon and Pierre Laborie (Toulouse: Privat, 1995), 42.

4 Laborie, *Les Français des années troubles*, 86.

5 François Marcot, "Pour une sociologie de la Résistance: Intentionnalité et fonctionnalité," in *La Résistance, une histoire sociale*, ed. Antoine Prost (Éditions de l'Atelier, 1997), 23.

6 Jean-Marie Guillon and Pierre Laborie, "Pour une histoire de la Résistance," in Guillon and Laborie, *Mémoire et histoire*, 16.

7 Henri Noguères, Marcel Degliame-Fouché, and Jean-Louis Vigier, *Histoire de la Résistance en France*, vol. 1: *Juin 1940–juin 1941* (Robert Laffont, 1967), 15, my emphasis.

8 Lucien Febvre, foreword to Henri Michel and Boris Mirkine-Guetzevitch, *Les idées politiques et sociales de la Résistance* (PUF, 1954), xi.

9 Pierre Laborie, "Qu'est-ce que la Résistance?," in *Dictionnaire historique de la Résistance*, ed. François Marcot (Robert Laffont, 2006), 34.

10 François Bédarida, "Sur le concept de Résistance," in Guillon and Laborie, *Mémoire et histoire*, 45.

### CHAPTER 1: THE CALL

1 Jean-Louis Crémieux-Brilhac, "Du 18 juin aux 18 juin," *Espoir* 123 (2000).

2 Colonel Passy, *Souvenirs: 10, Duke Street Londres (le BCRA)* (Monte Carlo: Solar, 1948), 104–105.

3 Jean-François Muracciole, *Les Français libres: L'autre Résistance* (Tallandier, 2009), 135.

4 Aurélie Luneau, *Radio-Londres, 1940–1944: Les voix de la liberté* (Perrin, 2005), 17–18.

5 Ibid., 21 and 23.

6 Communiqué broadcast on the BBC on June 28, 1940, quoted in Jean-Louis Crémieux-Brilhac, *La France libre: De l'appel du 18 juin à la Libération* (Gallimard, 1996), 63.

7 Luneau, *Radio-Londres*, 48–49.

8 Crémieux-Brilhac, *La France libre*, 225.

9 Ibid., 229.

10 Luneau, *Radio-Londres*, 78.

11 Ibid., 37.

12 Ibid., 113–114.

13 Renée Poznanski, *Propagandes et persécutions: La Résistance et le 'problème juif' (1940–1944)* (Fayard, 2008), 103.

14 Quoted in Luneau, *Radio-Londres*, 109.

15 Crémieux-Brilhac, *La France libre*, 215.

16 Luneau, *Radio-Londres*, 69.

17 Ibid., 101ff.

18 Dominique Veillon, "La ville comme creuset de la Résistance," in *La Résistance et les Français: Villes, centres et logiques de décision*, ed. Laurent Douzou, Robert Frank, Denis Peschanski, and Dominique Veillon (Cachan: École Normale Supérieure, 1995), 145.

19 Christine Levisse-Touzé, "Le rôle particulier de Paris pendant la Seconde Guerre mondiale," in Douzou et al., *La Résistance et les Français*, 187.

20 Michel Boivin and Jean Quellien, "La Résistance en Basse-Normandie: Définition et sociologie," in *La Résistance et les Français: Enjeux stratégiques et environnement social*, ed. Jacqueline Sainclivier and Christian Bougeard (Rennes: Presses Universitaires de Rennes, 1995), 169.

21 Luneau, *Radio-Londres*, 105.

22 Danielle Tartakowsky, "Géographie des manifestations de rue," in Douzou et al., *La Résistance et les Français*, 119.

23 Luneau, *Radio-Londres*, 121.

24 Boivin and Quellien, "La Résistance en Basse-Normandie," 169.

25 Colonel Passy, *Souvenirs: 2e Bureau, Londres* (Monte Carlo: Solar, 1947), 54.

26 Paul Paillole, *Services spéciaux (1935–1945)* (Robert Laffont, 1975), 432.

27 Colonel Passy, *Souvenirs: 2e Bureau*, 53.

28 Sébastien Albertelli, *Les Services secrets du général de Gaulle: Le BCRA (1940–1944)* (Perrin, 2009), 42.

29 Ibid., 43.

30 Colonel Passy, *Souvenirs: 2e Bureau*, 54–55.

31 Yves Le Maner, "La propagande britannique par tracts aériens en France (1940–1944)," paper presented at the conference *La Résistance et les Européens du Nord*, Brussels, November 23–25, 1994, typescript, 118.

32 David Reynolds, *From World War to Cold War* (Oxford: Oxford University Press, 2006), 114–115.

33 Michael R. D. Foot, *SOE in France: An Account of the Work of the British Special Operations Executive in France, 1940–1944* (London: Her Majesty's Stationery Office, 1966), 151.

34 Ibid., 154–156.

35 Alya Aglan, *Mémoires résistantes: Histoire du réseau Jade-Fitzroy, 1940–1944* (Cerf, 1994), 20ff.

36 Foot, *SOE in France*, 57–59.

37 Charles Portal to Gladwyn Jebb, February 1, 1941, quoted in Mark Seaman, "RAF Air Support to Resistance Groups in Western Europe," in *La Résistance et les Européens du Nord*, ed. R. Frank and J. Gotovitch (Brussels: Centre de recherches et d'études historiques de la Seconde Guerre mondiale / Institut d'histoire du temps présent, 1994), 136.

38 Charles Portal to H. N. Sporborg, quoted ibid.

39 Albertelli, *Les Services secrets*, 41.

40 Quoted ibid, 71.

41 Foot, *SOE in France*, 158.

42 Albertelli, *Les Services secrets*, 88.

43 Ibid., 68.

44 Quoted in Luneau, *Radio-Londres*, 118.

45 Henri Noguères, Marcel Degliame-Fouché, and Jean-Louis Vigier, *Histoire de la Résistance en France*, vol. 1: *Juin 1940–juin 1941* (Robert Laffont, 1967), 135.

46 Quoted in Albertelli, *Les Services secrets*, 100.

47 Quoted ibid., 105.

48 Ibid., 108.

49 Quoted ibid., 110.

50 Daniel Cordier, *Alias Caracalla* (Gallimard, 2009), 223.

51 Jean-Marie Guillon, "La Résistance dans le Var: Essai d'histoire politique," 3 vols. (PhD thesis, Université de Provence, Aix-en-Provence, 1989), 1:64.

52 Claude Bourdet, *L'aventure incertaine: De la Résistance à la Restauration* (Stock, 1975), 95.

53 Albertelli, *Les Services secrets*, 120.

54 Quoted ibid., 121.

## CHAPTER 2: PARTIES AND LABOR UNIONS

1 Philippe Pétain, message of October 30, 1940, quoted in Marshal Pétain, *La France nouvelle: Principes de la communauté, suivis des appels et messages, 17 juin 1940–17 juin 1941* (Fasquelle, 1941), 88.

2 Quoted in Olivier Wieviorka, *Orphans of the Republic: The Nation's Legislators in Vichy France*, trans. George Holoch (Cambridge, MA: Harvard University Press, 2009; French ed., 2001), 48.

3 Ibid.

4 Stéphane Courtois and Marc Lazar, *Histoire du Parti communiste français* (Presses Universitaires de France, 2001; 1st ed., 1995), 176.

5 Annette Wieviorka, *Maurice et Jeannette: Biographie du couple Thorez* (Fayard, 2010), 268.

6 Stéphane Courtois and Denis Peschanski, "La dominante de l'Internationale et les tournants du PCF," in *Le Parti communiste français des années sombres, 1938–1941*, ed. Jean-Pierre Azéma, Antoine Prost, and Jean-Pierre Rioux (Seuil, 1986), 263.

7 Jean-Marie Guillon, "La Résistance dans le Var: Essai d'histoire politique," 3 vols. (PhD thesis, Université de Provence, Aix-en-Provence, 1989), 87.

8 Quoted in Stéphane Courtois, *Le PCF dans la guerre: De Gaulle, la Résistance, Staline . . .* (Ramsay, 1980), 139.

9 Maurice Thorez, "Les vrais traîtres," quoted ibid., 146.

10 Quoted ibid., 162.

11 Daniel Virieux, "Le Front national de lutte pour la liberté et l'indépendance de la France: Un mouvement de Résistance, période clandestine (mai 1941–août 1944)," 5 vols. (PhD thesis, Paris-VIII, 1995), 18.

12 Benoît Frachon, in *Cahiers du bolchevisme*, 1st quarter (1941), quoted in Courtois, *Le PCF dans la guerre*, 169.

13 Ibid., 175.

14 Danielle Tartakowsky, *Les manifestations de rue en France, 1918–1968* (Publications de la Sorbonne, 1997), 461.

15 Danielle Tartakowsky, "Géographie des manifestations de rue," in *La Résistance et les Français: Villes, centres et logiques de décision*, ed. Laurent Douzou, Robert Frank, Denis Peschanski, and Dominique Veillon (Cachan: École Normale Supérieure, 1995), 124.

16 Jean-Louis Cuvelliez, "Les débuts de la Résistance à Toulouse et dans la région," in *Mémoire et histoire: La Résistance*, ed. Jean-Marie Guillon and Pierre Laborie (Toulouse: Privat, 1995), 122.

17 Alain Monchablon, "La manifestation à l'Étoile du 11 novembre 1940: Histoire et mémoires," *Vingtième siècle: Revue d'histoire* 110 (April–June 2011): 71.

18 Ibid., 72.

19 Quoted ibid., 77.

20 Quoted in Charles Tillon, *On chantait rouge: Mémoires pour l'Histoire d'un ouvrier breton devenu révolutionnaire professionnel, chef de guerre et ministre* (Robert Laffont, 1977), 301–302.

21 Jean-Marc Berlière and Franck Liaigre, *L'Affaire Guy Môquet: Enquête sur une mystification officielle* (Larousse, 2009), 76.

22 Quoted ibid., 77.

23 Daniel Borzeix, "Les débuts de Guingouin," in *Genèse et développement de la Résistance en R5, 1940–1943*, ed. Pascal Plas (Brive-la-Gaillarde: Éditions Les Monédières), 127ff.

24 Georges Guingouin, *4 ans de lutte sur le sol limousin* (Limoges: Lucien Souny, 1991), 26.

25 Quoted in Berlière and Liaigre, *L'Affaire*, 80.

26 Courtois and Peschanski, "La dominante de l'Internationale," 263.

27 On this point, see Gabriel Gorodetsky, *Grand Delusion: Stalin and the German Invasion of Russia* (New Haven, CT: Yale University Press, 1999).

28 Courtois, *Le PCF dans la guerre*, 162.

29 Quoted in Courtois and Lazar, *Histoire*, 183.

30 Virieux, "Le Front national," 19.

31 Quoted in Courtois, *Le PCF dans la guerre*, 191–192.

32 Étienne Dejonghe and Yves Le Maner, *Le Nord-Pas-de-Calais dans la main allemande* (Lille: La Voix du Nord, 1999), 194.

33 Ibid., 195.

34 Olivier Wieviorka, *Divided Memory: French Recollections of World War II from the Liberation to the Present*, trans. George Holoch (Stanford, CA: Stanford University Press, 2012; French ed., 2010), 61.

35 Quoted in Olivier Wieviorka, *Orphans of the Republic*, 120.

36 Paul Rives, Charles Spinasse, and Eugène Gaillard, "Lettre à Maxence Roldes," August 3, 1940, quoted ibid., 139.

37 Marc Sadoun, *Les Socialistes sous l'Occupation: Résistance et collaboration* (Presses de Sciences-Po, 1982), 110.

38 For a detailed chronology, see ibid., 114ff.

39 Ibid., 116.

40 *Le Populaire*, southern zone, June 15, 1942, quoted ibid., 117.

41 Quoted ibid., 159.

42 Quoted ibid., 128.

43 Quoted in Olivier Wieviorka, *Nous entrerons dans la carrière: De la Résistance à l'exercice du pouvoir* (Seuil, 1994), 48.

44 Jean-Marie Guillon, "Les socialistes en résistance: Un comportement politique," in Douzou et al., *La Résistance et les Français*, 382.

45 Quoted in Jean Texcier, *Un homme libre* (Albin Michel, 1960), 101–102.

46 "Manifeste du syndicalisme français," November 15, 1940, quoted in Christian Pineau, *La simple vérité: 1940–1945* (Phalanx, 1983; 1st ed., 1960), 594ff.

47 Oreste Capocci, François (alias "Léon") Chevalme, Albert Gazier, Eugène Jaccoud, Robert Lacoste, Pierre Neumeyer, Christian Pineau, Louis Saillant, and Victor Vandeputte.

48 Maurice Bouladoux, Gaston Tessier, and Jules Zirnheld.

49 Jacques Julliard, "La Charte du travail," in Fondation Nationale des Sciences Politiques, *Le gouvernement de Vichy, 1940–1942* (Presses de Sciences-Po, 1971), 164.

50 Alya Aglan, *La Résistance sacrifiée: Histoire du mouvement Libération-nord* (Champs-Flammarion, 2005; 1st ed., 1999), 40.

51 Ibid., 46–47.

52  Quoted ibid., 51.

53  Ibid., 59.

54  Diana Cooper-Richet, "Les ouvriers, l'Église et la Résistance," in *La Résistance et les Français: Enjeux stratégiques et environnement social*, ed. Jacqueline Sainclivier and Christian Bougeard (Rennes: Presses Universitaires de Rennes, 1995), 133.

55  Ibid.

56  Eugen Weber, *Action Française: Royalism and Reaction in Twentieth Century France* (Stanford, CA: Stanford University Press, 1962), 436.

57  Bruno Goyet, *Charles Maurras* (Presses de Sciences-Po, 2000), 84.

58  Quoted ibid., 85.

59  Weber, *Action Française*, 448.

60  Jacques Nobécourt, *Le Colonel de la Rocque, 1885–1946, ou les pièges du nationalisme chrétien* (Fayard, 1996), 707.

61  Quoted ibid., 725.

CHAPTER 3: BIRTH OF THE MOVEMENTS

1  Julien Blanc, *Au commencement de la Résistance: Du côté du musée de l'Homme, 1940–1941* (Seuil, 2010), 66.

2  Quoted in Alya Aglan, *La Résistance sacrifiée: Histoire du mouvement Libération-nord* (Champs-Flammarion, 2005; 1st ed., 1999), 66.

3  Quoted in Alya Aglan, *Le temps de la Résistance* (Arles: Actes Sud, 2008), 55.

4  Jacques Sémelin, "Jalons pour une histoire de la France résistante," in *La Résistance et les Français: Villes, centres et logiques de décision*, ed. Laurent Douzou, Robert Frank, Denis Peschanski, and Dominique Veillon (Cachan: École Normale Supérieure, 1995), 463.

5  Blanc, *Au commencement de la Résistance*, 67.

6  Quoted in Olivier Wieviorka, *Nous entrerons dans la carrière: De la Résistance à l'exercice du pouvoir* (Seuil, 1994), 73–74.

7  Claude Bourdet, *L'aventure incertaine: De la Résistance à la Restauration* (Stock, 1975), 89.

8  Henri Michel, *Histoire de la Résistance* (PUF, 1984; 1st ed., 1950), 61.

9  Olivier Wieviorka, *Une certaine idée de la Résistance: Défense de la France, 1940–1949* (Seuil, 1995), 21ff.

10  Jacques Lusseyran, *Et la lumière fut* (Chatou: Les Trois Arches, 1987), 285–286.

11  Dominique Veillon, *Le Franc-Tireur: Un journal clandestin, un mouvement de résistance, 1940–1944* (Flammarion, 1977), 48.

12  Jacques Baumel, *Résister: Histoire secrète des années d'occupation* (Albin Michel, 1999), 71.

13  Veillon, *Le Franc-Tireur*, 52.

14  Laurent Douzou, *La désobéissance: Histoire du mouvement Libération-sud* (Odile Jacob, 1995), 31ff.

15  Baumel, *Résister,* 70.

16  Ibid.

17  Marcel Prélôt and Paul Vignaux, quoted in Renée Bédarida, *Les armes de l'esprit: Témoignage chrétien (1941–1944)* (Éditions Ouvrières, 1977), 31.

18  Ibid., 41.

19  Quoted ibid., 43.

20  In the expression of Chaillet in 1946, quoted ibid., 54–55.

21  Quoted ibid., 58ff.

22  Harry R. Kedward, *Resistance in Vichy France: A Study of Ideas and Motivations in the Southern Zone, 1940–1942* (Oxford: Oxford University Press, 1978), 126–127.

23  Bourdet, *L'aventure incertaine,* 99–100.

24  Aglan, *La Résistance,* 74.

25  Jean-Pierre Levy, comments quoted in *La presse clandestine: 1940–1944* (Avignon: Conseil Général du Vaucluse, 1985), 94–95.

26  Philippe Viannay, *Du bon usage de la France: Résistance, Journalisme, Glénans* (Ramsay, 1988), 34.

27  Henri Frenay, *La nuit finira: Mémoires de Résistance,* vol. 1: *1940–1943* (Livre de poche, 1974; 1st ed., 1973), 110.

28  Bourdet, *L'aventure incertaine,* 72.

29  Veillon, *Le* Franc-Tireur, 70.

30  Christian Bougeard, "Le poids de la ville dans la Résistance en Bretagne et dans la France de l'Ouest," in Douzou et al., *La Résistance et les Français,* 249.

31  Cécile Vast, "Pantagruel," in *Dictionnaire historique de la Résistance,* ed. François Marcot (Robert Laffont, 2006), 741.

32  Marie Ducoudray, *Ceux de "Manipule": Un réseau de renseignement dans la Résistance en France* (Tirésias, 2001), 30.

33  Blanc, *Au commencement de la Résistance,* 202–203.

34  Ibid., 238.

35  Blanc, "Musée de l'Homme," in Marcot, *Dictionnaire historique de la Résistance,* 134–135.

36  Arthur Calmette, *L' "OCM," Histoire d'un mouvement de résistance de 1940 à 1946* (Presses Universitaires de France, 1961), 12.

37  On the genesis of the OCM and its first developments, see ibid., 11ff.

38  Henri Noguères, Marcel Degliame-Fouché, and Jean-Louis Vigier, *Histoire de la Résistance en France,* vol. 1: *Juin 1940–juin 1941* (Robert Laffont, 1967), 1:95.

39  Baumel, *Résister,* 63.

40  Ibid., 75.

41  Frenay, *La nuit finira,* 1:44.

42 Laurent Douzou and Dominique Veillon, "Comment les mouvements de la Résistance non communiste de zone sud ont-ils intégré la lutte armée dans leur stratégie?," in *La Résistance et les Français: Lutte armée et maquis*, ed. François Marcot (Besançon: Annales Littéraires de l'Université de Franche-Comté, 1996), 85.

43 Frenay, *La nuit finira*, 1:121–122.

44 Ibid., 159.

45 Jean Gemähling, *Souvenirs*, vol. 1, published by the author, n.d. (1999), 18ff.

46 Viannay, *Du bon usage*, 99.

47 On the beginnings of Combat, see Frenay, *La nuit finira*, vol. 1; and Robert Belot, *Henri Frenay: De la Résistance à l'Europe* (Seuil, 2003).

48 Laurent Douzou and Dominique Veillon, "Liberté," in Marcot, *Dictionnaire historique de la Résistance*, 129.

49 Frenay, *La nuit finira*, 1:199.

50 Bourdet, *L'aventure incertaine*, 70.

51 Quoted in Noguères et al., *Histoire de la Résistance en France*, 1:125.

52 Alban Vistel, *La nuit sans ombre: Histoire des mouvements unis de résistance, leur rôle dans la libération du Sud-Est* (Fayard, 1970), 47.

53 Quoted in Henri Michel, *Les courants de pensée de la Résistance* (Presses Universitaires de France, 1962), 135.

54 *Les Petites Ailes de France*, no. 5, quoted ibid., 136.

55 Indomitus (P. Viannay), "L'Allemand," *Défense de la France*, no. 12, March 20, 1942, quoted in Marie Granet, *Le journal* Défense de la France (Presses Universitaires de France, 1961), 66.

56 Jean Texcier, *Lettres à François*, quoted in Michel, *Les courants de pensée*, 139.

57 Vistel, *La nuit sans ombre*, 81.

58 Quoted in Jean-Louis Cuvelliez, "Les débuts de la Résistance à Toulouse et dans la région," in *Mémoire et histoire: La Résistance*, ed. Jean-Marie Guillon and Pierre Laborie (Toulouse: Privat, 1995), 131–132.

59 Veillon, *Le* Franc-Tireur, 74–75.

60 This claim was reiterated numerous times by many witnesses at the seminar conducted by Jean-Pierre Azéma, Claude Lévy, and Dominique Veillon at the Institut d'Histoire du Temps Présent.

61 Cuvelliez, "Les débuts de la Résistance à Toulouse," 134.

62 Michel, *Les courants de pensée*, 223.

63 Quoted in Vistel, *La nuit sans ombre*, 43.

64 Quoted in Pierre Laborie, "La Résistance et le sort des juifs: 1940–1942," in Guillon and Laborie, *Mémoire et histoire*, 252.

65 Quoted ibid.

66 Ibid., 249.

67 Quoted ibid., 251.

68 Maurice Ripoche, manifesto, October 1940, quoted in François Marcot, "Réflexions sur les valeurs de la Résistance," in Guillon and Laborie, *Mémoire et histoire*, 83.

69 *Les Petites Ailes de France*, no. 6, February 1941, quoted in Bénédicte Vergez-Chaignon, *Les Vichysto-résistants de 1940 à nos jours* (Perrin, 2008), 64.

70 Calmette, *L'"OCM,"* 28.

71 Indomitus (P. Viannay), *Défense de la France*, no. 9, January 25, 1942, quoted in Granet, *Le journal*, 45.

72 Laborie, "La Résistance et le sort des juifs: 1940–1942," in Guillon and Laborie, *Mémoire et histoire*, 250.

73 Agnès Humbert, *Notre guerre: Souvenirs de résistance* (Tallandier, 2004; 1st ed., 1946), 110.

74 Indomitus (P. Viannay), "Les derniers actes du maréchal," *Défense de la France*, no. 8, January 13, 1942, quoted in Granet, *Le journal*, 41.

75 Manifesto of November 1940, quoted in Daniel Cordier, *Jean Moulin: L'inconnu du Panthéon*, vol. 1: *Une ambition pour la République, Juin 1899–Juin 1936* (JC Lattès, 1989), 25.

76 Ibid.

77 Johanna Barasz, "De Vichy à la Résistance: Les vichysto-résistants, 1940–1944," 3 vols. (PhD thesis, Institut d'Études Politiques-Paris, 2010), 12.

78 Ibid., 194–195.

79 Claude d'Abzac-Epezy, *L'armée de l'air des années noires: Vichy 1940–1944* (Economica, 1998), 220ff.

80 Olivier Forcade, "Services spéciaux militaires," in Marcot, *Dictionnaire historique de la Résistance*, 211–212.

81 Ibid., 213.

82 Noguères et al., *Histoire de la Résistance en France*, 1:70ff.

83 Simon Kitson, *Vichy et la chasse aux espions nazis: Complexités de la politique de collaboration* (Autrement, 2005), 100 [English translation: *The Hunt for Nazi Spies: Fighting Espionage in Vichy France* (Chicago: University of Chicago Press, 2008)].

84 Abzac-Epezy, *L'armée de l'Air*, 363–364.

85 Jean Delmas, "Camouflage du matériel," in Marcot, *Dictionnaire historique de la Résistance*, 169.

86 Barasz, "De Vichy à la Résistance," 356.

87 Noguères et al., *Histoires de la Résistance en France*, 1:236.

88 Barasz, "De Vichy à la Résistance," 359. [Chantiers de la Jeunesse, founded in 1940, was a paramilitary organization aimed at organizing and training young people—trans.]

89 Vergez-Chaignon, *Les Vichysto-résistants*, 31.

90 Ibid., 112.

91 Barasz, "De Vichy à la Résistance," 60.

92 Vergez-Chaignon, *Les Vichysto-résistants*, 140.

93 Johanna Barasz, "Un vichyste en Résistance, le général de La Laurencie," *Vingtième siècle: Revue d'histoire* 94 (April–June 2007): 173.

94 Frenay, *La nuit finira*, 1:194.

95 Barasz, "Un vichyste," 180.

96 Abzac-Epezy, *L'armée de l'Air*, 232.

97 Vergez-Chaignon, *Les Vichysto-résistants*, 56.

98 Ibid., 36.

99 Frenay, *La nuit finira*, 1:86.

100 Noguères et al., *Histoire de la Résistance en France*, 1:239.

101 Abzac-Epezy, *L'armée de l'Air*, 223.

102 Douzou, *La désobéissance*, 88.

103 Ibid., 86ff.


CHAPTER 4: ENGAGEMENT

1 Pierre Laborie, *Le chagrin et le venin: La France sous l'Occupation, mémoire et idées reçues* (Bayard, 2011), 61.

2 Pierre Laborie, "Qu'est-ce que la Résistance?," in *Dictionnaire historique de la Résistance*, ed. François Marcot (Robert Laffont, 2006), 33.

3 François Bédarida, "L'histoire de la Résistance: Lecture d'hier, chantiers de demain," *Vingtième siècle: Revue d'histoire* 11 (July–September 1986): 80.

4 Laborie, "Qu'est-ce que la Résistance?," 34.

5 Foreword to Marcot, *Dictionnaire historique de la Résistance*, vii.

6 Bernard Comte, *L'honneur et la conscience: Catholiques français en Résistance (1940–1944)* (Éditions de l'Atelier, 1998), 9.

7 François Marcot, "Combien étaient-ils?," in Marcot, *Dictionnaire de la Résistance*, 339.

8 François Marcot, "Pour une sociologie de la Résistance: Intentionnalité et fonctionnalité," in *La Résistance, une histoire sociale*, ed. Antoine Prost (Éditions de l'Atelier, 1997), 26.

9 Marcot, "Combien étaient-ils?," 342.

10 Jean Anouilh, *L'orchestre* (Gallimard, "Folio," 1982; 1st ed., 1962), 110.

11 Raul Hilberg, *The Politics of Memory: The Journey of a Holocaust Historian* (Chicago: Ivan R. Dee, 1996), 136.

12 Claude Bourdet, *L'aventure incertaine: De la Résistance à la Restauration* (Stock, 1975), 321.

13 André Malraux, speech of May 10, 1975, in André Malraux, *La politique, la culture: Discours, articles, entretiens (1925–1975)*, ed. Janine Mossuz-Lavau (Gallimard, 1996), 373.

14 André Malraux, speech of November 23, 1975, ibid., 391.

15 Charles d'Aragon, *La Résistance sans héroïsme* (Seuil, 1977), 8.

16 Ibid., 215.

17 Philippe Burrin's expression in *La France à l'heure allemande* (Seuil, 1995) [English translation: *France under the Germans: Collaboration and Compromise*, trans. Janet Lloyd (New York: New Press, 1996)].

18 Marcot, "Pour une sociologie de la Résistance," 23.

19 François Marcot, *La Résistance dans le Jura* (Besançon: Cêtre, 1985), 72.

20 Henri Michel, "Rapport général," typescript, first lecture on the history of the resistance, 1958.

21 Marc Sadoun, *Les Socialistes sous l'Occupation: Résistance et collaboration* (Presses de Sciences-Po, 1982), 110.

22 Forces Françaises de l'Intérieur (French Forces of the Interior).

23 Interview quoted in Olivier Wieviorka, *Une certaine idée de la Résistance: Défense de la France, 1940–1949* (Seuil, 1995), 146.

24 Interview quoted ibid., 144.

25 Alain-René Michel, *La JEC face au nazisme et à Vichy* (Lillle: Presses Universitaires de Lille), 32ff.

26 Fabienne Federini, *Écrire ou combattre: Des intellectuels prennent les armes (1942–1944)* (La Découverte, 2006), 112–113.

27 Renée Bédarida, *Les armes de l'esprit: Témoignage chrétien (1941–1944)* (Éditions Ouvrières, 1977), 40.

28 Bourdet, *L'aventure incertaine*, 28–29.

29 Renaud Jean, "Carnets," *Communisme* 55–56 (1998): 126.

30 Benjamin Jung, "Marcel Gitton et le Parti ouvrier et paysan français (1939–1941): La voie d'un national-communisme de collaboration," paper prepared for the Institut d'Études Politiques-Paris, 2000.

31 Bourdet, *L'aventure incertaine*, 43.

32 Ibid., 56.

33 Ibid., 89.

34 Federini, *Écrire ou combattre*, 259.

35 Henri Becquart, letter to Marshal Pétain, October 1, 1940, quoted in Olivier Wieviorka, *Orphans of the Republic*, 168.

36 Henri Becquart, telegram to Marshal Pétain, October 24, 1940, quoted ibid., 159.

37 Alban Vistel, *La nuit sans ombre: Histoire des mouvements unis de résistance, leur rôle dans la libération du Sud-Est* (Fayard, 1970), 28.

38 Yves de Montcheuil, "Vers le soulèvement de la nation," *Cahiers du Témoignage Chrétien*, May 1944, quoted in Bédarida, *Les armes de l'esprit*, 352.

39 Interview quoted in Olivier Wieviorka, *Une certaine idée*, 184.

40 Claude Lanzmann, *Le lièvre de Patagonie: Mémoires* (Gallimard, 2009), 40.

41 Bourdet, *L'aventure incertaine*, 71.

42 Olivier Todd, *André Malraux: Une vie* (Gallimard, 2001), 313.

43 Jean Lacouture, *André Malraux: Une vie dans le siècle* (Seuil, 1973), 278.

44 André Malraux, *La condition humaine* (Gallimard, 1976; 1st ed., 1933), 54–55.

45 André Malraux, *L'espoir* (Gallimard, 1996; 1st. ed., 1937), 128.

46  Bourdet, *L'aventure incertaine*, 72–73.

47  Thomas Pouty, "Les fusillés en France, 1940–1944: Étude d'un panel de 1 000 victimes," in *La répression en France, 1940–1945*, ed. Bernard Garnier, Jean-Luc Leleu, and Jean Quellien (Caen: Centre de Recherche d'Histoire Quantitative, 2007), 208.

48  Delphine Kazandjian, "La déportation de répression organisée après le Débarquement au départ de la 'zone occupée,'" in Garnier et al., *La répression en France*, 239–240 and 247.

49  Aragon, *La Résistance sans héroïsme*, 56.

50  Ibid., 75. [The "blue line of the Vosges" refers to the borderline between France and German-occupied Alsace after 1870, hence to the Revanche.—trans.]

51  Raphaël Spina, "La France et les Français devant le Service du travail obligatoire" (PhD thesis, École Normale Supérieure de Cachan, 2012), 23.

52  Ibid., 806.

53  Ibid., 808.

54  Nicolas Mariot and Claire Zalc, *Face à la persécution: 991 juifs dans la guerre* (Odile Jacob, 2010), 181.

55  Ibid., 91.

56  Ibid.

57  Ibid., 114–115.

58  Burrin, *La France à l'heure allemande*, 322–328.

59  Alice Kaplan, *The Collaborator: The Trial and Execution of Robert Brasillach* (Chicago: University of Chicago, 2000), 33.

60  Federini, *Écrire ou combattre*, 215.

61  Ingrid Galster, *Sartre, Vichy et les intellectuels* (L'Harmattan, 2001), 12.

62  Ibid.; see the chapter titled "Historiographie ou hagiographie" for a detailed account of the event. The quotation is mentioned on p. 105.

63  Jacques Ion, "Interventions sociales, engagements bénévoles et mobilisation des expériences personnelles," in *Engagement public et exposition de la personne*, ed. Michel Peroni (Édition de l'Aube, 1997), 81.

64  Olivier Wieviorka, "À la recherche de l'engagement (1940–1944)," *Vingtième siècle: Revue d'histoire* 60 (1998): 62ff.

65  Bourdet, *L'aventure incertaine*, 70.

66  Vistel, *La nuit sans ombre*, 17.

67  Ibid.

68  Quoted in Olivier Wieviorka, *Une certaine idée*, 173–174.

69  Charles Tilly, *The Contentious French* (Cambridge, MA: Harvard University Press, 1986), 390.

70  Ibid.

71  Colonel Rémy, *Mémoires d'un agent secret de la France libre: Juin 1940–juin 1942* (Aux Trois Couleurs et Raoul Solar, 1946), 107.

72  Colonel Rémy, *Les soldats du silence: Mémoires d'un agent secret de la France libre*, vol. 2 (France-Empire, 1998), 68.

73   Jean-Marie Guillon, "Le maquis, une résurgence du banditisme social?," *Provence historique* 147 (1986): 57–67.

74   Jean-Marie Guillon, "La Résistance dans le Var: Essai d'histoire politique," 3 vols. (PhD thesis, Université de Provence, Aix-en-Provence, 1989), 57.

75   Gérard Bollon, "La tradition d'accueil avant la guerre," in *Le Plateau Vivarais-Lignon: Accueil et Résistance 1939–1944*, ed. Pierre Bolle (Le Chambon-sur-Lignon: Société d'histoire de la Montagne, 1992), 151.

76   Michel Fabreguet, "Réfractaires, maquisards et communautés protestantes des Cévennes et du Vivarais," quoted in Spina, "La France et les Français," 674.

77   Michael R. D. Foot, *SOE in France: An Account of the Work of the British Special Operations Executive in France, 1940–1944* (London: Her Majesty's Stationery Office, 1966), 189.

78   Marcot, *La Résistance dans le Jura*, 27.

79   Pierre Guillain de Bénouville, *Le sacrifice du matin* (Robert Laffont, 1946), 515.

80   Alya Aglan, *La Résistance sacrifiée: Histoire du mouvement Libération-nord* (Champs-Flammarion, 2005; 1st ed., 1999), 152.

81   Indomitus (P. Viannay), "Le devoir de tuer," *Défense de la France* 44, March 15, 1944, quoted in Marie Granet, *Le journal* Défense de la France (Presses Universitaires de France, 1961), 246–247.

82   Olivier Wieviorka, *Une certaine idée*, 182.

83   Henri Noguères, *La vie quotidienne des résistants de l'armistice à la libération (1940–1945)* (Hachette, 1984), 43.

84   Ibid., 13.

85   Rémy, *Les soldats du silence*, 2:189.

86   Circular mentioned in Marcot, *La Résistance dans le Jura*, 78.

87   In accordance with the famous model established by Albert Hirschman, *Exit, Voice, and Loyalty: Responses to Decline in Firms, Organizations, and States* (Cambridge, MA: Harvard University Press, 1970).

88   Robert Belot, *Aux frontières de la liberté: Vichy-Madrid-Alger-Londres: S'évader de France sous l'Occupation* (Fayard, 1998), 679.

89   Ibid., 661–662.

90   Olivier Wieviorka, *Une certaine idée*, 187.

91   Ibid., 160.

92   Boris Vildé, *Journal et lettres de prison, 1941–1942* (Allia, 1997), 62–63.

93   Colonel Rémy, *Les soldats du silence*, 239.

94   Fernand Grenier, *C'était ainsi . . . La résistance, Châteaubriand, Londres, Alger, le Vercors, Dachau* (Éditions Sociales, 1970), 172–173.

95   Bourdet, *L'aventure incertaine*, 27.

96   Pierre Péan, *Vies et morts de Jean Moulin* (Fayard, 1998), 357ff.

97   Foot, *SOE in France*, 159.

98   Colonel Rémy, *Mémoires*, 459.

99   Ibid., 465 and 467.

100   Ibid., 485.

101   Grenier, *C'était ainsi*, 172.

102   Quoted in Noguères, *La vie quotidienne des résistants*, 61–62.

103   Noguères, *La vie quotidienne des résistants*, 190.

104   Francis-Louis Closon, *Le temps des passions: De Jean Moulin à la Libération, 1943–1945* (Geneva: Famot, 1976; 1st ed., 1974), 212.

105   Daniel Cordier, *Alias Caracalla* (Gallimard, 2009), 533.

106   Jean Cassou, *La mémoire courte* (Mille et Une Nuits, 2011; 1st ed., 1953), 41–42.

107   Closon, *Le temps des passions*, 213–214.

108   Noguères, *La vie quotidienne des résistants*, 210.

109   Ibid., 58.

110   Colonel Rémy, *Mémoires*, 483.

111   Bourdet, *L'aventure incertaine*, 238.

112   Aragon, *La Résistance sans héroïsme*, 59.

113   Bourdet, *L'aventure incertaine*, 118.

114   Jacques Bingen, letter of April 14, 1944, quoted in Henri Noguères and Marcel Degliame-Fouché, *Histoire de la Résistance en France*, vol. 4: *Formez vos bataillons! Octobre 1943–mai 1944* (Robert Laffont, 1976), 632.

115   Milan Kundera, *Les testaments trahis* (Gallimard, 1993), 26. My thanks to my daughter Sophie for this information.

116   Harry R. Kedward, *Resistance in Vichy France: A Study of Ideas and Motivations in the Southern Zone, 1940–1942* (Oxford: Oxford University Press, 1978), 78.

## CHAPTER 5: GAME CHANGE

1   Colonel Passy, *Mémoires du chef des services secrets de la France libre* (Odile Jacob, 2000; 1st ed., 1947), 196.

2   Daniel Virieux, "Le Front national de lutte pour la liberté et l'indépendance de la France: Un mouvement de Résistance, période clandestine (mai 1941–août 1944)," 5 vols. (PhD thesis, Paris-VIII, 1995), 76.

3   Vladislav Smirnov, "L'Union soviétique, le Komintern et la Résistance française en 1940–1941," in *La Résistance et les Français: Villes, centres et logiques de décision*, ed. Laurent Douzou, Robert Frank, Denis Peschanski, and Dominique Veillon (Cachan: École Normale Supérieure, 1995), 510.

4   G. Dimitrov, telegram to Clément, July 1, 1941, quoted in Mikhaïl Narinski, "L'URSS, le Komintern et la lutte armée en France," in *La Résistance et les Français: Lutte armée et maquis*, ed. François Marcot (Besançon: Annales Littéraires de l'Université de Franche-Comté, 1996), 361.

5   M. Thorez, A. Marty, and G. Dimitrov, telegram to Clément for J. Duclos, August 8, 1941, quoted ibid., 362.

6   Franck Liaigre, "Bataillons de la jeunesse," in *Dictionnaire historique de la Résistance*, ed. François Marcot (Robert Laffont, 2006), 167.

7   Roger Bourderon, "Francs-tireurs et partisans français," in Marcot, *Dictionnaire historique de la Résistance*, 189.

8   Jacqueline Sainclivier, *La Résistance en Ille-et-Vilaine, 1940–1944* (Rennes: Presses Universitaires de Rennes, 1993), 58.

9   Virieux, "Le Front national," 163.

10  Quoted in Stéphane Courtois, *Le PCF dans la guerre: De Gaulle, la Résistance, Staline . . .* (Ramsay, 1980), 20.

11  Quoted ibid., 210.

12  Jean-Pierre Le Crom, "Syndicalisme et résistance," in Douzou, *La Résistance et les Français*, 406.

13  Quoted in Courtois, *Le PCF*, 212.

14  Danielle Tartakowsky, *Les manifestations de rue en France, 1918–1968* (Publications de la Sorbonne, 1997), 461.

15  Lise London, *La Mégère de la rue Daguerre: Souvenirs de résistance* (Seuil, 1995), 152.

16  Ibid, 161.

17  Tartakowsky, *Les manifestations*, 463.

18  Ibid., 467.

19  Jean-Marc Berlière and Franck Liaigre, *Liquider les traîtres: La face cachée du PCF, 1941–1943* (Robert Laffont, 2007), 142.

20  Report of Otto von Stülpnagel, quoted in Ahlrich Meyer, *L'Occupation allemande en France, 1940–1944* (Toulouse: Privat, 2002), 41.

21  Denis Peschanski, "21 août 1941: Attentat du métro Barbès," in Marcot, *Dictionnaire historique de la Résistance*, 607–608.

22  Quoted in Henri Noguères, Marcel Degliame-Fouché, and Jean-Louis Vigier, *Histoire de la Résistance en France de 1940 à 1945*, vol. 2: *L'armée de l'ombre: Juillet 1941–octobre 1942* (Robert Laffont, 1969), 161.

23  Christian Pineau, *La simple vérité: 1940–1945* (Phalanx, 1983; 1st ed., 1960), 180.

24  Denis Peschanski, "Attentats individuels contre les Allemands," in Marcot, *Dictionnaire historique de la Résistance*, 703.

25  Charles de Gaulle, speech of October 23, 1941, in *Discours et messages* (hereafter cited as *DM*), vol. 1: *Pendant la guerre, 1940–1946* (Plon, 1970), 122–123.

26  Henri Frenay, *La nuit finira: Mémoires de Résistance*, vol. 1: *1940–1943* (Livre de poche, 1974; 1st ed., 1973), 278.

27  Quoted in Noguères et al., *Histoire de la Résistance en France*, 2:73.

28  Berlière and Liaigre, *Liquider les traîtres*, 104 and 149.

29  Ibid., 171.

30  Ibid., 172.

31  Quoted in Noguères et al., *Histoire de la Résistance en France*, 2:159.

32 Sébastien Albertelli, *Les Services secrets du général de Gaulle: Le BCRA (1940–1944)* (Perrin, 2009), 120.

33 Ibid., 146.

34 Michael R. D. Foot, *SOE in France: An Account of the Work of the British Special Operations Executive in France, 1940–1944* (London: Her Majesty's Stationery Office, 1966), 149.

35 Daniel Cordier, *Alias Caracalla* (Gallimard, 2009), 238–239.

36 Ibid., 239.

37 Albertelli, *Les Services secrets*, 154.

38 Quoted in Noguères et al., *Histoire de la Résistance en France*, 2:318.

39 Ibid., 224–225.

40 Albertelli, *Les Services secrets*, 158.

41 Foot, *SOE in France*, 231.

42 For an overview, see François Kersaudy, *Churchill and de Gaulle* (London: Collins, 1981).

43 Jean-François Muracciole, *Les Français libres* (Tallandier, 2009), 136.

44 Ibid., 143.

45 Ibid.

46 Foot, *SOE in France*, 197.

47 Ibid.

48 Ibid., 203.

49 Ibid., 212–213.

50 For an overview, see Thomas Rabino, *Le réseau Carte: Histoire d'un réseau de la Résistance antiallemand, antigaulliste, anticommuniste et anticollaborationniste* (Perrin, 2008).

51 Quoted ibid., 151.

52 Quoted ibid., 195.

53 Quoted ibid., 197.

54 Foot, *SOE in France*, 206.

55 Rabino, *Le réseau Carte*, 301.

56 Ibid., 207.

57 Jacques Baumel, *Résister: Histoire secrète des années d'occupation* (Albin Michel, 1999), 58.

58 Rabino, *Le réseau Carte*, 217.

59 Ibid., 236.

60 Ibid., 247.

61 Albertelli, *Les Services secrets*, 88.

62 Ibid., 227.

63 Ibid., 161–162.

64 Daniel Cordier, *Jean Moulin: La République des Catacombes* (Gallimard, 1999), 51.

65 Ibid., 88.

66 For an overview, see Alya Aglan, *La Résistance sacrifiée: Histoire du mouvement Libération-nord* (Champs-Flammarion, 2005; 1st ed., 1999).

67  Ibid., 155.

68  Ibid., 156.

69  Ibid., 175.

70  Olivier Wieviorka, *Une certaine idée*, 34ff.

71  Défense de la France, "Les derniers actes du maréchal," *Défense de la France*, no. 8, January 13, 1942.

72  Indomitus (P. Viannay), "La France commande," *Défense de la France*, no. 4, December 1941 (?).

73  Philippe Viannay, *Du bon usage de la France: Résistance, Journalisme, Glénans* (Ramsay, 1988), 51.

74  Olivier Wieviorka, *Une certaine idée*, 79.

75  R. Tenaille (R. Salmon), "Résistance," *Défense de la France*, no. 2, September 10, 1941.

76  Indomitus (P. Viannay), "Vérités rudes," *Défense de la France*, no. 11, February 15, 1942.

77  Indomitus (P. Viannay), "Lettres à la jeunesse," *Défense de la France*, no. 18, June 17, 1942.

78  Étienne Dejonghe and Yves Le Maner, *Le Nord-Pas-de-Calais dans la main allemande* (Lille: La Voix du Nord, 1999), 186–187.

79  Claire Andrieu, "Ceux de la Libération," in Marcot, *Dictionnaire historique de la Résistance*, 115.

80  Arthur Calmette, *L' "OCM," Histoire d'un mouvement de résistance de 1940 à 1946* (Presses Universitaires de France, 1961), 102ff.

81  Quoted ibid., 53–54.

82  OCM, "Du côté de chez Pétain," June 1942, quoted in Calmette, *L' "OCM,"* 47.

83  Ibid., 49.

84  Ibid., 137.

85  Quoted in Laurent Douzou, *La désobéissance: Histoire du mouvement Libération-sud* (Odile Jacob, 1995), 87.

86  Baumel, *Résister*, 70.

87  Laurent Douzou, "Hervé Pierre," in Marcot, *Dictionnaire historique de la Résistance*, 442–443.

88  Quoted in Douzou, *La désobéissance*, 268.

89  Quoted ibid., 293.

90  Ibid., 165.

91  Quoted ibid., 191.

92  Quoted ibid., 195.

93  Ibid., 212.

94  Ibid., 197.

95  Dominique Veillon, *Le Franc-Tireur: Un journal clandestin, un mouvement de résistance, 1940–1944* (Flammarion, 1977), 164.

96  Ibid., 94.

97  Ibid., 97.

98  Ibid., 272.

99  *Franc-Tireur*, January 1942, quoted in Veillon, *Le* Franc-Tireur, 276.

100  *Franc-Tireur*, March 1942, quoted ibid., 299.

101  *Franc-Tireur*, April 1942, quoted ibid., 293.

102  *Franc-Tireur*, September 1942, quoted ibid.

103  *Franc-Tireur*, September 1942, quoted ibid. 294.

104  Ibid., 117.

105  Ibid., 213.

106  Claude Bourdet, *L'aventure incertaine: De la Résistance à la Restauration* (Stock, 1975), 104.

107  Frenay, *La nuit finira*, 1:166.

108  Ibid., 205–206.

109  Robert Belot, *Henri Frenay: De la Résistance à l'Europe* (Seuil, 2003), 256.

110  Cécile Vast, "Ceux de la Résistance," in Marcot, *Dictionnaire historique de la Résistance*, 116.

111  Frenay, *La nuit finira*, 1:188.

112  Ibid., 192.

113  Ibid., 178.

114  Jacques Soustelle, *Envers et contre tout: Souvenirs et documents sur la France libre*, 2 vols. (Robert Laffont, 1947–50), 1:309.

115  Belot, *Henri Frenay*, 275.

116  Ibid., 252.

117  Ibid., 193.

118  Ibid., 255ff.

119  Bourdet, *L'aventure incertaine*, 120.

120  Belot, *Henri Frenay*, 277.

121  Colonel Passy, *Souvenirs: 10, Duke Street Londres (le BCRA)* (Monte Carlo: Solar, 1948), 102.

122  Douzou, *La désobéissance*, 103.

123  Quoted in Frenay, *La nuit finira*, 1:271.

124  *Les Petites Ailes de France*, May 1941, quoted in Bénédicte Vergez-Chaignon, *Les Vichysto-résistants de 1940 à nos jours* (Perrin, 2008), 68.

125  Bourdet, *L'aventure incertaine*, 63.

CHAPTER 6: RALLYING BEHIND DE GAULLE

1  Jean-Louis Crémieux-Brilhac, *La France libre: De l'appel du 18 juin à la Libération* (Gallimard, 1996), 241.

2  Sébastien Albertelli, *Les Services secrets du général de Gaulle: Le BCRA (1940–1944)* (Perrin, 2009), 129.

3  Ibid., 135.

4  Ibid., 163.

5  Ibid., 167.

6   Ibid.

7   Ibid.

8   Orders (political and military) of November 5, 1941, quoted in Daniel Cordier, *Jean Moulin: La République des Catacombes* (Gallimard, 1999), 143.

9   Cordier, *Jean Moulin: La République*, 144.

10  Henri Frenay, *La nuit finira: Mémoires de Résistance*, vol. 1: *1940–1943* (Livre de poche, 1974; 1st ed., 1973), 217.

11  Jean-Marc Binot and Bernard Boyer, *L'argent de la Résistance* (Larousse, 2010), 37.

12  Albertelli, *Les Services secrets*, 175–176.

13  Frenay, *La nuit finira*, 1:216.

14  Quoted in Cordier, *Jean Moulin: La République*, 166.

15  Bruno Leroux, "Bureau d'information et de presse," in *Dictionnaire historique de la Résistance*, ed. François Marcot (Robert Laffont, 2006), 168.

16  On Pierre Brossolette, see Guillaume Piketty, *Pierre Brossolette: Un héros de la Résistance* (Odile Jacob, 1998).

17  Interview with the author in Olivier Wieviorka, *Nous entrerons dans la carrière: De la Résistance à l'exercice du pouvoir* (Seuil, 1994), 253–254.

18  Christian Pineau, *La simple vérité: 1940–1945* (Phalanx, 1983; 1st ed., 1960), 158.

19  Ibid., 159.

20  Ibid., 184.

21  Quoted in Cordier, *Jean Moulin: La République*, 201.

22  Frenay, *La nuit finira*, 1:223.

23  Ibid., 357.

24  Cordier, *Jean Moulin: La République*, 201.

25  De Gaulle, personal and secret instructions for action in France, October 29, 1942, quoted ibid., 200–201.

26  Frenay, *La nuit finira*, 1:390.

27  Jacques Soustelle, *Envers et contre tout: Souvenirs et documents sur la France libre*, 2 vols. (Robert Laffont, 1947–50), 1:312.

28  P. Brossolette, report of April 28, 1942, quoted in Piketty, *Pierre Brossolette*, 187.

29  Soustelle, *Envers et contre tout*, 1:312.

30  Piketty, *Pierre Brossolette*, 166.

31  Pierre Brossolette, report of May 8, 1942, quoted ibid., 189.

32  Piketty, *Pierre Brossolette*, 194.

33  Jean-Jaurès group, session of October 4, 1941, quoted in Marc Sadoun, *Les Socialistes sous l'Occupation: Résistance et collaboration* (Presses de Sciences-Po, 1982), 185.

34  Léon Blum, letter to the French people from London, May 5, 1942, in Léon Blum, *La prison, le procès, la déportation: Mémoires et correspondance* (Albin Michel, 1955), 349.

35  Sadoun, *Les Socialistes*, 143.

36  Léon Blum, note sent to General de Gaulle for President Roosevelt and Prime Minister Churchill, in Blum, *La prison*, 383.

37  Pierre Brossolette, political report of April 28, 1942, quoted in Piketty, *Pierre Brossolette*, 182.

38  Charles Vallin, comments on the BBC, September 17, 1942, quoted in Piketty, *Pierre Brossolette*, 206.

39  Piketty, *Pierre Brossolette*, 210.

40  Bénédicte Vergez-Chaignon, *Les Vichysto-résistants de 1940 à nos jours* (Perrin, 2008), 231.

41  Piketty, *Pierre Brossolette*, 207.

42  According to Claude Bourdet, *L'aventure incertaine: De la Résistance à la Restauration* (Stock, 1975), 152.

43  For a general account, see André Kaspi, "La 'comédie' d'Alger," *L'Histoire* 88 (April 1986): 50–58.

44  Ibid., 58.

45  Vergez-Chaignon, *Les Vichysto-résistants*, 292.

46  Interview quoted in Henri Noguères and Marcel Degliame-Fouché, *Histoire de la Résistance en France*, vol. 3: *Et du Nord au Midi, novembre 1942–septembre 1943* (Robert Laffont, 1972), 26.

47  Vergez-Chaignon, *Les Vichysto-résistants*, 258.

48  Johanna Barasz, "De Vichy à la Résistance: Les vichysto-résistants, 1940–1944," 3 vols. (PhD thesis, Institut d'Études Politiques-Paris, 2010), 398.

49  Interview quoted in Noguères and Degliame-Fouché, *Histoire de la Résistance en France*, 3:38.

50  Raymond Aubrac, *Où la mémoire s'attarde* (Odile Jacob, 1996), 85.

51  Ibid., 86.

52  Interview quoted in Noguères and Degliame-Fouché, *Histoire de la Résistance en France*, 3:40.

53  Barasz, "De Vichy à la Résistance," 411.

54  Ibid., 470.

55  Paul Paillole, *Services spéciaux (1935–1945)* (Robert Laffont, 1975), 399.

56  Vergez-Chaignon, *Les Vichysto-résistants*, 282.

57  Ibid., 275.

58  Barasz, "De Vichy à la Résistance," 475.

59  Ibid., 480.

60  Ibid., 487.

61  Quoted in Noguères and Degliame-Fouché, *Histoire de la Résistance en France*, 3:51.

62  Barasz, "De Vichy à la Résistance," 537.

63  Jean Delmas, "Organisation de résistance de l'armée," in Marcot, *Dictionnaire historique de la Résistance*, 201.

64  Simon Kitson, *Vichy et la chasse aux espions nazis: Complexités de la politique de collaboration* (Autrement, 2005), 93 [English translation: *The Hunt for Nazi Spies: Fighting Espionage in Vichy France* (Chicago: University of Chicago Press, 2008)].

65  Paillole, *Services spéciaux*, 421.

66  Indomitus (P. Viannay), "Un seul drapeau," *Défense de la France*, January 1, 1943, quoted in Olivier Wieviorka, *Une certaine idée*, 201.

67  *Défense de la France, Pantagruel, La France continue, Chantecler, Franc-Tireur, Libération, Combat, Résistance*, "Lettre ouverte aux généraux Giraud et de Gaulle," *Défense de la France*, January 20, 1943.

68  Cordier, *Jean Moulin: La République*, 284.

69  Ibid.

70  Ibid., 285.

71  Quoted by Stéphane Courtois, *Le PCF dans la guerre: De Gaulle, la Résistance, Staline . . .* (Ramsay, 1980), 304.

72  Cordier, *Jean Moulin: La République*, 292.

73  Courtois, *Le PCF dans la guerre*, 305.

74  Jacques Duclos, *Mémoires*, vol. 2: *Dans la bataille clandestine, Deuxième partie: 1943–1945: De la victoire de Stalingrad à la capitulation de Berlin* (Fayard, 1970), 83.

75  Courtois, *Le PCF dans la guerre*, 324.

76  Quoted in Piketty, *Pierre Brossolette*, 212.

77  Cordier, *Jean Moulin: La République*, 288.

## CHAPTER 7: FIGHTING THE SAME BATTLE?

1  Quoted in Aurélie Luneau, *Radio-Londres, 1940–1944: Les voix de la liberté* (Perrin, 2005), 154.

2  Charles de Gaulle, speech of April 30, 1942, in *DM*, 1:184.

3  Henri Frenay, *La nuit finira: Mémoires de Résistance*, vol. 1: *1940–1943* (Livre de poche, 1974; 1st ed., 1973), 277.

4  Unpublished recollections of Yvon Morandat, quoted in Luneau, *Radio-Londres*, 153.

5  According to the report in the newspaper *Libération*, no. 12, May 18, 1942, quoted in Alban Vistel, *La nuit sans ombre: Histoire des mouvements unis de résistance, leur rôle dans la libération du Sud-Est* (Fayard, 1970), 113.

6  Luneau, *Radio-Londres*, 155.

7  Danielle Tartakowsky, *Les manifestations de rue en France, 1918–1968* (Publications de la Sorbonne, 1997), 472.

8  Speech by Maurice Schumann, quoted in Luneau, *Radio-Londres*, 158.

9  Pierre Laborie, *L'opinion française sous Vichy* (Seuil, 1990), 253.

10  Ibid., 265.

11  Tartakowsky, *Les manifestations*, 473.

12  Luneau, *Radio-Londres*, 160–161.

13  Tartakowsky, *Les manifestations*, 467.

14  Ian Kershaw, *The End: The Defiance and Destruction of Hitler's Germany, 1944–1945* (New York: Penguin, 2011).

15  Patrice Arnaud and Helga Bories-Sawala, "Les Français et Françaises volontaires pour le travail en Allemagne: Recrutement et dimensions statistiques, images et représentations, mythes et réalités," in *La main-d'oeuvre française exploitée par le IIIe Reich*, ed. Bernard Garnier and Jean Quellien (Caen: Centre de Recherche d'Histoire Quantitative, 2003), 112.

16  Bernd Zielinski, "L'exploitation de la main-d'oeuvre française par l'Allemagne et la politique de collaboration (1940–1944)," in Garnier and Quellien, *La main-d'oeuvre*, 55.

17  Jean Quellien, "Les travailleurs forcés en Allemagne: Essai d'approche statistique," in Garnier and Quellien, *La main-d'oeuvre*, 75.

18  Antoine Prost, "Jeunesse et société dans la France de l'entre-deux-guerres," *Vingtième siècle: Revue d'histoire* 13 (1987): 35ff.

19  For an overview, see Xavier Vigna, *Histoire des ouvriers en France au XXe siècle* (Perrin, 2010), 143ff.

20  Hubert Desvages, "Les ouvriers de l'Isère," in *Les ouvriers en France pendant la Seconde Guerre mondiale*, ed. Denis Peschanski and Jean-Louis Robert (Cahiers de l'Institut d'Histoire du Temps Présent, 1992), 203.

21  Fabrice Sugier, "La politique ouvrière des pouvoirs publics dans le bassin houiller du Gard," in Peschanski and Robert, *Les ouvriers en France*, 289.

22  François Marcot, "Les ouvriers de Peugeot, le patronat et l'État," in Peschanski and Robert, *Les ouvriers en France*, 248.

23  Ibid., 252.

24  Christian Chevandier, "Clivages et continuités dans les perceptions et les comportements ouvriers: Les ateliers d'Oullins de la SNCF," in Peschanski and Robert, *Les ouvriers en France*, 433.

25  Olivier Kourchid, "Répressions et résistances: Les ouvriers des mines du Nord-Pas-de-Calais," in Peschanski and Robert, *Les ouvriers en France*, 215.

26  Forez (François Mauriac), *Cahier noir* (Éditions de Minuit, 1943), quoted in Vigna, *Histoires des ouvriers*, 154.

27  Zielinski, "L'exploitation de la main-d'oeuvre," 56–58.

28  Raphaël Spina, "La France et les Français devant le Service du travail obligatoire" (PhD thesis, École Normale Supérieure de Cachan, 2012), 500.

29  Quellien, "Les travailleurs forcés en Allemagne," 71.

30  Desvages, "Les ouvriers de l'Isère," 205.

31  Spina, "La France et les Français," 253.

32  Ibid., 263.

33  Marcot, "Les ouvriers de Peugeot," 250.

34  Sugier, "La politique ouvrière des pouvoirs publics," 289.

35  Spina, "La France et les Français," 280–283.

36  Ibid., 323.

37  Ibid., 909.

38  Desvages, "Les ouvriers de l'Isère," 203.

39  Michel Hau, "Les entreprises alsaciennes," in *La vie des entreprises sous l'Occupation*, ed. Alain Beltran, Robert Frank, and Henry Rousso (Belin, 1994), 244.

40  Ibid., 245.

41  Spina, "La France et les Français," 252–253.

42  Jean-Marie Guillon, "Y a-t-il un comportement ouvrier spécifique? Les ouvriers varois," in Peschanski and Robert, *Les ouvriers en France*, 471.

43  Arne Radtke-Delacor, "La place des commandes allemandes à l'industrie française dans les stratégies de guerre nazie de 1940 à 1944," in Beltran et al., *La vie des entreprises*, 23.

44  Spina, "La France et les Français," 307–308.

45  Ibid., 420.

46  Ibid., 938.

47  Ibid., 23.

48  H. R. Kedward, *In Search of the Maquis: Rural Resistance in Southern France, 1942–1944* (Oxford: Clarendon Press, 1993), 30.

49  Jean-Pierre Azéma, *Jean Moulin: Le rebelle, le patriote, le résistant* (Perrin, 2003), 356.

50  Tract distributed on October 16, 1942, in the factories of the Lyon region, quoted in Colonel Passy, *Souvenirs: Missions secrètes en France* (Plon, 1951), 301.

51  "Français! Debout contre l'esclavage," *Franc-Tireur*, no. 16, March 20, 1943, quoted in Dominique Veillon, *Le Franc-Tireur: Un journal clandestin, un mouvement de résistance, 1940–1944* (Flammarion, 1977), 295.

52  Robert Tenaille (R. Salmon), "Mots d'ordre," *Défense de la France*, no. 27, February 5, 1943, quoted in Granet, *Le journal*, 131.

53  "Déclaration commune des groupements français de résistance," *Défense de la France*, no. 28, February 20, 1943, quoted in in Marie Granet, *Le journal* Défense de la France (Presses Universitaires de France, 1961), 136.

54  Georges Guingouin, *4 ans de lutte sur le sol limousin* (Limoges: Lucien Souny, 1991), 75.

55  Frenay, *La nuit finira*, 1:438–439.

56  François Marcot, "Maquis," in *Dictionnaire historique de la Résistance*, ed. François Marcot (Robert Laffont, 2006), 675–676.

57  Frenay, *La nuit finira*, 1:483.

58  Spina, "La France et les Français," 874–876.

59  Telegram from the MUR to General de Gaulle, March 3, 1943, received March 20, 1943, quoted in Daniel Cordier, *Jean Moulin: La République des Catacombes* (Gallimard, 1999), 322.

60  Azéma, *Jean Moulin*, 358.

61  Cordier, *Jean Moulin: La République*, 323.
62  Quoted ibid., 333.
63  Ibid., 334.
64  Colonel Passy, *Souvenirs: Missions*, 73.
65  Cordier, *Jean Moulin: La République*, 352.
66  Jean Moulin, report of June 4, 1943, quoted in Colonel Passy, *Souvenirs: Missions*, 196.
67  Frenay, *La nuit finira*, 1:456.
68  Spina, "La France et les Français," 881.
69  Claude Bourdet, *L'aventure incertaine: De la Résistance à la Restauration* (Stock, 1975), 192.
70  Azéma, *Jean Moulin*, 360.
71  Gilles Vergnon, *Le Vercors: Histoire et mémoire d'un maquis* (Éditions de l'Atelier, 2002), 44–45.
72  Kedward, *In Search of the Maquis*, 29.
73  Bourdet, *L'aventure incertaine*, 225.
74  Spina, "La France et les Français," 937.
75  Ibid., 939.
76  Ibid., 953.
77  Guingouin, *4 ans de lutte*, 85.
78  François Marcot, *La Résistance dans le Jura* (Besançon: Cêtre, 1985), 196.
79  Ibid., 182.
80  Kedward, *In Search of the Maquis*, 34.
81  Plan quoted in Vergnon, *Le Vercors*, 47.
82  Vergnon, *Le Vercors*, 49.
83  Ibid., 52.

## CHAPTER 8: RESPONSES TO PERSECUTION OF THE JEWS

1  For an overview, see André Kaspi, *Les Juifs pendant l'Occupation* (Seuil, 1991).
2  Renée Poznanski, *Être juif en France pendant la Seconde Guerre mondiale* (Hachette, 1994), 265–268.
3  Serge Klarsfeld, *La Shoah en France*, vol. 3: *Le calendrier de la persécution des juifs de France, septembre 1942–août 1944* (Fayard, 2001), 1916–1918.
4  Serge Klarsfeld, *La Shoah en France*, vol. 1: *Vichy-Auschwitz: La "solution finale" de la question juive en France* (Fayard, 2001; 1st ed., 1983), 370.
5  Quoted ibid., 121.
6  In addition to the victims of deportation, there were those who died in French camps or prisons, the hostages who were shot, and the men, women, and children massacred on French soil by the Milice, for example.

7   Klarlsfeld, *La Shoah en France*, 1:368.

8   Renée Poznanski, *Propagandes et persécutions: La Résistance et le 'problème juif' (1940–1944)* (Fayard, 2008), 43.

9   Quoted ibid., 135.

10  Quoted ibid., 195–196.

11  Quoted ibid., 164.

12  Quoted ibid., 200.

13  *L'Humanité*, item of September 10, 1940, quoted ibid., 161.

14  Poznanski, *Propagandes et persécutions*, 161ff.

15  Annette Wieviorka, "Les années noires," in *Les Juifs de France, de la Révolution française à nos jours*, ed. Jean-Jacques Becker and Annette Wieviorka (Liana Levi, 1998), 230.

16  Quoted in Renée Bédarida, *Les armes de l'esprit: Témoignage chrétien (1941–1944)* (Éditions Ouvrières, 1977), 30.

17  Quoted ibid., 56–57.

18  "Le national-socialisme, mystique antichrétienne," 1st *Cahier* of Témoignage Chrétien, November 1941, in *Cahiers clandestins du Témoignage chrétien* (Éditions du Témoignage Chrétien, 1946), 15.

19  "Application et résultats en France," 1st *Cahier* of Témoignage Chrétien, November 1941, ibid., 35.

20  "Le sens de notre témoignage," 6th and 7th *Cahiers* of Témoignage Chrétien, April–May 1942, ibid., 194.

21  Ibid.

22  "Racistes français, valet d'Hitler," *Libération*, no. 6, February 15, 1942, quoted in Laurent Douzou, *La désobéissance: Histoire du mouvement Libération-sud* (Odile Jacob, 1995), 270–271.

23  Poznanski, *Propagandes et persécutions*, 194.

24  Asher Cohen, *Persécutions et sauvetages: Juifs et Français sous l'Occupation et sous Vichy* (Éditions du Cerf, 1993), 206.

25  Renée Poznanski, "Comité Amelot," in *Dictionnaire historique de la Résistance*, ed. François Marcot (Robert Laffont, 2006), 173–174.

26  Cohen, *Persécutions*, 103.

27  Ibid., 105.

28  Ibid., 215.

29  Police prefecture report of July 17, 1942, quoted in Klarsfeld, *La Shoah en France*, vol. 2: *Le calendrier de la persécution* (Fayard, 2001), 523.

30  Poznanski, *Propagandes et persécutions*, 286.

31  Francis-Louis Closon, *Le temps des passions: De Jean Moulin à la Libération, 1943–1945* (Geneva: Famot, 1976; 1st ed., 1974), 201.

32  Quoted in Cohen, *Persécutions*, 305.

33  Cohen, *Persécutions*, 307.

34  Ibid., 310.

35  Ibid., 377.

36  Patrick Cabanel, "Trocmé, André," in Marcot, *Dictionnaire historique de la Résistance*, 536–537.

37  Denis Peschanski, "Amitié chrétienne," in Marcot, *Dictionnaire historique de la Résistance*, 163–164.

38  Henri Moizet, "Juifs et Aveyronnais: Des rapports ambigus," in *La Résistance et les Européens du Sud*, ed. Jean-Marie Guillon and Robert Mencherini (L'Harmattan, 1999), 133.

39  Martine Lemalet, "L'OSE, une oeuvre dans le siècle," in Becker and Annette Wieviorka, *Les Juifs de France*, 234; entries on "Bergon, soeur Denise" and "Roques, Marguerite," in *Dictionnaire des Justes de France*, ed. Israel Gutman (Jerusalem: Yad Vashem, 2003), 85 and 500.

40  Gutman, *Dictionnaire des Justes de France*, 28.

41  Annette Wieviorka, "Les années noires," 228.

42  Poznanski, *Propagandes et persécutions*, 399.

43  Annette Wieviorka, "Les années noires," 236.

44  Quoted in Poznanski, *Propagandes et persécutions*, 386–387.

45  Quoted ibid., 322.

46  Poznanski, *Propagandes et persécutions*, 367–368.

47  Quoted ibid., 459.

48  Poznanski, *Propagandes et persécutions*, 460.

49  Ibid., 459.

CHAPTER 9: THE INTERNAL RESISTANCE IN 1943

1  Laurent Douzou, *La désobéissance: Histoire du mouvement Libération-sud* (Odile Jacob, 1995), 100.

2  Henri Michel, *Histoire de la Résistance en France* (Presses Universitaires de France, 1984; 1st ed., 1950), 29.

3  Marie Granet, *Ceux de la Résistance (1940–1944)* (Éditions de Minuit, 1964), 38.

4  Henri Frenay, *La nuit finira: Mémoires de Résistance*, vol. 1: *1940–1943* (Livre de poche, 1974; 1st ed., 1973), 445.

5  Ibid., 475.

6  Remarks reported in Olivier Wieviorka, *Une certaine idée de la Résistance: Défense de la France, 1940–1949* (Seuil, 1995), 134.

7  Charles d'Aragon, *La Résistance sans héroïsme* (Seuil, 1977), 38.

8  Douzou, *La désobéissance*, 136–137.

9  Alya Aglan, *La Résistance sacrifiée: Histoire du mouvement Libération-nord* (Champs-Flammarion, 2005; 1st ed., 1999), 191.

10  Ibid., 488.

11  Douzou, *La désobéissance*, 133.

12  F. Bourrée, "Védy, Gilbert," in *Dictionnaire historique de la Résistance*, ed. François Marcot (Robert Laffont, 2006), 539.

13  Michel, *Histoire de la Résistance*, 27.

14  Olivier Wieviorka, *Une certaine idée*, 67.

15  Ibid., 69.

16  Arthur Calmette, *L' "OCM," Histoire d'un mouvement de résistance de 1940 à 1946* (Presses Universitaires de France, 1961), 79.

17  Ibid., 86.

18  Granet, *Ceux de la Résistance*, 110.

19  Aglan, *La Résistance*, 205–210.

20  Interview with Pierre Cochery, quoted in Olivier Wieviorka, *Une certaine idée*, 71.

21  Dominique Veillon, *Le Franc-Tireur: Un journal clandestin, un mouvement de résistance, 1940–1944* (Flammarion, 1977), 329.

22  Cécile Vast, "*Le coq enchaîné* (Lyon)," in Marcot, *Dictionnaire historique de la Résistance*, 714.

23  Granet, *Ceux de la Résistance*, 31.

24  Douzou, *La désobéissance*, 163ff.

25  Laurent Douzou and Dominique Veillon, "Bollier, André," in Marcot, *Dictionnaire historique de la Résistance*, 369–370.

26  Olivier Wieviorka, *Une certaine idée*, 99–102.

27  Veillon, *Le Franc-Tireur*, 156.

28  Douzou, *La désobéissance*, 182.

29  Francis-Louis Closon, *Le temps des passions: De Jean Moulin à la Libération, 1943–1945* (Geneva: Famot, 1976; 1st ed., 1974), 216–217.

30  Wieviorka, *Une certaine idée*, 118–122.

31  Jean Gemähling, *Souvenirs*, vol. 1, published by the author, n.d. (1999), 36.

32  Quoted in Aglan, *La Résistance sacrifiée*, 190.

33  Veillon, *Le Franc-Tireur*, 145.

34  Laurent Douzou and Dominique Veillon, "Renouvin, Jacques," in Marcot, *Dictionnaire historique de la Résistance*, 514–515.

35  Jacques Soustelle, *Envers et contre tout: Souvenirs et documents sur la France libre*, 2 vols. (Paris: Robert Laffont, 1947–50), 1:313.

36  Douzou, *La désobéissance*, 189.

37  Frenay, *La nuit finira*, 1:446.

38  Veillon, *Le Franc-Tireur*, 154.

39  Jacques Debû-Bridel, *Les Éditions de Minuit: Historique*, quoted in Anne Simonin, *Les Éditions de Minuit, 1942–1955: Le devoir d'insoumission* (Institut Mémoires de l'Édition Contemporaine, 1994), 83.

40  Simonin, *Les Éditions de Minuit*, 87.

41  Ibid., 88.

42  Ibid., 89.

43  Ibid., 95.

44  Veillon, *Le Franc-Tireur*, 97.

45  Douzou, *La désobéissance*, 165.

46  Philippe Buton, "La France atomisée," in *La France des années noires,* vol. 2: *De l'Occupation à la Libération,* ed. Jean-Pierre Azéma and François Bédarida (Seuil, 2000; 1st ed., 1993), 421.

47  Olivier Wieviorka, *Une certaine idée,* 104.

48  Such was the assessment that Philippe Viannay, for example, quickly made for the DF; interview with the author.

49  Olivier Wieviorka, *Une certaine idée,* 41.

50  Michèle Cointet and Jean-Paul Cointet, *La France à Londres* (Brussels: Complexe, 1990), 213.

51  Jean-Baptiste Duroselle, *L'abîme, 1939–1945* (Imprimerie Nationale, 1983), 438.

52  In *Franc-Tireur,* September 30, 1943; and in *Combat,* August 1, 1943, for example.

53  On September 11, 1943, the radio station Le Poste National Français, for example, hailed the open distribution of *Défense de la France* in the Paris metro; see Olivier Wieviorka, "La presse clandestine," in *Mélanges de l'École française de Rome* 108 (1996): 130.

54  *La France continue,* no. 8, November 20, 1941, quoted in Henri Michel, *Les courants de pensée de la Résistance* (Presses Universitaires de France, 1962), 164.

55  *Franc-Tireur,* June 1, 1943, quoted ibid., 166.

56  *Cahiers* of the OCM, no. 4, September 1943, quoted ibid., 226.

57  *Combat,* no. 33, August 1942.

58  "La Résistance plus forte que jamais," *Franc-Tireur,* May 6, 1944.

59  "À guerre totale, résistance totale," *Combat,* March 1944.

60  Jean-Louis Crémieux-Brilhac, "Ici Londres: L'arme radiophonique," in *Paris 1944: Les enjeux de la libération,* ed. Christine Levisse-Touzé (Albin Michel, 1994), 161ff.

61  Marc Sadoun, "Le parti socialiste dans la Résistance," in *Les Socialistes en résistance: 1940–1944,* ed. Pierre Guidoni and Robert Verdier (Seli Arslan, 1999), 27.

62  Marc Sadoun, *Les Socialistes sous l'Occupation: Résistance et collaboration* (Presses de Sciences-Po, 1982), 208.

63  Ibid., 211–215.

64  Ibid., 215.

65  Ibid., 204.

66  Léon Blum, letter to General de Gaulle, March 15, 1943, in Léon Blum, *La prison, le procès, la déportation: Mémoires et correspondance* (Albin Michel, 1955), 398.

67  *Cahiers politiques,* no. 3, August 1943, quoted in Michel, *Les courants de pensée,* 368.

68  *Libérer et Fédérer,* nos. 15–16, April–May 1944, quoted ibid., 371.

69  Sadoun, *Les Socialistes,* 216.

70 Stéphane Courtois, *Le PCF dans la guerre: De Gaulle, la Résistance, Staline . . .* (Ramsay, 1980), 358.

71 Ibid.

72 Sadoun, *Les Socialistes*, 194.

73 Quoted in Henri Noguères and Marcel Degliame-Fouché, *Histoire de la Résistance en France*, vol. 3: *Et du Nord au Midi, novembre 1942–septembre 1943* (Robert Laffont, 1972), 129.

74 Daniel Virieux, "Le Front national de lutte pour la liberté et l'indépendance de la France: Un mouvement de Résistance, période clandestine (mai 1941–août 1944)" (PhD thesis, Paris-VIII, 1995), 250.

75 Front National, *Manifeste*, April 1943, quoted ibid., 310.

76 Jean-Marie Guillon, "La Résistance dans le Var: Essai d'histoire politique," 3 vols. (PhD thesis, Université de Provence, Aix-en-Provence, 1989), 487.

77 Courtois, *Le PCF dans la guerre*, 341–342.

78 Ibid., 348.

79 Guillon, "La Résistance dans le Var," 526–527.

80 Ibid., 537.

81 Cécile Vast, *"L'Humanité,"* in Marcot, *Dictionnaire historique de la Résistance*, 729.

82 Cécile Vast, *"France d'abord,"* ibid., 271.

83 Cécile Vast, *"La Pensée libre,"* ibid., 743.

84 Cécile Vast, *"La vie ouvrière,"* ibid., 768.

85 Jacqueline Sainclivier, *La Résistance en Ille-et-Vilaine, 1940–1944* (Rennes: Presses Universitaires de Rennes, 1993), 210.

86 Quoted in Noguères and Degliame-Fouché, *Histoire de la Résistance en France*, 3:95.

87 Note by Georges Marrane, June 1943, quoted in Virieux, "Le Front national," 334.

88 Georges Ternet, report of June 20, 1944, quoted ibid.

89 Pierre Hervé, report of May 9, 1943, quoted ibid., 338–339.

90 Letter from Jacques Duclos to Pierre Villon, January 18, 1944, quoted ibid., 707.

91 Laurent Douzou, "Libération-sud," in Marcot, *Dictionnaire historique de la Résistance*, 128.

92 *Franc-Tireur*, February 1942, quoted in Michel, *Les courants de pensée*, 268.

93 *Libération*-sud, no. 30, July 1, 1943, quoted ibid., 269.

94 Michel, *Les courants de pensée*, 272–273.

95 Calmette, *L'"OCM,"* 109.

96 Granet, *Ceux de la Résistance*, 42.

97 Calmette, *L'"OCM,"* 96.

98 Sainclivier, *La Résistance en Ille-et-Vilaine*, 217.

99 Veillon, *Le Franc-Tireur*, 183.

100 Daniel Borzeix, "Les débuts de Guingouin," in *Genèse et développement de la Résistance en R5, 1940–1943*, ed. Pascal Plas (Brive-la-Gaillarde: Éditions Les Monédières), 135.

101 Jean-Marc Berlière and Franck Liaigre, *Liquider les traîtres: La face cachée du PCF, 1941–1943* (Robert Laffont, 2007), 150.

102 Ibid., 151–154.

103 Christian Bougeard, "Le poids de la ville dans la Résistance en Bretagne et dans la France de l'Ouest," in *La Résistance et les Français: Villes, centres et logiques de décision*, ed. Laurent Douzou, Robert Frank, Denis Peschanski, and Dominique Veillon (Cachan: École Normale Supérieure, 1995), 251.

104 Renée Poznanski, "Résistance juive, résistants juifs: Retour à l'histoire," in *Mémoire et histoire: La Résistance*, ed. Jean-Marie Guillon and Pierre Laborie (Toulouse: Privat, 1995), 243.

105 Sainclivier, *La Résistance en Ille-et-Vilaine*, 220.

106 Jean-Marie Guillon, "La lutte armée et ses interprétations," in *La Résistance et les Français: Lutte armée et maquis*, ed. François Marcot (Besançon: Annales Littéraires de l'Université de Franche-Comté, 1996), 149–150.

107 Guillon, "La Résistance dans le Var," 355–356.

108 Ibid., 360–361.

109 Berlière and Liaigre, *Liquider les traîtres*, 171.

110 Ibid., 150.

111 Guillon, "La Résistance dans le Var," 361.

112 Jean-Claude Granhay, "Les maquis haut-saônois dans leur environnement social," in Marcot, *La Résistance et les Français*, 282.

CHAPTER 10: THE LONG ROAD TO UNITY

1 Sébastien Albertelli, *Les Services secrets du général de Gaulle: Le BCRA (1940–1944)* (Perrin, 2009), 158.

2 François Marcot, *La Résistance dans le Jura* (Besançon: Cêtre, 1985), 158.

3 Albertelli, *Les Services secrets*, 264.

4 Guillaume Piketty, *Pierre Brossolette: Un héros de la Résistance* (Odile Jacob, 1998), 243–245.

5 Albertelli, *Les Services secrets*, 278.

6 Quoted ibid., 276.

7 Daniel Cordier, *Jean Moulin: La République des Catacombes* (Gallimard, 1999), 284.

8 Charles de Gaulle, orders, January 24, 1943, quoted in Piketty, *Pierre Brossolette*, 250.

9 Charles de Gaulle, orders, February 9, 1943, quoted in Colonel Passy, *Souvenirs: Missions secrètes en France* (Plon, 1951), 63.

10 Colonel Passy, *Souvenirs: Missions*, 149.

11  Cordier, *Jean Moulin: La République*, 301.

12  Jean-Pierre Azéma, *Jean Moulin: Le rebelle, le patriote, le résistant* (Perrin, 2003), 276.

13  Colonel Passy, *Souvenirs: Missions*, 77.

14  Ibid., 84.

15  Alya Aglan, "Cohors-Asturies," in *Dictionnaire historique de la Résistance*, ed. François Marcot (Robert Laffont, 2006), 146.

16  Christian Bougeard, "Fana-Service B," in Marcot, *Dictionnaire historique de la Résistance*, 150.

17  Jean-Philippe Meyssonnier, "Le réseau Gallia, 1943–1944" (thesis for the Diplôme d'Études Approfondies, Institut d'Études politiques de Paris, 1994), 24ff.

18  Colonel Passy, *Souvenirs: Missions*, 91.

19  Ibid., 336.

20  Marie Ducoudray, *Ceux de "Manipule": Un réseau de renseignement dans la Résistance en France* (Tirésias, 2001), 64–65.

21  Ibid., 169–171.

22  Colonel Passy, *Souvenirs: Missions*, 104.

23  Colonel Passy and Pierre Brossolette, report ARQ1-BRU4, quoted in Piketty, *Pierre Brossolette*, 276.

24  Cordier, *Jean Moulin: La République*, 367.

25  Colonel Passy and Pierre Brossolette, report ARQ2-BRU5, quoted in Piketty, *Pierre Brossolette*, 287.

26  Piketty, *Pierre Brossolette*, 287–288.

27  Azéma, *Jean Moulin*, 320.

28  Ibid., 248.

29  Ibid., 320.

30  Ibid., 315.

31  Letter from the CAS to General de Gaulle, January 13, 1943, quoted in Piketty, *Pierre Brosselette*, 222.

32  Christian Pineau, report of January 15, 1943, quoted ibid., 224.

33  Azéma, *Jean Moulin*, 321.

34  Instructions of February 21, 1943, quoted ibid., 327.

35  Cordier, *Jean Moulin: La République*, 313.

36  Emmanuel d'Astier de La Vigerie, memorandum, April 1943, quoted in Azéma, *Jean Moulin*, 331.

37  Piketty, *Pierre Brossolette*, 228.

38  Ibid., 272.

39  Telegram of March 12, 1943, quoted in Azéma, *Jean Moulin*, 256–257.

40  Cordier, *Jean Moulin: La République*, 376.

41  Piketty, *Pierre Brossolette*, 287.

42  Cordier, *Jean Moulin: La République*, 366.

43  Ibid., 378.

44  Piketty, *Pierre Brossolette*, 284.

45  André Philip, note for Jean Moulin, April 1943, quoted in Azéma, *Jean Moulin*, 326.
46  Colonel Passy, *Souvenirs: Missions*, 180.
47  Ibid., 183.
48  Jean Moulin, letter to André Philip, June 4, 1943, quoted in Cordier, *Jean Moulin: La République*, 388.
49  Motion introduced by Georges Bidault, May 27, 1943, quoted ibid., 389.
50  Henri Giraud, quoted ibid., 329.
51  Cordier, *Jean Moulin: La République*, 314.
52  Jean Moulin, telegram of May 8, 1943, quoted ibid., 392.
53  Jean Moulin, report to André Philip, June 4, 1943, quoted in Azéma, *Jean Moulin*, 348.
54  Charles de Gaulle, *Mémoires de guerre: L'unité* (Presses Pocket, 1980; 1st ed., 1956), 122.
55  Cordier, *Jean Moulin: La République*, 337.
56  Ibid., 340.
57  Henri Frenay, letter to Jean Moulin, April 8, 1943, quoted ibid., 343.
58  Jean Moulin, report to General de Gaulle, May 7, 1943, quoted ibid., 345.
59  Report ARQ2-BRU5, quoted ibid., 335.
60  Cordier, *Jean Moulin: La République*, 390.
61  Jean Moulin, report of May 7, 1943, quoted in Olivier Wieviorka, *Une certaine idée de la Résistance: Défense de la France, 1940–1949* (Seuil, 1995), 218.

### CHAPTER 11: CALUIRE AND ITS REPERCUSSIONS

1  Henri Noguères and Marcel Degliame-Fouché, *Histoire de la Résistance en France*, vol. 3: *Et du Nord au Midi, novembre 1942–septembre 1943* (Robert Laffont, 1972), 420.
2  Ibid., 424.
3  Interview quoted ibid., 429.
4  Daniel Cordier, *Jean Moulin: La République des Catacombes* (Gallimard, 1999), 441.
5  Jean-Pierre Azéma, *Jean Moulin: Le rebelle, le patriote, le résistant* (Perrin, 2003), 420.
6  Quoted ibid., 419.
7  Pierre Péan, *Vies et morts de Jean Moulin* (Fayard, 1998), 544–545.
8  Jean Moulin, letter to General de Gaulle, June 15, 1943, quoted in Cordier, *Jean Moulin: La République*, 443–446.
9  Combat, note on security, January 31, 1943, quoted ibid., 451–452.
10  Azéma, *Jean Moulin*, 413.
11  Ibid., 415.
12  Ibid.

13  Statement quoted in Cordier, *Jean Moulin: La République*, 456–457.

14  Noguères and Degliame-Fouché, *Histoire de la Résistance en France*, 3:470.

15  Péan, *Vies et morts de Jean Moulin*, 553–555 and 562.

16  Statement quoted in Cordier, *Jean Moulin: La République*, 467.

17  Cordier, *Jean Moulin: La République*, 470.

18  Ibid., 474.

19  Noguères and Degliame-Fouché, *Histoire de la Résistance en France*, 3:469.

20  Dominique Veillon and Jean-Pierre Azéma, "Le point sur Caluire," in *Jean Moulin et la Résistance en 1943*, ed. Jean-Pierre Azéma, François Bédarida, and Robert Frank, *Cahiers de l'Institut d'Histoire du Temps Présent* 27 (June 1994): 140.

21  Noguères and Degliame-Fouché, *Histoire de la Résistance en France*, 3:478.

22  Joseph Zimet, "Claude Bouchinet-Serreulles," in *Dictionnaire de la France libre*, ed. François Broche et al. (Robert Laffont, 2010), 181.

23  Claude Bouchinet-Serreulles, *Nous étions faits pour être libres: La résistance avec de Gaulle et Jean Moulin* (Grasset, 2000), 304.

24  Cordier, *Jean Moulin: La République*, 488.

25  Guillaume Piketty, *Pierre Brossolette: Un héros de la Résistance* (Odile Jacob, 1998), 306–307.

26  Ibid., 311.

27  Jean-Marc Binot and Bernard Boyer, *L'argent de la Résistance* (Larousse, 2010), 14.

28  Jean-Claude Daumas, "Le travail," in *La France pendant la Seconde Guerre mondiale: Atlas historique*, ed. Jean-Luc Leleu, Françoise Passera, Jean Quellien, and Michel Daeffler (Fayard/Ministère de la Défense, 2010), 104.

29  Binot and Boyer, *L'argent de la Résistance*, 22.

30  Ibid., 23.

31  Ibid., 62.

32  Ibid., 55.

33  Ibid., 38.

34  Colonel Passy, *Souvenirs: Missions secrètes en France* (Plon, 1951), 380–384.

35  Binot and Boyer, *L'argent de la Résistance*, 50.

36  Ibid., 58.

37  Ibid., 59.

38  Azéma, *Jean Moulin*, 368.

39  Jacques Baumel, *Résister: Histoire secrète des années d'occupation* (Albin Michel, 1999), 278.

40  Binot and Boyer, *L'argent de la Résistance*, 40–41.

41  Ibid., 42.

42  Jean-Pierre Levy (with the collaboration of Dominique Veillon), *Mémoires d'un franc-tireur: Itinéraire d'un résistant (1940–1944)* (Brussels: Complexe, 1998), 81.

43 For an overview, see Robert Belot, *Henri Frenay: De la Résistance à l'Europe* (Seuil, 2003), 355ff. For a more in-depth study, but one favorable to Frenay, see Robert Belot and Gilbert Karpman, *L'Affaire suisse: La Résistance a-t-elle trahi de Gaulle?* (Armand Colin, 2009). For a viewpoint favorable to Moulin, see Cordier, *Jean Moulin: La République*, 350ff.

44 Henri Frenay, *La nuit finira: Mémoires de Résistance*, vol. 1: *1940–1943* (Livre de poche, 1974; 1st ed., 1973), 472.

45 Quoted in Cordier, *Jean Moulin: La République*, 357.

46 Sébastien Albertelli, *Les Services secrets du général de Gaulle: Le BCRA (1940–1944)* (Perrin, 2009), 313.

47 Cordier, *Jean Moulin: La République*, 358.

48 Baumel, *Résister*, 240.

49 Daniel Cordier, *Jean Moulin: L'inconnu du Panthéon*, vol. 1: *Une ambition pour la République, juin 1899–juin 1936* (JC Lattès, 1989), 214.

50 Jean Moulin, letter to General de Gaulle, May 7, 1943, quoted in Belot and Karpman, *L'Affaire suisse*, 130.

51 Cordier, *Jean Moulin: La République*, 361.

52 Belot, *Henri Frenay*, 393.

53 Claude Bourdet, *L'aventure incertaine: De la Résistance à la Restauration* (Stock, 1975), 200.

54 Ibid., 206.

55 Ibid., 209.

56 Henri Frenay, report of May 10, 1943, quoted in Noguères and Degliame-Fouché, *Histoire de la Résistance en France*, 3:377.

57 Emmanuel d'Astier de La Vigerie, memorandum, April 1943, quoted in Cordier, *Jean Moulin: L'inconnu*, 1:225–226.

58 Charles de Gaulle, instructions of May 21, 1943, quoted in Colonel Passy, *Souvenirs: Missions*, 189–190.

59 Pascal Copeau, letter to Emmanuel d'Astier, June 4, 1943, quoted in Cordier, *Jean Moulin: L'inconnu*, 1:241.

60 Cordier, *Jean Moulin: L'inconnu*, 1:264.

61 Comité Français de la Libération Nationale (French Committee of National Liberation), the committee established on June 3, 1943, to divide up powers between de Gaulle and Giraud.

62 Jean de Vogüé, plan of June 28, 1943, quoted in Olivier Wieviorka, *Une certaine idée de la Résistance: Défense de la France, 1940–1949* (Seuil, 1995), 235–236.

63 Bouchinet-Serreulles, *Nous étions faits pour être libres*, 312.

64 Bourdet, *L'aventure incertaine*, 222.

65 Ibid.

66 Noguères and Degliame-Fouché, *Histoire de la Résistance en France*, 3:503–504.

67 Appeal to the Nation, August 2, 1943, quoted in Cordier, *Jean Moulin: L'inconnu*, 1:270.

68  Piketty, *Pierre Brossolette*, 318.

69  Bouchinet-Serreulles, *Nous étions faits pour être libres*, 336.

70  Noguères and Degliame-Fouché, *Histoire de la Résistance en France*, 3:613–614.

71  Cordier, *Jean Moulin: La République*, 510.

72  Pierre Brossolette, letter to Colonel Passy, November 5, 1943, quoted in Noguères and Degliame-Fouché, *Histoire de la Résistance en France*, 3:614.

73  Piketty, *Pierre Brossolette*, 331–333.

74  Ibid., 337–338.

75  Pascal Copeau, statement quoted in Noguères and Degliame-Fouché, *Histoire de la Résistance*, 3:509.

CHAPTER 12: POWER STRUGGLES IN ALGIERS AND
THEIR CONSEQUENCES

1  Olivier Wieviorka, *Normandy: The Landings to the Liberation of Paris*, trans. M. B. BeDevoise (Cambridge, MA: Harvard University Press, 2008; French ed., 2007).

2  Jean-Louis Crémieux-Brilhac, *La France libre: De l'appel du 18 juin à la Libération* (Gallimard, 1996), chap. 16.

3  Olivier Wieviorka, *Orphans of the Republic: The Nation's Legislators in Vichy France*, trans. George Holoch (Cambridge, MA: Harvard University Press, 2009; French ed., 2001), 248.

4  Crémieux-Brilhac, *La France libre*, 603.

5  Bénédicte Vergez-Chaignon, *Les Vichysto-résistants de 1940 à nos jours* (Perrin, 2008), 326.

6  Christian Bachelier, "La nouvelle armée française," in *La France des années noires*, vol. 2: *De l'Occupation à la Libération*, ed. Jean-Pierre Azéma and François Bédarida (Seuil, 2000; 1st ed., 1993), 256.

7  Vergez-Chaignon, *Les Vichysto-résistants*, 472–473.

8  General Verneau, situation of the ORA, August 1943, quoted in Bachelier, "La nouvelle armée française," 121.

9  Vergez-Chaignon, *Les Vichysto-résistants*, 473.

10  Ibid., 353.

11  Ibid., 354.

12  François Marcot, *La Résistance dans le Jura* (Besançon: Cêtre, 1985), 87.

13  General Revers, report, November 1943, quoted in Bachelier, "La nouvelle armée française," 123.

14  Vergez-Chaignon, *Les Vichysto-résistants*, 362.

15  Sébastien Albertelli, *Les Services secrets du général de Gaulle: Le BCRA (1940–1944)* (Perrin, 2009), 317.

16  Ibid., 254.
17  Sébastien Laurent, "La guerre des services spéciaux en Afrique du Nord," in Louis Rivet, *Carnets du chef des services secrets: 1936–1944* (Nouveau Monde Éditions, 2010), 546.
18  Ibid., 552.
19  Ibid., 551.
20  Quoted in Albertelli, *Les Services secrets*, 344.
21  Sébastien Albertelli, "André Pélabon," in *Dictionnaire de la France libre*, ed. François Broche et al. (Robert Laffont, 2010), 1146–1147.
22  Claude d'Abzac-Epezy, "Gabriel Cochet," in *Dictionnaire historique de la Résistance*, ed. François Marcot (Robert Laffont, 2006), 391–392.
23  Albertelli, *Les Services secrets*, 371.
24  Ibid., 377–381.
25  Ibid., 422.
26  Ibid., 424.
27  Jean-Philippe Meyssonnier, "Le réseau Gallia, 1943–1944" (thesis for the Diplôme d'Études Approfondies, Institut d'Études politiques de Paris, 1994), 48–58.
28  Marie Ducoudray, *Ceux de "Manipule": Un réseau de renseignement dans la Résistance en France* (Tirésias, 2001), 177–178.
29  Albertelli, *Les Services secrets*, 158.
30  Michael R. D. Foot, *SOE in France: An Account of the Work of the British Special Operations Executive in France, 1940–1944* (London: Her Majesty's Stationery Office, 1966), 248.
31  Henri Noguères and Marcel Degliame-Fouché, *Histoire de la Résistance en France*, vol. 4: *Formez vos bataillons! Octobre 1943–mai 1944* (Robert Laffont, 1976), 33–34.
32  Foot, *SOE in France*, 262.
33  Ibid., 263.
34  Ibid., 266.
35  Jacqueline Sainclivier, *La Résistance en Ille-et-Vilaine, 1940–1944* (Rennes: Presses Universitaires de Rennes, 1993), 202.
36  Marie Granet, *Ceux de la Résistance (1940–1944)* (Éditions de Minuit, 1964), 103.
37  Sainclivier, *La Résistance en Ille-et-Vilaine*, 240.
38  Noguères and Degliame-Fouché, *Histoire de la Résistance en France*, 4:116–117.
39  Sainclivier, *La Résistance en Ille-et-Vilaine*, 254.
40  Raphaël Spina, "La France et les Français devant le Service du travail obligatoire" (PhD thesis, École Normale Supérieure de Cachan, 2012), 919.
41  Noguères and Degliame-Fouché, *Histoire de la Résistance en France*, 4:23.

42 Georges Guingouin, *4 ans de lutte sur le sol limousin* (Limoges: Lucien Souny, 1991), 89.

43 H. Romans-Petit, *Les maquis de l'Ain* (Hachette, 1974), 89.

44 Ibid., 33.

45 Harry R. Kedward, *Resistance in Vichy France: A Study of Ideas and Motivations in the Southern Zone, 1940–1942* (Oxford: Oxford University Press, 1978), 83.

46 Ibid., 63.

47 Jacques Bingen, report, January 1944, quoted in Daniel Cordier, *Jean Moulin: La République des Catacombes* (Gallimard, 1999), 600.

48 Statement of Paul Deserces, undated, quoted in Jacques Deserces, "Le maquis de Brigueil: Formation, composition et développement d'un maquis," in *Genèse et développement de la Résistance en R5, 1940–1943*, ed. Pascal Plas (Brive-la-Gaillarde: Éditions Les Monédières), 174.

49 Roger Racloz, "Souvenirs de maquisards de la moyenne Vallée de l'Arve (Les Marches: La Fontaine de Siloé, 1994), quoted in Claude Barbier, "Des 'événements de Haute-Savoie,' à Glières, mars 1943–mai 1944: Action et répression du maquis savoyard" (PhD thesis, Paris-I, 2011), 180.

50 André Jacquelin, *Lettres de mon maquis* (Roblot, 1975; 1st ed., 1947), 224–225.

51 Romans-Petit, *Les maquis de l'Ain*, 39–40.

52 Sainclivier, *La Résistance en Ille-et-Vilaine*, 231–232.

53 Noguères and Degliame-Fouché, *Histoire de la Résistance en France*, 4:312.

54 Quoted in Stéphane Courtois, *Le PCF dans la guerre: De Gaulle, la Résistance, Staline . . .* , 390.

55 Courtois, *Le PCF*, 396.

56 Ibid., 398.

57 These episodes are retraced in Henri Noguères and Marcel Degliame-Fouché, *Histoire de la Résistance en France*, vol. 3: *Et du Nord au Midi, novembre 1942–septembre 1943* (Robert Laffont, 1972), and in Crémieux-Brilhac, *La France libre*, 575ff.

58 Quoted in Noguères and Degliame-Fouché, *Histoire de la Résistance en France*, 3:601.

59 Crémieux-Brilhac, *La France libre*, 576.

60 Jean-Éric Callon, "La libération de la Corse: André Philip et le rétablissement de la légalité républicaine," in *Le rétablissement de la légalité républicaine*, ed. Fondation Charles-de-Gaulle (Brussels: Complexe, 1996), 57.

61 Noguères and Degliame-Fouché, *Histoire de la Résistance en France*, 3:603–605.

62 Courtois, *Le PCF*, 376.

63 Crémieux-Brilhac, *La France libre*, 578–581.

64 Quoted in Philippe Buton, *Les lendemains qui déchantent: Le Parti communiste français à la Libération* (Presses de Sciences-Po, 1993), 28.

65  Crémieux-Brilhac, *La France libre*, 577.

66  André Philip, letter to Baudouin, October 1943, quoted in Callon, "La libération de la Corse," 60.

67  Courtois, *Le PCF*, 388.

68  Buton, *Les lendemains qui déchantent*, 20.

69  Courtois, *Le PCF*, 381.

70  Buton, *Les lendemains qui déchantent*, 26–30.

71  Jacques Duclos, *Mémoires*, vol. 2: *Dans la bataille clandestine, Deuxième partie: 1943–1945: De la victoire de Stalingrad à la capitulation de Berlin* (Fayard, 1970), 132.

72  Courtois, *Le PCF*, 421.

73  Ibid., 375.

74  Duclos, *Mémoires*, 2:103.

75  Buton, *Les lendemains qui déchantent*, 37.

76  Courtois, *Le PCF*, 373.

77  Francis-Louis Closon, report of April 1, 1944, quoted in Buton, *Les lendemains qui déchantent*, 49.

78  Buton, *Les lendemains qui déchantent*, 59–60.

79  Courtois, *Le PCF*, 437.

80  Buton, *Les lendemains qui déchantent*, 69.

81  Ibid., 70.

82  Conversation between Daniel Mayer and Auguste Gillot of September 24, 1943, quoted in Marc Sadoun, *Les Socialistes sous l'Occupation: Résistance et collaboration* (Presses de Sciences-Po, 1982), 198.

83  Remarks quoted ibid., 222.

84  Sadoun, *Les Socialistes*, 202.

85  Proclamation of January 15, 1944, quoted in Olivier Wieviorka, *Une certaine idée de la Résistance: Défense de la France, 1940–1949* (Seuil, 1995), 241.

86  Philippe Viannay, *Du bon usage de la France: Résistance, Journalisme, Glénans* (Ramsay, 1988), 100.

87  Pierre Hervé ["Chardon"], report, late 1943, quoted in Olivier Wieviorka, *Une certaine idée*, 245.

88  Letter from Yvon Morandat to Emmanuel d'Astier de La Vigerie, May 30, 1944, quoted ibid., 248.

89  Letter from Copeau to Frenay, April 19, 1944, quoted ibid., 250.

90  Quoted ibid., 251–252.

91  Claude Bourdet, *L'aventure incertaine: De la Résistance à la Restauration* (Stock, 1975), 299–300.

92  Interview with the author, quoted in Olivier Wieviorka, *Une certaine idée*, 253.

93  Pascal Copeau, cable for Emmanuel d'Astier de La Vigerie, May 31, 1944, quoted ibid., 255.

CHAPTER 13: IN ORDER OF BATTLE

1  Claude Barbier, "Des 'événements de Haute-Savoie' à Glières, mars 1943–mai 1944: Action et répression du maquis savoyard" (PhD thesis, Paris-I, 2011), 139.

2  Quoted ibid., 145.

3  Barbier, "Des 'événements de Haute-Savoie' à Glières," 153.

4  Ibid., 167–171.

5  Ibid., 226ff.

6  Ibid., 404.

7  Ibid., 399.

8  Ibid., 406.

9  Ibid., 461–468.

10  Ibid., 527.

11  Ibid., 512.

12  Maurice Schumann, appeal of February 6, 1944, quoted ibid., 412.

13  Sébastien Albertelli, *Les Services secrets du général de Gaulle: Le BCRA (1940–1944)* (Perrin, 2009), 449.

14  Barbier, "Des 'événements de Haute-Savoie' à Glières," 552.

15  Statement quoted ibid, 542.

16  Jean Rosenthal, telegram to the BCRA, March 2, 1944, quoted ibid., 552.

17  Barbier, "Des 'événements de Haute-Savoie' à Glières," 590.

18  Ibid., 751.

19  Ibid., 507.

20  Ibid., 512.

21  Ibid., 634.

22  William Donovan, memo to the president, April 6, 1945, National Archives and Records Administration, Washington, DC (hereafter cited as NARA), microfilm 1642, roll 25.

23  Michael R. D. Foot, *SOE in France: An Account of the Work of the British Special Operations Executive in France, 1940–1944* (London: Her Majesty's Stationery Office, 1966), 87.

24  Sébastien Albertelli, "Les officiers du BCRA, Londres, 1940–1944 Essai d'étude prosopographique" (thesis for the Diplôme d'Études Approfondies, Paris, Institut d'Études Politiques, 1999), 1035.

25  Foot, *SOE in France*, 280.

26  Ibid., 344.

27  Ibid., 75.

28  Philippe André, "Les ambassadeurs de l'ombre: Les délégués militaires régionaux (DMR) du général de Gaulle, septembre 1943–septembre 1944" (M2 thesis, Paris-I, 2011), 120–121.

29  Ibid., 121.

30  Albertelli, *Les Services secrets*, 303.

31 Daniel Cordier, *Jean Moulin: La République des Catacombes* (Gallimard, 1999), 580.

32 Quoted in Foot, *SOE in France*, 360.

33 General Morgan, Operation Overlord, report and evaluation, July 15, 1943, NARA RG 331, entry 35, box 226.

34 Jean-Louis Crémieux-Brilhac, *La France libre: De l'appel du 18 juin à la Libération* (Gallimard, 1996), 773–774.

35 Emmanuel d'Astier de La Vigerie, *Sept fois sept jours* (10/18, 1963; 1st ed., 1961), 128.

36 SOE, memorandum of October 23, 1943, quoted in Albertelli, *Les Services secrets*, 340.

37 Colonel Passy, *Mémoires*, vol. 4, typescript, quoted in Albertelli, "Le BCRA," 792.

38 André, "Les ambassadeurs de l'ombre," 5.

39 Ibid., 49.

40 Maurice Chevance-Bertin, note relating to the plan for implementation of the FFI, observations, May 20, 1944, quoted ibid., 259.

41 André, "Les ambassadeurs de l'ombre," 69.

42 Maurice Bourgès-Manoury, correspondence of December 31, 1943, quoted ibid., 122.

43 André, "Les ambassadeurs de l'ombre," 179.

44 Ibid., 6.

45 BCRA, report of the meeting of April 5, 1944, quoted ibid., 227.

46 André, "Les ambassadeurs de l'ombre," 104.

47 Ibid., 106.

48 Ibid., 332.

49 Ibid., 236.

50 Ibid., 249.

51 Ibid., 243.

52 Ibid., 238.

53 Crémieux-Brilhac, *La France libre*, 775.

54 Charles de Gaulle, speech of April 18, 1942, in *DM*, 182.

55 Emmanuel d'Astier de La Vigerie, telegram to Parodi, May 29, 1944, quoted in Olivier Wieviorka, "La résistance intérieure et la libération de Paris," in *Paris 1944: Les enjeux de la libération*, ed. Christine Levisse-Touzé (Albin Michel, 1994), 138.

56 Philippe Buton, *Les lendemains qui déchantent: Le Parti communiste français à la Libération* (Presses de Sciences-Po, 1993), 99.

57 Olivier Wieviorka, "La résistance intérieure," 141.

58 Albertelli, *Les Services secrets*, 329–330.

59 André, "Les ambassadeurs de l'ombre," 54.

60 Ibid., 276.

61 Ibid., 323.

62 Ibid., 312.

63  Ibid., 318.

64  Ibid., 315.

65  Pierre-Henri Teitgen, letter to François de Menthon, November 3, 1943, quoted in Cordier, *Jean Moulin: La République*, 550.

66  Pascal Copeau, letter to Emmanuel d'Astier de La Vigerie, January 24, 1944, quoted ibid., 549.

67  Georges Bidault, telegram to Algiers, April 4, 1944, quoted ibid., 546.

68  Francis-Louis Closon, *Le temps des passions: De Jean Moulin à la Libération, 1943–1945* (Geneva: Famot, 1976; 1st ed., 1974), 175.

69  Jean-François Muracciole, "Parodi Alexandre," in *Dictionnaire de la France libre*, ed. François Broche et al. (Robert Laffont, 2010), 1122.

70  Jacques Bingen, letter of April 14, 1944, quoted in Cordier, *Jean Moulin: La République*, 569–570.

71  Cordier, *Jean Moulin: La République*, 571.

72  François Marcot, "Comité d'action militaire," in *Dictionnaire historique de la Résistance*, ed. François Marcot (Robert Laffont, 2006), 175.

73  Ibid.

74  Ibid.

75  Olivier Wieviorka, *Normandy: The Landings to the Liberation of Paris*, trans. M. B. BeDevoise (Cambridge, MA: Harvard University Press, 2008; French ed., 2007), 312–313.

76  Closon, *Le temps des passions*, 252.

77  Jacques Duclos, *Mémoires*, vol. 2: *Dans la bataille clandestine, Deuxième partie: 1943–1945: De la victoire de Stalingrad à la capitulation de Berlin* (Fayard, 1970), 235.

78  Closon, *Le temps des passions*, 176.

79  Jérôme Perrier, "Entre administration et politique: Michel Debré (1912–1948)" (PhD thesis, Institut d'Études Politiques-Paris, 2012), 486.

80  Charles-Louis Foulon, *Le pouvoir en province à la Libération: Les commissaires de la République 1943–1946* (Presses de Sciences-Po, 1975), 68.

81  Ibid., 76.

82  Perrier, "Entre administration et politique," 526.

83  Jean Morin, "La préparation du Comité général d'études," in *Le rétablissement de la légalité républicaine*, ed. Fondation Charles-de-Gaulle (Brussels: Complexe, 1996), 221.

84  Foulon, *Le pouvoir en province à la libération*, 72.

85  Émile Laffon, report, September 19, 1943, quoted ibid., 68.

86  Decree regarding the division of metropolitan territory into regional commissionships of the Republic and the creation of regional commissioners of the Republic, January 10, 1944, quoted ibid., 591.

87  Closon, *Le temps des passions*, 179.

88  Decree of April 21, 1944, quoted ibid., 230.

89  Closon, *Le temps des passions*, 225.

90  Ibid., 226.

91  Ibid., 183.
92  Ibid., 228.
93  Ibid., 194.
94  Ibid., 202.
95  Ibid., 243.
96  Diane de Bellescize, "L'intérim gouvernemental des secrétaires généraux," in Fondation Charles-de-Gaulle, *Le rétablissement*, 136.
97  Ibid., 139.
98  Pierre Péan, *Une jeunesse française: François Mitterrand, 1934–1947* (Fayard, 1994).
99  Charles de Gaulle, speech of July 14, 1943, in *DM*, 312.
100 Diane de Bellescize, "Comité général d'études," in Marcot, *Dictionnaire historique de la Résistance*, 178–179.
101 On this point, see Richard Kuisel, *Capitalism and the State in Modern France: Renovation and Economic Management in the Twentieth Century* (New York: Cambridge University Press, 1981), 187–218.
102 Claire Andrieu, *Le programme commun de la résistance: Des idées dans la guerre* (Éditions de l'Érudit, 1984), 37–38.
103 Ibid., 53.
104 Buton, *Les lendemains qui déchantent*, 53.
105 Andrieu, *Le programme commun de la résistance*, 60–63.
106 Plan of action for the resistance, March 15, 1944, quoted ibid., 162–165.
107 Jacques Duclos therefore gave his article the title "La peur du peuple et la trahison de la patrie" ("The Fear of the People and the Betrayal of the Nation"), in *L'Humanité*, March 15, 1944; see Andrieu, *Le programme commun de la résistance*, 70.
108 Andrieu, *Le programme commun de la résistance*, 70–71.
109 Plan of action for the resistance, March 15, 1944, quoted ibid., 165–166.
110 Buton, *Les lendemains qui déchantent*, 54.
111 Andrieu, *Le programme commun de la résistance*, 77.
112 Ibid., 76.
113 Ibid., 96.


CHAPTER 14: FORMEZ VOS BATAILLONS!

1  Charles de Gaulle, speech of June 6, 1944, in *DM*, 407.
2  Christine Levisse-Touzé, "État-Major des Forces françaises de l'intérieur (Londres)," in *Dictionnaire historique de la Résistance*, ed. François Marcot (Robert Laffont, 2006), 243–244.
3  Arthur L. Funk, "L'état-major interallié face à la lutte armée en France," in *La Résistance et les Français: Lutte armée et maquis*, ed. François Marcot (Besançon: Annales Littéraires de l'Université de Franche-Comté, 1996), 373–376.

4   Jean-Louis Crémieux-Brilhac, *La France libre: De l'appel du 18 juin à la Libération* (Gallimard, 1996), 862–863.
5   Ibid., 864.
6   Sébastien Albertelli, *Les Services secrets du général de Gaulle: Le BCRA (1940–1944)* (Perrin, 2009), 472.
7   Ibid., 473.
8   Crémieux-Brilhac, *La France libre*, 856–857.
9   Michael R. D. Foot, *SOE in France: An Account of the Work of the British Special Operations Executive in France, 1940–1944* (London: Her Majesty's Stationery Office, 1966), 388.
10  Crémieux-Brilhac, *La France libre*, 856.
11  Philippe André, "Les ambassadeurs de l'ombre: Les délegués militaires régionaux (DMR) du général de Gaulle, septembre 1943–septembre 1944" (M2 thesis, Paris-I, 2011), 332.
12  Koenig to d'Astier de La Vigerie, n.d., quoted in Jean-Marc Binot and Bernard Boyer, *L'argent de la Résistance* (Larousse, 2010), 155–156.
13  Jérôme Perrier, "Entre administration et politique: Michel Debré (1912–1948)" (PhD thesis, Institut d'Études Politiques-Paris, 2012), 512–516.
14  Binot and Boyer, *L'argent de la Résistance*, 94.
15  Ibid., 99–101.
16  Crémieux-Brilhac, *La France libre*, 866.
17  André, "Les ambassadeurs de l'ombre," 338.
18  Ibid., 342.
19  François Marcot, *La Résistance dans le Jura* (Besançon: Cêtre, 1985), 159.
20  BCRA to "Fantassin" [Valentin Abeille], January 24, 1944, quoted in Olivier Wieviorka, *Une certaine idée de la Résistance: Défense de la France, 1940–1949* (Seuil, 1995), 314.
21  Funk, "L'état-major interallié face à la lutte armée en France," 379.
22  Will Irwin, *The Jedburghs: The Secret History of the Allied Special Forces, France 1944* (New York: Public Affairs, 2005).
23  André, "Les ambassadeurs de l'ombre," 374.
24  Funk, "L'état-major interallié face à la lutte armée en France," 382.
25  Report by Hamish, quoted ibid., 385.
26  André, "Les ambassadeurs de l'ombre," 380–381.
27  Foot, *SOE in France*, 389.
28  Ibid.
29  Crémieux-Brilhac, *La France libre*, 857.
30  Marcot, *La Résistance dans le Jura*, 153.
31  "French Resistance during the First Ten Days of the Operations in Normandy," NARA RG 226, microfilm 1642, roll 103, frame 826.
32  SHAEF, "The Value of SOE Operations in the Supreme Commander's Sphere," July 13, 1945, NA HS8/378.
33  Albertelli, *Les Services secrets*, 498.

34 Olivier Wieviorka, *Normandy: The Landings to the Liberation of Paris*, trans. M. B. BeDevoise (Cambridge, MA: Harvard University Press, 2008; French ed., 2007), 246.

35 Luc Capdevilla, *Les Bretons au lendemain de l'Occupation: Imaginaire et comportement d'une sortie de guerre 1944–1945* (Rennes: Presses Universitaires de Rennes, 1999), 31.

36 Olivier Wieviorka, *Normandy*, 242.

37 Jeanne Bohec, *La plastiqueuse à bicyclette* (Édition du Félin, 1999; 1st ed., 1975), 135.

38 Claire Chevrillon, *Code Name Christiane Clouet: A Woman in the French Resistance* (College Station: Texas A&M University Press, 1995), 205.

39 Claude Bourdet, *L'aventure incertaine: De la Résistance à la Restauration* (Stock, 1975), 339.

40 Alban Vistel, *La nuit sans ombre: Histoire des mouvements unis de résistance, leur rôle dans la libération du Sud-Est* (Fayard, 1970), 447.

41 Colonel Henri Zeller, report, August 1944, quoted in Philippe Buton, *La joie douloureuse: La Libération de la France* (Brussels: Complexe, 2004), 61.

42 Philippe Buton, "La France atomisée," *La France des années noires*, vol. 2: *De l'Occupation à la Libération*, ed. Jean-Pierre Azéma and François Bédarida (Seuil, 2000; 1st ed., 1993), 429.

43 Buton, *La joie douloureuse*, 62.

44 Orders of the SAS brigade, May 21, 1944, quoted in Foot, *SOE in France*, 406.

45 Quoted in Crémieux-Brilhac, *La France libre*, 868.

46 Roger Leroux, "Le combat de Saint-Marcel," *Revue d'histoire de la Deuxième Guerre mondiale* 54 (1964): 11–12.

47 Quoted in Henri Noguères and Marcel Degliame-Fouché, *Histoire de la Résistance en France*, vol. 5: *Au grand soleil de la Libération, 1er juin 1944–15 mai 1945* (Robert Laffont, 1981), 76–77.

48 Leroux, "Le combat de Saint-Marcel," 15.

49 Ibid., 16.

50 Foot, *SOE in France*, 407.

51 Jacqueline Sainclivier, "Saint-Marcel (maquis de)," in Marcot, *Dictionnaire historique de la Résistance*, 762.

52 Capdevila, *Les Bretons au lendemain de l'Occupation*, 33.

53 Sainclivier, "Saint-Marcel (maquis de)," 762.

54 Foot, *SOE in France*, 407.

55 Leroux, "Le combat de Saint-Marcel," 26.

56 Henri Noguères and Marcel Degliame-Fouché, *Histoire de la Résistance en France*, vol. 4: *Formez vos bataillons! Octobre 1943–mai 1944* (Robert Laffont, 1976), 436–437.

57 Eugène Martres, "Mont-Mouchet (maquis du)," in Marcot, *Dictionnaire historique de la Résistance*, 740.

58 Ibid.

59  Quoted in Noguères and Degliame-Fouché, *Histoire de la Résistance en France*, 5:141.

60  Martres, "Mont-Mouchet (maquis du)," in Marcot, *Dictionnaire historique de la Résistance*, 740.

61  Quoted in Gilles Vergnon, "Vercors (maquis du)," in Marcot, *Dictionnaire historique de la Résistance*, 767.

62  Ibid.

63  Quoted in Noguères and Degliame-Fouché, *Histoire de la Résistance en France*, 5:101.

64  Ibid., 103.

65  Gilles Vergnon, *Le Vercors: Histoire et mémoire d'un maquis* (Éditions de l'Atelier, 2002), 90.

66  Ibid., 86–87.

67  Quoted in Crémieux-Brilhac, *La France libre*, 860.

68  Charles Tillon, *On chantait rouge: Mémoires pour l'Histoire d'un ouvrier breton devenu révolutionnaire professionnel, chef de guerre et ministre* (Robert Laffont, 1977), 375.

69  Quoted in Noguères and Degliame-Fouché, *Histoire de la Résistance en France*, 5:178.

70  Vergnon, *Le Vercors*, 102.

71  Ibid., 106.

72  Vergnon, "Vercors (maquis du)," in Marcot, *Dictionnaire historique de la Résistance*, 767.

73  Quoted in Noguères and Degliame-Fouché, *Histoire de la Résistance en France*, 5:380–381.

74  Vergnon, *Le Vercors*, 108.

75  Fernand Grenier, *C'était ainsi . . . La résistance, Châteaubriand, Londres, Alger, le Vercors, Dachau* (Éditions Sociales, 1970), 252.

76  Ibid., 253.

77  Philippe Viannay to the steering committee of the MLN, August 10, 1944, quoted in Olivier Wieviorka, *Une certaine idée*, 278.

78  Olivier Wieviorka, *Une certaine idée*, 282–283.

79  Ibid., 297–298.

80  Ibid., 300–302.

81  Noguères and Degliame-Fouché, *Histoire de la Résistance en France*, 5:124–125.

82  Eberhard Jäckel, *La France dans l'Europe de Hitler* (Fayard, 1968; German ed., 1966), 459.

83  Noguères and Degliame-Fouché, *Histoire de la Résistance*, 5:129.

84  Philippe Buton, *Les lendemains qui déchantent: Le Parti communiste français à la Libération* (Presses de Sciences-Po, 1993), 93.

85  H. Romans-Petit, *Les maquis de l'Ain* (Hachette, 1974), 137.

86  Ibid., 138.

87  Maurice Kriegel-Valrimont, *La Libération: Les archives du Comac (mai–août 1944)* (Éditions de Minuit, 1964), 15.

88  Ibid., 16.
89  Maurice Kriegel-Valrimont, *Mémoires rebelles* (Odile Jacob, 1999), 62–63.
90  COMAC, operations order, June [14,] 1944, quoted in Kriegel-Valrimont, *La Libération*, 45–47.
91  Report on the telegrams received on May 11 from the civilian mission, London, quoted in André, "Les ambassadeurs de l'ombre," 154.
92  Maurice Kriegel-Valrimont, plan submitted to the COMAC, August 7, 1944, quoted in Kriegel-Valrimont, *La Libération*, 158.
93  Agreement of August 14, 1944, quoted ibid., 45–47.
94  Crémieux-Brilhac, *La France libre*, 873.
95  Robert Aron, *Histoire de la libération de la France: Juin 1944–mai 1945* (Brussels: Marabout, 1984; 1st ed., 1959), 180.
96  Ibid., 207.
97  Crémieux-Brilhac, *La France libre*, 882–883.
98  Ibid., 883.
99  Aron, *Histoire de la libération de la France*, 544–545.
100  Jäckel, *La France dans l'Europe de Hitler*, 488.
101  Ibid., 490.
102  John Keegan, *Six Armies in Normandy: From D-Day to the Liberation of Paris* (London: Penguin, 1994; 1st ed., 1982), 285.
103  Buton, *Les lendemains qui déchantent*, 99.
104  Ibid., 100.
105  Ibid., 104.
106  Dwight D. Eisenhower, *Crusade in Europe* (Garden City, NY: Doubleday, 1948), 296.
107  COMAC, minutes of the meeting of July 3, 1944, summarized in Kriegel-Valrimont, *La Libération*, 71.
108  Manuel, telegram to Soustelle, August 24, 1944, quoted in Olivier Wieviorka, "La résistance intérieure et la libération de Paris," in *Paris 1944: Les enjeux de la libération*, ed. Christine Levisse-Touzé (Albin Michel, 1994), 146.
109  Adrien Dansette, *Histoire de la libération de Paris* (Fayard, 1946), 164.
110  Colonel Rol-Tanguy and Roger Bourderon, *Libération de Paris: Les cent documents* (Hachette, 1994), 189.
111  Ibid., 186.
112  Klaus-Jurgen Müller, "Le développement des opérations du groupe d'armées B fin juillet–fin août 1944," in Levisse-Touzé, *Paris 1944*, 102.
113  Quoted in Hans Umbreit, "La libération de Paris et la grande stratégie du IIIe Reich," in Levisse-Touzé, *Paris 1944*, 102.
114  Colonel Rol-Tanguy and Bourderon, *Libération de Paris*, 222.
115  Ibid., 229.
116  Charles de Gaulle, speech of August 25, 1944, in *DM*, 440.
117  Charles de Gaulle, *Mémoires de guerre: L'unité* (Presses Pocket, 1980; 1st ed., 1956), 361.

118  Ibid., 365.

119  Olivier Wieviorka, "La résistance intérieure et la libération de Paris," 146.

120  Quoted in Colonel Rol-Tanguy and Bourderon, *Libération de Paris*, 158a.

121  Rol-Tanguy, directive of August 24, 1944, Service Historique de l'Armée de Terre (Historical Archives of the Land Army), Château de Vincennes, 13 P 42.

122  Summary of the interview with Chaban, telegram from the Commission for the Interior (London) to the Commission for the Interior (Algiers), arrival date, August 11, 1944, AN 72 AJ 1901.

123  Jean-Louis Crémieux-Brilhac, "Ici Londres, l'arme radiophonique," in Levisse-Touzé, *Paris 1944*, 161.

124  Quoted in Keegan, *Six Armies in Normandy*, 306.

125  Georges Boris, telegram to d'Astier, August 11, 1944, AN F1A 3717.

126  "Idées sur le soulèvement national à Paris," August 14, 1944, AN 72 AJ 1901.

127  The estimates vary. In "Le général de Gaulle et la libération de Paris," in Levisse-Touzé, *Paris 1944*, 171, André Martel puts forward the figure of 130 dead for the Second Armored Division, 1,000 dead—including those who were executed—for the FFI, 582 dead for civilians; the Fondation Charles-de-Gaulle lists 76 dead for the Second Armored Division and 901 in the ranks of the FFI, figures comparable to those proposed by the Fondation de la France Libre.

128  Alain Brossat, *Libération, fête folle* (Autrement, 1994), 113.

129  Claude Roy, *Saison violente: Les yeux fermés dans Paris apaisé* (Julliard, 1945), quoted in Brossat, *Libération, fête folle*, 136.

130  Henry Rousso, "L'épuration, une histoire inachevée," in *Vichy, l'événement, la mémoire* (Gallimard, 2001), 501.

131  Ibid., 500.

132  Fabrice Virgili, *Shorn Women: Gender and Punishment in Liberation France* (Oxford: Berg, 2002; French ed., 2000).

133  Olivier Wieviorka, "Guerre civile à la française? Le cas des années sombres (1940–1945)," *Vingtième siècle: Revue d'histoire* 85 (January–March 2005): 5–19.

134  Philippe Pétain, message of June 6, 1944, quoted in Marc Ferro, *Pétain* (Fayard, 1987), 562.

135  Philippe Pétain, message of June 14, 1944, quoted ibid.

136  Jean-Paul Cointet and Michèle Cointet, "L'hypothèque de Vichy," in *Le rétablissement de la légalité républicaine*, ed. Fondation Charles-de-Gaulle (Brussels: Complexe, 1996), 287ff.

137  Quoted in Charles-Louis Foulon, "La Résistance et le pouvoir de l'État dans la France libérée," ibid., 189–190.

138  Olivier Wieviorka, *Une certaine idée*, 317.

139 Claude Bouchinet-Serreulles, report of September 6, 1944, quoted in Charles-Louis Foulon, "La Résistance et le pouvoir de l'État dans la France libérée," in Fondation Charles-de-Gaulle, *Le rétablissement*, 198.

CHAPTER 15: SOCIAL COMPONENTS

1 Michel Boivin and Jean Quellien, "La Résistance en Basse-Normandie," in *La Résistance et les Français: Enjeux stratégiques et environnement social*, ed. Jacqueline Sainclivier and Christian Bougeard (Rennes: Presses Universitaires de Rennes, 1995), 172.

2 Jacqueline Sainclivier, *La Résistance en Ille-et-Vilaine, 1940–1944* (Rennes: Presses Universitaires de Rennes, 1993), 96.

3 Boivin and Quellien, "La Résistance en Basse-Normandie," 172.

4 Raphaël Spina, "La France et les Français devant le Service du travail obligatoire" (PhD thesis, École Normale Supérieure de Cachan, 2012), 506.

5 Philippe Buton, "Les ouvriers et le Parti communiste français (1936–1947)," in *Les ouvriers en France pendant la Seconde Guerre mondiale*, ed. Denis Peschanski and Jean-Louis Robert (Cahiers de l'Institut d'Histoire du Temps Présent, 1992), 325.

6 Ibid., 321.

7 François Marcot, "Les ouvriers de Peugeot, le patronat et l'État," in Peschanski and Robert, *Les ouvriers en France*, 251.

8 Jean-Marie Guillon, "Y a-t-il un comportement ouvrier spécifique? Les ouvriers varois," ibid., 476.

9 Sainclivier, *La Résistance en Ille-et-Vilaine*, 114.

10 Michelle Perrot, *Jeunesse de la grève: France 1871–1890* (Seuil, 1984).

11 François Marcot, "Pour une sociologie de la Résistance: Intentionnalité et fonctionnalité," in *La Résistance, une histoire sociale*, ed. Antoine Prost (Éditions de l'Atelier, 1997), 29.

12 Jean-Marc Berlière and Laurent Chabrun, *Les policiers français sous l'Occupation* (Perrin, 2001), 139.

13 Ibid., 211–212.

14 Christian Chevandier, "Clivages et continuités dans les perceptions et les comportements ouvriers: Les ateliers d'Oullins de la SNCF," in Peschanski and Robert, *Les ouvriers en France*, 436.

15 Marcot, "Les ouvriers de Peugeot, le patronat et l'État," 252.

16 Guillon, "Y a-t-il un comportement ouvrier spécifique?" 471–472.

17 Jean-Marie Guillon, "Résistance et classe moyenne en zone sud," in Prost, *La Résistance, une histoire sociale*, 98.

18 Dominique Veillon, *Le Franc-Tireur: Un journal clandestin, un mouvement de résistance, 1940–1944* (Flammarion, 1977), 249.

19 Alya Aglan, *La Résistance sacrifiée: Histoire du mouvement Libération-nord* (Champs-Flammarion, 2005; 1st ed., 1999), 221.

20 Sainclivier, *La Résistance en Ille-et-Vilaine*, 96.

21 Henri Noguères, *La vie quotidienne des résistants de l'armistice à la libération (1940–1945)* (Hachette, 1984), 71.

22 Guillon, "Résistance et classe moyenne en zone sud," 101.

23 Serge Berstein, "Les classes moyennes devant l'histoire," *Vingtième siècle: Revue d'histoire* 37 (1993): 7.

24 Marcot, "Pour une sociologie de la Résistance," 27.

25 Ibid.

26 Noguères, *La vie quotidienne des résistants*, 29–30.

27 Sainclivier, *La Résistance en Ille-et-Vilaine*, 119.

28 Guillon, "Résistance et classe moyenne en zone sud," 110.

29 François Mauriac, letter to Claude Morgan, December 13, 1944, quoted in Anne Simonin, *Les Éditions de Minuit, 1942–1955: Le devoir d'insoumission* (Institut Mémoires de l'Édition Contemporaine, 1994), 154.

30 Marc Olivier Baruch, *Servir l'État français: L'administration en France de 1940 à 1944* (Fayard, 1997), 454.

31 Philippe Burrin, *La France à l'heure allemande* (Seuil, 1995), 433 [English translation: *France under the Germans: Collaboration and Compromise*, trans. Janet Lloyd (New York: New Press, 1996)].

32 Statistics compiled by Marcot, "Pour une sociologie de la Résistance," 33.

33 Marie Ducoudray, *Ceux de "Manipule": Un réseau de renseignement dans la Résistance en France* (Tirésias, 2001), 232.

34 Aglan, *La Résistance sacrifiée*, 221.

35 Olivier Wieviorka, *Une certaine idée de la Résistance: Défense de la France, 1940–1949* (Seuil, 1995), 189.

36 Spina, "La France et les Français," 308.

37 Marcot, "Pour une sociologie de la Résistance," 26.

38 Jean-Marie Guillon, "La Résistance dans le Var: Essai d'histoire politique," 3 vols. (PhD thesis, Université de Provence, Aix-en-Provence, 1989), 353.

39 Marcot, "Les ouvriers de Peugeot, le patronat et l'État," 248.

40 Fabrice Sugier, "La politique ouvrière des pouvoirs publics dans le bassin houiller du Gard," in Peschanski and Robert, *Les ouvriers en France*, 289.

41 Marc Sadoun, *Les Socialistes sous l'Occupation: Résistance et collaboration* (Presses de Sciences-Po, 1982), 176.

42 Bernard Comte, *L'honneur et la conscience: Catholiques français en Résistance (1940–1944)* (Éditions de l'Atelier, 1998), 92.

43 Denis Peschanski, "Espagnols," in *Dictionnaire historique de la Résistance*, ed. François Marcot (Robert Laffont, 2006), 880.

44  Janine Ponty, "Polonais," ibid., 905–906.

45  Ibid.

46  Comte, *L'honneur de la conscience*, 46.

47  Ibid., 88.

48  Spina, "La France et les Français," 679.

49  René Rémond, "De la Résistance spirituelle à la lutte armée," in *Églises et chrétiens dans la Seconde Guerre mondiale*, ed. Xavier de Montclos et al. (Lyon: Presses Universitaires de Lyon, 1982), 411.

50  Comte, *L'honneur de la conscience*, 88.

51  Rémond, "De la Résistance spirituelle à la lutte armée," 416.

52  This movement was created by Marc Sangnier to reconcile the church and the republic and to narrow the gap between workers and Christianity.

53  Diana Cooper-Richet and Guy Groux, "Les ouvriers, l'Église, la Résistance," in Sainclivier and Bougeard, *La Résistance et les Français*, 133.

54  Comte, *L'honneur et la conscience*, 107.

55  Quoted in Alain-René Michel, *La JEC face au nazisme et à Vichy* (Lille: Presses Universitaires de Lille), 112.

56  Renée Bédarida, *Les armes de l'esprit: Témoignage chrétien (1941–1944)* (Éditions Ouvrières, 1977), 109.

57  Étienne Fouilloux, "La Résistance spirituelle," in Sainclivier and Bougeard, *La Résistance et les Français*, 78.

58  Comte, *L'honneur et la conscience*, 177.

59  Ibid.

60  Alban Vistel, *La nuit sans ombre: Histoire des mouvements unis de résistance, leur rôle dans la libération du Sud-Est* (Fayard, 1970), 541.

61  Ibid., 541–542.

62  Pierre Bolle, "Rapport général," in *Le Plateau Vivarais-Lignon: Accueil et Résistance 1939–1944*, ed. Pierre Bolle (Le Chambon-sur-Lignon: Société d'histoire de la Montagne, 1992), 336.

63  Michel Fabreguet, "Les réfugiés et l'accueil," in Bolle, *Le Plateau Vivarais-Lignon*, 135.

64  Noguères, *La vie quotidienne des résistants*, 83.

65  Marc Boegner, letter to Marshal Pétain, January 10, 1941, quoted in Bolle, "Rapport général," 331.

66  Patrick Weil, "De l'affaire Dreyfus à l'Occupation," in *Les Juifs de France, de la Révolution française à nos jours*, ed. Jean-Jacques Becker and Annette Wieviorka (Liana Levi, 1998), 134.

67  Ibid., 118.

68  Jean Lacouture, *Pierre Mendès France* (Seuil, 1981), 117.

69  Ibid., 128.

70  Quoted in Renée Poznanski, *Être juif en France pendant la Seconde Guerre mondiale* (Hachette, 1994), 132.

71  Quoted ibid., 143.

72  Poznanski, *Être juif en France*, 144–145.

73  Ibid., 156.
74  Renée Poznanski, "Juifs dans la Résistance," in Marcot, *Dictionnaire historique de la Résistance*, 897.
75  Annie Kriegel, *Communismes au miroir français: Temps, cultures et sociétés en France devant le communisme* (Gallimard, 1974), 180.
76  Ibid., 183.
77  Ibid., 188.
78  Poznanski, *Être juif en France*, 501.
79  Bruno Leroux, "Gamzon, Robert," in Marcot, *Dictionnaire historique de la Résistance*, 422.
80  Veillon, *Le* Franc-Tireur, 253.
81  Olivier Wieviorka, *Une certaine idée*, 164.
82  Ducoudray, *Ceux de "Manipule,"* 229.
83  Sainclivier, *La Résistance en Ille-et-Vilaine*, 91.
84  Claude Bourdet, *L'aventure incertaine: De la Résistance à la Restauration* (Stock, 1975), 26.
85  Antoine Prost and Gérard Vincent, *Histoire de la vie privée*, vol. 5 (Seuil, 1999), 79.
86  This analysis relies on the files of resistance fighters who were arrested, which are often more accurate than those kept by the organization; see Olivier Wieviorka, *Une certaine idée*, 179.
87  Ducoudray, *Ceux de "Manipule,"* 230–231.
88  Veillon, *Le* Franc-Tireur, 256.
89  Olivier Wieviorka, *Une certaine idée*, 164–165.
90  Sainclivier, *La Résistance en Ille-et-Vilaine*, 89.
91  Boivin and Quellien, "La Résistance en Basse-Normandie," 171.
92  Claire Andrieu, "Les résistantes: Perspectives de recherche," in Prost, *La Résistance, une histoire sociale*, 74.
93  Ibid., 73.
94  Olivier Wieviorka, *Divided Memory: French Recollections of World War II from the Liberation to the Present*, trans. George Holoch (Stanford, CA: Stanford University Press, 2012; French ed., 2010).
95  Andrieu, "Les résistantes," 74.
96  Olivier Wieviorka, *Une certaine idée*, 165.
97  Noguères, *La vie quotidienne des résistants*, 74.
98  Andrieu, "Les résistantes," 74.
99  Christine Bard, *Les femmes dans la société française au XXe siècle* (Armand Colin, 2004; 1st ed., 2001), 60–61.
100  Olivier Wieviorka, *Une certaine idée*, 166–167.
101  Lise London, *La Mégère de la rue Daguerre: Souvenirs de résistance* (Seuil, 1995), 142.
102  Ibid., 7–8.
103  Remarks quoted in Margaret Collins Weitz, *Sisters in the Resistance: How Women Fought to Free France, 1940–1945* (New York: J. Wiley, 1995), 136.

104  Ducoudray, *Ceux de "Manipule,"* 231.

105  Olivier Wieviorka, *Une certaine idée*, 179.

106  Noguères, *La vie quotidienne des résistants*, 74.

107  Alix Heiniger, "Engagement et identité: Les militants antifascistes des organisations Freies Deutschland de l'exil à l'Ouest (Belgique, France, Suisse) à la RDA des années 1970 (1943–1957)" (PhD thesis, Université de Genève/École Normale Supérieure de Cachan, 2012), 54 and 96.

108  Remarks quoted in Weitz, *Sisters in the Resistance*, 113.

109  Bard, *Les femmes dans la société française*, 140.

110  Vistel, *La nuit sans ombre*, 251.

111  Olivier Wieviorka, *Une certaine idée*, 135.

112  Francis-Louis Closon, *Le temps des passions: De Jean Moulin à la Libération, 1943–1945* (Geneva: Famot, 1976; 1st ed., 1974), 213.

113  Luc Capdevila, François Rouquet, Fabrice Virgili, and Danièle Voldman, *Hommes et femmes dans la France en guerre (1914–1945)* (Payot, 2003), 92.

114  Ibid., 100.

115  Bard, *Les femmes dans la société française*, 144.

116  J.-F. Muracciole, *Les Français libres* (Tallandier, 2009).

117  Harry R. Kedward, *Resistance in Vichy France: A Study of Ideas and Motivations in the Southern Zone, 1940–1942* (Oxford: Oxford University Press, 1978), 77.

118  Guillon, "La Résistance dans le Var," 335–336.

119  Marcot, "Pour une sociologie de la Résistance," 25.

120  François Marcot, "Combien étaient-ils?," in Marcot, *Dictionnaire historique de la Résistance*, 340.

121  Ibid.

122  Statistics supplied by the Veteran Affairs Administration, Caen branch, reproduced in Olivier Wieviorka, *Divided Memory*, 116.

123  By contrast, 185,000 requests were declined in 2008; see ibid.

124  Marcot, "Combien étaient-ils?," 342.

125  Interview by Hanna Diamond, "L'expérience des femmes toulousaines," *Clio: Histoire, femmes et sociétés* 1 (1995), quoted in Bard, *Les femmes dans la société française*, 140.

126  François Marcot, *La Résistance dans le Jura* (Besançon: Cêtre, 1985), 175.

127  Ibid., 201.

128  Lucie Aubrac, *Ils partiront dans l'ivresse: Lyon, mai 1943, Londres, février 1944* (Seuil, 1984), 243 [English translation: *Outwitting the Gestapo*, trans. Konrad Bieber with the assistance of Betsy Wing (Lincoln: University of Nebraska Press, 1993)].

129  Jean Guéhenno, *Journal des années noires* (1947), entry of February 22, 1943, quoted in Spina, "La France et les Français," 315.

130  Pierre Laborie, *L'opinion française sous Vichy* (Seuil, 1990), 313.

131  Marcot, *La Résistance dans le Jura*, 204.

CHAPTER 16: THE REPRESSION

1 Gaël Eismann, *Hôtel Majestic: Ordre et sécurité en France occupée* (Tallandier, 2010), 134.

2 Report of the MbF for June–July 1941, quoted in Eberhard Jäckel, *La France dans l'Europe de Hitler* (Fayard, 1968; German ed., 1966), 268.

3 Eismann, *Hôtel Majestic*, 161–162.

4 Ibid., 210.

5 Ibid., 214.

6 Ibid., 220.

7 Virginie Sansico, *La justice du pire: Les cours martiales sous Vichy* (Payot, 2003), 31.

8 Ibid., 31.

9 Ibid., 86.

10 Eismann, *Hôtel Majestic*, 263.

11 Ahlrich Meyer, *L'Occupation allemande en France, 1940–1944* (Toulouse: Privat, 2002), 109.

12 Quoted by Ahlrich Meyer, "Les débuts du 'cycle attentats-répression' en automne 1941," in *La Résistance et les Français: Villes, centres et logiques de décision*, ed. Laurent Douzou, Robert Frank, Denis Peschanski, and Dominique Veillon (Cachan: École Normale Supérieure, 1995), 491.

13 Eismann, *Hôtel Majestic*, 355.

14 Ibid., 290.

15 Otto von Stülpnagel, report quoted in Meyer, "Les débuts du 'cycle attentats-répression' en automne 1941," 491.

16 To borrow the terms of the notice of December 14, 1941, quoted in Meyer, *L'Occupation allemande en France*, 34.

17 Otto von Stülpnagel, letter to Marshal Keitel, February 15, 1942, quoted in Jean Solchany, "Le commandement militaire en France face au fait résistant," in Douzou et al., *La Résistance et les Français*, 527.

18 Eismann, *Hôtel Majestic*, 354.

19 Ibid., 349.

20 Denis Peschanski, *Vichy 1940–1944: Contrôle et exclusion* (Brussels: Complexe, 1997), 61.

21 Ibid., 63.

22 Eismann, *Hôtel Majestic*, 232.

23 Peschanski, *Vichy 1940–1944*, 76.

24 Jean-Marc Berlière, "Les 'polices' de l'État français: Genèse et construction d'un appareil répressif," in *La répression en France, 1940–1945*, ed. Bernard Garnier, Jean-Luc Leleu, and Jean Quellien (Caen: Centre de Recherche d'Histoire Quantitative, 2007), 122.

25 Eismann, *Hôtel Majestic*, 361.

26 Jean-Marc Berlière and Laurent Chabrun, *Les policiers français sous l'Occupation* (Perrin, 2001), 148.

27  Ibid., 181.

28  Ibid., 95.

29  Ibid., 206.

30  Peschanski, *Vichy 1940–1944*, 76.

31  René Bousquet, letter to the regional prefects, undated, 1942, quoted in Berlière and Chabrun, *Les policiers français sous l'Occupation*, 33.

32  Meyer, *L'Occupation allemande en France*, 37.

33  Eismann, *Hôtel Majestic*, 399.

34  Report of the military administration, March 15, 1942, quoted in Jäckel, *La France dans l'Europe de Hitler*, 284.

35  Eismann, *Hôtel Majestic*, 389.

36  Ibid., 431.

37  Ibid., 430.

38  Ibid., 437.

39  Ibid.

40  Meyer, *L'Occupation allemande en France*, 161.

41  Eismann, *Hôtel Majestic*, 445.

42  Ibid.

43  Quoted ibid., 447–448.

44  Peter Lieb and Robert Paxton, "Maintenir l'ordre en France occupée: Combien de divisions?," *Vingtième siècle: Revue d'histoire* 112 (October–December 2011): 121–122.

45  Jean-Luc Leleu, "D'une politique répressive à une politique terroriste: Oradour," in Garnier et al., *La répression en France*, 305.

46  Ibid.

47  Ibid.

48  Meyer, *L'Occupation allemande en France*, 179.

49  Solchany, "Le commandement militaire en France face au fait résistant," 518.

50  Jochen Böhler, " 'Mythe du franc-tireur' et atrocités de guerre: Une constante de la conduite allemande de la guerre lors des deux conflits mondiaux," in Garnier et al., *La répression en France*, 33.

51  Solchany, "Le commandement militaire en France face au fait résistant," 518.

52  Sansico, *La justice du pire*, 43.

53  Virginie Sansico, "Les cours martiales de Vichy en 1944: Un cas extrême de justice d'exception," in Garnier et al., *La répression en France*, 277.

54  Ibid., 281.

55  Thomas Pouty, "Les fusillés en France occupée, 1940–1944: Étude d'un panel de 1 000 victimes," in Garnier et al., *La répression en France*, 206.

56  Peter Lieb's estimate, quoted in Eismann, *Hôtel Majestic*, 442.

57  Yves Lescure, "L'enquête de la Fondation pour la Mémoire de la Déportation," in Garnier et al., *La répression en France*, 162.

58  Jäckel, *La France dans l'Europe de Hitler*, 434.

59  Delphine Kazandjian, "La déportation de répression organisée après le débarquement au départ de 'zone occupée,'" in Garnier et al., *La répression en France*, 239–240.

60  Pouty, "Les fusillés en France occupée, 1940–1944," 210.

61  Eismann, *Hôtel Majestic*, 442.

62  Pouty, "Les fusillés en France occupée, 1940–1944," 208.

63  Alya Aglan, "Comment meurent les réseaux," in Garnier et al., *La répression en France*, 228.

64  Olivier Wieviorka, *Une certaine idée de la Résistance: Défense de la France, 1940–1949* (Seuil, 1995), 341.

65  Hélène Guillon, "Approche de la répression extrajudiciaire à l'été 1944," in Garnier et al., *La répression en France*, 228.

66  Michael R. D. Foot, *SOE in France: An Account of the Work of the British Special Operations Executive in France, 1940–1944* (London: Her Majesty's Stationery Office, 1966), 425.

67  Olivier Wieviorka, *Une certaine idée*, 341.

68  Jean Quellien, "Motifs d'arrestation et de déportation," in Garnier et al., *La répression en France*, 164.

69  Ibid., 165.

70  Ibid., 165–166.

71  Raphaël Spina, "La France et les Français devant le Service du travail obligatoire" (PhD thesis, École Normale Supérieure de Cachan, 2012), 809.

72  Quellien, "Motifs d'arrestation et de déportation," 167.

73  Meyer, *L'Occupation allemande en France*, 143.

74  Quellien, "Motifs d'arrestation et de déportation," 170.

75  Peter Lieb, "La 157e division de réserve et la lutte contre le maquis dans le Jura et les Alpes françaises," in Garnier et al., *La répression en France*, 296.

76  Jean-Pierre Azéma, introduction to Garnier et al., *La répression en France*, 9.

77  Peter Lieb's estimate, cited in Eismann, *Hôtel Majestic*, 442.

78  Quellien, "Motifs d'arrestation et de déportation," 170.

79  Claude Bourdet, *L'aventure incertaine: De la Résistance à la Restauration* (Stock, 1975), 337–338.

80  Olivier Wieviorka, *Une certaine idée*, 335–336.

81  Bourdet, *L'aventure incertaine*, 325ff.

82  Stéphane Hessel, *Danse avec le siècle* (Seuil, 1997), 80.

83  Gilles Perrault, *L'Orchestre rouge* (Livre de Poche, 1972).

84  Bourdet, *L'aventure incertaine*, 329.

85  Jean-Marc Berlière and Franck Liaigre, *Liquider les traîtres: La face cachée du PCF, 1941–1943* (Robert Laffont, 2007), 246–247.

86  Hessel, *Danse avec le siècle*, 81.

87  Francis-Louis Closon, *Le temps des passions: De Jean Moulin à la Libération, 1943–1945* (Geneva: Famot, 1976; 1st ed., 1974), 244.

88  Jäckel, *La France dans l'Europe de Hitler*, 466.

89  Eismann, *Hôtel Majestic*, 375.

90  Lieb and Paxton, "Maintenir l'ordre en France occupée," 121.

91  Berlière and Chabrun, *Les policiers français sous l'Occupation*, 35.

92  Tract quoted ibid., 51.

93  Renée Poznanski, *Être juif en France pendant la Seconde Guerre mondiale* (Hachette, 1994), 665.

94  Laurent Joly, *L'antisémitisme de bureau: Enquête au coeur de la préfecture de police de Paris et du commissariat général aux Questions juives (1940–1944)* (Grasset, 2011), 241.

95  Berlière and Liaigre, *Liquider les traîtres*, 256.

96  Ibid., 220.

97  Ibid., 167.

98  Berlière and Chabrun, *Les policiers français sous l'Occupation*, 190.

99  Sansico, *La justice du pire*, 52.

100  Joseph Darnand, speech of February 10, 1944, quoted in Jean-Pierre Azéma, "La Milice," *Vingtième siècle: Revue d'histoire* 28 (1990): 101.

101  Raymond Clemoz, note to the forces of law and order, quoted ibid., 101.

102  Pierre Giolitto, *Histoire de la Milice* (Perrin, 1997), 287–291.

103  Jacques Delperrie de Bayac, *Histoire de la Milice (1918–1945)* (Fayard, 1969), 411–414.

104  Ibid., 435–442 and 450–458.

105  Berlière and Chabrun, *Les policiers français sous l'Occupation*, 116.

106  Philippe Aziz, *Tu trahiras sans vergogne: Histoire de deux "collabos": Bonny et Lafont* (Livre de Poche, 1973; 1st ed., 1970), 15.

## CHAPTER 17: INCOMPLETE VICTORY

1  Charles de Gaulle, speech of April 20, 1943, in *DM*, 280–281.

2  Défense de la France, "Le Mouvement de la libération nationale," *Défense de la France* 43, January 15, 1944.

3  *Le Monde*, November 1, 1945.

4  Robert Mencherini, "Les changements des rapports de force politiques," in *Les élites locales dans la tourmente: Du Front populaire aux années cinquante*, ed. Denis Peschanski and Gilles Le Béguec (Centre National de la Recherche Scientifique Éditions, 2000), 40.

5  Henri Frenay, *La nuit finira: Mémoires de Résistance*, vol. 2: *1940–1943* (Livre de poche, 1974; 1st ed., 1973), 277–278.

6  Philippe Buton, "Le PCF et la Résistance sous la IVe République," in *Résistance et politique sous la IVe République*, ed. Bernard Lachaise (Bordeaux: Presses Universitaires de Bordeaux, 2004), 97ff.

7   Ibid.
8   On that political itinerary, see Anne-Laure Ollivier, "Gaston Defferre: Un socialiste face au pouvoir, de Marseille à l'élection présidentielle de 1969," 2 vols. (PhD thesis, École Normale Supérieure, Cachan, 2011).
9   Noëlline Castagnez, *Socialistes en République: Les parlementaires SFIO de la IVe République* (Rennes: Presses Universitaires de Rennes, 2004), 97.
10  Ibid., 104–105.
11  Noëlline Castagnez and Gilles Morin, "Résistance et socialisme: Brève rencontre," in Lachaise, *Résistance et politique*, 116.
12  Ibid., 121.
13  Castagnez, *Socialistes et République*, 109.
14  Gilles Morin, "Les élections locales de 1945: La normalisation de la vie politique," *La IVe République: Histoire, recherches et archives* 357–358 (1997): 231.
15  Gilles Richard, "Les droites et le Parlement, 1944–1948: Essai de mesure globale," in *La recomposition des droites en France à la Libération, 1944–1948,* ed. Gilles Richard and Jacqueline Sainclivier (Rennes: Presses Universitaires de Rennes, 2004), 56ff.
16  Ibid., 51.
17  Note du Jury d'honneur, June 5, 1945, archives du Jury d'honneur.
18  Richard Kuisel, *Capitalism and the State in Modern France: Renovation and Economic Management in the Twentieth Century* (New York: Cambridge University Press, 1981), 224.
19  Philip Nord, *France's New Deal, from the Thirties to the Postwar Era* (Princeton, NJ: Princeton University Press, 2011), 154.
20  Ibid., 207.
21  Ibid., 161.
22  Ibid., 89.
23  Ibid., 106.
24  Ibid., 157–158.
25  Ibid., 211.
26  Kuisel, *Capitalism and the State in Modern France*, 209.
27  For an overview, see Olivier Wieviorka, "La presse," in *Les pouvoirs en France à la Libération*, ed. Philippe Buton and Jean-Marie Guillon (Belin, 1994), 140–158.
28  Jean Mottin, "Histoire politique de la presse (1944–1949)," *Bilans hebdomadaires* (1949): 52.
29  Claude Bellanger et al., *Histoire générale de la presse française* (Presses Universitaires de France, 1975), 374.
30  Ibid., 356.
31  Charles d'Aragon, *La Résistance sans héroïsme* (Seuil, 1977), 160.

CHAPTER 18: A DIVIDED MEMORY

1 Olivier Wieviorka, "Les avatars du statut de résistant," *Vingtième siècle: Revue d'histoire* 50 (April–June 1996): 55–66.

2 Law of March 3, 1945, my emphasis.

3 Émile Fournier, debate of June 8, 1948, *Journal Officiel du Conseil de la République*, June 9, 1948, 1395.

4 Robert Bétolaud, remarks at the Conseil de la République, debate of February 1, 1949, *Journal Officiel du Conseil de la République*, 92.

5 Minutes of the national commission on resistance deportees-internees, February 5, 1954, Ministry of Veterans Affairs, Caen, dossier 11.

6 Minutes of the national commission on resistance deportees-internees, January 31, 1964, Ministry of Veterans Affairs, Caen, dossier 11.

7 Quoted in Pieter Lagrou, *Mémoires patriotiques et occupation nazie* (Brussels: Complexe, 2003), 222.

8 André Méric, remarks to the Assemblée Nationale, debate of May 2, 1989, *Journal Officiel de l'Assemblée Nationale* (1989): 587.

9 Louis Mexandeau, remarks to the Assemblée Nationale, debate of December 19, 1992, *Journal Officiel de l'Assemblée Nationale* (1992): 6830.

10 For an overview, see Olivier Wieviorka, *Divided Memory: French Recollections of World War II from the Liberation to the Present*, trans. George Holoch (Stanford, CA: Stanford University Press, 2012; French ed., 2010).

11 Charles de Gaulle, speech of November 3, 1943, in *DM*, 337–338.

12 Fernand Grenier, *C'était ainsi . . . La résistance, Châteaubriand, Londres, Alger, le Vercors, Dachau* (Éditions Sociales, 1970), 268.

13 Jacques Duclos, *Mémoires: Dans la bataille clandestine*, vol. 1: *De la drôle de guerre à la ruée vers Stalingrad* (Fayard, 1970), 85.

14 Colonel Passy, *Souvenirs: Missions secrètes en France* (Plon, 1951), 5.

15 Philippe Oulmont, "L'hommage municipal: Continuité et fluctuations, 1940–2007," in *Les voies "de Gaulle" en France: Le Général dans l'espace et la mémoire des communes*, ed. Philippe Oulmont, *Cahiers de la Fondation Charles-de-Gaulle* 17 (2009): 22.

16 Sylvie Lindeperg, *Les écrans de l'ombre: La Second Guerre mondiale dans le cinéma français, 1944–1969* (Centre National de la Recherche Scientifique Éditions, 1997), 79–83.

17 Ibid., 35off.

18 Quoted in Henry Rousso, *Le syndrome de Vichy de 1944 à nos jours* (Seuil, 1990; 1st ed., 1987), 131.

19 Henri Frenay, *La nuit finira: Mémoires de Résistance*, vol. 1: *1940–1943* (Livre de poche, 1974; 1st ed., 1973); Claude Bourdet, *L'aventure incertaine: De la Résistance à la Restauration* (Stock, 1975).

20 Passy, *Souvenirs: Missions*, 413.

21 Henri Frenay, *L'énigme Jean Moulin* (Robert Laffont, 1977).

22 Thierry Wolton, *Le grand recrutement* (Grasset, 1993).

23 Pierre Péan, *Une jeunesse française: François Mitterrand, 1934–1947* (Fayard, 1994).

24 Gérard Chauvy, *Aubrac: Lyon 1943* (Albin Michel, 1997).

25 Jean-Pierre Azéma, "Il n'y a pas d'affaire Aubrac," *L'Histoire* 211 (June 1997): 82.

26 Nicolas Sarkozy, speech in Lyon, April 5, 2007.

27 Jan Patočka, *Essais hérétiques* (Lagasse: Verdier, 1981; Czech ed., 1975), 144.

28 Pierre Laborie, "Mémoire de la résistance," in *Dictionnaire historique de la Résistance*, ed. François Marcot (Robert Laffont, 2006), 832.

29 Jean-Pierre Azéma, *De Munich à la Libération, 1983–1944* (Seuil, 1979), 169.

## CONCLUSION

1 Charles de Gaulle, "Appel du 18 juin," in *DM*, 4.

# CHRONOLOGY

1940

June 17  Edmond Michelet (in Brive) and Charles Tillon (in Bordeaux) distribute their first tracts.

June 18  Charles de Gaulle launches his appeal from London; emissaries from the PCF begin to negotiate with Otto Abetz for the right to once more publish *L'Humanité*.

June 20  Étienne Achavanne sabotages telephone lines.

June 22  Signing of the armistice with Germany.

June 25  The armistice with Germany and Italy goes into effect.

July  Winston Churchill creates the SOE, whose aim is to "set Europe ablaze."

The Socialist Jean Texcier composes his "Conseils à l'occupé" ("Guidelines for the Occupied").

July 1  André Dewavrin, known as "Passy," is named head of the Second and Third Bureaus.

July 10  The Parliament meeting in Vichy grants full powers to Marshal Pétain.

Appeal (backdated) launched by the PCF.

July 14  Premier broadcast on the BBC of *Les Français parlent aux Français (French Speaking to the French)*.

July 18  Beginning of radio broadcasts from Free France carried on the BBC.

August 7  Churchill-de Gaulle accords: Great Britain acknowledges the FFL.

September 6  General Cochet's call to prepare for the Revanche.

October  Maurice Ripoche distributes the manifesto that creates the CDLL movement.

Distribution in the north of *L'homme libre*, created by Jean Lebas; publication of the first issue of *Pantagruel*.

October 3  First Statute on Jews.

October 27  Formation of the CDE in Brazzaville by Charles de Gaulle.

November  Henry Frenay's manifesto announcing the creation of the MLN; creation of France-Liberté, the future Franc-Tireur; publication of the *Petites Ailes* of Nord-Pas-de-Calais; publication of *L'Université libre*.

November 9  Dissolution of the management/union confederations.

November 11  Demonstration by lycée and university students at the Étoile and on the Champs-Élysées.

November 15  Labor union manifesto.

November 25  First issue of *Liberté*.

December  Creation of the OCM.

First piece of mail sent to London by Rémy.

December 1  Christian Pineau puts out the first issue of *Libération*-nord.

December 15  First issue of *Résistance*, organ of the Musée de l'Homme network.

December 19  Five Communist parliamentarians ask to testify for the prosecution at the court of Riom.

December 22  Honoré d'Estienne d'Orves disembarks in Brittany.

December 23  De Gaulle calls for the French to desert the streets.


1941

January  Creation of the CAS for the occupied zone.

First issue of *Valmy*.

January 14  Beginning of the "V" graffiti campaign.

January 21  Arrest of d'Estienne d'Orves.

January 24  Frenay places himself on "armistice leave."

February  Dismantlement of the Musée de l'Homme network.

March 15  Operation Savannah.

March 30  Formation of the CAS in the southern zone.

April 23  Law on the nationalization of the police forces.

May  Creation of the Alliance network of the British Intelligence Service.

May 6  Arrival by parachute of the first F Section agent of the SOE.

May 15  Appeal of the PCF (backdated) encouraging the creation of an FN.

May 27  Beginning of the miners' strike in Nord-Pas-de-Calais.

June  Publication of the first *Bulletin des Volontaires de la Liberté*.

June 2  Second Statute on Jews.

June 10  Full resumption of work in the mines of Nord-Pas-de-Calais.

June 22  Operation Barbarossa.

July  First issue of *Libération*-sud.

July 14  First issue of *Défense de la France*.

August 12  Pétain delivers what becomes known as the "ill wind" speech.

August 14  Creation (backdated) of the Special Sections.

August 21  Attack by "Fabien" at the Barbès-Rochechouart metro station.

August 27  The Special Section in Paris retroactively sentences three Communists to death.

September 24  De Gaulle forms the CNF.

September 28  Code on Hostages.

October 20  Jean Moulin arrives in London.

October 21  Execution of forty-eight hostages following attacks committed in Nantes and Bordeaux.

October 23  Over the radio, de Gaulle condemns the strategy of attacks on individuals.

October 25  First meeting between de Gaulle and Moulin.

November  Merger of Liberté and Libération Nationale to form a movement that will take its name from that of its newspaper, *Combat*.

First issue of the *Cahiers du Témoignage chrétien*.

November 6–7  Arrival by parachute of Yvon Morandat.

December  First issues of *Franc-Tireur* and *Combat*.

December 7  The United States enters the war, following the Japanese attack on Pearl Harbor.

December 7 and 12  Night and Fog decree.


1942

January 2  Moulin arrives by parachute in the southern zone.

January 29  First meeting between Frenay and Pierre Pucheu.

February  *L'Humanité* announces the creation of the FTP.

February 19  Beginning of the trial of Riom, to judge those supposedly responsible for the defeat.

February 20 Éditions de Minuit publishes Vercors's *Le silence de la mer*.

February 27–28 Destruction of the Bruneval radar tracking station.

February 28 Christian Pineau departs for London.

March 27 The first convoy of Jewish deportees leaves for Auschwitz.

April 7 Beginning of the trial at the Maison de la Chimie.

April 14 The trial of Riom is suspended.

April 17 Escape of General Giraud.

April 18 Pierre Laval's return to power.

April 28 Return of Christian Pineau, who brings with him de Gaulle's political manifesto.

May Arrival in London of Félix Gouin, SFIO representative to Free France.

May 1 Demonstrations in the free zone.

May 5 Arrival of Karl Oberg in Paris.

May 15 Publication in the southern zone of the first issue of *Le Populaire*.

June Publication of the first *Cahier* of the OCM.

June 1 Oberg officially assumes his duties.

June 22 Laval announces the Relève and declares he wishes for "the victory of Germany."

July 14 Popular demonstrations in the southern zone.

Free France renames itself "Fighting France."

July 28 The Socialist André Philip becomes commissioner for the interior.

July 29 Oberg-Bousquet accord.

August 1 Housewives' demonstration on rue Daguerre in Paris.

August 23 Pastoral letter from Monsignor Saliège protesting the roundups of Jews.

September Creation of the CDLR.

September 4 First Vichy law on the requisition of the labor force.

September 17 Arrival in London of Charles Vallin of the PSF.

September 26 Frenay and Emmanuel d'Astier de La Vigerie arrive in London.

October Agreement in London between Free France and the southern movements to form a CC and the AS (under General Delestraint's command).

October 13  Strikes protesting the "deportation" of laborers.

November  Establishment of the CCZS.

Creation of the SOAM.

November 5  Colonel Rivet leaves for Algiers.

November 8  Anglo-American landing in North Africa.

November 11  The Germans invade the southern zone.

November 27  The French fleet scuttles itself in Toulon.

December  Creation of the OMA, the future ORA.

December 24  Execution of Admiral Darlan.

December 26  Giraud named high commissioner, civilian and military commander in North Africa.


## 1943

January 1  The École des Cadres d'Uriage is closed down.

January 6  Incidents of Montluçon.

January 11  Fernand Grenier, representative of the PCF, arrives in London.

January 13  Beginning of the Anfa Conference.

January 26  The three major movements in the southern zone federate, creating the MUR.

January 26–27  Pierre Brossolette arrives in the French metropolis.

January 30  Creation of the Milice.

February  Beginning of the Swiss affair.

February 2  German surrender at Stalingrad.

February 16  Vichy mobilizes three age cohorts for the STO.

February 21  Giving new instructions, de Gaulle orders the creation of the CNR.

February 26–27  Colonel Passy's arrival in France; beginning of the Brumaire-Arquebuse mission.

March 14  General Giraud delivers the first republican speech of his life.

March 26  Brossolette creates the CCZN.

April  Creation of the BOA.

April 17  Le Perreux accords sealing the reunification of the CGT.

May 27  First meeting of the CNR in Paris.

May 30  De Gaulle arrives in Algiers.

June 2  Creation of the Franc-Garde of the Milice.

June 3  Creation of the CFLN.

June 9  Arrest of General Delestraint.

June 21  At Caluire, arrest of Moulin and of several top leaders of the resistance.

June 25  Creation of the CCDMR.

August  Francis-Louis Closon, charged with setting up the CDLs, arrives in France.

August 15–16  Jacques Bingen arrives in France.

August 25  Directive on the DMRs.

August 30  Georges Bidault elected president of the CNR.

September  First DMR envoys.

September 2  First sabotage operations of Operation Armada.

September 9  Uprising of Corsican partisans.

September 17  Decree convening the ACP.

September 25  Affair of rue de la Pompe.

September 28  Execution of Julius Ritter by the FTP-MOI.

October 4  Liberation of Corsica.

November 3  Inaugural session of the ACP.

November 6–9  Giraud is ousted from the CFLN; Frenay, d'Astier de La Vigerie, and François de Menthon join it.

November 11  Demonstrations, notably in Oyonnax.

November 13  In Grenoble, destruction of the artillery Polygone.

November 20  Creation in Algiers of the DGSS, resulting in the merger of the Gaullist and Giraudist secret services.


## 1944

January  Several resistance movements federate to form the MLN.

January 15  *Défense de la France* prints 450,000 copies of its issue 43.

January 20  The Vichy regime creates courts-martial to judge resistance fighters.

February  Maquisards ascend the Glières plateau.

February 1  Creation of the FFI.

February 2  Emile Bollaert and Brossolette attempt to reach England by sea.

February 3  Sperrle Decree.

February 21  Execution of twenty-two FTP-MOI, including Missak Manouchian.

February 25  Destruction of STO files in Paris.

March 10  Alexandre Parodi named delegate general of the CFLN.

March 15  The program of the CNR is adopted.

March 22  Suicide of Brossolette; execution of Pucheu.

March 26  The Germans undertake an offensive reconnaissance of the Glières plateau.

April 2  Massacre of Ascq in retaliation for a railroad sabotage operation.

April 4  Fernand Grenier and François Billoux join the CFLN.

April 21  Decree of the CFLN defining the organization of the government upon liberation.

May 13  The COMAC is incorporated into the CNR.

May 30  General Koenig acknowledged by the Allies to be commander in chief of the FFI.

June 3  The CFLN becomes the GPRF.

June 6  Allied landing in Normandy; the resistance implements the plans in place.

June 8–9  The maquis of the Vercors is sealed off.

June 9  Hangings in Tulle.

June 10  Koenig orders slowdown of the guerilla war; the Germans attack the maquis of Mont-Mouchet; the Das Reich Division commits the massacre of Oradour-sur-Glane.

June 14  De Gaulle visits the beachhead in Normandy and goes to Bayeux.

June 18  German attack on the maquis of Saint-Marcel, which disperses.

June 28  An MLN commando executes Philippe Henriot.

July 3  Proclamation of the republic of the Vercors.

July 21  Beginning of the German assault on the Vercors.

July 25  Beginning of Operation Cobra in Cotentin, followed by the breakthrough into Avranches.

August 4  Liberation of Rennes.

August 10  Beginning of the railroad workers' strike in Paris.

August 15  Franco-American landing in Provence; beginning of the Paris police force strike.

August 16  Adolf Hitler orders retreat.

August 17  The last convoy of Jews leaves for the east.

August 18  The labor unions launch the order for general strike in Paris.

August 19  Beginning of the Paris insurrection.

August 20  Liberation of Toulouse.

August 21  Insurrection in Marseilles; Georges Guingouin's forces liberate Limoges.

August 22  Liberation of Grenoble.

August 25  The Germans surrender in Paris.

August 26  Liberation parade in Paris.

September 3  Liberation of Lyon; liberation of Lille.

September 9  Formation of the new de Gaulle government.

September 10  Surrender of the Elster column.

September 12  The troops coming from Normandy and Provence join together in Burgundy.

September 30  Law regarding the press.

October 23  The Allies recognize de jure the GPRF.

October 28  Dissolution of the Milices Patriotiques.

November 23  Liberation of Strasbourg.

November 26  Constituent Congress of the MRP.

December 16  The Germans launch a major offensive in the Ardennes.


## 1945

January 16  Nationalization of the Renault factories.

January 23–28  First national congress of the MLN.

February 6  Execution of Robert Brasillach.

April 6  Decree regarding the purge of the political staff.

April 9  Nationalization of Air France and of Gnome-et-Rhône.

April 29  First round of the municipal elections.

May 8 German surrender.

May 13 Second round of the municipal elections.

June 25 Creation of the UDSR.

October 4–19 Laws creating Social Security.

October 21 Referendum and elections for the Constituent Assembly.

November 21 Formation of the new de Gaulle government.

December 2 Nationalization of credit banks and the Banque de France.

# SELECTED BIBLIOGRAPHY

Unless otherwise indicated, the city of publication is Paris.

MEMOIRS

Aragon, Charles d'. *La Résistance sans héroïsme*. Seuil, 1977.

Astier de La Vigerie, Emmanuel d'. *Sept fois sept jours*. 10/18, 1963.

———. *Seven Times Seven Days*. Translated by Humphrey Hare. London: Macgibbon and Kee, 1958.

Aubrac, Raymond. *Où la mémoire s'attarde*. Odile Jacob, 1996.

Baumel, Jacques. *Résister: Histoire secrète des années d'occupation*. Albin Michel, 1999.

Bouchinet-Serreulles, Claude. *Nous étions faits pour être libres: La Résistance avec de Gaulle et Jean Moulin*. Grasset, 2000.

Bourdet, Claude. *L'aventure incertaine: De la Résistance à la Restauration*. Stock, 1975.

Closon, Francis-Louis. *Le temps des passions: De Jean Moulin à la Libération, 1943–1945*. Geneva: Famot, 1976; 1st ed., 1974.

Cordier, Daniel. *Alias Caracalla*. Gallimard, 2009.

Duclos, Jacques. *Mémoires: Dans la bataille clandestine*. Part 1: *1940–1942: De la drôle de guerre à la ruée vers Stalingrad*. Part 2: *1943–1945: De la victoire de Stalingrad à la capitulation de Berlin*. Fayard, 1970.

Frenay, Henri. *La nuit finira: Mémoires de Résistance*. Vol. 1: *1940–1943*. Vol. 2: *1943–1945*. Livre de Poche, 1974; 1st. ed., 1973.

Gaulle, Charles de. *Mémoires de guerre*. Vol. 1: *L'appel: 1940–1942* (1st ed., 1954). Vol. 2: *L'unité: 1942–1944* (1st ed., 1956). Vol. 3: *Le salut: 1944–1946* (1st ed., 1959). Presses Pocket, 1980.

———. *The Complete War Memoirs, 1940–1946*. Vol. 1: *The Call to Honor, 1940–1942*. Vol. 2: *Unity, 1942–1944*. Vol. 3: *Salvation, 1944–1946*. New York: Simon and Schuster, 1964.

Gemähling, Jean. *Souvenirs*. 2 vols. Typescript, 2000.

Guillain de Bénouville, Pierre. *Le sacrifice du matin*. Robert Laffont, 1946.

Guingouin, Georges. *4 ans de lutte sur le sol limousin*. Limoges: Lucien Souny, 1991.

Humbert, Agnès. *Notre guerre: Souvenirs de Résistance*. Tallandier, 2004; 1st ed., 1946.

Kriegel-Valrimont. *Mémoires rebelles*. Odile Jacob, 1999.

Lanzmann, Claude. *Le lièvre de Patagonie: Mémoires*. Gallimard, 2009.

———. *The Patagonian Hare: A Memoir*. Translated by Frank Wynne. New York: Farrar, Straus and Giroux, 2012.

Levy, Jean-Pierre, with the collaboration of Dominique Veillon. *Mémoires d'un franc-tireur: Itinéraire d'un résistant (1940–1944)*. Brussels: Complexe, 1998.

London, Lise. *La mégère de la rue Daguerre: Souvenirs de Résistance*. Seuil, 1995.

Paillole, Paul. *Services spéciaux (1935–1945)*. Robert Laffont, 1975.

Passy, Colonel. *Souvenirs*. Vol. 1: *2e Bureau, Londres*. Monte Carlo: Solar, 1947. Vol. 2: *10 Duke Street*. Monte Carlo: Solar, 1948. Vol. 3: *Missions secrètes en France*. Plon, 1951. These three titles were reprinted under the title *Mémoires du chef des services secrets de la France libre*. Odile Jacob, 2000.

Pineau, Christian. *La simple vérité: 1940–1945*. Phalanx, 1983; 1st ed., 1960.

Romans-Petit, Henri. *Les maquis de l'Ain*. Hachette, 1974.

Tillon, Charles. *On chantait rouge: Mémoires pour l'Histoire d'un ouvrier breton devenu révolutionnaire professionnel, chef de guerre et ministre*. Robert Laffont, 1977.

Viannay, Philippe. *Du bon usage de la France: Résistance, journalisme, Glénans*. Ramsay, 1988.

Vistel, Alban. *La nuit sans ombre: Histoire des mouvements unis de Résistance, leur rôle dans la libération du Sud-Est*. Fayard, 1970.

Wieviorka, Olivier. *Nous entrerons dans la carrière: De la Résistance à l'exercice du pouvoir*. Seuil, 1994.

OVERVIEWS

Aglan, Alya. *Le temps de la Résistance*. Arles: Actes Sud, 2008.

Association pour l'Histoire des Chemins de Fer en France. *Une entreprise publique dans la guerre: La SNCF, 1939–1945*. Presses Universitaires de France, 2001.

Azéma, Jean-Pierre. *De Munich à la Libération*. Seuil, 1979.

———. *From Munich to the Liberation, 1938–1944*. Translated by Janet Lloyd. Cambridge: Cambridge University Press, 1984.

Bédarida, François. "L'histoire de la Résistance: Lecture d'hier, chantiers de demain." *Vingtième siècle: Revue d'histoire* 11 (July–September 1986): 75–89.

Binoit, Jean-Marc, and Bertrand Boyer. *L'argent de la Résistance*. Larousse, 2010.

Broche, François, Georges Caïtucoli, and Jean-François Muracciole, eds. *Dictionnaire de la France libre*. Robert Laffont, 2010.

Cohen, Asher. *Persécutions et sauvetages: Juifs et Français sous l'Occupation et sous Vichy*. Le Cerf, 1993.

Douzou, Laurent, Robert Frank, Denis Peschanski, and Dominique Veillon, eds. *La Résistance et les Français: Villes, centres et logiques de décision*. Cachan: École Normale Supérieure, 1995.

Federini, Fabienne. *Écrire ou combattre: Des intellectuels prennent les armes (1942–1944)*. La Découverte, 2006.

Guillon, Jean-Marie, and Pierre Laborie, eds. *Mémoire et histoire: La Résistance.* Toulouse: Privat, 1995.

Guillon, Jean-Marie, and Robert Mencherini, eds. *La Résistance et les Européens du Sud.* L'Harmattan, 1999.

Jackson, Julian. *France: The Dark Years, 1940–1944.* Oxford: Oxford University Press, 2001.

Kedward, Harry Roderick. *The Resistance in Vichy France: A Study of Ideas and Motivations in the Southern Zone, 1940–1942.* Oxford: Oxford University Press, 1978.

———. *In Search of the Maquis: Rural Resistance in Southern France, 1942–1944.* Oxford: Clarendon Press, 1993.

Laborie, Pierre. *L'opinion française sous Vichy.* Seuil, 1990.

———. *Les Français des années troubles: De la guerre d'Espagne à la Libération.* Seuil, 2003; 1st ed., 2001.

*La Résistance et les Européens du Nord.* 2 vols. Proceedings of the Colloquium of Brussels, 1994.

Leleu, Jean-Luc, Françoise Passera, Jean Quellien, and Michel Daeffler, eds. *La France pendant la Seconde Guerre mondiale: Atlas historique.* Fayard/Ministère de la Défense, 2010.

Marcot, François, ed. *La Résistance et les Français: Lutte armée et maquis.* Besançon: Annales Littéraires de l'Université de Franche-Comté, 1996.

———, ed. *Dictionnaire historique de la Résistance.* Robert Laffont, 2006.

Michel, Henri. *Histoire de la Résistance.* Presses Universitaires de France, 1984; 1st ed., 1950.

———. *Les courants de pensée de la Résistance.* Presses Universitaires de France, 1962.

Monchablon, Alain. "La manifestation à l'Étoile du 11 novembre 1940: Histoire et mémoires." *Vingtième siècle: Revue d'histoire* 110 (April–June 2011): 67–81.

Moore, Bob, ed. *Resistance in Western Europe.* Oxford: Berg, 2000.

Noguères, Henri. *La vie quotidienne des résistants de l'armistice à la libération (1940–1945).* Hachette, 1984.

Noguères, Henri, Marcel Degliame-Fouché, and Jean-Louis Vigier. *Histoire de la Résistance en France.* Vol. 1: *Juin 1940–juin 1941.* Vol. 2: *L'armée de l'ombre: Juillet 1941–octobre 1942.* Vol. 3: *Et du Nord au Midi: Novembre 1942–septembre 1943.* Vol. 4: *Formez vos bataillons! Octobre 1943–mai 1944.* Vol. 5: *Au grand soleil de la Libération.* Robert Laffont, 1967–1981.

Sainclivier, Jacqueline, and Christian Bougeard. *La Résistance et les Français: Enjeux stratégiques et environnement social.* Rennes: Presses Universitaires de Rennes, 1995.

Sémelin, Jacques. *Sans armes face à Hitler: La Résistance civile en Europe, 1939–1943.* Payot, 1989.

Tartakowsky, Danielle. *Les manifestations de rue en France, 1918–1968.* Publications de la Sorbonne, 1997.

Wieviorka, Olivier. "La presse clandestine." *Mélanges de l'École Française de Rome* 108 (1996): 125–136.

———. "À la recherche de l'engagement." *Vingtième siècle: Revue d'histoire* 60 (October–December 1998): 58–70.

## ON THE MOVEMENTS AND NETWORKS

Aglan, Alya. *La Résistance sacrifiée: Histoire du mouvement Libération-nord.* Champs-Flammarion, 2005; 1st ed., 1999.

———. *Mémoires résistantes: Histoire du réseau Jade-Fitzroy 1940–1944.* Cerf, 1994.

Bédarida, Renée. *Les armes de l'esprit: Témoignage chrétien (1941–1944).* Éditions ouvrières, 1977.

Blanc, Julien. *Au commencement de la Résistance: Du côté du musée de l'Homme, 1940–1941.* Seuil, 2010.

Calmette, Arthur. *L' "OCM": Histoire d'un mouvement de résistance de 1940 à 1946.* Presses Universitaires de France, 1961.

Douzou, Laurent. *La désobéissance: Histoire du mouvement Libération-sud.* Odile Jacob, 1995.

Ducoudray, Marie. *Ceux de "Manipule": Un réseau de renseignement dans la Résistance en France.* Éditions Tirésias, 2001.

Foot, Michael R. D. *SOE in France: An Account of the Work of the British Special Operations Executive in France, 1940–1944.* London: Her Majesty's Stationery Office, 1966.

Granet, Marie. *Ceux de la Résistance (1940–1944).* Éditions de Minuit, 1964.

Meyssonier, Jean-Philippe. "Le réseau Gallia." Thesis for the Diplôme d'Études Approfondies, Institut d'Études Politiques-Paris, 1994.

Rabino, Thomas. *Le réseau Carte: Histoire d'un réseau de la Résistance antiallemand, antigaulliste, anticommuniste et anticollaborationniste.* Perrin, 2008.

Simonin, Anne. *Les Éditions de Minuit, 1942–1955: Le devoir d'insoumission.* Institut Mémoires de l'Édition Contemporaine, 1994.

Veillon, Dominique, *Le Franc-Tireur: Un journal clandestin, un mouvement de Résistance, 1940–1944.* Flammarion, 1977.

Virieux, Daniel. "Le Front national de lutte pour la liberté et l'indépendance de la France: Un mouvement de Résistance, période clandestine (mai 1941– août 1944)." 5 vols. PhD thesis, Paris-VIII, 1995.

Wieviorka, Olivier. *Une certaine idée de la Résistance: Défense de la France, 1940– 1949.* Seuil, 1995.

## ON FREE FRANCE

Albertelli, Sébastien. *Les Services secrets du général de Gaulle: Le BCRA 1940–1944.* Perrin, 2009.

André, Philippe. "Les ambassadeurs de l'ombre: Les délégués militaires régionaux (DMR) du général de Gaulle: Septembre 1943–septembre 1944." M2 thesis, Paris-I, 2011.

———. *La Résistance confisquée? Les délégués militaires du général de Gaulle de Londres à la Libération.* Perrin, 2013.

Crémieux-Brilhac, Jean-Louis. *La France libre: De l'appel du 18 juin à la Libération.* Gallimard, 1996.

Fondation de la France Libre/Fondation Charles-de-Gaulle. *La France libre: Actes du colloque international tenu à l'Assemblée nationale les 15 et 16 juin 2004.* Limoges: Lavauzelle, 2005.

Luneau, Aurélie. *Radio Londres, 1940–1944: Les voix de la liberté.* Perrin, 2005.

Murraciole, Jean-François. *Les Français libres: L'autre Résistance.* Tallandier, 2009.


## ON POLITICAL FORCES AND CURRENTS

Azéma, Jean-Pierre, Antoine Prost, and Jean-Pierre Rioux, eds. *Le Parti communiste français des années sombres, 1938–1941.* Seuil, 1986.

Barasz, Johanna. "De Vichy à la Résistance: Les vichysto-résistants, 1940–1944." 3 vols. PhD thesis, Institut d'Études Politiques-Paris, 2010.

Berlière, Jean-Marc, and Franck Liaigre. *Liquider les traîtres: La face cachée du PCF, 1941–1943.* Robert Laffont, 2007.

Buton, Philippe. *Les lendemains qui déchantent: Le Parti communiste français à la Libération.* Presses de Sciences-Po, 1993.

Castagnez, Noëlline. *Socialistes en République: Les parlementaires SFIO de la IVe République.* Rennes: Presses Universitaires de Rennes, 2004.

Courtois, Stéphane. *Le PCF dans la guerre: De Gaulle, la Résistance, Staline . . .* Ramsay, 1980.

Guidoni, Pierre, and Robert Verdier, eds. *Les Socialistes en Résistance, 1940–1944.* Seli Arslan, 1999.

Sadoun, Marc. *Les Socialistes sous l'Occupation: Résistance et collaboration.* Presses de Sciences-Po, 1982.

Vergez-Chaignon, Bénédicte. *Les Vichysto-résistants de 1940 à nos jours.* Perrin, 2008.

Wieviorka, Olivier. *Les orphelins de la République: Destinées des députés et sénateurs français, 1940–1945.* Seuil, 2001.

———. *Orphans of the Republic: The Nation's Legislators in Vichy France.* Translated by George Holoch. Cambridge, MA: Harvard University Press, 2009.


## ON INSTITUTIONS, GROUPS, AND SOCIAL CLASSES

Abzac-Épezy, Claude d'. *L'armée de l'air des années noires: Vichy 1940–1944.* Economica, 1998.

Andrieu, Claire. *Le programme commun de la Résistance: Des idées dans la guerre.* Éditions de l'Érudit, 1984.

Baruch, Marc Olivier. *Servir l'État français: L'administration en France de 1940 à 1944.* Fayard, 1997.

Comte, Bernard. *L'honneur et la conscience: Catholiques français en Résistance (1940–1944).* Éditions de l'Atelier, 1998.

Peschanski, Denis, and Jean-Louis Robert, eds. *Les ouvriers en France pendant la Seconde Guerre mondiale.* Cahiers de l'Institut d'Histoire du Temps Présent, 1992.

Poznanski, Renée. *Être juif en France pendant la Seconde Guerre mondiale.* Hachette, 1995.

———. *Propagandes et persécutions: La Résistance et le "problème juif": 1940–1944.* Fayard, 2008.

Prost, Antoine, ed. *La Résistance, une histoire sociale.* Éditions de l'Atelier, 1997.

Spina, Raphaël. "La France et les Français devant le Service du travail obligatoire (1942–1945)." PhD thesis, École Normale Supérieure, Cachan, 2012.

Weitz, Margaret Collins. *Sisters in the Resistance: How Women Fought to Free France, 1940–1945.* New York: J. Wiley, 1995.

## THE GERMAN OCCUPATION AND THE REPRESSIVE FORCES

Berlière, Jean-Marc, and Laurent Chabrun. *Les policiers français sous l'Occupation.* Perrin, 2001.

Eismann, Gaël. *Hôtel Majestic: Ordre et sécurité en France occupée (1940–1944).* Tallandier, 2010.

Garnier, Bernard, Jean-Luc Leleu, and Jean Quellien, eds. *La répression en France, 1940–1945.* Caen: Centre de Recherche d'Histoire Quantitative, 2007.

Jäckel, Eberhard. *La France dans l'Europe de Hitler.* Translated by Denise Meunier. Fayard, 1968; German ed., 1966.

Kitson, Simon. *The Hunt for Nazi Spies: Fighting Espionage in Vichy France.* Translated by Catherine Tihanyi. Chicago: University of Chicago Press, 2008.

———. *Vichy et la chasse aux espions nazis: Complexités de la politique de collaboration.* Autrement, 2005.

Meyer, Ahlrich. *L'Occupation allemande en France, 1940–1944.* Toulouse: Privat, 2002.

Peschanski, Denis. *Vichy 1940–1944: Contrôle et exclusion.* Brussels: Complexe, 1997.

Sansico, Virginie. *La justice du pire: Les cours martiales sous Vichy.* Payot, 2003.

## BIOGRAPHIES

Azéma, Jean-Pierre. *Jean Moulin: Le rebelle, le patriote, le résistant.* Perrin, 2003.

Belot, Robert. *Henri Frenay: De la Résistance à l'Europe.* Seuil, 2003.

Cordier, Daniel. *Jean Moulin: La République des Catacombes*. Gallimard, 1999.

Nobécourt, Jacques. *Le Colonel de La Rocque, 1885–1946, ou les pièges du nationalisme chrétien*. Fayard, 1996.

Piketty, Guillaume. *Pierre Brossolette: Un héros de la Résistance*. Odile Jacob, 1998.

## REGIONAL STUDIES

Barbier, Claude. "Des 'événements de Haute-Savoie' à Glières, mars 1943–mai 1944: Action et répression du maquis savoyard." PhD thesis, Paris-I, 2011.

———. *Le maquis de Glières: Mythe et réalité*. Perrin, 2014.

Dejonghe, Étienne, and Yves Le Maner. *Le Nord-Pas-de-Calais dans la main allemande*. Lille: La Voix du Nord, 1999.

Guillon, Jean-Marie. "La Résistance dans le Var: Essai d'histoire politique." 3 vols. PhD thesis, Aix-en-Provence, 1989.

Marcot, François. *La Résistance dans le Jura*. Besançon: Cêtre, 1985.

Plas, Pascal, ed. *Genèse et développement de la Résistance en R5, 1940–1943*. Brive-la-Gaillarde: Éditions Les Monédières.

Sainclivier, Jacqueline. *La Résistance en Ille-et-Vilaine, 1940–1944*. Rennes: Presses Universitaires de Rennes, 1993.

Vergnon, Gilles. *Le Vercors: Histoire et mémoire d'un maquis*. Éditions de l'Atelier, 2002.

## ON THE LIBERATION

Aron, Robert. *Histoire de la libération de la France, juin 1944–mai 1945*. Brussels: Marabout, 1984; 1st ed., 1959.

———. *France Reborn: The History of the Liberation, June 1944–May 1945*. Translated by Humphrey Hare. New York: Charles Scribner's Sons, 1964.

Brossat, Alain. *Libération, fête folle, 6 juin 1944–8 mai 1945: Mythes et rites ou le grand théâtre des passions populaires*. Autrement, 1994.

Buton, Philippe. *La joie douloureuse: La Libération de la France*. Brussels: Complexe, 2004.

Buton, Philippe, and Jean-Marie Guillon, eds. *Les pouvoirs en France à la Libération*. Belin, 1994.

Capdevila, Luc. *Les Bretons au lendemain de l'Occupation: Imaginaire et comportement d'une sortie de guerre, 1944–1945*. Rennes: Presses Universitaires de Rennes, 1999.

Fondation Charles-de-Gaulle. *Le rétablissement de la légalité républicaine*. Brussels: Complexe, 1996.

Foulon, Charles-Louis. *Le pouvoir en province à la Libération: Les commissaires de la République, 1943–1946*. Presses de Sciences-Po, 1975.

Irwin, Will. *The Jedburghs: The Secret History of the Allied Special Forces, France 1944*. New York: Public Affairs, 2005.

Kriegel-Valrimont, Maurice. *La Libération: Les archives du Comac (mai–août 1944)*. Éditions de Minuit, 1964.

Kuisel, Richard. *Capitalism and the State in Modern France: Renovation and Economic Management in the Twentieth Century*. Cambridge: Cambridge University Press, 1981.

Lachaise, Bernard, ed. *Résistance et politique sous la IVe République*. Bordeaux: Presses Universitaires de Bordeaux, 2004.

Levisse-Touzé, Christine, ed. *Paris 1944: Les enjeux de la libération*. Albin Michel, 1994.

Nord, Philip. *France's New Deal, from the Thirties to the Postwar Era*. Princeton, NJ: Princeton University Press, 2011.

Peschanski, Denis, and Gilles Le Béguec, eds. *Les élites locales dans la tourmente: Du Front populaire aux années cinquante*. Centre National de la Recherche Scientifique Éditions, 2000.

Richard, Gilles, and Jacqueline Sainclivier, eds. *La recomposition des droites en France à la Libération, 1944–1948*. Rennes: Presses Universitaires de Rennes, 2004.

Wieviorka, Olivier. "Guerre civile à la française? Le cas des années sombres (1940–1945)." *Vingtième siècle: Revue d'histoire* 85 (January–March 2005): 5–19.

## ON MEMORY

Boursier, Jean-Yves, ed. *Musées de guerre et mémoriaux*. Éditions de la Maison des Sciences de l'Homme, 2005.

Conan, Éric, and Henry Rousso. *Vichy, un passé qui ne passe pas*. Fayard, 1994.

Courtois, Stéphane. "Luttes politiques et élaboration d'une histoire: Le PCF historien du PCF dans la Deuxième Guerre mondiale." *Communisme* 4 (1983): 5–26.

Douzou, Laurent. *La Résistance française, une histoire périlleuse: Essai d'historiographie*. Seuil, 2005.

Gacon, Stéphane. *L'amnistie: De la commune à la guerre d'Algérie*. Seuil, 2002.

Lagrou, Pieter. *The Legacy of Nazi Occupation: Patriotic Memory and National Recovery in Western Europe, 1945–1965*. Cambridge: Cambridge University Press, 2000.

———. *Mémoires patriotiques et occupation nazie*. Brussels: Complexe, 2003.

Lavabre, Marie-Claire. *Le fil rouge: Sociologie de la mémoire communiste*. Presses de Sciences-Po, 1994.

Lindeperg, Sylvie. *Les écrans de l'ombre: La Seconde Guerre mondiale dans le cinéma français, 1944–1969*. Centre National de la Recherche Scientifique Éditions, 1997.

Namer, Gérard. *Batailles pour la mémoire: La commémoration en France de 1945 à nos jours*. Papyrus, 1983.

Nora, Pierre. "Gaullistes et communistes." In *Les lieux de mémoire*, edited by Pierre Nora, 2:2489–2532. Gallimard, 1997.

Rousso, Henry. *Le syndrome de Vichy de 1944 à nos jours*. Seuil, 1990; 1st ed., 1987.

———. *The Vichy Syndrome: History and Memory in France since 1944*. Translated by Arthur Goldhammer. Cambridge, MA: Harvard University Press, 1991.

Vergnon, Gilles, and Michèle Battesti, eds. *Les associations d'anciens résistants et la fabrique de la mémoire de la SGM*. Cahiers du Centre d'Études d'Histoire de la Défense 28, 2006.

Wieviorka, Olivier. "Du bon usage du passé: Résistance, politique, mémoire." *Mots* 32 (September 1992): 67–79.

———. *La mémoire désunie: Le souvenir politique des années sombres, de la Libération à nos jours*. Seuil, 2010.

———. *Divided Memory: French Recollections of World War II from the Liberation to the Present*. Translated by George Holoch. Stanford, CA: Stanford University Press, 2012.

———. "Les avatars du statut de résistant en France (1945–1992)." *Vingtième siècle: Revue d'histoire* 50 (April–June 1996): 55–66.

# ACKNOWLEDGMENTS

This book owes a great deal to the sympathetic and exacting readings of family, friends, and colleagues. I would like to express here my profound gratitude to Sébastien Albertelli, Raphaëlle Branche, Philippe Buton, Gaël Eismann, Alain Geismar, and Fabrice Virgili.

At Éditions Perrin, Benoît Yvert and Nicolas Gras-Payen spared no effort to see this book to its successful conclusion.

My mother, with her usual kindness, agreed to compile the index for the original French edition.

This history would have taken longer to complete had I not had the honor of joining the Institut Universitaire de France, which provides its members with extraordinary conditions for pursuing their research.

Regarding the English-language version, published by Harvard University Press, I would like to thank Kathleen McDermott for her confidence and also Patrice Higonnet, to whom I owe so much—not to neglect, of course, Jane Marie Todd, who took on the difficult task of translating this work.

My thanks to one and all.

# INDEX

Abwehr (German military intelligence), 81, 180, 272, 431, 437

Action Française, 17, 34, 138, 157, 393; loyalty to Vichy, 51; opposition to Third Republic, 395; youth organization of, 231

Albertelli, Sébastien, 16, 132, 139, 165, 304, 326

Albrecht, Berty, 68, 93, 153, 159, 405

Algeria, 16, 175, 461, 466; independence of, 463; torture used by French forces in, 465, 471

Alsace-Lorraine, *xiv*, 11, 31, 142, 484n50

Anglo-American Allies, 161, 201, 205, 470; advance into France, 373; attitudes toward French resistance, 328–332; de Gaulle's distrust of, 165; North African landings, 31, 160, 175–176, 259, 296, 312. *See also* Normandy (D-Day) landings

Anti-Fascism, 38, 39, 68, 93, 388, 394; disowned by PCF leaders, 40; of foreigners in resistance, 393; vagaries of Communist Party line and, 34, 123

Anti-Semitism, 32, 43, 143, 146, 402, 459; intensification of persecution, 215; racial persecution of Jews and, 209–210; in resistance groups, 77; resistance reactions to, 210–214; SS in charge of persecution, 422; trade union rejection of, 49; of Vichy regime, 51, 52, 399–400

Aragon, Charles d', 71, 91, 101, 117, 223, 453

Army of shadows, 4, 78, 197, 198; Anglo-American Allies' view of, 353; anonymity favored by, 33–34; conflicts over operational command, 371–373; defined against Vichy, 53; de Gaulle's leadership and, 221, 462; emergence of, 7; lack of historical precedents for, 467; legend of French majority involved in, 88; middle- and upper-class supporters of, 390; number of actions carried out by, 250; political parties absent from, 240; postwar political reform and, 449; scandals about soldiers of, 463–464. *See also* Resistance, internal

AS (Armée Secrète), 97, 108, 153, 170, 181; Caluire affair and, 271–272, 274, 277; confusion in free zone during Nazi invasion, 180; de Gaulle and control of, 340; dispute over command of, 267–268, 289; formation of, 169; Frenay's claim to leadership of, 285, 288; French soldiers in, 300; FTP merged with, 317, 340; German and Vichy attacks on, 364; maquis and, 202, 205; military actions of, 311; ORA and, 301

Aubrac, Lucie, 110, 113, 148, 149, 403, 405; in leadership position, 407; on peasants' aid to resistance, 412; scandal concerning Caluire affair and, 464

Aubrac, Raymond, 179, 231, 245, 274, 288, 343, 403; Jewish identity of, 401; paramilitary sector assigned to, 149; scandal concerning Caluire affair and, 464

Barbie, Klaus, 103, 271, 272–273, 275–276, 464

BBC (British Broadcasting Corporation), 8, 9, 14–15, 25, 99, 137; cautious support for French resistance, 13, 29; de Gaulle and, 11, 12, 187, 439; Glières tragedy and, 323; liberation of Paris and, 380, 381; on maquis activities, 205; on persecution of Jews, 218, 219; underground press and, 235–236, 237; women addressed by, 408

BCRA (Bureau Central de Renseignement et d'Action), 131–133, 139, 149, 271, 294, 360; Allied landing plans and, 336, 337; Anglo-American Allies and, 328; Brumaire-Arquebuse Mission and,